Heritage
of Western
Civilization

Heritage of Western Civilization

SIXTH EDITION

VOLUME I

Edited by

JOHN L. BEATTY

OLIVER A. JOHNSON

University of California, Riverside

PRENTICE-HALL, INC., *Englewood Cliffs, New Jersey 07632*

Library of Congress Cataloging-in-Publication Data

Heritage of western civilization.

  1. Civilization, Occidental—History—Sources.
2. Civilization—History—Sources. I. Beatty, John
Louis, 1922–1975. II. Johnson, Oliver A.
CB245.H428 1987   909'.09821   86–20507
ISBN 0–13–387275–0 (v. 1)

Cover design: Wanda Lubelska
Manufacturing buyer: Ray Keating

© 1987, 1982, 1977, 1971, 1966, 1958 by Prentice-Hall, Inc.
A division of Simon & Schuster
Englewood Cliffs, New Jersey 07632

Printed in the United States of America

10 9 8 7 6 5 4

ISBN 0-13-387275-0   01

Prentice-Hall International (UK) Limited, *London*
Prentice-Hall of Australia Pty. Limited, *Sydney*
Prentice-Hall Canada Inc., *Toronto*
Prentice-Hall Hispanoamericana, S.A., *Mexico*
Prentice-Hall of India Private Limited, *New Delhi*
Prentice-Hall of Japan, Inc., *Tokyo*
Prentice-Hall of Southeast Asia Pte. Ltd., *Singapore*
Editora Prentice-Hall do Brasil, Ltda., *Rio de Janeiro*

Contents

RENAISSANCE AND REFORMATION

367

Preface to the Sixth Edition

As a result mainly of suggestions made to me by those who have used *Heritage of Western Civilization* as a text, I have made a number of changes and—I hope—improvements in the sixth edition. These include adding selections from *The Enchiridion* of Epictetus, *The Dialogue* of St. Catherine of Siena, *A Pilgrimage for Religion's Sake* of Erasmus, *The Progress of the Human Mind* of Condorcet, *A Discourse on the Moral Effects of the Arts and Sciences* of Rousseau, *Evolutionary Socialism* of Bernstein, and *The Effects of Atomic Bombs on Hiroshima and Nagasaki*. Because of space constraints, my inclusion of these new selections has had to be accompanied by the deletion of works by Marcus Aurelius, Tacitus, Kant, and Webb as well as Rousseau's *Social Contract* and Erasmus's *Praise of Folly*. I have also introduced a new and better translation of Einhard's *Life of Charlemagne*.

I appreciate the help given me by many readers of *Heritage*, now as in the past, in shaping the contents of both volumes. I am particularly indebted to my colleague, Professor Norman Ravitch, for his valuable suggestions.

Oliver A. Johnson

Heritage
of Western
Civilization

King Hammurabi of Babylon receiving the laws from the sun god, Marduk. (*Culver Pictures, Inc.*)

THE ANCIENT NEAR EAST

The source of Western civilization, the ancient Near East, lies in a relatively small area of land where three continents—Asia, Africa, and Europe—come together. Although our heritage is a long one, it is difficult to state with precision just when it began. Two quite different kinds of problems stand in the way of dating accurately the beginnings of our civilization. An obvious difficulty is that in the very early centuries people had not developed the art of writing and so could not preserve a detailed or reliable account of their deeds. A more formidable obstacle lies in determining just what constitutes "civilization." Clearly we cannot decide when a civilization began until after we have determined what a civilization is. Historians, generally, have solved this problem by dating the birth of civilization from the time when people first began to live together in cities. Accepting this criterion, we can date the beginning of Western Civilization in the fifth millennium B.C., when inhabitants of the ancient Near East began drifting down from the hills into the fertile river bottoms, abandoning their nomadic existence as herdsmen for a more settled life in towns.

Some historians, however, believe that civilization demands more than city life; in particular, they insist on the necessity of permanent, accurate records. This criterion implies the ability to write. Those who base civilization on the existence of written records have an additional point in their argument, for almost concurrent with the invention of writing at the end of the fourth millennium B.C. there occurred a second event of epochal significance. Usually called the "copper revolution," this development is important not only because it introduced a metal as the main constituent of arms and implements in place of stone, but also because it led to a vast expansion of commerce. Since few localities possessed copper deposits, it was necessary to transport the supplies long distances from their sources to their destinations. Extensive commerce required larger political units, more complex commercial organization, and better means of transportation and communication. All of these are basic ingredients of civilized life.

Whether we accept the notion that civilized life begins with life in the city or only with the development of a written language, we must recognize a fact often overlooked—that the temporal portion of Western history occupied by the civilizations of the ancient Near East is a large one indeed. If we take the year 500 B.C., when the first truly European civilization, classical Greece, entered its period of greatness, as a dividing line, we find that we have cut Western civilization almost exactly in half, the last twenty-five hundred years belonging to the world of European and American history and the first twenty-five hundred years belonging to the history of the ancient Near East. And if we mark the beginning of civilization by the development of city life, we must tip the temporal balance in favor of the pre-Greek world.

Our knowledge of the ancient Near East comes from many sources. Important among these, of course, are written records. The Old Testament, for instance, is a treasure house of information about every facet of life in ancient times, revealing intimate details of the daily life not only of the tribes of Israel but also of their neighbors from Egypt to Mesopotamia. For those periods of history in which no written records exist, our most important sources of information are the findings of archeologists. Since the romantic discovery of the city of Troy a century ago by the German amateur, Heinrich Schliemann, archeologists have systematically dug up the sites where ancient people had built. They have been aided in their researches in various unexpected ways. For example, the most essential item in an ancient household, the clay pot, is almost indestructible. Although it may be broken and cast on a dump heap, the shards remain through the millennia waiting to be put together again. When the archeologist of the twentieth century has reassembled this humble object, he can learn much about its original owners from its composition, its shape, and its decoration. In addition, he can make shrewd deductions about the time it was originally molded from the relative depth of the layer in the dump from which he dug it up.

Again, the archeologist is greatly indebted in particular to the ancient Egyptians for their faith in immortality. Believing in a life after death much like that on earth, they filled the tombs of their deceased with everything necessary for a prosperous, happy existence. Preserved intact through the ages in the dry air of the Egyptian desert, ancient tombs like that of the pharaoh Tutenkhamon, who reigned in the fourteenth century B.C., have yielded dazzling treasures to the picks and shovels of modern diggers.

Because it spanned several millennia, the history of the ancient Near East is a complex affair. Nevertheless it is possible to distinguish four major Near Eastern centers of civilization: Mesopotamia, Egypt, Asia Minor and Syria, and the eastern Mediterranean Sea. Mesopotamia is generally conceded to have the oldest civilization. At a very early date people were attracted by the deep, rich soils created by the annual flooding of the two great rivers, the Tigris and Euphrates, as they flowed in a generally eastward direction to their ultimate destination in the Persian Gulf. The long history of Mesopotamia witnessed a succession of different groups of people gaining political domination over the land, only to be overcome and superseded by another group. A twofold reason lies behind this turbulent history. The land, because of its fertility, was extremely attractive and hence considered a worthy prize. In addition, it was very difficult to defend against invasions because it offered few natural barriers to deter attackers.

To reap maximum benefit from the fertile soil of the river valley, it was necessary to develop extensive systems of irrigation. Such an endeavor required large-scale cooperation, which in turn encouraged the development of legal relationships. The result was an early elaboration of a complex legal system, which was codified by the Babylonian king Hammurabi around 1700 B.C. and became one of the most important bequests of Mesopotamia to Western civilization.

Ancient Egypt, like Mesopotamia, was a civilization based on a river. To reach its mouth where it empties into the southeast corner of the Mediterranean Sea, the Nile meanders for nearly a thousand miles from its first cataract in upper Egypt. Most of the life of ancient Egypt was concentrated in a narrow strip of fertile land, ten to twenty miles wide, along the banks of the river. Egypt differed from Mesopotamia, however, in having a relatively tranquil history. Indeed, it was one of the most stable societies in the history of the world. The reason, again, was mainly geographical. Relatively isolated and protected from potential invaders by barriers of mountain and desert, the Egyptians were able to go about their affairs century after century unmolested by foreign intruders.

The third general area of the ancient Near East, Asia Minor and Syria, is more difficult to characterize briefly because its history was quite diverse. Including the Anatolian peninsula between the eastern Mediterranean and the Black Seas as well as the narrow strip of land between the eastern end of the Mediterranean and the desert of Arabia, this land was the home of many very diverse groups of people. Because of their strategic location along the shores of the Mediterranean and astride the main overland routes connecting Egypt and Mesopotamia, the peoples of the area turned naturally to trade as a way of life. One group, the Phoenicians, took to the sea, sending their ships far and wide across the Mediterranean and even venturing beyond the Straits of Gibraltar into the Atlantic. Others turned to trade by land; a group known as Aramaeans dominated commerce in the Near East from their trading city of Damascus for centuries. Among the smallest, weakest, yet most influential of all Near Eastern peoples was a group of wandering tribes who presumably originated near the mouth of the Tigris and Euphrates and, after many vicissitudes, settled in the land of Canaan, on a thin coastal strip at the southeast corner of the Mediterranean. These were the Jewish people; their contribution to Western civilization requires no explanation.

The final important ancient Near Eastern civilization had its center in the islands of the eastern Mediterranean and the Aegean seas and along the coastal strips of the adjacent mainland, in Greece and Asia Minor. Of particular significance was the island of Crete, just off the southern tip of Greece. Here an advanced society developed, especially at the city of Cnossus, where an enormous and elaborate palace was built to house the royal family and their retainers. The Minoans, as the members of this civilization are generally called, naturally took to the sea and for centuries dominated the commerce of the Aegean area, from seaports on Crete, on other islands, and on the mainland. Although Minoan civilization declined after some unknown force attacked and destroyed the great palace at Cnossus around 1400 B.C., this city and the civilization it represented achieved a high level of wealth, splendor, and sophistication. In addition, it provided a link between the older civilizations in the ancient Near East and the first of European civilizations, classical Greece.

During the last thousand years of its period of greatness, civilization in the ancient Near East was characterized by the appearance of successive empires. Among the first of these was the Babylonian Empire of Hammurabi, which took shape in Mesopotamia around 1700 B.C. There followed an Egyptian Empire and an Empire of the Hittites with its center in Anatolia. Overshadowing all of these in extent and influence were the last two imperial powers, first the Assyrians and then the Persians. Under their great leaders, Cyrus and Darius, the Persians gained control of all the ancient Near East from the Mediterranean shores in the West to the banks of the Indus River in India in the East. Around 500 B.C. they began to move across the Straits of the Dardanelles into Europe. Here they were met by the Greeks in a series of decisive encounters which were to shape the course of Western history to our own day.

Egyptian Religious Hymns

The religion of ancient Egypt is an extremely complex subject. One authority, W. M. F. Petrie (writing in Hastings' *Encyclopedia of Religion and Ethics*, volume V), distinguishes six main strata of Egyptian theology: (1) pure animal worship, (2) animal-headed gods with human bodies, (3) human gods of the Osiris cycle, (4) cosmic gods of the Rä cycle, (5) abstract gods of principles, and (6) gods brought in from foreign sources. Such diversity, although suggesting that the Egyptians were fickle and inconstant in their religious allegiances, is probably more truly understood as a natural development of religious consciousness taking place over a period of five thousand years, from prehistoric times to the beginning of the Christian era.

Long as Petrie's list is, however, it still fails to include one important and historically pervasive facet of Egyptian religious worship. This is animism, or the deification of forces of nature—a type of religion found in most early civilizations. The selections that follow illustrate two forms of Egyptian animism: worship of the Nile and worship of the sun. Why the people of Egypt selected these two natural forces for deification is understandable. Each formed a necessary condition for the sustenance of life in the valley, the Nile by annually inundating the land and nourishing the soil, and the sun because its warmth caused the crops to grow. Without the presence of both, the Nile valley would have been either a desert or a swamp in which Egyptian civilization as we know it would probably never have developed. The *Hymn to the Sun* has, in addition, another claim to our attention, for many scholars hold it to be the first clear statement in Western civilization of monotheism, or the belief in a single god.

The two hymns presented here come from different historical epochs. The exact date of the *Hymn to the Nile* is not known but scholars believe that it was composed for a festival held in Thebes celebrating the annual flooding of the land by the river. The *Hymn to the Sun* was composed by King Ikhnaton, probably around 1370 B.C. It is interesting to compare it with the 104th Psalm, written several hundred years later. Both of the hymns that follow, particularly the first, have come to us mutilated through the ravages of time. Parts that are missing have either been reconstructed by the translators or are indicated by ellipses.

Hymn to the Nile

Praise to thee, O Nile, that issueth from the earth, and cometh to nourish Egypt. Of hidden nature, a darkness in the daytime. . . .

That watereth the meadows, he that Rē[1] hath created to nourish all cattle. That giveth drink to the desert places, which are far from water; it is his dew that falleth from heaven.

Beloved of Kēb,[2] director of the corn-god; that maketh to flourish every workshop of Ptah.[3]

Lord of fish, that maketh the water-fowl to go upstream. . . .

That maketh barley and createth wheat, so that he may cause the temples to keep festivals.

If he be sluggish,[4] the nostrils are stopped up,[5] and all men are impoverished; the victuals of the gods are diminished, and millions of men perish.

If he be niggardly the whole land is in terror and great and small lament. . . . Khnum[6] hath fashioned him. When he riseth, the land is in exultation and every body is in joy.

All jaws begin to laugh and every tooth is revealed.

He that bringeth victuals and is rich in food, that createth all that is good. The revered, sweet-smelling. . . . That createth herbage for the cattle, and giveth sacrifice to every god, be he in the underworld, in heaven, or upon earth. . . . That filleth the storehouses, and maketh wide the granaries, that giveth things to the poor.

He that maketh trees to grow according to every wish, and men have no lack thereof; the ship is built by his power, for there is no joinery with stones. . . .

. . . thy young folk and thy children shout for joy over thee, and men hail thee as king. Unchanging of laws, when he cometh forth in the presence of Upper and Lower Egypt. Men drink the water. . . .

He that was in sorrow is become glad, and every heart is joyful. Sobk, the child of Neith,[7] laugheth, and the divine Ennead, that is in thee, is glorious.

Thou that vomitest forth, giving the fields to drink and making strong the people. He that maketh the one rich and loveth the other. He maketh no distinctions, and boundaries are not made for him.

Thou light, that cometh from the

---

[1] The sun-god.

[2] The earth-god.

[3] Ptah, the craftsman, who fashions everything, could effect nothing without the Nile.

[4] On the occasion of a deficient inundation.

[5] Men no longer breathe and live.

[6] The ram-headed god, who fashions all that is.

[7] Sobk has the form of a crocodile and will originally have been a water-god, who rejoices in the inundation.

Adolph Erman, *The Literature of the Ancient Egyptians*, trans. A. M. Blackman (London: Methuen & Co., Ltd., 1927), pp. 146–49. Courtesy of Methuen & Co., Ltd.

darkness! Thou fat for his cattle! He is a strong one, that createth. . . .

. . . one beholdeth the wealthy as him that is full of care, one beholdeth each one with his implements. . . . None that (otherwise) goeth clad, is clad,[8] and the children of notables are unadorned. . . .

He that establisheth right, whom men love. . . . It would be but lies to compare thee with the sea, that bringeth no corn. . . . no bird descendeth in the desert. . . .

Men begin to play to thee on the harp, and men sing to thee with the hand.[9] Thy young folk and thy children shout for joy over thee, and deputations to thee are appointed.

He that cometh with splendid things and adorneth the earth! That causeth the ship to prosper before men; that quickeneth the hearts in them that are with child; that would fain have there be a multitude of all kinds of cattle.

When thou art risen in the city of the sovereign, then men are satisfied with a goodly list.[10] "I would

---

[8] For hard work, clothes are taken off.

[9] It is an old custom to beat time with the hand while singing.

[10] *I.e.*, a multitude of good things.

like lotus flowers," saith the little one, "and all manner of things," saith the . . . commander, "and all manner of herbs," say the children. Eating bringeth forgetfulness of him.[11] Good things are scattered over the dwelling. . . .

When the Nile floodeth, offering is made to thee, cattle are slaughtered for thee, a great oblation is made for thee. Birds are fattened for thee, antelopes are hunted for thee in the desert. Good is recompensed unto thee.

Offering is also made to every other god, even as is done for the Nile, with incense, oxen, cattle, and birds (upon) the flame. The Nile hath made him his cave in Thebes, and his name shall be known no more in the underworld. . . .

All ye men, extol the Nine Gods, and stand in awe of the might which his son, the Lord of All, hath displayed, even he that maketh green the Two River-banks. Thou art verdant, O Nile, thou art verdant. He that maketh man to live on his cattle, and his cattle on the meadow! Thou art verdant, thou art verdant; O Nile, thou art verdant.

---

[11] The Nile.

Hymn to the Sun

Thy dawning is beautiful in the horizon of heaven,
O living Aton,[1] Beginning of life!
When thou risest in the eastern horizon of heaven,
Thou fillest every land with thy beauty;
For thou art beautiful, great, glittering, high over the earth;
Thy rays, they encompass the lands, even all thou hast made.
Thou art Rē, and thou hast carried them all away captive;
Thou bindest them by thy love.
Though thou art afar, thy rays are on earth;
Though thou art on high, thy footprints are the day.

When thou settest in the western horizon of heaven,
The world is in darkness like the dead.
They sleep in their chambers,
Their heads are wrapt up,
Their nostrils stopped, and none seeth the other.
Stolen are all their things, that are under their heads,
While they know it not.
Every lion cometh forth from his den,
All serpents, they sting.
Darkness reigns,
The world is in silence,
He that made them has gone to rest in his horizon.

Bright is the earth,
When thou risest in the horizon,
When thou shinest as Aton by day.
The darkness is banished,
When thou sendest forth thy rays,
The Two Lands[2] are in daily festivity,
Awake and standing upon their feet,

For thou hast raised them up.
Their limbs bathed, they take their clothing;
Their arms uplifted in adoration to thy dawning.
Then in all the world, they do their work.

All cattle rest upon their herbage,
All trees and plants flourish,
The birds flutter in their marshes.
Their wings uplifted in adoration to thee.
All the sheep dance upon their feet,
All winged things fly,
They live when thou hast shone upon them.

The barques sail up-stream and down-stream alike.
Every highway is open because thou hast dawned.
The fish in the river leap up before thee,
And thy rays are in the midst of the great sea.

Thou art he who createst the man-child in woman,
Who makest seed in man,
Who giveth life to the son in the body of his mother,
Who soothest him that he may not weep,
A nurse even in the womb.
Who giveth breath to animate every one that he maketh.
When he cometh forth from the body,
. . . on the day of his birth,
Thou openest his mouth in speech,
Thou suppliest his necessities.

When the chicklet crieth in the eggshell,
Thou givest him breath therein, to preserve him alive.
When thou hast perfected him
That he may pierce the egg,
He cometh forth from the egg,

---

[1] [One of the names given to the sun-god—*Ed.*]

[2] [Upper and Lower Egypt—*Ed.*]

Trans. James H. Breasted.

10

To chirp with all his might;
He runneth about upon his two feet,
When he hath come forth therefrom.
How manifold are all thy works!
They are hidden from before us,
O thou sole god, whose powers no other
    possesseth.
Thou didst create the earth according
    to thy desire.
While thou wast alone:
Men, all cattle large and small,
All that are upon the earth,
That go about upon their feet;
All that are on high,
That fly with their wings.
The countries of Syria and Nubia,
The land of Egypt;
Thou settest every man in his place,
Thou suppliest their necessities.
Every one has his possessions,
And his days are reckoned.
Their tongues are divers in speech,
Their forms likewise and their skins,
For thou divider, hast divided the peo-
    ples.

Thou makest the Nile in the Nether
    World,
Thou bringest it at thy desire, to pre-
    serve the people alive.
O lord of them all, when feebleness is
    in them,
O lord of every house, who risest for
    them,
O son of day, the fear of every distant
    land,
Thou makest also their life.
Thou has set a Nile in heaven,
That it may fall for them,
Making floods upon the mountains, like
    the great sea;
And watering their fields among their
    towns.
How excellent are thy designs, O lord
    of eternity!
The Nile in heaven is for the strangers,
And for the cattle of every land, that go
    upon their feet;
But the Nile, it cometh from the Nether
    World for Egypt.

Thus thy rays nourish every garden,
When thou risest they live, and grow by
    thee.

Thou makest the seasons, in order to
    create all thy works:
Winter bringing them coolness,
And the heat of summer likewise.
Thou hast made the distant heaven to
    rise therein,
In order to behold all that thou didst
    make,
While thou wast alone,
Rising in thy form as living Aton,
Dawning, shining afar off and return-
    ing.
Thou makest the beauty of form,
    through thyself alone.
Cities, towns and settlements,
On highway or on river,
All eyes see thee before them.
For thou art Aton of the day over the
    earth.

Thou art in my heart,
There is no other that knoweth thee,
Save thy son Ikhnaton.
Thou hast made him wise in thy designs
And in thy might.
The world is in thy hand,
Even as thou hast made them.
When thou hast risen, they live:
When thou settest, they die.
For thou art duration, beyond thy mere
    limbs,
By thee man liveth,
And their eyes look upon thy beauty.
Until thou settest.
All labour is laid aside,
When thou settest in the west;
When thou risest, they are made to grow
. . . for the king.

Since thou didst establish the earth,
Thou has raised them up for thy son,
Who came forth from thy limbs,
The king, living in truth,
The lord of the Two Lands Nefer-khe-
    pru-Rë, Wan-Rë,
The son of Rë, living in truth, lord of
    diadems,
Ikhnaton, whose life is long;
And for the great royal wife, his be-
    loved,
Mistress of the Two Lands, Nefer nefru
    aton, Nofretete,
Living and flourishing for ever and
    ever.

The Code of Hammurabi

At the turn of the twentieth century a French archeological expedition unearthed one of the most magnificent finds of our times—a stele, or tablet, on which was inscribed the entire Code of Hammurabi. Found at Susa in western Persia where it had been taken by an Elamite king as war booty in the twelfth century B.C., the stele is of stone, about eight feet tall, and contains approximately thirty-six hundred lines of writing. Although the stone has been damaged slightly, most of the writing, in cuneiform script, is legible. At the top of the stele is a well-executed carving showing Hammurabi receiving the laws from Marduk, the Sun God of Babylonia. After its discovery the stele was transported to Paris and placed in the Louvre, where it remains on display.

Hammurabi, an Amorite (a tribe occupying the middle Euphrates valley), established himself in power and founded the city of Babylon along the lower river, then reigned as king of Babylonia for forty-three years, from 1728 to 1686 B.C. Although he was responsible for formulating and publishing the Code, he did not originate the laws that it contains. Rather, the Code is a compilation and revision of older laws of the Sumerians and Akkadians (tribes occupying the same general region). These deal with almost every facet of life in the ancient Near East, including marriage and the family, the relationships among social classes, the regulations of land and business, labor relations, military service, religion, and crime. They are important not only for the light they shed on the society of that time but also for the influence they had on later Near Eastern law codes. In this regard it is instructive to compare the Code with the Mosaic law as it appears in the Old Testament. Both reveal, particularly in their sanction of the *lex talionis*, something of the cruelty and violence that was endemic throughout the ancient world.

For the selection that follows we have chosen the most important legal provisions of the Code, eliminating regulations of minor significance.

The Code of Hammurabi

1. If a seignior[1] accused another seignior and brought a charge of murder against him, but has not proved it, his accuser shall be put to death.

2. If a seignior brought a charge of sorcery against another seignior, but has not proved it, the one against whom the charge of sorcery was brought, upon going to the river,[2] shall throw himself into the river, and if the river has then overpowered him, his accuser shall take over his estate; if the river has shown that seignior to be innocent and he has accordingly come forth safe, the one who brought the charge of sorcery against him shall be put to death, while the one who threw himself into the river shall take over the estate of his accuser.

3. If a seignior came forward with false testimony in a case, and has not proved the word which he spoke, if that case was a case involving life, that seignior shall be put to death.

4. If he came forward with false testimony concerning grain or money, he shall bear the penalty of that case.

5. If a judge gave a judgment, rendered a decision, deposited a sealed document, but later has altered his judgment, they shall prove that the judge altered the judgment which he gave and he shall pay twelvefold the claim which holds in that case; furthermore, they shall expel him in the assembly from his seat of judgment and he shall never again sit with the judges in a case.

6. If a seignior stole the property of church or state, that seignior shall be put to death; also the one who received the stolen goods from his hand shall be put to death.

• • •

14. If a seignior has stolen the young son of another seignior, he shall be put to death.

15. If a seignior has helped either a male slave of the state or a female slave of the state or a male slave of a private citizen or a female slave of a private citizen to escape through the city-gate, he shall be put to death.

16. If a seignior has harbored in his house either a fugitive male or female slave belonging to the state or to a private citizen and has not brought him forth at the summons

---

[1] *awēlum* seems to be used in at least three senses: (1) sometimes to indicate a man of the higher class, a noble; (2) sometimes a free man of any class, high or low; and (3) occasionally a man of any class, from king to slave. I follow the ambiguity of the original and use the rather general term "seignior," as employed in Italian and Spanish, to indicate any free man of standing. [This and following notes are by the translator—*Ed.*]

[2] The river (the Euphrates) as judge in the case was regarded as god.

James B. Pritchard, ed. *Ancient Near East: An Anthology of Texts and Pictures.* Copyright © 1958 by Princeton University Press. Scattered excerpts reprinted by permission of Princeton University Press.

of the police, that householder shall be put to death.

• • •

22. If a seignior committed robbery and has been caught, that seignior shall be put to death.

23. If the robber has not been caught, the robbed seignior shall set forth the particulars regarding his lost property in the presence of god, and the city and governor, in whose territory and district the robbery was committed, shall make good to him his lost property.

• • •

25. If fire broke out in a seignior's house and a seignior, who went to extinguish it, cast his eye on the goods of the owner of the house and has appropriated the goods of the owner of the house, that seignior shall be thrown into that fire.

26. If either a private soldier or a commissary,[3] whose despatch on a campaign of the king was ordered, did not go or he hired a substitute and has sent him in his place, that soldier or commissary shall be put to death, while the one who was hired by him shall take over the estate.

27. In the case of either a private soldier or a commissary who was carried off while in the armed service of the king, if after his disappearance they gave his field and

orchard to another and he has looked after his feudal obligations—if he has returned and reached his city, they shall restore his field and orchard to him and he shall himself look after his feudal obligations.

28. In the case of either a private soldier or a commissary, who was carried off while in the armed service of the king, if his son is able to look after the feudal obligations, the field and orchard shall be given to him and he shall look after the feudal obligations of his father.

29. If his son is so young that he is not able to look after the feudal obligations of his father, one-third of the field and orchard shall be given to his mother in order that his mother may rear him.

• • •

34. If either a sergeant or a captain has appropriated the household goods of a soldier, has wronged a soldier, has let a soldier for hire, has abandoned a soldier to a superior in a lawsuit, has appropriated the grant which the king gave to a soldier, that sergeant or captain shall be put to death.

35. If a seignior has bought from the hand of a soldier the cattle or sheep which the king gave to the soldier, he shall forefeit his money.

36. In no case is the field, orchard, or house belonging to a soldier, a commissary, or a feudatory salable.

• • •

42. If a seignior rented a field for cultivation, but has not produced grain in the field, they shall prove that he did no work on the

---

[3] The exact meaning of the two military terms used here, *redum* and *ba'irum*, is uncertain. The former means literally "follower" and is regularly used for the ordinary foot-soldier; the latter means literally "fisher, hunter," hence "commissary" here.

field and he shall give grain to the owner of the field on the basis of those adjoining it.

• • •

45. If a seignior let his field to a tenant and has already received the rent of his field, and later Adad has inundated the field or a flood has ravaged it, the loss shall be the tenant's.

46. If he has not received the rent of the field, whether he let the field for one-half or one-third the crop, the tenant and the owner of the field shall divide proportionately the grain which is produced in the field.

• • •

53. If a seignior was too lazy to make the dike of his field strong and did not make his dike strong and a break has opened up in his dike and he has accordingly let the water ravage the farmland, the seignior in whose dike the break was opened shall make good the grain that he let get destroyed.

54. If he is not able to make good the grain, they shall sell him and his goods, and the farmers whose grain the water carried off shall divide the proceeds.

• • •

98. If a seignior gave money to another seignior for a partnership, they shall divide equally in the presence of god the profit or loss which was incurred.

99. If a merchant lent money at interest to a trader for the purpose of trading and making purchases and sent him out on the road, the

trader shall . . . on the road the money which was entrusted to him.

100. If he has realized a profit where he went, he shall write down the interest on the full amount of money that he borrowed and they shall count up the days against him and he shall repay his merchant.

101. If he has not realized a profit where he went, the trader shall repay to the merchant double the money that he borrowed.

102. If a merchant has lent money to a trader as a favor and he has experienced a loss where he went, he shall pay back the principal of the money to the merchant.

103. If, when he went on the road, an enemy has made him give up whatever he was carrying, the trader shall so affirm by god and then he shall go free.

• • •

106. If a trader borrowed money from a merchant and has then disputed the fact with his merchant, that merchant in the presence of god and witnesses shall prove that the trader borrowed the money and the trader shall pay to the merchant threefold the full amount of money that he borrowed.

107. When a merchant entrusted something to a trader and the trader has returned to his merchant whatever the merchant gave him, if the merchant has then disputed with him whatever the trader gave him, that trader shall prove it against the merchant in the presence of god and witnesses and the merchant shall pay to the trader sixfold whatever he received because he had a dispute with his trader.

108. If a woman wine seller, instead of receiving grain for the price

of a drink, has received money by the large weight and so has made the value of the drink less than the value of the grain, they shall prove it against that wine seller and throw her into the water.

109. If outlaws have congregated in the establishment of a woman wine seller and she has not arrested those outlaws and did not take them to the palace, that wine seller shall be put to death.

110. If a hierodule,[4] a nun, who is not living in a convent, has opened the door of a wineshop or has entered a wineshop for a drink, they shall burn that woman.

• • •

120. If a seignior deposited his grain in another seignior's house for storage and a loss has then occurred at the granary or the owner of the house opened the storage-room and took grain or he has denied completely the receipt of the grain which was stored in his house, the owner of the grain shall set forth the particulars regarding his grain in the presence of god and the owner of the house shall give to the owner of the grain double the grain that he took.

• • •

122. If a seignior wishes to give silver, gold, or any sort of thing to another seignior for safekeeping, he shall show to witnesses the full amount that he wishes to give, ar-

range the contracts, and then commit it to safekeeping.

123. If he gave it for safekeeping without witnesses and contracts and they have denied its receipt to him at the place where he made the deposit, that case is not subject to claim.

124. If a seignior gave silver, gold, or any sort of thing for safekeeping to another seignior in the presence of witnesses and he has denied the fact to him, they shall prove it against that seignior and he shall pay double whatever he denied.

125. If a seignior deposited property of his for safekeeping and at the place where he made the deposit his property has disappeared along with the property of the owner of the house, either through breaking in or through scaling the wall, the owner of the house, who was so careless that he let whatever was given to him for safekeeping get lost, shall make it good and make restitution to the owner of the goods, while the owner of the house shall make a thorough search for his lost property and take it from its thief.

126. If the seignior's property was not lost, but he has declared, "My property is lost," thus deceiving his city council, his city council shall set forth the facts regarding him in the presence of god, that his property was not lost, and he shall give to his city council double whatever he laid claim to.

• • •

128. If a seignior acquired a wife, but did not draw up the contracts for her, that woman is no wife.

---

[4] The exact meaning of the term used here, *nadītum*, is unknown, but it indicates some kind of religious functionary.

129. If the wife of a seignior has been caught while lying with another man, they shall bind them and throw them into the water. If the husband of the woman wishes to spare his wife, then the king in turn may spare his subject.

130. If a seignior bound the betrothed wife of another seignior, who had had no intercourse with a male and was still living in her father's house, and he has lain in her bosom and they have caught him, that seignior shall be put to death, while that woman shall go free.

131. If a seignior's wife was accused by her husband, but she was not caught while lying with another man, she shall make affirmation by god and return to her house.

132. If the finger was pointed at the wife of a seignior because of another man, but she has not been caught while lying with the other man, she shall throw herself into the river[5] for the sake of her husband.

• • •

138. If a seignior wishes to divorce his wife who did not bear him children, he shall give her money to the full amount of her marriage-price and he shall also make good to her the dowry which she brought from her father's house and then he may divorce her.

139. If there was no marriage-price, he shall give her one mina of silver as the divorce-settlement.

140. If he is a peasant, he shall give her one-third mina of silver.

141. If a seignior's wife, who was living in the house of the seignior, has made up her mind to leave in order that she may engage in business, thus neglecting her house and humiliating her husband, they shall prove it against her; and if her husband has then decided on her divorce, he may divorce her, with nothing to be given her as her divorce-settlement upon her departure. If her husband has not decided on her divorce, her husband may marry another woman, with the former woman living in the house of her husband like a maidservant.

142. If a woman so hated her husband that she has declared, "You may not have me," her record shall be investigated at her city council; and if she was careful and was not at fault, even though her husband has been going out and disparaging her greatly, that woman, without incurring any blame at all, may take her dowry and go off to her father's house.

143. If she was not careful, but was a gadabout, thus neglecting her house and humiliating her husband, they shall throw that woman into the water.

• • •

150. If a seignior, upon presenting a field, orchard, house, or goods to his wife, left a sealed document with her, her children may not enter a claim against her after the death of her husband, since the mother may give her inheritance to that son of hers whom she likes, but she may not give it to an outsider.

151. If a woman, who was living in a seignior's house, having made a contract with her husband that a creditor of her husband may not distrain her, has then had him deliver a written statement; if there

---

[5] *I.e.*, submit to the water ordeal, with the river as divine judge.

was a debt against that seignior before he married that woman, his creditors may not distrain his wife; also, if there was a debt against that woman before she entered the seignior's house her creditors may not distrain her husband.

152. If a debt has developed against them after that woman entered the seignior's house, both of them shall be answerable to the merchant.

153. If a seignior's wife has brought about the death of her husband because of another man, they shall impale that woman on stakes.

154. If a seignior has had intercourse with his daughter, they shall make that seignior leave the city.

155. If a seignior chose a bride for his son and his son had intercourse with her, but later he himself has lain in her bosom and they have caught him, they shall bind that seignior and throw him into the water.

156. If a seignior chose a bride for his son and his son did not have intercourse with her, but he himself has lain in her bosom, he shall pay to her one-half mina of silver and he shall also make good to her whatever she brought from her father's house in order that the man of her choice may marry her.

157. If a seignior has lain in the bosom of his mother after the death of his father, they shall burn both of them.

•   •   •

159. If a seignior, who had the betrothal-gift brought to the house of his prospective father-in-law and paid the marriage-price, has then fallen in love with another woman and has said to his prospective fa-

ther-in-law, "I will not marry your daughter," the father of the daughter shall keep whatever was brought to him.

160. If a seignior had the betrothal-gift brought to the house of the prospective father-in-law and paid the marriage-price, and the father of the daughter has then said, "I will not give my daughter to you," he shall pay back double the full amount that was brought to him.

•   •   •

162. If, when a seignior acquired a wife, she bore him children and that woman has then gone to her fate, her father may not lay claim to her dowry, since her dowry belongs to her children.

163. If a seignior acquired a wife and that woman has gone to her fate without providing him with children, if his father-in-law has then returned to him the marriage-price which that seignior brought to the house of his father-in-law, her husband may not lay claim to the dowry of that woman, since her dowry belongs to her father's house.

•   •   •

168. If a seignior, having made up his mind to disinherit his son, has said to the judges, "I wish to disinherit my son," the judges shall investigate his record, and if the son did not incur wrong grave enough to be disinherited, the father may not disinherit his son.

169. If he has incurred wrong against his father grave enough to be disinherited, they shall let him off the first time; if he has incurred grave wrong a second time, the father may disinherit his son.

170. When a seignior's first wife bore him children and his female slave also bore him children, if the father during his lifetime has ever said "My children!" to the children whom the slave bore him, thus having counted them with the children of the first wife, after the father has gone to his fate, the children of the first wife and the children of the slave shall share equally in the goods of the paternal estate, with the first-born, the son of the first wife, receiving a preferential share.

171. However, if the father during his lifetime has never said "My children!" to the children whom the slave bore him, after the father has gone to his fate, the children of the slave may not share in the goods of the paternal estate along with the children of the first wife; freedom for the slave and her children shall be effected, with the children of the first wife having no claim at all against the children of the slave for service; the first wife shall take her dowry and the marriage-gift which her husband, upon giving it to her, wrote down on a tablet for her, and living in the home of her husband, she shall have the usufruct of it as long as she lives, without ever selling it, since her heritage belongs to her children.

·   ·   ·

175. If either a palace or a private citizen's slave married the daughter of a seignior and she has borne children, the owner of the slave may not lay claim to the children of the seignior's daughter for service.

176. Furthermore, if a palace slave or a private citizen's slave married the daughter of a seignior and when he married her she entered the house of the palace slave or the private citizen's slave with the dowry from her father's house and after they were joined together they set up a household and so acquired goods, but later either the palace slave or the private citizen's slave has gone to his fate, the seignior's daughter shall take her dowry, but they shall divide into two parts whatever her husband and she acquired after they were joined together and the owner of the slave shall take one-half, with the seignior's daughter taking one-half for her children.

176a. If the seignior's daughter has no dowry, they shall divide into two parts whatever her husband and she acquired after they were joined together and the owner of the slave shall take one-half, with the seignior's daughter taking one-half for her children.

177. If a widow, whose children are minors, has made up her mind to enter the house of another, she may not enter without the consent of the judges; when she wishes to enter the house of another, the judges shall investigate the condition of her former husband's estate and they shall entrust her former husband's estate to her later husband and that woman and they shall have them deposit a tablet to the effect that they will look after the estate and also rear the young children, without ever selling the household goods, since the purchaser who purchases the household goods of a widow's children shall forfeit his money, with the goods reverting to their owner.

·   ·   ·

181. If a father dedicated his

daughter to deity as a hierodule, a sacred prostitute, or a devotee and did not present a dowry to her, after the father has gone to his fate, she shall receive as her share in the goods of the paternal estate her one-third patrimony, but she shall have only the usufruct of it as long as she lives, since her heritage belongs to her brothers.

.   .   .

185. If a seignior adopted a boy in his own name and has reared him, that foster child may never be reclaimed.

186. If a seignior, upon adopting a boy, seeks out his father and mother when he had taken him, that foster child may return to his father's house.

.   .   .

188. If a member of the artisan class took a son as a foster child and has taught him his handicraft, he may never be reclaimed.

189. If he has not taught him his handicraft, that foster child may return to his father's house.

.   .   .

195. If a son has struck his father, they shall cut off his hand.

196. If a seignior has destroyed the eye of a member of the aristocracy, they shall destroy his eye.

197. If he has broken another seignior's bone, they shall break his bone.

198. If he has destroyed the eye of a commoner or broken the bone of a commoner, he shall pay one mina of silver.

199. If he has destroyed the eye

of a seignior's slave or broken the bone of a seignior's slave, he shall pay one-half his value.

200. If a seignior has knocked out a tooth of a seignior of his own rank, they shall knock out his tooth.

201. If he has knocked out a commoner's tooth, he shall pay one-third mina of silver.

.   .   .

209. If a seignior struck another seignior's daughter and has caused her to have a miscarriage, he shall pay ten shekels of silver for her fetus.

210. If that woman has died, they shall put his daughter to death.

.   .   .

215. If a physician performed a major operation on a seignior with a bronze lancet and has saved the seignior's life, or he opened up the eye-socket of a seignior with a bronze lancet and has saved the seignior's eye, he shall receive ten shekels of silver.

.   .   .

218. If a physician performed a major operation on a seignior with a bronze lancet and has caused the seignior's death, or he opened up the eye-socket of a seignior and has destroyed the seignior's eye, they shall cut off his hand.

.   .   .

224. If a veterinary surgeon performed a major operation on either an ox or an ass and has saved its life, the owner of the ox or ass shall

give to the surgeon one-sixth shekel of silver as his fee.

225. If he performed a major operation on an ox or an ass and has caused its death, he shall give to the owner of the ox or ass one-fourth its value.

226. If a brander cut off the slave-mark of a slave not his own without the consent of the owner of the slave, they shall cut off the hand of that brander.

• • •

229. If a builder constructed a house for a seignior, but did not make his work strong, with the result that the house which he built collapsed and so has caused the death of the owner of the house, that builder shall be put to death.

230. If it has caused the death of a son of the owner of the house, they shall put the son of that builder to death.

231. If it has caused the death of a slave of the owner of the house, he shall give slave for slave to the owner of the house.

232. If it has destroyed goods, he shall make good whatever it destroyed; also, because he did not make the house strong which he built and it collapsed, he shall reconstruct the house which collapsed at his own expense.

• • •

236. If a seignior let his boat for hire to a boatman and the boatman was so careless that he has sunk or wrecked the boat, the boatman shall make good the boat to the owner of the boat.

237. When a seignior hired a boatman and a boat and loaded it with grain, wool, oil, dates, or any kind of freight, if that boatman was so careless that he has sunk the boat and lost what was in it as well, the boatman shall make good the boat which he sank and whatever he lost that was in it.

• • •

244. If a seignior hired an ox or an ass and a lion has killed it in the open, the loss shall be its owner's.

245. If a seignior hired an ox and has caused its death through carelessness or through beating, he shall make good ox for ox to the owner of the ox.

• • •

249. If a seignior hired an ox and god struck it and it has died, the seignior who hired the ox shall so affirm by god and then he shall go free.

250. If an ox, when it was walking along the street, gored a seignior to death, the case is not subject to claim.

251. If a seignior's ox was a gorer and his city council made it known to him that it was a gorer, but he did not pad its horns or tie up his ox, and that ox gored to death a member of the aristocracy, he shall give one-half mina of silver.

• • •

265. If a shepherd, to whom cattle or sheep were given to pasture, became unfaithful and hence has altered the cattlemark or has sold them, they shall prove it against him and he shall make good in cattle and sheep to their owner tenfold what he stole.

266. If a visitation of god has occurred in a sheepfold or a lion has made a kill, the shepherd shall prove himself innocent in the presence of god, but the owner of the sheepfold shall receive from him the animal stricken in the fold.

267. If the shepherd was careless and has let lameness develop in the fold, the shepherd shall make good in cattle and sheep the loss through the lameness which he let develop in the fold and give them to their owner.

•   •   •

278. If a seignior purchased a male or female slave and when his month was not yet complete, epilepsy attacked him, he shall return him to his seller and the purchaser shall get back the money which he paid out.

279. If a seignior purchased a male or female slave and he has then received a claim against him, his seller shall be responsible for the claim.

280. If a seignior has purchased in a foreign land the male or female slave of another seignior and when he has arrived home the owner of the male or female slave has identified either his male or his female slave, if that male and female slave are natives of the land, their freedom shall be effected without any money payment.

281. If they are natives of another land, the purchaser shall state in the presence of god what money he paid out and the owner of the male or female slave shall give to the merchant the money he paid out and thus redeem his male or female slave.

282. If a male slave has said to his master, "You are not my master," his master shall prove him to be his slave and cut off his ear.

The Old Testament

The Old Testament unquestionably ranks among the greatest creations of the mind of man. That it should have been produced at all is extraordinary; that it was the work of a weak, relatively insignificant nation which was regularly exploited and overrun by its more powerful neighbors is well-nigh incredible. Although we usually think of the Old Testament as a religious document, it is much more than that. In its pages are recorded, in infinite variety and rich detail, the full range of the historical experience of a remarkable people.

Because it is impossible to encompass the wealth of the Old Testament in a selection of a length appropriate for this book, we have chosen for illustration two of its main themes. These themes—the belief in one God (monotheism) and the concept of God as a moral being standing in definite moral relationships to humanity—are probably the most important contributions made by the ancient Jewish people to Western civilization. That the Old Testament books present views on these two subjects that are often inconsistent with each other should be neither surprising nor disconcerting, for these books reveal the gradually developing moral and religious consciousness of their authors. It is particularly instructive to compare one of the most mature expressions of moral consciousness in the ancient world as it appears in the selection from Ezekiel with the doctrine of "original sin" as it is first stated by St. Paul in his Epistle to the Romans and later developed by the Christian theologians St. Augustine and John Calvin. The source for this Christian doctrine of original sin is found in the book of Genesis, with its account of God's creation of the universe, his creation of Adam and Eve in his own image, his placing them in the idyllic Garden of Eden, and of their sin of disobedience against him. A second moral problem of the most profound significance is found in the Book of Job. The issue concerns the question of divine justice. Why, Job asks, should the wicked of this world so often prosper and the just suffer? It is interesting, too, to note the contrast between Hebraic and Greek religious attitudes as revealed in the Job story and in the myths of the Greek heroes. Whereas Job suffered in patience every plague from heaven, submitting his will to divine judgment, the mythical heroes of Greece were in constant rebellion against the decrees from Olympus.

The following selections have been taken from the King James Version of the Bible; however, their form has been altered slightly to make them more readable.

Genesis

In the beginning God created the heaven and the earth. And the earth was without form, and void; and darkness was upon the face of the deep. And the Spirit of God moved upon the face of the waters. And God said, "Let there be light": and there was light. And God saw the light, that it was good and God divided the light from the darkness. And God called the light Day, and the darkness he called Night. And the evening and the morning were the first day.

And God said, "Let there be a firmament in the midst of the waters, and let it divide the waters from the waters." And God made the firmament, and divided the waters which were under the firmament from the waters which were above the firmament: and it was so. And God called the firmament Heaven. And the evening and the morning were the second day.

And God said, "Let the waters under the heaven be gathered together unto one place, and let the dry land appear": and it was so. And God called the dry land Earth; and the gathering together of the waters called he Seas: and God saw that it was good. And God said, "Let the earth bring forth grass, the herb yielding seed, and the fruit tree yielding fruit after his kind, whose seed is in itself, upon the earth": and it was so. And the earth brought forth grass, and herb yielding seed after his kind, and the tree yielding fruit, whose seed was in itself, after his kind: and God saw that it was good. And the evening and the morning were the third day.

And God said, "Let there be lights in the firmament of the heaven to divide the day from the night; and let them be for signs, and for seasons, and for days, and years: and let them be for lights in the firmament of the heaven to give light upon the earth": and it was so. And God made two great lights; the greater light to rule the day, and the lesser light to rule the night: he made the stars also. And God set them in the firmament of the heaven to give light upon the earth. And to rule over the day and over the night, and to divide the light from the darkness: and God saw that it was good. And the evening and the morning were the fourth day.

And God said, "Let the waters bring forth abundantly the moving creature that hath life, and fowl that may fly above the earth in the open firmament of heaven." And God created great whales, and every living creature that moveth, which the waters brought forth abundantly, after their kind, and every winged fowl after his kind: and God saw that it was good. And God blessed them, saying, "Be fruitful, and multiply, and fill the water in the seas, and let fowl multiply in the earth." And the evening and the morning were the fifth day.

And God said, "Let the earth bring forth the living creature after

Chapters 1, 2, 3.

his kind, cattle, and creeping thing, and beast of the earth after his kind": and it was so. And God made the beast of the earth after his kind, and cattle after their kind, and every thing that creepeth upon the earth after his kind: and God saw that it was good.

And God said, "Let us make man in our image, after our likeness: and let them have dominion over the fish of the sea, and over the fowl of the air, and over the cattle, and over all the earth, and over every creeping thing that creepeth upon the earth." So God created man in his own image, in the image of God created he him: male and female created he them. And God blessed them, and God said unto them, "Be fruitful, and multiply, and replenish the earth, and subdue it: and have dominion over the fish of the sea, and over the fowl of the air, and over every living thing that moveth upon the earth."

And God said, "Behold, I have given you every herb bearing seed, which is upon the face of all the earth, and every tree, in the which is the fruit of a tree yielding seed; to you it shall be for meat. And to every beast of the earth, and to every fowl of the air, and to every thing that creepeth upon the earth, wherein there is life, I have given every green herb for meat": and it was so. And God saw every thing that he had made, and, behold, it was very good. And the evening and the morning were the sixth day.

Thus the heavens and the earth were finished, and all the host of them. And on the seventh day God ended his work which he had made; and he rested on the seventh day from all his work which he had made. And God blessed the seventh day, and sanctified it: because that in it he had rested from all his work which God created and made.

These are the generations of the heavens and of the earth when they were created, in the day that the LORD God made the earth and the heavens. And every plant of the field before it was in the earth, and every herb of the field before it grew: for the LORD God had not caused it to rain upon the earth, and there was not a man to till the ground. But there went up a mist from the earth, and watered the whole face of the ground. And the LORD God formed man of the dust of the ground, and breathed into his nostrils the breath of life; and man became a living soul.

And the LORD God planted a garden eastward in Eden; and there he put the man whom he had formed. And out of the ground made the LORD God to grow every tree that is pleasant to the sight, and good for food; the tree of life also in the midst of the garden, and the tree of knowledge of good and evil. And a river went out of Eden to water a garden; and from thence it was parted, and became into four heads. The name of the first is Pison: that is it which compasseth the whole land of Havilah, where there is gold; and the gold of that land is good: there is bdellium and the onyx stone. And the name of the second river is Gihon: the same is it that compasseth the whole land of Ethiopia. And the name of the third river is Hiddekel: that is it which goeth toward the east of Assyria. And the fourth river is Euphrates. And the LORD God took the man, and put him into the garden of Eden to dress it and to keep it. And the LORD God commanded the man, saying, "Of every tree of the garden thou mayest freely eat: But of the tree of the knowledge of good and evil, thou shalt not eat of it: for in the day that thou eatest thereof thou shalt surely die."

And the LORD God said, "It is not good that the man should be alone; I will make an help meet for him." And out of the ground the LORD God formed every beast of the field, and every fowl of the air; and brought them unto Adam to see what he would call them: and whatsoever Adam called every living creature, that was the name thereof. And Adam gave names to all cattle, and to the fowl of the air, and to every beast of the field; but for Adam there was not found an help meet for him. And the LORD God caused a deep sleep to fall upon Adam, and he slept: and he took one of his ribs, and closed up the flesh instead thereof. And the rib, which the LORD God had taken from man, made he a woman, and brought her unto the man. And Adam said, "This is now bone of my bones, and flesh of my flesh: she shall be called Woman, because she was taken out of Man. Therefore shall a man leave his father and his mother, and shall cleave unto his wife: and they shall be one flesh." And they were both naked, the man and his wife, and were not ashamed.

Now the serpent was more subtil than any beast of the field which the LORD God had made. And he said unto the woman, "Yea, hath God said, 'Ye shall not eat of every tree of the garden'?" And the woman said unto the serpent, "We may eat of the fruit of the trees of the garden: But of the fruit of the tree which is in the midst of the garden God hath said, 'Ye shall not eat of it, neither shall ye touch it, lest ye die.'" And the serpent said unto the woman, "Ye shall not surely die: For God doth know that in the day ye eat thereof, then your eyes shall be opened, and ye shall be as gods, knowing good and evil." And when the woman saw that the tree was good for food, and that it was pleasant to the eyes, and a tree to be desired to make one wise, she took of the fruit thereof, and did eat, and gave also unto her husband with her and he did eat. And the eyes of them both were opened, and they knew that they were naked; and they sewed fig leaves together, and made themselves aprons.

And they heard the voice of the LORD God walking in the garden in the cool of the day: and Adam and his wife hid themselves from the presence of the LORD God amongst the trees of the garden. And the LORD God called unto Adam, and said unto him, "Where art thou?" And he said, "I heard thy voice in the garden, and I was afraid, because I was naked; and I hid myself." And he said, "Who told thee that thou wast naked? Hast thou eaten of the tree, whereof I commanded thee that thou shouldest not eat?" And the man said, "The woman whom thou gavest to be with me, she gave me of the tree, and I did eat. " And the LORD God said unto the woman, "What is this that thou hast done?" And the woman said, "The serpent beguiled me, and I did eat." And the LORD God said unto the serpent, "Because thou hast done this, thou art cursed above all cattle, and above every beast of the field; upon thy belly shalt thou go, and dust shalt thou eat all the days of thy life: And I will put enmity between thee and the woman, and between thy seed and her seed; it shall bruise thy head, and thou shalt bruise his heel." Unto the woman he said, "I will greatly multiply thy sorrow and thy conception; in sorrow thou shalt bring forth children; and thy desire shall be to thy husband, and he shall rule over thee." And unto Adam he said, "Because thou hast harkened unto the voice of thy wife, and hast eaten of the tree, of which I commanded thee, saying 'Thou shalt not eat of it': cursed is the ground for thy sake; in sorrow shalt thou eat of it all the days of thy life; thorns also and thistles shall it bring forth to thee; and thou shalt eat the herb of the field; in the sweat of thy face shalt thou eat bread, till thou return unto the ground; for out of it wast thou taken: for dust thou art, and unto dust shalt thou return." And Adam called his wife's name Eve; because she was the mother of all living. Unto Adam also and to his wife did the LORD God make coats of skins, and clothed them.

And the LORD God said, "Behold, the man is become as one of us, to know good and evil: and now, lest he put forth his hand, and take also of the tree of life, and eat, and live for ever": Therefore the LORD God sent him forth from the garden of Eden, to till the ground from whence he was taken. So he drove out the man; and he placed at the east of the garden of Eden Cherubim and a flaming sword which turned every way, to keep the way of the tree of life.

Exodus

•   •   •

In the third month, when the children of Israel were gone forth out of the land of Egypt, the same day came they into the wilderness of Sinai. For they were departed from Rephidim, and were come to the desert of Sinai, and had pitched in the wilderness; and there Israel camped before the mount. And Moses went up unto God, and the LORD called unto him out of the mountain, saying, "Thus shalt thou say to the house of Jacob, and tell the children of Israel; 'Ye have seen what I did unto the Egyptians, and how I bare you on eagles' wings, and brought you unto myself. Now, therefore, if ye will obey my voice indeed, and keep my covenant, then ye shall be a peculiar treasure unto me above all people: for all the earth is mine: And ye be unto me a kingdom of priests, and an holy nation.' These are the words which thou shalt speak unto the children of Israel."

And Moses came and called for the elders of the people, and laid before their faces all these words which the LORD commanded him. And all the people answered together, and said, "All that the LORD

Chapters 19; 20:1–17; 21:1–25.

hath spoken we will do." And Moses returned the words of the people unto the LORD. And the LORD said unto Moses, "Lo, I come unto thee in a thick cloud, that the people may hear when I speak with thee, and believe thee for ever." And Moses told the words of the people unto the LORD.

And the LORD said unto Moses, "Go unto the people, and sanctify them to day and to morrow, and let them wash their clothes. And be ready against the third day: for the third day the LORD will come down in the sight of all the people upon mount Sinai. And thou shalt set bounds unto the people round about, saying 'Take heed to yourselves, that ye go not up into the mount, or touch the border of it: whosoever toucheth the mount shall be surely put to death: There shall not an hand touch it, but he shall surely be stoned, or shot through; whether it be beast or man, it shall not live: when the trumpet soundeth long, they shall come up to the mount.'"

And Moses went down from the mount unto the people, and sanctified the people; and they washed their clothes. And he said unto the people, "Be ready against the third day: come not at your wives."

And it came to pass on the third day in the morning, that there were thunders and lightnings, and a thick cloud upon the mount, and the voice of the trumpet exceeding loud; so that all the people that was in the camp trembled. And Moses brought forth the people out of the camp to meet with God; and they stood at the nether part of the mount. And mount Sinai was altogether on a smoke, because the LORD descended upon it in fire:

and the smoke thereof ascended as the smoke of a furnace, and the whole mount quaked greatly. And when the voice of the trumpet sounded long, and waxed louder and louder, Moses spake and God answered him by a voice. And the LORD came down upon the mount Sinai, on the top of the mount: and the LORD called Moses up to the top of the mount; and Moses went up. And the LORD said unto Moses, "Go down, charge the people, lest they break through unto the LORD to gaze, and many of them perish. Let the priests also, which come near to the LORD, sanctify themselves, lest the LORD break forth upon them." And Moses said unto the LORD, "The people cannot come up to mount Sinai: for thou chargest us, saying, 'Set bounds about the mount, and sanctify it.'" And the LORD said unto him, "Away, get thee down, and thou shalt come up, thou, and Aaron with thee: but let not the priests and the people break through to come up unto the LORD, lest he break forth upon them." So Moses went down unto the people, and spake unto them.

And God spake all these words, saying, "I am the LORD thy God, which have brought thee out of the land of Egypt, out of the house of bondage. Thou shalt have no other gods before me. Thou shall not make unto thee any graven image, or any likeness of any thing that is in heaven above, or that is in the earth beneath, or that is in the water under the earth. Thou shalt not bow down thyself to them, nor serve them: for I the LORD thy God am a jealous God, visiting the iniquity of the fathers upon the children unto the third and fourth generation of them that hate me: And shewing mercy unto thousands of them that love me, and keep my commandments. Thou shalt not take the name of the LORD thy God in vain; for the LORD will not hold him guiltless that taketh his name in vain. Remember the sabbath day, to keep it holy. Six days shalt thou labour, and do all thy work: But the seventh day is the sabbath of the LORD thy God; in it thou shalt not do any work, thou, nor thy son, nor thy daughter, thy manservant, nor thy maidservant, nor thy cattle, nor the stranger that is within thy gates. For in six days the LORD made heaven and earth, the sea, and all that in them is, and rested the seventh day: wherefore the LORD blessed the sabbath day, and hallowed it. Honour thy father and thy mother: that thy days may be long upon the land which the LORD thy God giveth thee. Thou shalt not kill. Thou shalt not commit adultery. Thou shalt not steal. Thou shalt not bear false witness against thy neighbour. Thou shalt not covet thy neighbour's house, thou shalt not covet thy neighbour's wife, nor his manservant, nor his maidservant, nor his ox, nor his ass, nor any thing that is thy neighbour's.

• • •

"Now these are the judgments which thou shalt set before them.

"If thou buy an Hebrew servant, six years he shall serve: and in the seventh he shall go out free for nothing. If he came in by himself, he shall go out by himself: if he were married, then his wife shall go out with him. If his master have given him a wife, and she have borne him sons or daughters; the wife and her children shall be her master's, and he shall go out by himself. And if the servant shall plainly say, 'I love my master, my wife, and my children; I will not go out free': Then his master shall bring him unto the judges; he shall also bring him to the door, or unto the door post; and his master shall bore his ear through with an awl; and he shall serve him for ever.

"And if a man sell his daughter to be a maidservant, she shall not go out as the menservants do. If she please not her master, who hath betrothed her to himself, then shall he let her be redeemed: to sell her unto a strange nation he shall have no power, seeing he hath dealt deceitfully with her. And if he have betrothed her unto his son, he shall deal with her after the manner of daughters. If he take him another wife; her food, her raiment, and her duty of marriage, shall he not diminish. And if he do not these three unto her, then shall she go out free without money.

"He that smiteth a man so that he die, shall be surely put to death. And if a man lie not in wait, but God deliver him into his hand; then I will appoint thee a place whither he shall flee. But if a man come presumptuously upon his neighbour to slay him with guile; thou shalt take him from mine altar, and he may die.

"And he that smiteth his father, or his mother, shall be surely put to death.

"And he that stealeth a man, and selleth him, or if he be found in his hand, he shall surely be put to death.

"And he that curseth his father, or his mother, shall surely be put to death.

"And if men strive together, and one smite another with a stone, or with his fist, and he die not, but keepeth his bed: If he rise again, and walk abroad upon his staff, then shall he that smote him be quit: only he shall pay for the loss of his time, and shall cause him to be thoroughly healed.

"And if a man smite his servant, or his maid, with a rod, and he die under his hand; he shall be surely punished. Notwithstanding, if he continue a day or two, he shall not be punished: for he is his money.

"If men strive, and hurt a woman with child, so that her fruit depart from her, and yet no mischief follow: he shall be surely punished, according as the woman's husband will lay upon him; and he shall pay as the judges determine. And if any mischief follow, then thou shalt give life for life. Eye for eye, tooth for tooth, hand for hand, foot for foot. Burning for burning, wound for wound, stripe for stripe."

The First Book of Kings

• • •

And it came to pass after many days, that the word of the LORD came to Elijah in the third year, saying, "Go shew thyself unto Ahab; and I will send rain upon the earth." And Elijah went to shew himself unto Ahab. And there was a sore famine in Samaria. And Ahab called Obadiah, which was the governor of his house. (Now Obadiah feared the LORD greatly: For it was so, when Jezebel cut off the prophets of the LORD, that Obadiah took an hundred prophets, and hid them by fifty in a cave, and fed them with bread and water.) And Ahab said unto Obadiah, "Go into the land, unto all fountains of water, and unto all brooks: peradventure we may find grass to save the horses and mules alive, and we lose not all the beasts." So they divided the land between them to pass throughout it: Ahab went one way by himself, and Obadiah went another way by himself.

And as Obadiah was in the way, behold, Elijah met him: and he knew him, and fell on his face, and said, "Art thou that my lord Elijah?" And he answered him, "I am: go, tell thy lord, 'Behold, Elijah is here.'" And he said, "What have I sinned, that thou wouldest deliver thy servant into the hand of Ahab, to slay me? As the LORD thy God liveth, there is no nation or kingdom, whither my lord hath not sent to seek thee: and when they said, 'He is not there'; he took an oath of the kingdom and nation, that they found thee not. And now thou sayest, 'Go, tell thy lord, "Behold, Elijah is here."' And it shall come to pass, as soon as I am gone from thee, that the spirit of the LORD shall carry thee whither I know not; and so when I come and tell Ahab, and he

Chapter 18:1–45.

cannot find thee, he shall slay me: but I thy servant fear the LORD from my youth. Was it not told my lord what I did when Jezebel slew the prophets of the LORD, how I hid an hundred men of the LORD's prophets by fifty in a cave, and fed them with bread and water? And now thou sayest, 'Go, tell thy lord, "Behold, Elijah is here"'; and he shall slay me."

And Elijah said, "As the LORD of hosts liveth, before whom I stand, I will surely shew myself unto him to day." So Obadiah went to meet Ahab, and told him: and Ahab went to meet Elijah.

And it came to pass, when Ahab saw Elijah, that Ahab said unto him, "Art thou he that troubleth Israel?" And he answered, "I have not troubled Israel; but thou, and thy father's house, in that ye have forsaken the commandments of the LORD, and thou hast followed Baalim. Now therefore send, and gather to me all Israel unto mount Carmel, and the prophets of Baal four hundred and fifty, and the prophets of the groves four hundred, which eat at Jezebel's table."

So Ahab sent unto all the children of Israel, and gathered the prophets together unto mount Carmel. And Elijah came unto all the people, and said, "How long halt ye between two opinions? If the LORD be God, follow him: but if Baal, then follow him." And the people answered him not a word. Then said Elijah unto the people, "I, even I only, remain a prophet of the LORD; but Baal's prophets are four hundred and fifty men. Let them therefore give us two bullocks; and let them choose one bullock for themselves, and cut it in pieces, and lay it on wood, and put no fire under: and I will dress the other bullock, and lay it on wood, and put no fire under: And call ye on the name of your gods, and I will call on the name of the LORD: and the God that answereth by fire, let him be God." And all the people answered and said, "It is well spoken."

And Elijah said unto the prophets of Baal, "Choose you one bullock for yourselves, and dress it first; for ye are many; and call on the name of your gods, but put no fire under." And they took the bullock which was given them, and they dressed it, and called on the name of Baal from morning even until noon, saying, "O Baal, hear us." But there was no voice, nor any that answered. And they leaped upon the alter which was made. And it came to pass at noon, that Elijah mocked them, and said, "Cry aloud: for he is a god; either he is talking, or he is pursuing, or he is in a journey, or peradventure he sleepeth, and must be awaked." And they cried aloud, and cut themselves after their manner with knives and lancets, till the blood gushed out upon them. And it came to pass, when midday was past, and they prophesied until the time of the offering of the evening sacrifice, that there was neither voice, nor any to answer, nor any that regarded.

And Elijah said unto all the people, "Come near unto me." And all the people came near unto him. And he repaired the altar of the LORD that was broken down. And Elijah took twelve stones, according to the number of the tribes of the sons of Jacob, unto whom the word of the LORD came, saying, "Israel shall be thy name": And with the stones he built an altar in the name of the LORD: and he made a trench about the altar, as great as would contain two measures of seed. And he put the wood in order, and cut the bullock in pieces, and laid him on the wood, and said, "Fill four barrels with water, and pour it on the burnt sacrifice, and on the wood." And he said, "Do it the second time." And they did it the second time. And he said, "Do it the third time." And they did it the third time. And the water ran round about the altar; and he filled the trench also with water. And it came to pass at the time of the offering of the evening sacrifice, that Elijah the prophet came near, and said, "LORD God of Abraham, Isaac, and of Israel, let it be known this day that thou art God in Israel, and that I am thy servant, and that I have done all these things at thy word. Hear me, O LORD, hear me, that this people may know that thou art the LORD God, and that thou hast turned their heart back again."

Then the fire of the LORD fell, and consumed the burnt sacrifice, and the wood, and the stones, and the dust, and licked up the water that was in the trench. And when all the people saw it, they fell on their faces: and they said, "The LORD, he is the God; the LORD, he is the God." And Elijah said unto them, "Take the prophets of Baal; let not one of them escape." And they took them: and Elijah brought them down to the brook Kishon, and slew them there.

And Elijah said unto Ahab, "Get thee up, eat and drink; for there is a sound of abundance of rain." So Ahab went up to eat and to drink. And Elijah went up to the top of Carmel: and he cast himself down upon the earth, and put his face between his knees. And said to his servant, "Go up now, look toward the sea." And he went up and looked, and said, "There is nothing." And he said, "Go again and seven more times." And it came to pass at the seventh time, that he said, "Behold there ariseth a little cloud, out of the sea, like a man's hand." And he said, "Go up, say unto Ahab, 'Prepare thy chariot, and get thee down, that the rain stop thee not.'" And it came to pass in the mean while, that the heaven was black with clouds and wind, and there was a great rain.

Isaiah

• • •

"Yet now hear, O Jacob my servant; and Israel, whom I have chosen: Thus saith the LORD that made thee, and formed thee from the

womb, which will help thee; 'Fear not, O Jacob, my servant; and thou, Jesurun, whom I have chosen. For I will pour water upon him that is thirsty, and floods upon the dry ground: I will pour my spirit upon

Chapters 44:1–19; 45:5–25.

thy seed, and my blessing upon thine offspring: And they shall spring up as among the grass, as willows by the water courses. One shall say, "I am the LORD's"; and another shall call himself by the name of Jacob; and another shall subscribe with his hand unto the LORD, and surname himself by the name of Israel.' Thus saith the LORD the King of Israel, and his redeemer the LORD of hosts; 'I am the first, and I am the last; and beside me there is no God. And who, as I, shall call, and shall declare it, and set it in order to me, since I appointed the ancient people? And the things that are coming, and shall come, let them shew unto them. Fear ye not, neither be afraid: have not I told thee from that time, and have declared it? Ye are even my witnesses. Is there a God beside me? Yea, there is no God; I know not any.

'They that make a graven image are all of them vanity; and their delectable things shall not profit; and they are their own witnesses; they see not, nor know; that they may be ashamed. Who hath formed a god, or molten a graven image that is profitable for nothing? Behold, all his fellows shall be ashamed: and the workmen, they are of men: let them all be gathered together, let them stand up; yet they shall fear, and they shall be ashamed together. The smith with the tongs both worketh in the coals, and fashioneth it with hammers, and worketh it with the strength of his arms: yea, he is hungry, and his strength faileth: he drinketh no water, and is faint. The carpenter stretcheth out his rule; he marketh it out with a line; he fitteth it with planes, and he marketh it out with the compass, and maketh it after the figure of a man, according to the beauty of a man; that it may remain in the house. He heweth him down cedars, and taketh the cypress and the oak, which he strengtheneth for himself among the trees of the forest: he planteth an ash, and the rain doth nourish it. Then shall it be for a man to burn: for he will take thereof, and warm himself; yea, he kindleth it and baketh bread; yea, he maketh a god, and worshippeth it; he make it a graven image, and falleth down thereto. He burneth part thereof in the fire; with part thereof he eateth flesh; he roasteth roast, and is satisfied: yea, he warmeth himself, and saith "Aha, I am warm, I have seen the fire." And the residue thereof he maketh a god, even his graven image: he falleth down unto it, and worshippeth it, and prayeth unto it, and saith, "Deliver me; for thou art my god." They have not known or understood: for he hath shut their eyes, that they cannot see; and their hearts, that they cannot understand. And none considereth in his heart, neither is there knowledge nor understanding to say, "I have burned part of it in the fire; yea, also I have baked bread upon the coals thereof; I have roasted flesh, and eaten it: and shall I make the residue thereof an abomination? shall I fall down to the stock of a tree?"

• • •

'I am the LORD, and there is none else, there is no God beside me: I girded thee, though thou hast not known me: That they may know from the rising of the sun, and from the west, that there is none beside me. I am the LORD, and there is none else. I form the light, and create darkness: I make peace, and create evil: I the LORD do all these things. Drop down, ye heavens, from above, and let the skies pour down righteousness: let the earth open, and let them bring forth salvation, and let righteousness spring up together: I the LORD have created it. Woe unto him that striveth with his Maker! Let the potsherd strive with the potsherds of the earth. Shall the clay say to him that fashioneth it, "What makest thou?" or thy work, "He hath no hands?" Woe unto him that saith unto his father, "What begettest thou?" or to the woman, "What hast thou brought forth?"

"Thus saith the LORD, the Holy One of Israel, and his Maker, 'Ask me of things to come concerning my sons, and concerning the work of my hands command ye me. I have made the earth, and created man upon it: I, even my hands, have stretched out the heavens, and all their host have I commanded. I have raised him up in righteousness, and I will direct all his ways: he shall build my city, and he shall let go my captives, not for price nor reward,' saith the LORD of hosts.

"Thus saith the LORD, 'The labour of Egypt, and merchandise of Ethiopia and of the Sabeans, men of stature, shall come over unto thee, and they shall be thine: they shall come after thee; in chains they shall come over, and they shall fall down unto thee, they shall make supplication unto thee, saying, "Surely God is in thee; and there is none else, there is no God. Verily thou art a God that hidest thyself,

O God of Israel, the Saviour." They shall be ashamed, and also confounded, all of them they shall go to confusion together that are makers of idols. But Israel shall be saved in the LORD with an everlasting salvation: ye shall not be ashamed nor confounded world without end.' For thus saith the LORD that created the heavens; God himself that formed the earth and made it; he hath established it, he created it not in vain, he formed it to be inhabited: 'I am the LORD: and there is none else. I have not spoken in secret, in a dark place of the earth: I said not unto the seed of Jacob, "Seek ye me in vain": I the LORD speak righteousness, I declare things that are right.

'Assemble yourselves and come; draw near together, ye that are escaped of the nations: they have no knowledge that set up the wood of their graven image, and pray unto a god that cannot save. Tell ye, and bring them near; yea, let them take counsel together; who hath declared this from ancient time? Who hath told it from that time? Have not I the LORD? And there is no God else beside me; a just God and a Saviour; there is none beside me. Look unto me, and be ye saved, all the ends of the earth: for I am God, and there is none else. I have sworn by myself, the word is gone out of my mouth in righteousness, and shall not return, that unto me every knee shall bow, every tongue shall swear. "Surely," shall one say, "in the LORD have I righteousness and strength": even to him shall men come; and all that are incensed against him shall be ashamed. In the LORD shall all the seed of Israel be justified, and shall glory.'"

Ezekiel

• • •

The word of the LORD came unto me again, saying, "What mean ye, that ye use this proverb concerning the land of Israel, saying, 'The fathers have eaten sour grapes, and the children's teeth are set on edge'?"

"As I live," saith the LORD God, "ye shall not have occasion any more to use this proverb in Israel. Behold, all souls are mine; as the soul of the father, so also the soul of the son is mine: the soul that sinneth, it shall die. But if a man be just, and do that which is lawful and right, and hath not eaten upon the mountains, neither hath lifted up his eyes to the idols of the house of Israel, neither hath defiled his neighbour's wife, neither hath come near to a menstruous woman, and hath not oppressed any, but hath restored to the debtor his pledge, hath spoiled none by violence, hath given his bread to the hungry, and hath covered the naked with a garment; he that hath not given forth upon usury, neither hath taken any increase, that hath withdrawn his hand from iniquity, hath executed true judgment between man and man, hath walked in my statutes, and hath kept my judgments, to deal truly; he is just, he shall surely live," saith the LORD God.

"If he beget a son that is a robber, a shedder of blood, and that doeth the like to any one of these things, and that doeth not any of those duties, but even hath eaten upon the mountains and defiled his neighbour's wife, hath oppressed the poor and needy, hath spoiled by violence, hath not restored the pledge, and hath lifted up his eyes to the idols, hath committed abomination, hath given forth upon usury, and hath taken increase; shall he then live? He shall not live: he hath done all these abominations; he shall surely die; his blood shall be upon him.

"Now, lo, if he beget a son, that seeth all his father's sins which he hath done, and considereth, and doeth not such like, that hath not eaten upon the mountains, neither hath lifted up his eyes to the idols of the house of Israel, hath not defiled his neighbour's wife, neither hath oppressed any, hath not withholden the pledge, neither hath spoiled by violence, but hath given his bread to the hungry, and hath covered the naked with a garment, that hath taken off his hand from the poor, that hath not received usury nor increase, hath executed my judgments, hath walked in my statutes; he shall not die for the iniquity of his father, he shall surely live. As for his father, because he cruelly oppressed, spoiled his brother by violence, and did that which is not good among his people, lo, even he shall die in his iniquity.

"Yet ye say, 'Why? doth not the son bear the iniquity of the father?' When the son hath done that which is lawful and right, and hath kept all my statutes, and hath done them,

Chapter 18.

he shall surely live. The soul that sinneth, it shall die. The son shall not bear the iniquity of the father, neither shall the father bear the iniquity of the son: the righteousness of the righteous shall be upon him, and the wickedness of the wicked shall be upon him. But if the wicked will turn from all his sins that he hath committed, and keep all my statutes, and do that which is lawful and right he shall surely live, he shall not die. All his transgressions that he hath committed, they shall not be mentioned unto him: in his righteousness that he hath done he shall live.

"Have I any pleasure at all that the wicked should die?" saith the LORD God: "and not that he should return from his ways, and live? But when the righteous turneth away from his righteousness, and committeth iniquity, and doeth according to all the abominations that the wicked man doeth, shall he live? All his righteousness that he hath done shall not be mentioned: in his trespass that he hath trespassed, and in his sin that he hath sinned, in them shall he die.

"Yet ye say, 'The way of the LORD is not equal.' Hear now, O house of Israel; Is not my way equal? Are not your ways unequal? When a righteous man turneth away from his righteousness, and committeth iniquity, and dieth in them; for his iniquity that he hath done shall he die. Again, when the wicked man turneth away from his wickedness that he hath committed, and doeth that which is lawful and right, he shall save his soul alive. Because he considereth, and turneth away from all his transgressions that he hath committed, he shall surely live, he shall not die. Yet saith the house of Israel, 'The way of the Lord is not equal,' O house of Israel, are not my ways equal? Are not your ways unequal? Therefore I will judge you, O house of Israel, every one according to his ways," saith the LORD God. "Repent, and turn yourselves from all your transgressions; so iniquity shall not be your ruin. Cast away from you all your transgressions; whereby ye have transgressed; and make you a new heart and a new spirit: for why will ye die, O house of Israel? For I have no pleasure in the death of him that dieth," saith the LORD God: "wherefore turn yourselves, and live ye."

The Book of Job

There was a man in the land of Uz, whose name was Job; and that man was perfect and upright, and one that feared God, and eschewed evil. And there were born unto him seven sons and three daughters. His substance also was seven thousand sheep, and three thousand camels, and five hundred yoke of oxen, and five hundred she asses, and a very great household; so that this man was the greatest of all the men of

Chapters 1; 2:1–10; 10; 21:7–15; 23:2–12; 38; 40:1–14; 42:1–6, 10–17.

the east. And his sons went and feasted in their houses, every one his day; and sent and called for their three sisters to eat and to drink with them. And it was so, when the days of their feasting were gone about, that Job sent and sanctified them, and rose up early in the morning, and offered burnt offerings according to the number of them all: for Job said, "It may be that my sons have sinned, and cursed God in their hearts." Thus did Job continually.

Now there was a day when the sons of God came to present themselves before the LORD, and Satan came also among them. And the LORD said unto Satan, "Whence comest thou?" Then Satan answered the LORD, and said, "From going to and fro in the earth, and from walking up and down in it." And the LORD said unto Satan, "Hast thou considered my servant Job, that there is none like him in the earth, a perfect and an upright man, one that feareth God, and escheweth evil?" Then Satan answered the LORD, and said, "Doth Job fear God for nought? Hast not thou made an hedge about him, and about his house, and about all that he hath on every side? Thou hast blessed the work of his hands, and his substance is increased in the land. But put forth thine hand now, and touch all that he hath and he will curse thee to thy face." And the LORD said unto Satan, "Behold, all that he hath is in thy power; only upon himself put not forth thine hand." So Satan went forth from the presence of the LORD.

And there was a day when his sons and his daughters were eating and drinking wine in their eldest brother's house. And there came a messenger unto Job, and said, "The oxen are plowing, and the asses feeding beside them: And the Sabeans fell upon them, and took them away; yea, they have slain the servants with the edge of the sword; and I only am escaped alone to tell thee." While he was yet speaking, there came also another, and said, "The fire of God is fallen from heaven, and hath burned up the sheep, and the servants, and consumed them; and I only escaped alone to tell thee." While he was yet speaking, there came also another, and said, "The Chaldeans made out three bands, and fell upon the camels, and have carried them away, yea, and slain the servants with the edge of the sword; and I only am escaped alone to tell thee." While he was yet speaking, there came also another, and said, "Thy sons and thy daughters were eating and drinking wine in their eldest brother's house: And, behold, there came a great wind from the wilderness, and smote the four corners of the house, and it fell upon the young men, and they are dead; and I only am escaped alone to tell thee." Then Job arose, and rent his mantle, and shaved his head, and fell down upon the ground, and worshipped. And said, "Naked came I out of my mother's womb, and naked shall I return thither: the LORD gave, and the LORD hath taken away; blessed be the name of the LORD." In all this Job sinned not, nor charged God foolishly.

Again there was a day when the sons of God came to present themselves before the LORD, and Satan came also among them to present himself before the LORD. And the LORD said unto Satan, "From whence comest thou?" And Satan answered the LORD, and said, "From going to and fro in the earth, and from walking up and down in it." And the LORD said unto Satan, "Hast thou considered my servant Job, that there is none like him in the earth, a perfect and an upright man, one that feareth God, and escheweth evil? And still he holdeth fast his integrity, although thou movedst me against him, to destroy him without cause." And Satan answered the LORD, and said, "Skin for skin, yea, all that a man hath will he give for his life. But put forth thine hand now, and touch his bone and his flesh, and he will curse thee to thy face." And the LORD said unto Satan, "Behold, he is in thine hand; but save his life."

So went Satan forth from the presence of the LORD, and smote Job with sore boils from the sole of his foot unto his crown. And he took him a potsherd to scrape himself withal; and he sat down among the ashes.

Then said his wife unto him, "Dost thou still retain thine integrity? Curse God, and die." But he said unto her. "Thou speakest as one of the foolish women speaketh. What? shall we receive good at the hand of God, and shall we not receive evil?" In all this did not Job sin with his lips.

• • •

[*And Job spake, and said*] "My soul is weary of my life; I will leave my complaint upon myself; I will speak in the bitterness of my soul. I will say unto God, 'Do not condemn me; shew me wherefore thou contendest with me. Is it good unto thee that thou shouldest oppress, that thou shouldest despise the work of thine hands, and shine upon the counsel of the wicked? Hast thou eyes of flesh? or seest thou as man seeth? Are thy days as the days of man? Are thy years as man's days, that thou enquirest after mine iniquity, and searchest after my sin? Thou knowest that I am not wicked; and there is none that can deliver out of thine hand. Thine hands have made me and fashioned me together round about; yet thou dost destroy me. Remember, I beseech thee, that thou hast made me as the clay; and wilt thou bring me into dust again? Hast thou not poured me out as milk, and curdled me like cheese? Thou hast clothed me with skin and flesh, and hast fenced me with bones and sinews. Thou hast granted me life and favour, and thy visitation hath preserved my spirit. And these things hast thou hid in thine heart; I know that this is with thee.

'If I sin, then thou markest me, and thou wilt not acquit me from mine iniquity. If I be wicked, woe unto me; and if I be righteous, yet will I not lift up my head. I am full of confusion; therefore see thou mine affliction; for it increaseth. Thou huntest me as a fierce lion: and again thou shewest thyself marvellous upon me. Thou renewest thy witnesses against me, and increasest thine indignation upon me; changes and war are against me. Wherefore then hast thou brought me forth out of the womb? Oh that I had given up the ghost, and no eye had seen me! I should have been as though I had not been; I should have been carried from the womb to the grave. Are not my days few? Cease then, and let me alone, that I may take comfort a little, before I go whence I shall not return, even to the land of darkness and the shadow of death; a land of darkness, as darkness itself; and of the shadow of death, without any order, and where the light is as darkness.'

• • •

"Wherefore do the wicked live, become old, yea, are mighty in power? Their seed is established in their sight with them, and their offspring before their eyes. Their houses are safe from fear, neither is the rod of God upon them. Their bull gendereth, and faileth not; their cow calveth, and casteth not her calf. They send forth their little ones like a flock, and their children dance. They take the timbrel and harp, and rejoice at the sound of the organ. They spend their days in wealth, and in a moment go down to the grave. Therefore they say unto God, 'Depart from us; for we desire not the knowledge of thy ways. What is the Almighty, that we should serve him? And what profit should we have, if we pray unto him?'

• • •

"Even to day is my complaint bitter: my stroke is heavier than my groaning. Oh that I knew where I might find him! that I might come even unto his seat! I would order my cause before him, and fill my mouth with arguments. I would know the words which he would answer me, and understand what he would say unto me. Will he plead against me with his great power? No, but he would put strength in me. There the righteous might dispute with him; so should I be delivered for ever from my judge. Behold, I go forward, but he is not

there; and backward, but I cannot perceive him: On the left hand, where he doth work, but I cannot behold him: he hideth himself on the right hand, that I cannot see him. But he knoweth the way that I take: when he hath tried me, I shall come forth as gold. My foot hath held his steps, his way have I kept, and not declined. Neither have I gone back from the commandment of his lips; I have esteemed the words of his mouth more than my necessary food."

• • •

Then the LORD answered Job out of the whirlwind, and said "Who is this that darkeneth counsel by words without knowledge? Gird up now thy loins like a man; for I will demand of thee, and answer thou me. Where wast thou when I laid the foundations of the earth? Declare, if thou hast understanding. Who hath laid the measures thereof, if thou knowest? Or who hath stretched the line upon it? Whereupon are the foundations thereof fastened? Or who laid the corner stone thereof; when the morning stars sang together, and all the sons of God shouted for joy? Or who shut up the sea with doors, when it brake forth, as if it had issued out of the womb? When I made the cloud the garment thereof, and thick darkness a swaddling band for it, and brake up for it my decreed place, and set bars and doors, and said, 'Hitherto shalt thou come, but no further: and here shall thy proud waves be stayed'? Hast thou commanded the morning since thy days; and caused the dayspring to know his place; that it might take hold of the end of the earth, that the wicked might be shaken out of it? It is turned as clay to the seal; and they stand as a garment. And from the wicked their light is withholden, and the high arm shall be broken. Hast thou entered into the springs of the sea? Or hast thou walked in the search of the depth? Have the gates of death been opened unto thee? Or hast thou seen the doors of the shadow of death? Hast thou perceived the breadth of the earth? Declare if thou knowest it all.

"Where is the way where light dwelleth? And as for darkness, where is the place thereof, that thou shouldest take it to the bound thereof, and that thou shouldest know the paths to the house thereof? Knowest thou it, because thou wast then born? Or because the number of thy days is great? Hast thou entered into the treasures of the snow? Or hast thou seen the treasures of the hail, which I have reserved against the time of trouble, against the day of battle and war? By what way is the light parted, which scattereth the east wind upon the earth? Who hath divided a watercourse for the overflowing of waters, or a way for the lightning or thunder; to cause it to rain on the earth, where no man is; on the Wilderness, wherein there is no man; to satisfy the desolate and waste ground; and to cause the bud of the tender herb to spring forth? Hath the rain a father? Or who hath begotten the drops of dew? Out of whose womb came the ice? And the hoary frost of heaven, who hath gendered it? The waters are hid as with a stone, and the face of the deep is frozen.

"Canst thou bind the sweet influences of Pleiades, or loose the bonds of Orion? Canst thou bring forth Massaroth in his season? Or canst thou guide Arcturus with his sons? Knowest thou the ordinances of heaven? Canst thou set the dominion thereof in the earth? Canst thou lift up thy voice to the clouds, that abundance of waters may cover thee? Canst thou send lightnings, that they may go, and say unto thee, 'Here we are'? Who hath put wisdom in the inward parts? Or who hath given understanding to the heart? Who can number the clouds in wisdom? Or who can stay the bottles of heaven, when the dust groweth into hardness, and the clods cleave fast together? Wilt thou hunt the prey for the lion? Or fill the appetite of the young lions, when they couch in their dens, and abide in the covert to lie in wait? Who provideth for the raven his food? When his young ones cry unto God, they wander for lack of meat."

• • •

Moreover, the LORD answered Job, and said, "Shall he that contendeth with the Almighty instruct him? He that reproveth God, let him answer it."

Then Job answered the LORD, and said, "Behold, I am vile; what shall I answer thee? I will lay mine hand upon my mouth. Once have I spoken; but I will not answer: yea, twice; but I will proceed no further."

Then answered the LORD unto Job out of the whirlwind, and said, "Gird up thy loins now like a man: I will demand of thee, and declare thou unto me. Wilt thou also disannul my judgment? Wilt thou condemn me, that thou mayest be righteous? Hast thou an arm like God? Or canst thou thunder with a voice like him? Deck thyself now with majesty and excellency; and array thyself with glory and beauty. Cast abroad the rage of thy wrath: and behold every one that is proud, and abase him. Look on every one that is proud, and bring him low; and tread down the wicked in their place. Hide them in the dust together; and bind their faces in secret. Then will I also confess unto thee that thine own right hand can save thee."

•   •   •

Then Job answered the LORD, and said, "I know that thou canst do every thing, and that no thought can be witholden from thee. Who is he that hideth counsel without knowledge? Therefore have I uttered that I understood not; things too wonderful for me, which I knew not. Hear, I beseech thee, and I will speak: I will demand of thee, and declare thou unto me. I have heard of thee by the hearing of the ear: but now mine eye seeth thee. Wherefore I abhor myself, and repent in dust and ashes."

•   •   •

And the LORD turned the captivity of Job, when he prayed for his friends: also the LORD gave Job twice as much as he had before. Then came there unto him all his brethren, and all his sisters, and all they that had been of his acquaintance before, and did eat bread with him in his house: and they bemoaned him, and comforted him over all the evil that the LORD had brought upon him: every man also gave him a piece of money, and every one an earring of gold. So the LORD blessed the latter end of Job more than his beginning: for he had fourteen thousand sheep, and six thousand camels, and a thousand yoke of oxen, and a thousand she asses. He had also seven sons and three daughters. And he called the name of the first, Jemima; and the name of the second, Kezia; and the name of the third, Kerenhappuch. And in all the land were no women found so fair as the daughters of Job: and their father gave them inheritance among their brethren. After this lived Job an hundred and forty years, and saw his sons, and his son's sons, even four generations. So Job died, being old and full of days.

The death of Socrates. (*Culver Pictures, Inc.*)

GREECE

The naval engagement fought between the Greeks and Persians off the island of Salamis in 480 B.C. must be ranked as one of the truly decisive battles of Western history. For at Salamis the Greeks, following up their victory at Marathon ten years earlier, succeeded in halting the imperial march of Xerxes to the west and hence in gaining a century and a half of security from foreign conquest. This relatively brief respite was brought to a close by the armies of Philip of Macedon and his son, Alexander the Great, in the latter part of the fourth century. But while it lasted, the Greeks perfected a civilization whose achievements still stand as objects of admiration and inspiration for the Western world.

The center of classical Greek civilization was the *polis*, or city-state. Ancient Greece was divided into hundreds of *poleis*, each a tiny unit politically independent and culturally unique. Athens, for example, one of the largest of the *poleis*, had a total population of just over 300 thousand and an area roughly equal to that of Rhode Island. The forms of government varied widely from *polis* to *polis*, and even within the same *polis* at different times.

By far the most important form—at least as far as later Western history is concerned—was the Athenian democracy, particularly as it appeared in the Age of Pericles during the fifth century B.C. Although the Athenians shared with us the belief that democratic government means rule by the people, their democracy differed from ours in one important respect: Because of the very size and complexity of the nation in which we live, we must exercise our sovereignty through representatives, but in Athens the people could rule directly. Every adult male citizen was a member of the Assembly, the sole legislative body of the city-state. From the ranks of the assembly a Council of Five Hundred was chosen annually to supervise the administrative affairs of the *polis*. From the Council, in turn, an executive committee of fifty was chosen to conduct the day-to-day business of administration for a term lasting one-tenth of a year. One member of this committee was then chosen as chairman for each twenty-four-hour period. Since all these selections were made by lot, any citizen of the *polis* might be called on to serve as the chief administrative officer of Athens for a day.

But for the average Greek the *polis* was more than just the political unit within which he happened to live. It was also the center of his social, intellectual, aesthetic, and religious life. Aristotle, in the beginning of his work on political theory, the *Politics*, takes a typically Greek attitude toward the *polis* in the statement which is usually translated, "Man is a political animal," but which in the original Greek reads, "Man is by nature an animal intended to live in a *polis*." Here Aristotle is implying that only within the *polis* can one live a truly human life. The philosopher Socrates expresses a similar feeling toward the *polis*. Though unjustly condemned to death by an Athenian court, he rejected a chance to escape from prison, insisting that, because he owed his very being to his *polis*, he must accept whatever Athens decreed for him, even execution.

Some scholars have been convinced that Athens in the fifth century B.C. represents the high point of Western civilization. In the words of the contemporary historian, H. D. F. Kitto, Athens "was clearly the most civilized society that has yet existed." Whether or not we accept this evaluation, it is true that today, over two thousand years later, the world still finds the accomplishments of the Athenians—in art and architecture, poetry, drama, history, political theory, science, mathematics, philosophy, and religion—a source of instruction and enjoyment.

One of the finest appreciations of Athens' achievements was made by a great Athenian leader—Pericles. The occasion was a funeral oration that he delivered in 431 B.C. just outside the city walls, to honor the Athenian soldiers who had fallen in the first year of the Peloponnesian War. For Pericles, the highest honor that could be paid to the dead was to say that they "were worthy of Athens." By Athens he referred not just to the city in which they had lived, but to the way of life that they, as Athenians, had shared. The Athenians, Pericles told his audience, are "lovers of the beautiful." The truth of Pericles' claim was self-evident; anyone listening to him could have verified it simply by turning his head and gazing back at the city itself. Had he done so he would have found the view dominated by the Acropolis, rising high above the plain and crowned with temples. In the center stood the Parthenon, completed less than a decade before Pericles delivered his oration. Dedicated to Athena, goddess of wisdom and protectress of Athens, the Parthenon embodied an ideal of beauty based on architectural symmetry or balance.

The ideal of balance so completely realized in the Parthenon was pursued in all forms of Greek art. And, outside the aesthetic realm, it was an ideal that pervaded Greek civilization. Just as the Greek experienced pleasure in a well-proportioned building, so he delighted in a well-balanced personality and tried in his life to follow the path of moderation. The life of moderation is summed up in Aristotle's famous doctrine of the Golden Mean, perhaps the most closely reasoned defense ever made of a civilization and its way of life. Behind the Greek ideal of moderation and balance stands the belief that the universe is a rational order, operating according to fixed laws. The orderliness of the universe, the Greeks argued, is good, hence order anywhere must be good, and disorder must be evil. When the Greeks translated this belief into aesthetic and moral terms, they found their ideal of beauty in the ordered symmetry of the Parthenon, and their conception of the good life in the moderation of the Golden Mean.

Because they were convinced that mankind is capable of reasoning, the Greeks concluded that we can comprehend the world in which we live. This faith—that people can understand the universe—along with the conclusions the Greeks reached in their attempts to do so, is probably the greatest single contribution of the Greeks to Western civilization. The Greek faith in reason permeated their entire intellectual and cultural life. To take the most obvious example, it made possible their phenomenal achievements in science. Earlier civilizations in the ancient Near East had developed advanced technologies, but the Greeks were the first theoretical scientists in Western history. What set them apart from their predecessors was their ability to generalize, to see an object or event not simply in its individuality but as an instance of a universal rule or pattern. They were led to seek the general laws governing natural events—in other words, to become theoretical scientists—by their conviction that people can, by the use of their reasoning powers, discover the rational pattern of the universe.

This tendency to generalize shows itself over and over again in Greek thought. Thucydides, in the introduction to his *History of the Peloponnesian War*, states that he is interested not just in recounting the events of the war but in revealing the general pattern of war. The Greek tragedians attempted to trace the patterns in which universal moral law revealed itself in people's lives. This emphasis on universal law in Greek tragedy led the twentieth-century philosopher A. N. Whitehead to conclude that the tragic poets must be considered the originators of scientific thought. Greek generalization reached its highest expression in Plato's Form of the Good, one of the most difficult concepts in Western thought. For Plato's belief that the Form of the Good is the heart of reality is really a philosophical formulation of the Greek faith in the ultimate unity, rationality, and goodness of the universe.

Yet the Greeks failed to generalize in one crucial area, that of practical politics, and it was this failure that led to their downfall. Loyalty to their own *polis* and jealousy of all the others prevented the Greeks from ever uniting to form a single nation. The unwillingness of the Greeks to cooperate in a common cause nearly led to disaster as early as the Persian Wars; for, as Herodotus makes clear, the Athenian naval commander at the battle of Salamis had to deceive his Peloponnesian allies to keep them from fleeing the enemy. The political disunity of the Greeks reached its climax a half century later, in the Peloponnesian War between Athens and Sparta. This war (431–404 B.C.) marked the turning point in the history of Greece. Though the Greeks produced much of value, particularly in science and philosophy, in later years, the great period of Greek civilization was ended by this long and costly struggle. The resources of the Greek *poleis*, of defeated Athens in particular, were dissipated, and in the fourth century the proud city-states fell easy prey to the invading Macedonians from the north. Thus ended one of the most brilliant episodes in the history of Western civilization.

Herodotus

History is the art of telling the most complicated and fascinating story ever related—the story of the human race and its past. Since history is essentially storytelling, the person who tells the story best, who is the ablest *raconteur*, is obviously the best historian. This does not mean that history is simply imaginative literature, however, for the records and the factual foundation of the past are the very warp and woof of the story. Thus, the storyteller must respect those qualities that are the essence of good historical writing: accuracy in assembling and presenting facts, right reason in analyzing the facts, and sobriety and judgment in interpreting the facts. But even the possession of these qualities will not ensure that an author will write good history, for storytelling is above all an act of communication, and an author who fails to communicate fails to tell the story. History is written to be read, and the best historian is the one who tells his tale with wit and imagination, using every literary device at his command to carry the reader along on the stream of his narrative.

The first historian to measure up to these demanding standards was Herodotus (484–c.424 B.C.), a citizen of the Greek city-state of Halicarnassus in Asia Minor. In the latter part of the fifth century B.C. Herodotus undertook to record the history of the wars between the city-states of Greece and the great Persian Empire. His purpose, he tells us, was to preserve the memory of the great events that had occurred during the wars and of the heroic deeds that had been performed on both sides. He skillfully unfolded his tale in nine books, each named for one of the nine muses of Greek mythology. Herodotus was the first writer to go beyond simply ticking off events in chronological sequence. He analyzed motives and searched for relationships between events, trying to generalize and to work out a broad pattern into which individual happenings could be fitted. For this reason he is often called "the father of history."

The following selections are from the first, seventh, and eighth books of the *History of the Persian Wars*. The first is a brief passage taken from Herodotus' general introduction. The second recounts the heroic but futile defense of the pass at Thermopylae, near the north coast of the Greek mainland, by a small band of Spartans under their leader Leonidas against the Persian army in 480 B.C. The final selection describes the decisive naval battle fought off the island of Salamis, just opposite Athens, a little later, in which the Greeks under the astute leadership of Themistocles routed the enemy fleet and ended the Persian advance into Europe.

The History of Herodotus

These are the researches of Herodotus of Halicarnassus, which he publishes, in the hope of thereby preserving from decay the remembrance of what men have done, and of preventing the great and wonderful actions of the Greeks and the Barbarians from losing their due meed of glory; and withal to put on record what were their grounds of feud.

. . .

*THE SEVENTH BOOK ENTITLED
"POLYMNIA"*

**[The Battle of
Thermopylae]**

. . .

The Greek forces at Thermopylae, when the Persian army drew near to the entrance of the pass, were seized with fear; and a council was held to consider about a retreat. It was the wish of the Peloponnesians generally that the army should fall back upon the Peloponnese, and there guard the Isthmus. But Leonidas, who saw with what indignation the Phocians and Locrians heard of this plan, gave his voice for remaining where they were, while they sent envoys to the several cities to ask for help, since they were too few to make a stand against an army like that of the Medes.

While this debate was going on, Xerxes sent a mounted spy to observe the Greeks, and note how many they were, and see what they were doing. He had heard, before he came out of Thessaly, that a few men were assembled at this place, and that at their head were certain Lacedaemonians, under Leonidas, a descendant of Hercules. The horseman rode up to the camp, and looked about him, but did not see the whole army; for such as were on the further side of the wall (which had been rebuilt and was now carefully guarded) it was not possible for him to behold; but he observed those on the outside, who were encamped in front of the rampart. It chanced that at this time the Lacedaemonians held the outer guard, and were seen by the spy, some of them engaged in gymnastics exercises, others combing their long hair. At this the spy greatly marvelled, but he counted their number, and when he had taken accurate note of everything, he rode back quietly; for no one pursued after him, nor paid any heed to his visit. So he returned and told Xerxes all that he had seen.

Upon this, Xerxes, who had no means of surmising the truth—namely, that the Spartans were preparing to do or die manfully—but thought it laughable that they should be engaged in such employments, sent and called to his presence Demaratus the son of Ariston, who still remained with the army.

The History of Herodotus, trans. G. Rawlinson.

48

When he appeared Xerxes told him all that he had heard, and questioned him concerning the news, since he was anxious to understand the meaning of such behaviour on the part of the Spartans. Then Demaratus said—

"I spake to thee, O king! concerning these men long since, when we had but just begun our march upon Greece; thou, however, didst only laugh at my words, when I told thee of all this, which I saw would come to pass. Earnestly do I struggle at all times to speak truth to thee, sire; and now listen to it once more. These men have come to dispute the pass with us; and it is for this that they are now making ready. 'Tis their custom, when they are about to hazard their lives, to adorn their heads with care. Be assured, however, that if thou canst subdue the men who are here and the Lacedaemonians who remain in Sparta, there is no other nation in all the world which will venture to lift a hand in their defence. Thou hast now to deal with the first kingdom and town in Greece, and with the bravest men."

Then Xerxes, to whom what Demaratus said seemed altogether to surpass belief, asked further, "how it was possible for so small an army to contend with his?"

"O king!" Demaratus answered, "let me be treated as a liar, if matters fall not out as I say."

But Xerxes was not persuaded any the more. Four whole days he suffered to go by, expecting that the Greeks would run away. When, however, he found on the fifth that they were not gone, thinking that their firm stand was merely impudence and recklessness, he grew wroth, and sent against them the Medes and Cissians, with orders to take them alive and bring them into his presence. Then the Medes rushed forward and charged the Greeks, but fell in vast numbers: others however took the places of the slain, and would not be beaten off, though they suffered terrible losses. In this way it became clear to all, and especially to the king, that though he had plenty of combatants, he had but very few warriors. The struggle, however, continued during the whole day.

Then the Medes, having met so rough a reception, withdrew from the fight; and their place was taken by the band of Persians under Hydarnes, whom the king called his "Immortals": they, it was thought would soon finish the business. But when they joined battle with the Greeks, 'twas with no better success than the Median detachment— things went much as before—the two armies fighting in a narrow space, and the barbarians using shorter spears than the Greeks, and having no advantage from their numbers. The Lacedaemonians fought in a way worthy of note, and showed themselves far more skilful in fight than their adversaries, often turning their backs, and making as though they were all flying away, on which the barbarians would rush after them with much noise and shouting, when the Spartans at their approach would wheel round and face their pursuers, in this way destroying vast numbers of the enemy. Some Spartans likewise fell in these encounters, but only a very few. At last the Persians, finding that all their efforts to gain the pass availed nothing, and that, whether they attacked by divisions or in any other way, it was to no purpose, withdrew to their own quarters.

During these assaults, it is said that Xerxes, who was watching the battle, thrice leaped from the throne on which he sat, in terror for his army.

Next day the combat was renewed, but with no better success on the part of the barbarians. The Greeks were so few that the barbarians hoped to find them disabled, by reason of their wounds, from offering any further resistance; and so they once more attacked them. But the Greeks were drawn up in detachments according to their cities, and bore the brunt of the battle in turns,—all except the Phocians, who had been stationed on the mountain to guard the pathway. So, when the Persians found no difference between that day and the preceding, they again retired to their quarters.

Now, as the king was in a great strait, and knew not how he should deal with the emergency, Ephialtes, the son of Eurydemus, a man of Malis, came to him and was admitted to a conference. Stirred by the hope of receiving a rich reward at the king's hands, he had come to tell him of the pathway which led across the mountain to Thermopylae; by which disclosure he brought destruction on the band of Greeks who had there withstood the barbarians.

* * *

Great was the joy of Xerxes on this occasion; and as he approved highly of the enterprise which Ephialtes undertook to accomplish, he forthwith sent upon the errand Hydarnes, and the Persians under

him. The troops left the camp about the time of the lighting of the lamps. The pathway along which they went was first discovered by the Malians of these parts, who soon afterwards led the Thessalians by it to attack the Phocians, at the time when the Phocians fortified the pass with a wall, and so put themselves under cover from danger. And ever since, the path has always been put to an ill use by the Malians.

The course which it takes is the following:—Beginning at the Asopus, where that stream flows through the cleft in the hills, it runs along the ridge of the mountain, which is called, like the pathway over it, Anopaea, and ends at the city of Alpenus—the first Locrian town as you come from Malis—by the stone called Melampygus and the seats of the Cercopians. Here it is as narrow as at any other point.

The Persians took this path, and, crossing the Asopus, continued their march through the whole of the night, having the mountains of Ceta on their right hand, and on their left those of Trachis. At dawn of day they found themselves close to the summit. Now the hill was guarded, as I have already said, by a thousand Phocian men-at-arms, who were placed there to defend the pathway, and at the same time to secure their own country. They had been given the guard of the mountain path, while the other Greeks defended the pass below, because they had volunteered for the service, and had pledged themselves to Leonidas to maintain the post.

The ascent of the Persians became known to the Phocians in the following manner:—During all the time that they were making their way up, the Greeks remained unconscious of it, inasmuch as the whole mountain was covered with groves of oak; but it happpened that the air was very still, and the leaves which the Persians stirred with their feet made, as it was likely they would, a loud rustling, whereupon the Phocians jumped up and flew to seize their arms. In a moment the barbarians came in sight, and, perceiving men arming themselves, were greatly amazed; for they had fallen in with an enemy when they expected no opposition. Hydarnes, alarmed at the sight, and fearing lest the Phocians might be Lacedaemonians, inquired of Ephialtes to what nation these troops belonged. Ephialtes told him the exact truth, whereupon he arrayed his Persians for battle. The Phocians, galled by the showers of arrows to which they were exposed, and imagining themselves the special object of the Persian attack, fled hastily to the crest of the mountain, and there made ready to meet death; but while their mistake continued, the Persians, with Ephialtes and Hydarnes, not thinking it worth their while to delay on account of Phocians, passed on and descended the mountain with all possible speed.

The Greeks at Thermopylae received the first warning of the destruction which the dawn would bring on them from the seer Megistias, who read their fate in the victims as he was sacrificing. After this deserters came in, and brought the news that the Persians were marching round by the hills: it was still night when these men arrived. Last of all, the scouts came running down from the heights, and brought in the same accounts, when the day was just beginning to break. Then the Greeks held a council to consider what they should do, and here opinions were divided: some were strong against quitting their post, while others contended to the contrary. So when the council had broken up, part of the troops departed and went their ways homeward to their several states; part however resolved to remain, and to stand by Leonidas to the last.

• • •

At sunrise Xerxes made libations, after which he waited until the time when the forum is wont to fill, and then began his advance. Ephialtes had instructed him thus, as the descent of the mountain is much quicker, and the distance much shorter, than the way round the hills, and the ascent. So the barbarians under Xerxes began to draw nigh; and the Greeks under Leonidas, as they now went forth determined to die, advanced much further than on previous days, until they reached the more open portion of the pass. Hitherto they had held their station within the wall, and from this had gone forth to fight at the point where the pass was the narrowest. Now they joined battle beyond the defile, and carried slaughter among the barbarians, who fell in heaps. Behind them the captains of the squadrons, armed with whips, urged their men forward with continual blows. Many were thrust into the sea, and there perished; a still greater number were trampled to death by their own soldiers; no one heeded the dying. For the Greeks, reckless of their own safety and desperate, since they knew that, as the mountain had been crossed, their destruction was nigh at hand, exerted themselves with the most furious valour against the barbarians.

By this time the spears of the greater number were all shivered, and with their swords they hewed down the ranks of the Persians; and here, as they strove, Leonidas fell fighting bravely, together with many other famous Spartans, whose names I have taken care to learn on account of their great worthiness, as indeed I have those of all the three hundred. There fell too at the same time very many famous Persians: among them, two sons of Darius, Abrocomes and Hyperanthes, his children by Phratagune, the daughter of Artanes. Artanes was brother of King Darius, being a son of Hystaspes, the son of Arsames; and when he gave his daughter to the king, he made him heir likewise of all his substance; for she was his only child.

Thus two brothers of Xerxes here fought and fell. And now there arose a fierce struggle between the Persians and the Lacedaemonians over the body of Leonidas, in which the Greeks four times drove back the enemy, and at last by their great bravery succeeded in bearing off the body. This combat was scarcely ended when the Persians with Ephialtes approached; and the Greeks, informed that they drew nigh, made a change in the manner of their fighting. Drawing back into the narrowest part of the pass, and retreating even behind the cross wall, they posted themselves upon a hillock, where they stood all drawn up together in one close body except only the Thebans. The hillock whereof I speak is at the entrance of the straits, where the stone lion stands which was set up in honour of Leon-

idas. Here they defended themselves to the last, such as still had swords using them, and the others resisting with their hands and teeth; till the barbarians, who in part had pulled down the wall and attacked them in front, in part had gone round and now encircled them upon every side, overwhelmed and buried the remnant which was left beneath showers of missile weapons.

THE EIGHTH BOOK, ENTITLED "URANIA"

[The Battle of Salamis]

• • •

Meanwhile, at Salamis,[1] the Greeks no sooner heard what had befallen the Athenian citadel, than they fell into such alarm that some of the captains did not even wait for the council to come to a vote, but embarked hastily on board their vessels, and hoisted sail as though they would take to flight immediately. The rest, who stayed at the council board, came to a vote that the fleet should give battle at the Isthmus. Night now drew on, and the captains, dispersing from the meeting, proceeded on board their respective ships.

Themistocles, as he entered his own vessel, was met by Mnesiphilus, an Athenian, who asked him what the council had resolved to do. On learning that the resolve was to stand away from the Isthmus,

[1] [Several days after the battle of Thermopylae and immediately following the sacking of Athens by the Persians—*Ed.*]

and there give battle on behalf of the Peloponnese, Mnesiphilus exclaimed:—

If these men shall sail way from Salamis, thou will have no fight at all for the one fatherland; for they will scatter themselves to their own homes; and neither Eurybiades nor any one else will be able to hinder them, or to stop the breaking up of the armament. Thus will Greece be brought to ruin through evil counsels. But haste thee now; and, if there be any possible way, seek to unsettle these resolves—mayhap thou mightest persuade Eurybiades to change his mind, and continue here.

The suggestion greatly pleased Themistocles; and without answering a word, he went straight to the vessel of Eurybiades. Arrived there, he let him know that he wanted to speak with him on a matter touching the public service. So Eurybiades bade him come on board, and say whatever he wished. Then Themistocles, seating himself at his side, went over all the arguments which he had heard from Mnesiphilus, pretending as if they were his own, and added to them many new ones besides; until at last he persuaded Eurybiades, by his importunity, to quit his ship and again collect the captains to council.

As soon as they were come, and before Eurybiades had opened to them his purpose in assembling them together, Themistocles, as men are wont to do when they are very anxious, spoke much to divers of them; whereupon the Corinthian captain, Adeimantus, the son of Ocytus, observed—"Themistocles, at the games they who start too soon are scourged." "True," rejoined the other in his excuse, "but they who wait too late are not crowned."

Thus he gave the Corinthian at this time a mild answer; and towards Eurybiades himself he did not use any of those arguments which he had urged before, or say aught of the allies betaking themselves to flight if once they broke up from Salamis; it would have been ungraceful for him, when the confederates were present, to make accusation against any; but he had recourse to quite a new sort of reasoning, and addressed him as follows:—

With thee it rests, O! Eurybiades, to save Greece, if thou wilt only hearken unto me, and give the enemy battle here, rather than yield to the advice of those among us, who would have the fleet withdrawn to the Isthmus. Hear now, I beseech thee, and judge between the two courses. At the Isthmus thou wilt fight in an open sea, which is greatly to our disadvantage, since our ships are heavier and fewer in number than the enemy's; and further, thou wilt in any case lose Salamis, Megara, and Egina, even if all the rest goes well with us. The land and sea force of the Persians will advance together; and thy retreat will but draw them towards the Peloponnese, and so bring all Greece into peril. If, on the other hand, thou doest as I advise, these are the advantages which thou wilt so secure: in the first place, as we shall fight in a narrow sea with few ships against many, if the war follows the common course, we shall gain a great victory: for to fight in a narrow space is favorable to us—in an open sea, to them. Again, Salamis will in this case be preserved, where we have placed our wives and children. Nay, that very point by which ye set most store, is secured as much by the other: for whether we fight here or at the Isthmus, we shall equally give battle in defense of the Peloponnese. Assuredly ye will not do wisely to draw the Persians upon that region. For if things turn out as I anticipate, and we beat them by sea, then we shall have kept your Isthmus free from the barbarians, and they will have advanced no further than Attica, but from thence have fled back in disorder; and we shall, moreover, have saved Megara, Egina, and Salamis itself, where an oracle has said that we are to overcome our enemies. When men counsel reasonably, reasonable success ensues; but when in their counsels they reject reason, God does not choose to follow the wonderings of human fancies.

When Themistocles had thus spoken, Adeimantus the Corinthian again attacked him, and bade him be silent, since he was a man without a city; at the same time, he called on Eurybiades not to put the question at the instance of one who had no country, and urged that Themistocles should show of what state he was envoy, before he gave his voice with the rest. This reproach he made, because the city of Athens had been taken, and was in the hands of the barbarians. Hereupon Themistocles spake many bitter things against Adeimantus and the Corinthians generally; and for proof that he had a country, reminded the captains, that with two hundred ships at his command all fully manned for battle, he had both city and territory as good as theirs; since there was no Grecian state which could resist his men if they were to make a descent.

After this declaration, he turned to Eurybiades, and addressing him with greater warmth and earnestness—"If thou wilt stay here," he said, "and behave like a brave man, all will be well—if not, thou will bring Greece to ruin. For the whole fortune of the war depends on our ships. Be thou persuaded by my words. If not, we will take our families on board, and go, just as we are, to Siris in Italy, which is ours from of old, and which the prophecies declare we are to colonise some day or other. You then, when you have lost allies like us, will hereafter call to mind what I have now said."

At these words of Themistocles, Eurybiades changed his determination; principally, as I believe, because he feared that if he withdrew the fleet to the Isthmus, the Athenians would sail away, and knew that without the Athenians, the rest of their ships could be no match for the fleet of the enemy. He therefore decided to remain, and give battle at Salamis. And now, the different chiefs, notwithstanding their skirmish of words, on learning the decision of Eurybiades, at once made ready for the fight.

•   •   •

The men belonging to the fleet of Xerxes, after they had seen the Spartan dead at Thermopylae, and crossed the channel from Trachis to Histiaca, waited there by the space of three days, and then sailing down through the Euripus, in three more came to Phalêrum. In my judgment, the Persian forces both by land and sea when they invaded Attica, were not less numerous than they had been on their arrival at Sêpias and Thermopylae. For against the Persian loss in the storm and at Thermopylae, and again in the sea-fights off Artemisium, I set the various nations which had since joined the king—as the Malians, the Dorians, the Locrians, and the Boeotians—each serving full force in his army except the last, who did not number in their ranks either the Thespians or the Plataeans; and together with these, the Carystians, the Andrians, the Tenians, and the other people of the islands, who all fought on this side except the five states already mentioned. For as the Persians penetrated further into

Greece, they were joined continually by fresh nations.

Reinforced by the contingents of all these various states, except Paros, the barbarians reached Athens. As for the Parians, they tarried at Cythnus, waiting to see how the war would go. The rest of the sea forces came safe to Phalêrum, where they were visited by Xerxes, who had conceived a desire to go aboard and learn the wishes of the fleet. So he came and sate in a seat of honour; and the sovereigns of the nations, and the captains of the ships, were sent for to appear before him, and as they arrived took their seats according to the rank assigned them by the king. In the first seat sate the king of Sidon; after him, the king of Tyre; then the rest in their order. When the whole had taken their places, one after another, and were set down in orderly array, Xerxes, to try them, sent Mardonius and questioned each, whether a sea-fight should be risked or no.

Mardonius accordingly went round the entire assemblage, beginning with the Sidonian monarch, and asked this question; to which all gave the same answer, advising to engage the Greeks, except only Artemisia, who spake as follows:—

Say to the king, Mardonius, that these are my words to him: I was not the least brave of those who fought at Euboea, nor were my achievements there among the meanest; it is my right, therefore, O my lord, to tell thee plainly, what I think to be most for thy advantage now. This then is my advice. Spare thy ships, and do not risk a battle; for these people are as much superior to thy people in seamanship, as men to women. What so great need is there for thee to incur hazard at sea? Art thou not master of Athens, for which thou didst undertake thy expedition? Is not Greece subject to thee? Not a soul now resists thy advance. They who once

resisted, were handled even as they deserved. Now learn how I expect that affairs will go with thy adversaries. If thou art not over-hasty to engage with them by sea, but wilt keep thy fleet near the land, then whether thou abidest as thou art, or marchest forward towards the Peloponnese, thou wilt easily accomplish all for which thou art come hither. The Greeks cannot hold out against thee very long; thou wilt soon part them asunder, and scatter them to their several homes. In the island where they lie, I hear they have no food in store; nor is it likely, if thy land force begins its march towards the Peloponnese, that they will remain quietly where they are—at least such as come from that region. Of a surety they will not greatly trouble themselves to give battle on behalf of the Athenians. On the other hand, if thou art hasty to fight, I tremble lest the defeat of thy sea force bring harm likewise to thy land army. This, too, thou shouldst remember, O king; good masters are apt to have bad servants; and bad masters good ones. Now, as thou art the best of men, thy servants must needs be a sorry set. These Egyptians, Cyprians, Cilicians, and Pamphylians, who are counted in the number of thy subject-allies, of how little service are they to thee!

As Artemisia spake, they who wished her well were greatly troubled concerning her words, thinking that she would suffer some hurt at the king's hands, because she exhorted him not to risk a battle; they, on the other hand, who disliked and envied her, favoured as she was by the king above all the rest of the allies, rejoiced at her declaration, expecting that her life would be the forfeit. But Xerxes, when the words of the several speakers were reported to him, was pleased beyond all others with the reply of Artemisia; and whereas, even before this, he had always esteemed her much, he now praised her more than ever. Nevertheless, he gave orders that the advice of the greater number should be followed; for he thought that at Euboea the fleet had not done its best, because he himself was not there to see—whereas this time he resolved that he would be an eye-witness of the combat.

Orders were now given to stand out to sea; and the ships proceeded towards Salamis, and took up the stations to which they were directed, without let or hindrance from the enemy. The day, however, was too far spent for them to begin the battle, since night already approached: so they prepared to engage upon the morrow. The Greeks, meanwhile, were in great distress and alarm, more especially those of the Peloponnese; who were troubled that they had been kept at Salamis to fight on behalf of the Athenian territory; and feared that, if they should suffer defeat, they would be pent up and besieged in an island, while their own country was left unprotected.

.   .   .

At first they conversed together in low tones, each man with his fellow, secretly, and marvelled at the folly shown by Eurybiades; but presently the smothered feeling broke out, and another assembly was held; whereat the old subjects provoked much talk from the speakers, one side maintaining that it was best to sail to the Peloponnese and risk battle for that, instead of abiding at Salamis and fighting for a land already taken by the enemy; while the other, which consisted of the Athenians, Eginetans, and Megarians, was urgent to remain and have the battle fought where they were.

Then Themistocles, when he saw that the Peloponnesians would carry the vote against him, went out secretly from the council, and instructing a certain man what he should say, sent him on board a merchant ship to the fleet of the Medes. The man's name was Sicinnus; he was one of Themistocles' household slaves, and acted as tutor to his sons; in after times, when the Thespians were admitting persons to citizenship, Themistocles made him a Thespian, and a rich man to boot. The ship brought Sicinnus to the Persian fleet, and there he delivered his message to the leaders in these words:—

The Athenian commander has sent me to you privily, without the knowledge of the other Greeks. He is a well-wisher to the king's cause, and would rather success attend on you than on his countrymen; wherefore he bids me tell you, that fear has seized the Greeks and they are meditating a hasty flight. Now then it is open to you to achieve the best work that ever ye wrought, if only ye will hinder their escaping. They no longer agree among themselves, so that they will not now make any resistance—nay, 'tis likely ye may see a fight already begun between such as favour and such as oppose your cause.

The Messenger, when he had thus expressed himself, departed and was seen no more.

Then the captains, believing all that the messenger had said, proceeded to land a large body of Persian troops on the islet of Psyttaleia, which lies between Salamis and the mainland; after which, about the hour of midnight, they advanced their western wing towards Salamis, so as to inclose the Greeks. At the same time the force stationed about Ceos and Cynosura moved forward, and filled the whole strait as far as Munychia with their ships. This advance was made to prevent the

Greeks from escaping by flight, and to block them up in Salamis, where it was thought that vengeance might be taken upon them for the battles fought near Artemisium. The Persian troops were landed on the islet of Psyttaleia, because, as soon as the battle began, the men and wrecks were likely to be drifted thither, as the isle lay in the very path of the coming fight,—and they would thus be able to save their own men and destroy those of the enemy. All these movements were made in silence, that the Greeks might have no knowledge of them; and they occupied the whole night, so that the men had no time to get their sleep.

I cannot say that there is no truth in prophecies, or feel inclined to call in question those which speak with clearness, when I think of the following:—

When they shall bridge with their ships to the sacred strand of Diana, Girt with the golden falchion, and eke to marine Cynosura, Mad hope swelling their hearts at the downfall of beautiful Athens—Then shall godlike Right extinguish haughty Presumption, Insult's furious offspring, who thinketh to overthrow all things. Brass with brass shall mingle, and Mars with blood shall empurple Ocean's waves. Then—then shall the day of Grecia's freedom Come from Victory fair, and Saturn's son all-seeing.

When I look to this, and perceive how clearly Bacis spoke, I neither venture myself to say anything against prophecies, nor do I approve of others impugning them.

Meanwhile, among the captains at Salamis, the strife of words grew fierce. As yet they did not know that they were encompassed, but imagined that the barbarians remained in the same places where they had seen them the day before.

In the midst of their contention, Aristides, the son of Lysimachus, who had crossed from Egina, arrived in Salamis. He was an Athenian, and had been ostracised by the commonality, yet I believe, from what I have heard concerning his character, that there was not in all Athens a man so worthy or so just as he. He now came to the council, and standing outside, called for Themistocles. Now Themistocles was not his friend, but his most determined enemy. However, under the pressure of the great dangers impending, Aristides forgot their feud, and called Themistocles out of the council, since he wished to confer with him. He had heard before his arrival of the impatience of the Peloponnesians to withdraw the fleet to the Isthmus. As soon therefore as Themistocles came forth, Aristides addressed him in these words:—

Our rivalry at all times, and especially at the present season, ought to be a struggle, which of us shall most advantage our country. Let me then say to thee, that so far as regards the departure of the Peloponnesians from this place, much talk and little will be found precisely alike. I have seen with my own eyes that which I now report; that, however much the Corinthians or Eurybiades himself may wish it, they cannot now retreat; for we are enclosed on every side by the enemy. Go in to them, and make this known.

"Thy advice is excellent," answered the other, "and thy tidings are also good. That which I earnestly desired to happen, thine eyes have beheld accomplished. Know that what the Medes have now done was at my instance; for it was necessary, as our men would not fight here at their own free will, to make them fight whether they would or no. But come now, as thou hast brought the good news, go in and tell it. For if I speak to them, they will think it a feigned tale, and will not believe that the barbarians have inclosed us around. Therefore do thou go to them, and inform them how matters stand. If they believe thee, 'twill be for the best; but if otherwise, it will not harm. For it is impossible that they should now flee away, if we are indeed shut in on all sides, as thou sayest."

Then Aristides entered the assembly, and spoke to the captains: he had come, he told them, from Egina, and had but barely escaped the blockading vessels—the Greek fleet was entirely inclosed by the ships of Xerxes—and he advised them to get themselves in readiness to resist the foe. Having said so much, he withdrew. And now another contest arose, for the greater part of the captains would not believe the tidings.

But while they still doubted, a Tenian trireme, commanded by Paneatius the son of Sôsimenes, deserted from the Persians and joined the Greeks, bringing full intelligence. For this reason the Tenians were inscribed upon the tripod at Delphi among those who overthrew the barbarians. With this ship, which deserted to their side at Salamis, and the Lemnian vessel which came over before at Artemisium, the Greek fleet was brought to the full number of 380 ships; otherwise it fell short by two of that amount.

The Greeks now, not doubting what the Tenians told them, made ready for the coming fight. At dawn of day, all the men-at-arms were assembled together, and speeches were made to them, of which the best was that of Themistocles; who throughout contrasted what was noble with what was base, and bade them, in all that came within the range of man's nature and constitution, *always* to make choice of the nobler part. Having thus wound up his discourse, he told them to go at once on board their ships, which they accordingly did; and about this time the trireme, that had been sent to Egina for the Æacidae, returned; whereupon the Greeks put to sea with all their fleet.

The fleet had scarce left the land when they were attacked by the barbarians. At once most of the Greeks began to back water, and were about touching the shore, when Ameinias of Pallené, one of the Athenian captains, darted forth in front of the line, and charged a ship of the enemy. The two vessels became entangled, and could not separate, whereupon the rest of the fleet came up to help Ameinias, and engaged with the Persians. Such is the account which the Athenians give of the way in which the battle began; but the Eginetans maintain that the vessel which had been to Egina for the Æacidae, was the one that brought on the fight. It is also reported, that a phantom in the form of a woman appeared to the Greeks, and, in a voice that was heard from end to end of the fleet, cheered them on to the fight; first, however, rebuking them, and saying—"Strange men, how long are ye going to back water?"

Against the Athenians, who held the western extremity of the line towards Eleusis, were placed the Phoenicians; against the Lacedaemonians, whose station was eastward towards the Piraeus, the Ionians. Of these last a few only followed the advice of Themistocles, to fight backwardly; the greater number did far otherwise. I could mention here the names of many trierarchs who took vessels from the Greeks, but I shall pass over all excepting Theomêstor the son of Androdamas, and Phylacus the son of Histiaeus, both Samians. I show this preference to them, inasmuch as for this service Theomêstor was made tyrant of Samos by the Persians, while Phylacus was enrolled among the king's benefactors, and presented with a large estate in land. In the Persian tongue the king's benefactors are called Orosangs.

Far the greater number of the Persian ships engaged in this battle were disabled—either by the Athenians or by the Eginetans. For as the Greeks fought in order and kept their line, while the barbarians were in confusion and had no plan in anything that they did, the issue of the battle could scarce be other than it was. Yet the Persians fought far more bravely here than at Euboea, and indeed surpassed themselves; each did his utmost through fear of Xerxes, for each thought that the king's eye was upon himself.

What part the several nations, whether Greek or barbarian, took in the combat, I am not able to say for certain; Artemisia, however, I know, distinguished herself in such a way as raised her even higher than she stood before in the esteem of the king. For after confusion had spread throughout the whole of the king's fleet, and her ship was closely pursued by an Athenian trireme, she, having no way to fly, since in front of her were a number of friendly vessels, and she was nearest of all the Persians to the enemy,

resolved on a measure which in fact proved her safety. Pressed by the Athenian pursuer, she bore straight against one of the ships of her own party, a Calyndian, which had Damasithymus, the Calyndian king, himself on board. I cannot say whether she had had any quarrel with the man while the fleet was at the Hellespont, or not—neither can I decide whether she of set purpose attacked his vessel, or whether it merely chanced that the Calyndian ship came in her way—but certain it is that she bore down upon his vessel and sank it, and that thereby she had the good fortune to procure herself a double advantage. For the commander of the Athenian trireme, when he saw her bear down on one of the enemy's fleet, thought immediately that her vessel was a Greek, or else had deserted from the Persians, and was now fighting on the Greek side; he therefore gave up the chase, and turned away to attack others.

Thus in the first place she saved her life by the action, and was enabled to get clear off from the battle; while further, it fell out that in the very act of doing the king an injury she raised herself to a greater height than ever in his esteem. For as Xerxes beheld the fight, he remarked (it is said) the destruction of the vessel, whereupon the bystanders observed to him—"Seest thou, master, how well Artemisia fights, and how she has just sunk a ship of the enemy?" Then Xerxes asked if it were really Artemisia's doing; and they answered, "Certainly, for they knew her ensign": while all made sure that the sunken vessel belonged to the opposite side. Everything, it is said, conspired to prosper the queen—it was especially fortunate for her, that not one of those on board the Calyndian ship survived to become her accuser. Xerxes, they say, in reply to the remarks made to him, observed—"My men have behaved like women, and my women like men!"

There fell in this combat Ariabignes, one of the chief commanders of the fleet, who was son of Darius and brother of Xerxes, and with him perished a vast number of men of high repute, Persians, Medes, and allies. Of the Greeks there died only a few; for as they were able to swim, all those that were not slain outright by the enemy escaped from the sinking vessels and swam across to Salamis. But on the side of the barbarians more perished by drowning than in any other way, since they did not know how to swim. The great destruction took place when the ships which had been first engaged began to fly; for they who were stationed in the rear, anxious to display their valour before the eyes of the king, made every effort to force their way to the front, and thus became entangled with such of their own vessels as were retreating.

In this confusion the following event occurred: certain Phoenicians belonging to ships which had thus perished made their appearance before the king, and laid the blame of their loss on the Ionians, declaring that they were traitors, and had willfully destroyed the vessels. But the upshot of this complaint was, that the Ionian captains escaped the death which threatened them, while their Phoenician accusers received death as their reward. For it happened that, exactly as they spoke, a Samothracian vessel bore down on an Athenian and sank it, but was attacked and crippled immediately by one of the Eginetan squadron. Now the Samothracians were expert with the javelin, and aimed their weapons so well, that they cleared the deck of the vessel which had disabled their own, after which they sprang on board, and took it. This saved the Ionians. Xerxes, when he saw the exploit, turned fiercely on the Phoenicians—(he was ready, in his extreme vexation, to find fault with any one)—and ordered their heads to be cut off, to prevent them, he said, from casting the blame of their own misconduct upon braver men. During the whole time of the battle Xerxes sate at the base of the hill called Ægaleôs, over against Salamis; and whenever he saw any of his own captains perform any worthy exploit he inquired concerning him; and the man's name was taken down by his scribes, together with the names of his father and his city. Ariarammes too, a Persian, who was a friend of the Ionians, and present at the time whereof I speak, had a share in bringing about the punishment of the Phoenicians.

When the rout of the barbarians began, and they sought to make their escape to Phalêrum, the Eginetans, awaiting them in the channel, performed exploits worthy to be recorded. Through the whole of the confused struggle the Athenians employed themselves in destroying such ships as either made resistance or fled to shore, while the Eginetans dealt with those which endeavoured to escape down the straits; so that the Persian vessels were no sooner clear of the Athenians than straightway they fell into the hands of the Eginetan squadron.

It chanced here that there was a meeting between the ship of Themistocles, which was hasting in pursuit of the enemy, and that of Polycritus, son of Crius the Eginetan, which had just charged a Sidonian trireme. The Sidonian vessel was the same that captured the Eginetan guard-ship off Sciathus, which had Pytheas, the son of Ischenous, on board—that Pytheas, I mean, who fell covered with wounds, and whom the Sidonians kept on board their ship, from admiration of his gallantry. This man afterwards returned in safety to Egina, for when the Sidonian vessel with its Persian crew fell into the hands of the Greeks, he was still found on board. Polycritus no sooner saw the Athenian trireme than knowing at once whose vessel it was, as he observed that it bore the ensign of the admiral, he shouted to Themistocles jeeringly, and asked him, in a tone of reproach, if the Eginetans did not show themselves rare friends to the Medes. At the same time, while he thus reproached Themistocles, Polycritus bore straight down on the Sidonian. Such of the barbarian vessels as escaped from the battle fled to Phalêrum, and there sheltered themselves under the protection of the land army.

The Greeks who gained the greatest glory of all in the seafight of Salamis were the Eginetans, and after them the Athenians. The individuals of most distinction were Polycritus the Eginetan, and two Athenians, Eumenes of Anayrus, and Aminias of Pallené; the latter of whom had pressed Artemisia so hard. And assuredly, as he had known that the vessel carried Artemisia on board, he would never have given over the chase till he had either succeeded in taking her, or else been taken himself. For the Athenian captains had received special orders touching the queen, and moreover a reward of ten thousand drachmas had been proclaimed for any one who should make her prisoner; since there was great indignation felt that a woman should appear in arms against Athens. However, as I said before, she escaped; and so did some others whose ships survived the engagement; and these were all now assembled at the port of Phalêrum.

• • •

As soon as the sea-fight was ended, the Greeks drew together to Salamis all the wrecks that were to be found in that quarter, and prepared themselves for another engagement, supposing that the king would renew the fight with the vessels still remained to him. Many of the wrecks had been carried away by a westerly wind to the coast of Attica, where they were thrown upon the strip of shore called Côlias. Thus not only were the prophecies of Bacis and Musaeus concerning this battle fulfilled completely, but likewise, by the place to which the wrecks were drifted, the prediction of Lysistratus, an Athenian soothsayer, uttered many years before these events, and quite forgotten at the time by all the Greeks, was fully accomplished. The words were:—

Then shall the sight of the oars fill Colian dames with amazement.

Sophocles

The life of Sophocles, the tragic poet, spanned the fifth century. Born in 496 B.C., he was just old enough to remember the battle of Marathon, and in 480 he led a chorus of Athenian youths in the ceremonial celebration of the naval victory at Salamis. He reached the height of his creative powers in the Age of Pericles. His *Antigone* was produced in 441, three years before the completion of the Parthenon, and his *King Oedipus* was produced around 430, the year before the death of Pericles. Sophocles died in 406 at the age of ninety, two years before the Athenian defeat in the Peloponnesian War.

To understand the tragic drama *Antigone*, we must realize that, according to Greek religion, the body of a deceased person had to be buried before the soul could enter Hades. Thus, Antigone had a sacred duty to bury her brother, a duty that she believed took precedence over all others, even obedience to the decrees of the state. The tragedy, therefore, can be interpreted as a clash between divine law, championed by Antigone, and human or political law, championed by Creon. Such an interpretation, however, does not exhaust the meaning of the play. Viewed as a dramatic portrayal of human character, the tragedy that destroys both Antigone and Creon becomes the inevitable result of a clash between two strong-willed individuals, each dedicated to an ideal in itself good, but neither willing to make any compromise between his ideal and that held by the other.

Antigone

CHARACTERS

ISMENE ⎫ *daughters of*
ANTIGONE ⎭ *Oedipus*

CREON, *King of Thebes*
HAEMON, *son of* CREON
TEIRESIAS, *a blind prophet*
SENTRY

MESSENGER
EURYDICE, *wife of* CREON
CHORUS *of Theban elders*
King's attendants
Queen's attendants
BOY *leading* TEIRESIAS
SOLDIERS

SCENE: Before the Palace at Thebes
Enter ISMENE *from the central door of the Palace.* ANTIGONE *follows, anxious and urgent; she closes the door carefully, and comes to join her sister.*

ANTIGONE: O sister! Ismene dear, dear sister Ismene!
You know how heavy the hand of God is upon us;
How we who are left must suffer for our father, Oedipus.
There is no pain, no sorrow, no suffering, no dishonour
We have not shared together, you and I.
And now there is something more. Have you heard this order,
This latest order that the King has proclaimed to the city?
Have you heard how our dearest are being treated like enemies?
ISMENE: I have heard nothing about any of those we love,
Neither good nor evil—not, I mean, since the death
Of our two brothers, both fallen in a day.
The Argive army, I hear, was withdrawn last night.

I know no more to make me sad or glad.
ANTIGONE: I thought you did not. That's why I brought you out here,
Where we shan't be heard, to tell you something alone.
ISMENE: What is it, Antigone? Black news, I can see already.
ANTIGONE: O Ismene, what do you think? Our two dear brothers . . .
Creon has given funeral honours to one,
And not to the other; nothing but shame and ignominy.
Eteocles has been buried, they tell me, in state,
With all honourable observances due to the dead.
But Polynices, just as unhappily fallen—the order
Says he is not to be buried, not to be mourned;
To be left unburied, unwept, a feast of flesh
For keen-eyed carrion birds. The noble Creon!
It is against you and me he has made this order.

Sophocles, "Antigone," in *The Theban Plays*, trans. E. F. Watling (Harmondsworth, Middlesex: Penguin Books, Ltd., 1947), pp. 126–62. Courtesy of Penguin Books, Ltd.

Yes, against me. And soon he will be here himself

To make it plain to those that have not heard it,

And to enforce it. This is no idle threat;

The punishment for disobedience is death by stoning.

So now you know. And now is the time to show

Whether or not you are worthy of your high blood.

ISMENE: My poor Antigone, if this is really true,

What more can I do, or undo, to help you?

ANTIGONE: Will you help me? Will you do something with me? Will you?

ISMENE: Help you do what, Antigone? What do you mean?

ANTIGONE: Would you help me lift the body . . . you and me?

ISMENE: You cannot mean . . . to bury him? Against the order?

ANTIGONE: Is he not my brother, and yours, whether you like it

Or not? I shall never desert him, never.

ISMENE: How could you dare, when Creon has expressly forbidden it?

ANTIGONE: He has no right to keep me from my own.

ISMENE: O sister, sister, do you forget how our father

Perished in shame and misery, his awful sin

Self-proved, blinded by his own self-mutilation?

And then his mother, his wife—for she was both—

Destroyed herself in a noose of her own making

And now our brothers, both in a single day

Fallen in an awful exaction of death for death,

Blood for blood, each slain by the other's hand.

Now we two left; and what will be the end of us,

If we transgress the law and defy our king?

O think, Antigone; we are women; it is not for us

To fight against men; our rulers are stronger than we,

And we must obey in this, or in worse than this.

May the dead forgive me, I can do no other

But as I am commanded; to do more is madness.

ANTIGONE: No; then I will not ask you for your help.

Nor would I thank you for it, if you gave it.

Go your own way; I will bury my brother;

And if I die for it, what happiness!

Convicted of reverence—I shall be content

To lie beside a brother whom I love.

We have only a little time to please the living,

But all eternity to love the dead.

There I shall lie for ever. Live, if you will;

Live, and defy the holiest laws of heaven.

ISMENE: I do not defy them; but I cannot act

Against the State. I am not strong enough.

ANTIGONE: Let that be your excuse, then I will go

And heap a mound of earth over my brother.

ISMENE: I fear for you, Antigone; I fear—

ANTIGONE: You need not fear for me. Fear for yourself.

ISMENE: At least be secret. Do not breathe a word.

I'll not betray your secret.

ANTIGONE: Publish it

To all the world! Else I shall hate
  you the more.
ISMENE: Your heart burns! Mine is
  frozen at the thought.
ANTIGONE: I know my duty, where
  true duty lies.
ISMENE: If you can do it; but you're
  bound to fail.
ANTIGONE: When I have tried and
  failed, I shall have failed.
ISMENE: No sense in starting on a
  hopeless task.
ANTIGONE: Oh, I shall hate you if you
  talk like that!
And he will hate you, rightly. Leave
  me alone
With my own madness. There is no
  punishment
Can rob me of my honourable
  death.
ISMENE: Go then, if you are determined,
  to your folly.
But remember that those who love
  you . . . love you still.
ISMENE *goes into the Palace.*
ANTIGONE *leaves the stage by a side exit.*
Enter the CHORUS *of Theban elders.*
CHORUS: Hail the sun! the brightest of
  all that ever
Dawned on the City of Seven Gates,
  City of Thebes!
Hail the golden dawn over Dirce's
  river
Rising to speed the flight of the
  white invaders
Homeward in full retreat!
The army of Polynices was gathered
  against us,
In angry dispute his voice was lifted
  against us.
Like a ravening bird of prey he
  swooped around us
With white wings flashing, with
  flying plumes,
With armed hosts ranked in
  thousands.
At the threshold of seven gates in a
  circle of blood

His swords stood round us, his jaws
  were opened against us;
But before he could taste our blood,
  or consume us with fire,
He fled, fled with the roar of the
  dragon behind him
And thunder of war in his ears.
The Father of Heaven abhors the
  proud tongue's boasting;
He marked the oncoming torrent,
  the flashing stream
Of their golden harness, the clash of
  their battle gear;
He heard the invader cry Victory
  over our ramparts,
And smote him with fire to the
  ground.
Down to the ground from the crest
  of his hurricane onslaught
He swung, with the fiery brands of
  his hate brought low:
Each and all to their doom of
  destruction appointed
By the god that fighteth for us.
Seven invaders at seven gates, seven
  defenders
Spoiled of their bronze for a tribute
  to Zeus; save two
Luckless brothers in one fight
  matched together
And in one death laid low.
Great is the victory, great be the joy
In the city of Thebes, the city of
  chariots.
Now is the time to fill the temples
With glad thanksgiving for warfare
  ended;
Shake the ground with the night-
  long dances,
Bacchus afoot and delight
  abounding.
But see, the King comes here,
Creon, the son of Menoeceus,
Whom the gods have appointed for
  us
In our recent change of fortune.
What matter is it, I wonder,
That has led him to call us together

By his special proclamation?

The central door is opened, and
CREON *enters.*

CREON: My councillors: now that the gods have brought our city
Safe through a storm of trouble to tranquillity,
I have called you especially out of all my people
To conference together, knowing that you
Were loyal subjects when King Laius reigned,
And when King Oedipus so wisely ruled us,
And again, upon his death, faithfully served
His sons, till they in turn fell—both slayers, both slain,
Both stained with brother-blood, dead in a day—
And I, their next of kin, inherited
The throne and kingdom which I now possess.
No other touchstone can test the heart of a man,
The temper of his mind and spirit, till he be tried
In the practice of authority and rule.
For my part, I have always held the view,
And hold it still, that a king whose lips are sealed
By fear, unwilling to seek advice, is damned.
And no less damned is he who puts a friend
Above his country: I have no good word for him.
As God above is my witness, who sees all,
When I see any danger threatening my people,
Whatever it may be, I shall declare it.
No man who is his country's enemy
Shall call himself my friend. Of this I am sure—
Our country is our life; only when she
Rides safely, have we any friends at all
Such is my policy for our common weal.
In pursuance of this, I have made a proclamation
Concerning the sons of Oedipus, as follows:
Eteocles, who fell fighting in defense of the city,
Fighting gallantly, is to be honoured with burial
And with all the rites due to the noble dead.
The other—you know whom I mean—his brother Polynices,
Who came back from exile intending to burn and destroy
His fatherland and the gods of his fatherland,
To drink the blood of his kin, to make them slaves—
He is to have no grave, no burial,
No mourning from anyone; it is forbidden.
He is to be left unburied, left to be eaten
By dogs and vultures, a horror for all to see.
I am determined that never, if I can help it,
Shall evil triumph over good. Alive
Or dead, the faithful servant of his country
Shall be rewarded.

CHORUS: Creon, son of Menoeceus,
You have given your judgment for the friend and for the enemy.
As for those that are dead, so for us who remain,
Your will is law.

CREON: See then that it be kept.

CHORUS: My lord, some younger would be fitter for that task.

CREON: Watchers are already set over the corpse.

CHORUS: What other duty then remains for us?

CREON: Not to connive at any disobedience.

CHORUS: If there were any so mad as to ask for death—

CREON: Ay, that is the penalty. There is always someone
Ready to be lured to ruin by hope of gain.

He turns to go. A SENTRY *enters from the side of the stage.*
CREON *pauses at the Palace door.*

SENTRY: My lord: if I am out of breath, it is not from haste.
I have not been running. On the contrary, many a time
I stopped to think and loitered on the way,
Saying to myself 'Why hurry to your doom,
Poor fool?' and then I said 'Hurry, you fool.
If Creon hears this from another man,
Your head's as good as off.' So here I am,
As quick as my unwilling haste could bring me;
In no great hurry, in fact. So now I am here . . .
But I'll tell my story . . . though it may be nothing after all.
And whatever I have to suffer, it can't be more
Than what God wills, so I cling to that for my comfort.

CREON: Good heavens, man, whatever is the matter?

SENTRY: To speak of myself first—I never did it, sir;
Nor saw who did; no one can punish me for that.

CREON: You tell your story with a deal of artful precaution.
It's evidently something strange.

SENTRY: It is.
So strange, it's very difficult to tell.

CREON: Well, out with it, and let's be done with you.

SENTRY: It's this, sir, The corpse . . . someone has just
Buried it and gone. Dry dust over the body
They scattered, in the manner of holy burial.

CREON: What! Who dared to do it?

SENTRY: I don't know, sir.
There was no sign of a pick, no scratch of a shovel;
The ground was hard and dry—no trace of a wheel;
Whoever it was has left no clues behind him.
When the sentry on the first watch showed it us,
We were amazed. The corpse was covered from sight—
Not with a proper grave—just a layer of earth—
As it might be, the act of some pious passer-by.
There were no tracks of an animal either, a dog
Or anything that might have come and mauled the body.
Of course we all started pitching in to each other,
Accusing each other, and might have come to blows,
With no one to stop us; for anyone might have done it,
But it couldn't be proved against him, and all denied it.
We were all ready to take hot iron in hand
And go through fire and swear by God and heaven
We hadn't done it, nor knew of anyone
That could have thought of doing it, much less done it.
Well, we could make nothing of it. Then one of our men

Said something that made all our
  blood run cold—
Something we could neither refuse
  to do, nor do,
But at our own risk. What he said
  was 'This
Must be reported to the King; we
  can't conceal it.'
So it was agreed. We drew lots for
  it, and I,
Such is my luck, was chosen. So here
  I am,
As much against my will as yours,
  I'm sure;
A bringer of bad news expects no
  welcome.

CHORUS: My lord, I fear—I feared it
  from the first—
That this may prove to be an act of
  the gods.

CREON: Enough of that! Or I shall lose
  my patience.
Don't talk like an old fool, old
  though you be.
Blasphemy, to say the gods could
  give a thought
To carrion flesh! Held him in high
  esteem,
I suppose, and buried him like a
  benefactor—
A man who came to burn their
  temples down,
Ransack their holy shrines, their
  land, their laws?
Is that the sort of man you think
  gods love?
Not they. No. There's a party of
  malcontents
In the city, rebels against my word
  and law,
Shakers of heads in secret, impatient
  of rule;
They are the people, I see it well
  enough,
Who have bribed their instruments
  to do this thing.
Money! Money's the curse of man,
  none greater.

That's what wrecks cities, banishes
  men from home,
Tempts and deludes the most well-
  meaning soul,
Pointing out the way to infamy and
  shame.
Well, they shall pay for their success.
  (*To the* SENTRY)
See to it!
See to it, you! Upon my oath, I
  swear,
As Zeus is my god above: either you
  find
The perpetrator of this burial
And bring him here into my sight,
  or death—
No, not your mere death shall pay
  the reckoning,
But, for a living lesson against such
  infamy,
You shall be racked and tortured till
  you tell
The whole truth of this outrage; so
  you may learn
To seek your gain where gain is
  yours to get,
Not try to grasp it everywhere. In
  wickedness
You'll find more loss than profit.

SENTRY: May I say more?

CREON: No more; each word you say
  but stings me more.

SENTRY: Stings in your ears, sir, or in
  your deeper feelings?

CREON: Don't bandy words, fellow,
  about my feelings.

SENTRY: Though I offend your ears,
  sir, it is not I
But he that's guilty that offends
  your soul.

CREON: Oh, born to argue, were you?

SENTRY: Maybe so;
But still not guilty in this business.

CREON: Doubly so, if you have sold
  your soul for money.

SENTRY: To think that thinking men
  should think so wrongly!

CREON: Think what you will. But if you fail to find
The doer of this deed, you'll learn one thing:
Ill-gotten gain brings no one any good.
He goes into the Palace.
SENTRY: Well, heaven send they find him.
But whether or no,
They'll not find me again, that's sure. Once free,
Who never thought to see another day,
I'll thank my lucky stars, and keep away.
Exit.
CHORUS: Wonders are many on earth, and the greatest of these
Is man, who rides the ocean and takes his way
Through the deeps, through wind-swept valleys of perilous seas
That surge and sway.
He is master of ageless Earth, to his own will bending
The immortal mother of gods by the sweat of his brow,
As year succeeds to year; with toil unending
Of mule and plough.
He is lord of all things living: birds of the air,
Beasts of the field, all creatures of sea and land
He taketh, cunning to capture and ensnare
With sleight of hand;
Hunting the savage beast from the upland rocks,
Taming the mountain monarch in his lair,
Teaching the wild horse and the roaming ox
His yoke to bear.
The use of language, the wind-swift motion of brain

He learnt; found out the laws of living together
In cities, building him shelter against the rain
And wintry weather.
There is nothing beyond his power. His subtlety
Meeteth all chance, all danger conquereth.
For every ill he hath found its remedy,
Save only death.
O wondrous subtlety of man, that draws
To good or evil ways! Great honour is given
And power to him who upholdeth his country's laws.
And the justice of heaven.
But he that, too rashly daring, walks in sin
In solitary pride to his life's end,
At door of mine shall never enter in
To call me friend.
(Severally, seeing some persons approach from a distance)
O gods! a wonder to see!
Surely it cannot be—
It is no other—
Antigone!
Unhappy maid—
Unhappy Oedipus' daughter; it is she they bring.
Can she have rashly disobeyed
The order of our King?
Enter the SENTRY, *bringing* ANTIGONE *guarded by two more soldiers.*
SENTRY: We've got her. Here's the woman that did the deed.
We found her in the act of burying him. Where's the King?
CHORUS: He is just coming out of the palace now.
Enter CREON.
CREON: What's this? What am I just in time to see?
SENTRY: My lord, an oath's a very dangerous thing.

Second thoughts may prove us liars.
  Not long since
I swore I wouldn't trust myself again
To face your threats; you gave me a
  drubbing the first time.
But there's no pleasure like an
  unexpected pleasure,
Not by a long way. And so I've
  come again,
Though against my solemn oath.
  And I've brought this lady,
Who's been caught in the act of
  setting that grave in order.
And no casting lots for it this time—
  the prize is mine
And no one else's. So take her;
  judge and convict her.
I'm free, I hope, and quit of the
  horrible business.
CREON: How did you find her? Where
  have you brought her from?
SENTRY: She was burying the man with
  her own hands, and that's the
  truth.
CREON: Are you in your senses? Do
  you know what you are saying?
SENTRY: I saw her myself, burying the
  body of the man
  Whom you said not to bury. Don't I
  speak plain?
CREON: How did she come to be seen
  and taken in the act?
SENTRY: It was this way.
  After I got back to the place,
  With all your threats and curses
  ringing in my ears,
  We swept off all the earth that
  covered the body,
  And left it a sodden naked corpse
  again;
  Then sat up on the hill, on the
  windward side,
  Keeping clear of the stench of him,
  as far as we could;
  All of us keeping each other up to
  the mark,
  With pretty sharp speaking, not to
  be caught napping this time.

So this went on some hours, till the
  flaming sun
Was high in the top of the sky, and
  the heat was blazing.
Suddenly a storm of dust, like a
  plague from heaven,
Swept over the ground, stripping
  the trees stark bare,
Filling the sky; you had to shut your
  eyes
To stand against it. When at last it
  stopped,
There was the girl, screaming like
  an angry bird,
When it finds its nest left empty and
  little ones gone.
Just like that she screamed, seeing
  the body
Naked, crying and cursing the ones
  that had done it.
Then she picks up the dry earth in
  her hands,
And pouring out of a fine bronze
  urn she's brought
She makes her offering three times
  to the dead.
Soon as we saw it, down we came
  and caught her.
She wasn't at all frightened. And so
  we charged her
With what she'd done before, and
  this. She admitted it,
I'm glad to say—though sorry too,
  in a way.
It's good to save your own skin, but
  a pity
To have to see another get into
  trouble,
Whom you've no grudge against.
  However, I can't say
I've ever valued anyone else's life
More than my own, and that's the
  honest truth.
CREON (*to* ANTIGONE): Well, what do
  you say—you, hiding your head
  there:
  Do you admit, or do you deny the
  deed?

ANTIGONE: I do admit it. I do not deny it.

CREON (*to the* SENTRY): You—you may go. You are discharged from blame.

Exit SENTRY.

Now tell me, in as few words as you can,

Did you know the order forbidding such an act?

ANTIGONE: I knew it, naturally. It was plain enough.

CREON: And yet you dared to contravene it?

ANTIGONE: Yes.

That order did not come from God. Justice,

That dwells with the gods below, knows no such law.

I did not think your edicts strong enough

To overrule the unwritten unalterable laws

Of God and heaven, you being only a man.

They are not of yesterday or to-day, but everlasting,

Though where they came from, none of us can tell.

Guilty of their transgression before God

I cannot be, for any man on earth.

I knew that I should have to die, of course,

With or without your order. If it be soon,

So much the better. Living in daily torment

As I do, who would not be glad to die?

This punishment will not be any pain.

Only if I had let my mother's son

Lie there unburied, then I could not have borne it.

This I can bear. Does that seem foolish to you?

Or is it you that are foolish to judge me so?

CHORUS: She shows her father's stubborn spirit: foolish

Not to give way when everything's against her.

CREON: Ah, but you'll see. The over-obstinate spirit

Is soonest broken; as the strongest iron will snap

If over-tempered in the fire to brittleness.

A little halter is enough to break

The wildest horse. Proud thoughts do not sit well

Upon subordinates. This girl's proud spirit

Was first in evidence when she broke the law;

And now, to add insult to her injury,

She gloats over her deed. But, as I live,

She shall not flout my orders with impunity.

My sister's child—ay, were she even nearer,

Nearest and dearest, she should not escape

Full punishment—she, and her sister too,

Her partner, doubtless, in this burying.

Let her be fetched! She was in the house just now;

I saw her, hardly in her right mind either.

Often the thoughts of those who plan dark deeds

Betray themselves before the deed is done.

The criminal who being caught still tries

To make a fair excuse, is damned indeed.

ANTIGONE: Now you have caught, will you do more than kill me?

CREON: No, nothing more; that is all I
    could wish.
ANTIGONE: Why then delay? There is
    nothing that you can say
That I should wish to hear, as
    nothing I say
Can weigh with you. I have given
    my brother burial.
What greater honour could I wish?
    All these
Would say that what I did was
    honourable,
But fear locks up their lips. To
    speak and act
Just as he likes is a king's
    prerogative.
CREON: You are wrong. None of my
    subjects thinks as you do.
ANTIGONE: Yes, sir, they do; but dare
    not tell you so.
CREON: And you are not only alone,
    but unashamed.
ANTIGONE: There is no shame in
    honouring my brother.
CREON: Was not his enemy, who died
    with him, your brother?
ANTIGONE: Yes, both were brothers,
    both of the same parents.
CREON: You honour one, and so insult
    the other.
ANTIGONE: He that is dead will not
    accuse me of that.
CREON: He will, if you honour him no
    more than the traitor.
ANTIGONE: It was not a slave, but his
    brother, that died with him.
CREON: Attacking his country, while
    the other defended it.
ANTIGONE: Even so, we have a duty to
    the dead.
CREON: Not to give equal honour to
    good and bad.
ANTIGONE: Who knows? In the country
    of the dead that may be the law.
CREON: An enemy can't be a friend,
    even when dead.
ANTIGONE: My way is to share my love,
    not share my hate.

CREON: Go then, and share your love
    among the dead.
We'll have no woman's law here,
    while I live.
Enter ISMENE *from the Palace.*
CHORUS: Here comes Ismene, weeping
    In sisterly sorrow; a darkened brow,
    Flushed face, and the fair cheek
    marred
With flooding rain.
CREON: You crawling viper! Lurking in
    my house
To suck my blood! Two traitors
    unbeknown
Plotting against my throne. Do you
    admit
To a share in this burying, or deny
    all knowledge?
ISMENE: I did it—yes—if she will let
    me say so.
I am as much to blame as she is.
ANTIGONE: No.
That is not just. You would not lend
    a hand
And I refused your help in what I
    did.
ISMENE: But I am not ashamed to
    stand beside you
Now in the hour of trial, Antigone.
ANTIGONE: Whose was the deed, Death
    and the dead are witness.
I love no friend whose love is only
    words.
ISMENE: O sister, sister, let me share
    your death,
Share in the tribute of honour to
    him that is dead.
ANTIGONE: You shall not die with me.
    You shall not claim
That which you would not touch.
    One death is enough.
ISMENE: How can I bear to live, if you
    must die?
ANTIGONE: Ask Creon. Is not he the
    one you care for?
ISMENE: You do yourself no good to
    taunt me so.

ANTIGONE: Indeed no: even my jests are bitter pains.

ISMENE: But how, O tell me, how can I still help you?

ANTIGONE: Help yourself. I shall not stand in your way.

ISMENE: For pity, Antigone—can I not die with you?

ANTIGONE: You chose; life was your choice, when mine was death.

ISMENE: Although I warned you that it would be so.

ANTIGONE: Your way seemed right to some, to others mine.

ISMENE: But now both in the wrong, and both condemned.

ANTIGONE: No, no. You live. My heart was long since dead,
So it was right for me to help the dead.

CREON: I do believe the creatures both are mad,
One lately crazed, the other from her birth.

ISMENE: Is it not likely, sir? The strongest mind
Cannot but break under misfortune's blows.

CREON: Yours did, when you threw in your lot with hers.

ISMENE: How could I wish to live without my sister?

CREON: You have no sister. Count her dead already.

ISMENE: You could not take her—kill your own son's bride?

CREON: Oh, there are other fields for him to plough.

ISMENE: No truer troth was ever made than theirs.

CREON: No son of mine shall wed so vile a creature.

ANTIGONE: O Haemon, can your father spite you so?

CREON: You and your paramour, I hate you both.

CHORUS: Sir, would you take her from your own son's arms?

CREON: Not I, but death shall take her.

CHORUS: Be it so.
Her death, it seems, is certain.

CREON: Certain it is.
No more delay. Take them, and keep them within—
The proper place for women. None so brave
As not to look for some way of escape
When they see life stand face to face with death.

The women are taken away.

CHORUS: Happy are they who know not the taste of evil.
From a house that heaven hath shaken
The curse departs not
But falls upon all of the blood,
Like the restless surge of the sea when the dark storm drives
The black sand hurled from the deeps
And the Thracian gales boom down
On the echoing shore.
In life and in death is the house of Labdacus stricken.
Generation to generation,
With no atonement,
It is scourged by the wrath of a god.
And now for the dead dust's sake is the light of promise,
The tree's last root, crushed out
By pride of heart and the sin
Of presumptuous tongue.
For what presumption of man can match thy power,
O Zeus, that art not subject to sleep or time
Or age, living for ever in bright Olympus?
To-morrow and for all time to come,
As in the past,
This law is immutable:
For mortals greatly to live is greatly to suffer.

Roving ambition helps many a man
    to good,
And many it falsely lures to light
    desires,
Till failure trips them unawares, and
    they fall
On the fire that consumes them.
    Well was it said,
Evil seems good
To him who is doomed to suffer;
And short is the time before that
    suffering comes.
    But here comes Haemon,
Your youngest son.
Does he come to speak his sorrow
For the doom of his promised bride,
The loss of his marriage hopes?
CREON: We shall know it soon, and
    need no prophet to tell us.
    Enter HAEMON.
Son, you have heard, I think, our
    final judgment
On your late betrothed. No angry
    words, I hope?
Still friends, in spite of everything,
    my son?
HAEMON: I am your son, sir; by your
    wise decisions
My life is ruled, and them I shall
    always obey.
I cannot value any marriage-tie
Above your own good guidance.
CREON: Rightly said.
Your father's will should have your
    heart's first place.
Only for this do fathers pray for
    sons
Obedient, loyal, ready to strike
    down
Their father's foes, and love their
    fathers' friends.
To be the father of unprofitable
    sons
Is to be the father of sorrows, a
    laughingstock
To all one's enemies. Do not be
    fooled, my son,

By lust and the wiles of a woman.
    You'll have bought
Cold comfort if your wife's a
    worthless one.
No wound strikes deeper than love
    that is turned to hate.
This girl's an enemy; away with her,
And let her go and find a mate in
    Hades.
Once having caught her in a
    flagrant act—
The one and only traitor in our
    State—
I cannot make myself a traitor too;
So she must die. Well may she pray
    to Zeus,
The God of Family Love. How, if I
    tolerate
A traitor at home, shall I rule those
    abroad?
He that is a righteous master of his
    house
Will be a righteous statesman. To
    transgress
Or twist the law to one's own
    pleasures, presume
To order where one should obey, is
    sinful,
And I will have none of it.
He whom the State appoints must
    be obeyed
To the smallest matter, be it right—
    or wrong.
And he that rules his household,
    without a doubt,
Will make the wisest king, or, for
    that matter,
The staunchest subject. He will be
    the man
You can depend on in the storm of
    war,
The faithfullest comrade in the day
    of battle.
There is no more deadly peril than
    disobedience;
States are devoured by it, homes
    laid in ruins,

Armies defeated, victory turned to
   rout.
While simple obedience saves the
   lives of hundreds
Of honest folk. Therefore, I hold to
   the law,
And will never betray it—least of all
   for a woman.
Better be beaten, if need be, by a
   man,
Than let a woman get the better of
   us.
CHORUS: To me, as far as an old man
   can tell,
   It seems your Majesty has spoken
   well.
HAEMON: Father, man's wisdom is the
   gift of heaven,
   The greatest gift of all. I neither am
   Nor wish to be clever enough to
   prove you wrong,
   Though all men might not think the
   same as you do.
   Nevertheless, I have to be your
   watchdog,
   To know what others say and what
   they do,
   And what they find to praise and
   what to blame.
   Your frown is a sufficient silencer
   Of any word that is not for your
   ears.
   But I hear whispers spoken in the
   dark;
   On every side I hear voices of pity
   For this poor girl, doomed to the
   cruellest death,
   And most unjust, that ever woman
   suffered
   For an honourable action—burying
   a brother
   Who was killed in a battle, rather
   than leave him naked
   For dogs to maul and carrion birds
   to peck at.
   Has she not rather earned a crown
   of gold?—

Such is the secret talk about the
   town.
Father, there is nothing I can prize
   above
Your happiness and well-being.
   What greater good
Can any son desire? Can any father
Desire more from his son?
   Therefore I say,
Let not your first thought be your
   only thought.
Think if there cannot be some other
   way.
Surely, to think your own the only
   wisdom,
And yours the only word, the only
   will,
Betrays a shallow spirit, an empty
   heart.
It is no weakness for the wisest man
To learn when he is wrong, know
   when to yield.
So, on the margin of a flooded river
Trees bending to the torrent live
   unbroken,
While those that strain against it are
   snapped off.
A sailor has to tack and slacken
   sheets
Before the gale, or find himself
   capsized.
So, father, pause, and put aside
   your anger.
I think, for what my young
   opinion's worth,
That, good as it is to have infallible
   wisdom,
Since this is rarely found, the next
   best thing
Is to be willing to listen to wise
   advice.
CHORUS: There is something to be
   said, my lord, for his point of
   view,
   And for yours as well; there is much
   to be said on both sides.
CREON: Indeed! Am I to take lessons
   at my time of life

From a fellow of his age?

HAEMON: No lesson you need to be
  ashamed of.
  It isn't a question of age, but of
  right and wrong.

CREON: Would you call it right to
  admire an act of disobedience?

HAEMON: Not if the act were also
  dishonourable.

CREON: And was not this woman's
  action dishonourable?

HAEMON: The people of Thebes think
  not.

CREON: The people of Thebes!
  Since when do I take my orders
  from the people of Thebes?

HAEMON: Isn't that rather a childish
  thing to say?

CREON: No, I am king, and responsible
  only to myself.

HAEMON: A one-man state? What sort
  of a state is that?

CREON: Why, does not every state
  belong to its ruler?

HAEMON: You'd be an excellent king—
  on a desert island.

CREON: Of course, if you're on the
  woman's side—

HAEMON: No, no—
  Unless you're the woman. It's you
  I'm fighting for.

CREON: What, villain, when every word
  you speak is against me?

HAEMON: Only because I know you are
  wrong, wrong.

CREON: Wrong? To respect my own
  authority?

HAEMON: What sort of respect
  tramples on all that is holy?

CREON: Despicable coward! No more
  will than a woman!

HAEMON: I have nothing to be
  ashamed of.

CREON: Yet you plead her cause.

HAEMON: No, yours, and mine, and
  that of the gods of the dead.

CREON: You'll never marry her this
  side of death.

HAEMON: Then, if she dies, she does
  not die alone.

CREON: Is that a threat, you
  impudent—

HAEMON: Is it a threat
  To try to argue against wrong-
  headedness?

CREON: You'll learn what wrong-
  headedness is, my friend, to your
  cost.

HAEMON: O father, I could call you
  mad, were you not my father.

CREON: Don't toady me, boy; keep that
  for your lady-love.

HAEMON: You mean to have the last
  word then?

CREON: I do.
  And what is more, by all the gods in
  heaven,
  I'll make you sorry for your
  impudence.
  (*Calling to those within*)
  Bring out that she-devil, and let her
  die
  Now, with her bridegroom by to see
  it done!

HAEMON: That sight I'll never see. Nor
  from this hour
  Shall you see me again. Let those
  that will
  Be witness of your wickedness and
  folly.
  Exit.

CHORUS: He is gone, my lord, in very
  passionate haste.
  And who shall say what a young
  man's wrath may do?

CREON: Let him go! Let him do! Let
  him rage as never man raged,
  He shall not save those women from
  their doom.

CHORUS: You mean, then sire, to put
  them both to death?

CREON: No, not the one whose hand
  was innocent.

CHORUS: And to what death do you
  condemn the other?

CREON: I'll have her taken to a desert place
Where no man ever walked, and there walled up
Inside a cave, alive, with food enough
To acquit ourselves of the blood-guiltiness
That else would lie upon our commonwealth.
There she may pray to Death, the god she loves,
And ask release from death; or learn at last
What hope there is for those who worship death.

Exit.

CHORUS:
Where is the equal of Love?
Where is the battle he cannot win,
The power he cannot outmatch?
In the farthest corners of earth, in the midst of the sea,
He is there; he is here
In the bloom of a fair face
Lying in wait;
And the grip of his madness
Spares not god or man,
   Marring the righteous man,
Driving his soul into mazes of sin
And strife, dividing a house,
For the light that burns in the eyes of a bride of desire
Is a fire that consumes.
At the side of the great gods
Aphrodite immortal
Works her will upon all.

The doors are opened and ANTIGONE *enters, guarded.*

But here is a sight beyond all bearing,
At which my eyes cannot but weep;
Antigone forth faring
To her bridal-bower of endless sleep.

ANTIGONE: You see me, countrymen, on my last journey,
Taking my last leave of the light of day;
Going to my rest, where death shall take me
Alive across the silent river.
No wedding-day; no marriage-music;
Death will be all my bridal dower.

CHORUS: But glory and praise go with you, lady,
To your resting-place. You go with your beauty
Unmarred by the hand of consuming sickness,
Untouched by the sword, living and free,
As none other that ever died before you.

ANTIGONE: The daughter of Tantalus, a Phrygian maid,
Was doomed to a piteous death on the rock
Of Sipylos, which embraced and imprisoned her,
Merciless as the ivy; rain and snow
Beat down upon her, mingled with her tears,
As she wasted and died. Such was her story,
And such is the sleep that I shall go to.

CHORUS: She was a goddess of immortal birth,
And we are mortals; the greater the glory,
To share the fate of a god-born maiden,
A living death, but a name undying.

ANTIGONE: Mockery, mockery! By the gods of our fathers,
Must you make me a laughing-stock while I yet live?
O lordly sons of my city! O Thebes!
Your valley of rivers, your chariots and horses!
No friend to weep at my banishment
To a rock-hewn chamber of endless durance,

In a strange cold tomb alone to
  linger
Lost between life and death for
  ever.
CHORUS: My child, you have gone your
  way
To the outermost limit of daring
And have stumbled against Law
  enthroned.
This is the expiation
You must make for the sin of your
  father.
ANTIGONE: My father—the thought
  that sears my soul—
The unending burden of the house
  of Labdacus.
Monstrous marriage of mother and
  son . . .
My father . . . my parents . . . O
  hideous shame!
Whom now I follow, unwed, curse-
  ridden,
Doomed to this death by the ill-
  starred marriage
That marred my brother's life.
CHORUS: An act of homage is good in
  itself, my daughter;
But authority cannot afford to
  connive at disobedience.
You are the victim of your own self-
  will.
ANTIGONE: And must go the way that
  lies before me.
No funeral hymn; no marriage-
  music;
No sun from this day forth, no light,
No friend to weep at my departing.
Enter CREON.
CREON: Weeping and wailing at the
  door of death!
There'd be no end of it, if it had
  force
To buy death off. Away with her at
  once,
And close her up in rock-vaulted
  tomb.
Leave her and let her die, if die she
  must,

Or live within her dungeon. Though
  on earth
Her life is ended from this day, her
  blood
Will not be on our hands.
ANTIGONE: So to my grave,
My bridal-bower, my everlasting
  prison,
I go, to join those many of my
  kinsmen
Who dwell in the mansions of
  Persephone,
Last and unhappiest, before my
  time.
Yet I believe my father will be there
To welcome me, my mother greet
  me gladly,
And you, my brother, gladly see me
  come.
Each one of you my hands have laid
  to rest,
Pouring the due libations on your
  graves.
It was by this service to your dear
  body, Polynices,
I earned the punishment which now
  I suffer,
Though all good people know it was
  for your honour.
O but I would not have done the
  forbidden thing
For any husband or for any son.
For why? I could have had another
  husband
And by him other sons, if one were
  lost;
But, father and mother lost, where
  would I get
Another brother? For thus
  preferring you
My brother, Creon condemns me
  and hales me away,
Never a bride, never a mother,
  unbefriended,
Condemned alive to solitary death.
What law of heaven have I
  transgressed? What god

Can save me now? What help or hope have I,
In whom devotion is deemed sacrilege?
If this is God's will, I shall learn my lesson
In death; but if my enemies are wrong,
I wish them no worse punishment than mine.

CHORUS: Still the same tempest in the heart
Torments her soul with angry gusts.

CREON: The more cause then have they that guard her
To hasten their work; or they too suffer.

CHORUS: Alas, that word had the sound of death.

CREON: Indeed there is no more to hope for.

ANTIGONE: Gods of our fathers, my city, my home,
Rulers of Thebes! Time stays no longer.
Last daughter of your royal house
Go I, his prisoner, because I honoured
Those things to which honour truly belongs.

ANTIGONE *is led away.*

CHORUS: Such was the fate, my child, of Danae
Locked in a brazen bower,
A prison secret as a tomb,
Where was no day.
Daughter of kings, her royal womb
Garnered the golden shower
Of life from Zeus. So strong is Destiny,
No wealth, no armoury, no tower,
No ship that rides the angry sea
Her mastering hand can stay.
And Dryas' son, the proud Edonian king,
Pined in a stony cell
At Dionysus' bidding pent
To cool his fire

Till, all his full-blown passion spent,
He came to know right well
What god his ribald tongue was challenging
When he would break the fiery spell
Of the wild Maenads' revelling
And vex the Muses' choir.
It was upon the side
Of Bosporus, where the Black Rocks stand
By Thracian Salmydessus over the twin tide,
That Thracian Ares laughed to see
How Phineus' angry wife most bloodily
Blinded his two sons' eyes that mutely cried
For vengeance; crazed with jealousy
The woman smote them with the weaving-needle in her hand.
Forlorn they wept away
Their sad step-childhood's misery
Predestined from their mother's ill-starred marriage-day.
She was of old Erechtheid blood,
Cave-dwelling daughter of the North-wind God;
On rocky steeps, as mountain ponies play,
The wild winds nursed her maidenhood.
On her, my child, the grey Fates laid hard hands, as upon thee.

Enter TEIRESIAS, *the blind prophet, led by a boy.*

TEIRESIAS: Gentlemen of Thebes, we greet you, my companion and I,
Who share one pair of eyes on our journeys together—
For the blind man goes where his leader tells him to.

CREON: You are welcome, father Teiresias. What's your news?

TEIRESIAS: Ay, news you shall have; and advice, if you can heed it.

CREON: There was never a time when I failed to heed it, father.

TEIRESIAS: And thereby have so far steered a steady course.

CREON: And gladly acknowledge the debt we owe to you.

TEIRESIAS: Then mark me now; for you stand on a razor's edge.

CREON: Indeed? Grave words from your lips, good priest. Say on.

TEIRESIAS: I will; and show you all that my skill reveals,
At my seat of divination, where I sit
These many years to read the signs of heaven,
An unfamiliar sound came to my ears
Of birds in vicious combat, savage cries
In strange outlandish language, and the whirr
Of flapping wings; from which I well could picture
The gruesome warfare of their deadly talons.
Full of foreboding then I made the test
Of sacrifice upon the altar fire.
There was no answering flame; only rank juice
Oozed from the flesh and dripped among the ashes,
Smouldering and sputtering; the gall vanished in a puff,
And the fat ran down and left the haunches bare.
Thus (through the eyes of my young acolyte,
Who sees for me, that I may see for others)
I read the signs of failure in my quest.
And why? The blight upon us is your doing.
The blood that stains altars and our shrines,
The blood that dogs and vultures have licked up,
It is none other than the blood of Oedipus
Spilled from the veins of his ill-fated son.
Our fires, our sacrifices, and our prayers
The gods abominate. How should the birds
Give any other than ill-omened voices,
Gorged with the dregs of blood that man has shed?
Mark this, my son: all men fall into sin.
But sinning, he is not for ever lost
Hapless and helpless, who can make amends
And has not set his face against repentance.
Only a fool is governed by self-will.
Pay to the dead his due. Wound not the fallen.
It is no glory to kill and kill again.
My words are for your good, as is my will,
And should be acceptable, being for your good.

CREON: You take me for your target, reverend sir,
Like all the rest. I know your art of old,
And how you make your commodity
To trade and traffic in for your advancement.
Trade as you will; but all the silver of Sardis
And all the gold of India will not buy
A tomb for yonder traitor. No. Let the eagles
Carry his carcass up to the throne of Zeus;
Even that would not be sacrilege enough
To frighten me from my determination
Not to allow this burial. No man's act
Has power enough to pollute the goodness of God.

But great and terrible is the fall,
Teiresias,
Of mortal men who seek their own
advantage
By uttering evil in the guise of
good.
TEIRESIAS: Ah, is there any wisdom in
the world?
CREON: Why, what is the meaning of
that wide-flung taunt?
TEIRESIAS: What prize outweighs the
priceless worth of prudence?
CREON: Ay, what indeed? What
mischief matches the lack of it?
TEIRESIAS: And there you speak of
your own symptom, sir.
CREON: I am loth to pick a quarrel
with you, priest.
TEIRESIAS: You do so, calling my
divination false.
CREON: I say all prophets seek their
own advantage.
TEIRESIAS: All kings, say I, seek gain
unrighteously.
CREON: Do you forget to whom you
say it?
TEIRESIAS: No.
Our king and benefactor, by my
guidance.
CREON: Clever you may be, but not
therefore honest.
TEIRESIAS: Must I reveal my yet
unspoken mind?
CREON: Reveal all; but expect no gain
from it.
TEIRESIAS: Does that still seem to you
my motive, then?
CREON: Nor is my will for sale, sir, in
your market.
TEIRESIAS: Then hear this. Ere the
chariot of the sun
Has rounded once or twice his
wheeling way,
You shall have given a son of your
own loins
To death, in payment for death—
two debts to pay:

One for the life that you have sent
to death,
The life you have abominably
entombed;
One for the dead still lying above
ground
Unburied, unhonoured, unblest by
the gods below.
You cannot alter this. The gods
themselves
Cannot undo it. It follows of
necessity
From what you have done. Even
now the avenging Furies,
The hunters of hell that follow and
destroy,
Are lying in wait for you, and will
have their prey,
When the evil you have worked for
others fall on you.
Do I speak this for my gain? The
time shall come,
And soon, when your house will be
filled with the lamentation
Of men and women; and every
neighboring city
Will be goaded to fury against you,
for upon them
Too the pollution falls when the
dogs and vultures
Bring the defilement of blood to
their hearths and altars.
I have done. You pricked me, and
these shafts of wrath
Will find their mark in your heart.
You cannot escape
The sting of their sharpness.
Lead me home, my boy.
Let us leave him to vent his anger
on younger ears,
Or school his mind and tongue to a
milder mood
Than that which now possesses him.
Lead on.
Exit.
CHORUS: He has gone, my lord. He
has prophesied terrible things.

And for my part, I that was young and now am old
Have never known his prophecies proved false.

CREON: It is true enough; and my heart is torn in two.
It is hard to give way, and hard to stand and abide
The coming of the curse. Both ways are hard.

CHORUS: If you would be advised, my good lord Creon—

CREON: What must I do? Tell me, and I will do it.

CHORUS: Release the woman from her rocky prison.
Set up a tomb for him that lies unburied.

CREON: Is it your wish that I consent to this?

CHORUS: It is, and quickly. The gods do not delay
The stroke of their swift vengeance on the sinner.

CREON: It is hard, but I must do it. Well I know
There is no armour against necessity.

CHORUS: Go. Let your own hand do it, and no other.

CREON: I will go this instant.
Slaves there! One and all.
Bring spades and mattocks out on the hill!
My mind is made; 'twas I imprisoned her,
And I will set her free. Now I believe
It is by the laws of heaven that man must live.
Exit.

CHORUS:
O Thou whose name is many.
Son of the Thunderer, dear child of his Cadmean bride,
Whose hand is mighty
In Italia,
In the hospitable valley
of Eleusis,
And in Thebes,
The mother-city of thy worshippers,
Where sweet Ismenus gently watereth
The soil whence sprang the harvest of the dragon's teeth;
Where torches on the crested mountains gleam,
And by Castalia's stream
The nymph-train in thy dance rejoices,
When from the ivy-tangled glens
Of Nysa and from vine-clad plains
Thou comest to Thebes where the immortal voices
Sing thy glad strains.
Thebes, where thou lovest most to be,
With her, thy mother, the fire-stricken one,
Sickens for need of thee.
Healer of all her ills;
Come swiftly o'er the high Parnassian hills,
Come o'er the sighing sea.
The stars, whose breath is fire, delight
To dance for thee; the echoing night
Shall with thy praises ring.
Zeus-born, appear! With Thyiads revelling
Come, bountiful
Iacchus, King!
Enter a MESSENGER, *from the side of the stage.*

MESSENGER: Hear, men of Cadmus' city, hear and attend,
Men of the house of Amphion, people of Thebes!
What is the life of man? A thing not fixed
For good or evil, fashioned for praise or blame.
Chance raises a man to the heights, chance casts him down,

And none can foretell what will be
from what is.
Creon was once an enviable man;
He saved his country from her
enemies,
Assumed the sovereign power, and
bore it well,
The honoured father of a royal
house.
Now all is lost; for life without life's
joys
Is living death; and such a life is his.
Riches and rank and show of
majesty
And state, where no joy is, are
empty, vain
And unsubstantial shadows, of no
weight
To be compared with happiness of
heart.
CHORUS: What is your news? Disaster
in the royal house?
MESSENGER: Death; and the guilt of it
on living heads.
CHORUS: Who dead? And by what
hand?
MESSENGER: Haemon is dead,
Slain by his own—
CHORUS: His father?
MESSENGER: His own hand.
His father's act it was that drove
him to it.
CHORUS: Then all has happened as the
prophet said.
MESSENGER: What's next to do, your
worships will decide.
The Palace door opens.
CHORUS: Here comes the Queen,
Eurydice.
Poor soul,
It may be she has heard about her
son.
Enter EURYDICE, *attended by women.*
EURYDICE: My friends, I heard
something of what you were
saying
As I came to the door. I was on my
way to prayer

At the temple of Pallas, and had
barely turned the latch
When I caught your talk of some
near calamity.
I was sick with fear and reeled in
the arms of my women.
But tell me what is the matter, what
have you heard?
I am not unacquainted with grief,
and I can bear it.
MESSENGER: Madam, it was I that saw
it, and will tell you all.
To try to make it any lighter now
Would be to prove myself a liar.
Truth
Is always best.
It was thus. I attended your
husband,
The King, to the edge of the field
where lay the body
Of Polynices, in pitiable state,
mauled by the dogs.
We prayed for him to the Goddess
of the Roads, and to Pluto,
That they might have mercy upon
him. We washed the remains
In holy water, and on a fire of
fresh-cut branches
We burned all that was left of him,
and raised
Over his ashes a mound of his
native earth.
That done, we turned towards the
deep rock-chamber
Of the maid that was married with
death.
Before we reached it,
One that stood near the accursed
place had heard
Loud cries of anguish, and came to
tell King Creon.
As he approached, came strange
uncertain sounds
Of lamentation, and he cried aloud:
'Unhappy wretch! Is my foreboding
true?
Is this the most sorrowful journey
that ever I went?

My son's voice greets me. Go, some
of you, quickly
Through the passage where the
stones are thrown apart,
Into the mouth of the cave, and see
if it be
My son, my own son Haemon that I
hear.
If not, I am the sport of gods.'
We went
And looked, as bidden by our
anxious master.
There in the furthest corner of the
cave
We saw her hanging by the neck.
The rope
Was of the woven linen of her dress.
And, with his arms about her, there
stood he
Lamenting his lost bride, his luckless
love,
His father's cruelty.
When Creon saw them,
Into the cave he went, moaning
piteously.
'O my unhappy boy,' he cried again,
'What have you done? What
madness brings you here
To your destruction? Come away,
my son,
My son, I do beseech you, come
away!'
His son looked at him with one
angry stare,
Spat in his face, and then without a
word
Drew sword and struck out. But his
father fled
Unscathed. Whereon the poor
demented boy
Leaned on his sword and thrust it
deeply home
In his own side, and while his life
ebbed out
Embraced the maid in loose-
enfolding arms,
His spurting blood staining her pale
cheeks red.
EURYDICE *goes quickly back into the*
Palace.

Two bodies lie together, wedded in
death,
Their bridal sleep a witness to the
world
How great calamity can come to
man
Through man's perversity.
CHORUS: But what is this?
The Queen has turned and gone
without a word.
MESSENGER: Yes. It is strange. The best
that I can hope
Is that she would not sorrow for her
son
Before us all, but vents her grief in
private
Among her women. She is too wise,
I think,
To take a false step rashly.
CHORUS: It may be.
Yet there is danger in unnatural
silence
No less than in excess of
lamentation.
MESSENGER: I will go in and see,
whether in truth
There is some fatal purpose in her
grief.
Such silence, as you say, may well be
dangerous.
He goes in.
Enter Attendants preceding the King.
CHORUS: The King comes here.
What the tongue scarce dares to tell
Must now be known
By the burden that proves too well
The guilt, no other man's
But his alone.
Enter CREON *with the body of* HAEMON.
CREON: The sin, the sin of the erring
soul
Drives hard unto death.
Behold the slayer, the slain,
The father, the son.
O the curse of my stubborn will!
Son, newly cut off in the newness of
youth,
Dead for my fault, not yours.
CHORUS: Alas, too late you have seen
the truth.

CREON: I learn in sorrow. Upon my
head God has delivered this heavy
punishment,
Has struck me down in the ways of
wickedness,
And trod my gladness under foot.
Such is the bitter affliction of mortal
man.
Enter the MESSENGER *from the Palace.*
MESSENGER: Sir, you have this and
more than this to bear.
Within there's more to know, more
to your pain.
CREON: What more? What pain can
overtop this pain?
MESSENGER: She is dead—your wife,
the mother of him that is dead—
The death-wound fresh in her
heart. Alas, poor lady!
CREON: Insatiable Death, wilt thou
destroy me yet?
What say you, teller of evil?
I am already dead,
And is there more?
Blood upon blood?
More death? My wife?
*The central doors open, revealing the
body of* EURYDICE.
CHORUS: Look then, and see; nothing
is hidden now.
CREON: O second horror!
What fate awaits me now?
My child here in my arms . . . and
there, the other . . .
The son . . . the mother . . .
MESSENGER: There at the altar with the
whetted knife
She stood, and as the darkness
dimmed her eyes
Called on the dead, her elder son
and this,
And with her dying breath cursed
you, their slayer.
CREON: O horrible . . .
Is there no sword for me,
To end this misery?
MESSENGER: Indeed you bear the
burden of two deaths.

It was her dying word.
CREON: And her last act?
MESSENGER: Hearing her son was dead,
with her own hand
She drove the sharp sword home
into her heart.
CREON: There is no man can bear this
guilt but I.
It is true, I killed him.
Lead me away, away, I live no
longer.
CHORUS: 'Twere best, if anything is
best in evil times.
What's soonest done, is best, when
all is ill.
CREON: Come, my last hour and
fairest,
My only happiness . . . come soon.
Let me not see another day.
Away . . . away . . .
CHORUS: The future is not to be
known; our present care
Is with the present; the rest is in
other hands.
CREON: I ask no more than I have
asked.
CHORUS: Ask nothing.
What is to be, no mortal can escape.
CREON: I am nothing. I have no life.
Lead me away . . .
That have killed unwittingly
My son, my wife.
I know not where I should turn,
Where look for help.
My hands have done amiss, my head
is bowed
With fate too heavy for me.
Exit.
CHORUS: Of happiness the crown
And chiefest part
Is wisdom, and to hold
The gods in awe.
This is the law
That, seeing the stricken heart
Of pride brought down,
We learn when we are old.
Exeunt.

Thucydides

Thucydides (c.471–c.396 B.C.) was the greatest of classical historians, perhaps the greatest historian in Western civilization. Although not the equal of Herodotus as a relator of fascinating stories, he had a style of presentation that carries the reader along easily and gracefully. Thucydides' primary concern was to present the true history of the Peloponnesian War between Athens and Sparta, a war in which he himself was an active participant. As a general in the Athenian army he failed to prevent a Spartan force from capturing an important military stronghold, and was banished from Athens for twenty years. Much of this time he spent traveling in enemy territory and observing the course of the struggle.

In his search for truth, Thucydides imposed on himself certain critical techniques and methods. He ruthlessly discarded any story that could not be verified by documentary evidence or eyewitness accounts, or that failed to stand the test of a logical analysis. As a result, the History of the Peloponnesian War is an extraordinarily trustworthy source of knowledge about fifth-century Greece. There is one qualification, however: Thucydides often put speeches into the mouths of historical personages. Thus, the Melian Dialogue and Pericles' Funeral Oration reproduced here appear as direct quotations, although they were actually written by Thucydides himself. Thucydides was careful to emphasize that this was simply a dramatic technique, however, and that he was trying only to convey the accurate meaning or general sense of what was said and not the full text of the speech as it was delivered.

Thucydides' contributions to the art of history include a careful use of source materials, an emphasis on rational and natural explanations of history and a denial of supernatural explanations, an understanding of military and naval strategy, and an awareness of the economic basis of military strength. Even his reason for writing the History is noteworthy. Herodotus had written, as he himself says, to preserve the memory of great events. But Thucydides wrote to instruct, to teach others the causes of events and the motivations behind people's actions, so that future generations might be able, by studying the record that he made available, to avoid the mistakes of the Greeks and the terrible consequences to which those mistakes had ultimately led.

History of the Peloponnesian War

BOOK I

1. Thucydides, an Athenian, wrote the history of the war in which the Peloponnesians and the Athenians fought against one another. He began to write when they first took up arms, believing that it would be great and memorable above any previous war.[1] For he argued that both states were then at the full height of their military power, and he saw the rest of the Hellenes either siding or intending to side with one or other of them. No movement ever stirred Hellas more deeply than this; it was shared by many of the Barbarians, and might be said even to affect the world at large.

• • •

22. As to the speeches which were made either before or during the war, it was hard for me, and for others who reported them to me, to recollect the exact words. I have therefore put into the mouth of each speaker the sentiments proper to the occasion, expressed as I thought he would be likely to express them, while at the same time I endeavored, as nearly as I could, to give the general purport of what was actually said. Of the events of the war I have not ventured to speak from any chance information, nor according to any notion of my own; I have described nothing but what I either saw myself, or learned from others of whom I made the most careful and particular inquiry. The task was a laborious one, because eye-witnesses of the same occurrences gave different accounts of them, as they remembered or were interested in the actions of one side or the other. And very likely the strictly historical character of my narrative may be disappointing to the ear. But if he who desires to have before his eyes a true picture of the events which have happened, and of the like events which may be expected to happen hereafter in the order of human things, shall pronounce what I have written to be useful, then I shall be satisfied. My history is an everlasting possession, not a prize composition which is heard and forgotten.

• • •

BOOK II

• • •

34. During the same winter,[2] in accordance with an old national custom, the funeral of those who first fell in this war was celebrated by the

---

[1] [Thucydides is here referring to himself in the third person.—*Ed.*]

[2] [After the first year of the Peloponnesian War, 431 B.C.—*Ed.*]

Thucydides, trans. B. Jowett, 2nd ed.

Athenians at the public charge. The ceremony is as follows: Three days before the celebration they erect a tent in which the bones of the dead are laid out, and every one brings to his own dead any offering which he pleases. At the time of the funeral the bones are placed in chests of cypress wood, which are conveyed on hearses; there is one chest for each tribe. They also carry a single empty litter decked with a pall for all whose bodies are missing, and cannot be recovered after the battle. The procession is accompanied by any one who chooses, whether citizen or stranger, and the female relatives of the deceased are present at the place of interment and make lamentation. The public sepulchre is situated in the most beautiful spot outside the walls; there they always bury those who fall in war; only after the battle of Marathon the dead, in recognition of their pre-eminent valor, were interred on the field. When the remains have been laid in the earth, some man of known ability and high reputation, chosen by the city, delivers a suitable oration over them; after which the people depart. Such is the manner of interment; and the ceremony was repeated from time to time throughout the war. Over those who were the first buried Pericles was chosen to speak. At the fitting moment he advanced from the sepulchre to a lofty stage, which had been erected in order that he might be heard as far as possible by the multitude, and spoke as follows:—

Funeral Speech

35. "Most of those who have spoken here before me have commended the law-giver who added this oration to our other funeral customs; it seemed to them a worthy thing that such an honor should be given at their burial to the dead who have fallen on the field of battle. But I should have preferred that, when men's deeds have been brave, they should be honored in deed only, and with such an honor as this public funeral, which you are now witnessing. Then the reputation of many would not have been imperilled on the eloquence or want of eloquence of one and their virtues believed or not as he spoke well or ill. For it is difficult to say neither too little nor too much; and even moderation is apt not to give the impression of truthfulness. The friend of the dead who knows the facts is likely to think that the words of the speaker fall short of his knowledge and of his wishes; another who is not so well informed, when he hears of anything which surpasses his own powers, will be envious and will suspect exaggeration. Mankind are tolerant of the praises of others so long as each hearer thinks that he can do as well or nearly as well himself, but, when the speaker rises above him, jealousy is aroused and he begins to be incredulous. However, since our ancestors have set the seal of their approval upon the practice, I must obey, and to the utmost of my power shall endeavor to satisfy the wishes and beliefs of all who hear me.

36. "I will speak first of our ancestors, for it is right and becoming that now, when we are lamenting the dead, a tribute should be paid to their memory. There has never been a time when they did not inhabit this land, which by their valor they have handed down from generation to generation, and we

have received from them a free state. But if they were worthy of praise, still more were our fathers, who added to their inheritance, and after many a struggle transmitted to us their sons this great empire. And we ourselves assembled here today, who are still most of us in the vigor of life, have chiefly done the work of improvement, and have richly endowed our city with all things, so that she is sufficient for herself both in peace and war. Of the military exploits by which our various possessions were acquired, or of the energy with which we or our fathers drove back the tide of war, Hellenic or Barbarian, I will not speak; for the tale would be long and is familiar to you. But before I praise the dead, I should like to point out by what principles of action we rose to power, and under what institutions and through what manner of life our empire became great. For I conceive that such thoughts are not unsuited to the occasion, and that this numerous assembly of citizens and strangers may profitably listen to them.

37. "Our form of government does not enter into rivalry with the institutions of others. We do not copy our neighbors, but are an example to them. It is true that we are called a democracy, for the administration is in the hands of the many and not of the few. But while the law secures equal justice to all alike in their private disputes, the claim of excellence is also recognized; and when a citizen is in any way distinguished, he is preferred to the public service, not as a matter of privilege, but as the reward of merit. Neither is poverty a bar, but a man may benefit his country whatever

be the obscurity of his condition. There is no exclusiveness in our public life, and in our private intercourse we are not suspicious of one another, nor angry with our neighbor if he does what he likes; we do not put on sour looks at him which, though harmless, are not pleasant. While we are thus unconstrained in our private intercourse, a spirit of reverence pervades our public acts; we are prevented from doing wrong by respect for authority and for the laws, having an especial regard to those which are ordained for the protection of the injured as well as those unwritten laws which bring upon the transgressor of them the reprobation of the general sentiment.

38. "And we have not forgotten to provide for our weary spirits many relaxations from toil; we have regular games and sacrifices throughout the year; at home the style of our life is refined; and the delight which we daily feel in all these things helps to banish melancholy. Because of the greatness of our city the fruits of the whole earth flow in upon us; so that we enjoy the goods of other countries as freely as of our own.

39. "Then, again, our military training is in many respects, superior to that of our adversaries. Our city is thrown open to the world, and we never expel a foreigner or prevent him from seeing or learning anything of which the secret if revealed to an enemy might profit him. We rely not upon management or trickery, but upon our own hearts and hands. And in the matter of education, whereas they from early youth are always undergoing laborious exercises which are to make them brave, we live at ease, and yet

are equally ready to face the perils which they face. And here is the proof. The Lacedaemonians come into Attica not by themselves, but with their whole confederacy following; we go alone into a neighbor's country; and although our opponents are fighting for their homes and we on a foreign soil, we have seldom any difficulty in overcoming them. Our enemies have never yet felt our united strength; the care of a navy divides our attention, and on land we are obliged to send our own citizens everywhere. But they, if they meet and defeat a part of our army, are as proud as if they had routed us all, and when defeated they pretend to have been vanquished by us all.

40. "If then we prefer to meet danger with a light heart but without laborious training, and with a courage which is gained by habit and not enforced by law, are we not greatly the gainers? Since we do not anticipate the pain, although, when the hour comes, we can be as brave as those who never allow themselves to rest; and thus too our city is equally admirable in peace and in war. For we are lovers of the beautiful, yet simple in our tastes, and we cultivate the mind without a loss of manliness. Wealth we employ, not for talk and ostentation, but when there is a real use for it. To avow poverty with us is no disgrace: the true disgrace is in doing nothing to avoid it. An Athenian citizen does not neglect the state because he takes care of his own household; and even those of us who are engaged in business have a very fair idea of politics. We alone regard a man who takes no interest in public affairs, not as a harmless, but as a useless character; and if few of us

are originators, we are all sound judges of a policy. The great impediment to action is, in our opinion, not discussion, but the want of that knowledge which is gained by discussion preparatory to action. For we have a peculiar power of thinking before we act and of acting too, whereas other men are courageous from ignorance but hesitate upon reflection. And they are surely to be esteemed the bravest spirits who, having the clearest sense both of the pains and pleasures of life, do not on that account shrink from danger. In doing good, again, we are unlike others; we make our friends by conferring, not by receiving favors. Now, he who confers a favor is the firmer friend, because he would fain by kindness keep alive the memory of an obligation; but the recipient is colder in his feelings, because he knows that in requiting another's generosity he will not be winning gratitude, but only paying a debt. We alone do good to our neighbors not upon a calculation of interest, but in the confidence of freedom and in a frank and fearless spirit.

41. "To sum up: I say that Athens is the school of Hellas, and that the individual Athenian in his own person seems to have the power of adapting himself to the most varied forms of action with the utmost versatility and grace. This is no passing and idle word, but truth and fact; and the assertion is verified by the position to which these qualities have raised the state. For in the hour of trial Athens alone among her contemporaries is superior to the report of her. No enemy who comes against her is indignant at the reverses which he sustains at the hands of such a city; no subject

complains that his masters are unworthy of him. And we shall assuredly not be without witnesses; there are mighty monuments of our power which will make us the wonder of this and of succeeding ages; we shall not need the praises of Homer or of any other panegyrist whose poetry may please for the moment, although his representation of the facts will not bear the light of day. For we have compelled every land and every sea to open a path for our valor, and have everywhere planted eternal memorials of our friendship and of our enmity. Such is the city for whose sake these men nobly fought and died; they could not bear the thought that she might be taken from them; and every one of us who survive should gladly toil on her behalf.

42. "I have dwelt upon the greatness of Athens because I want to show you that we are contending for a higher prize than those who enjoy none of these privileges, and to establish by manifest proof the merit of these men whom I am now commemorating. Their loftiest praise has been already spoken. For in magnifying the city I have magnified them, and men like them whose virtues made her glorious. And of how few Hellenes can it be said as of them, that their deeds when weighted in the balance have been found equal to their fame! Methinks that a death such as theirs has been gives the true measure of a man's worth; it may be the first revelation of his virtues, but is at any rate their final seal. For even those who come short in other ways may justly plead the valor with which they have fought for their country; they have blotted out the evil with the good, and have bene-fited the state more by their public services than they have injured her by their private actions. None of these men were enervated by wealth or hesitated to resign the pleasures of life; none of them put off the evil day in the hope, natural to poverty, that a man, though poor, may one day become rich. But, deeming that the punishment of their enemies was sweeter than any of these things, and that they could fall in no nobler cause, they determined at the hazard of their lives to be honorably avenged, and to leave the rest. They resigned to hope their unknown chance of happiness; but in the face of death they resolved to rely upon themselves alone. And when the moment came they were minded to resist and suffer, rather than to fly and save their lives; they ran away from the word of dishonor, but on the battle-field their feet stood fast, and in an instant, at the height of their fortune, they passed away from the scene, not of their fear, but of their glory.

43. "Such was the end of these men; they were worthy of Athens, and the living need not desire to have a more heroic spirit, although they may pray for a less fatal issue. The value of such a spirit is not to be expressed in words. Any one can discourse to you forever about the advantage of a brave defence which you know already. But instead of listening to him I would have you day by day fix your eyes upon the greatness of Athens, until you become filled with the love of her; and when you are impressed by the spectacle of her glory, reflect that this empire has been acquired by men who knew their duty and had the courage to do it, who in the hour of conflict had the fear of dishonor

always present to them, and who, if ever they failed in an enterprise, would not allow their virtues to be lost to their country, but freely gave their lives to her as the fairest offering which they could present at her feast. The sacrifice which they collectively made was individually repaid to them; for they received again each one for himself a praise which grows not old, and the noblest of all sepulchres—I speak not of that in which their remains are laid, but of that in which their glory survives, and is proclaimed always and on every fitting occasion both in word and deed. For the whole earth is the sepulchre of famous men; not only are they commemorated by columns and inscriptions in their own country, but in foreign lands there dwells also an unwritten memorial of them, graven not on stone but in the hearts of men. Make them your examples, and, esteeming courage to be freedom and freedom to be happiness, do not weigh too nicely the perils of war. The unfortunate who has no hope of a change for the better has less reason to throw away his life than the prosperous who, if he survives, is always liable to a change for the worse, and to whom any accidental fall makes the most serious difference. To a man of spirit, cowardice and disaster coming together are far more bitter than death, striking him unperceived at a time when he is full of courage and animated by the general hope.

44. "Wherefore I do not now commiserate the parents of the dead who stand here; I would rather comfort them. You know that your life has been passed amid manifold vicissitudes; and that they may be deemed fortunate who have gained most honor, whether an honorable death like theirs, or an honorable sorrow like yours, and whose days have been so ordered that the term of their happiness is likewise the term of their life. I know how hard it is to make you feel this, when the good fortune of others will too often remind you of the gladness which once lightened your hearts. And sorrow is felt at the want of those blessings, not which a man never knew, but which were a part of his life before they were taken from him. Some of you are of an age at which they may hope to have other children, and they ought to bear their sorrow better; not only will the children who may hereafter be born make them forget their own lost ones, but the city will be doubly a gainer. She will not be left desolate, and she will be safer. For a man's counsel cannot have equal weight or worth, when he alone has no children to risk in the general danger. To those of you who have passed their prime, I say; 'Congratulate yourselves that you have been happy during the greater part of your days; remember that your life of sorrow will not last long, and be comforted by the glory of those who are gone. For the love of honor alone is ever young, and not riches, as some say, but honor is the delight of men when they are old and useless.'

45. "To you who are the sons and brothers of the departed, I see that the struggle to emulate them will be an arduous one. For all men praise the dead, and, however preeminent your virtue may be, hardly will you be thought, I do not say to equal, but even to approach them. The living have their rivals and detractors, but when a man is

out of the way, the honor and good-will which he receives is unalloyed. And, if I am to speak of womanly virtues to those of you who will henceforth be widows, let me sum them up in one short admonition: To a woman not to show more weakness than is natural to her sex is a great glory, and not to be talked about for good or for evil among men.

46. "I have paid the required tribute, in obedience to the law, making use of such fitting words as I had. The tribute of deeds has been paid in part; for the dead have been honorably interred, and it remains only that their children should be maintained at the public charge until they are grown up; this is the solid prize with which, as with a garland, Athens crowns her sons living and dead, after a struggle like theirs. For where the rewards of virtue are greatest, there the noblest citizens are enlisted in the service of the state. And now, when you have duly lamented, every one his own dead, you may depart."

. . .

BOOK III

. . .

82. For not long afterwards[3] nearly the whole Hellenic world was in commotion; in every city the chiefs of the democracy and of the oligarchy were struggling, the one to bring in the Athenians, the other the Lacedaemonians. Now, in time of peace, men would have had no

---

[3] [In 427 B.C., or four years after Pericles' Funeral Oration.—*Ed.*]

excuse for introducing either, and no desire to do so, but when they were at war and both sides could easily obtain allies to the hurt of their enemies and the advantage of themselves, the dissatisfied party were only too ready to invoke foreign aid. And revolution brought upon the cities of Hellas many terrible calamities, such as have been and always will be while human nature remains the same, but which are more or less aggravated and differ in character with every new combination of circumstances. In peace and prosperity both states and individuals are actuated by high motives, because they do not fall under the dominion of imperious necessities; but war which takes away the comfortable provision of daily life is a hard master, and tends to assimilate men's characters to their conditions.

When troubles had once begun in the cities, those who followed carried the revolutionary spirit further and further, and determined to outdo the report of all who had preceded them by the ingenuity of their enterprises and the atrocity of their revenges. The meaning of words had no longer the same relation to things, but was changed by them as they thought proper. Reckless daring was held to be loyal courage; prudent delay was the excuse of a coward; moderation was the disguise of unmanly weakness; to know everything was to do nothing. Frantic energy was the true quality of man. A conspirator who wanted to be safe was a recreant in disguise. The lover of violence was always trusted, and his opponent suspected. He who succeeded in a plot was deemed knowing, but a still greater master in craft was he who detected one. On the other hand, he who plotted from the first to have nothing to do with plots was a breaker up of parties and a poltroon who was afraid of the enemy. In a word, he who could outstrip another in a bad action was applauded, and so was he who encouraged to evil one who had no idea of it. The tie of party was stronger than the tie of blood, because a partisan was more ready to dare without asking why. (For party associations are not based upon established law, nor do they seek the public good; they are formed in defiance of the laws and from self-interest.) The seal of good faith was not divine law, but fellowship in crime. If any enemy when he was in the ascendant offered fair words, the opposite party received them, not in a generous spirit, but by a jealous watchfulness of his actions. Revenge was dearer than self-preservation. Any agreements sworn to by either party, when they could do nothing else, were binding as long as both were powerless. But he who on a favorable opportunity first took courage and struck at his enemy when he saw him off his guard, had greater pleasure in a perfidious than he would have had in an open act of revenge; he congratulated himself that he had taken the safer course, and also that he had over-reached his enemy and gained the prize of superior ability. In general, the dishonest more easily gain credit for cleverness than the simple for goodness; men take a pride in the one, but are ashamed of the other.

The cause of all these evils was the love of power originating in avarice and ambition, and the party-spirit which is engendered by them when men were fairly embarked in a contest. For the leaders on either side used specious names, the one party professing to uphold the constitutional equality of the many, the other the wisdom of an aristocracy, while they made the public interests, to which in name they were devoted, in reality their prize. Striving in every way to overcome each other, they committed the most monstrous crimes; yet even these were surpassed by the magnitude of their revenges which they pursued to the very utmost, neither party observing any definite limits either of justice or public expediency, but both alike making the caprice of the moment their law. Either by the help of an unrighteous sentence, or grasping power with the strong hand, they were eager to satiate the impatience of party-spirit. Neither faction cared for religion; but any fair pretence which succeeded in effecting some odious purpose was greatly lauded. And the citizens who were of neither party fell a prey to both; either they were disliked because they held aloof, or men were jealous of their surviving.

83. Thus revolution gave birth to every form of wickedness in Hellas. The simplicity which is so large an element in a noble nature was laughed to scorn and disappeared. An attitude of perfidious antagonism everywhere prevailed; for there was no word binding enough, nor oath terrible enough to reconcile enemies. Each man was strong only in the conviction that nothing was secure; he must look to his own safety, and could not afford to trust others. Inferior intellects generally succeeded best. For, aware of their own deficiencies, and fearing the capacity of their opponents, for whom they were no match in powers

of speech, and whose subtle wits were likely to anticipate them in contriving evil, they struck boldly and at once. But the clever sort, presuming in their arrogance that they would be aware in time, and disdaining to act when they could think, were taken off their guard and easily destroyed.

• • •

BOOK V

• • •

84. In the ensuing summer, Alcibiades sailed to Argos with twenty ships, and seized any of the Argives who were still suspected to be of the Lacedaemonian faction, three hundred in number; and the Athenians deposited them in the subject islands near at hand. The Athenians next made an expedition against the island of Melos[4] with thirty ships of their own, six Chian, and two Lesbian, twelve hundred hoplites and three hundred archers besides twenty mounted archers of their own, and about fifteen hundred hoplites furnished by their allies in the islands. The Melians are colonists of the Lacedaemonians who would not submit to Athens like the other islanders. At first they were neutral and took no part. But when the Athenians tried to coerce them by ravaging their lands they were driven into open hostilities. The generals, Cleomedes the son of Lycomedes and Tisias the son of Tisimachus, encamped with the Athenian forces on the island. But before they did the country any

---

[4] [In 416 B.C.—Ed.]

harm they sent envoys to negotiate with the Melians. Instead of bringing these envoys before the people, the Melians desired them to explain their errand to the magistrates and to the chief men. They spoke as follows—

85. "Since we are not allowed to speak to the people, lest, forsooth, they should be deceived by seductive and unanswerable arguments which they would hear set forth in a single uninterrupted oration (for we are perfectly aware that this is what you mean in bringing us before a select few), you who are sitting here may as well make assurance yet surer. Let us have no set speeches at all, but do you reply to each several statement of which you disapprove, and criticise it at once. Say first of all how you like this mode of proceeding."

86. The Melian representatives answered:—"The quiet interchange of explanations is a reasonable thing, and we do not object to that. But your warlike movements, which are present not only to our fears but to our eyes, seem to belie your words. We see that, although you may reason with us, you mean to be our judges; and that at the end of the discussion if the justice of our cause prevail and we therefore refuse to yield, we may expect war; if we are convinced by you, slavery."

87. ATHENIAN: Nay, but if you are only going to argue from fancies about the future, or if you meet us with any other purpose than that of looking your circumstances in the face and saving your city, we have done; but if this is your intention we will proceed.

88. MELIAN: It is an excusable and natural thing that men in our position should have much to say

and should indulge in many fancies. But we admit that this conference has met to consider the question of our preservation; and therefore let the argument proceed in the manner which you propose.

89. ATHENIAN: Well, then, we Athenians will use no fine words; we will not go out of our way to prove at length that we have a right to rule, because we overthrew the Persians; or that we attack you now because we are suffering any injury at your hands. We should not convince you if we did; nor must you expect to convince us by arguing that, although a colony of the Lacedaemonians, you have taken no part in their expeditions, or that you have never done us any wrong. But you and we should say what we really think, and aim only at what is possible, for we both alike know that into the discussion of human affairs, the question of justice only enters where the pressure of necessity is equal, and that the powerful exact what they can, and the weak grant what they must.

90. MELIAN: Well, then, since you set aside justice and invite us to speak of expediency, in our judgment it is certainly expedient that you should respect a principle which is for the common good; and that to every man when in peril a reasonable claim should be accounted a claim of right, and any plea which he is disposed to urge, even if failing of the point a little, should help his cause. Your interest in this principle is quite as great as ours, inasmuch as you, if you fall, will incur the heaviest vengeance, and will be the most terrible example to mankind.

91. ATHENIAN: The fall of our empire, if it should fall, is not an event to which we look forward with dismay; for ruling states such as Lacedaemon are not cruel to their vanquished enemies. And we are fighting not so much against the Lacedaemonians as against our own subjects who may some day rise up and overcome their former masters. But this is a danger which you may leave to us. And we will now endeavor to show that we have come in the interests of our empire, and that in what we are about to say we are only seeking the preservation of your city. For we want to make you ours with the least trouble to ourselves, and it is for the interests of us both that you should not be destroyed.

92. MELIAN: It may be your interest to be our masters, but how can it be ours to be your slaves?

93. ATHENIAN: To you the gain will be that by submission you will avert the worst; and we shall be all the richer for your preservation.

94. MELIAN: But must we be your enemies? Will you not receive us as friends if we are neutral and remain at peace with you?

95. ATHENIAN: No, your enmity is not half so mischievous to us as your friendship; for the one is in the eyes of our subjects an argument of our power, the other of our weakness.

96. MELIAN: But are your subjects really unable to distinguish between states in which you have no concern, and those which are chiefly your own colonies, and in some cases have revolted and been subdued by you?

97. ATHENIAN: Why, they do not doubt that both of them have a good deal to say for themselves on the score of justice, but they think that states like yours are left free because they are able to defend themselves,

and that we do not attack them because we dare not. So that your subjection will give us an increase of security, as well as an extension of empire. For we are masters of the sea, and you who are islanders, and insignificant islanders too, must not be allowed to escape us.

98. MELIAN: But do you not recognise another danger? For once more, since you drive us from the plea of justice and press upon us your doctrine of expediency, we must show you what is for our interest, and, if it be for yours also, may hope to convince you:—Will you not be making enemies of all who are now neutrals? When they see how you are treating us they will expect you some day to turn against them; and if so, are you not strengthening the enemies whom you already have, and bringing upon you others who, if they could help, would never dream of being your enemies at all?

99. ATHENIAN: We do not consider our really dangerous enemies to be any of the peoples inhabiting the mainland who, secure in their freedom, may defer indefinitely any measures of precaution which they take against us, but islanders who, like you, happen to be under no control, and all who may be already irritated by the necessity of submission to our empire—these are our real enemies, for they are the most reckless and most likely to bring themselves as well as us into a danger which they cannot but foresee.

100. MELIAN: Surely then, if you and your subjects will brave all this risk, you to preserve your empire and they to be quit of it, how base and cowardly it would be in us, who retain our freedom, not to do and

suffer anything rather than be your slaves.

101. ATHENIAN: Not so, if you calmly reflect: for you are not fighting against equals to whom you cannot yield without disgrace, but you are taking counsel whether or not you shall resist an overwhelming force. The question is not one of honor but of prudence.

102. MELIAN: But we know that the fortune of war is sometimes impartial, and not always on the side of numbers. If we yield now all is over; but if we fight there is yet a hope that we may stand upright.

103. ATHENIAN: Hope is a good comforter in the hour of danger, and when men have something else to depend upon, although hurtful, she is not ruinous. But when her spendthrift nature has induced them to stake their all, they see her as she is in the moment of their fall, and not till then. While the knowledge of her might enable them to beware of her, she never fails. You are weak and a single turn of the scale might be your ruin. Do not you be thus deluded; avoid the error of which so many are guilty, who, although they might still be saved if they would take the natural means, when visible grounds of confidence forsake them, have recourse to the invisible, to prophecies and oracles and the like, which ruin men by the hopes which they inspire in them.

104. MELIAN: We know only too well how hard the struggle must be against your power, and against fortune, if she does not mean to be impartial. Nevertheless we do not despair of fortune, for we hope to stand as high as you in the favor of heaven, because we are righteous, and you against whom we contend are unrighteous; and we are satis-

fied that our deficiency in power will be compensated by the aid of our allies the Lacedaemonians; they cannot refuse to help us, if only because we are their kinsmen, and for the sake of their own honor. And therefore our confidence is not so utterly blind as you suppose.

105. ATHENIAN: As for the Gods, we expect to have quite as much of their favor as you: for we are not doing or claiming anything which goes beyond common opinion about divine or men's desires about human things. For of the Gods we believe, and of men we know, that by a law of their nature wherever they can rule they will. This law was not made by us, and we are not the first who have acted upon it; we did but inherit it, and shall bequeath it to all time, and we know that you and all mankind, if you were as strong as we are, would do as we do. So much for the Gods; we have told you why we expect to stand as high in their good opinion as you. And then as to the Lacedaemonians—when you imagine that out of very shame they will assist you, we admire the simplicity of your idea, but we do not envy you the folly of it. The Lacedaemonians are exceedingly virtuous among themselves, and according to their national standard of morality. But in respect of their dealings with others, although many things might be said, a word is enough to describe them—of all men whom we know they are the most notorious for identifying what is pleasant with what is honorable, and what is expedient with what is just. But how inconsistent is such a character with your present blind hope of deliverance!

106. MELIAN: That is the very reason why we trust them; they will look to their interest, and therefore will not be willing to betray the Melians, who are their own colonists, lest they should be distrusted by their friends in Hellas and play into the hands of their enemies.

107. ATHENIAN: But do you not see that the path of expediency is safe, whereas justice and honor involve danger in practice, and such dangers the Lacedaemonians seldom care to face?

108. MELIAN: On the other hand we think that whatever perils there may be, they will be ready to face them for our sakes, and will consider danger less dangerous where we are concerned. For if they need our aid we are close at hand, and they can better trust our loyal feeling because we are their kinsmen.

109. ATHENIAN: Yes, but what encourages men who are invited to join in a conflict is clearly not the goodwill of those who summon them to their side, but a decided superiority in real power. To this no men look more keenly than the Lacedaemonians; so little confidence have they in their own resources that they only attack their neighbors when they have numerous allies, and therefore they are not likely to find their way by themselves to an island, when we are masters of the sea.

110. MELIAN: But they may send their allies: the Cretan sea is a large place; and the masters of the sea will have more difficulty in overtaking vessels which want to escape than the pursued in escaping. If the attempt should fail, they may invade Attica itself, and find their way to allies of yours whom Brasidas did not reach; and then you will have to fight, not for the conquest of a land in which you have no concern,

but nearer home, for the preservation of your confederacy and of your own territory.

111. ATHENIAN: Help may come from Lacedaemon to you as it has come to others, and should you ever have actual experience of it, then you will know that never once have the Athenians retired from a siege through fear of a foe elsewhere. You told us that the safety of your city would be your first care, but we remark that, in this long discussion, not a word has been uttered by you which would give a reasonable man expectation of deliverance. Your strongest grounds are hopes deferred, and what power you have is not to be compared with that which is already arrayed gainst you. Unless after we have withdrawn you mean to come, as even now you may, to a wiser conclusion, you are showing a great want of sense. For surely you cannot dream of flying to that false sense of honor which has been the ruin of so many when danger and dishonor were staring them in the face. Many men with their eyes still open to the consequences have found the word 'honor' too much for them, and have suffered a mere name to lure them on, until it has drawn down upon them real and irretrievable calamities; through their own folly they have incurred a worse dishonor than fortune would have inflicted upon them. If you are wise you will not run this risk; you ought to see that there can be no disgrace in yielding to a great city which invites you to become her ally on reasonable terms, keeping your own land, and merely paying tribute, and that you will certainly gain no honor if, having to choose between two alternatives, safety and war, you obstinately prefer the worse. To maintain our rights against equals, to be politic with superiors, and to be moderate towards inferiors is the path of safety. Reflect once more when we have withdrawn, and say to yourselves over and over again that you are deliberating about your one and only country, which may be saved or may be destroyed by a single decision.

112. The Athenians left the conference: the Melians, after consulting among themselves, resolved to persevere in their refusal, and made answer as follows:—"Men of Athens, our resolution is unchanged; and we will not in a moment surrender that liberty which our city, founded seven hundred years ago, still enjoys; we will trust to the good-fortune which by the favor of the Gods has hitherto preserved us, and for human help to the Lacedaemonians, and endeavor to save ourselves. We are ready however to be your friends, and the enemies neither of you nor of the Lacedaemonians, and we ask you to leave our country when you have made such a peace as may appear to be in the interest of both parties."

113. Such was the answer of the Melians; the Athenians, as they quitted the conference, spoke as follows:—"Well, we must say, judging from the decision at which you have arrived, that you are the only men who deem the future to be more certain than the present, and regard things unseen as already realized in your fond anticipation, and that the more you cast yourselves upon the Lacedaemonians and fortune, and hope, and trust them, the more complete will be your ruin."

114. The Athenian envoys returned to the army, and the generals, when they found that the Me-

lians would not yield, immediately commenced hostilities. They surrounded the town of Melos with a wall, dividing the work among the several contingents. They then left troops of their own and of the allies to keep guard both by land and by sea, and retired with the greater part of their army; the remainder carried on the blockade.

•   •   •

116. ... The place was now closely invested, and there was treachery among the citizens themselves. So the Melians were induced to surrender at discretion. The Athenians thereupon put to death all who were of military age, and made slaves of the women and children. They then colonised the island, sending thither five hundred settlers of their own.

The Last Days of Socrates

Although Socrates (c.470–399 B.C.) was an influential philosopher and teacher, he wrote nothing. Therefore, we must rely on secondary accounts for information about his life and beliefs. Such accounts, particularly the writings of his most famous disciple, Plato, make it possible to reconstruct the broad outlines of his career. Socrates was born in Athens, the son of a stonecutter. Instead of learning his father's trade, he began early in life to frequent the Athenian marketplace, where he listened to the intellectuals of the city argue questions of politics, art, morality, and philosophy.

Before long, he had acquired a reputation as a man of wisdom and had gathered about himself a group of young disciples, who were intrigued by the unusual manner in which he taught. Unlike the sophists ("wise men"), the professional teachers of the day who were willing to teach anyone anything for a suitable fee, Socrates professed to be completely ignorant. Instead of attempting to teach, he wandered about Athens seeking wisdom by asking questions of everyone he met, including the city's leading politicians, generals, artists, and philosophers. As might be expected, under Socrates' questioning many of the self-styled sages of Athens

proved to be without wisdom. Although Socrates' unflinching quest for wisdom and truth won him many loyal followers, it inevitably aroused the enmity of those whose ignorance he unmasked. Through their influence in Athens, his enemies succeeded in having him brought to trial and condemned to death. But they were unable to silence him, for his words live on in the Dialogues of Plato.

Although he professed to have no wisdom of his own, Socrates did have a positive philosophy. The basic premise of his philosophy was the doctrine that *virtue is knowledge*, or that the good life is the life of wisdom. To gain knowledge and, hence, virtue, he believed, education is necessary. But knowledge is not something that can be poured into an individual from the outside. Rather, it is something that lies deep within each person and needs only to be drawn out. Socrates' method for bringing this inborn knowledge to the surface was to ask a series of questions, a technique that is known as the *dialectic method*.

The selections that follow are an account of the last days of Socrates written by Plato some time after the events described. Socrates had been hauled into court by a group of accusers, a sort of "un-Athenian activities committee," who charged him with being an atheist and a corrupter of youth. In Plato's *Apology*, Socrates is represented as replying to the charges with a general defense of his way of life. In the *Crito*, Plato pictures Socrates waiting in prison for his execution and arguing with a friend (who has arranged for his escape) about whether he would be justified in running away, even though he has been unjustly convicted. The extract from the *Phaedo* records Socrates' death. These selections give us a fresh and living portrait of Socrates the man, a fairly comprehensive account of his philosophy, and a glimpse of the social and legal structure of the Athens of his day.

The Apology

SCENE: The Court of Justice

I cannot tell what impression my accusers have made upon you, Athenians: for my own part, I know that they nearly made me forget who I was, so plausible were they; and yet they have scarcely uttered one single word of truth. But of all their many falsehoods, the one which astonished me most, was when they said that I was a clever speaker, and that you must be careful not to let me mislead you. I thought that it was most imprudent of them not to be ashamed to talk in that way; for as soon as I opened my mouth the lie will be exposed, and I shall prove that I am not a clever speaker in any way at all: unless, indeed, by a clever speaker they mean a man who speaks the truth. If that is their meaning, I agree with them that I am a much greater orator than they. My accusers, then I repeat, have said little or nothing that is true: but from me you shall hear the whole truth. Certainly you will not hear an elaborate speech, Athenians, drest up, like theirs, with words and phrases. I will say to you what I have to say, without preparation, and in the words which come first, for I believe that my cause is just; so let none of you expect anything else. Indeed, my friends, it would hardly be seemly for me, at my age, to come before you like a young man with his specious falsehoods. But there is one thing, Athenians, which I do most earnestly beg and entreat of you. Do not be surprised and do not interrupt, if in my defence I speak in the same way that I am accustomed to speak in the marketplace, at the tables of the money-changers, where many of you have heard me, and elsewhere. The truth is this: I am more than seventy years old, and this is the first time that I have ever come before a Court of Law; so your manner of speech here is quite strange to me. If I had been really a stranger, you would have forgiven me for speaking in the

Trans. F. J. Church.

language and the fashion of my native country: and so now I ask you to grant me what I think I have a right to claim. Never mind the style of my speech—it may be better or it may be worse—give your whole attention to the question, Is what I say just, or is it not? That is what makes a good judge, as speaking the truth makes a good advocate.

I have to defend myself Athenians, first against the old false charges of my old accusers, and then against the later ones of my present accusers. For many men have been accusing me to you, and for very many years, who have not uttered a word of truth: and I fear them more than I fear Anytus and his companions, formidable as they are. But, my friends, those others are still more formidable; for they got hold of most of you when you were children, and they have been more persistent in accusing me with lies, and in trying to persuade you that there is one Socrates, a wise man, who speculates about the heavens, and who examines into all things that are beneath the earth, and who can "make the worse appear the better reason." These men, Athenians, who spread abroad this report, are the accusers whom I fear; for their hearers think that persons who pursue such inquiries never believe in the gods. And then they are many, and their attacks have been going on for a long time: and they spoke to you when you were at the age most readily to believe them: for you were all young, and many of you were children: and there was no one to answer them when they attacked me. And the most unreasonable thing of all is that commonly I do not even know their names: I cannot tell you who they are, except in the case of the comic poets. But all the rest who have been trying to prejudice you against me, from motives of spite and jealousy, and sometimes, it may be, from conviction, are the enemies whom it is hardest to meet. For I cannot call any one of them forward in Court, to cross-examine him: I have, as it were, simply to fight with shadows in my defence, and to put questions which there is no one to answer. I ask you, therefore, to believe that, as I say, I have been attacked by two classes of accusers—first by Meletus and his friends, and then by those older ones of whom I have spoken. And, with your leave, I will defend myself first against my old enemies; for you heard their accusations first, and they were much more persistent than my present accusers are.

Well, I must make my defence, Athenians, and try in the short time allowed me to remove the prejudice which you have had against me for a long time. I hope that I may manage to do this, if it be good for you and for me, and that my defence may be successful, but I am quite aware of the nature of my task, and I know that it is a difficult one. Be the issue, however, as God wills, I must obey the law, and make my defence.

Let us begin again, then, and see what is the charge which has given rise to the prejudice against me, which was what Meletus relied on when he drew his indictment. What is the calumny which my enemies have been spreading about me? I must assume that they are formally accusing me, and read their indictment. It would run somewhat in this fashion: "Socrates is an evil-doer, who meddles with inquiries into things beneath the earth, and in heaven, and who 'makes the worse appear the better reason,' and who teaches others these same things." That is what they say; and in the Comedy of Aristophanes you yourselves saw a man called Socrates swinging round in a basket, and saying that he walked the air, and talking a great deal of nonsense about matters of which I understand nothing, either more or less. I do not mean to disparage that kind of knowledge, if there is any man who possesses it. I trust Meletus may never be able to prosecute me for that. But, the truth is, Athenians, I have nothing to do with these matters, and almost all of you are yourselves my witnesses of this. I beg all of you who have heard me converse, and they are many, to inform your neighbors and tell them if any of you ever heard me conversing about such matters, either more or less. That will show you that the other common stories about me are as false as this one.

But, the fact is, that not one of these stories is true; and if you have heard that I undertake to educate men, and exact money from them for so doing, that is not true either; though I think that it would be a fine thing to be able to educate men, as Gorgias of Leontini, and Prodicus of Ceos, and Hippias of Elis do. For each of them, my friends, can go into any city, and persuade the young men to leave the society of their fellow-citizens, with any of whom they might associate for nothing, and to be only too glad to be allowed to pay money for the privilege of associating with themselves. And I believe that there is another wise man from Paros residing in Athens at this moment. I happened

to meet Callias, the son of Hipponicus, a man who has spent more money on the Sophists than every one else put together. So I said to him—he has two sons—"Callias, if your two sons had been foals or calves, we could have hired a trainer for them who would have made them perfect in the excellence which belongs to their nature. He would have been either a groom or a farmer. But whom do you intend to take to train them, seeing that they are men? Who understands the excellence which belongs to men and to citizens? I suppose that you must have thought of this, because of your sons. Is there such a person," said I, "or not?" "Certainly there is," he replied. "Who is he," said I, "and where does he come from, and what is his fee?" "His name is Evenus, Socrates," he replied. "He comes from Paros, and his fee is five minae." Then I thought that Evenus was a fortunate person if he really understood this art and could teach so cleverly. If I had possessed knowledge of that kind, I should have given myself airs and prided myself on it. But, Athenians, the truth is that I do not possess it.

Perhaps some of you may reply: "But, Socrates, what is this pursuit of yours? Whence come these calumnies against you? You must have become engaged in some pursuit out of the common. All these stories and reports of you would never have gone about, if you had not been in some way different from other men. So tell us what your pursuits are, that we may not give our verdict in the dark." I think that that is a fair question, and I will try to explain to you what it is that has raised these calumnies against me, and given me this name. Listen, then: some of you perhaps will think that I am jesting, but I assure you that I will tell you the whole truth. I have gained this name, Athenians, simply by reason of a certain wisdom. But by what kind of wisdom? It is by just that wisdom which is, I believe, possible to men. In that, it may be, I am really wise. But the men of whom I was speaking just now must be wise in a wisdom which is greater than human wisdom, or in some way which I cannot describe, for certainly I know nothing of it myself, and if any man says that I do, he lies and wants to slander me. Do not interrupt me, Athenians, even if you think that I am speaking arrogantly. What I am going to say is not my own: I will tell you who says it, and he is worthy of your credit. I will bring the god of Delphi to be the witness of the fact of my wisdom and of its nature. You remember Chaerephon. From youth upwards he was my comrade; and he went into exile with the people,[1] and with the people he returned. And you remember, too, Chaerephon's character; how vehement he was in carrying through whatever he took in hand. Once he went to Delphi and ventured to put this question to the oracle,—I entreat you again, my friends, not to cry out,—he asked if there was any man who was wiser than I: and the priestess answered that there was no man. Chaerephon himself is dead, but his brother here will confirm what I say.

Now see why I tell you this. I am going to explain to you the origin of my unpopularity. When I heard of the oracle I began to reflect: What

can God mean by this dark saying? I know very well that I am not wise, even in the smallest degree. Then what can he mean by saying that I am the wisest of men? It cannot be that he is speaking falsely, for he is a god and cannot lie. And for a long time I was at a loss to understand his meaning: then, very reluctantly, I turned to seek for it in this manner. I went to a man who was reputed to be wise, thinking that there, if anywhere, I should prove the answer wrong, and meaning to point out to the oracle its mistake, and to say, "You said that I was the wisest of men, but this man is wiser than I am." So I examined the man—I need not tell you his name, he was a politician—but this was the result, Athenians. When I conversed with him I came to see that, though a great many persons, and most of all he himself, thought that he was wise, yet he was not wise. And then I tried to prove to him that he was not wise, though he fancied that he was: and by so doing I made him, and many of the bystanders, my enemies. So when I went away, I thought to myself, "I am wiser than this man: neither of us probably knows anything that is really good, but he thinks he has knowledge, when he has not, while I, having no knowledge, do not think that I have. I seem at any rate, to be a little wiser than he is on this point: I do not think that I know what I do not know." Next I went to another man who was reputed to be still wiser than the last, with exactly the same result. And there again I made him, and many other men, my enemies.

Then I went on to one man after another, seeing that I was making enemies every day, which caused

---

[1] [At the time of the oligarchy of the Thirty, 404 B.C.—*Trans.*]

me much unhappiness and anxiety: still I thought that I must set God's command above everything. So I had to go to every man who seemed to possess any knowledge, and search for the meaning of the oracle: and, Athenians, I must tell you the truth; verily, by the dog of Egypt, this was the result of the search which I made at God's bidding. I found that the men, whose reputation for wisdom stood highest, were nearly the most lacking in it; while others, who were looked down on as common people, were much better fitted to learn. Now, I must describe to you the wanderings which I undertook, like a series of Heraclean labours, to make full proof of the oracle. After the politicians, I went to the poets, tragic, dithyrambic, and others, thinking that there I should find myself manifestly more ignorant than they. So I took up the poems on which I thought that they had spent most pains, and asked them what they meant, hoping at the same time to learn something from them. I am ashamed to tell you the truth, my friends, but I must say it. Almost any one of the bystanders could have talked about the works of these poets better than the poets themselves. So I soon found that it is not by wisdom that the poets create their works, but by a certain natural power and by inspiration, like soothsayers and prophets, who say many fine things, but who understand nothing of what they say. The poets seemed to me to be in a similar case. And at the same time I perceived that, because of their poetry, they thought that they were the wisest of men in other matters too, which they were not. So I went away again, thinking that I had the same advantage over the poets that I had over the politicians.

Finally, I went to the artizans, for I knew very well that I possessed no knowledge at all, worth speaking of, and I was sure that I should find that they knew many fine things. And in that I was not mistaken. They knew what I did not know, and so far they were wiser than I. But, Athenians, it seemed to me that the skilled artizans made the same mistake as the poets. Each of them believed himself to be extremely wise in matters of the greatest importance, because he was skilful in his own art: and this mistake of theirs threw their real wisdom into the shade. So I asked myself, on behalf of the oracle, whether I would choose to remain as I was, without either their wisdom or their ignorance, or to possess both, as they did. And I made answer to myself and to the oracle that it was better for me to remain as I was.

By reason of this examination, Athenians, I have made many enemies of a very fierce and bitter kind, who have spread abroad a great number of calumnies about me, and people say that I am "a wise man." For the bystanders always think that I am wise myself in any matter wherein I convict another man of ignorance. But, my friends, I believe that only God is really wise: and that by this oracle he meant that men's wisdom is worth little or nothing. I do not think that he meant that Socrates was wise. He only made use of my name, and took me as an example, as though he would say to men, "He among you is the wisest, who, like Socrates, knows that in very truth his wisdom is worth nothing at all." And therefore I still go about testing and examining every man whom I think wise, whether he be a citizen or a stranger, as God has commanded me; and whenever I find that he is not wise, I point out to him on the part of God that he is not wise. And I am so busy in this pursuit that I have never had leisure to take any part worth mentioning in public matters, or to look after my private affairs. I am in very great poverty by reason of my service to God.

And besides this, the young men who follow me about, who are the sons of wealthy persons and have a great deal of spare time, take a natural pleasure in hearing men cross-examined: and they often imitate me among themselves: then they try their hands at cross-examining other people. And, I imagine, they find a great abundance of men who think that they know a great deal, when in fact they know little or nothing. And then the persons who are cross-examined get angry with me instead of with themselves, and say that Socrates is an abominable fellow who corrupts young men. And when they are asked, "Why, what does he do? what does he teach?" they do not know what to say; but, not to seem at a loss, they repeat the stock charges against all philosophers, and allege that he investigates things in the air and under the earth, and that he teaches people to disbelieve in the gods, and "to make the worse appear the better reason." For, I fancy, they would not like to confess the truth, which is that they are shown up as ignorant pretenders to knowledge that they do not possess. And so they have been filling your ears with their bitter calumnies for a long time, for they are zealous and numerous and bitter against me; and they are well disciplined and plausible in speech. On these grounds Meletus and Anytus and Lycon have attacked me. Meletus is indignant with me on the part of the poets, and Anytus on the part of the artizans and politicians, and Lycon on the part of the orators. And so, as I said at the beginning, I shall be surprised if I am able, in the short time allowed me for my defence, to remove from your minds this prejudice which has grown so strong. What I have told you, Athenians, is the truth: I neither conceal, nor do I suppress anything, small or great. And yet I know that it is just this plainness of speech which makes me enemies. But that is only a proof that my words are true, and that the prejudice against me, and the causes of it, are what I have said. And whether you look for them now or hereafter, you will find that they are so.

[*Socrates then cross-examines and discredits his chief accuser*—Ed.]

•   •   •

Perhaps some one will say: "Are you not ashamed, Socrates, of following pursuits which are very likely now to cause your death?" I should answer him with justice, and say: My friend, if you think that a man of any worth at all ought to reckon the chances of life and death when he acts, or that he ought to think of anything but whether he is acting rightly or wrongly, and as a good or a bad man would act, you are grievously mistaken. According to you, the demigods who died at Troy would be men of no great worth, and among them the son of Thetis, who thought nothing of danger when the alternative was disgrace. For when his mother, a goddess, addressed him, as he was burning to slay Hector, I suppose in this fashion, "My son, if thou avengest the death of thy comrade Patroclus, and slayest Hector, thou wilt die thyself, for 'fate awaits thee straightway after Hector's death'"; he heard what she said, but he scorned danger and death; he feared much more to live a coward, and not to avenge his friend. "Let me punish the evil-doer and straightway die," he said, "that I may not remain here by the beaked ships, a scorn of men, encumbering the earth." Do you suppose that he thought of danger or of death? For this, Athenians, I believe to be the truth. Wherever a man's post is, whether he has chosen it of his own will, or whether he has been placed at it by his commander, there it is his duty to remain and face the danger, without thinking of death, or of any other thing, except dishonour.

When the generals whom you chose to command me, Athenians, placed me at my post at Potidaea, and at Amphipholis, and at Delium, I remained where they placed me, and ran the risk of death, like other men: and it would be very strange conduct on my part if I were to desert my post now from fear of death or of any other thing, when God has commanded me, as I am persuaded that he has done, to spend my life searching for wisdom, and in examining myself and others. That would indeed be a very strange thing: and then certainly I might with justice be brought to trial for not believing in the gods: for I should be disobeying the oracle, and fearing death, and thinking myself wise, when I was not wise. For to fear death, my friends, is only to think ourselves wise, without being wise: for it is to think that we know what we do not know. For anything that men can tell, death may be the greatest good that can happen to them: but they fear it as if they knew quite well that it was the greatest of evils. And what is this but that shameful ignorance of thinking that we know what we do not know? In this manner too, my friends, perhaps I am different from the mass of mankind: and if I were to claim to be at all wiser than others, it would be because I do not think that I have any clear knowledge about the other world, when, in fact, I have none. But I do know very well that it is evil and base to do wrong, and to disobey my superior, whether he be man or god. And I will never do what I know to be evil, and shrink in fear from what, for all that I can tell, may be a good. And so, even if you acquit me now, and do not listen to Anytus' argument that, if I am to be acquitted, I ought never to have been brought to trial at all; and that, as it is, you are bound to put me to death, because, as he said, if I escape, all your children will forthwith be utterly corrupted by practising what Socrates teaches; if you were therefore to say to me, "Socrates, this time we will not listen to Anytus: we will let you go; but on this condition, that you cease from carrying on this search of yours, and from philosophy; if you are found following those pursuits again, you shall die": I say, if you offered to let me go on these terms, I should reply:—"Athenians, I hold you in the highest regard and love; but I will obey God rather than you: and as long as I have breath and strength I will not cease from philosophy, and from exhorting you, and declaring the truth to everyone of you whom I meet, saying, as I am wont, 'My excellent friend, you are a citizen of Athens, a city which is very great and very famous for wisdom and power of mind; are you not ashamed of caring so much for the making of money, and for reputation, and for honour? Will you not think or care about wisdom, and truth, and the perfection of your soul?'" And if he disputes my words, and says that he does care about these things, I shall not forthwith release him and go away: I shall question him and cross-examine him and test him: and if I think that he has not virtue, though he says that he has, I shall reproach him for setting the lower value on the most important things, and a higher value on those that are of less account. This I shall do to every one whom I meet, young or old, citizen or stranger: but more especially to the citizens, for they are more nearly akin to me. For, know well, God has commanded me to do so. And I think that no better piece of fortune has ever befallen you in Athens than my service to God. For I spend my whole life in going about and persuading you all to give your first and chiefest care to the perfection of your souls, and not till you have done that to think of your bodies, or your wealth; and telling you that virtue does not come from wealth, but that wealth, and every other good thing which men have, whether in public, or in private, comes from virtue. If then I corrupt the youth by this teaching, the mischief is great: but if any man says that I teach anything else, he speaks falsely. And therefore, Athenians, I say, either listen to Anytus, or do not listen to him: either acquit me, or do not acquit me: but be sure that I shall not alter my way of life; no, not if I have to die for it many times.

Do not interrupt me, Athenians. Remember the request which I made to you, and listen to my words. I think that it will profit you to hear them. I am going to say something more to you, at which you may be inclined to cry out: but do not do that. Be sure that if you put me to death, who am what I have told you that I am, you will do yourselves more harm than me. Meletus and Anytus can do me no harm: that is impossible: for I am sure that God will not allow a good man to be injured by a bad one. They may indeed kill me, or drive me into exile, or deprive me of my civil rights; and perhaps Meletus and others think those things great evils. But I do not think so: I think that it is a much greater evil to do what he is doing now, and to try to put a man to death unjustly. And now, Athenians, I am not arguing in my own defence at all, as you might expect me to do: I am trying to persuade you not to sin against God, by condemning me, and rejecting his gift to you. For if you put me to death, you will not easily find another man to fill my place. God has sent me to attack the city, as if it were a great and noble horse, to use a quaint simile, which was rather sluggish from its size, and which needed to be aroused by a gadfly: and I think that I am the gadfly that God has sent to the city to attack it; for I never cease from settling upon you, as it were, at every point, and rousing, and exhorting, and reproaching each man of you all day long. You will not easily find any one else, my friends, to fill my place:

and if you take my advice, you will spare my life. You are vexed, as drowsy persons are, when they are awakened, and of course, if you listen to Anytus, you could easily kill me with a single blow, and then sleep on undisturbed for the rest of your lives, unless God were to care for you enough to send another man to arouse you. And you may easily see that it is God who has given me to your city: a mere human impulse would never have led me to neglect all my own interests, or to endure seeing my private affairs neglected now for so many years, while it made me busy myself unceasingly in your interests, and go to each man of you by himself, like a father, or an elder brother, trying to persuade him to care for virtue. There would have been a reason for it, if I had gained any advantage by this conduct, or if I had been paid for my exhortations; but you see yourselves that my accusers, though they accuse me of everything else without blushing, have not had the effrontery to say that I ever either extracted or demanded payment. They could bring no evidence of that. And I think that I have sufficient evidence of the truth of what I say in my poverty.

Perhaps it may seem strange to you that, though I am so busy in going about in private with my counsel, yet I do not venture to come forward in the assembly, and take part in the public councils. You have often heard me speak of my reason for this, and in many places: it is that I have a certain divine sign from God, which is the divinity that Meletus has caricatured in his indictment. I have had it from childhood: it is a kind of voice, which whenever I hear it, always turns me

back from something which I was going to do, but never urges me to act. It is this which forbids me to take part in politics. And I think that it does well to forbid me. For, Athenians, it is quite certain that if I had attempted to take part in politics, I should have perished at once and long ago, without doing any good either to you or to myself. And do not be vexed with me for telling the truth. There is no man who will preserve his life for long, either in Athens or elsewhere, if he firmly opposes the wishes of the people, and tries to prevent the commission of much injustice and illegality in the State. He who would really fight for justice, must do so as a private man, not in public, if he means to preserve his life, even for a short time.

I will prove to you that this is so by very strong evidence, not by mere words, but by what you value highly, actions. Listen then to what has happened to me, that you may know that there is no man who could make me consent to do wrong from the fear of death; but that I would perish at once rather than give way. What I am going to tell you may be a commonplace in the Courts of Law; nevertheless it is true. The only office that I ever held in the State, Athenians, was that of Senator. When you wished to try the ten generals, who did not rescue their men after the battle of Arginusae, in a body, which was illegal, as you all came to think afterwards, the tribe Antiochis, to which I belong, held the presidency. On that occasion I alone of all the presidents opposed your illegal action, and gave my vote against you. The speakers were ready to suspend me and arrest me; and you were clamouring against me, and crying out to me to submit. But I thought that I ought to face the danger out in the cause of law and justice, rather than join with you in your unjust proposal, from fear of imprisonment or death. That was before the destruction of the democracy. When the oligarchy came, the Thirty sent for me, with four others, to the Council-Chamber and ordered us to bring over Leon the Salaminian from Salamis, that they might put him to death. They were in the habit of frequently giving similar orders to many others, wishing to implicate as many men as possible in their crimes. But then I again proved, not by mere words, but by my actions, that, if I may use a vulgar expression, I do not care a straw for death; but that I do care very much indeed about not doing anything against the laws of God or man. That government with all its power did not terrify me into doing anything wrong, but when we left the Council-Chamber, the other four went over to Salamis, and brought Leon across to Athens; and I went away home: and if the rule of the Thirty had not been destroyed soon afterwards, I should very likely have been put to death for what I did then. Many of you will be my witnesses in this matter.

Now do you think that I should have remained alive all these years, if I had taken part in public affairs, and had always maintained the cause of justice like an honest man, and had held it a paramount duty, as it is, to do so? Certainly not, Athenians, nor any other man either. But throughout my whole life, both in private, and in public, whenever I have had to take part in public affairs, you will find that I have never yielded a single point in a question of right and wrong to any man; no, not to those whom my enemies falsely assert to have been my pupils. But I was never any man's teacher. I have never withheld myself from any one, young or old, who was anxious to hear me converse while I was about my mission; neither do I converse for payment, and refuse to converse without payment: I am ready to ask questions of rich and poor alike, and if any man wishes to answer me, and then listen to what I have to say, he may. And I cannot justly be charged with causing these men to turn out good or bad citizens: for I never either taught, or professed to teach any of them any knowledge whatever. And if any man asserts that he ever learnt or heard any thing from me in private, which every one else did not hear as well as he, be sure that he does not speak the truth.

Why is it, then, that people delight in spending so much time in my company? You have heard why, Athenians. I told you the whole truth when I said that they delight in hearing me examine persons who think that they are wise when they are not wise. It is certainly very amusing to listen to that. And, I say, God has commanded me to examine men in oracles, and in dreams, and in every way in which the divine will was ever declared to man. This is the truth, Athenians, and if it were not the truth, it would be easily refuted. For if it were really the case that I have already corrupted some of the young men, and I am now corrupting others, surely some of them, finding as they grew older that I had given them evil counsel in their youth, would have come forward to-day to accuse me and take their revenge. Or if they were unwilling to do so themselves, surely their kinsmen, their fathers, or brothers, or other relatives, would, if I had done them any harm, have remembered it, and taken their revenge. Certainly I see many of them in Court. Here is Crito, of my own deme and of my own age, the father of Critobulus; here is Lysanias of Sphettus, the father of Aeschinus: here is also Antiphon of Cephisus, the father of Epigenes. Then here are others, whose brothers have spent their time in my company; Nicostratus, the son of Theozotides, and brother of Theodotus—and Theodotus is dead, so he at least cannot entreat his brother to be silent: here is Paralus, the son of Demodocus, and the brother of Theages: here is Adeimantus, the son of Ariston, whose brother is Plato here: and Aeantodorus, whose brother is Aristodorus. And I can name many others to you, some of whom Meletus ought to have called as witnesses in the course of his own speech: but if he forgot to call them then, let him call them now—I will stand aside while he does so—and tell us if he has any such evidence. No, on the contrary, my friends, you will find all these men ready to support me, the corrupter, the injurer of their kindred, as Meletus and Anytus call me. Those of them who have been already corrupted might perhaps have some reason for supporting me: but what reason can their relatives, who are grown up, and who are uncorrupted, have, except the reason of truth and justice, that they know very well that Meletus is a liar, and that I am speaking the truth?

Well, my friends, this, together it may be with other things of the same nature, is pretty much what I have to say in my defence. There may be some one among you who will be vexed when he remembers how, even in a less important trial than this, he prayed and entreated the judges to acquit him with many tears, and brought forward his children and many of his friends and relatives in Court, in order to appeal to your feelings; and then finds that I shall do none of these things, though I am in what he would think the supreme danger. Perhaps he will harden himself against me when he notices this: it may make him angry, and he may give his vote in anger. If it is so with any of you—I do not suppose that it is, but in case it should be so—I think that I should answer him reasonably if I said: "My friend, I have kinsmen too, for in the words of Homer, 'I am not born of sticks and stones,' but of woman"; and so, Athenians, I have kinsmen, and I have three sons, one of them a lad, and the other two still children. Yet I will not bring any of them forward before you, and implore you to acquit me. And why will I do none of these things? It is not from arrogance, Athenians, nor because I hold you cheap: whether or not I can face death bravely is another question: but for my own credit, and for your credit, and for the credit of our city, I do not think it well, at my age, and with my name, to do anything of that kind. Rightly or wrongly, men have made up their minds that in some way Socrates is different from the mass of mankind. And it will be a shameful thing if those of you who are thought to excell in wisdom, or in bravery, or in any other virtue, are going to act in this fashion. I have often seen men with a reputation behaving in a strange way at their trial, as if they thought it a terrible fate to be killed, and as though they expected to live for ever, if you did not put them to death. Such men seem to me to bring discredit on the city: for any stranger would suppose that the best and most eminent Athenians, who are selected by their fellow-citizens to hold office, and for other honours, are no better than women. Those of you, Athenians, who have any reputation at all, ought not to do these things: and you ought not to allow us to do them: you should show that you will be much more merciless to men who make the city ridiculous by these pitiful pieces of acting, than to men who remain quiet.

But apart from the question of credit, my friends, I do not think that it is right to entreat the judge to acquit us, or to escape condemnation in that way. It is our duty to convince his mind by reason. He does not sit to give away justice to his friends, but to pronounce judgment: and he has sworn not to favour any man whom he would like to favour, but to decide questions according to law. And therefore we ought not to teach you to forswear yourselves; and you ought not to allow yourselves to be taught, for then neither you nor we would be acting righteously. Therefore, Athenians, do not require me to do these things, for I believe them to be neither good nor just nor holy; and, more especially do not ask me to do them today, when Meletus is prosecuting me for impiety. For were I to be successful, and to prevail on you by my prayers to break your oaths, I should be clearly teach-ing you to believe that there are no gods; and I should be simply accusing myself by my defence of not believing in them. But, Athenians, that is very far from the truth. I do believe in the gods as no one of my accusers believes in them: and to you and to God I commit my cause to be decided as is best for you and for me.

[*He is found guilty by 281 votes to 220, and in a second vote is condemned to death*—Ed.]

• • •

You have not gained very much time, Athenians, and, as the price of it, you will have an evil name from all who wish to revile the city, and they will cast in your teeth that you put Socrates, a wise man, to death. For they will certainly call me wise, whether I am wise or not, when they want to reproach you. If you would have waited for a little while, your wishes would have been fulfilled in the course of nature; for you see that I am an old man, far advanced in years, and near to death. I am speaking not to all of you, only to those who have voted for my death. And now I am speaking to them still. Perhaps, my friends, you think that I have been defeated because I was wanting in the arguments by which I could have persuaded you to acquit me, if, that is, I had thought it right to do or to say anything to escape punishment. It is not so. I have been defeated because I was wanting, not in arguments, but in overboldness and effrontery: because I would not plead before you as you would have liked to hear me plead, or appeal to you with weeping and wailing, or say and do many other things, which

I maintain are unworthy of me, but which you have been accustomed to from other men. But when I was defending myself, I thought that I ought not to do anything unmanly because of the danger which I ran, and I have not changed my mind now. I would very much rather defend myself as I did, and die, than as you would have had me do, and live. Both in a law suit, and in war, there are some things which neither I nor any other man may do in order to escape from death. In battle a man often sees that he may at least escape from death by throwing down his arms and falling on his knees before the pursuer to beg for his life. And there are many other ways of avoiding death in every danger, if a man will not scruple to say and to do anything. But, my friends, I think that it is a much harder thing to escape from wickedness than from death; for wickedness is swifter than death. And now I, who am old and slow, have been overtaken by the slower pursuer: and my accusers, who are clever and swift, have been overtaken by the swifter pursuer, which is wickedness. And now I shall go hence, sentenced by you to death; and they will go hence, sentenced by truth to receive the penalty of wickedness and evil. And I abide by this award as well as they. Perhaps it was right for these things to be so: and I think that they are fairly measured.

And now I wish to prophesy to you, Athenians who have condemned me. For I am going to die, and that is the time when men have most prophetic power. And I prophesy to you who have sentenced me to death, that a far severer punishment than you have inflicted on me, will surely overtake you as I am dead. You have done this thing, thinking that you will be relieved from having to give an account of your lives. But I say that the result will be very different from that. There will be more men who will call you to account, whom I have held back, and whom you did not see. And they will be harder masters to you than I have been, for they will be younger, and you will be more angry with them. For if you think that you will restrain men from reproaching you for your evil lives by putting them to death, you are very much mistaken. That way of escape is hardly possible, and it is not a good one. It is much better, and much easier, not to silence reproaches, but to make yourselves as perfect as you can. This is my parting prophecy to you who have condemned me.

With you who have acquitted me I should like to converse touching this thing that has come to pass, while the authorities are busy, and before I go to the place where I have to die. So, I pray you, remain with me until I go hence: there is no reason why we should not converse with each other while it is possible. I wish to explain to you, as my friends, the meaning of what has befallen me. A wonderful thing has happened to me, judges—for you I am right in calling judges. The prophetic sign, which I am wont to receive from the divine voice, has been constantly with me all through my life till now, opposing me in quite small matters if I were not going to act rightly. And now you yourselves see what has happened to me; a thing which might be thought, and which is sometimes actually reckoned, the supreme evil. But the sign of God did not withstand me when I was leaving my house in the morning, nor when I was coming up hither to the Court, nor at any point in my speech, when I was going to say anything: though at other times it has often stopped me in the very act of speaking. But now, in this matter, it has never once withstood me, either in my words or my actions. I will tell you what I believe to be the reason of that. This thing that has come upon me must be a good: and those of us who think that death is an evil must needs be mistaken. I have a clear proof that that is so; for my accustomed sign would certainly have opposed me, if I had not been going to fare well.

And if we reflect in another way we shall see that we may well hope that death is a good. For the state of death is one of two things: either the dead man wholly ceases to be, and loses all sensation; or, according to the common belief, it is a change and migration of the soul unto another place. And if death is the absence of all sensation, and like the sleep of one whose slumbers are unbroken by any dreams, it will be a wonderful gain. For if a man had to select that night in which he slept so soundly that he did not even see any dreams, and had to compare with it all the other nights and days of his life, and then had to say how many days and nights in his life he had spent better and more pleasantly than this night, I think that a private person, nay, even the great King himself, would find them easy to count, compared with the others. If that is the nature of death, I for one count it a gain. For then it appears that eternity is nothing more than a single night. But if death is a journey to another place,

and the common belief be true, that there are all who have died, what good could be greater than this, my judges? Would a journey not be worth taking, at the end of which, in the other world, we should be released from the self-styled judges who are here, and should find the true judges, who are said to sit in judgment below, such as Minos, and Rhadamanthus, and Aeacus, and Triptolemus, and the other demigods who were just in their lives? Or what would you not give to converse with Orpheus and Musaeus and Hesiod and Homer? I am willing to die many times, if this be true. And for my own part I should have a wonderful interest in meeting there Palamedes, and Ajax the son of Telamon, and the other men of old who have died through an unjust judgment, and in comparing my experiences with theirs. That I think would be no small pleasure. And, above all, I could spend my time in examining those who are there, as I examine men here, and in finding out which of them is wise, and which of them thinks himself wise, when he is not wise. What would we not give, my judges, to be able to examine the leader of the great expedition against Troy, or Odysseus, or Sisyphus, or countless other men and women whom we could name? It would be an infinite happiness to converse with them, and to live with them, and to examine them. Assuredly there they do not put men to death for doing that. For besides the other ways in which they are happier than we are, they are immortal, at least if the common belief be true.

And you too, judges, must face death with a good courage, and believe this as a truth, that no evil can happen to a good man, either in life, or after death. His fortunes are not neglected by the gods; and what has come to me to-day has not come by chance. I am persuaded that it was better for me to die now, and to be released from trouble: and that was the reason why the sign never turned me back. And so I am hardly angry with my accusers, or with those who have condemned me to die. Yet it was not with this mind that they accused me and condemned me, but meaning to do me an injury. So far I may find fault with them.

Yet I have one request to make of them. When my sons grow up, visit them with punishment, my friends, and vex them in the same way that I have vexed you, if they seem to you to care for riches, or for any other thing, before virtue: and if they think that they are something, when they are nothing at all, reproach them, as I have reproached you, for not caring for what they should, and for thinking that they are great men when in fact they are worthless. And if you will do this, I myself and my sons will have received our deserts at your hands.

But now the time has come, and we must go hence; I to die, and you to live. Whether life or death is better is known to God, and to God only.

Crito

SCENE: The Prison of Socrates

SOCRATES: Why have you come at this hour, Crito? Is it not still early?

CRITO: Yes, very early.

SOCRATES: About what time is it?

CRITO: It is just day-break.

SOCRATES: I wonder that the jailor was willing to let you in.

CRITO: He knows me now, Socrates, I come here so often; and besides, I have done him a service.

SOCRATES: Have you been here long?

CRITO: Yes; some time.

SOCRATES: Then why did you sit down without speaking? Why did you not wake me at once?

CRITO: Indeed, Socrates, I wish that I myself were not so sleepless and sorrowful. But I have been wondering to see how sweetly you sleep. And I purposely did not wake you, for I was anxious not to disturb your repose. Often before, all through your life, I have thought that your temper was a happy one; and I think so more than ever now, when I see how easily and calmly you bear the calamity that has come to you.

SOCRATES: Nay Crito, it would be absurd if at my age I were angry at having to die.

CRITO: Other men as old are overtaken by similar calamities, Socrates; but their age does not save them from being angry with their fate.

SOCRATES: That is so: but tell me, why are you here so early?

CRITO: I am the bearer of bitter

Trans. F. J. Church.

news, Socrates: not bitter, it seems, to you; but to me, and to all your friends, both bitter and grievous: and to none of them, I think, is it more grievous than to me.

SOCRATES: What is it? Has the ship come from Delos, at the arrival of which I am to die?

CRITO: No, it has not actually arrived: but I think that it will be here to-day, from the news which certain persons have brought from Sunium, who left it there. It is clear from their news that it will be here to-day; and then, Socrates, to-morrow your life will have to end.

SOCRATES: Well, Crito, may it end fortunately. Be it so, if so the gods will. But I do not think that the ship will be here to-day.

CRITO: Why do you suppose not?

SOCRATES: I will tell you. I am to die on the day after the ship arrives, am I not?

CRITO: That is what the authorities say.

SOCRATES: Then I do not think that it will come to-day, but to-morrow. I judge from a certain dream which I saw a little while ago in the night: so it seems to be fortunate that you did not wake me.

CRITO: And what was this dream?

SOCRATES: A fair and comely woman, clad in white garments, seemed to come to me, and call me and say, "O Socrates—
The third day hence shall thou fair Phthia reach."

CRITO: What a strange dream, Socrates!

SOCRATES: But its meaning is clear; at least to me, Crito.

CRITO: Yes, too clear, it seems. But, O my good Socrates, I beseech you for the last time to listen to me and save yourself. For to me your death will be more than a single disaster: not only shall I lose a friend the like of whom I shall never find again, but many persons, who do not know you and me well, will think that I might have saved you if I had been willing to spend money, but that I neglected to do so. And what character could be more disgraceful than the character of caring more for money than for one's friends? The world will never believe that we were anxious to save you, but that you yourself refused to escape.

SOCRATES: But, my excellent Crito, why should we care so much about the opinion of the world? The best men, of whose opinion it is worth our while to think, will believe that we acted as we really did.

CRITO: But you see, Socrates, that it is necessary to care about the opinion of the world too. This very thing that has happened to you proves that the multitude can do a man not the least, but almost the greatest harm, if he be falsely accused to them.

SOCRATES: I wish that the multitude were able to do a man the greatest harm, Crito, for then they would be able to do him the greatest good too. That would have been well. But, as it is, they can do neither. They cannot make a man either wise or foolish: they act wholly at random.

CRITO: Well, be it so. But tell me this, Socrates. You surely are not anxious about me and your other friends, and afraid lest, if you escape, the informers should say that we stole you away, and get us into trouble, and involve us in a great deal of expense, or perhaps in the loss of all of our property, and, it may be, bring some other punishment upon us besides? If you have any fear of that kind, dismiss it. For of course we are bound to run those risks, and still greater risks than those if necessary, in saving you. So do not, I beseech you, refuse to listen to me.

SOCRATES: I am anxious about that, Crito, and about much besides.

CRITO: Then have no fear on that score. There are men who, for no very large sum, are ready to bring you out of prison into safety. And then, you know, these informers are cheaply bought, and there would be no need to spend much upon them. My fortune is at your service, and I think that it is sufficient: and if you have any feeling about making use of my money, there are strangers in Athens, whom you know, ready to use theirs, and one of them, Simmias of Thebes, has actually brought enough for this very purpose. And Cebes and many others are ready too. And therefore, I repeat, do not shrink from saving yourself on that ground. And do not let what you said in the Court, that if you went into exile you would not know what to do with yourself, stand in your way; for there are many places for you to go to, where you will be welcomed. If you choose to go to Thessaly, I have friends there who will make much of you, and shelter you from any annoyance from the people of Thessaly.

And besides, Socrates, I think that you will be doing what is wrong, if you abandon your life when you might preserve it. You are simply playing the game of your enemies; it is exactly the game of those who wanted to destroy you. And what is more, to me you seem to be abandoning your children too: you will leave them to take their chance in life, as far as you are concerned, when you might bring them up and educate them. Most likely their fate will be the usual fate of children who are left orphans. But you ought not to beget children unless you mean to take the trouble of bringing them up and educating them. It seems to me that you are choosing the easy way, and not the way of a good and brave man, as you ought, when you have been talking all your life long of the value that you set upon virtue. For my part, I feel ashamed both for you, and for us who are your friends. Men will think that the whole of this thing which has happened to you—your appearance in court to take your trial, when you need not have appeared at all; the very way in which the trial was conducted; and then lastly this, for the crowning absurdity of the whole affair, is due to our cowardice. It will look as if we had shirked the danger out of miserable cowardice; for we did not save you, and you did not save yourself, when it was quite possible to do so, if we had been good for anything at all. Take care, Socrates, lest these things be not evil only, but also dishonourable to you and to us. Consider then; or rather the time for consideration is past; we must resolve; and there is only one plan possible. Everything must be done to-night. If we delay any longer, we are lost. O Socrates, I implore you not to refuse to listen to me.

SOCRATES: My dear Crito, if your anxiety to save me be right, it is most valuable: but if it be not right, its greatness makes it all the more dangerous. We must consider then whether we are to do as you say, or not; for I am still what I always have been, a man who will listen to no voice but the voice of the reasoning which on consideration I find to be truest. I cannot cast aside my former arguments because this misfortune has come to me. They seem to me to be as true as ever they were, and I hold exactly the same ones in honour and esteem as I used to: and if we have no better reasoning to substitute for them, I certainly shall not agree to your proposal, not even though the power of the multitude should scare us with fresh terrors, as children are scared with hobgoblins, and inflict upon us new fines, and imprisonments, and deaths. How then shall we most fitly examine the question? Shall we go back first to what you say about the opinions of men, and ask if we used to be right in thinking that we ought to pay attention to some opinions, and not to others? Used we to be right in saying so before I was condemned to die, and has it now become apparent that we were talking at random, and arguing for the sake of argument, and that it was really nothing but play and nonsense? I am anxious, Crito, to examine our former reasoning with your help, and to see whether my present position will appear to me to have affected its truth in any way, or not; and whether we are to set it aside, or to yield assent to it. Those of us who thought at all seriously, used always to say, I think, exactly what I said just now, namely, that we ought to esteem some of the opinions which men form highly, and not others. Tell me, Crito, if you please, do you not think that they were right? For you, humanly speaking, will not have to die tomorrow, and your judgment will not be biased by that circumstance. Consider then: do you not think it reasonable to say that we should not esteem all the opinions of men, but only some, nor the opinions of all

men, but only of some men? What do you think? Is not this true?

CRITO: It is.

SOCRATES: And we should esteem the good opinions, and not the worthless ones?

CRITO: Yes.

SOCRATES: But the good opinions are those of the wise, and the worthless ones those of the foolish?

CRITO: Of course.

SOCRATES: And what used we to say about this? Does a man who is in training, and who is in earnest about it, attend to the praise and blame and opinion of all men, or of the one man only who is a doctor or a trainer?

CRITO: He attends only to the opinion of the one man.

SOCRATES: Then he ought to fear the blame and welcome the praise of this one man, not of the many?

CRITO: Clearly.

SOCRATES: Then he must act and exercise, and eat and drink in whatever way the one man who is his master, and who understands the matter, bids him; not as others bid him?

CRITO: That is so.

SOCRATES: Good. But if he disobeys this one man, and disregards his opinion and his praise, and esteems instead what the many, who understand nothing of the matter, say, will he not suffer for it?

CRITO: Of course he will.

SOCRATES: And how will he suffer? In what direction, and in what part of himself?

CRITO: Of course in his body. That is disabled.

SOCRATES: You are right. And, Crito, to be brief, is it not the same, in everything? And, therefore, in questions of right and wrong, and of the base and the honourable, and of good and evil, which we are now considering, ought we to follow the opinion of the many and fear that, or the opinion of the one man who understands these matters (if we can find him), and feel more shame and fear before him than before all other men? For if we do not follow him, we shall cripple and maim that part of us which, we used to say, is improved by right and disabled by wrong. Or is this not so?

CRITO: No, Socrates, I agree with you.

SOCRATES: Now, if, by listening to the opinions of those who do not understand, we disable that part of us which is improved by health and crippled by disease, is our life worth living, when it is crippled? It is the body, is it not?

CRITO: Yes.

SOCRATES: Is life worth living with the body crippled and in a bad state?

CRITO: No, certainly not.

SOCRATES: Then is life worth living when that part of us which is maimed by wrong and benefited by right is crippled? Or do we consider that part of us, whatever it is, which has to do with right and wrong to be of less consequence than our body?

CRITO: No, certainly not.

SOCRATES: But more valuable?

CRITO: Yes, much more so.

SOCRATES: Then, my excellent friend, we must not think so much of what the many will say of us; we must think of what the one man, who understands right and wrong, and of what Truth herself will say of us. And so you are mistaken to begin with, when you invite us to regard the opinion of the multitude concerning the right and the honourable and the good, and their opposites. But, it may be said, the multitude can put us to death?

CRITO: Yes, that is evident. That may be said, Socrates.

SOCRATES: True. But, my excellent friend, to me it appears that the conclusion which we have just reached, is the same as our conclusion of former times. Now consider whether we still hold to the belief, that we should set the highest value, not on living, but on living well?

CRITO: Yes, we do.

SOCRATES: And living well and honourably and rightly mean the same thing: do we hold to that or not?

CRITO: We do.

SOCRATES: Then, starting from these premises, we have to consider whether it is right or not right for me to try to escape from prison, without the consent of the Athenians. If we find that it is right, we will try: if not, we will let it alone. I am afraid that considerations of expense, and of reputation, and of bringing up my children, of which you talk, Crito, are only the reflections of our friends, the many, who lightly put men to death, and who would, if they could, as lightly bring them to life again, without a thought. But reason, which is our guide, shows us that we can have nothing to consider but the question which I asked just now: namely, shall we be doing right if we give money and thanks to the men who are to aid me in escaping, and if we ourselves take our respective parts in my escape? Or shall we in truth be doing wrong, if we do all this? And if we find that we should be doing wrong, then we must not take any account either of death, or of any other evil that may be the consequence of remaining quietly here, but only of doing wrong.

CRITO: I think that you are right, Socrates. But what are we to do?

SOCRATES: Let us consider that together, my good sir, and if you can contradict anything that I say, do so, and I will be convinced: but if you cannot, do not go on repeating to me any longer, my dear friend, that I should escape without the consent of the Athenians. I am very anxious to act with your approval: I do not want you to think me mistaken. But now tell me if you agree with the doctrine from which I start, and try to answer my questions as you think best.

CRITO: I will try.

SOCRATES: Ought we never to do wrong intentionally at all; or may we do wrong in some ways, and not in others? Or, as we have often agreed in former times, is it never either good or honourable to do wrong? Have all our former conclusions been forgotten in these few days? Old men as we were, Crito, did we not see, in days gone by, when we were gravely conversing with each other, that we were no better than children? Or is not what we used to say most assuredly the truth, whether the world agrees with us or not? Is not wrong-doing an evil and a shame to the wrong-doer in every case, whether we incur a heavier or a lighter punishment than death as the consequence of doing right? Do we believe that?

CRITO: We do.

SOCRATES: Then we ought never to do wrong at all?

CRITO: Certainly not.

SOCRATES: Neither, if we ought never to do wrong at all, ought we to repay wrong with wrong, as the world thinks we may?

CRITO: Clearly not.

SOCRATES: Well then, Crito, ought we to do evil to any one?

CRITO: Certainly I think not, Socrates.

SOCRATES: And is it right to repay evil with evil, as the world thinks, or not right?

CRITO: Certainly it is not right.

SOCRATES: For there is no difference, is there, between doing evil to a man, and wronging him?

CRITO: True.

SOCRATES: Then we ought not to repay wrong with wrong or do harm to any man, no matter what we may have suffered from him. And in conceding this, Crito, be careful that you do not concede more than you mean. For I know that only a few men hold, or ever will hold this opinion. And so those who hold it, and those who do not, have no common ground of argument; they can of necessity only look with contempt on each other's belief. Do you therefore consider very carefully whether you agree with me and share my opinion. Are we to start in our inquiry from the doctrine that it is never right either to do wrong, or to repay wrong with wrong, or to avenge ourselves on any man who harms us, by harming him in return? Or do you disagree with me and dissent from my principle? I myself have believed in it for a long time, and I believe in it still. But if you differ in any way, explain to me how. If you still hold to our former opinion, listen to my next point.

CRITO: Yes, I hold to it, and I agree with you. Go on.

SOCRATES: Then, my next point, or rather my next question, is this: Ought a man to perform his just agreements, or may he shuffle out of them?

CRITO: He ought to perform them.

SOCRATES: Then consider. If I escape without the State's consent, shall I be injuring those whom I ought least to injure, or not? Shall I be abiding by my just agreements or not?

CRITO: I cannot answer your question, Socrates. I do not understand it.

SOCRATES: Consider it in this way. Suppose the laws and the commonwealth were to come and appear to me as I was preparing to run away (if that is the right phrase to describe my escape) and were to ask, "Tell us, Socrates, what have you in your mind to do? What do you mean by trying to escape, but to destroy us, the laws, and the whole city, so far as in you lies? Do you think that a state can exist and not be overthrown, in which the decisions of law are of no force, and are disregarded and set at nought by private individuals?" How shall we answer questions like that, Crito? Much might be said, especially by an orator, in defence of the law which makes judicial decisions supreme. Shall I reply, "But the state has injured me: it has decided my cause wrongly." Shall we say that?

CRITO: Certainly we will, Socrates.

SOCRATES: And suppose the laws were to reply, "Was that our agreement? or was it that you would submit to whatever judgments the state should pronounce?" And if we were to wonder at their words, perhaps they would say, "Socrates, wonder not at our words, but answer us; you yourself are accustomed to ask questions and to answer them. What complaint have you against us and the city, that you are trying to destroy us? Are we not, first, your parents? Through us your father took your mother and begat you. Tell us, have you any fault to find with those of us that are the laws of marriage?" "I have none," I should reply. "Or have you any fault to find with those of us that regulate the nurture and education of the child, which you, like others, received? Did not we do well in bidding your father educate you in music and gymnastic?" "You did," I should say. "Well then, since you were brought into the world and nurtured and educated by us, how, in the first place, can you deny that you are our child and our slave, as your fathers were before you? And if this be so, do you think that your rights are on a level with ours? Do you think that you have a right to retaliate upon us if we should try to do anything to you? You had not the same rights that your father had, or that your master would have had, if you had been a slave. You had no right to retaliate upon them if they ill-treated you, or to answer them if they reviled you, or to strike them back if they struck you, or to repay them evil with evil in any way. And do you think that you may retaliate on your country and its laws? If we try to destroy you, because we think it right, will you in return do all that you can to destroy us, the laws, and your country, and say that in so doing you are doing right, you, the man, who in truth thinks so much of virtue? Or are you too wise to see that your country is worthier, and more august, and more sacred, and holier and held in higher honour both by the gods and by all men of understanding, than your father and your mother and all your other ancestors; and that it is your bounden duty to reverence it, and to submit to it, and to approach it more humbly than you would approach your father, when it is angry with you; and either to do whatever it bids you to do or to persuade it to excuse you; and to obey in silence if it orders you to endure stripes or imprisonment, or if it send you to battle to be wounded or to die? That is what is your duty. You must not give way, nor retreat, nor desert your post. In war, and in the court of justice, and everywhere, you must do whatever your city and your country bid you do, or you must convince them that their commands are unjust. But it is against the law of God to use violence to your father or to your mother; and much more so is it against the law of God to use violence to your country." What answer shall we make, Crito? Shall we say that the laws speak truly, or not?

CRITO: I think that they do.

SOCRATES: "Then consider, Socrates," perhaps they would say, "if we are right in saying that by attempting to escape you are attempting to injure us. We brought you into the world, we nurtured you, we educated you, we gave you and every other citizen a share of all the good things we could. Yet we proclaim that if any man of the Athenians is dissatisfied with us, he may take his goods and go away whithersoever he pleases: we give that permission to every man who chooses to avail himself of it, so soon as he has reached man's estate, and sees us, the laws, and the administration of our city. No one of us stands in his way or forbids him to take his goods and go wherever he likes, whether it be to an Athenian colony, or to any foreign country, if he is dissatisfied with us and with the city. But we say that every man of you who remains here, seeing how we administer justice, and how we govern the city in other matters, has agreed, by the very fact of remaining here, to do whatsoever we bid him. And, we say, he who disobeys us, does a threefold wrong: he disobeys us who are his parents, and he disobeys us who fostered him, and he disobeys us after he has agreed to obey us, without persuading us that we are wrong. Yet we did not bid him sternly to do whatever we told him. We offered him an alternative; we gave him his choice, either to obey us, or to convince us that we were wrong: but he does neither.

"These are the charges, Socrates, to which we say that you will expose yourself, if you do what you intend; and that not less, but more than other Athenians." And if I were to ask, "And why?" they might retort with justice that I have bound myself by the agreement with them more than other Athenians. They would say, "Socrates, we have very strong evidence that you were satisfied with us and with the city. You would not have been content to stay at home in it more than other Athenians, unless you had been satisfied with it more than they. You never went away from Athens to the festivals, save once to the Isthmian games, nor elsewhere except on military service; you never made other journeys like other men; you had no desire to see other cities or other laws; you were contented with us and our city. So strongly did you prefer us, and agree to be governed by us: and what is more, you begat children in this city, you found it so pleasant. And besides, if you had wished, you might at your trial have offered to go into exile. At that time you could have done with the State's consent, what you are trying now to do without it. But then you gloried in being willing to die. You said that you preferred death to exile. And now you are not ashamed of those words; you do not respect us the laws, for you are trying to destroy us: and you are acting just as a miserable slave would act, trying to run away, and breaking the covenant and agreement which you made to submit to our government. First, therefore, answer this question. Are we right, or are we wrong, in saying that you have agreed not in mere words, but in reality to live under our government?" What are we to say, Crito? Must we not admit that it is true?

CRITO: We must, Socrates.

SOCRATES: Then they would say, "Are you not breaking your covenants and agreements with us? And you were not led to make them by force or by fraud: you had not to make up your mind in a hurry. You had seventy years in which you might have gone away, if you had been disatisfied with us, or if the agreement had seemed to you unjust. But you preferred neither Lacedaemon nor Crete, though you are fond of saying that they are well governed, nor any other state, either of the Hellenes, or the Bar-

barians. You went away from Athens less than the lame and the blind and the cripple. Clearly you, far more than other Athenians, were satisfied with the city, and also with us who are its laws: for who would be satisfied with a city which had no laws? And now will not you abide by your agreement? If you take our advice, you will, Socrates: then you will not make yourself ridiculous by going away from Athens.

"For consider: what good will you do yourself or your friends by thus transgressing, and breaking your agreement? It is tolerably certain that they, on their part, will at least run the risk of exile, and of losing their civil rights, or of forfeiting their property. For yourself, you might go to one of the neighbouring cities, to Thebes or to Megara for instance—for both of them are well governed—but, Socrates, you will come as an enemy to these commonwealths; and all who care for their city will look askance at you, and think that you are a subverter of law. And you will confirm the judges in their opinion, and make it seem that their verdict was a just one. For a man who is a subverter of law, may well be supposed to be a corrupter of the young and thoughtless. Then will you avoid well-governed states and civilised men? Will life be worth having, if you do? Or will you consort with such men, and converse without shame—about what, Socrates? About the things which you talk of here? Will you tell them that virtue, and justice, and institutions, and law are the most precious things that men can have? And do you not think that that will be a shameful thing in Socrates? You ought to think so.

But you will leave these places; you will go to the friends of Crito in Thessaly: for there there is most disorder and license: and very likely, they will be delighted to hear of the ludicrous way in which you escaped from prison, dressed up in peasant's clothes, or in some other disguise which people put on when they are running away, and with your appearance altered. But will no one say how you, an old man, with probably only a few more years to live, clung so greedily to life that you dared to transgress the highest laws? Perhaps not, if you do not displease them. But if you do, Socrates, you will hear much that will make you blush. You will pass your life as the flatterer and the slave of all men; and what will you be doing but feasting in Thessaly? It will be as if you had made a journey to Thessaly for an entertainment. And where will be all our old sayings about justice and virtue then? But you wish to live for the sake of your children? You want to bring them up and educate them? What? Will you take them with you to Thessaly, and bring them up and educate them there? Will you make them strangers to their own country, that you may bestow this benefit on them too? Or supposing that you leave them in Athens, will they be brought up and educated better if you are alive, though you are not with them? Yes; your friends will take care of them. Will your friends take care of them if you make a journey to Thessaly, and not if you make a journey to Hades? You ought not to think that, at least if those who call themselves your friends are good for anything at all.

"No, Socrates, be advised by us who have fostered you. Think neither of children, nor of life, nor of any other thing before justice, that when you come to the other world you may be able to make your defence before the rulers who sit in judgment there. It is clear that neither you nor any of your friends will be happier, or juster, or holier in this life, if you do this thing, nor will you be happier after you are dead. Now you will go away wronged, not by us, the laws, but by men. But if you repay evil with evil, and wrong with wrong in this shameful way, and break your agreements and covenants with us, and injure those whom you should least injure, yourself, and your friends, and your country, and us, and so escape, then we shall be angry with you while you live, and when you die our brethren, the laws in Hades, will not receive you kindly; for they will know that on earth you did all that you could to destroy us. Listen then to us, and let not Crito persuade you to do as he says."

Know well, my dear friend Crito, that this is what I seem to hear, as the worshippers of Cybele seem, in their frenzy, to hear the music of flutes: and the sound of these words rings loudly in my ears, and drowns all other words. And I feel sure that if you try to change my mind you will speak in vain; nevertheless, if you think that you will succeed, say on.

CRITO: I can say no more, Socrates.

SOCRATES: Then let it be, Crito: and let us do as I say, seeing that God so directs us.

Phaedo

SCENE: The Prison of Socrates

• • •

When he had finished speaking Crito said, "Be it so, Socrates. But have you any commands for your friends or for me about your children, or about other things? How shall we serve you best?"

"Simply by doing what I always tell you, Crito. Take care of your own selves, and you will serve me and mine and yourselves in all that you do, even though you make no promises now. But if you are careless of your own selves, and will not follow the path of life which we have pointed out in our discussions both today and at other times, all your promises now, however profuse and earnest they are, will be of no avail."

"We will do our best," said Crito. "But how shall we bury you?"

"As you please," he answered; "only you must catch me first, and not let me escape you." And then he looked at us with a smile and said, "My friends, I cannot convince Crito that I am the Socrates who has been conversing with you, and arranging his arguments in order. He thinks that I am the body which he will presently see a corpse, and he asks how he is to bury me. All the arguments which I have used to prove that I shall not remain with you after I have drunk the poison, but that I shall go away to the happiness of the blessed, with which I tried to comfort you and myself, have been thrown away on him. Do you therefore be my sureties to him, as he was my surety at the trial, but in a different way. He was surety for me then that I would remain; but you must be my sureties to him that I shall go away when I am dead, and not remain with you: then he will feel my death less; and when he sees my body being burnt or buried, he will not be grieved because he thinks that I am suffering dreadful things: and at my funeral he will not say that it is Socrates whom he is laying out, or bearing to the grave, or burying." "For, dear Crito," he continued, "you must know that to use words wrongly is not only a fault in itself; it also creates evil in the soul. You must be of good cheer, and say that you are burying my body: and you must bury it as you please, and as you think right."

With these words he rose and went into another room to bathe himself: Crito went with him and told us to wait. So we waited, talking of the argument, and discussing it, and then again dwelling on the greatness of the calamity which had fallen upon us: it seemed as if we were going to lose a father, and to be orphans for the rest of our life. When he had bathed, and his children had been brought to him,—he had two sons quite little, and one grown up,—and the women of his family were come, he spoke with them in Crito's presence, and gave them his last commands; then he

Trans. F. J. Church.

sent the women and children away, and returned to us. By that time it was near the hour of sunset, for he had been a long while within. When he came back to us from the bath he sat down, but not much was said after that. Presently the servant of the Eleven came and stood before him and said, "I know that I shall not find you unreasonable like other men, Socrates. They are angry with me and curse me when I bid them drink the poison because the authorities make me do it. But I have found you all along the noblest and gentlest and best man that has ever come here; and now I am sure that you will not be angry with me, but with those who you know are to blame. And so farewell, and try to bear what must be as lightly as you can; you know why I have come." With that he turned away weeping, and went out.

Socrates looked up at him, and replied, "Farewell: I will do as you say." Then he turned to us and said, "How courteous the man is! And the whole time that I have been here, he has constantly come in to see me, and sometimes he has talked to me, and has been the best of men; and now, how generously he weeps for me! Come, Crito, let us obey him: let the poison be brought if it is ready; and if it is not ready, let it be prepared."

Crito replied, "Nay, Socrates, I think that the sun is still upon the hills; it has not set. Besides, I know that other men take the poison quite late, and eat and drink heartily, and even enjoy the company of their chosen friends, after the announcement has been made. So do not hurry; there is still time."

Socrates replied, "And those whom you speak of, Crito, naturally do so; for they think that they will be gainers by so doing. And I naturally shall not do so; for I think that I should gain nothing by drinking the poison a little later, but my own contempt for so greedily saving up a life which is already spent. So do not refuse to do as I say."

Then Crito made a sign to his slave who was standing by; and the slave went out, and after some delay returned with the man who was to give the poison, carrying it prepared in a cup. When Socrates saw him, he asked, "You understand these things, my good sir, what have I to do?"

"You have only to drink this," he replied, "and to walk about until your legs feel heavy, and then lie down; and it will act of itself." With that he handed the cup to Socrates, who took it quite cheerfully, without trembling, and without any change of colour or of feature, and looked up at the man with that fixed glance of his, and asked, "What say you to making a libation from this draught? May I, or not?" "We only prepare so much as we think sufficient, Socrates," he answered. "I understand," said Socrates. "But I suppose that I may, and must, pray to the gods that my journey hence may be prosperous: that is my prayer; be it so." With these words he put the cup to his lips and drank the poison quite calmly and cheerfully. Till then most of us had been able to control our grief fairly well; but when we saw him drinking, and then the poison finished, we could do so no longer: my tears came fast in spite of myself, and I covered my face and wept for myself: it was not for him, but at my own misfortune at losing such a friend. Even before that Crito had been unable to restrain his tears, and had gone away; and Apollodorus, who had never once ceased weeping the whole time, burst into a loud cry, and made us one and all break down by his sobbing and grief, except only Socrates himself. "What are you doing, my friends?" he exclaimed. "I sent away the women chiefly in order that they might not offend in this way; for I have heard that a man should die in silence. So calm yourselves and bear up." When we heard that we were ashamed, and we ceased from weeping. But he walked about, until he said that his legs were getting heavy, and then he lay down on his back, as he was told. And the man who gave the poison began to examine his feet and legs, from time to time: then he pressed his foot hard, and asked if there was any feeling in it; and Socrates said, "No": and then his legs, and so higher and higher, and showed us that he was cold and stiff. And Socrates felt himself, and said that when it came to his heart, he should be gone. He was already growing cold about the groin, when he uncovered his face, which had been covered, and spoke for the last time. "Crito," he said, "I owe a cock to Asclepius: do not forget to repay it." "It shall be done," replied Crito. "Is there anything else that you wish?" He made no answer to this question; but after a short interval there was a movement, and the man uncovered him, and his eyes were fixed. Then Crito closed his mouth and his eyes.

Such was the end of our friend, a man, I think, who was the wisest and justest, and the best man that I have ever known.

Plato

Among the host of handsome and brilliant young men who dogged the footsteps of Socrates about Athens, one youth stood out from the rest, both physically and intellectually. His real name was Aristocles, but he soon acquired the nickname Plato ("the broad-shouldered one"). The son of a wealthy and noble family—on his mother's side he was descended from the great law-giver, Solon—Plato (427–347 B.C.) was preparing for a career in politics when the trial and execution of Socrates changed the course of his life. He abandoned his political career and turned to philosophy, opening a school on the outskirts of Athens dedicated to the Socratic search for wisdom. Plato's school, known as the Academy, was the first university in the history of the West. It continued in operation for over nine hundred years, from 387 B.C. until it was closed by an edict of the Roman Emperor Justinian in A.D. 529.

Unlike Socrates, Plato was a writer as well as a teacher. His writings are in the form of dialogues, with Socrates as the principal speaker. In the selection that follows, the "Allegory of the Cave" (perhaps the most famous passage in all his works), Plato describes symbolically the predicament in which man finds himself and proposes a way of salvation. In addition, the Allegory presents, in brief form, most of Plato's major philosophical theories: his belief that the world revealed by our senses is not the real world but only a poor copy of it, and that the real world can be apprehended only intellectually; his idea that knowledge cannot be transferred from teacher to student, but rather that education consists in directing the student's mind toward what is real and important and allowing him to apprehend it for himself; his faith that the universe ultimately is good; his conviction that enlightened men have an obligation to the rest of society, and that a good society must be one in which truly wise men are the rulers. Woven into these themes is a defense of the life of Socrates and a condemnation of Athenian society for having executed him.

The Allegory is from Book VII of Plato's best-known work, *The Republic*, which represents a conversation between Socrates and some friends on the nature of justice, and which includes Plato's plan for an ideal state ruled by philosophers.

The Republic

[THE ALLEGORY OF THE CAVE]

Next, said I [Socrates], here is a parable to illustrate the degrees in which our nature may be enlightened or unenlightened. Imagine the condition of men living in a sort of cavernous chamber underground, with an entrance open to the light and a long passage all down the cave. Here they have been from childhood, chained by the leg and also by the neck, so that they cannot move and can see only what is in front of them, because the chains will not let them turn their heads. At some distance higher up is the light of a fire burning behind them; and between the prisoners and the fire is a track with a parapet built along it, like the screen at a puppet-show, which hides the performers while they show their puppets over the top.

I see, said he.

Now behind this parapet imagine persons carrying along various artificial objects, including figures of men and animals in wood or stone or other materials, which project above the parapet. Naturally, some of these persons will be talking, others silent.[1]

It is a strange picture, he said, and a strange sort of prisoners.

Like ourselves, I replied; for in the first place prisoners so confined would have seen nothing of themselves or of one another, except the shadows thrown by the fire-light on the wall of the Cave facing them, would they?

Not if all their lives they had been prevented from moving their heads.

And they would have seen as little of the objects carried past.

Of course.

Now, if they could talk to one another, would they not suppose that their words referred only to those passing shadows which they saw?

Necessarily.

And suppose their prison had an echo from the wall facing them? When one of the people crossing behind them spoke, they could only suppose that the sound came from the shadow passing before their eyes.

No doubt.

[1] [A modern Plato would compare his Cave to an underground cinema, where the audience watch the play of shadows thrown by the film passing before a light at their backs. The film itself is only an image of "real" things and events in the world outside the cinema. For the film Plato has to substitute the clumsier apparatus of a procession of artificial objects carried on their heads by persons who are merely part of the machinery, providing for the movement of the objects and the sounds whose echo the prisoners hear. The parapet prevents these persons' shadows from being cast on the wall of the Cave.—Trans.]

The Republic of Plato, trans. F. H. Cornford (Oxford: The Clarendon Press, 1941), pp. 227–235. Reprinted by permission of Oxford University Press.

In every way, then, such prisoners would recognize as reality nothing but the shadows of those artificial objects.

Inevitably.

Now consider what would happen if their release from the chains and the healing of their unwisdom should come about in this way. Suppose one of them set free and forced suddenly to stand up, turn his head, and walk with eyes lifted to the light; all these movements would be painful, and he would be too dazzled to make out the objects whose shadows he had been used to see. What do you think he would say, if someone told him that what he had formerly seen was meaningless illusion, but now, being somewhat nearer to reality and turned towards more real objects, he was getting a truer view? Suppose further that he were shown the various objects being carried by and were made to say, in reply to questions, what each of them was. Would he not be perplexed and believe the objects now shown him to be not so real as what he formerly saw?

Yes, not nearly so real.

And if he were forced to look at the firelight itself, would not his eyes ache, so that he would try to escape and turn back to the things which he could see distinctly, convinced that they really were clearer than these other objects now being shown to him?

Yes.

And suppose someone were to drag him away forcibly up the steep and rugged ascent and not let him go until he had hauled him out into the sunlight, would he not suffer pain and vexation at such treatment, and, when he had come out into the light, find his eyes so full of its radiance that he could not see a single one of the things that he was now told were real?

Certainly he would not see them all at once.

He would need, then, to grow accustomed before he could see things in that upper world. At first it would be easiest to make out shadows, and then the images of men and things reflected in water, and later on the things themselves. After that, it would be easier to watch the heavenly bodies and the sky itself by night, looking at the light of the moon and stars rather than the Sun and the Sun's light in the daytime.

Yes, surely.

Last of all, he would be able to look at the Sun and contemplate its nature, not as it appears when reflected in water or any alien medium, but as it is in itself in its own domain.

No doubt.

And now he would begin to draw the conclusion that it is the Sun that produces the seasons and the course of the year and controls everything in the visible world, and moreover is in a way the cause of all that he and his companions used to see.

Clearly he would come at last to that conclusion.

Then if he called to mind his fellow prisoners and what passed for wisdom in his former dwelling-place, he would surely think himself happy in the change and be sorry for them. They may have had a practice of honouring and commending one another, with prizes for the man who had the keenest eye for the passing shadows and the best memory for the order in which they followed or accompanied one another, so that he could make a good guess as to which was going to come next. Would our released prisoner be likely to covet those prizes or to envy the men exalted to honour and power in the Cave? Would he not feel like Homer's Achilles, that he would far sooner "be on earth as a hired servant in the house of a landless man" or endure anything rather than go back to his old beliefs and live in the old way?

Yes, he would prefer any fate to such a life.

Now imagine what would happen if he went down again to take his former seat in the Cave. Coming suddenly out of the sunlight, his eyes would be filled with darkness. He might be required once more to deliver his opinion on those shadows, in competition with the prisoners who had never been released, while his eyesight was still dim and unsteady; and it might take some time to become used to the darkness. They would laugh at him and say that he had gone up only to come back with his sight ruined; it was worth no one's while even to attempt the ascent. If they could lay hands on the man who was trying to set them free and lead them up, they would kill him.[2]

Yes, they would.

Every feature in this parable, my dear Glaucon, is meant to fit our earlier analysis. The prison dwelling corresponds to the region revealed to us through the sense of sight, and the fire-light within it to the power of the Sun. The ascent to see the things in the upper world you may take as standing for the upward journey of the soul into the region of the intelligible; then you will be

in possession of what I surmise, since that is what you wish to be told. Heaven knows whether it is true; but this, at any rate, is how it appears to me. In the world of knowledge, the last thing to be perceived and only with great difficulty is the essential Form of Goodness. Once it is perceived, the conclusion must follow that, for all things, this is the cause of whatever is right and good; in the visible world it gives birth to light and to the lord of light, while it is itself sovereign in the intelligible world and the parent of intelligence and truth. Without having had a vision of this Form no one can act with wisdom, either in his own life or in matters of state.

So far as I can understand, I share your belief.

Then you may also agree that it is no wonder if those who have reached this height are reluctant to manage the affairs of men. Their souls long to spend all their time in that upper world—naturally enough, if here once more our parable holds true. Nor, again, is it at all strange that one who comes from the contemplation of divine things to the miseries of human life should appear awkward and ridiculous when, with eyes still dazed and not yet accustomed to the darkness, he is compelled, in a lawcourt or elsewhere, to dispute about the shadows of justice or the images that cast those shadows, and to wrangle over the notions of what is right in the minds of men who have never beheld Justice itself.

It is not at all strange.

No; a sensible man will remember that the eyes may be confused in two ways—by a change from light to darkness or from darkness to light; and he will recognize that the

[2] [An allusion to the fate of Socrates.—*Trans.*]

same thing happens to the soul. When he sees it troubled and unable to discern anything clearly, instead of laughing thoughtlessly, he will ask whether, coming from a brighter existence, its unaccustomed vision is obscured by the darkness, in which case he will think its condition enviable and its life a happy one; or whether, emerging from the depths of ignorance, it is dazzled by excess of light. If so, he will rather feel sorry for it; or, if he were inclined to laugh, that would be less ridiculous than to laugh at the soul which has come down from the light.

That is a fair statement.

If this is true, then, we must conclude that education is not what it is said to be by some, who profess to put knowledge into a soul which does not possess it, as if they could put sight into blind eyes. On the contrary, our own account signifies that the soul of every man does possess the power of learning the truth and the organ to see with; and that, just as one might have to turn the whole body round in order that the eye should see light instead of darkness, so that entire soul must be turned away from this changing world, until its eye can bear to contemplate reality and that supreme splendour which we have called the Good. Hence there may well be an art whose aim would be to effect this very thing, the conversion of the soul, in the readiest way; not to put the power of sight into the soul's eye, which already has it, but to ensure that, instead of looking in the wrong direction, it is turned the way it ought to be.

Yes, it may well be so.

It looks, then, as though wisdom were different from those ordinary virtues, as they are called, which are not far removed from bodily qualities, in that they can be produced by habituation and exercise in a soul which has not possessed them from the first. Wisdom, it seems, is certainly the virtue of some diviner faculty, which never loses its power, though its use for good or harm depends on the direction towards which it is turned. You must have noticed in dishonest men with a reputation for sagacity the shrewd glance of a narrow intelligence piercing the objects to which it is directed. There is nothing wrong with their power of vision, but it has been forced into the service of evil, so that the keener its sight, the more harm it works.

Quite true.

And yet if the growth of a nature like this had been pruned from earliest childhood, cleared of those clinging overgrowths which come of gluttony and all luxurious pleasure and, like leaden weights charged with affinity to this mortal world, hang upon the soul, bending its vision downwards; if, freed from these, the soul were turned round towards true reality, then this same power in these very men would see the truth as keenly as the objects it is turned to now.

Yes, very likely.

Is it not also likely, or indeed certain after what has been said, that a state can never be properly governed either by the uneducated who know nothing of truth or by men who are allowed to spend all their days in the pursuit of culture? The ignorant have no single mark before their eyes at which they must aim in all the conduct of their own lives and of affairs of state; and the others will not engage in action if they can help it, dreaming that, while still alive, they have been translated to the Islands of the Blest.

Quite true.

It is for us, then, as founders of a commonwealth, to bring compulsion to bear on the noblest natures. They must be made to climb the ascent to the vision of Goodness, which we called the highest object of knowledge; and, when they have looked upon it long enough, they must not be allowed, as they now are, to remain on the heights, refusing to come down again to the prisoners or to take any part in their labours and rewards, however much or little these may be worth.

Shall we not be doing them an injustice, if we force on them a worse life than they might have?

You have forgotten again, my friend, that the law is not concerned to make any one class specially happy, but to ensure the welfare of the commonwealth as a whole. By persuasion or constraint it will unite the citizens in harmony, making them share whatever benefits each class can contribute to the common good; and its purpose in forming men of that spirit was not that each should be left to go his own way, but that they should be instrumental in binding the community into one.

True, I had forgotten.

You will see, then, Glaucon, that there will be no real injustice in compelling our philosophers to watch over and care for the other citizens. We can fairly tell them that their compeers in other states may quite reasonably refuse to collaborate: there they have sprung up, like a self-sown plant, in despite of their country's institutions; no one has fostered their growth, and they cannot be expected to show gratitude for a care they have never

received. "But," we shall say, "it is not so with you. We have brought you into existence for your country's sake as well as for your own, to be like leaders and kingbees in a hive; you have been better and more thoroughly educated than those others and hence you are more capable of playing your part both as men of thought and as men of action. You must go down, then, each in his turn, to live with the rest and let your eyes grow accustomed to the darkness. You will then see a thousand times better than those who live there always; you will recognize every image for what it is and know what it represents, because you have seen justice, beauty, and goodness in their reality; and so you and we shall find life in our commonwealth no mere dream, as it is in most existing states, where men live fighting one another about shadows and quarrelling for power, as if that were a great prize; whereas in truth government can be at its best and free from dissension only where the destined rulers are least desirous of holding office."

Quite true.

Then will our pupils refuse to listen and to take their turns at sharing in the work of the community, though they may live together for most of their time in a purer air?

No; it is a fair demand, and they are fair-minded men. No doubt, unlike any ruler of the present day, they will think of holding power as an unavoidable necessity.

Yes, my friend; for the truth is that you can have a well-governed society only if you can discover for your future rulers a better way of life than being in office; then only will power be in the hands of men who are rich, not in gold, but in wealth that brings happiness, a good and wise life. All goes wrong when, starved for lack of anything good in their own lives, men turn to public affairs hoping to snatch from thence the happiness they hunger for. They set about fighting for power, and this internecine conflict ruins them and their country. The life of true philosophy is the only one that looks down upon offices of state; and access to power must be confined to men who are not in love with it; otherwise rivals will start fighting. So whom else can you compel to undertake the guardianship of the commonwealth, if not those who, besides understanding best the principles of government, enjoy a nobler life than the politician's and look for rewards of a different kind?

There is indeed no other choice.

Aristotle

Aristotle (384–322 B.C.) was a native of Macedonia. At the age of eighteen he journeyed to Athens and enrolled as a student in the Academy (see page 129), where he remained for twenty years until the death of Plato. He then moved to Asia Minor to become political advisor to the ruler of a small kingdom. While there he married the king's niece. It is said that he spent his honeymoon gathering seashells for use in scientific studies. From Asia Minor he was called back to his native Macedonia to serve as tutor to Alexander (later "the Great"), who was then a boy of twelve. When Alexander set out to conquer the world, Aristotle returned to Athens and established a school of his own, the Lyceum, as a rival to the Academy. For the next eleven years he divided his time among teaching, public lecturing, and writing. His philosophical system is known as the *peripatetic* (or "walking") philosophy, a title derived from his habit of pacing back and forth as he lectured. At the death of Alexander in 323 B.C., Aristotle, because of his former association with the conqueror, found himself unpopular in Athens. Fearing the anger of the mob and remembering the fate of Socrates, he fled the city, not wishing, as he put it, "to give the Athenians a second chance of sinning against philosophy." He died in exile the following year.

Aristotle was a remarkably productive writer. His extant works include major treatises on physics, astronomy, zoology, biology, botany, psychology, logic, ethics, metaphysics, political theory, constitutional history, rhetoric, and the theory of art. His influence on the intellectual history of the West has been at least equal to that of Plato. Wherever his works have been studied, there has been intellectual ferment, activity, and development. Partly as a result of Aristotle's influence, the Moslems of the Near East enjoyed an intellectual golden age while Europe was still deep in the Dark Ages. The rediscovery of Aristotle by Europeans, through their contact with the Moslems, contributed directly to the cultural awakening in Europe that culminated in the high Middle Ages of the thirteenth century. Since the rise of modern science, the philosophy of Aristotle has come under increasingly sharp attack; nevertheless many of his main concepts and theories remain alive and vigorous in our own century.

The following selection is from one

of Aristotle's major works, *The Politics*. His views, in *The Politics*, on the social nature of man, the purpose of government, and the most desirable kind of society, have formed the basis, along with Plato's *Republic*, for almost all subsequent political theory in the West.

The Politics

BOOK I

Observation shows us, first, that every polis (or state) is a species of association, and secondly, that all associations are instituted for the purpose of attaining some good—for all men do all their acts with a view to achieving something which is, in their view, a good. We may therefore hold on the basis of what we actually observe that all associations aim at some good; and we may also hold that the particular association which is the most sovereign of all, and includes all the rest, will pursue this aim most, and will thus be directed to the most sovereign of all goods. This most sovereign and inclusive association is the polis, as it is called, or the political association.

It is a mistake to believe that the "statesman" is the same as the monarch of a kingdom, or the manager of a household, or the master of a number of slaves. Those who hold this view consider that each of these persons differs from the others not with a difference of kind, but merely with a difference of degree, and according to the number, or the paucity, of the persons with whom he deals. On this view a man who is concerned with few persons is a master: one who is concerned with more is the manager of a household: one who is concerned with still more is a "statesman," or a monarch. This view abolishes any real differences between a large household and a small polis; and it also reduces the difference between the "statesman" and the monarch to the one fact that the latter has an uncontrolled and sole authority, while the former exercises his authority in conformity with the rules imposed by the art of statesmanship and as one who rules and is ruled in turn. But this is a view which cannot be accepted as correct. There is an *essential* difference between these persons, and between the associations with which they are concerned.

Our point will be made clear if we proceed to consider the matter according to our normal method of analysis. Just as, in all other fields, a compound should be analyzed until we reach its simple and uncompounded elements (or, in other

The Politics of Aristotle, trans. E. Barker (Oxford: The Clarendon Press, 1946), pp. 1–7, 110–25, 129–34, 180–83. Reprinted by permission of Oxford University Press.

words, the smallest atoms of the whole which it constitutes), so we must also consider analytically the elements of which a polis is composed. We shall then gain a better insight into the difference from one another of the persons and associations just mentioned; and we shall also be in a position to discover whether it is possible to attain a systematic view of the general issues involved.

If, accordingly, we begin at the beginning, and consider things in the process of their growth, we shall best be able, in this as in other fields, to attain scientific conclusions by the method we employ. First of all, there must necessarily be a union or pairing of those who cannot exist without one another. Male and female must unite for the reproduction of the species—not from deliberate intention, but from the natural impulse, which exists in animals generally as it also exists in plants, to leave behind them something of the same nature as themselves. Next, there must necessarily be a union of the naturally ruling element with the element which is naturally ruled, for the preservation of both. The element which is able, by virtue of its intelligence, to exercise forethought, is naturally a ruling and master element; the element which is able, by virtue of its bodily power, to do what the other element plans, is a ruled element, which is naturally in a state of slavery; and master and slave have accordingly as they thus complete one another a common interest. The female and the slave, we may pause to note, are naturally distinguished from one another. Nature makes nothing in a spirit of stint, as smiths do when they make the Delphic knife to serve

a number of purposes: she makes each separate thing for a separate end; and she does so because each instrument has the finest finish when it serves a single purpose and not a variety of purposes. Among the barbarians, however, contrary to the order of nature the female and the slave occupy the same position—the reason being that no naturally ruling element exists among them, and conjugal union thus comes to be a union of a female who is a slave with a male who is also a slave. This is why our poets have said,

Meet it is that barbarous peoples should be governed by the Greeks

—the assumption being that barbarian and slave are by nature one and the same.

The first result of these two elementary associations of male and female, and of master and slave is the household or family. Hesiod spoke truly in the verse,

First house, and wife, and ox to draw the plough,

for oxen serve the poor in lieu of household slaves. The first form of association naturally instituted for the satisfaction of daily recurrent needs is thus the family; and the members of the family are accordingly termed by Charondas "associates of the bread-chest," as they are also termed by Epimenides the Cretan "associates of the manger." The next form of association—which is also the *first* to be formed from more households than one, and for the satisfaction of something more than daily recurrent needs—is the village. The most natural form of the village appears to be that of a colony or offshoot from a family; and some have thus called the members of the village by the name of "sucklings of the same milk," or, again, of "sons and the sons of sons." This, it may be noted, is the reason why each Greek polis was originally ruled—as the peoples of the barbarian world still are—by kings. They were formed of persons who were already monarchically governed, *i.e.* they were formed from households and villages, and households are always monarchically governed by the eldest of the kin, just as villages, when they are offshoots from the household, are similarly governed in virtue of the kinship between their members. This primitive kinship is what Homer describes, in speaking of the Cyclopes:

Each of them ruleth
Over his children and wives,

a passage which shows that they lived in scattered groups, as indeed men generally did in ancient times. The fact that men generally were governed by kings in ancient times, and that some still continue to be governed in that way, is the reason that leads us all to assert that the gods are also governed by a king. We make the lives of the gods in the likeness of our own—as we also make their shapes.

When we come to the final and perfect association, formed from a number of villages, we have already reached the polis—an association which may be said to have reached the height of full self-sufficiency; or rather to speak more exactly we may say that while it *grows* for the sake of mere life and is so far, and at that stage, still short of full self-sufficiency, it *exists* when once it is fully grown for the sake of a good life and is therefore fully self-sufficient.

Because it is the completion of associations existing by nature, every polis exists by nature, having itself the same quality as the earlier associations from which it grew. It is the end or consummation to which those associations move, and the "nature" of things consists in their end or consummation; for what each thing is when its growth is completed we call the nature of that thing, whether it be a man or a horse or a family. Again, and this is a second reason for regarding the state as natural, the end, or final cause, is the best. Now self-sufficiency which is the object of the state to bring about is the end, and so the best; and on this it follows that the state brings about the best, and is therefore natural, since nature always aims at bringing about the best.

From these considerations it is evident that the polis belongs to the class of things that exist by nature, and that man is by nature an animal intended to live in a polis. He who is without a polis, by reason of his own nature and not of some accident, is either a poor sort of being, or a being higher than man: he is like the man of whom Homer wrote in denunciation:

"Clanless and lawless and heartless is he."

The man who is such by nature, *i.e.* unable to join in the society of a polis, at once plunges into a passion for war; he is in the position of a solitary advanced piece in a game of draughts.

The reason why man is a being meant for political association, in a higher degree than bees or other gregarious animals can ever associate, is evident. Nature, according to our theory, makes nothing in vain; and man alone of the animals is furnished with the faculty of language. The mere making of sounds serves to indicate pleasure and pain, and is thus a faculty that belongs to animals in general: their nature enables them to attain the point at which they have perceptions of pleasure and pain, and can signify those perceptions to one another. But language serves to declare what is advantageous and what is the reverse, and it therefore serves to declare what is just and what is unjust. It is the peculiarity of man, in comparison with the rest of the animal world, that he alone possesses a perception of good and evil, of the just and the unjust, and of other similar qualities; and it is association in a common perception of these things which makes a family and a polis.

We may now proceed to add that though the individual and the family are prior in the order of time the polis is prior in the order of nature to the family and the individual. The reason for this is that the whole is necessarily prior in nature to the part. If the whole body be destroyed, there will not be a foot or a hand, except in that ambiguous sense in which one uses the same word to indicate a different thing, as when one speaks of a "hand" made of stone; for a hand, when destroyed by the destruction of the whole body, will be no better than a stone "hand." All things derive their essential character from their function and their capacity; and it follows that if they are no longer fit to discharge their function, we ought not to say that they are still the same things, but only that, by an ambiguity, they still have the same names.

We thus see that the polis exists by nature and that it is prior to the individual. The proof of both propositions is the fact that the polis is a whole, and that individuals are simply its parts. Not being self-sufficient when they are isolated, all individuals are so many parts all equally depending on the whole which alone can bring about self-sufficiency. The man who is isolated—who is unable to share in the benefits of political association, or has no need to share because he is already self-sufficient—is no part of the polis, and must therefore be either a beast or a god. Man is thus intended by nature to be a part of a political whole, and there is therefore an immanent impulse in all men towards an association of this order. But the man who first *constructed* such an association was none the less the greatest of benefactors. Man, when perfected, is the best of animals; but if he be isolated from law and justice he is the worst of all. Injustice is all the graver when it is armed injustice; and man is furnished from birth with arms such as, for instance, language which are intended to serve the purposes of moral prudence and virtue, but which may be used in preference for opposite ends. That is why, if he be without virtue, he is a most unholy and savage being, and worse than all others in the indulgence of lust and gluttony. Justice which is his salvation belongs to the polis;

for justice, which is the determination of what is just, is an ordering of the political association.

•   •   •

BOOK III

•   •   •

We have next to consider the subject of constitutions. Is there a single type, or are there a number of types? If there are a number of types, what are these types; how many of them are there; and how do they differ? A constitution (or polity) may be defined as "the organization of a polis, in respect of its offices generally, but especially in respect of that particular office which is sovereign in all issues." The civic body is everywhere the sovereign of the state; in fact the civic body is the polity (or constitution) itself. In democratic states, for example, the people is sovereign: in oligarchies, on the other hand, the few have that position; and this difference of the sovereign bodies is the reason why we say that the two types of constitution differ—as we may equally apply the same reasoning to other types besides these.

It is thus evident that there are a number of types of constitution, but before we discuss their nature we must first ascertain two things—the nature of the end for which the state exists, and the various kinds of authority to which men and their associations are subject. So far as the first of these things is concerned, it has already been stated, in our first book (where we were concerned with the management of the household and the control of

slaves), that "man is an animal impelled by nature to live in a polis." A *natural impulse* is thus one reason why men desire to live a social life even when they stand in no need of mutual succour; but they are also drawn together by a *common interest*, in proportion as each attains a share in good life through the union of all in a form of political association. The good life is the chief end, both for the community as a whole and for each of us individually. But men also come together, and form and maintain political associations, merely for the sake of life, for perhaps there is some element of the good even in the simple act of living, so long as the evils of existence do not preponderate too heavily. It is an evident fact that most men cling hard enough to life to be willing to endure a good deal of suffering, which implies that life has in it a sort of healthy happiness and a natural quality of pleasure.

So far of the end for which the state exists. As regards the second question, it is easy enough to distinguish the various kinds of rule or authority of which men commonly speak; and indeed we have often had occasion to define them ourselves in works intended for the general public. The rule of a master is one kind; and here, though there is really a common interest which unites the natural master and the natural slave, the fact remains that the rule is primarily exercised with a view to the master's interest, and only incidentally with a view to that of the slave, who must be preserved in existence if the rule itself is to remain. Rule over wife and children, and over the household generally, is a second kind of rule, which we have called by the name of household management. Here the rule is either exercised in the interest of the ruled or for the attainment of some advantage common to both ruler and ruled. Essentially it is exercised in the interest of the ruled, as is also plainly the case with other arts besides that of ruling, such as medicine and gymnastics—though an art may incidentally be exercised for the benefit of its practitioner, and there is nothing to prevent (say) a trainer from becoming occasionally a member of the class he instructs, in the same sort of way as a steersman is always one of the crew. Thus a trainer or steersman primarily considers the good of those who are subject to his authority; but when he becomes one of them personally, he incidentally shares in the benefit of that good— the steersman thus being also a member of the crew, and the trainer (though still a trainer) becoming also a member of the class which he instructs.

This principle also applies to a third kind of rule—that exercised by the holders of political office. When the constitution of a state is constructed on the principle that its members are equals and peers, the citizens think it proper that they should hold office by turns which implies that the office of ruler is primarily intended for the benefit of the ruled and is therefore a duty to be undertaken by each in turn, though incidentally the ruler shares in the general benefit by virtue of being himself a member of the citizen body. At any rate this is the natural system, and the system which used to be followed in the days when men believed that they ought to serve by turns, and each assumed that others would take over

the duty of considering his benefit, just as he had himself, during his term of office, considered the interest of others. Today the case is altered. Moved by the profits to be derived from office and the handling of public property, men want to hold office continuously. It is as if the holders of office were sick men, who got the benefit of permanent health by being permanently in office: at any rate their ardour for office is just what it would be if that were the case. The conclusion which follows is clear. Those constitutions which consider the common interest are *right* constitutions, judged by the standard of absolute justice. Those constitutions which consider only the personal interest of the rulers are all *wrong* constitutions, or perversions of the right forms. Such perverted forms are despotic whereas the polis is an association of freemen.

Now that these matters have been determined, the next subject for consideration is the number and nature of the different constitutions. We may first examine the class of right constitutions and consider its different species; the different perversions will at once be apparent when the right constitutions have been determined. The term "constitution" signifies the same thing as the term "civic body." The civic body in every polis is the sovereign; and the sovereign must necessarily be either One, or Few, or Many. On this basis we may say that when the One, or the Few, or the Many, rule with a view to the common interest, the constitutions under which they do so must necessarily be right constitutions. On the other hand the constitutions directed to the personal interest of the One, or the

Few, or the Masses, must necessarily be perversions. They deviate from the true standard by not regarding the interest of all, and are thus involved in a dilemma: either the name of citizen cannot be given to persons who share in the constitution but whose interests are not regarded, or, if the name is to be given, they must have their share of the benefits. Among forms of government by a single person Kingship, in the general use of language, denotes the species which looks to the common interest. Among forms of government by a few persons (but more than one) Aristocracy denotes the species which similarly looks to that interest—that name being given to this species either because the best are the rulers, or because its object is what is best for the state and its members. Finally, when the masses govern the state with a view to the common interest, the name used for this species is the generic name common to all constitutions (or polities)—the name of "Polity." There is a good reason for the usage which gives to this form the generic name, and not a special name which connotes, as the name "Aristocracy" does, a special excellence. It is possible for one man, or a few, to be of outstanding excellence; but when it comes to a large number, we can hardly expect a fine edge of all the varieties of excellence. What we can expect particularly is the military kind of excellence, which is the kind that shows itself in a mass. This is the reason why the defence forces are the most sovereign body under this constitution, and those who possess arms are the persons who enjoy constitutional rights.

These are the three subdivisions of the class of right constitutions.

Three perversions correspond to them. Tyranny is the perversion of Kingship; Oligarchy of Aristocracy; and Democracy of Polity. Tyranny is a government by a single person directed to the interest of that person; Oligarchy is directed to the interest of the well-to-do; Democracy is directed to the interest of the poorer classes. None of the three is directed to the advantage of the whole body of citizens.

We must treat at somewhat greater length of the nature of each of these last constitutions. There are certain difficulties involved; and when one is pursuing a philosophical method of inquiry in any branch of study, and not merely looking to practical considerations, the proper course is to set out the truth about every particular with no neglect or omission. Tyranny, as has just been said, is single-person government of the political association on the lines of despotism, *i.e.* treating the citizens as a master treats slaves; oligarchy exists where those who have property are the sovereign authority of the constitution; and conversely democracy exists where the sovereign authority is composed of the poorer classes, and not of the owners of property. The first difficulty which arises concerns the definition just given of democracy and oligarchy. We have defined democracy as the sovereignty of numbers; but we can conceive a case in which the majority who hold the sovereignty in a state are the well-to-do. Similarly oligarchy is generally stated to be the sovereignty of a small number; but it might conceivably happen that the poorer classes were fewer in number than the well-to-do, and yet—in virtue of superior vigour—were the sovereign authority of the constitution. In neither case could the definition previously given of these constitutions be regarded as true. We might attempt to overcome the difficulty by combining both of the factors—wealth with paucity of numbers, and poverty with mass. On this basis oligarchy might be defined as the constitution under which the rich, being also few in number, hold the offices of the state; and similarly democracy might be defined as the constitution under which the poor, being also many in number, are in control. But this involves us in another difficulty. If our new definition is exhaustive, and there are no forms of oligarchy and democracy other than those enumerated in that definition, what names are we to give to the constitutions just suggested as conceivable—those where the wealthy form a majority and the poor a minority, and where the wealthy majority in the one case, and the poor minority in the other, are the sovereign authority of the constitution? The course of the argument thus appears to show that the factor of number—the small number of the sovereign body in oligarchies, or the large number in democracies—is an accidental attribute, due to the simple fact that the wealthy are generally few and the poor are generally numerous. Therefore the causes originally mentioned, *i.e.* small and large numbers, are not in fact the real causes of the difference between oligarchies and democracies. The real ground of the difference between oligarchy and democracy is poverty and riches. It is inevitable that any constitution should be an oligarchy if the rulers under it are rulers in virtue of riches, whether they are few or many; and it is equally inevitable that a constitution under which the poor rule should be a democracy.

It happens, however, as we have just remarked, and this is why number becomes an accidental attribute of both of these constitutions, that the rich are few and the poor are numerous. It is only a few who have riches, but all alike share in free status; and these are the real grounds on which the two parties, the oligarchical and the democratic, dispute the control of the constitution.

We must next ascertain, now that we have discovered the social ground on which they rest, what are the distinctive principles attributed by their advocates to oligarchy and democracy, and what are the oligarchical and the democratic conceptions of justice. Both oligarchs and democrats have a hold on a sort of conception of justice; but they both fail to carry it far enough, and neither of them expresses the true conception of justice in the whole of its range. In democracies, for example, justice is considered to mean equality in the distribution of office. It does mean equality—but equality for those who are equal, and not for all. In oligarchies, again, inequality in the distribution of office is considered to be just; and indeed it is—but only for those who are unequal, and not for all. The advocates of oligarchy and democracy both refuse to consider this factor—who are the persons to whom their principles properly apply—and they both make erroneous judgments. The reason is that they are judging *in their own case*; and most men, as a rule, are bad judges where their own interests are involved. Justice is relative to persons; and a just distribution is one in which the relative values of the things given correspond to those of the persons receiving—a point which has already been made in the *Ethics*. It follows that a just distribution of offices among a number of different persons will involve a consideration of the personal values, or merits, of each of those persons. But the advocates of oligarchy and democracy, while they agree about what constitutes equality in the *thing*, disagree about what constitutes it in *persons*. The main reason for this is the reason just stated—they are judging, and judging erroneously, in their own case; but there is also another reason—they are misled by the fact that they are professing a sort of conception of justice, and professing it up to a point, into thinking that they profess one which is absolute and complete. The oligarchs think that superiority on one point—in their case wealth—means superiority on all: the democrats believe that equality in one respect—for instance, that of free birth—means equality all round.

Both sides, however, fail to mention the really cardinal factor, *i.e.* the nature of the end for which the state exists. If property were the end for which men came together and formed an association, men's share in the offices and honours of the state would be proportionate to their share of property; and in that case the argument of the oligarchical side—that it is not just for a man who has contributed one pound to share equally in a sum of a hundred pounds (or, for that matter, in the interest accruing upon that sum) with the man who has contributed all the rest—would appear to be a strong argument. But the end of the state is not mere life; it is, rather, a good quality of life. If mere life were the end, there might be a state of slaves, or even a state of animals; but in the world as we know it any such state is impossible, because slaves and animals do not share in true felicity and free choice, *i.e.* the attributes of a good quality of life. Similarly, it is not the end of the state to provide an alliance for mutual defence against all injury, or to ease exchange and promote economic intercourse. If that had been the end, the Etruscans and the Carthaginians, who are united by such bonds, would be in the position of belonging to a single state; and the same would be true of all peoples who have commercial treaties with one another. It is true that such peoples have agreements about imports and exports; treaties to ensure just conduct in the course of trade; and written terms of alliance for mutual defence. On the other hand they have no common offices of state to deal with these matters; each, on the contrary, has its own offices, confined to itself. Neither of the parties concerns itself to ensure a proper quality of character among the members of the other; neither of them seeks to ensure that all who are included in the scope of the treaties shall be free from injustice and from any form of vice; and neither of them goes beyond the aim of preventing its own members from committing injustice in the course of trade against the members of the other. But it is the cardinal issue of goodness or badness in the life of the polis which always engages the attention of any state that concerns itself to secure a system of good laws well obeyed. The conclusion which clearly follows is that any polis which is truly so called, and is not merely one in name, must devote itself to the end of encouraging goodness. Otherwise, a political association sinks into a mere alliance, which only differs in space, *i.e.* in the contiguity of its members, from other forms of alliance where the members live at a distance from one another. Otherwise, too, law becomes a mere covenant—or (in the phrase of the Sophist Lycophron) "a guarantor of men's rights against one another"—instead of being, as it should be, a rule of life such as will make the members of a polis good and just.

That this is the case, *i.e.* that a polis is truly a polis only when it makes the encouragement of goodness its end, may be readily proved. If two different sites could be united in one, so that the polis of Megara and that of Corinth were embraced by a single wall, that would not make a single polis. If the citizens of two cities intermarried with one another, that would not make a single polis—even though intermarriage is one of the forms of social life which are characteristic of a polis. Nor would it make a polis if a number of persons—living at a distance from one another, but not at so great a distance but that they could still associate—had a common system of laws to prevent their injuring one another in the course of exchange. We can imagine, for instance, one being a carpenter, another a farmer, a third a shoemaker, and others producing other goods; and we can imagine a total number of as many as 10,000. But if these people were associated in nothing further than matters such as exchange and alliance, they would still

have failed to reach the stage of a polis. Why should this be the case? It cannot be ascribed to any lack of contiguity in such an association. The members of a group so constituted might come together on a single site; but if that were all—if each still treated his private house as if it were a state, and all of them still confined their mutual assistance to action against aggressors (as if it were only a question of a defensive alliance)—if, in a word, the spirit of their intercourse were still the same after their coming together as it had been when they were living apart—their association, even on its new basis, could not be deemed by any accurate thinker to be a polis. It is clear, therefore, that a polis is not an association for residence on a common site, or for the sake of preventing mutual injustice and easing exchange. These are indeed conditions which must be present before a polis can exist; but the presence of all these conditions is not enough, in itself, to constitute a polis. What constitutes a polis is an association of households and clans in a good life, for the sake of attaining a perfect and self-sufficing existence. This consummation, however, will not be reached unless the members inhabit one and the self-same place and practise intermarriage. It was for this reason, *i.e.* to provide these necessary conditions, that the various institutions of a common social life—marriage-connexions, kin-groups, religious gatherings, and social pastimes generally—arose in cities. But these institutions are the business of friendship and not the purpose of the polis. It is friendship and not a polis which consists in the pursuit of a common social life. The end and purpose of a polis is the good life, and the institutions of social life are means to that end. A polis is constituted by the association of families and villages in a perfect and self-suffing existence; and such an existence, on our definition, consists in a life of true felicity and goodness.

It is therefore for the sake of good actions, and not for the sake of social life, that political associations must be considered to exist. This conclusion enables us to attain a proper conception of justice. Those who contribute most to an association of this character, *i.e.* who contribute most to good action, have a greater share in the polis and should therefore, in justice, receive a larger recognition from it than those who are equal to them (or even greater) in free birth and descent, but unequal in civic excellence, or than those who surpass them in wealth but are surpassed by them in excellence. From what has been said it is plain that both sides to the dispute about constitutions, *i.e.* both the democratic and the oligarchical side, profess only a partial conception of justice.

A difficulty arises when we turn to consider what body of persons should be sovereign in the polis. We can imagine five alternatives: the people at large; the wealthy; the better sort of men; the one man who is best of all; the tyrant. But all these alternatives appear to involve unpleasant results: indeed, how can it be otherwise? Take, for example, the first alternative. What if the poor, on the ground of their being a majority, proceed to divide among themselves the possessions of the wealthy—will not this be unjust? "No, by heaven" (a democrat may

reply); "it has been justly decreed so by the sovereign." "But if this is not the extreme of injustice" (we may reply in turn), "what *is?*" Whenever a majority of any sort, irrespective of wealth or poverty, divides among its members the possessions of a minority, that majority is obviously ruining the state. But goodness can never ruin anything that has goodness, nor can justice, in its nature, be ruinous to a state. It is therefore clear that a law of this kind, *i.e.* a law of spoliation passed by a majority of any sort, cannot possibly be just. To treat such a law as just is really to justify tyranny. The tyrant's acts too, on the principle alleged by the democrats that any decree of the sovereign is just, must necessarily be just; for he too uses coercion by virtue of superior power in just the same sort of way as the people coerce the wealthy. We may now take the alternative that the wealthy are sovereign. Is it just that a minority composed of the wealthy should rule? If they too behave like the others—if they plunder and confiscate the property of the people—can their action be called just? If it can, the action of the people, in the converse case, must equally be termed just. It is clear that all these acts of oppression, whether by the people, the tyrant, or the wealthy are mean and unjust. But what of the next alternative? Should the better sort of men have authority and be sovereign in all matters? In that case, the rest of the citizens will necessarily be debarred from honours, since they will not enjoy the honour of holding civic office. We speak of offices as honours; and when a single set of persons hold office permanently, the rest of the community must necessarily be debarred from all honours. We come to a last alternative. Is it better than any of the other alternatives that the one best man should rule? This is still more oligarchical than the rule of the wealthy few or the few of the better sort because the number of those debarred from honours is even greater. It may perhaps be urged that there is still another alternative; that it is a poor sort of policy to vest sovereignty in any person or body of persons, subject as persons are to the passions that beset men's souls; and that it is better to vest it in law. But this does not solve the difficulty. The law itself may incline either towards oligarchy or towards democracy; and what difference will the sovereignty of law then make in the problems which have just been raised? The consequences already stated will follow just the same.

The other alternatives may be reserved for a later inquiry; but the first of the alternatives suggested— that the people at large should be sovereign rather than the few best— would appear to be defensible, and while it presents some difficulty it perhaps also contains some truth. There is this to be said for the Many. Each of them by himself may not be of a good quality; but when they all come together it is possible that they may surpass—collectively and as a body, although not individually—the quality of the few best. Feasts to which many contribute may excel those provided at one man's expense. In the same way, when there are many who contribute to the process of deliberation, each can bring his share of goodness and moral prudence; and when all meet together the people may thus become something in the nature of a single person, who—as he has many feet, many hands, and many senses—may also have many qualities of character and intelligence. This is the reason why the Many are also better judges than the few of music and the writing of poets: some appreciate one part, some another, and all together appreciate all. We may note that this combination of qualities, which gives the Many their merit, can also be traced in cases of *individual* merit. The thing which makes a good man differ from a unit in the crowd—as it is also the thing which is generally said to make a beautiful person differ from one who is not beautiful, or an artistic representation differ from ordinary reality—is that elements which are elsewhere scattered and separate are here combined in a unity. It is this unity which counts; for if you take the elements separately, you may say of an artistic representation that it is surpassed by the eye of this person or by some other feature of that.

It is not clear, however, that this combination of qualities, which we have made the ground of distinction between the many and the few best, is true of all popular bodies and all large masses of men. Perhaps it may be said, "By heaven, it is clear that there are some bodies of which it cannot possibly be true; for if you included them, you would, by the same token, be found to include a herd of beasts. That would be absurd; and yet what difference is there between these bodies and a herd of beasts?" All the same, and in spite of this objection, there is nothing to prevent the view we have stated from being true of *some* popular bodies.

It would thus seem possible to solve, by the considerations we have advanced, both the problem raised in the previous chapter "What body of *persons* should be sovereign?" and the further problem which follows upon it, "What are the *matters* over which freemen, or the general body of citizens—men of the sort who neither have wealth nor can make any claim on the ground of goodness—should properly exercise sovereignty?" It may be argued, from one point of view, that it is dangerous for men of this sort to share in the highest offices, as injustice may lead them into wrongdoing, and thoughtlessness into error. But it may also be argued, from another point of view, that there is serious risk in not letting them have *some* share in the enjoyment of power; for a state with a body of disfranchised citizens who are numerous and poor must necessarily be a state which is full of enemies. The alternative left is to let them share in the deliberative and judicial functions; and we thus find Solon, and some of the other legislators, giving the people the two general functions of electing the magistrates to office and of calling them to account at the end of their tenure of office, but *not* the right of holding office themselves in their individual capacity. There is wisdom in such a policy. When they all meet together, the people display a good enough gift of perception, and combined with the better class they are of service to the state (just as impure food, when it is mixed with pure, makes the whole concoction more nutritious than a small amount of the pure would be); but each of them is imperfect in the judgments he forms by himself. . . .

In all arts and sciences the end in view is some good. In the most sovereign of all the arts and sciences—and this is the art and science of politics—the end in view is the greatest good and the good which is most pursued. The good in the sphere of politics is justice; and justice consists in what tends to promote the common interest. General opinion makes it consist in some sort of equality. Up to a point this general opinion agrees with the philosophical inquiries which contain our conclusions on ethics. In other words, it holds that justice involves two factors—things, and the persons to whom things are assigned—and it considers that persons who are equal should have assigned to them equal things. But here there arises a question which must not be overlooked, Equals and unequals—yes; but equals and unequals *in what?* This is a question which raises difficulties, and involves us in philosophical speculation on politics. It is possible to argue that offices and honours ought to be distributed unequally, *i.e.* that superior amounts should be assigned to superior persons, on the basis of superiority *in any respect whatsoever*—even though there were similarity, and no shadow of any difference, in every other respect; and it may be urged, in favour of this argument, that where people differ from one another there must be a difference in what is just and proportionate to their merits. If this argument were accepted, the mere fact of a better complexion, or greater height, or any other such advantage, would establish a claim for a greater share of political rights to be given to its possessor. But is not the argument obviously wrong?

To be clear that it is, we have only to study the analogy of the other arts and sciences. If you were dealing with a number of flute-players who were equal in their art, you would not assign them flutes on the principle that the better born should have a greater amount. Nobody will play the better for being better born; and it is to those who are better at the job that the better supply of tools should be given. If our point is not yet plain, it can be made so if we push it still further. Let us suppose a man who is superior to others in flute-playing, but far inferior in birth and beauty. Birth and beauty may be greater goods than the ability to play the flute, and those who possess them may, upon balance, surpass the flute-player more in these qualities than he surpasses them in his flute-playing; but the fact remains that *he* is the man who ought to get the better supply of flutes. If it is to be recognized in connexion with a given function, superiority in quality such as birth—or for that matter wealth—ought to contribute something to the performance of that function; and here these qualities contribute nothing to such performance.

There is a further objection. If we accept this argument that offices and honours should be assigned on the basis of excellence in *any* respect, every quality will have to be commensurable with every other. You will begin by reckoning a given degree of (say) height as superior to a given degree of some other quality, and you will thus be driven to pit height in general against (say) wealth and birth in general. But on this basis—i.e. that, *in a given case*, A is counted as excelling in height

to a greater degree than B does in goodness, and that, *in general*, height is counted as excelling to a greater degree than goodness does—qualities are made commensurable. We are involved in mere arithmetic; for if amount X of some quality is "better" than amount Y of some other, some amount which is other than X must clearly be equal to it, *i.e.* must be *equally* good. This is impossible because things that differ in quality cannot be treated in terms of quantity, or regarded as commensurable. It is therefore clear that in matters political just as in matters belonging to other arts and sciences there is no good reason for basing a claim to the exercise of authority on any and every kind of superiority. Some may be swift and others slow; but this is no reason why one should have more political rights, and the others less. It is in athletic contests that the superiority of the swift receives its reward. Claims to political rights must be based on the ground of contribution to the elements which constitute the being of the state. There is thus good ground for the claims to honour and office which are made by persons of good descent, free birth, or wealth. Those who hold office must necessarily be free men and taxpayers: a state could not be composed entirely of men without means, any more than it could be composed entirely of slaves. But we must add that if wealth and free birth are necessary elements, the temper of justice and a martial habit are also necessary. These too are elements which must be present if men are to live together in a state. The one difference is that the first two elements are necessary to the simple existence of a state, and the last two for its good life.

If we are thinking in terms of contribution to the state's existence, all of the elements mentioned, or at any rate several of them, may properly claim to be recognized in the award of honours and office; but if we are thinking in terms of contribution to its good life, then culture and goodness, as we have noted already, may be regarded as having the justest claim. On the other hand—and following our principle that it is not right for men who are equal in one respect, and only in one, to have an equal share of all things as the democrats claim, or for men who are superior in one respect to have a superior share of everything as the oligarchs claim—we are bound to consider all constitutions which recognize such claims as perverted forms. We have noted already that there is a certain sense in which all the contributors of the different elements are justified in the claims they advance, though none of them is absolutely justified. (a) The rich are so far justified that they have a larger share of the land, which is a matter of public interest: they are also, as a rule, more reliable in matters of contract. (b) The free and the nobly born who both contribute the element of birth may claim recognition together as being closely connected. The better-born are citizens to a greater extent than the low-born; and good birth has always honour in its own country. In addition and apart from any honour paid them the descendants of better men are likely to be intrinsically better; good birth means goodness of the whole stock. (c) Similarly we may also allow that goodness of character has a just claim; for in our view the virtue of justice, which is necessarily accompanied by all the other virtues and which may thus be identified with *general* virtue or goodness is a virtue which acts in social relations and is therefore one of the elements essential to the existence of a political society. (d) But there is a further claim that may also be urged. Besides the claim of individuals, based on their having the particular attribute of wealth or birth or goodness, there is the claim of the people at large, based on its having, collectivley, still more of all these attributes. The many may urge their claims against the few: taken together and compared with the few they are stronger, richer, and better.

Let us suppose three rival claimants—for example, the good, the wealthy and well-born, and some sort of general body of citizens—all living together in a single state. Will they fall to disputing which of them is to govern, or will they agree? This issue is not a matter of dispute in any of the constitutions mentioned in our previous classification. These constitutions differ in virtue of different groups being sovereign: one of them is distinguished by sovereignty being vested in the wealthy; another by its being vested in the good; and so with each of the rest. But the question we are discussing is different. It is a question of determining who is to govern when the claims of different groups are simultaneously present. Suppose, for example, that the good are exceedingly few in number: how are we to settle their claim? Must we only have regard to the fact that they are few for the function they have to discharge; and must we therefore inquire whether they will be able to manage a state, or numerous enough to compose one? Here there arises a difficulty which applies not only to the good, but to all the different claimants for political office and honour. It may equally be held that there is no justice in the claim of a few to rule on the ground of their greater wealth, or on that of their better birth; and there is an obvious reason for holding this view. If there is any *one* man who in turn is richer than all the rest, this one man must rule over all on the very same ground of justice which the few rich plead for *their* right to rule; and similarly any one man who is preeminent in point of good birth must carry the say over those who claim on the ground of birth. In aristocracies, too, the same logic may be applied in the matter of merit or goodness. If some one man be a better man than all the other good men who belong to the civic body, this one man should be sovereign on the very same ground of justice which the other men plead in defence of *their* right to govern. Even the claims of the Many may be challenged by this line of argument. If the reason why they should be sovereign is their being stronger than the Few, we are logically driven to conclude that where one man is stronger than all the rest—or a group of more than one, but fewer than the Many, is stronger—that one man or group must be sovereign instead of the Many.

All these considerations would seem to prove that none of the principles, wealth, birth, goodness, and the strength of numbers, in virtue of which men claim to rule and to have all others subject to their rule, is a proper principle.

Take, for example, those who claim to be sovereign over the citizen body on the ground of goodness; or take, again, those who base their claim on the ground of wealth. The claims of both may be justly challenged by the masses; for there is nothing whatever to prevent the Many—collectively if not individually—from being better, or richer, than the Few. This last reflection enables us to take another step, and to meet a difficulty which is sometimes raised and discussed. The difficulty is this. Suppose that the Many are actually better, taken as a whole, than the Few: what, in that case, is the proper policy for a lawgiver who wishes to enact right laws to the best of his power? Should he direct his legislation to the benefit of the better sort, or should he direct it to that of the majority? We may reply that the benefit of neither ought to be considered exclusively; that what is "right" should be understood as what is "equally right"; and what is "equally right" is what is for the benefit of the whole state and for the common good of its citizens. Citizens, in the common sense of that term, are *all* who share in the civic life of ruling and being ruled in turn. In the particular sense of the term, they vary from constitution to constitution; and under an ideal constitution they must be those who are able and willing to rule and be ruled with a view to attaining a way of life according to goodness.

• • •

BOOK IV

• • •

We have now to consider what is the best constitution and the best way of life for the *majority* of states and men. In doing so we shall not employ, for the purpose of measuring "the best," a standard of excellence above the reach of ordinary men, or a standard of education requiring exceptional endowments and equipment, or the standard of a constitution which attains an ideal height. We shall only be concerned with the sort of life which most men are able to share and the sort of constitution which it is possible for most states to enjoy. The "aristocracies," so called, of which we have just been treating, will not serve us for this purpose: they either lie, at one extreme, beyond the reach of most states, or they approach, at the other, so closely to the constitution called "polity" that they need not be considered separately and must be treated as identical with it. The issues we have just raised can all be decided in the light of one body of fundamental principles. If we adopt as true the statements made in the *Ethics*—(1) that a truly happy life is a life of goodness lived in freedom from impediments, and (2) that goodness consists in a mean[1]—it follows that the best way of life for the *majority* of men is one which consists in a mean, and a mean of the kind attainable by every individual. Further, the same criteria which determine whether the citizen-body, *i.e.* all its members, considered as *individuals*, have a good or bad way of life must also apply to the constitution; for a constitution is the way of life of a citizen-body. In all states there may be distinguished three parts, or classes, of the citizen-body—the very rich; the very poor;

---

[1] [Following a middle path between excess and deficiency—*Ed.*]

and the middle class which forms the mean. Now it is admitted, as a general principle, that moderation and the means are always best. We may therefore conclude that in the ownership of all gifts of fortune a middle condition will be the best. Men who are in this condition are the most ready to listen to reason. Those who belong to either extreme—the over-handsome, the over-strong, the over-noble, the over-wealthy; or at the opposite end the over-poor, the over-weak, the utterly ignoble—find it hard to follow the lead of reason. Men in the first class tend more to violence and serious crime: men in the second tend too much to roguery and petty offences; and most wrong-doing arises either from violence or roguery. It is a further merit of the middle class that its members suffer least from ambition, which both in the military and the civil sphere is dangerous to states. It must also be added that those who enjoy too many advantages—strength, wealth, connexions, and so forth—are both unwilling to obey and ignorant how to obey. This is a defect which appears in them from the first, during childhood and in home-life: nurtured in luxury, they never acquire a habit of discipline, even in the matter of lessons. But there are also defects in those who suffer from the opposite extreme of a lack of advantages: they are far too mean and poor-spirited. We have thus, on the one hand, people who are ignorant how to rule and only know how to obey, as if they were so many slaves, and, on the other hand, people who are ignorant how to obey any sort of authority and only know how to rule as if they were masters of slaves.

The result is a state, not of freemen, but only of slaves and of masters: a state of envy on the one side and on the other contempt. Nothing could be further removed from the spirit of friendship or the temper of a political community. Community depends on friendship; and when there is enmity instead of friendship, men will not even share the same path. A state aims at being, as far as it can be, a society composed of equals and peers who, as such, can be friends and associates; and the middle class, more than any other, has this sort of composition. It follows that a state which is based on the middle class is bound to be the best constituted in respect of the elements, *i.e.* equals and peers, of which, in our view, a state is naturally composed. The middle classes besides contributing, in this way, to the security of the state enjoy a greater security themselves than any other class. They do not, like the poor, covet the goods of others; nor do others covet their possessions, as the poor covet those of the rich. Neither plotting against others, nor plotted against themselves, they live in freedom from danger; and we may well approve the prayer of Phocylides

Many things are best for the middling:
Fain would I be of the state's middle
    class.

It is clear from our argument, first, that the best form of political society is one where power is vested in the middle class, and, secondly, that good government is attainable in those states where there is a large middle class—large enough, if possible, to be stronger than both of the other classes, but at any rate large enough to be stronger than either of them singly; for in that case its addition to either will suffice to turn the scale, and will prevent either of the opposing extremes from becoming dominant. It is therefore the greatest of blessings for a state that its members should possess a moderate and adequate property. Where some have great possessions, and others have nothing at all, the result is either an extreme democracy or an unmixed oligarchy; or it may even be—indirectly, and as a reaction against both of these extremes—a tyranny. Tyranny is a form of government which may grow out of the headiest type of democracy, or out of oligarchy; but it is much less likely to grow out of constitutions of the middle order, or those which approximate to them, *e.g.* moderate oligarchies. We shall explain the reason later when we come to treat of revolutions and constitutional change.

Meanwhile, it is clear that the middle type of constitution is best for the *majority* of states. It is the one type free from faction; where the middle class is large, there is least likelihood of faction and dissension among the citizens. Large states are generally more free from faction just because they have a large middle class. In small states, on the other hand, it is easy for the whole population to be divided into only two classes; nothing is left in the middle, and all—or almost all—are either poor or rich. The reason why democracies are generally more secure and more permanent than oligarchies is the character of their middle class, which is more numerous, and is allowed a larger share in the government, than it is in oligarchies. Where democracies have no middle class, and the poor are greatly superior in number, trouble ensues, and they are speedily ruined. It must also be considered a proof of its value that the best legislators have come from the middle class. Solon was one, as his own poems prove; Lycurgus was another (and not, as is sometimes said, a member of the royal family); and the same is true of Charondas and most of the other legislators.

Plutarch

Little is known of the life of Plutarch; there are many legends but few verifiable facts. He was a Greek, born in Boeotia around A.D. 40, and educated in Athens. He spent much of his life in the service of his native city-state, although he seems to have found time for considerable travel, including several brief visits to Rome, where he devoted himself to study. He died, highly honored, in Boeotia around A.D. 120.

It is difficult to consider Plutarch as anything other than a moralist. Although his fame rests firmly on the merits of his major work, *The Parallel Lives*, he was neither a great biographer nor a good historian. In his biographies he does not attempt to provide complete accounts of the lives of his subjects; rather, he carefully selects details and anecdotes to point up the good or bad qualities in the character and the actions of the person. As history, *The Parallel Lives* gives only imperfect accounts of an age, with no attempt to recount events systematically.

Even the organization of the book reveals the moralist at work. The lives are arranged in pairs, with the biography of a prominent Greek followed by the biography of a distinguished Roman. Frequently a pair of parallel lives is accompanied by a chapter in which the two are compared. It is in these comparisons that Plutarch reveals his penchant for drawing moral conclusions.

The following selection is from the life of Alexander. In *The Parallel Lives* this brief biography is followed, for obvious reasons, by the life of Julius Caesar. This particular translation was made in the seventeenth century by the English poet John Dryden.

Alexander

It being my purpose to write the lives of Alexander the king, and of Caesar, by whom Pompey was destroyed, the multitude of their great actions affords so large a field that I were to blame if I should not by

Plutarch's Lives, trans. John Dryden.

way of apology forewarn my reader that I have chosen rather to epitomize the most celebrated parts of their story, than to insist at large on every particular circumstance of it. It must be borne in mind that my design is not to write histories, but lives. And the most glorious exploits do not always furnish us with the clearest discoveries of virtue or vice in men; sometimes a matter of less moment, an expression or a jest, informs us better of their characters and inclinations, than the most famous sieges, the greatest armaments, or the bloodiest battles whatsoever. Therefore as portrait-painters are more exact in the lines and features of the face, in which the character is seen, than in the other parts of the body, so I must be allowed to give my more particular attention to the marks and indications of the souls of men, and while I endeavor by these to portray their lives, may be free to leave more weighty matters and great battles to be treated of by others.

• • •

Alexander was born the sixth of Hecatombaeon, which month the Macedonians call Lous, the same day that the temple of Diana at Ephesus was burnt; which Hegesias of Magnesia makes the occasion of a conceit, frigid enough to have stopped the conflagration. The temple, he says, took fire and was burnt while its mistress was absent, assisting at the birth of Alexander. And all the Eastern soothsayers who happened to be then at Ephesus, looking upon the ruin of this temple to be the forerunner of some other calamity, ran about the town, beating their faces, and crying, that this day had brought forth something that would prove fatal and destructive to all Asia.

Just after Philip had taken Potidaea, he received these three messages at one time, that Parmenio had overthrown the Illyrians in a great battle, that his race-horse had won the course at the Olympic games, and that his wife had given birth to Alexander; with which being naturally well pleased, as an addition to his satisfaction, he was assured by the diviners that a son, whose birth was accompanied with three successes, could not fail of being invincible.

The statues that gave the best representation of Alexander's person, were those of Lysippus (by whom alone he would suffer his image to be made), those peculiarities which many of his successors afterwards and his friends used to affect to imitate, the inclination of his head a little on one side towards his left shoulder, and his melting eye, having been expressed by this artist with great exactness. But Apelles, who drew him with thunderbolts in his hand, made his complexion browner and darker than it was naturally; for he was fair and of light color, passing into ruddiness in his face and upon his breast. Aristoxenus in his Memoirs tells us that a most agreeable odor exhaled from his skin, and that his breath and body all over was so fragrant as to perfume the clothes which he wore next him; the cause of which might probably be the hot and adust temperament of his body. For sweet smells, Theophrastus conceives, are produced by the concoction of moist humours by heat, which is the reason that those parts of the world which are driest and most burnt up, afford spices of the best kind, and in the greatest quantity; for the heat of the sun exhausts all the superfluous moisture which lies in the surface of bodies, ready to generate putrefaction. And this hot constitution, it may be, rendered Alexander so addicted to drinking, and so choleric. His temperance, as to the pleasures of the body, was apparent in him in his very childhood, as he was with much difficulty incited to them, and always used them with great moderation; though in other things he was extremely eager and vehement, and in his love of glory, and the pursuit of it, he showed a solidity of high spirit and magnanimity far above his age. For he neither sought nor valued it upon every occasion, as his father Philip did (who affected to show his eloquence almost to a degree of pedantry, and took care to have the victories of his racing chariots at the Olympic games engraven on his coin), but when he was asked by some about him, whether he would run a race in the Olympic games, as he was very swift-footed, he answered, he would, if he might have kings to run with him. Indeed, he seems in general to have looked with indifference, if not with dislike, upon the professed athletes. He often appointed prizes, for which not only tragedians and musicians, pipers and harpers, but rhapsodists also, strove to outvie one another; and delighted in all manner of hunting and cudgel-playing, but never gave any encouragement to contests either of boxing or of the pancratium.[1]

While he was yet very young, he

---

[1] [A combination of boxing and wrestling—*Ed.*]

entertained the ambassadors from the king of Persia, in the absence of his father, and entering much into conversation with them, gained so much upon them by his affability, and the questions he asked them, which were far from being childish or trifling (for he inquired of them the length of the ways, the nature of the road into inner Asia, the character of their king, how he carried himself to his enemies, and what forces he was able to bring into the field), that they were struck with admiration of him, and looked upon the ability so much famed of Philip, to be nothing in comparison with the forwardness and high purpose that appeared thus early in his son. Whenever he heard Philip had taken any town of importance, or won any signal victory, instead of rejoicing at it altogether, he would tell his companions that his father would anticipate every thing, and leave him and them no opportunities of performing great and illustrious actions. For being more bent upon action and glory than either upon pleasure or riches, he esteemed all that he should receive from his father as a diminution and prevention of his own future achievements; and would have chosen rather to succeed to a kingdom involved in troubles and wars, which would have afforded him frequent exercise of his courage, and a large field of honor, than to one already flourishing and settled, where his inheritance would be an inactive life, and the mere enjoyment of wealth and luxury.

The care of his education, as it might be presumed, was committed to a great many attendants, preceptors, and teachers, over the whole of whom Leonidas, a near kinsman of Olympias, a man of an austere temper, presided, who did not indeed himself decline the name of what in reality is a noble and honorable office, but in general his dignity, and his near relationship, obtained him from other people the title of Alexander's foster father and governor. But he who took upon him the actual place and style of his pedagogue, was Lysimachus the Acarnanian, who, though he had nothing specially to recommend him, but his lucky fancy of calling himself Phoenix, Alexander Achilles, and Philip Peleus, was therefore well enough esteemed, and ranged in the next degree after Leonidas.

Philonicus the Thessalian brought the horse Bucephalas to Philip, offering to sell him for thirteen talents; but when they went into the field to try him, they found him so very vicious and unmanageable, that he reared up when they endeavored to mount him, and would not so much as endure the voice of any of Philip's attendants. Upon which, as they were leading him away as wholly useless and untractable, Alexander, who stood by, said, "What an excellent horse do they lose, for want of address and boldness to manage him!" Philip at first took no notice of what he said; but when he heard him repeat the same thing several times, and saw that he was much vexed to see the horse sent away, "Do you reproach," said he to him, "those who are older than yourself, as if you knew more, and were better able to manage him than they?" "I could manage this horse," replied he, "better than others do." "And if you do not," said Philip, "what will you forfeit for your rashness?" "I will pay," answered Alexander, "the whole price of the horse." At this the whole company fell a laughing; and as soon as the wager was settled amongst them, he immediately ran to the horse, and taking hold of the bridle, turned him directly towards the sun, having, it seems, observed that he was disturbed at and afraid of the motion of his own shadow; then letting him go forward a little, still keeping the reins in his hand, and stroking him gently when he found him begin to grow eager and fiery, he let fall his upper garment softly, and with one nimble leap securely mounted him, and when he was seated, by little and little drew in the bridle, and curbed him without either striking or spurring him. Presently, when he found him free from all rebelliousness, and only impatient for the course, he let him go at full speed, inciting him now with a commanding voice, and urging him also with his heel. Philip and his friends looked on at first in silence and anxiety for the result, till seeing him turn at the end of his career, and come back rejoicing and triumphing for what he had performed, they all burst out into acclamations of applause; and his father, shedding tears, it is said, for joy, kissed him as he came down from his horse, and in his transport, said, "O my son, look thee out a kingdom equal to and worthy of thyself, for Macedonia is too little for thee."

After this, considering him to be of a temper easy to be led to his duty by reason, but by no means to be compelled, he always endeavored to persuade rather than to command or force him to any thing; and now looking upon the instruction and tuition of his youth to be of greater difficulty and importance, than to be wholly trusted to the ordinary masters in music and poetry, and the common school subjects, and to require, as Sophocles says,

The bridle and the rudder too,

he sent for Aristotle, the most learned and most celebrated philosopher of his time, and rewarded him with a munificence proportionable to and becoming the care he took to instruct his son. For he repeopled his native city Stagira, which he had caused to be demolished a little before, and restored all the citizens who were in exile or slavery, to their habitations. As a place for the pursuit of their studies and exercises, he assigned the temple of the Nymphs, near Mieza, where, to this very day, they show you Aristotle's stone seats, and the shady walks which he was wont to frequent. It would appear that Alexander received from him not only his doctrines of Morals, and of Politics, but also something of those more abstruse and profound theories which these philosophers, by the very names they gave them, professed to reserve for oral communication to the initiated, and did not allow many to become acquainted with. For when he was in Asia, and heard Aristotle had published some treatises of that kind, he wrote to him, using very plain language to him in behalf of philosophy, the following letter:

Alexander to Aristotle greeting. You have not done well to publish your books of oral doctrine; for what is there now that we excel others in, if those things which we have been particularly instructed in be laid open to all? For my part, I assure you, I had rather excel others in the knowledge of what is excellent, *than in the extent of my power and dominion. Farewell.*

And Aristotle, soothing this passion for preeminence, speaks, in his excuse for himself, of these doctrines, as in fact both published and not published; as indeed, to say the truth, his books on metaphysics are written in a style which makes them useless for ordinary teaching, and instructive only, in the way of memoranda, for those who have been already conversant in that sort of learning.

Doubtless also it was to Aristotle, that he owed the inclination he had, not to the theory only, but likewise to the practice of the art of medicine. For when any of his friends were sick, he would often prescribe them their course of diet, and medicines proper to their disease, as we may find in his epistles. He was naturally a great lover of all kinds of learning and reading; and Onesicritus informs us, that he constantly laid Homer's *Iliad*, according to the copy corrected by Aristotle, called the casket copy, with his dagger under his pillow, declaring that he esteemed it a perfect portable treasure of all military virtue and knowledge. When he was in the upper Asia, being destitute of other books, he ordered Harpalus to send him some; who furnished him with Philistus's History, a great many of the plays of Euripides, Sophocles, and Aeschylus, and some dithyrambic odes, composed by Telestes and Philoxenus. For awhile he loved and cherished Aristotle no less, as he was wont to say himself, than if he had been his father, giving this reason for it, that as he had received life from the one, so the other had taught him to live well. But afterwards, upon some mistrust of him, yet not so great as to make him do him any hurt, his familiarity and friendly kindness to him abated so much of its former force and affectionateness, as to make it evident he was alienated from him. However, his violent thirst after and passion for learning, which were once implanted, still grew up with him, and never decayed; as appears by his veneration of Anaxarchus, by the present of fifty talents which he sent to Xeonocrates, and his particular care and esteem of Dandamis and Calanus.

• • •

Soon after, the Grecians, being assembled at the Isthmus, declared their resolution of joining with Alexander in the war against the Persians, and proclaimed him their general. While he stayed here, many public ministers and philosophers came from all parts to visit him, and congratulated him on his election, but contrary to his expectation, Diogenes of Sinope,[2] who then was living at Corinth, thought so little of him, that instead of coming to compliment him, he never so much as stirred out of the suburb called the Cranium, where Alexander found him lying alone in the sun. When he saw so much company near him, he raised himself a little, and vouchsafed to look upon Alexander; and when he kindly asked him whether he wanted any thing, "Yes," said he, "I would have you stand from between me and the sun." Alexander was so struck at this answer, and surprised at the greatness of the man, who had taken so little notice of him, that as he went away, he told his followers who were laughing at the moroseness of the philosopher, that if he were not Alexander, he would choose to be Diogenes.

Then he went to Delphi, to consult Apollo concerning the success of the war he had undertaken, and happening to come on one of the forbidden days, when it was esteemed improper to give any answers from the oracle, he sent messengers to desire the priestess to do her office; and when she refused, on the plea of a law to the contrary, he went up himself, and began to draw her by force into the temple, until tired and overcome with his importunity, "My son," said she, "thou art invincible." Alexander taking hold of what she spoke, declared he had received such an answer as he wished for, and that it was needless to consult the god any further. Among other prodigies that attended the departure of his army, the image of Orpheus at Libethra, made by cypresswood, was seen to sweat in great abundance, to the discouragement of many. But Aristander told him, that far from presaging any ill to him, it signified he should perform acts so important and glorious as would make the poets and musicians of future ages labor and sweat to describe and celebrate them.

His army, by their computation who make the smallest amount, consisted of thirty thousand foot, and four thousand horse; and those who make the most of it, speak but of forty-three thousand foot, and three thousand horse. Aristobulus says, he had not a fund of above seventy talents for their pay, nor had he more than thirty days' provision, if

---

[2] [A famous Greek philosopher, who lived in a tub and went about carrying a lighted lantern, "in search of an honest man."—Ed.]

we may believe Duris; Onesicritus tells us, he was two hundred talents in debt. However narrow and disproportionable the beginnings of so vast an undertaking might seem to be, yet he would not embark his army until he had informed himself particularly what means his friends had to enable them to follow him, and supplied what they wanted, by giving good farms to some, a village to one, and the revenue of some hamlet or harbor town to another. So that at last he had portioned out or engaged almost all the royal property; which giving Perdiccas an occasion to ask him what he would leave himself, he replied, his hopes. "Your soldiers," replied Perdiccas, "will be your partners in those," and refused to accept of the estate he had assigned him. Some others of his friends did the like, but to those who willingly received, or desired assistance of him, he liberally granted it, as far as his patrimony in Macedonia would reach, the most part of which was spent in these donations.

With such vigorous resolutions, and his mind thus disposed, he passed the Hellespont, and at Troy sacrificed to Minerva, and honored the memory of the heroes who were buried there, with solemn libations; especially Achilles, whose gravestone he anointed, and with his friends, as the ancient custom is, ran naked about his sepulchre, and crowned it with garlands, declaring how happy he esteemed him, in having while he lived so faithful a friend, and when he was dead, so famous a poet to proclaim his actions. While he was viewing the rest of the antiquities and curiosities of the place, being told he might see Paris's harp, if he pleased, he said,

he thought it not worth looking on, but he should be glad to see that of Achilles, to which he used to sing the glories and great actions of brave men.

In the mean time Darius's captains having collected large forces, were encamped on the further bank of the river Granicus, and it was necessary to fight, as it were, in the gate of Asia for an entrance into it. The depth of the river, with the unevenness and difficult ascent of the opposite bank, which was to be gained by main force, was apprehended by most, and some pronounced it an improper time to engage, because it was unusual for the kings of Macedonia to march with their forces in the month called Daesius. But Alexander broke through these scruples, telling them they should call it a second Artemisium. And when Parmenio advised him not to attempt any thing that day, because it was late, he told him that he should disgrace the Hellespont, should he fear the Granicus. And so without more saying, he immediately took the river with thirteen troops of horse, and advanced against whole showers of darts thrown from the steep opposite side, which was covered with armed multitudes of the enemy's horse and foot, notwithstanding the disadvantage of the ground and the rapidity of the stream; so that the action seemed to have more of frenzy and desperation in it, than of prudent conduct. However, he persisted obstinately to gain the passage, and at last with much ado making his way up the banks, which were extremely muddy and slippery, he had instantly to join in a mere confused hand-to-hand combat with the enemy, before he could draw up his men, who were still passing over, into any order. For the enemy pressed upon him with loud and warlike outcries; and charging horse against horse, with their lances, after they had broken and spent these, they fell to it with their swords. And Alexander, being easily known by his buckler, and a large plume of white feathers on each side of his helmet, was attacked on all sides, yet escaped wounding, though his cuirass was pierced by a javelin in one of the joinings. And Rhoesaces and Spithridates, two Persian commanders, falling upon him at once, he avoided one of them, and struck at Rhoesaces, who had a good cuirass on, with such force, that his spear breaking in his hand, he was glad to betake himself to his dagger. While they were thus engaged, Spithridates came up on one side of him, and raising himself upon his horse, gave him such a blow with his battle-axe on the helmet, that he cut off the crest of it, with one of his plumes, and the helmet was only just so far strong enough to save him, that the edge of the weapon touched the hair of his head. But as he was about to repeat his stroke, Clitus, called the black Clitus, prevented him, by running him through the body with his spear. At the same time Alexander despatched Rhoesaces with his sword. While the horse were thus dangerously engaged, the Macedonian phalanx passed the river, and the foot on each side advanced to fight. But the enemy hardly sustained the first onset, soon gave ground and fled, all but the mercenary Greeks, who, making a stand upon a rising ground, desired quarter, which Alexander, guided rather by passion than judgment,

refused to grant, and charging them himself first, had his horse (not Bucephalas, but another) killed under him. And this obstinacy of his to cut off these experienced desperate men, cost him the lives of more of his own soldiers than all the battle before, besides those who were wounded. The Persians lost in this battle twenty thousand foot, and two thousand five hundred horse. On Alexander's side, Aristobulus says there were not wanting above four and thirty, of whom nine were foot-soldiers; and in memory of them he caused so many statues of brass, of Lysippus's making, to be erected. And that the Grecians might participate the honor of his victory, he sent a portion of the spoils home to them, particularly to the Athenians three hundred bucklers, and upon all the rest he ordered this inscription to be set: "Alexander the son of Philip, and the Grecians, except the Lacedaemonians, won these from the barbarians who inhabit Asia." All the plate and purple garments, and other things of the same kind that he took from the Persians, except a very small quantity which he reserved for himself, he sent as a present to his mother.

This battle presently made a great change of affairs to Alexander's advantage. For Sardis itself, the chief seat of the barbarian's power in the maritime provinces, and many other considerable places were surrendered to him; only Halicarnassus and Miletus stood out, which he took by force, together with the territory about them. After which he was a little unsettled in his opinion how to proceed. Sometimes he thought it best to find out Darius as soon as he could, and put all to the hazard of a battle; another while he looked upon it as a more prudent course to make an entire reduction of the seacoast, and not to seek the enemy till he had first exercised his power here and made himself secure of the resources of these provinces. While he was thus deliberating what to do, it happened that a spring of water near the city of Xanthus in Lycia, of its own accord swelled over its banks, and threw up a copper plate upon the margin, in which was engraven in ancient characters, that the time would come, when the Persian empire should be destroyed by the Grecians. Encouraged by this accident, he proceeded to reduce the maritime parts of Cilicia and Phoenicia, and passed his army along the seacoasts of Pamphylia with such expedition that many historians have described and extolled it with that height of admiration, as if it were no less than a miracle, and an extraordinary effect of divine favor, that the waves which usually come rolling in violently from the main, and hardly ever leave so much as a narrow beach under the steep, broken cliffs at any time uncovered, should on a sudden retire to afford him passage. Menander, in one of his comedies, alludes to this marvel when he says:

Was Alexander ever favored more?
Each man I wish for meets me at my
    door,
And should I ask for passage through
    the sea,
The sea I doubt not would retire for
    me.

But Alexander himself in his epistles mentioned nothing unusual in this at all, but says he went from Phaselis, and passed through what they call the Ladders. At Phaselis he stayed some time, and finding the statue of Theodectes, who was a native of this town and was now dead, erected in the marketplace, after he had supped, having drunk pretty plentifully, he went and danced about it, and crowned it with garlands, honoring not ungracefully in his sport, the memory of a philosopher whose conversation he had formerly enjoyed, when he was Aristotle's scholar.

• • •

Darius was by this time upon his march from Susa, very confident, not only in the number of his men, which amounted to six hundred thousand, but likewise in a dream, which the Persian soothsayers interpreted rather in flattery to him, than according to the natural probability. He dreamed that he saw the Macedonian phalanx all on fire, and Alexander waiting on him, clad in the same dress which he himself had been used to wear when he was courier to the late king; after which, going into the temple of Belus, he vanished out of his sight. The dream would appear to have supernaturally signified to him the illustrious actions the Macedonians were to perform, and that as he from a courier's place had risen to the throne, so Alexander should come to be master of Asia, and not long surviving his conquests, conclude his life with glory. Darius's confidence increased the more, because Alexander spent so much time in Cilicia, which he imputed to his cowardice. But it was sickness that detained him there, which some say he contracted from his fatigues, others from bathing in the river Cydnus, whose waters were exceedingly cold. However it happened, none of his physicians would venture to give him any remedies, they thought his case so desperate, and were so afraid of the suspicions and ill-will of the Macedonians if they should fail in the cure; till Philip, the Acarnanian, seeing how critical his case was, but relying on his own well-known friendship for him, resolved to try the last efforts of his art, and rather hazard his own credit and life, than suffer him to perish for want of physic, which he confidently administered to him, encouraging him to take it boldly, if he desired a speedy recovery, in order to prosecute the war. At this very time, Parmenio wrote to Alexander from the camp, bidding him have a care of Philip, as one who was bribed by Darius to kill him, with great sums of money, and a promise of his daughter in marriage. When he had perused the letter, he put it under his pillow, without showing it so much as to any of his most intimate friends, and when Philip came in with the potion, he took it with great cheerfulness and assurance, giving him meantime the letter to read. This was a spectacle well worth being present at, to see Alexander take the draught, and Philip read the letter at the same time, and then turn and look upon one another, but with different sentiments; for Alexander's looks were cheerful and open, to show his kindness to and confidence in his physician, while the other was full of surprise and alarm at the accusation, appealing to the gods to witness his innocence, sometimes lifting up his hands to heaven, and then throwing himself down by the bedside, and beseeching Alexander to lay aside all fear, and follow his directions without apprehension. For the medicine at first worked so strongly as to drive, so to say, the vital forces into the interior, he lost his speech, and falling into a swoon, had scarce any sense of pulse left. However, in no long time, by Philip's means, his health and strength returned, and he showed himself in public to the Macedonians, who were in continual fear and dejection until they saw him abroad again.

•   •   •

In his diet, also, he was most temperate, as appears, omitting many other circumstances, by what he said to Ada, whom he adopted, with the title of mother, and afterwards created queen of Garia. For when she out of kindness sent him every day many curious dishes, and sweetmeats, and would have furnished him with some cooks and pastry-men, who were thought to have great skill, he told her he wanted none of them, his preceptor, Leonidas, having already given him the best, which were a night march to prepare for breakfast, and a moderate breakfast to create an appetite for supper. Leonidas also, he added, used to open and search the furniture of his chamber, and his wardrobe, to see if his mother had left him any thing that was delicate or superfluous. He was much less addicted to wine than was generally believed; that which gave people occasion to think so of him, was, that when he had nothing else to do, he loved to sit long and talk, rather than drink, and over every cup hold a long conversation. For when his affairs called upon him, he would not be detained, as other generals often were, either by wine, or sleep, nuptial solemnities, spectacles, or any other diversion whatsoever; a convincing argument of which is, that in the short time he lived, he accomplished so many and so great actions. When he was free from employment, after he was up, and had sacrificed to the gods, he used to sit down to breakfast, and then spend the rest of the day in hunting, or writing memoirs, giving decisions on some military questions, or reading. In marches that required no great haste, he would practise shooting as he went along, or to mount a chariot, and alight from it in full speed. Sometimes, for sport's sake, as his journals tell us, he would hunt foxes and go fowling. When he came in for the evening, after he had bathed and was anointed, he would call for his bakers and chief cooks, to know if they had his dinner ready. He never cared to dine till it was pretty late and beginning to be dark, and was wonderfully circumspect at meals that every one who sat with him should be served alike and with proper attention; and his love of talking, as was said before, made him delight to sit long at his wine. And then, though otherwise no prince's conversation was ever so agreeable, he would fall into a temper of ostentation and soldierly boasting, which gave his flatterers a great advantage to ride him, and made his better friends very uneasy. For though they thought it too base to strive who should flatter him most, yet they found it hazardous not to do it; so that between the shame and the danger, they were in great strait how to behave themselves. After such an entertainment, he was wont to bathe, and then perhaps he would sleep till noon,

and sometimes all day long. He was so very temperate in his eating, that when any rare fish or fruits were sent him, he would distribute them among his friends, and often reserve nothing for himself. His table, however, was always magnificent, the expense of it still increasing with his good fortune, till it amounted to ten thousand drachmas a day, to which sum he limited it, and beyond this he would suffer none to lay out in any entertainment where he himself was the guest.

• • •

After he had reduced all Asia on this side of the Euphrates, he advanced towards Darius, who was coming down against him with a million of men. In his march, a very ridiculous passage happened. The servants who followed the camp, for sport's sake divided themselves into two parties, and named the commander of one of them Alexander, and of the other Darius. At first they only pelted one another with clods of earth, but presently took to their fists, and at last, heated with the contention, they fought in good earnest with stones and clubs, so that they had much ado to part them; till Alexander, upon hearing of it, ordered the two captains to decide the quarrel by single combat, and armed him who bore his name himself, while Philotas did the same to him who represented Darius. The whole army were spectators of this encounter, willing from the event of it to derive an omen of their own future success. After they had fought stoutly a pretty long while, at last he who was called Alexander had the better, and for a reward of his prowess, had twelve villages given him, with leave to wear the Persian dress. So we are told by Eratosthenes.

But the great battle of all that was fought with Darius, was not, as most writers tell us, at Arbela, but at Gaugamela. . . . The oldest of his commanders, and chiefly Parmenio, when they beheld all the plain between Niphates and the Gordyaean mountains shining with the lights and fires which were made by the barbarians, and heard the uncertain and confused sound of voices out of their camp, like the distant roaring of a vast ocean, were so amazed at the thoughts of such a multitude, that after some conference among themselves, they concluded it an enterprise too difficult and hazardous for them to engage so numerous an enemy in the day, and therefore meeting the king as he came from sacrificing, besought him to attack Darius by night, that the darkness might conceal the danger of the ensuing battle. To this he gave them the celebrated answer, "I will not steal a victory," which though some at the time thought a boyish and inconsiderate speech, as if he played with danger, others, however, regarded as an evidence that he confided in his present condition, and acted on a true judgment of the future, not wishing to leave Darius, in case he were worsted, the pretext of trying his fortune again, which he might suppose himself to have, if he could impute his overthrow to the disadvantage of the night, as he did before to the mountains, the narrow passages, and the sea. For while he had such numerous forces and large dominions still remaining, it was not any want of men or arms that could induce him to give up the war, but only the loss of all

courage and hope upon the conviction of an undeniable and manifest defeat.

After they were gone from him with this answer, he laid himself down in his tent and slept the rest of the night more soundly than was usual with him, to the astonishment of the commanders, who came to him early in the morning, and were fain themselves to give order that the soldiers should breakfast. But at last, time not giving them leave to wait any longer, Parmenio went to his bedside, and called him twice or thrice by his name, till he waked him, and then asked him how it was possible, when he was to fight the most important battle of all, he could sleep as soundly as if he were already victorious. "And are we not so, indeed," replied Alexander smiling, "since we are at last relieved from the trouble of wandering in pursuit of Darius through a wide and wasted country, hoping in vain that he would fight us?" And not only before the battle, but in the height of the danger, he showed himself great, and manifested the self-possession of a just foresight and confidence. For the battle for some time fluctuated and was dubious. The left wing, where Parmenio commanded, was so impetuously charged by the Bactrian horse that it was disordered and forced to give ground, at the same time that Mazaeus had sent a detachment round about to fall upon those who guarded the baggage, which so disturbed Parmenio, that he sent messengers to acquaint Alexander that the camp and baggage would be all lost unless he immediately relieved the rear by a considerable reinforcement drawn out of the front. This message being brought him just as he was giving the signal to those about him for the onset, he bade them tell Parmenio that he must have surely lost the use of his reason, and had forgotten, in his alarm, that soldiers, if victorious, become masters of their enemies' baggage; and if defeated, instead of taking care of their wealth or their slaves, have nothing more to do but to fight gallantly and die with honor. When he had said this, he put on his helmet, having the rest of his arms on before he came out of his tent, which were a coat of the Sicilian make, girt close about him, and over that a breast-piece of thickly quilted linen, which was taken among other booty at the battle of Issus. The helmet, which was made by Theophilus, though of iron, was so well wrought and polished, that it was as bright as the most refined silver. To this was fitted a gorget of the same metal, set with precious stones. His sword, which was the weapon he most used in fight, was given him by the king of the Citieans, and was of an admirable temper and lightness. The belt which he also wore in all engagements, was of much richer workmanship than the rest of his armor. It was a work of the ancient Helicon, and had been presented to him by the Rhodians, as a mark of their respect to him. So long as he was engaged in drawing up his men, or riding about to give orders or directions, or to view them, he spared Bucephalas, who was now growing old, and made use of another horse; but when he was actually to fight, he sent for him again, and as soon as he was mounted, commenced the attack.

He made the longest address that day to the Thessalians and other Greeks, who answered him with loud shouts, desiring him to lead them on against the barbarians, upon which he shifted his javelin into his left hand, and with his right lifted up towards heaven, besought the gods, as Callisthenes tells us, that if he was of a truth the son of Jupiter, they would be pleased to assist and strengthen the Grecians. At the same time the augur Aristander, who had a white mantle about him, and a crown of gold on his head, rode by and showed them an eagle that soared just over Alexander, and directed his flight towards the enemy; which so animated the beholders, that after mutual encouragements and exhortations, the horses charged at full speed, and were followed in a mass by the whole phalanx of the foot. But before they could well come to blows with the first ranks, the barbarians shrunk back, and were hotly pursued by Alexander, who drove those that fled before him into the middle of the battle, where Darius himself was in person, whom he saw from a distance over the foremost ranks, conspicuous in the midst of his lifeguard, a tall and fine-looking man, drawn in a lofty chariot, defended by an abundance of the best horse, who stood close in order about it, ready to receive the enemy. But Alexander's approach was so terrible, forcing those who gave back upon those who yet maintained their ground, that he beat down and dispersed them almost all. Only a few of the bravest and valiantest opposed the pursuit, who were slain in their king's presence, falling in heaps upon one another, and in the very pangs of death striving to catch hold of the horses. Darius now seeing all was lost, that those who were placed in front to defend him were broken and beat back upon him, that he could not turn or disengage his chariot without great difficulty, the wheels being clogged and entangled among the dead bodies, which lay in such heaps as not only stopped, but almost covered the horses, and made them rear and grow so unruly, that the frighted charioteer could govern them no longer, in this extremity was glad to quit his chariot and his arms, and mounting, it is said, upon a mare that had been taken from her foal, betook himself to flight. But he had not escaped so either, if Parmenio had not sent fresh messengers to Alexander, to desire him to return and assist him against a considerable body of the enemy which yet stood together, and would not give ground. For, indeed, Parmenio is on all hands accused of having been sluggish and unserviceable in this battle, whether age had impaired his courage, or that, as Callisthenes says, he secretly disliked and envied Alexander's growing greatness. Alexander, though he was not a little vexed to be so recalled and hindered from pursuing his victory, yet concealed the true reason from his men, and causing a retreat to be sounded, as if it were too late to continue the execution any longer, marched back towards the place of danger and by the way met with the news of the enemy's total overthrow and flight.

This battle being thus over, seemed to put a period to the Persian empire, and Alexander, who was now proclaimed king of Asia, returned thanks to the gods in magnificent sacrifices, and rewarded his friends and followers with great sums of money, and palaces, and governments of provinces. And eager to gain honor with the Grecians, he wrote to them that he would have all tyrannies abolished, that they might live free according to their own laws, and specially to the Plataeans, that their city should be rebuilt, because their ancestors had permitted their countrymen of old to make their territory the seat of the war, when they fought with the barbarians for their common liberty. He sent also part of the spoils into Italy, to the Crotoniats, to honor the zeal and courage of their citizen Phayllus, the wrestler, who, in the Median war, when the other Grecian colonies in Italy disowned Greece, that he might have a share in the danger, joined the fleet at Salamis, with a vessel set forth at his own charge. So affectionate was Alexander to all kind of virtue, and so desirous to preserve the memory of laudable actions.

• • •

At the taking of Susa, Alexander found in the palace forty thousand talents in money already coined, besides an unspeakable quantity of other furniture and treasure; amongst which was five thousand talents' worth of Hermionian purple, that had been laid up there an hundred and ninety years, and yet kept its color as fresh and lively as at first. The reason of which, they say, is that in dyeing the purple they made use of honey, and of white oil in the white tincture, both which after the like space of time preserve the clearness and brightness of their lustre. Dinon also relates that the Persian kings had water fetched from the Nile and the Danube, which they laid up in their treasuries as a sort of testimony of the greatness of their power and universal empire.

The entrance into Persia was through a most difficult country, and was guarded by the noblest of the Persians, Darius himself having escaped further. Alexander, however, chanced to find a guide in exact correspondence with what the Pythia had foretold when he was a child, that a lycus should conduct him into Persia. For by such an one, whose father was a Lycian, and his mother a Persian, and who spoke both languages, he was now led into the country, by a way something about, yet without fetching any considerable compass. Here a great many of the prisoners were put to the sword, of which himself gives this account, that he commanded them to be killed in the belief that it would be for his advantage. Nor was the money found here less, he says, than at Susa, besides other movables and treasure, as much as ten thousand pair of mules and five thousand camels could well carry away. Amongst other things he happened to observe a large statue of Xerxes thrown carelessly down to the ground in the confusion made by the multitude of soldiers pressing into the palace. He stood still, and accosting it as if it had been alive, "Shall we," said he, "neglectfully pass thee by, now thou art prostrate on the ground, because thou once invadedst Greece, or shall we erect thee again in consideration of the greatness of thy mind and thy other virtues?" But at last, after he had paused some time, and silently considered with himself, he went on without taking any further notice of it. In this place he took up his winter quarters, and stayed four months to refresh his soldiers. It is related that the first time he sat on the royal throne of Persia, under the canopy of gold, Demaratus, the Corinthian, who was much attached to him and had been one of his father's friends, wept, in an old man's manner, and deplored the misfortune of those Greeks whom death had deprived of the satisfaction of seeing Alexander seated on the throne of Darius.

From hence designing to march against Darius, before he set out, he diverted himself with his officers at an entertainment of drinking and other pastimes, and indulged so far as to let every one's mistress sit by and drink with them. The most celebrated of them was Thais, an Athenian, mistress of Ptolemy, who was afterwards king of Egypt. She, partly as a sort of well-turned compliment to Alexander, partly out of sport, as the drinking went on, at last was carried so far as to utter a saying, not misbecoming her native country's character, though somewhat too lofty for her own condition. She said it was indeed some recompense for the toils she had undergone in following the camp all over Asia, that she was that day treated in, and could insult over, the stately palace of the Persian monarchs. But, she added, it would please her much better, if while the king looked on, she might in sport, with her own hands, set fire to the court of that Xerxes who reduced the city of Athens to ashes, that it might be recorded to posterity, that the women who followed Alexander had taken a severer revenge on the Persians for the sufferings and affronts of Greece, than all the famed commanders had been able to do by sea or land. What she said was received with such universal liking and murmurs of applause, and so seconded by the encouragement and eagerness of the company, that the king himself, persuaded to be of the party, started from his seat, and with a chaplet of flowers on his head, and a lighted torch in his hand, led them the way, while they went after him in a riotous manner, dancing and making loud cries about the place; which when the rest of the Macedonians perceived, they also in great delight ran thither with torches; for they hoped the burning and destruction of the royal palace was an argument that he looked homeward, and had no design to reside among the barbarians. Thus some writers give their account of this action, while others say it was done deliberately; however, all agree that he soon repented of it, and gave order to put out the fire.

• • •

When he came into Persia, he distributed money among the women, as their own kings had been wont to do, who as often as they came thither, gave every one of them a piece of gold; on account of which custom, some of them, it is said, had come but seldom, and Ochus was so sordidly covetous, that to avoid this expense, he never visited his native country once in all his reign. Then finding Cyrus's sepulchre opened and rifled, he put Polymachus, who did it, to death, though he was a man of some distinction, a born Macedonian of Pella. And after he had read the inscription, he caused it to be cut again below the old one in Greek characters; the words being these: "O man, whosoever thou art, and from whencesoever thou comest (for I know thou wilt come), I am Cyrus, the founder of the Persian empire; do not grudge me this little earth which covers my body." The reading of this sensibly touched Alexander, filling him with the thought of the uncertainty and mutability of human affairs. . . .

At Susa, he married Darius' daughter Statira, and celebrated also the nuptials of his friends, bestowing the noblest of the Persian ladies upon the worthiest of them, at the same time making it an entertainment in honor of the other Macedonians whose marriages had already taken place. At this magnificent festival, it is reported, there were no less than nine thousand guests, to each of whom he gave a golden cup for the libations. Not to mention other instances of his wonderful magnificence, he paid the debts of his army, which amounted to nine thousand eight hundred and seventy talents. But Antigenes, who had lost one of his eyes, though he owned nothing, got his name set down in the list of those who were in debt, and bringing one who pretended to be his creditor, and to have supplied him from the bank, received the money. But when the cheat was found out, the king was so incensed at it, that he banished him from court, and took away his command, though he was an excellent soldier, and a man of great courage. For when he was but a youth, and served under Philip at the siege of Perinthus, where he was wounded in the eye by an arrow shot out of an engine, he would neither let the arrow be taken out, nor be persuaded to quit the field, till he had bravely repulsed the enemy and forced them to retire into the town. Accordingly he was not able to support such a disgrace with any patience, and it was plain that grief and despair would have made him kill himself, but that the king fearing it, not only pardoned him, but let him also enjoy the benefit of his deceit.

The thirty thousand boys whom he left behind him to be taught and disciplined, were so improved at his return, both in strength and beauty, and performed their exercises with such dexterity and wonderful agility, that he was extremely pleased with them, which grieved the Macedonians, and made them fear he would have the less value for them. And when he proceeded to send down the infirm and maimed soldiers to the sea, they said they were unjustly and infamously dealt with, after they were worn out in his service upon all occasions, now to be turned away with disgrace and sent home into their country among their friends and relations, in a worse condition than when they came out; therefore they desired him to dismiss them one and all, and to account his Macedonians useless, now he was so well furnished with a set of advancing boys, with whom, if he pleased, he might go on and conquer the world. These speeches so incensed Alexander, that after he had given them a great deal of reproachful language in his passion, he drove them away, and committed the watch to Persians, out of whom he chose his guards and attendants. When the Mace-

donians saw him escorted by these men, and themselves excluded and shamefully disgraced, their high spirits fell, and conferring with one another, they found that jealousy and rage had almost distracted them. But at last coming to themselves again, they went without their arms, with only their undergarments on, crying and weeping, to offer themselves at his tent, and desired him to deal with them as their baseness and ingratitude deserved. However, this would not prevail; for though his anger was already somewhat mollified, yet he would not admit them into his presence, nor would they stir from thence, but continued two days and nights before his tent, bewailing themselves, and imploring him as their lord to have compassion on them. But the third day he came out to them, and seeing them very humble and penitent, he wept himself a great while, and after a gentle reproof spoke kindly to them, and dismissed those who were unserviceable with magnificent rewards, and with this recommendation to Antipater, that when they came home, at all public shows and in the theatres, they should sit on the best and foremost seats, crowned with chaplets of flowers. He ordered, also, that the children of those who had lost their lives in his service, should have their fathers' pay continued to them.

• • •

As he was upon his way to Babylon, Nearchus, who had sailed back out of the ocean up the mouth of the river Euphrates, came to tell him he had met with some Chaldaean diviners, who had warned him against Alexander's going thither. Alexander, however, took no thought of it, and went on, and when he came near the walls of the place, he saw a great many crows fighting with one another, some of whom fell down just by him. After this, being privately informed that Apollodorus, the governor of Babylon, had sacrificed, to know what would become of him, he sent for Pythagoras, the soothsayer, and on his admitting the thing, asked him, in what condition he found the victim; and when he told him the liver was defective in its lobe, "A great presage indeed!" said Alexander. However, he offered Pythagoras no injury, but was sorry that he had neglected Nearchus's advice, and stayed for the most part outside the town, removing his tent from place to place, and sailing up and down the Euphrates. Besides this, he was disturbed by many other prodigies. A tame ass fell upon the biggest and handsomest lion that he kept, and killed him by a kick. And one day after he had undressed himself to be anointed, and was playing at ball, just as they were going to bring his clothes again, the young men who played with him perceived a man clad in the king's robes, with a diadem upon his head, sitting silently upon his throne. They asked him who he was, to which he gave no answer a good while, till at last coming to himself, he told them his name was Dionysius, that he was of Messenia, that for some crime of which he was accused, he was brought thither from the sea-side, and had been kept long in prison, that Serapis appeared to him, had freed him from his chains, con-

ducted him to that place, and commanded him to put on the king's robe and diadem, and to sit where they found him, and to say nothing. Alexander, when he heard this, by the direction of his soothsayers, put the fellow to death, but he lost his spirits, and grew diffident of the protection and assistance of the gods, and suspicious of his friends. His greatest apprehension was of Antipater and his sons, one of whom, Iolaus, was his chief cupbearer; and Cassander, who had lately arrived, and had been bred up in Greek manners, the first time he saw some of the barbarians adore the king, could not forbear laughing at it aloud, which so incensed Alexander, that he took him by the hair with both hands, and dashed his head against the wall. Another time, Cassander would have said something in defence of Antipater to those who accused him, but Alexander interrupting him, said, "What is it you say? Do you think people, if they had received no injury, would come such a journey only to calumniate your father?" To which when Cassander replied, that their coming so far from the evidence was a great proof of the falseness of their charges, Alexander smiled, and said those were some of Aristotle's sophisms, which would serve equally on both sides; and added, that both he and his father should be severely punished, if they were found guilty of the least injustice towards those who complained. All which made such a deep impression of terror in Cassander's mind, that long after, when he was king of Macedonia, and master of Greece, as he was walking up and down at Delphi, and looking at the statues, at the sight of that of Alexander he was suddenly struck with alarm, and shook all over, his eyes rolled, his head grew dizzy, and it was long before he recovered himself.

When once Alexander had given way to fears of supernatural influence, his mind grew so disturbed and so easily alarmed, that if the least unusual or extraordinary thing happened, he thought it a prodigy or a presage, and his court was thronged with diviners and priests whose business was to sacrifice and purify and foretell the future. So miserable a thing is incredulity and contempt of divine power on the one hand, and so miserable, also, superstition on the other, which like water, where the level has been lowered, flowing in and never stopping, fills the mind with slavish fears and follies, as now in Alexander's case. But upon some answers which were brought him from the oracle concerning Hephaestion, he laid aside his sorrow, and fell again to sacrificing and drinking, and having given Nearchus a splendid entertainment, after he had bathed, as was his custom, just as he was going to bed, at Medius's request he went to supper with him. Here he drank all the next day, and was attacked with a fever, which seized him, not as some write, after he had drunk of the bowl of Hercules; nor was he taken with any sudden pain in his back, as if he had been struck with a lance, for these are the inventions of some authors who thought it their duty to make the last scene of so great an action as tragical and moving as they could. Aristobulus tells us, that in the rage of his fever and a violent thirst, he took a draught of wine upon which he fell into delirium, and died on the thirtieth day of the month Daesius.

But the journals give the following record. On the eighteenth of the month, he slept in the bathing-room on account of his fever. The next day he bathed and removed into his chamber, and spent his time in playing at dice with Medius. In the evening he bathed and sacrificed, and ate freely, and had the fever on him through the night. On the twentieth, after the usual sacrifices and bathing, he lay in the bathing-room and heard Nearchus's narrative of his voyage, and the observations he had made in the great sea. The twenty-first he passed in the same manner, his fever still increasing, and suffered much during the night. The next day the fever was very violent, and he had himself removed and his bed set by the great bath, and discoursed with his principal officers about finding fit men to fill up the vacant places in the army. On the twenty-fourth he was much worse, and was carried out of his bed to assist at the sacrifices, and gave order that the general officers should wait within the court, while the inferior officers kept watch without doors. On the twenty-fifth he was removed to his palace on the other side of the river, where he slept a little, but his fever did not abate, and when the generals came into his chamber, he was speechless, and continued so the following day. The Macedonians, therefore, supposing he was dead, came with great clamors to the gates, and menaced his friends so that they were forced to admit them, and let them pass through unarmed along by his bedside. The same day Python and Seleucus were despatched to the temple of Serapis to inquire if they should bring Alexander thither, and were answered by the god, that they should not remove him. On the twenty-eighth, in the evening, he died. This account is most of it word for word as it is written in the diary.

A conjectural restoration of Imperial Rome (*Culver Pictures, Inc.*)

ROME

One historian of classical civilization has stated flatly, "Far and away the most important and frequent events in ancient history are wars."[1] As we have seen, two of the great classical historians chose war as their theme—Herodotus with his description of the conflict between the Greeks and the Persians, and Thucydides with his analysis of the struggle of Greek against Greek in the Peloponnesian War. The inter-Greek wars were ended only by conquest from the north and the beginnings of the spectacular military career of Alexander the Great of Macedonia. While all these wars were occupying the attention of the eastern Mediterranean world, to the west another mighty military machine was being forged, a machine that was to sweep out from its homeland to conquer the civilized world. By 338 B.C., two years before the accession of Alexander, the first major step on the long road to empire had been taken by a city-state on the Tiber River known as Rome. Rome had conquered her Latin neighbors and incorporated them into the Roman state.

In the succeeding three hundred years, Rome enjoyed the most sustained series of military triumphs the world had ever seen. By 265 B.C., she had extended her rule over most of the Italian peninsula; by about 200 B.C., she had brought most of Spain, the rest of Italy, and Sicily, Corsica, and Sardinia under her dominion; during the next hundred years she conquered southern Gaul, the rest of Spain, parts of North Africa, Macedonia, Greece, and about half of Asia Minor; and by the time of the birth of Jesus, the rest of Asia Minor, Syria, Egypt, most of North Africa, and all of Gaul had been added to the Roman tribute lists. Of course, these remarkable conquests were not carried out without occasional reverses and defeats. Hannibal's invasion and occupation of the Italian peninsula from 218 B.C. to 203 B.C. was the most serious reversal. But, though Hannibal's success pointed to certain Roman weaknesses, it revealed the sources of Roman strength as well.

The long road to empire was engineered and paved by the Roman army. Seldom has there been a finer military machine than the one developed by the Republic of Rome. Quite early, Rome transformed her armed forces from an ill-trained mob into a professional, highly trained, rigorously disciplined body of citizen-soldiers who could be used at great distances from Rome and

---

[1] Michael Grant, *Ancient History* (London: Methuen & Co., Ltd., 1952), p. 128.

who served for long periods of time. The weapons of the Roman soldier were superior to those of his opponents, particularly after the adoption of a short cut-and-thrust sword which made him especially effective in close combat. The fundamental unit of the Roman army was the legion, an adaptation of the successful Macedonian phalanx. In its final form, the legion was composed of three thousand heavily armed infantrymen, all so dedicated to the honor and the reputation of the legion that the defeat of the legion or the loss of its eagles constituted an unthinkable disgrace. Reinforcing their devotion to the legion was a deep-seated loyalty to Rome.

Somehow the Romans managed to instill this devotion to Rome even into the peoples they conquered, and Roman citizenship became highly prized and eagerly sought. The leaders of the Roman Republic wisely offered the allies and former enemies of Rome a limited citizenship, with the possibility of full citizenship later on. Thus, all shared the hope of being able to say "*Civis Romanus sum*"—I am a Roman citizen. What a powerful phrase! The man who could say that was protected by the fear of the Roman law and of Roman justice; he shared in the glory that was Rome and the triumphs that were Roman; he contributed to the governance of the worldwide empire, for he could vote in its elections, serve in its courts, and act as an official in its administration.

If military success was a glory of the Roman Empire, it was also a curse. The creation of a world empire led to the creation of an imperial organization— an organization that the republican city-state of Rome was incapable of maintaining without undergoing violent internal change. The peasant-soldiers began to grumble over being kept away from the land year after year; the military leaders became too accustomed to commanding obedience; the mother-city became too used to triumph and success. All contributed to the final disappearance of the Republic. The citizen's loyalty to his legion and to the Republic was transformed into loyalty to his commander, and the legions became private armies. Plutarch may have admired his Caesar, but only because Caesar sought to restore political order to the chaos that had developed in the last century of the Roman Republic. The disappearance of the small landowner, the development of a wealthy class, corruption in government administration, and the evolution of a complex bureaucracy to administer the empire were all factors in the disintegration of the old system and the emergence of the Roman Empire.

The concept of empire—and of emperor—took several generations to emerge fully. But it was clearly present when Augustus took the title *princeps* (first citizen), even though he continued the fiction of republican rule after his triumph over both the Senate and the assassins of Julius Caesar. Happily for Rome, Augustus and his successor, Tiberius, were talented and powerful enough to resolve the civil difficulties and to stabilize the administration so that Rome was able to withstand the abuse and corruption of the regimes that followed. Not even madness, frivolity, and palace intrigue could disturb the quiet workings of the Empire—the civil administration functioned smoothly, the army maintained the peace, commerce was active, and industry continued prosperous. The *Pax Romana* lasted two hundred years, during which time the civilized world enjoyed a new freedom from the perennial warfare of the ancient world.

During these centuries of peace Roman civilization achieved the heights of its glory. Its accomplishments in architecture have rarely been matched. Recognizing the arch (which the Greeks had not appreciated) as a thing of beauty as well as utility, the Romans were able to bridge wide rivers, to supply the vast city of Rome with water from far-off hills and mountains, and to erect the Colosseum, which seated nearly fifty thousand spectators at the gladiatorial games and contests. The realistic portrait sculpture of the Romans has never been equaled. Perhaps this excellence was a reflection of the practical, hard, peasant virtues of the Roman citizen. But the greatest triumphs of Roman civilization lay not in art, architecture, literature, or speculative thought, but in the realm of the practical and the everyday. Law, military order, and civil administration were the accomplishments that were most truly Roman. And these three most clearly reveal the Roman genius—the desire for order and efficiency and the ability to attain them. This desire, together with the Roman dedication to duty, right, state, and honor, is manifest in the works of the philosopher Cicero.

The Roman world made its greatest contribution to Western civilization almost inadvertently, when an obscure province under Roman rule produced the man Jesus. Although his life and teachings have inspired millions in succeeding ages, Jesus himself would undoubtedly have questioned the organization that grew up to spread his beliefs. The first two centuries after Christ were a time of peace and tranquility, but also a time in which the common man felt lost and devoid of spiritual comfort. The Christian faith proffered security and balm for the difficulties of this world and salvation in the next. And as the faith spread, the Roman genius for order and efficiency again manifested itself; for the growing Church, with its increasingly complex activities, modeled its organization on that of the civil administration. Bishops established cathedrals in provincial urban centers, and local churches were set up in the smaller cities and towns. The capstone to this structure was natural, obvious, and logical: the bishop of Rome was to head the Church just as the emperor led the Empire.

But Rome could not solve the problems of world dominion. The Empire had stabilized the regime created by the Republic, but it had been unable to develop a solution to the basic problems raised by empire. How could a state maintain a great army without being dominated by it? Or, a different problem, how could a city-state maintain a very large army of citizen-soldiers without extending citizenship to them? And if citizenship were extended, how could it instill in these citizens the same dedication and devotion found in the native Roman? Whatever the problems were and whatever solutions to them hindsight might offer, one thing at least remains: the history and glory of Rome lasted over eight hundred years, a long time indeed in the recorded history of civilization.

Polybius

Any eyewitness account of an event has intrinsic value. When the witness is a person of intellectual and emotional detachment, his account is likely to be much more rewarding. Substance is added to the narrative, too, when the observer is a man with analytical powers of the first order. Such a person was the Greek historian Polybius, who continued the great tradition of Herodotus and Thucydides.

Polybius (c. 205–123 B.C.) was brilliantly equipped to write the history of his time, for he had had a literary education and was widely experienced in affairs of state. A leader in the Achaean League, a group of Greek city-states that were attempting to retain a measure of political autonomy in the face of Roman expansion into the Eastern Mediterranean, he favored a policy of cooperation with the Romans, even offering to lead a group of cavalry from his own city-state of Megalopolis in support of their campaign against Macedonia. When, however, the Roman legions had succeeded in conquering the Macedon-

ians, they turned their attention to the Achaean League cities to the south, quickly subduing them. To assure their political dominance of the area, they transported one thousand leading Achaeans, including Polybius, to Italy as hostages. Retired forcibly from an active public life, Polybius turned to writing his *Histories*. Through the intervention of a friend, he was able to spend most of his sixteen years of exile in Rome, where he could examine original documents and observe the workings of the Roman government at first hand. His circle of friends included many of the most powerful men of the time. In 150 B.C. he was permitted to return to Greece, where he bent all his efforts toward creating an atmosphere of understanding between the Greeks and the Romans. Polybius died at the age of eight-two, after falling from a horse.

The following selection reflects his experiences and observations while in Rome. Taken from Book VI of the *Histories*, it is, as Polybius says, "a disquisition on the Roman constitution."

The Histories

Preface

1. I am aware that some will be at a loss to account for my interrupting the course of my narrative for the sake of entering upon the following disquisition on the Roman constitution. But I think that I have already in many passages made it fully evident that this particular branch of my work was one of the necessities imposed on me by the nature of my original design; and I pointed this out with special clearness in the preface which explained the scope of my history. I there stated that the feature of my work which was at once the best in itself, and the most instructive to the students of it, was that it would enable them to know and fully realise in what manner, and under what kind of constitution, it came about that nearly the whole world fell under the power of Rome in somewhat less than fifty-three years—an event certainly without precedent. This being my settled purpose, I could see no more fitting period than the present for making a pause, and examining the truth of the remarks about to be made on this constitution. In private life if you wish to satisfy yourself as to the badness or goodness of particular persons, you would not, if you wish to get a genuine test, examine their conduct as a time of uneventful repose, but in the hour of brilliant success or conspicuous reverse. For the true test of a perfect man is the power of bearing with spirit and dignity violent changes of fortune. An examination of a constitution should be conducted in the same way: and therefore being unable to find in our day a more rapid or more signal change than that which has happened to Rome, I reserve my disquisition on its constitution for this place. . . .

What is really educational and beneficial to students of history is the clear view of the causes of events, and the consequent power of choosing the better policy in a particular case. Now in every practical undertaking by a state we must regard as the most powerful agent for success or failure the form of its constitution; for from this as from a fountainhead all conceptions and plans of action not only proceed, but attain their consummation. . . .

• • •

3. Of the Greek republics, which have again and again risen to greatness and fallen into insignificance, it is not difficult to speak, whether we recount their past history or venture an opinion on their future. For to report what is already known is an easy task, nor is it hard to guess what is to come from our knowledge of what has been. But in regard to the Romans it is neither an easy matter to describe their present state, owing to the complexity of their constitution; nor to speak with confidence of their future, from our

The Histories of Polybius, trans. Evelyn S. Shuckburgh.

inadequate acquaintance with their peculiar institutions in the past whether affecting their public or private life. It will require then no ordinary attention and study to get a clear and comprehensive conception of the distinctive features of this constitution.

Now, it is undoubtedly the case that most of those who profess to give us authoritative instruction on this subject distinguish three kinds of constitutions, which they designate *kingship, aristocracy, democracy.* But in my opinion the question may be fairly put to them, whether they name these as being the *only* ones, or as the best. In either case I think they are wrong. For it is plain that we must regard as the *best* constitution that which partakes of all these three elements. And this is no mere assertion, but has been proved by the example of Lycurgus, who was the first to construct a constitution—that of Sparta—on this principle. Nor can we admit that these are the only forms: for we have had before now examples of absolute and tyrannical forms of government, which, while differing as widely as possible from kingship, yet appear to have some points of resemblance to it; on which account all absolute rulers falsely assume and use, as far as they can, the title of king. Again there have been many instances of oligarchical governments having in appearance some analogy to aristocracies, which are, if I may say so, as different from them as it is possible to be. The same also holds good about democracy.

. . .

11. . . .I will now endeavour to describe [the constitution] of Rome at the period of their disastrous defeat at Cannae [in 216 B.C.]. . . .

As for the Roman constitution, it had three elements, each of them possessing sovereign powers: and their respective share of power in the whole state had been regulated with such a scrupulous regard to equality and equilibrium, that no one could say for certain, not even a native, whether the constitution as a whole were an aristocracy or democracy or despotism. And no wonder: for if we confine our observation to the power of the Consuls we should be inclined to regard it as despotic; if on that of the Senate, as aristocratic; and if finally one looks at the power possessed by the people it would seem a clear case of democracy. What the exact powers of these several parts were, and still, with slight modifications, are, I will now state.

12. The Consuls, before leading out the legions, remain in Rome and are supreme masters of the administration. All other magistrates, except the Tribunes, are under them and take their orders. They introduce foreign ambassadors to the Senate; bring matters requiring deliberation before it; and see to the execution of its decrees. If, again, there are any matters of state which require the authorisation of the people, it is their business to see to them, to summon the popular meetings, to bring the proposals before them, and to carry out the decrees of the majority. In the preparations for war, also, and in a word in the entire administration of a campaign, they have all but absolute power. It is competent to them to impose on the allies such levies as they think good, to appoint the Military Tribunes, to make up the

roll for soldiers and select those that are suitable. Besides they have absolute power of inflicting punishment on all who are under their command while on active service: and they have authority to expend as much of the public money as they choose, being accompanied by a quaestor who is entirely at their orders. A survey of these powers would in fact justify our describing the constitution as despotic,—a clear case of royal government. Nor will it affect the truth of my description, if any of the institutions I have described are changed in our time, or in that of our posterity: and the same remarks apply to what follows.

13. The Senate has first of all the control of the treasury, and regulates the receipts and disbursements alike. For the Quaestors cannot issue any public money for the various departments of the state without a decree of the Senate, except for the service of the Consuls. The Senate controls also what is by far the largest and most important expenditure, that, namely, which is made by the censors every lustrum for the repair or construction of public buildings; this money cannot be obtained by the censors except by the grant of the Senate. Similarly all crimes committed in Italy requiring a public investigation, such as treason, conspiracy, poisoning, or wilful murder, are in the hands of the Senate. Besides, if any individual or state among the Italian allies requires a controversy to be settled, a penalty to be assessed, help or protection to be afforded,—all this is the province of the Senate. Or again, outside Italy, if it is necessary to send an embassy to reconcile warring communities, or to remind them of their duty, or sometimes to impose requisitions upon them, or to receive their submission, or finally to proclaim war against them,—this too is the business of the Senate. In like manner the reception to be given foreign ambassadors in Rome, and the answers to be returned to them, are decided by the Senate. With such business the people have nothing to do. Consequently, if one were staying at Rome when the Consuls were not in town, one would imagine the constitution to be a complete aristocracy: and this has been the idea entertained by many Greeks, and by many kings as well, from the fact that nearly all the business they had to do with Rome was settled by the Senate.

14. After this one would naturally be inclined to ask what part is left for the people in the constitution, when the Senate has these various functions, especially the control of the receipts and expenditure of the exchequer; and when the Consuls, again, have absolute power over the details of military preparation, and an absolute authority in the field? There is, however, a part left the people, and it is a most important one. For the people is the sole fountain of honour and of punishment; and it is by these two things and these alone that dynasties and constitutions and, in a word, human society are held together: for where the distinction between them is not sharply drawn both in theory and practice, there no undertaking can be properly administered,—as indeed we might expect when good and bad are held in exactly the same honour. The people then is the only court to decide matters of life and death; and even in cases where the

penalty is money, if the sum to be assessed is sufficiently serious, and especially when the accused have held the higher magistracies. And in regard to this arrangement there is one point deserving especial commendation and record. Men who are on trial for their lives at Rome, while sentence is in process of being voted,—if even only one of the tribes whose votes are needed to ratify the sentence has not voted,— have the privilege at Rome of openly departing and condemning themselves to a voluntary exile. Such men are safe at Naples or Praeneste or at Tibur, and at other towns with which this arrangement has been duly ratified on oath.

Again, it is the people who bestow offices on the deserving, which are the most honourable rewards of virtue. It has also the absolute power of passing or repealing laws; and, most important of all, it is the people who deliberate on the question of peace and war. And when provisional terms are made for alliance, suspension of hostilities, or treaties, it is the people who ratify them or the reverse.

These considerations again would lead one to say that the chief power in the state was the people's, and that the constitution was a democracy.

15. Such, then, is the distribution of power between the several parts of the state. I must now show how each of these several parts can, when they choose, oppose or support each other.

The Consul, then, when he has started on an expedition with the powers I have described, is to all appearance absolute in the administration of the business in hand; still he has need of the support both of people and Senate, and, without them, is quite unable to bring the matter to a successful conclusion. For it is plain that he must have supplies sent to his legions from time to time; but without a decree of the Senate they can be supplied neither with corn, nor clothes, nor pay, so that all the plans of a commander must be futile, if the Senate is resolved either to shrink from danger or hamper his plans. And again, whether a Consul shall bring any undertaking to a conclusion or no depends entirely on the Senate: for it has absolute authority at the end of a year to send another Consul to supersede him, or to continue the existing one in his command. Again, even to the successes of the generals, the Senate has the power to add distinction and glory, and on the other hand to obscure their merits and lower their credit. For these high achievements are brought in tangible form before the eyes of the citizens by what are called "triumphs." But in these triumphs the commanders cannot celebrate with proper pomp, or in some cases celebrate at all, unless the Senate concurs and grants the necessary money. As for the people, the Consuls are pre-eminently obliged to court their favour, however distant from home may be the field of their operations; for it is the people, as I have said before, that ratifies, or refuses to ratify, terms of peace and treaties; but most of all because when laying down their office they have to give account of their administration before it. Therefore in no case is it safe for the Consuls to neglect either the Senate or the goodwill of the people.

16. As for the Senate, which possesses the immense power I have

neglect either the Senate or the goodwill of the people.

16. As for the Senate, which possesses the immense power I have described, in the first place it is obliged in public affairs to take the multitude into account, and respect the wishes of the people; and it cannot put into execution the penalty for offences against the republic, which are punishable with death, unless the people first ratifies its decrees. Similarly even in matters which directly affect the senators,— for instance, in the case of a law depriving senators of certain dignities and offices, or even actually cutting down their property,—even in such cases the people has the sole power of passing or rejecting the law. But most important of all is the fact that, if the Tribunes interpose their veto, the Senate not only is unable to pass a decree, but cannot even hold a meeting at all, whether formal or informal. Now, the Tribunes are always bound to carry out the decree of the people, and above all things to have regard for their wishes: therefore, for all these reasons the Senate stands in awe of the multitude, and cannot neglect the feelings of the people.

17. In like manner the people on its part is far from being independent of the Senate, and is bound to take its wishes into account both collectively and individually. For contracts, too numerous to count, are given out by the censors in all parts of Italy, for the repairs or construction of public buildings; there is also the collection of revenue from many rivers, harbours, gardens, mines, and land—everything, in a word, that comes under the control of the Roman government: and in all these the people at large are engaged; so that there is scarcely a man, so to speak, who is not interested either as a contractor or as being employed in the works. For some purchase the contracts from the censors for themselves; and others go partners with them; while others again go security for these contractors, or actually pledge their property to the treasury for them. Now over all these transactions the Senate has absolute control. It can grant an extension of time; and in case of unforeseen accident can relieve the contractors from a portion of their obligation, or release them from it altogether, if they are absolutely unable to fill it. And there are many details in which the Senate can inflict great hardships, or, on the other hand, grant great indulgences to the contractors: for in every case the appeal is to it. But the most important point of all is that the judges are taken from its members in the majority of trials, whether public or private, in which the charges are heavy. Consequently, all citizens are much at its mercy; and being alarmed at the uncertainty as to when they may need its aid, are cautious about resisting or actively opposing its will. And for a similar reason men do not rashly resist the wishes of the Consuls, because one and all may become subject to their absolute authority on a campaign.

18. The result of this power of the several estates for mutual help or harm is a union sufficiently firm for all emergencies, and a constitution than which it is impossible to find a better. For whenever any danger from without compels them to unite and work together, the strength which is developed by the State is so extraordinary, that every-

to secure that any determination come to should not fail for want of promptitude; while each individual works, privately and publicly alike, for the accomplishment of the business in hand. Accordingly, the peculiar constitution of the State makes it irresistible, and certain of obtaining whatever it determines to attempt. Nay, even when these external alarms are past, and the people are enjoying their good fortune and the fruits of their victories, and, as usually happens, growing corrupted by flattery and idleness, show a tendency to violence and arrogance,—it is in these circumstances, more than ever, that the constitution is seen to possess within itself the power of correcting abuses. For when any one of the three classes becomes puffed up, and manifests an inclination to be contentious and unduly encroaching, the mutual interdependency of all the three, and the possibility of the pretentions of any one being checked and thwarted by the others, must plainly check this tendency: and so the proper equilibrium is maintained by the impulsiveness of the one part being checked by its fear of the other.

• • •

The Roman Republic Compared with Others

43. Nearly all historians have recorded as constitutions of eminent excellence those of Lacedaemonia, Crete, Mantinea, and Carthage. Some have also mentioned those of Athens and Thebes. The former I may allow to pass; but I am convinced that little need be said of the Athenian and Theban constitutions:

their growth was abnormal, the period of their zenith brief, and the changes they experienced unusually violent. Their glory was a sudden and fortuitous flash, so to speak; and while they still thought themselves prosperous, and likely to remain so, they found themselves involved in circumstances completely the reverse. The Thebans got their reputation for valour among the Greeks, by taking advantage of the senseless policy of the Lacedaemonians, and the hatred of the allies toward them, owing to the valour of one, or at most two, men who were wise enough to appreciate the situation. Since fortune quickly made it evident that it was not the peculiarity of their constitution, but the valour of their leaders, which gave the Thebans their success. For the great power of Thebes notoriously took its rise, attained its zenith, and fell to the ground with the lives of Epaminondas and Pelopidas. We must therefore conclude that it was not its constitution, but its men, that caused the high fortune which it then enjoyed.

44. A somewhat similar remark applies to the Athenian constitution also. For though it perhaps had more frequent interludes of excellence, yet its highest perfection was attained during the brilliant career of Themistocles; and having reached that point it quickly declined, owing to its essential instability. For the Athenian demus is always in the position of a ship without a commander. In such a ship, if fear of the enemy, or the occurrence of a storm induce the crew to be of one mind and to obey the helmsman, everything goes well; but if they recover from this fear, and begin to treat their officers with

contempt, and to quarrel with each other because they are no longer of one mind,—one party wishing to continue the voyage, and the other urging the steersman to bring the ship to anchor; some letting out the sheets, and others hauling them in, and ordering the sails to be furled,—their discord and quarrels make a sorry show to lookers-on; and the position of affairs is full of risk to those on board engaged in the same voyage: and the result has often been that, after escaping the dangers of the wildest seas, and the most violent storms, they wreck their ship in harbour and close to shore. And this is what has often happened to the Athenian constitution. For, after repelling, on various occasions, the greatest and most formidable dangers by the valour of its people and their leaders, there have been times when, in periods of secure tranquillity, it has gratuitously and recklessly encountered disaster. Therefore I need say no more about either it, or the Theban constitution: in both of which a mob manages everything on its own unfettered impulse—a mob in the one city distinguished for headlong outburst of fiery temper, in the other trained in long habits of violence and ferocity.

45. Passing to the Cretan polity there are two points which deserve our consideration. The first is how such writers as Ephorus, Xenophon, Callisthenes and Plato—who are the most learned of the ancients—could assert that it was like that of Sparta; and secondly how they came to assert that it was at all admirable. I can agree with neither assertion; and I will explain why I say so. And first as to its dissimilarity with the Spartan constitution. The peculiar merit of the latter is said to be its land laws, by which no one possesses more than another, but all citizens have an equal share in the public land. The next distinctive feature regards the possession of money: for as it is utterly discredited among them, the jealous competition which arises from inequality of wealth is entirely removed from the city. A third peculiarity of the Lacedaemonian polity is that, of the officials by whose hands and with whose advice the whole government is conducted, the kings hold an hereditary office, while the members of the Gerusia are elected for life.

46. Among the Cretans the exact reverse of all these arrangements obtains. The laws allow them to possess as much land as they can get with no limitation whatever. Money is so highly valued among them, that its possession is not only thought to be necessary but in the highest degree creditable. And in fact greed and avarice are so native to the soil in Crete, that they are the only people in the world among whom no stigma attaches to any sort of gain whatever. Again all their offices are annual and on a democratic footing. I have therefore often felt at a loss to account for these writers speaking of the two constitutions, which are radically different, as though they were closely united and allied. But, besides overlooking these important differences, these writers have gone out of their way to comment at length on the legislation of Lycurgus: "He was the only important legislator," they say, "who saw the important points. For there being two things on which the safety of a commonwealth depends,—courage in the face of the enemy and con-

cord at home,—by abolishing covetousness, he with it removed all motive for civil broil and contest: whence it has been brought about that the Lacedaemonians are the best governed and most united people in Greece." Yet while giving utterance to these sentiments, and though they see that, in contrast to this, the Cretans by their ingrained avarice are engaged in countless public and private seditions, murders and civil wars, they yet regard these facts as not affecting their contention, but are bold enough to speak of the two constitutions as alike. Ephorus, indeed, putting aside names, employs expressions so precisely the same, when discoursing on the two constitutions, that, unless one noticed the proper names, there would be no means whatever of distinguishing which of the two he was describing.

47. In what the difference between them consists I have already stated. I will now address myself to showing that the Cretan constitution deserves neither praise nor imitation.

In my mind, then, there are two things fundamental to every state, in virtue of which its powers and constitution become desirable or objectionable. These are customs and laws. Of these the desirable are those which make men's private lives holy and pure, and the public character of the state civilised and just. The objectionable are those whose effect is the reverse. As, then, when we see good customs and good laws prevailing among certain people, we confidently assume that in consequence of them, the men and their civil constitution will be good also, so when we see private life full of covetousness, and public policy of injustice, plainly we have reason for asserting their laws, particular customs, and general constitution to be bad. Now, with few exceptions, you could find no habits prevailing in private life more steeped in treachery than those in Crete, and no public policy more inequitable. Holding, then, the Cretan constitution to be neither like the Spartan, nor worthy of choice or imitation, I reject it from the comparison which I have instituted.

Nor again would it be fair to introduce the Republic of Plato, which is also spoken of in high terms by some philosophers. For just as we refuse admission to the athletic contests to those actors or athletes who have not acquired a recognized position or trained for them, so we ought not to admit this Platonic constitution to the contest for the prize of merit unless it can first point to some genuine and practical achievement. Up to this time the notion of bringing it into comparison with the constitutions of Sparta, Rome, and Carthage would be like putting up a statue to compare with living and breathing men. Even if such a statue were faultless in point of art, the comparison of the lifeless with the living would naturally leave an impression of imperfection and incongruity upon the minds of the spectators.

48. I shall therefore omit these, and proceed with my description of the Laconian constitution. Now it seems to me that for securing unity among the citizens, for safeguarding the Laconian territory, and preserving the liberty of Sparta inviolate, the legislation and provisions of Lycurgus were so excellent, that I am forced to regard his wisdom as something superhuman. For the

equality of landed possessions, the simplicity in their food, and the practice of taking it in common, which he established, were well calculated to secure morality in private life and to prevent civil broils in the State; as also their training in the endurance of labours and dangers to make men brave and noble minded: but when both these virtues, courage and high morality, are combined in one soul or in one state, vice will not readily spring from such a soil, nor will such men easily be overcome by their enemies. By constructing his constitution therefore in this spirit, and of these elements, he secured two blessings to the Spartans—safety for their territory, and a lasting freedom for themselves after he was gone. He appears however to have made no one provision whatever, particular or general, for the acquisition of the territory of their neighbours; or for the assertion of their supremacy; or, in a word, for any policy of aggrandisement at all. What he had still to do was to impose such a necessity, or create such a spirit among the citizens, that, as he had succeeded in making their individual lives independent and simple, the public character of the state should also become independent and moral. But the actual fact is, that though he made them the most disinterested and sober-minded men in the world, as far as their own ways of life and their national institutions were concerned, he left them in regard to the rest of Greece ambitious, eager for supremacy, and encroaching in the highest degree.

49. For in the first place is it not notorious that they were the first Greeks to cast a covetous eye upon the territory of their neighbours,

and that accordingly they waged a war of subjugation on the Messenians? In the next place is it not related in all histories that in their dogged obstinacy they bound themselves with an oath never to desist from the siege of Messene until they had taken it? And lastly it is known to all that in their efforts for supremacy in Greece they submitted to do the bidding of those whom they had once conquered in war. For when the Persians invaded Greece, they conquered them, as champions of the liberty of the Greeks; yet when the invaders had retired and fled, they betrayed the cities of Greece into their hands by the peace of Antalcidas, for the sake of getting money to secure their supremacy over the Greeks. It was then that the defect in their constitution was rendered apparent. For as long as their ambition was confined to governing their immediate neighbours, or even the Peloponnesians only, they were content with the resources and supplies provided by Laconia itself, having all material of war ready to hand, and being able without much expenditure of time to return home or convey provisions with them. But directly they took in hand to despatch naval expeditions, or to go on campaigns by land outside the Peloponnese, it was evident that neither their iron currency, nor their use of crops for payment in kind, would be able to supply them with what they lacked if they abided by the legislation of Lycurgus; for such undertakings required money universally current, and goods from foreign countries. Thus they were compelled to wait humbly at Persian doors, impose tribute on the islanders, and exact contribution from all the Greeks:

knowing that, if they abided by the laws of Lycurgus, it was impossible to advance any claims upon any outside power at all, much less upon the supremacy in Greece.

50. My object, then, in this disgression is to make it manifest by actual fact that, for guarding their own country with absolute safety, and for preserving their own freedom, the legislation of Lycurgus was entirely sufficient; and for those who are content with these objects we must concede that there neither exists, nor ever has existed, a constitution and civil order preferable to that of Sparta. But if any one is seeking aggrandisement, and believes that to be a leader and ruler and despot of numerous subjects, and to have all looking and turning to him, is a finer thing than that,—in this point of view we must acknowledge that the Spartan constitution is deficient, and that of Rome superior and better constituted for obtaining power. And this has been proved by actual facts. For when the Lacedaemonians strove to possess themselves of the supremacy in Greece, it was not long before they brought their own freedom itself into danger. Whereas the Romans, after obtaining supreme power of the Italians themselves, soon brought the whole world under their rule,—in which achievement the abundance and availability of their supplies largely contributed to their success.

51. Now the Carthaginian constitution seems to me originally to have been well contrived in these most distinctively important particulars. For they had kings, and the Gerusia had the powers of an aristocracy, and the multitude were supreme in such things as affected them; and on the whole the adjustment of its several parts was very like that of Rome and Sparta. But about the period of its entering on the Hannibalian war the political state of Carthage was on the decline, that of Rome improving. For whereas there is in every body, or polity, or business a natural stage of growth, zenith, and decay; and whereas everything in them is best at the zenith; we may thereby judge of the difference between these two constitutions as they existed at that period. For exactly so far as the strength and prosperity of Carthage preceded that of Rome in point of time, by so much was Carthage then past its prime, while Rome was exactly at its zenith, as far as its political constituion was concerned. In Carthage therefore the influence of the people in the policy of the state had already risen to be supreme, while at Rome the Senate was at the height of its power: and so, as in the one measures were deliberated upon by the many, in the other by the best men, the policy of the Romans in all public undertakings proved the stronger; on which account, though they met with capital disasters, by force of prudent counsels they finally conquered the Carthaginians in the war.

52. If we look however at separate details, for instance at the provisions for carrying on a war, we shall find that whereas for a naval expedition the Carthaginians are the better trained and prepared,—as it is only natural with a people with whom it has been hereditary for many generations to practise this craft, and to follow the seaman's trade above all nations in the world,—yet, in regard to military service on land, the Romans train

themselves to a much higher pitch than the Carthaginians. The former bestow their whole attention upon this department: whereas the Carthaginians wholly neglect their infantry, though they do take some slight interest in the cavalry. The reason of this is that they employ foreign mercenaries, the Romans native and citizen levies. It is in this point that the latter policy is preferable to the former. They have their hopes of freedom ever resting on the courage of mercenary troops: the Romans on the valour of their own citizens and the aid of their allies. The result is that even if the Romans have suffered a defeat at first, they renew the war with undiminished forces, which the Carthaginians cannot do. For, as the Romans are fighting for country and children, it is impossible for them to relax the fury of their struggle; but they persist with obstinate resolution until they have overcome their enemies. What has happened in regard to their navy is an instance in point. In skill the Romans are much behind the Carthaginians, as I have already said; yet the upshot of the whole naval war has been a decided triumph for the Romans, owing to the valour of their men. For although nautical science contributes largely to success in seafights, still it is the courage of the marines that turns the scale most decisively in favour of victory. The fact is that Italians as a nation are by nature superior to Phoenicians and Libyans both in physical strength and courage; but still their habits also do much to inspire the youth with enthusiasm for such exploits. One example will be sufficient of the pains taken by the Roman state to turn out men ready to endure anything to win a reputation in their country for valour.

53. Whenever one of their illustrious men dies, in the course of his funeral, the body with all its paraphernalia is carried into the forum to the Rostra, as a raised platform there is called, and sometimes is propped upright upon it so as to be conspicuous, or, more rarely, is laid upon it. Then with all the people standing round, his son, if he has left one of full age and he is there, or, failing him, one of his relations, mounts the Rostra and delivers a speech concerning the virtues of the deceased, and the successful exploits performed by him in his lifetime. By these means the people are reminded of what has been done, and made to see it with their own eyes,—not only such as were engaged in the actual transactions but those also who were not;—and their sympathies are so deeply moved, that the loss appears not to be confined to the actual mourners, but to be a public one affecting the whole people. After the burial and all the usual ceremonies have been performed, they place the likeness of the deceased in the most conspicuous spot in his house, surmounted by a wooden canopy or shrine. This likeness consists of a mask made to represent the deceased with extraordinary fidelity both in shape and colour. These likenesses they display at public sacrifices adorned with much care. And when any illustrious member of the family dies, they carry these masks to the funeral, putting them on men whom they thought as like the originals as possible in height and other personal peculiarities. And these substitutes assume clothes according to the rank of the person represented;

if he was a consul or praetor, a toga with purple stripes; if a censor, whole purple; if he had also celebrated a triumph or performed any exploit of that kind, a toga embroidered with gold. These representatives also ride themselves in chariots, while the fasces and axes, and all the other customary insignia of the particular offices, lead the way, according to the dignity of the rank in the state enjoyed by the deceased in his lifetime; and on arriving at the Rostra they all take their seats on ivory chairs in their order. There could not easily be a more inspiring spectacle than this for a young man of noble ambitions and virtuous aspirations. For can we conceive any one to be unmoved at the sight of all the likenesses collected together of the men who have earned glory, all as it were living and breathing? Or what could be a more glorious spectacle?

54. Besides, the speaker over the body about to be buried, after having finished the panegyric of this particular person, starts upon the others whose representatives are present, beginning with the most ancient, and recounts the successes and achievements of each. By this means the glorious memory of brave men is continually renewed; the fame of those who have performed any noble deed is never allowed to die; and the renown of those who have done good service to their country becomes a matter of common knowledge to the multitude, and part of the heritage of posterity. But the chief benefit of the ceremony is that it inspires young men to shrink from no exertion for the general welfare, in the hope of obtaining the glory which awaits the brave. And what I

say is confirmed by this fact. Many Romans have volunteered to decide a whole battle by single combat; not a few have deliberately accepted certain death, some in time of war to secure the safety of the rest, some in time of peace to preserve the safety of the commonwealth. There have also been instances of men in office putting their own sons to death, in defiance of every custom and law, because they rated the interests of their country higher than those of natural ties even with their nearest and dearest. There are many stories of this kind, related of many men in Roman history; but one will be enough for our present purpose; and I will give the name as an instance to prove the truth of my words.

55. The story goes that Horatius Cocles, while fighting with two enemies at the head of the bridge over the Tiber, which is the entrance to the city on the north, seeing a large body of men advancing to support his enemies, and fearing that they would force their way into the city, turned round, and shouted to those behind him to hasten back to the other side and break down the bridge. They obeyed him: and whilst they were breaking the bridge, he remained at his post receiving numerous wounds, and checked the progress of the enemy: his opponents being panic stricken, not so much by his strength as by the audacity with which he held his ground. When the bridge had been broken down, the attack of the enemy was stopped; and Cocles then threw himself into the river with his armour on and deliberately sacrificed his life, because he valued the safety of his country and his own future reputation more highly

than his present life, and the years of existence that remained to him. Such is the enthusiasm and emulation for noble deeds that are engendered among the Romans by their customs.

56. Again the Roman customs and principles regarding money transactions are better than those of the Carthaginians. In the view of the latter nothing is disgraceful that makes for gain; with the former nothing is more disgraceful than to receive bribes and to make profit by improper means. For they regard wealth obtained from unlawful transactions to be as much a subject of reproach, as a fair profit from the most unquestioned source is of commendation. A proof of the fact is this. The Carthaginians obtain office by open bribery, but among the Romans the penalty for it is death. With such a radical difference, therefore, between the rewards offered to virtue among the two people, it is natural that the ways adopted for obtaining them should be different also.

But the most important difference for the better which the Roman commonwealth appears to me to display is in their religious beliefs. For I conceive that what in other nations is looked upon as a reproach, I mean a scrupulous fear of the gods, is the very thing which keeps the Roman Commonwealth together. To such an extraordinary height is this carried among them, both in private and public business, that nothing could exceed it. Many people might think this unaccountable; but in my opinion their object is to use it as a check upon the common people. If it were possible to form a state wholly of philosophers, such a custom would perhaps

be unnecessary. But seeing that every multitude is fickle, and full of lawless desires, unreasoning anger, and violent passion, the only resource is to keep them in check by mysterious terrors and scenic effects of this sort. Wherefore, to my mind, the ancients were not acting without purpose or at random, when they brought in among the vulgar those opinions about the gods, and the belief in the punishments in Hades: much rather do I think that men nowadays are acting rashly and foolishly in rejecting them. This is the reason why, apart from anything else, Greek statesmen, if entrusted with a single talent, though protected by ten checking-clerks, as many seals, and twice as many witnesses, yet cannot be induced to keep faith: whereas among the Romans, in their magistracies and embassies, men have the handling of a great amount of money, and yet from pure respect to their oath keep their faith intact. And, again, in other nations it is a rare thing to find a man who keeps his hands out of the public purse, and is entirely pure in such matters: but among the Romans it is a rare thing to detect a man in the act of committing such a crime. . . .

Recapitulation and Conclusion

57. That to all things, then, which exist there is ordained decay and change I think requires no further arguments to show: for the inexorable course of nature is sufficient to convince us of it.

But in all polities we observe two sources of decay existing from natural causes, the one external, the other internal and self-produced.

The external admits of no certain or fixed definition, but the internal follows a definite order. What kind of polity, then, comes naturally first, and what second, I have already stated in such a way, that those who are capable of taking in the whole drift of my argument can henceforth draw their own conclusions as to the future of the Roman polity. For it is quite clear, in my opinion. When a commonwealth, after warding off many great dangers, has arrived at a high pitch of prosperity and undisputed power, it is evident that, by the lengthened continuance of great wealth within it, the manner of life of its citizens will become more extravagant; and that the rivalry for office, and in other spheres of activity, will become fiercer than it ought to be. And as this state of things goes on more and more, the desire of office and the shame of losing reputation, as well as the ostentation and extravagance of living, will prove the beginning of a deterioration. And of this change the people will be credited with being the authors, when they become convinced that they are being cheated by some from avarice, and are puffed up with flattery by others from love of office. For when that comes about, in their passionate resentment and acting under the dictates of anger, they will refuse to obey any longer, or to be content with having equal powers with their leaders, but will demand to have all or far the greatest themselves. And when that comes to pass the constitution will receive a new name, which sounds better than any other in the world, liberty or democracy; but, in fact, it will become that worst of all governments, mob-rule.

Cicero

The philosophy of Stoicism, although it had been originated by Greeks, was carried to its full development by Romans. Indeed, it might well be called the "official" philosophy of classical Rome, for it numbered among its outstanding spokesmen such political leaders as the emperor Marcus Aurelius and the statesmen Seneca and Cicero. One might wonder that such men, engaged in practical politics, should find time for philosophizing; nevertheless, they must be credited with two contributions, both of great historical significance, to Stoic political and moral theory. The first of these is the doctrine of Natural Law: the theory that Nature (or the Universe), because it is the embodiment of an indwelling Reason, is governed by rational Laws and that people, being partakers of this universal Reason, are capable of discovering these Laws of Nature and ought, as rational beings, to live in accord with them. This doctrine, since its formulation by the Roman Stoics, has persisted as the dominant tradition in Western political theory, underlying the social structure of the Middle Ages and receiving its classic modern affirmation in the preamble to the American Declaration of Independence.

The second Roman contribution to Stoicism is the notion of "cosmopolitanism." The Law of Nature, being universal, stands above the edicts of any nation; hence individuals, whatever their nationality or status, are bound equally by this Law. As a rational being, everyone is "a citizen of the whole universe, considered as a single Commonwealth." Here the Roman philosophers made a complete break in theory from the political provincialism embodied in the traditional distinction between "Greek" and "barbarian," a break paralleling that in practice which the Roman Empire made from the political isolationism of the Greek city-state.

Cicero was one of the last political leaders of the Roman Republic, holding numerous offices in the government, including that of consul in 63 B.C. He was proscribed and executed in 43 B.C. by the Second Triumvirate. His dialogue *The Laws* is modeled after one of the same name written by Plato, whom he admired greatly. The three persons of the dialogue represent Cicero and his brothers, Marcus of course being Cicero himself. The selection included here is from Book I.

The Laws

MARCUS: The whole subject of universal law and jurisprudence must be comprehended in this discussion, in order that this which we call civil law, may be confined in some one small and narrow space of nature. For we shall have to explain the true nature of moral justice, which must be traced back from the nature of man. And laws will have to be considered by which all political states should be governed. And last of all, shall we have to speak of those laws and customs of nations which are framed for the use and convenience of particular countries (in which even our own people will not be omitted), which are known by the title of civil laws.

QUINTUS: You take a noble view of the subject, my brother, and go to the fountainhead, in order to throw light on the subject of our consideration; and those who treat civil law in any other manner, are not so much pointing out the paths of justice as those of litigation.

MARCUS: That is not quite the case, my Quintus. It is not so much the science of law that produces litigation, as the ignorance of it. But more of this by-and-by. At present let us examine the first principles of Right.

Now, many learned men have maintained that it springs from law. I hardly know if their opinion be not correct, at least according to their own definition; for "law," say they, "is the highest reason implanted in nature, which prescribes those things which ought to be done, and forbids the contrary." And when this same reason is confirmed and established in men's minds, it is then law.

They therefore conceive that prudence is a law, whose operation is to urge us to good actions, and restrain us from evil ones. And they think, too, that the Greek name for law, which is derived from the word, to distribute, implies the very nature of the thing, that is, to give every man his due. The Latin name, *lex*, conveys the idea of selections, *a legendo*. According to the Greeks, therefore, the name of law implies an equitable distribution: according to the Romans, an equitable selection. And, indeed, both characteristics belong peculiarly to law.

And if this be a correct statement, which it seems to me for the most part to be, then the origin of right is to be sought in the law. For this is the true energy of nature, this is the very soul and reason of a wise man, and the test of virtue and vice. But since all this discussion of ours relates to a subject, the terms of which are of frequent occurrence in the popular language of the citizens, we shall be sometimes obliged to use the same terms as the vulgar, and to call that law, which in its written enactments sanctions what it thinks fit by special commands or prohibitions.

Let us begin, then, to establish the principles of justice on that supreme law, which has existed from

Trans. C. D. Yonge.

all ages before any legislative enactments were drawn up in writing, or any political governments constituted.

QUINTUS: That will be more convenient, and more sensible with reference to the subject of the discussion which we have determined on.

MARCUS: Shall we, then, seek for the origin of justice at its fountainhead? when we have discovered which, we shall be in no doubt to what these questions which we are examining ought to be referred.

QUINTUS: Such is the course I would advise.

ATTICUS: I also subscribe to your brother's opinion.

MARCUS: Since, then, we wish to maintain and preserve the constitution of that republic which Scipio, in those six books which I have written under that title, has proved to be the best, and since all our laws are to be accommodated to the kind of political government there described, we must also treat of the general principles of morals and manners, and not limit ourselves on all occasions to written laws; but I purpose to trace back the origin of right from nature itself, who will be our best guide in conducting the whole discussion.

ATTICUS: You will do right, and when she is our guide it is absolutely impossible for us to err.

MARCUS: Do you then grant, my Atticus (for I know my brother's opinion already), that the entire universe is regulated by the power of the immortal Gods, that by their nature, reason, energy, mind, divinity, or some other word of clearer signification, if there be such, all things are governed and directed? for if you will not grant me this,

that is what I must begin by establishing.

ATTICUS: I grant you all you can desire. But owing to this singing of birds and babbling of water, I fear my fellow-learners can scarcely hear me.

MARCUS: You are quite right to be on your guard; for even the best men occasionally fall into a passion, and they will be very indignant if they hear you denying the first article of this notable book, entitled "The Chief Doctrines of Epicurus," in which he says "that God takes care of nothing, neither of himself nor of any other being!"

ATTICUS: Pray proceed, for I am waiting to know what advantage you mean to take of the concession I have made you.

MARCUS: I will not detain you long. This is the bearing which they have on our subject. This animal—prescient, sagacious, complex, acute, full of memory, reason, and counsel, which we call man—has been generated by the supreme God in a most transcendent condition. For he is the only creature among all the races and descriptions of animated beings who is endued with superior reason and thought, in which the rest are deficient. And what is there, I do not say in man alone, but in all heaven and earth, more divine than reason, which, when it becomes right and perfect, is justly termed wisdom?

There exists, therefore, since nothing is better than reason, and since this is the common property of God and man, a certain aboriginal rational intercourse between divine and human natures. But where reason is common, there right reason must also be common to the same parties; and since this right reason is what we call law, God and men must be considered as associated by law. Again, there must also be a communion of right where there is communion of law. And those who have law and right thus in common, must be considered members of the same commonwealth.

And if they are obedient to the same rule and the same authority, they are even much more so to this one celestial regency, this divine mind and omnipotent deity. So that the entire universe may be looked upon as forming one vast commonwealth of gods and men. And, as in earthly states certain ranks are distinguished with reference to the relationships of families, according to a certain principle which will be discussed in its proper place, that principle, in the nature of things, is far more magnificent and splendid by which men are connected with the Gods, as belonging to their kindred and nation.

For when we are reasoning on universal nature, we are accustomed to argue (and indeed the truth is just as it is stated in that argument) that in the long course of ages, and the uninterrupted succession of celestial revolutions, there arrived a certain ripe time for the sowing of the human race; and when it was sown and scattered over the earth, it was animated by the divine gift of souls. And as men retained from their terrestrial origin those other particulars by which they cohere together, which are frail and perishable, their immortal spirits were ingenerated by the Deity. From which circumstance it may be truly said, that we possess a certain consanguinity, and kindred, and fellowship with the heavenly powers. And

among all the varieties of animals, there is not one except man which retains any idea of the Divinity. And among men themselves, there is no nation so savage and ferocious as not to admit the necessity of believing in a God, however ignorant they may be what sort of God they ought to believe in. From whence we conclude that every man must recognise a Deity, who has any recollection and knowledge of his own origin.

Now, the law of virtue is the same in God and man, and in no other disposition besides them. This virtue is nothing else than a nature perfect in itself, and wrought up to the most consummate excellence. There exists, therefore, a similitude between God and man. And as this is the case, what connection can there be which concerns us more nearly, and is more certain?

Since, then, the Deity has been pleased to create and adorn man to be the chief and president of all terrestrial creatures, so it is evident, without further argument, that human nature has also made very great advances by its own intrinsic energy; that nature, which without any other instruction than her own, has developed the first rude principles of the understanding, and strengthened and perfected reason to all the appliances of science and art.

ATTICUS: Oh ye immortal Gods! to what a distance back are you tracing the principles of justice! However, you are discoursing in such a style that I will not show any impatience to hear what I expect you to say on the Civil Law. But I will listen patiently, even if you spend the whole day in this kind of discourse; for assuredly these, which perhaps you are embracing in your argument for the sake of others, are grander topics than even the subject itself for which they prepare the way.

MARCUS: You may well describe these topics as grand, which we are now briefly discussing. But of all the questions which are ever the subject of discussion among learned men, there is none which it is more important thoroughly to understand than this, that man is born for justice, and that law and equity have not been established by opinion, but by nature. This truth will become still more apparent if we investigate the nature of human association and society.

For there is no one thing so like or so equal to another, as in every instance man is to man. And if the corruption of customs, and the variation of opinions, did not induce an imbecility of minds, and turn them aside from the course of nature, no one would more nearly resemble than all men would resemble all men. Therefore, whatever definition we give of man, will be applicable to the whole human race. And this is a good argument that there is no dissimilarity of kind among men; because if this were the case, one definition could not include all men.

In fact, reason, which alone gives us so many advantages over beasts, by means of which we conjecture, argue, refute, discourse, and accomplish and conclude our designs, is assuredly common to all men; for the faculty of acquiring knowledge is similar in all human minds, though the knowledge itself may be endlessly diversified. By the same senses we all perceive the same objects, and those things which move the senses at all, do move in the same way the senses of all men. And those first rude elements of intelligence which, as I before observed, are the earliest developments of thought, are similarly impressed upon all men; and that faculty of speech which is the interpreter of the mind, agrees in the ideas which it conveys, though it may differ in the words by which it expresses them. And therefore there exists not a man in any nation, who, if he adopts nature for his guide, may not arrive at virtue.

Nor is this resemblance which all men bear to each other remarkable in those things only which are in accordance with right reason, but also in errors. For all men alike are captivated by pleasure, which, although it is a temptation to what is disgraceful, nevertheless bears some resemblance to natural good; for, as by its delicacy and sweetness it is delightful, it is through a mistake of the intellect adopted as something salutary.

And by error scarcely less universal, we shun death as if it were a dissolution of nature, and cling to life because it keeps us in that existence in which we were born. Thus, likewise, we consider pain as one of the greatest evils, not only on account of its present asperity, but also because it seems the precursor of mortality. Again, on account of the apparent resemblance between renown with honour, those men appear to us happy who are honoured, and miserable who happen to be inglorious. In like manner our minds are all similarly susceptible of inquietudes, joys, desires, and fears; nor if different men have different opinions, does it follow that those who deify dogs and cats, do not labour under superstition equally with other nations, though they may differ from them in the forms of its manifestation.

Again, what nation is there which has not a regard for kindness, benignity, gratitude, and mindfulness of benefits? What nation is there in which arrogance, malice, cruelty, and unthankfulness, are not reprobated and detested? And while this uniformity of opinions proves that the whole race of mankind is united together, the last point is that a system of living properly makes men better. If what I have said meets your approbation, I will proceed; or if any doubts occur to you, we had better clear them up first.

ATTICUS: There is nothing which strikes us, if I may reply for both of us.

MARCUS: It follows, then, that nature made us just that we might share our goods with each other, and supply each other's wants. You observe in this discussion, whenever I speak of nature, I mean nature in its genuine purity, but that there is, in fact, such corruption engendered by evil customs, that the sparks, as it were, of virtue which have been given by nature are extinguished, and that antagonist vices arise around it and become strengthened.

But if, as nature prompts them to, men would with deliberate judgments, in the words of the poet, "being men, think nothing that concerns mankind indifferent to them," then would justice be cultivated equally by all. For to those to whom nature has given reason, she has also given right reason, and therefore also law, which is nothing else than right reason enjoining what is good, and forbidding what is evil. And if nature has given us law, she hath also given us right. But she has

bestowed reason on all, therefore right has been bestowed on all. And therefore did Socrates deservedly execrate the man who first drew a distinction between utility and nature, for he used to complain that this error was the source of all human vices, to which this sentence of Pythagoras refers—"The things belonging to friends are common"—and that other, "Friendly equality." From whence it appears, that when a wise man has displayed this benevolence which is so extensively and widely diffused towards one who is endowed with equal virtue, then that phenomenon takes place which is altogether incredible to some people, but which is a necessary consequence, that he loves himself not more dearly than he loves his friends. For how can a difference of interests arise where all interests are similar? If there could be ever so minute a difference of interests, then there would be an end of even the nature of friendship, the real meaning of which is such, that there is no friendship at all the moment that a person prefers anything happening to himself rather than to his friend.

Now, these preliminary remarks have been put forward as a preparation for the rest of our discourse and argument, in order that you may more easily understand that nature herself is the foundation of justice. And when I have explained this a little more at large, then I will proceed to the consideration of that civil law from which all these arguments of mine are derived.

QUINTUS: Then you have not much to add, my brother, for the arguments you have already used have sufficiently proved to Atticus, or at all events to me, that nature is the fountain of justice. . . .

•   •   •

MARCUS: It is therefore an absurd extravagance in some philosophers to assert, that all things are necessarily just which are established by the civil laws and the institutions of nations. Are then the laws of tyrants just, simply because they are laws? Suppose the thirty tyrants of Athens had imposed certain laws on the Athenians? or suppose again that these Athenians were delighted with these tyrannical laws, would these laws on that account have been considered just? For my own part, I do not think such laws deserve any greater estimation than that passed during our own interregnum, which ordained that the dictator should be empowered to put to death with impunity whatever citizens he pleased, without hearing them in their own defence.

For there is but one essential justice which cements society, and one law which establishes this justice. This law is right reason, which is the true rule of all commandments and prohibitions. Whoever neglects this law, whether written or unwritten, is necessarily unjust and wicked.

But if justice consists in submission to written laws and national customs, and if, as the same school affirms, everything must be measured by utility alone, he who thinks that such conduct will be advantageous to him will neglect the laws, and break them if it is in his power. And the consequence is, that real justice has really no existence if it have not one by nature, and if that which is established as such on account of utility is overturned by some other utility.

But if nature does not ratify law, then all the virtues may lose their sway. For what becomes of generosity, patriotism, or friendship? Where will the desire of benefitting our neighbours, or the gratitude that acknowledges kindness, be able to exist at all? For all these virtues proceed from our natural inclination to love mankind. And this is the true basis of justice, and without this not only the mutual charities of men, but the religious services of the Gods, would be at an end; for these are preserved, as I imagine, rather by the natural sympathy which subsists between divine and human beings, than by mere fear and timidity.

But if the will of the people, the decrees of the senate, the adjudications of magistrates, were sufficient to establish rights, then it might become right to rob, right to commit adultery, right to substitute forged wills, if such conduct were sanctioned by the votes or decrees of the multitude. But if the opinions and suffrages of foolish men had sufficient weight to out-balance the nature of things, then why should they not determine among them, that what is essentially bad and pernicious should henceforth pass for good and beneficial? Or why, since law can make right out of injustice, should it not also be able to change evil into good?

But we have no other rule by which we may be capable of distinguishing between a good or a bad law than that of nature. Nor is it only right and wrong which are discriminated by nature, but generally all that is honourable is by this means distinguished from all that is shameful; for common sense has impressed in our minds the first principles of things, and has given us a general acquaintance with them; by which we connect with virtue every honourable quality, and with vice all that is disgraceful.

But to think that these differences exist only in opinion, and not in nature, is the part of an idiot. For even the virtue of a tree or a horse, in which expression there is an abuse of terms, does not exist in our opinion only, but in nature; and if that is the case, then what is honourable and disgraceful must also be discriminated by nature.

For if opinion could determine respecting the character of universal virtue, it might also decide respecting particular or partial virtues. But who will dare to determine that a man is prudent and cautious, not from his general conduct, but from some external appearances? For virtue evidently consists in perfect reason, and this certainly resides in nature. Therefore so does all honour and honesty in the same way.

For as what is true and false, creditable and discreditable, is judged of rather by their essential qualities than their external relations, so the consistent and perpetual course of life, which is virtue, and the inconsistency of life, which is vice, are judged of according to their own nature—and that inconstancy must necessarily be vicious.

We form an estimate of the opinions of youths, but not by their opinions. Those virtues and vices which reside in their moral natures must not be measured by opinions. And so of all moral qualities, we must discriminate between honour-

able and dishonourable by reference to the essential nature of the things themselves.

The good we commend, must needs contain in itself something commendable; for as I before stated, goodness is not a mode of opinion, but of nature. For if it were otherwise, opinion alone might constitute virtue and happiness, which is the most absurd of suppositions. And since we judge of good and evil by their nature, and since good and evil are the first principles of nature, certainly we should judge in the same manner of all honourable and all shameful things, referring them all to the law of nature.

But we are often too much disturbed by the dissensions of men and the variation of opinions. And because the same thing does not happen with reference to our senses, we look upon them as certain by nature. Those objects indeed, which sometimes present to us one appearance, sometimes another, and which do not always appear to the same people in the same way, we term fictions of the senses; but it is far otherwise. For neither parent, nor nurse, nor master, nor poet, nor drama, deceive our senses; nor do popular prejudices seduce them from the truth. But all kinds of snares are laid for the mind, either by those errors which I have just enumerated, which, taking possession of the young and uneducated, imbue them deeply, and bend them any way they please; or by that pleasure which is the imitator of goodness, being thoroughly and closely implicated with all our senses—the prolific mother of all evils. For she so corrupts us by her blandishments, that we no longer perceive some things which are essentially excellent because they have none of this deliciousness and pruriency.

It follows that I may now sum up the whole of this argument by asserting, as is plain to every one from these positions which have been already laid down, that all right and all that is honourable is to be sought for its own sake. In truth, all virtuous men love justice and equity for what they are in themselves; nor is it like a good man to make a mistake, and love that which does not deserve their affection. Right, therefore, is desirable and deserving to be cultivated for its own sake; and if this be true of right, it must be true also of justice. What then shall we say of liberality? Is it exercised gratuitously, or does it covet some reward and recompense? If a man does good without expecting any recompense for his kindness, then it is gratuitous: if he does expect compensation, it is a mere matter of traffic. Nor is there any doubt that he who truly deserves the reputation of a generous and kind-hearted man, is thinking of his duty, not of his interest. In the same way the virtue of justice demands neither emolument nor salary, and therefore we desire it for its own sake. And the case of all the moral virtues is the same, and so is the opinion of them.

Besides this, if we weigh virtue by the mere utility and profit that attend it, and not by its own merit, the one virtue which results from such an estimate will be in fact a species of vice. For the more a man refers all his actions especially to his own advantage, the further he recedes from probity; so that they who measure virtue by profit, acknowledge no other virtue than this,

which is a kind of vice. For who can be called benevolent, if no one ever acts kindly for the sake of another? And where are we to find a grateful person, if those who are disposed to be so can find no benefactor to whom they can show gratitude? What will become of sacred friendship, if we are not to love our friend for his own sake with all our heart and soul, as people say? if we are even to desert and discard him, as soon as we despair of deriving any further assistance or advantage from him. What can be imagined more inhuman than this conduct? But if friendship ought rather to be cultivated on its own account, so also for the same reason are society, equality, and justice desirable for their own sakes. If this be not so, then there can be no such thing as justice at all; for the most unjust thing of all is to seek a reward for one's just conduct.

What then shall we say of temperance, sobriety, continence, modesty, bashfulness, and chastity? Is it the fear of infamy, or the dread of judgments and penalties, which prevent men from being intemperate and dissolute? Do men then live in innocence and moderation, only to be well spoken of, and to acquire a certain fair reputation? Modest men blush even to speak of indelicacy. And I am greatly ashamed of those philosophers, who assert that there are no vices to be avoided but those which the laws have branded with infamy. For what shall I say? Can we call those persons truly chaste, who abstain from adultery merely for the fear of public exposure, and that disgrace which is only one of its many evil consequences? For what can be either praised or blamed with reason, if you depart from that great law and rule of nature, which makes the difference between right and wrong? Shall corporal defects, if they are remarkable, shock our sensibilities, and shall those of the soul make no impression on us?—of the soul, I say, whose turpitude is so evidently proved by its vices. For what is there more hideous than avarice, more brutal than lust, more contemptible than cowardice, more base than stupidity and folly? Well, then, are we to call those persons unhappy, who are conspicuous for one or more of these, on account of some injuries, or disgraces, or sufferings to which they are exposed, or on account of the moral baseness of their sins? And we may apply the same test in the opposite way to those who are distinguished for their virtue.

Lastly, if virtue be sought for on account of some other things, it necessarily follows that there is something better than virtue. Is it money, then? is it fame, or beauty, or health? all of which appear of little value to us when we possess them; nor can it be by any possibility certainly known how long they will last. Or is it (what it is shameful even to utter) that basest of all, pleasure? Surely not; for it is in the contempt and disdain of pleasure that virtue is most conspicuous. . . . But the real state of the case is, that since law ought to be both a correctress of vice and a recommender of virtue, the principles on which we direct our conduct ought to be drawn from her. And, thus it comes to pass wisdom is the mother of all the virtuous arts, from the love of which the Greeks have composed the word Philosophy; and which is beyond all contradiction the richest, the brightest, and the most excellent of the gifts which the Gods have bestowed on the life of mankind. For wisdom alone has taught us, among other things, the most difficult of all lessons, namely, *to know ourselves*, a precept so forcible and so comprehensive, that it has been attributed not to a man, but to the God of Delphi himself.

For he who knows himself must in the first place be conscious that he is inspired by a divine principle. And he will look upon his rational part as a resemblance to some divinity consecrated within him, and will always be careful that his sentiments as well as his external behavior be worthy of so inestimable a gift of God. And after he has thoroughly examined himself and tested himself in every way, he will become aware what signal advantages he has received from nature at his entrance into life, and with what infinite means and appliances he is furnished for the attainment and acquisition of wisdom, since in the very beginning of all things, he has, as it were, the intelligible principles of things delineated, as it were, on his mind and soul, by the enlightening assistance of which, and the guidance of wisdom, he sees that he shall become a good and consequently a happy man.

For what can be described or conceived more truly happy than the state of that man, whose mind having attained to an exact knowledge and perception of virtue, has entirely discarded all obedience to and indulgence of the body, and has trampled on voluptuousness as a thing unbecoming the dignity of his nature, and has raised himself above all fear of death or pain; who maintains a benevolent intercourse with his friends, and has learnt to look upon all who are united to him by nature as his kindred; who has learnt to preserve piety and reverence towards the Gods and pure religion; and who has sharpened and improved the perceptions of his mind, as well as of his eyesight, to choose the good and reject the evil, which virtue from its foreseeing things is called Prudence?

When this man shall have surveyed the heavens, the earth, and the seas, and studied the nature of all things, and informed himself from whence they have been generated, to what state they will return, and of the time and manner of their dissolution, and has learnt to distinguish what parts of them are mortal and perishable, and what divine and eternal—when he shall have almost attained to a knowledge of that Being who superintends and governs these things, and shall look on himself as not confined within the walls of one city, or as the member of any particular community, but as a citizen of the whole universe, considered as a single Commonwealth: amid such a grand magnificence of things as this, and such a prospect and knowledge of nature, what a knowledge of himself, O ye immortal Gods, will a man arrive at!

Suetonius

It is very doubtful that anyone, anywhere, at any time has ever claimed Suetonius' *Lives of the Caesars* to be a dispassionate, objective account of the careers of the men he chose to examine. As a matter of fact, this effective Roman polemicist was a very able practical psychologist, using a rather subtle literary device to undermine the reputations of those about whom he wrote. One clear example of the method can be seen in his allusions to the relationship between Julius Caesar and the king of Bithynia. But this should not obscure the real debt historians of Imperial Rome owe to this remarkable biographer. His work remains one of the major sources of information about his subjects, and his wealth of anecdotal detail has provided later writers with material obtainable nowhere else. Also, Suetonius' style or pattern of treatment was taken as the best possible by nearly all biographers from his time to the Renaissance. This pattern was rigid almost to the point of being tedious—first an account of the subject's family and lineage, next an account of his birth and education, then a strict chronological recital of his career, followed by a physical description and a character analysis, and lastly, the story of his death. Naturally, the character analysis section offered considerable scope for the moral commentary in which Suetonius seems to have delighted. To appreciate the influence of Suetonius on later biographers it is necessary only to compare the following selection with Einhard's *Life of Charlemagne* (see pp. 281–301).

Suetonius (Caius Suetonius Tranquillus) was born in the last third of the first century and died about the middle of the second century after Christ. One of the few firm facts known about his life is that he was for a time private secretary to the Emperor Hadrian. As such he may have had access to official documents and records, but whether he took advantage of this opportunity is not known. However, his influence cannot be denied. As a literary model and as an important source of information he takes his place with Plutarch (a contemporary) as a major figure in the historiography of the classical world. The selection that follows is from his biography of Julius Caesar.

The Lives of the Caesars

BOOK I

The Deified Julius

. . .

Caesar's very first enactment after becoming consul [in 59 B.C.] was, that the proceedings both of the senate and of the people should day by day be compiled and published. He also revived a by-gone custom, that during the months when he did not have the fasces an orderly should walk before him, while the lictors followed him. He brought forward an agrarian law too, and when his colleague announced adverse omens, he resorted to arms and drove him from the Forum; and when next day Bibulus made complaint in the senate and no one could be found who ventured to make a motion, or even to express an opinion about so high-handed a proceeding (although decrees had often been passed touching less serious breaches of the peace), Caesar's conduct drove him to such a pitch of desperation, that from that time until the end of his term he did not leave his house, but merely issued proclamations announcing adverse omens.

From that time on Caesar managed all the affairs of state alone and after his own pleasure; so that sundry witty fellows, pretending by way of jest to sign and seal testamentary documents, wrote, "Done in the consulship of Julius and Caesar," instead of "Bibulus and Caesar," writing down the same man twice, by name and by surname. Presently too the following verses were on everyone's lips:—

In Caesar's year, not Bibulus', an act took place of late;
For naught do I remember done in Bibulus' consulate.

The plain called Stellas, which had been devoted to public uses by the men of by-gone days, and the Campanian territory, which had been reserved to pay revenues for the aid of the government, he divided without casting lots among twenty thousand citizens who had three or more children each. When the publicans asked for relief, he freed them from a third part of their obligation, and openly warned them in contracting for taxes in the future not to bid too recklessly. He freely granted everything else that anyone took into his head to ask, either without opposition or by intimidating anyone who tried to object. Marcus Cato, who tried to delay proceedings, was dragged from the House by a lictor at Caesar's command and taken off to prison. When Lucius Lucullus was somewhat too outspoken in his opposition, he filled him with such fear of malicious prosecution, that Lucullus actually fell on his knees before him. Because Cicero, while pleading in court, deplored the state of the times, Caesar transferred the orator's enemy Publius Clodius that very same day from the patricians

Suetonius: The Lives of the Caesars, trans. J. C. Rolfe.

to the plebeians, a thing for which Clodius had for a long time been vainly striving; and that too at the ninth hour. Finally, taking action against all the opposition in a body, he bribed an informer to declare that he had been egged on by certain men to murder Pompey, and to come out upon the rostra and name the guilty parties according to a prearranged plot. But when the informer had named one or two to no purpose and not without suspicion of double-dealing, Caesar, hopeless of the success of his overhasty attempt, is supposed to have had him taken off by poison.

At about the same time he took to wife Calpurnia, daughter of Lucius Piso, who was to succeed him in the consulship, and affianced his own daughter Julia to Gnaeus Pompeius, breaking a previous engagement with Servilius Caepio, although the latter had shortly before rendered him conspicuous service in his contest with Bibulus. And after this new alliance he began to call upon Pompey first to give his opinion in the senate, although it had been his habit to begin with Crassus, and it was the rule for the consul in calling for opinions to continue throughout the year the order which he had established on the Kalends of January.

Backed therefore by his father-in-law and son-in-law, out of all the numerous provinces he made the Gauls his choice, as the most likely to enrich him and furnish suitable material for triumphs. At first, it is true, by the bill of Vatinius he received only Cisalpine Gaul with the addition of Illyricum; but presently he was assigned Gallia Comata as well by the senate, since the members feared that even if they should

refuse it, the people would give him this also. Transported with joy at this success, he could not keep from boasting a few days later before a crowded house, that having gained his heart's desire to the grief and lamentation of his opponents, he would therefore from that time mount on their heads; and when someone insultingly remarked that that would be no easy matter for any woman, he replied in the same vein that Semiramis too had been queen in Syria and the Amazons in days of old had held sway over a great part of Asia.

When at the close of his consulship the praetors Gaius Memmius and Lucius Domitius moved an inquiry into his conduct the previous year, Caesar laid the matter before the senate; and when they failed to take it up, and three days had been wasted in fruitless wrangling, went off to his province. Whereupon his quaestor was at once arraigned on several counts, as a preliminary to his own impeachment. Presently he himself too was prosecuted by Lucius Antistius, tribune of the commons, and it was only by appealing to the whole college that he contrived not to be brought to trial, on the ground that he was absent on public service. Then to secure himself for the future, he took great pains always to put the magistrates for the year under personal obligation, and not to aid any candidates or suffer any to be elected, save as guaranteed to defend him in his absence. And he did not hesitate in some cases to exact an oath to keep this pledge or even a written contract.

When however Lucius Domitius, candidate for the consulship, openly threatened to effect as consul what he had been unable to do as praetor, and to take his armies from him, Caesar compelled Pompeius and Crassus to come to Luca, a city in his province, where he prevailed on them to stand for a second consulship, to defeat Domitius; and he also succeeded through their influence in having his term as governor of Gaul made five years longer. Encouraged by this, he added to the legions which he had received from the state others at his own cost, one actually composed of men of Transalpine Gaul and bearing a Gallic name too (for it was called Alauda), which he trained in the Roman tactics and equipped with Roman arms; and later on he gave every man of it citizenship. After that he did not let slip any pretext for war, however unjust and dangerous it might be, picking quarrels as well with allied as with hostile and barbarous nations; so that once the senate decreed that a commission be sent to inquire into the condition of the Gallic provinces, and some even recommended that Caesar be handed over to the enemy. But as his enterprises prospered, thanksgivings were appointed in his honour oftener and for longer periods than for anyone before his time.

During the nine years of his command this is in substance what he did. All that part of Gaul which is bounded by the Pyrenees, the Alps and the Cevennes, and by the Rhine and Rhone rivers, a circuit of some thirty-two hundred miles, with the exception of some allied states which had rendered him good service, he reduced to the form of a province; and imposed upon it a yearly tribute of forty million sesterces. He was the first Roman to build a bridge and attack the Ger-

mans beyond the Rhine, and he inflicted heavy losses upon them. He invaded the Britons too, a people unknown before, vanquished them, and exacted moneys and hostages. Amid all these successes he met with adverse fortune but three times in all: in Britain, where his fleet narrowly escaped destruction in a violent storm; in Gaul, when one of his legions was routed at Gergovia; and on the borders of Germany, when his lieutenants Titurius and Aurunculeius were ambushed and slain.

Within this same space of time he lost first his mother, then his daughter, and soon afterwards his grandchild. Meanwhile, as the community was aghast at the murder of Publius Clodius, the senate had voted that only one consul should be chosen, and expressly named Gnaeus Pompeius. When the tribunes planned to make him Pompey's colleague, Caesar urged them rather to propose to the people that he be permitted to stand for a second consulship without coming to Rome, when the term of his governorship drew near its end, to prevent his being forced for the sake of the office to leave his province prematurely and without finishing the war. On the granting of this, aiming still higher and flushed with hope, he neglected nothing in the way of lavish expenditure or of favours to anyone, either in his public capacity or privately. He began a forum with the proceeds of his spoils, the ground for which cost more than a hundred million sesterces. He announced a combat of gladiators and a feast for the people in memory of his daughter, a thing quite without precedent. To raise the expectation of these events to the highest possible pitch, he had the material for the banquet prepared in part by his own household, although he had let contracts to the markets as well. He gave orders too that whenever famous gladiators fought without winning the favour of the people, they should be rescued by force and kept for him. He had the novices trained, not in a gladiatorial school by professionals, but in private houses by Roman knights and even by senators who were skilled in arms, earnestly beseeching them, as is shown by his own letters, to give the recruits individual attention and personally direct their exercises. He doubled the pay of the legions for all time. Whenever grain was plentiful, he distributed it to them without stint or measure, and now and then gave each man a slave from among the captives.

Moreover, to retain his relationship and friendship with Pompey, Caesar offered him his sister's granddaughter Octavia in marriage, although she was already the wife of Gaius Marcellus, and asked for the hand of Pompey's daughter, who was promised to Faustus Sulla. When he had put all Pompey's friends under obligation, as well as the great part of the senate, through loans made without interest or at a low rate, he lavished gifts on men of all other classes, both those whom he invited to accept his bounty and those who applied to him unasked, including even freedmen and slaves who were special favourites of their masters or patrons. In short, he was the sole and ever ready help of all who were in legal difficulties or in debt and of young spendthrifts, excepting only those whose burden of guilt or of poverty was so heavy, or who were so given up to riotous living, that even he could not save them; and to these he declared in the plainest terms that what they needed was a civil war.

He took no less pains to win the devotion of princes and provinces all over the world, offering prisoners to some by the thousand as a gift, and sending auxiliary troops to the aid of others whenever they wished, and as often as they wished, without the sanction of the senate or people, besides adorning the principal cities of Asia and Greece with magnificent public works, as well as those of Italy and the provinces of Gaul and Spain. At last, when all were thunderstruck at his actions and wondered what their purpose could be, the consul Marcus Claudius Marcellus, after first making proclamation that he purposed to bring before the senate a matter of the highest public moment, proposed that a successor to Caesar be appointed before the end of his term, on the ground that the war was ended, peace was established, and the victorious army ought to be disbanded; also that no account be taken of Caesar at the elections, unless he were present, since Pompey's subsequent action had not annulled the decree of the people. And it was true that when Pompey proposed a bill touching the privileges of officials, in the clause where he debarred absentees from candidacy for office he forgot to make a special exception in Caesar's case, and did not correct the oversight until the law had been inscribed on a tablet of bronze and deposited in the treasury. Not content with depriving Caesar of his provinces and his privilege, Marcellus also moved that the colonists whom Caesar had settled in Novum Comum by the bill of Vatinius should lose their citizenship, on the ground that it had been given from political motives and was not authorized by the law.

Greatly troubled by these measures, and thinking, as they say he was often heard to remark, that now that he was the leading man of the state, it was harder to push him down from the first place to the second than it would be from the second to the lowest, Caesar stoutly resisted Marcellus, partly through vetoes of the tribunes and partly through the other consul, Servius Sulpicius. When next year Gaius Marcellus, who had succeeded his cousin Marcus as consul, tried the same thing, Caesar by a heavy bribe secured the support of the other consul, Aemilius Paulus, and of Gaius Curio, the most reckless of the tribunes. But seeing that everything was being pushed most persistently, and that even the consuls-elect were among the opposition, he sent a written appeal to the senate, not to take from him the privilege which the people had granted, or else to compel the others in command of armies to resign also; feeling sure, it was thought, that he could more readily muster his veterans as soon as he wished, than Pompey his newly levied troops. He further proposed a compromise to his opponents, that after giving up eight legions and Transalpine Gaul, he be allowed to keep two legions and Cisalpine Gaul, or at least one legion and Illyricum, until he was elected consul.

But when the senate declined to interfere, and his opponents declared that they would accept no compromise in a matter affecting the public welfare, he crossed to Hither Gaul, and after holding all the assizes, halted at Ravenna, intending to resort to war if the senate took any drastic action against the tribunes of the commons who interposed vetoes in his behalf. Now this was his excuse for the civil war, but it is believed that he had other motives. Gnaeus Pompeius used to declare that since Caesar's own means were not sufficient to complete the works which he had planned, nor to do all that he had led the people to expect on his return, he desired a state of general unrest and turmoil. Others say that he dreaded the necessity of rendering an account for what he had done in his first consulship contrary to the auspices and the laws, and regardless of vetoes; for Marcus Cato often declared, and took oath too, that he would impeach Caesar the moment he had disbanded his army. It was openly said too that if he was out of office on his return, he would be obliged, like Milo, to make his defence in a court hedged about by armed men. The latter opinion is the more credible one in view of the assertion of Asinius Pollio, that when Caesar at the battle of Pharsalus saw his enemies slain or in flight, he said, word for word: "They would have it so. Even I, Gaius Caesar, after so many great deeds, should have been found guilty, if I had not turned to my army for help." Some think that habit had given him a love of power, and that weighing the strength of his adversaries against his own, he grasped the opportunity of usurping the despotism which had been his heart's desire from early youth. Cicero too was seemingly of this opinion, when he wrote in the third book of his *De Officiis* that Caesar ever had upon his lips these lines of Euripides, of which Cicero himself adds a version:—

If wrong may e'er be right, for a throne's sake
Were wrong most right:—be God in all else feared.

Accordingly, when word came that the veto of the tribunes had been set aside and they themselves had left the city, he at once sent on a few cohorts with all secrecy, and then, to disarm suspicion, concealed his purpose by appearing at a public show, inspecting the plans of a gladiatorial school which he intended building, and joining as usual in a banquet with a large company. It was not until after sunset that he set out very privily with a small company, taking the mules from a bakeshop hard by and harnessing them to a carriage; and when his lights went out and he lost his way, he was astray for some time, but at last found a guide at dawn and got back to the road on foot by narrow bypaths. Then, overtaking his cohorts at the river Rubicon, which was the boundary of his province, he paused for a while, and realising what a step he was taking, he turned to those about him and said: "Even yet we may draw back; but once cross yon little bridge, and the whole issue is with the sword."

As he stood in doubt, this sign was given him. On a sudden there appeared hard by a being of wondrous stature and beauty, who sat and played upon a reed; and when not only the shepherds flocked to hear him, but many of the soldiers left their posts, and among them some of the trumpeters, the appar-

ition snatched a trumpet from one of them, rushed to the river, and sounding the war-note with mighty blast, strode to the opposite bank. Then Caesar cried: "Take we the course which the signs of the gods and the false dealing of our foes point out. The die is cast," said he.

Accordingly, crossing with his army, and welcoming the tribunes of the commons, who had come to him after being driven from Rome, he harangued the soldiers with tears, and rending his robe from his breast besought their faithful service. It is even thought that he promised every man a knight's estate, but that came of a misunderstanding; for since he often pointed to the finger of his left hand as he addressed them and urged them on, declaring that to satisfy all those who helped him to defend his honour he would gladly tear his very ring from his hand, those on the edge of the assembly, who could see him better than they could hear his words, assumed that he said what his gesture seemed to mean; and so the report went about that he had promised them the right of the ring and four hundred thousand sesterces as well.

The sum total of his movements after that is, in their order, as follows: He overran Umbria, Picenum, and Etruria, took prisoner Lucius Domitius, who had been irregularly named his successor, and was holding Corfinium with a garrison, let him go free, and then proceeded along the Adriatic to Brundisium, where Pompey and the consuls had taken refuge, intending to cross the sea as soon as might be. After vainly trying by every kind of hindrance to prevent their sailing, he marched off to Rome, and after calling the senate together to discuss public business, went to attack Pompey's strongest forces, which were in Spain under command of three of his lieutenants—Marcus Petreius, Lucius Afranius, and Marcus Varro—saying to his friends before he left, "I go to meet an army without a leader, and I shall return to meet a leader without an army." And in fact, though his advance was delayed by the siege of Massilia, which had shut its gates against him, and by extreme scarcity of supplies, he nevertheless quickly gained a complete victory.

Returning thence to Rome, he crossed into Macedonia, and after blockading Pompey for almost four months behind mighty ramparts, finally routed him in the battle at Pharsalus, followed him in his flight to Alexandria, and when he learned that his rival had been slain, made war on King Ptolemy, whom he perceived to be plotting against his own safety as well; a war in truth of great difficulty, convenient neither in time nor place, but carried on during the winter season, within the walls of a well-provisioned and crafty foeman, while Caesar himself was without supplies of any kind and ill-prepared. Victor in spite of all, he turned over the rule of Egypt to Cleopatra and her young brother, fearing that if he made a province of it, it might one day under a headstrong governor be a source of revolution. From Alexandria he crossed to Syria, and from there went to Pontus, spurred on by the news that Pharnaces, son of Mithridates the Great, had taken advantage of the situation to make war, and was already flushed with numerous successes; but Caesar vanquished him in a single battle within

five days after his arrival and four hours after getting sight of him, often remarking on Pompey's good luck in gaining his principal fame as a general by victories over such feeble foemen. Then he overcame Scipio and Juba, who were patching up the remnants of their party in Africa, and the sons of Pompey in Spain.

In all the civil wars he suffered not a single disaster except through his lieutenants, of whom Gaius Curio perished in Africa, Gaius Antonius fell into the hands of the enemy in Illyricum, Publius Dolabella lost a fleet also off Illyricum, and Gnaeus Domitius Calvinus an army in Pontus. Personally he always fought with the utmost success, and the issue was never even in doubt save twice: once at Dyrrachium, where he was put to flight, and said of Pompey, who failed to follow up his success, that he did not know how to use a victory; again in Spain, in the final struggle, when, believing the battle lost, he actually thought of suicide.

Having ended the wars, he celebrated five triumphs, four in a single month, but at intervals of a few days, after vanquishing Scipio; and another on defeating Pompey's sons. The first and most splendid was the Gallic triumph, the next the Alexandrian, then the Pontic, after that the African, and finally the Spanish, each differing from the rest in its equipment and display of spoils. As he rode through the Velabrum on the day of his Gallic triumph, the axle of his chariot broke, and he was all but thrown out; and he mounted the Capitol by torchlight, with forty elephants bearing lamps on his right and his left. In his Pontic triumph he displayed among the show-pieces of the procession an inscription of but three words, "I came, I saw, I conquered," not indicating the events of the war, as the others did, but the speed with which it was finished.

To each and every foot-soldier of his veteran legions he gave twenty-four thousand sesterces by way of booty, over and above the two thousand apiece which he had paid them at the beginning of the civil strife. He also assigned them lands, but not side by side, to avoid dispossessing any of the former owners. To every man of the people, besides ten pecks of grain and the same number of pounds of oil, he distributed the three hundred sesterces which he had promised at first, and one hundred apiece to boot because of the delay. He also remitted a year's rent in Rome to tenants who paid two thousand sesterces or less, and in Italy up to five hundred sesterces. He added a banquet and a dole of meat, and after his Spanish victory two dinners; for deeming that the former of these had not been served with a liberality creditable to his generosity, he gave another five days later on a most lavish scale.

He gave entertainments of divers kinds: a combat of gladiators and also stage-plays in every ward all over the city, performed too by actors of all languages, as well as races in the circus, athletic contests, and a sham sea-fight. In the gladiatorial contest in the Forum Furius Leptinus, a man of praetorian stock, and Quintus Calpenus, a former senator and pleader at the bar, fought to a finish. A Pyrrhic dance was performed by the sons of the princes of Asia and Bithynia. During the plays Decimus Laberius, a Roman Knight, acted a farce of his own composition, and having been presented with five hundred thousand sesterces and a gold ring, passed from the stage through the orchestra and took his place in the fourteen rows. For the races the circus was lengthened at either end and a broad canal was dug all about it; then young men of the highest rank drove four-horse and two-horse chariots and rode pairs of horses, vaulting from one to the other. The game called Troy was performed by two troops, of younger and of older boys. Combats with wild beasts were presented on five successive days, and last of all there was a battle between two opposing armies, in which five hundred foot-soldiers, twenty elephants, and thirty horsemen engaged on each side. To make room for this, the goals were taken down and in their place two camps were pitched over against each other. The athletic competitions lasted for three days in a temporary stadium built for the purpose in the region of the Campus Martius. For the naval battle a pool was dug in the lesser Codeta and there was a contest of ships of two, three, and four banks of oars, belonging to the Tyrian and Egyptian fleets, manned by a large force of fighting men. Such a throng flocked to all these shows from every quarter, that many strangers had to lodge in tents pitched in the streets or along the roads, and the press was often such that many were crushed to death, including two senators.

Then turning his attention to the reorganisation of the state, he reformed the calendar, which the negligence of the pontiffs had long since so disordered, through their privilege of adding months or days at pleasure, that the harvest festivals did not come in summer nor those of the vintage in the autumn; and he adjusted the year to the sun's course by making it consist of three hundred and sixty-five days, abolishing the intercalary month, and adding one day every fourth year. Furthermore, that the correct reckoning of seasons might begin with the next Kalends of January, he inserted two other months between those of November and December; hence the year in which these arrangements were made was one of fifteen months, including the intercalary month, which belonged to that year according to the former custom.

He filled the vacancies in the senate, enrolled additional patricians, and increased the number of praetors, aediles, and quaestors, as well as of the minor officials; he reinstated those who had been degraded by official action of the censors or found guilty of bribery by verdict of the jurors. He shared the elections with the people on this basis: that except in the case of the consulship, half of the magistrates should be appointed by the people's choice, while the rest should be those whom he had personally nominated. And these he announced in brief notes like the following, circulated in each tribe: "Caesar the Dictator to this or that tribe. I commend to you so and so, to hold their positions by your votes." He admitted to office even the sons of those who had been proscribed. He limited the right of serving as jurors to two classes, the equestrian and senatorial orders, disqualifying the third class, the tribunes of the treasury.

He made the enumeration of the people neither in the usual manner nor place, but from street to street aided by the owners of blocks of houses, and reduced the number of those who received grain at public expense from three hundred and twenty thousand to one hundred and fifty thousand. And to prevent the calling of additional meetings at any future time for purposes of enrollment, he provided that the places of such as died should be filled each year by the praetors from those who were not on the list.

Moreover, to keep up the population of the city, depleted as it was by the assignment of eighty thousand citizens to colonies across the sea, he made a law that no citizen older than twenty or younger than forty, who was not detained by service in the army, should be absent from Italy for more than three successive years; that no senator's son should go abroad except as the companion of a magistrate or on his staff; and that those who made a business of grazing should have among their herdsmen at least one-third who were men of free birth. He conferred citizenship on all who practised medicine at Rome, and on all teachers of the liberal arts, to make them more desirous of living in the city and to induce others to resort to it.

As to debts, he disappointed those who looked for their cancellation, which was often agitated, but finally decreed that the debtors should satisfy their creditors according to a valuation of their possessions at the price which they had paid for them before the civil war, deducting from the principal whatever interest had been paid in cash or pledged through bankers; an arrangement which wiped out about a fourth part of their indebtedness. He dissolved all guilds, except those of ancient foundation. He increased the penalties for crimes; and inasmuch as the rich involved themselves in guilt with less hesitation because they merely suffered exile, without any loss of property, he punished murderers of freemen by the confiscation of all their goods, as Cicero writes, and others by the loss of one-half.

He administered justice with the utmost conscientiousness and strictness. Those convicted of extortion he even dismissed from the senatorial order. He annulled the marriage of an ex-praetor, who had married a woman the very day after her divorce, although there was no suspicion of adultery. He imposed duties on foreign wares. He denied the use of litters and the wearing of scarlet robes or pearls to all except to those of a designated position and age, and on set days. In particular he enforced the law against extravagance, setting watchmen in various parts of the market, to seize and bring to him dainties which were exposed for sale in violation of the law; and sometimes he sent his lictors and soldiers to take from a dining-room any articles which had escaped the vigilance of his watchmen, even after they had been served.

In particular, for the adornment and convenience of the city, also for the protection and extension of the Empire, he formed more projects and more extensive ones every day: first of all, to rear a temple to Mars, greater than any in existence, filling up and levelling the pool in which he had exhibited the sea-fight, and to build a theatre of vast size, sloping down from the Tarpeian rock; to reduce the civil code to fixed limits, and of the vast and prolix mass of statutes to include only the best and most essential in a limited number of volumes; to open to the public the greatest possible libraries of Greek and Latin books, assigning to Marcus Varro the charge of procuring and classifying them; to drain the Pomptine marshes; to let out the water from Lake Fucinus; to make a highway from the Adriatic across the summit of the Apennines as far as the Tiber; to cut a canal through the Isthmus; to check the Dacians, who had poured into Pontus and Thrace; then to make war on the Parthians by way of Lesser Armenia, but not to risk a battle with them until he had first tested their mettle.

All these enterprises and plans were cut short by his death. But before I speak of that, it will not be amiss to describe briefly his personal appearance, his dress, his mode of life, and his character, as well as his conduct in civil and military life.

He is said to have been tall of stature, with a fair complexion, shapely limbs, a somewhat full face, and keen black eyes; sound of health, except that towards the end he was subject to sudden fainting fits and to nightmare as well. He was twice attacked by the falling sickness during his campaigns. He was somewhat over-nice in the care of his person, being not only carefully trimmed and shaved, but even having superfluous hair plucked out, as some have charged; while his baldness was a disfigurement which troubled him greatly, since he found that it was often the subject of the gibes of his detractors. Because of it he used to comb forward his scanty locks from the crown of his head, and of all the honours voted him by the senate people there was none which he received or made use of more gladly than the privilege of wearing a laurel wreath at all times. They say, too, that he was remarkable in his dress; that he wore a senator's tunic with fringed sleeves reaching to the wrist, and always had a girdle over it, though rather a loose one; and this, they say, was the occasion of Sulla's *mot*, when he often warned the nobles to keep an eye on the ill-girt boy.

He lived at first in the Subura in a modest house, but after he became pontifex maximus, in the official residence of the Sacred Way. Many have written that he was very fond of elegance and luxury; that having laid the foundations of a country-house on his estate at Nemi and finished it at great cost, he tore it all down because it did not suit him in every particular, although at the time he was still poor and heavily in debt; and that he carried tessellated and mosaic floors about with him on his campaigns.

They say that he was led to invade Britain by the hope of getting pearls, and that in comparing their size he sometimes weighed them with his own hand; that he was always a most enthusiastic collector of gems, carvings, statues, and pictures by early artists; also of slaves of exceptional figure and training at enormous prices, of which he himself was so ashamed that he forbade their entry in his accounts.

It is further reported that in the provinces he gave banquets constantly in two dining-halls, in one of which his officers or Greek companions, in the other Roman civilians

and the more distinguished of the provincials reclined at table. He was so punctilious and strict in the management of his household, in small matters as well as in those of greater importance, that he put his baker in irons for serving him with one kind of bread and his guests with another; and he inflicted capital punishment on a favourite freedman for adultery with the wife of a Roman knight, although no complaint was made against him.

There was no stain on his reputation for chastity except his intimacy with King Nicomedes, but that was a deep and lasting reproach, which laid him open to insults from every quarter. I say nothing of the notorious lines of Licinius Calvus:

Whate'er Bithynia had, and Caesar's paramour.

I pass over, too, the invectives of Dolabella and the elder Curio, in which Dolabella calls him "the queen's rival, the inner partner of the royal couch," and Curio, "the brothel of Nicomedes and the stew of Bithynia." I take no account of the edicts of Bibulus, in which he posted his colleague as "the queen of Bithynia," saying that "of yore he was enamoured of a king, but now of a king's estate." At this same time, so Marcus Brutus declares, one Octavius, a man whose disordered mind made him somewhat free with his tongue, after saluting Pompey as "king" in a crowded assembly, greeted Caesar as "queen." But Gaius Memmius makes the direct charge that he acted as cup-bearer to Nicomedes with the rest of his wantons at a large dinner party, and that among the guests were some merchants from Rome, whose names Memmius gives. Cicero, indeed, is not content with having written in sundry letters that Caesar was led by the king's attendants to the royal apartments, that he lay on a golden couch arrayed in purple, and that the virginity of this son of Venus was lost in Bithynia; but when Caesar was once addressing the senate in defence of Nysa, daughter of Nicomedes, and was enumerating his obligations to the king, Cicero cried: "No more of that, pray, for it is well known what he gave you, and what you gave him in turn." Finally, in his Gallic triumph his soldiers, among the bantering songs which are usually sung by those who follow the chariot, shouted these lines, which became a by-word:—

All the Gauls did Caesar vanquish, Nicomedes vanquished him:
Lo! now Caesar rides in triumph, victor over all the Gauls,
Nicomedes does not triumph, who subdued the conqueror.

That he was unbridled and extravagant in his intrigues is the general opinion, and that he seduced many illustrious women, among them Postumia, wife of Servius Sulpicius, Lollia, wife of Aulus Gabinius, Tertulla, wife of Marcus Crassus, and even Gnaeus Pompey's wife, Mucia. At all events there is no doubt that Pompey was taken to task by the elder and that younger Curio, as well as by many others, because through a desire for power he had afterwards married the daughter of a man on whose account he divorced a wife who had borne him three children, and whom he had often referred to with a groan as an Aegisthus. But beyond

all others Caesar loved Servilla, the mother of Marcus Brutus, for whom in his first consulship he bought a pearl costing six million sesterces. During the civil war, too, besides other presents, he knocked down some fine estates to her in a public auction at a nominal price, and when some expressed their surprise at the low figure, Cicero wittily remarked: "It's a better bargain than you think, for there is a third off." And in fact it was thought that Servilla was prostituting her own daughter Tertia to Caesar.

That he did not refrain from intrigues in the provinces is shown in particular by this couplet, which was also shouted by the soldiers in his Gallic triumph:—

Men of Rome, keep close your consorts, here's a bald adulterer.
Gold in Gaul you spent in dalliance, which you borrowed here in Rome.

He had love affairs with queens too, including Eunoe the Moor, wife of Bogudes, on whom, as well as on her husband, he bestowed many splendid presents, as Naso writes; but above all with Cleopatra, with whom he often feasted until daybreak, and he would have gone through Egypt with her in her state-barge almost to Aethiopia, had not his soldiers refused to follow him. Finally he called her to Rome and did not let her leave until he had ladened her with high honours and rich gifts, and he allowed her to give his name to the child which she bore. In fact, according to certain Greek writers, this child was very like Caesar in looks and carriage. Mark Anthony declared to the senate that Caesar had really acknowledged the boy, and that Gaius Matius, Gaius Oppius, and other friends of Caesar knew this. Of these Gaius Oppius, as if admitting that the situation required apology and defence, published a book, to prove that the child whom Cleopatra fathered on Caesar was not his. Helvius Cinna, tribune of the commons, admitted to several that he had a bill drawn up in due form, which Caesar had ordered him to propose to the people in his absence, making it lawful for Caesar to marry what wives he wished, "for the purpose of begetting children." But to remove all doubt that he had an evil reputation for shameless vice and for adultery, I have only to add that the elder Curio in one of his speeches calls him "every woman's man and every man's woman."

That he drank very little wine not even his enemies denied. There is a saying of Marcus Cato that Caesar was the only man who undertook to overthrow the state when sober. Even in the matter of food Gaius Oppius tells us that he was so indifferent, that once when his host served stale oil instead of fresh, and the other guests would have none of it, Caesar partook even more plentifully than usual, not to seem to charge his host with carelessness or lack of manners.

Neither when in command of armies nor as a magistrate at Rome did he show a scrupulous integrity; for as certain men have declared in their memoirs, when he was proconsul in Spain, he not only begged money from the allies, to help pay his debts, but also attacked and sacked some towns of the Lusitanians although they did not refuse his terms and opened their gates to him on his arrival. In Gaul he pillaged shrines and temples of the gods filled with offerings, and oftener sacked towns for the sake of plunder than for any fault. In consequence he had more gold than he knew what to do with, and offered it for sale throughout Italy and the provinces at the rate of three thousand sesterces the pound. In his first consulship he stole three thousand pounds of gold from the Capitol, replacing it with the same weight of gilded bronze. He made alliances and thrones a matter of barter, for he extorted from Ptolemy alone in his own name and that of Pompey nearly six thousand talents, while later on he met the heavy expenses of the civil wars and of his triumphs and entertainments by the most barefaced pillage and sacrilege.

In eloquence and in the art of war he either equalled or surpassed the fame of their most eminent representatives. After his accusation of Dolabella, he was without question numbered with the leading advocates. At all events when Cicero reviews the orators in his *Brutus*, he says that he does not see to whom Caesar ought to yield the palm, declaring that his style is elegant as well as transparent, even grand and in a sense noble. Again in a letter to Cornelius Nepos he writes thus of Caesar: "Come now, what orator would you rank above him of those who have devoted themselves to nothing else? Who has cleverer or more frequent epigrams? Who is either more picturesque or more choice in diction?" He appears, at least in his youth, to have imitated the manner of Caesar Strabo, from whose speech entitled "For the Sardinians" he actually transferred some passages word for word to a trial address of his own. He is said to have delivered himself in a high-pitched voice with impassioned action and gestures, which were not without grace. He left several speeches, including some which are attributed to him on insufficient evidence. Augustus had good reason to think that the speech "For Quintus Metellus" was rather taken down by shorthand writers who could not keep pace with his delivery, than published by Caesar himself; for in some copies I find that even the title is not "For Metellus," but, "Which He Wrote for Metellus," although the discourse purports to be from Caesar's lips, defending Metellus and himself against the charges of their common detractors. Augustus also questions the authenticity of the address "To His Soldiers in Spain," although there are two sections of it, one purporting to have been spoken at the first battle, the other at the second, when Asinius Pollio writes that because of the sudden onslaught of the enemy he actually did not have time to make an harangue.

He left memoirs too of his deeds in the Gallic war and in the civil strife with Pompey; for the author of the Alexandrian, African, and Spanish Wars is unknown; some think it was Oppius, others Hirtius, who also supplied the final book of the Gallic War, which Caesar left unwritten. With regard to Caesar's memoirs Cicero, also in the *Brutus* speaks in the following terms: "He wrote memoirs which deserve the highest praise; they are naked in their simplicity, straightforward yet graceful, stripped of all rhetorical adornment, as of a garment; but while his purpose was to supply material to others, on which those who wished to write history might draw, he haply gratified silly folk,

who will try to use the curling-irons on his narrative, but he has kept men of any sense from touching the subject." Of these same memoirs Hirtius uses this emphatic language: "They are so highly rated in the judgment of all men, that he seems to have deprived writers of an opportunity, rather than given them one; yet our admiration for this feat is greater than that of others; for they know how well and faultlessly he wrote, while we know besides how easily and rapidly he finished his task." Asinius Pollio thinks that they were put together somewhat carelessly and without strict regard for truth; since in many cases Caesar was too ready to believe the accounts which others gave of their actions, and gave a perverted account of his own, either designedly or perhaps from forgetfulness; and he thinks that he intended to rewrite and revise them. He left besides a work in two volumes "On Analogy," the same number of "Speeches Criticising Cato," in addition to a poem, entitled "The Journey." He wrote the first of these works while crossing the Alps and returning to his army from Hither Gaul, where he had held the assizes; the second about the time of the battle of Munda, and the third in the course of a twenty-four days' journey from Rome to Farther Spain. Some letters of his to the senate are also preserved, and he seems to have been the first to reduce such documents to pages and the form of a notebook, whereas previously consuls and generals sent their reports written right across the sheet. There are also letters of his to Cicero, as well as to his intimates on private affairs, and in the latter, if he had anything confidential to say, he wrote it in cipher, that is, by so changing the order of the letters of the alphabet, that not a word could be made out. If anyone wishes to decipher these, and get at their meaning, he must substitute the fourth letter of the alphabet, namely D, for A, and so with the others. We also have mention of certain writings of his boyhood and early youth, such as the "Praises of Hercules," a tragedy "Oedipus," and a "Collection of Apophthegms"; but Augustus forbade the publication of all these minor works in a very brief and frank letter sent to Pompeius Macer, whom he had selected to set his libraries in order.

He was highly skilled in arms and horsemanship, and of incredible powers of endurance. On the march he headed his army, sometimes on horseback, but oftener on foot, bareheaded both in the heat of the sun and in the rain. He covered great distances with incredible speed, making a hundred miles a day in a hired carriage and with little baggage, swimming the rivers which barred his path or crossing them on inflated skins, and very often arriving before the messengers sent to announce his coming.

In the conduct of his campaigns it is a question whether he was more cautious or more daring, for he never led his army where ambuscades were possible without carefully reconnoitering the country, and he did not cross to Britain without making personal inquiries about the harbours, the course, and the approach to the island. But on the other hand, when news came that his camp in Germany was beleaguered, he made his way to his men through the enemies' pickets, disguised as a Gaul. He crossed from Brundisium to Dyrrachium in winter time, running the blockade of the enemy's fleets; and when the troops which he had ordered to follow him delayed to do so, and he had sent to fetch them many times in vain, at last in secret and alone he boarded a small boat at night with his head muffled up; and he did not reveal who he was, or suffer the helmsman to give way to the gale blowing in their teeth, until he was all but overwhelmed by the waves.

No regard for religion ever turned him from any undertaking, or even delayed him. Though the victim escaped as he was offering sacrifice, he did not put off his expedition against Scipio and Juba. Even when he had a fall as he disembarked, he gave the omen a favourable turn by crying: "I hold thee fast, Africa." Furthermore, to make the prophecies ridiculous which declared that the stock of the Scipios was fated to be fortunate and invincible in that province, he kept with him in camp a contemptible fellow belonging to the Cornelian family, to whom the nickname Salvito had been given as a reproach for his manner of life.

He joined battle, not only after planning his movements in advance but on a sudden opportunity, often immediately at the end of a march, and sometimes in the foulest weather, when one would least expect him to make a move. It was not until his later years that he became slower to engage, through a conviction that the oftener he had been victor, the less he ought to tempt fate, and that he could not possibly gain as much by success as he might lose by a defeat. He never put his enemy to flight without also driving him from his camp, thus giving him no respite in his panic. When the issue was doubtful, he used to send away the horses, and his own among the first, to impose upon his troops the greater necessity of standing their ground by taking away that aid to flight.

He rode a remarkable horse, too, with feet that were almost human; for its hoofs were cloven in such a way as to look like toes. This horse was foaled on his own place, and since the soothsayer had declared that it foretold the rule of the world for its master, he reared it with the greatest care, and was the first to mount it, for it would endure no other rider. Afterwards, too, he dedicated a statue of it before the temple of Venus Genetrix.

Epictetus

Although the philosophy of Stoicism (see p. 196) numbered among its spokesmen some of the greatest figures in the history of Rome, including the Emperor Marcus Aurelius, it was not confined to people in high places. Rather, one of its most influential advocates was a man named Epictetus, who was a slave. A native of Asia Minor, where he was born around the middle of the first century, A.D., Epictetus was captured by the Roman legions and transported to the capital, where he entered the household of a member of Nero's imperial guard. His masters, soon recognizing the talents of their young slave, wisely sent him to the best school in Rome. Here he was introduced to the Stoic philosophy to which later he was to contribute so much.

Unlike Cicero, who concerned himself with broad social and political issues, Epictetus devoted his attention to the problems human beings face in life as individuals. He was concerned with persons and the way in which they ought to live. Epictetus became famous as a teacher, first in Rome and later in Epirus, on the Greek mainland. Like Socrates, whom he desired to emulate, he wrote nothing; the selection that follows was edited from lecture notes taken by one of his students. Epictetus died in 120 A.D.

Some scholars believe that in Epictetus' home town in Asia Minor there was a community of the new religious sect called Christians and that Epictetus was influenced by their doctrines. This explanation could account for the similarities between his views and those of the Christian writers who were becoming active at his time. But so could the opposite assumption— that these writers were influenced by Epictetus. Whatever the exact historical relationship between Roman Stoicism and early Christianity, the parallels between many of their doctrines are sometimes quite striking.

The Enchiridion (or *Manual*), from which the following selection is taken, consists of sayings, admonitions, and general advice on the conduct of life intended by Epictetus for the guidance of his pupils. It exhibits in a marked degree a basic incongruity that permeates the Stoic view of life—on the one hand a faith in the ultimate goodness of the universe and on the other constant reminders of the apparent evils that beset humankind.

The Enchiridion

I

Of things some are in our power, and others are not. In our power are opinion, movement towards a thing, desire, aversion; and in a word, whatever are our own acts: not in our power are the body, property, reputation, offices, and in a word, whatever are not our own acts. And the things in our power are by nature free, not subject to restraint nor hindrance: but the things not in our power are weak, slavish, subject to restraint, in the power of others. Remember then that if you think the things which are by nature slavish to be free, and the things which are in the power of others to be your own, you will be hindered, you will lament, you will be disturbed, you will blame both gods and men: but if you think that only which is your own to be your own, and if you think that what is another's as it really is, belongs to another, no man will ever compel you, no man will hinder you, you will never blame any man, you will accuse no man, you will do nothing involuntarily, no man will harm you, you will have no enemy, for you will not suffer any harm.

If then you desire such great things, remember that you must not lay hold of them with a small effort; but you must leave alone some things entirely, and postpone others for the present. But if you wish for these things also, and power and wealth, perhaps you will not gain even these very things because you aim also at those former things: certainly you will fail in those things through which alone happiness and freedom are secured. Straightway then practise saying to every harsh appearance, You are an appearance, and in no manner what you appear to be. Then examine it by the rules which you possess, and by this first and chiefly, whether it relates to the things which are in our power or to things which are not in our power; and if it relates to anything which is not in our power, be ready to say, that it does not concern you.

II

Remember that desire contains in it the profession of obtaining that which you desire; and the profession in aversion is that you will not fall into that which you attempt to avoid: and he who fails in his desire is unfortunate; and he who falls into that which he would avoid, is unhappy. If then you attempt to avoid only the things contrary to nature which are within your power, you will not be involved in any of the things which you would avoid. But if you attempt to avoid disease or death or poverty, you will be unhappy. Take away then aversion from all things which are not in our power, and transfer it to the things contrary to nature which are in our

The Discourses of Epictetus, trans. G. Long (London, 1877).

power. But destroy desire completely for the present. For if you desire anything which is not in our power, you must be unfortunate: but of the things in our power, and which it would be good to desire, nothing yet is before you. But employ only the power of moving towards an object and retiring from it; and these powers indeed only slightly and with exceptions and with remission.

III

In every thing which pleases the soul, or supplies a want, or is loved, remember to add this to the description; what is the nature of each thing, beginning from the smallest? If you love an earthen vessel, say it is an earthen vessel which you love; for when it has been broken, you will not be disturbed. If you are kissing your child or wife, say that it is a human being whom you are kissing, for when the wife or child dies, you will not be disturbed.

IV

When you are going to take in hand any act, remind yourself what kind of an act it is. If you are going to bathe, place before yourself what happens in the bath: some splashing the water, others pushing against one another, others abusing one another, and some stealing: and thus with more safety you will undertake the matter, if you say to yourself, I now intend to bathe, and to maintain my will in a manner conformable to nature. And so you will do in every act: for thus if any

hindrance to bathing shall happen, let this thought be ready: it was not this only that I intended, but I intended also to maintain my will in a way conformable to nature; but I shall not maintain it so, if I am vexed at what happens.

V

Men are disturbed not by the things which happen, but by the opinions about the things: for example, death is nothing terrible, for if it were, it would have seemed so to Socrates; for the opinion about death, that it is terrible, is the terrible thing. When then we are impeded or disturbed or grieved, let us never blame others, but ourselves, that is, our opinions. It is the act of an ill-instructed man to blame others for his own bad condition; it is the act of one who has begun to be instructed, to lay the blame on himself; and of one whose instruction is completed, neither to blame another, nor himself.

VI

Be not elated at any advantage, which belongs to another. If a horse when he is elated should say, I am beautiful, one might endure it. But when you are elated, and say, I have a beautiful horse, you must know that you are elated at having a good horse. What then is your own? The use of appearances. Consequently when in the use of appearances you are conformable to nature, then you will be elated, for then you will be elated at something good which is your own.

VII

As on a voyage when the vessel has reached a port, if you go out to get water, it is an amusement by the way to pick up a shell fish or some bulb, but your thoughts ought to be directed to the ship, and you ought to be constantly watching if the captain should call, and then you must throw away all those things, that you may not be bound and pitched into the ship like sheep; so in life also, if there be given to you instead of a little bulb and a shell a wife and child, there will be nothing to prevent you from taking them. But if the captain should call, run to the ship, and leave all those things without regard to them. But if you are old, do not even go far from the ship, lest when you are called you make default.

VIII

Seek not that the things which happen should happen as you wish; but wish the things which happen to be as they are, and you will have a tranquil flow of life.

IX

Disease is an impediment to the body; but not to the will, unless the will itself chooses. Lameness is an impediment to the leg, but not to the will. And add this reflection on the occasion of every thing that happens; for you will find it an impediment to something else, but not to yourself.

X

On the occasion of every accident that befalls you, remember to turn to yourself and inquire what power you have for turning it to use. If you see a fair man or a fair woman, you will find that the power to resist is temperance. If labour be presented to you, you will find that it is endurance. If it be abusive words, you will find it to be patience. And if you have been thus formed to the proper habit, the appearances will not carry you along with them.

XI

Never say about any thing, I have lost it, but say I have restored it. Is your child dead? It has been restored. Is your wife dead? She has been restored. Has your estate been taken from you? Has not then this also been restored? But he who has taken it from me is a bad man. But what is it to you, by whose hands the giver demanded it back? So long as he may allow you, take care of it as a thing which belongs to another, as travellers do with their inn.

XII

If you intend to improve, throw away such thoughts as these: if I neglect my affairs, I shall not have the means of living: unless I chastise my slave, he will be bad. For it is better to die of hunger and so to be released from grief and fear than to live in abundance with perturbation; and it is better for your slave to be bad than for you to be unhappy. Begin then from little things.

Is the oil spilled? Is a little wine stolen? Say on the occasion, at such price is sold freedom from perturbation; at such price is sold tranquillity, but nothing is got for nothing. And when you call your slave, consider that it is possible that he does not hear; and if he does hear, that he will do nothing which you wish. But matters are not so well with him, but altogether well with you, that it should be in his power for you to be not disturbed.

XIII

If you would improve, submit to be considered without sense and foolish with respect to externals. Wish to be considered to know nothing: and if you shall seem to some to be a person of importance, distrust yourself. For you should know that it is not easy both to keep your will in a condition conformable to nature and to secure external things: but if a man is careful about the one, it is an absolute necessity that he will neglect the other.

XIV

If you would have your children and your wife and your friends to live for ever, you are silly; for you would have the things which are not in your power to be in your power, and the things which belong to others to be yours. So if you would have your slave to be free from faults, you are a fool; for you would have badness not to be badness, but something else. But if you wish not to fail in your desires, you are able to do that. Practise then this which you are able to do. He is the master of every man who has the power over the things, which another person wishes or does not wish, the power to confer them on him or to take them away. Whoever then wishes to be free, let him neither wish for any thing nor avoid anything which depends on others: if he does not observe this rule, he must be a slave.

XV

Remember that in life you ought to behave as at a banquet. Suppose that something is carried round and is opposite to you. Stretch out your hand and take a portion with decency. Suppose that it passes by you. Do not detain it. Suppose that it is not yet come to you. Do not send your desire forward to it, but wait till it is opposite to you. Do so with respect to children, so with respect to a wife, so with respect to magisterial offices, so with respect to wealth, and you will be some time a worthy partner of the banquets of the gods. But if you take none of the things which are set before you, and even despise them, then you will be not only a fellow banqueter with the gods, but also a partner with them in power. For by acting thus Diogenes and Heracleitus and those like them were deservedly divine, and were so called.

XVI

When you see a person weeping in sorrow either when a child goes abroad or when he is dead, or when the man has lost his property, take care that the appearance do not hurry you away with it, as if he were suffering in external things. But straightway make a distinction in your own mind, and be in readiness to say, it is not that which has happened that afflicts this man, for it does not afflict another, but it is the opinion about this thing which afflicts the man. So far as words then do not be unwilling to show him sympathy, and even if it happens so, to lament with him. But take care that you do not lament internally also.

XVII

Remember that thou art an actor in a play, of such a kind as the author may choose; if short, of a short one; if long, of a long one: if he wishes you to act the part of a poor man, see that you act the part naturally; if the part of a lame man, of a magistrate, of a private person, do the same. For this is your duty, to act well the part that is given to you; but to select the part, belongs to another.

XVIII

When a raven has croaked inauspiciously, let not the appearance hurry you away with it; but straightway make a distinction in your mind and say, None of these things is signified to me, but either to my poor body, or to my small property, or to my reputation, or to my children or to my wife: but to me all significations are auspicious if I choose. For whatever of these things results, it is in my power to derive benefit from it.

XIX

You can be invincible, if you enter into no contest in which it is not in your power to conquer. Take care then when you observe a man honoured before others or possessed of great power or highly esteemed for any reason, not to suppose him happy, and be not carried away by the appearance. For if the nature of the good is in our power, neither envy nor jealousy will have a place in us. But you yourself will not wish to be a general or senator or consul, but a free man: and there is only one way to this, to despise the things which are not in our power.

XX

Remember that it is not he who reviles you or strikes you, who insults you, but it is your opinion about these things as being insulting. When then a man irritates you, you must know that it is your own opinion which has irritated you. Therefore especially try not to be carried away by the appearance. For if you once gain time and delay, you will more easily master yourself.

XXI

Let death and exile and every other thing which appears dreadful be daily before your eyes; but most of all death: and you will never think of anything mean nor will you desire any thing extravagantly.

XXII

If you desire philosophy, prepare yourself from the beginning to be ridiculed, to expect that many will sneer at you, and say, He has all at once returned to us as a philosopher; and whence does he get this supercilious look for us? Do you not show a supercilious look; but hold on to the things which seem to you best as one appointed by God to this station. And remember that if you abide in the same principles, these men who first ridiculed will afterwards admire you: but if you shall have been overpowered by them, you will bring on yourself double ridicule.

XXIII

If it should ever happen to you to be turned to externals in order to please some person, you must know that you have lost your purpose in life. Be satisfied then in every thing with being a philosopher; and if you wish to seem also to any person to be a philosopher, appear so to yourself, and you will be able to do this.

XXIV

Let not these thoughts afflict you, I shall live unhonoured and be nobody nowhere. For if want of honour is an evil, you cannot be in evil through the means of another any more than you can be involved in any thing base. Is it then your business to obtain the rank of a magistrate, or to be received at a banquet? By no means. How then can this be want of honour? And how will you be nobody nowhere, when you ought to be somebody in those things only which are in your power, in which indeed it is permitted to you to be a man of the greatest worth? But your friends will be without assistance! What do you mean by being without assistance? They will not receive money from you, nor will you make them Roman citizens. Who then told you that these are among the things which are in our power, and not in the power of others? And who can give to another what he has not himself? Acquire money then, your friends say, that we also may have something. If I can acquire money and also keep myself modest, and faithful and magnanimous, point out the way, and I will acquire it. But if you ask me to lose the things which are good and my own, in order that you may gain the things which are not good, see how unfair and silly you are. Besides, which would you rather have, money or a faithful and modest friend? For this end then rather help me to be such a man, and do not ask me to do this by which I shall lose that character. But my country, you say, as far as it depends on me, will be without my help. I ask again, what help do you mean? It will not have porticoes or baths through you. And what does this mean? For it is not furnished with shoes by means of a smith, nor with arms by means of a shoemaker. But it is enough if every man fully discharges the work that is his own: and if you provided it with another citizen faithful and modest, would you not be useful to it? Yes. Then you also cannot be useless to it. What place then, you say, shall I hold in the city? Whatever you can, if you maintain at the same time your fidelity and modesty. But if when you wish to be useful to the state, you shall lose these qualities, what profit could you be to it, if you were made shameless and faithless?

XXV

Has any man been preferred before you at a banquet, or in being saluted, or in being invited to a consultation? If these things are good, you ought to rejoice that he has obtained them: but if bad, be not grieved because you have not obtained them; and remember that you cannot, if you do not the same things in order to obtain what is not in our own power, be considered worthy of the same things. For how can a man obtain an equal share with another when he does not visit a man's doors as that other man does, when he does not attend him when he goes abroad, as the other man does; when he does not praise him as another does? You will be unjust then and insatiable, if you do not part with the price, in return for which those things are sold, and if you wish to obtain them for nothing. Well, what is the price of lettuces? An obolus perhaps. If then a man gives us the obolus, and receives the lettuces, and if you do not give up the obolus and do not obtain the lettuces, do not suppose that you receive less than he who has got the lettuces; for as he has the lettuces, so you have the obolus which you did not give. In the same way then in the other matter also you have not been invited to a man's feast, for you did not give to the host the price at which the supper is sold; but he sells it for praise, he sells it for personal attention. Give then the price, if it is for your interest, for which it is sold. But if you wish both not to give the price and to obtain the things, you are insatiable and silly. Have you nothing then in place of the supper? You have indeed, you have the not flattering of him, whom you did not choose to flatter; you have the not enduring of the man when he enters the room.

XXVI

We may learn the will of nature from the things in which we do not differ from one another: for instance, when your neighbour's slave has broken his cup, or any thing else, we are ready to say forthwith, that it is one of the things which happen. You must know then that when your cup also is broken, you ought to think as you did when your neighbour's cup was broken. Transfer this reflection to greater things also. Is another man's child or wife dead? There is no one who would not say, this is an event incident to man. But when a man's own child or wife is dead, forthwith he calls out. Wo to me, how wretched I am. But we ought to remember how we feel when we hear that it has happened to others.

XXVII

As a mark is not set up for the purpose of missing the aim, so neither does the nature of evil exist in the world.

Juvenal

The Roman Juvenal was the greatest satiric poet who ever lived, asserts Gilbert Highet in the opening sentence of his book, *Juvenal the Satirist* (Oxford 1954). And Juvenal's Third Satire is commonly regarded as the most penetrating and the most incisive of all the sixteen satires published by this second-century Roman. In this brief essay Juvenal "describes" his city, with all its filth and corruption, its lavishness and decadence. In the course of his descriptions, Juvenal gives us a portrait of himself—a man who knew how to hate.

Juvenal was a latter-day elder Cato who wanted to resurrect the self-reliance, independence, maturity, and quiet self-confidence of an age past. In other words, he sought a return to the ideals of the Republic, which, it may be suspected, he tended to romanticize.

The speculations about Juvenal's life are many; the facts are few. He is thought to have been born in Aquinum some sixty miles southeast of Rome around 60 A.D., and to have died about 130. He may have had military experience; he may have been exiled to Egypt; he may have been the son of a freed slave; he may have lived on charity; he may have been wealthy. Such, at least, are some of the speculations that have sprung from diligent and thoughtful probings of his *Satires*, but very little can be claimed with assurance. Perhaps here Juvenal shows his real genius, since, even in this most personally revealing of literary *genres*, he has managed to conceal information concerning himself almost completely.

The satire, in a somewhat free translation by Rolfe Humphries, depicts a conversation in which a friend of Juvenal, who has decided to move into the country, describes, in vivid detail, living conditions in the city of Rome.

The Third Satire

Troubled because my old friend is
going, I still must commend him
For his decision to settle down in the
ghost town of Cumae,
Giving the Sibyl one citizen more. That's
the gateway to Baiae
There, a pleasant shore, a delightful
retreat. I'd prefer
Even a barren rock in that bay to the
brawl of Subura.
Where have we ever seen a place so
dismal and lonely
We'd not be better off there, than afraid,
as we are here, of fires,
Roofs caving in, and the thousand risks
of this terrible city
Where the poets recite all through the
dog days of August?

While they are loading his goods on one
little four-wheeled wagon,
Here he waits, by the old archways
which the aqueducts moisten.
This is where Numa, by night, came to
visit his goddess.
That once holy grove, its sacred spring,
and its temple,
Now are let out to the Jews, if they have
some straw and a basket.
Every tree, these days, has to pay rent
to the people.
Kick the Muses out; the forest is swarm-
ing with beggars.
So we go down to Egeria's vale, with its
modern improvements.
How much more close the presence
would be, were there lawns by the
water.
Turf to the curve of the pool, not this
unnatural marble!

Umbricius has much on his mind. "Since
there's no place in the city,"
He says, "For an honest man, and no
reward for his labors,
Since I have less today than yesterday,
since by tomorrow
That will have dwindled still more, I
have made my decision. I'm going
To the place where, I've heard, Dae-
dalus put off his wings,
While my white hair is still new, my old
age in the prime of its straightness,
While my fate spinner still has yarn on
her spool, while I'm able
Still to support myself on two good legs,
without crutches.
Rome, good-bye! Let the rest stay in the
town if they want to,
Fellows like A, B, and C, who make
black white at their pleasure,
Finding it easy to grab contracts for
rivers and harbors,
Putting up temples, or cleaning out sew-
ers, or hauling off corpses,
Or, if it comes to that, auctioning slaves
in the market.
Once they used to be hornblowers,
working the carneys;
Every wide place in the road knew their
puffed-out cheeks and their squeal-
ing.
Now they give shows of their own.
Thumbs up! Thumbs down! And the
killers
Spare or slay, and then go back to
concessions for private privies.
Nothing they won't take on. Why not?—
since the kindness of Fortune
(Fortune is out for laughs) has exalted
them out of the gutter.
"What should I do in Rome? I am no
good at lying.
If a book's bad, I can't praise it, or go
around ordering copies.

The Satires of Juvenal, trans. Rolfe Humphries (Bloomington: Indiana University
Press, 1958), pp. 33–45. Courtesy of Indiana University Press.

I don't know the stars; I can't hire out
as assassin
When some young man wants his father
knocked off for a price; I have never
Studied the guts of frogs, and plenty of
others know better
How to convey to a bride the gifts of
the first man she cheats with.
I am no lookout for thieves, so I cannot
expect a commission
On some governor's staff. I'm a useless
corpse, or a cripple.
Who has a pull these days, except your
yes men and stooges
With blackmail in their hearts, yet smart
enough to keep silent?
No honest man feels in debt to those he
admits to his secrets,
But your Verres must love the man who
can tattle on Verres
Any old time that he wants. Never let
the gold of the Tagus,
Rolling under its shade, become so important, so precious
You have to lie awake, take bribes that
you'll have to surrender,
Tossing in gloom, a threat to your
mighty patron forever.

"Now let me speak of the race that our
rich men dote on most fondly.
These I avoid like the plague, let's have
no coyness about it.
Citizens, I can't stand a Greekized
Rome. Yet what portion
Of the dregs of our town comes from
Achaia only?
Into the Tiber pours the silt, the mud
of Orontes,
Bringing its babble and brawl, its dis-
sonant harps and its timbrels,
Bringing also the tarts who display their
wares at the Circus.
Here's the place, if your taste is for
hatwearing whores, brightly colored!
What have they come to now, the simple
souls from the country
Romulus used to know? They put on
the *trechedipna*
(That might be called, in our tongue,
their running-to-dinner outfit),
Pin on their *niketeria* (medals), and smell
ceromatic

(Attar of wrestler). They come, trooping
from Samos and Tralles,
Adros, wherever that is, Azusa and Cu-
camonga,
Bound for the Esquiline or the hill we
have named for the vineyard,
Termites, into great halls where they
hope, some day, to be tyrants.
Desperate nerve, quick wit, as ready in
speech as Isaeus,
Also a lot more long-winded. Look over
there! See that fellow?
What do you take him for? He can be
anybody he chooses,
Doctor of science or letters, a vet or a
chiropractor,
Orator, painter, masseur, palmologist,
tightrope walker.
If he is hungry enough, your little Greek
stops at nothing.
Tell him to fly to the moon, and he runs
right off for his space ship.
Who flew first? Some Moor, some Turk,
some Croat, or some Slovene?
Not on your life, but a man from the
very center of Athens.

"Should I not run away from these
purple-wearing freeloaders?
Must I wait while they sign their names?
Must their couches always be softer?
Stowaways, that's how they got here, in
the plums and figs from Damascus.
I was here long before they were: my
boyhood drank in the sky
Over the Aventine hill; I was nourished
by Sabine olives.
Agh, what lackeys they are, what syco-
phants! See how they flatter
Some ignoramus's talk, or the looks of
some horrible eyesore,
Saying some Ichabod Crane's long neck
reminds them of muscles
Hercules strained when he lifted An-
taeus aloft on his shoulders,
Praising some cackling voice that really
sounds like a rooster's
When he's pecking a hen. We can praise
the same objects that they do,
Only, they are believed. Does an actor
do any better
Mimicking Thais, Alcestis, Doris without any clothes on?

It seems that a woman speaks, not a
mask; the illusion is perfect
Down to the absence of bulge and the
little cleft under the belly.
Yet they win no praise at home, for all
of their talent.
Why?—Because Greece is a stage, and
every Greek is an actor.
Laugh, and he splits his sides; weep,
and his tears flow in torrents
Though he's not sad; if you ask for a
little more fire in the winter
He will put on his big coat; if you say
'I'm hot,' he starts sweating.
We are not equals at all; he always has
the advantage,
Able, by night or day, to assume, from
another's expression,
This or that look, prepared to throw up
his hands, to cheer loudly
If his friend gives a good loud belch or
doesn't piss crooked,
Or if a gurgle comes from his golden
cup when inverted
Straight up over his nose—a good deep
swig, and no heeltaps!

"Furthermore, nothing is safe from his
lust, neither matron nor virgin,
Nor her affianced spouse, or the boy
too young for the razor.
If he can't get at these, he would just as
soon lay his friend's grandma.
(Anything, so he'll get in to knowing the
family secrets!)
Since I'm discussing the Greeks, let's
turn to their schools and professors,
The crimes of the hood and gown, Old
Dr. Egnatius, informant,
Brought about the death of Barea, his
friend and his pupil,
Born on that riverbank where the pi-
nion of Pegasus landed.
No room here, none at all, for any
respectable Roman
Where a Protogenes rules, or a Diphilus,
or a Hermarchus,
Never sharing their friends—a racial
characteristic!
Hands off! He puts a drop of his own,
or his countryside's poison
Into his patron's ear, an ear which is
only too willing

And I am kicked out of the house, and
all my years of long service
Count for nothing. Nowhere does the
loss of a client mean less.
"Let's not flatter ourselves. What's the
use of our service?
What does a poor man gain by hurrying
out in the nighttime,
All dressed up before dawn, when the
praetor nags at his troopers
Bidding them hurry along to convey his
respects to the ladies,
Barren, of course, like Albina, before
any others can get there?
Sons of men freeborn give right of way
to rich man's
Slave; a crack, once or twice, at Calvina
or Catiena
Costs an officer's pay, but if you like the
face of some floozy
You hardly have money enough to make
her climb down from her high chair.
Put on the stand, at Rome, a man with
a record unblemished,
No more a perjurer than Numa was, or
Metellus,
What will they question? His wealth,
right away, and possibly, later,
(Only possibly, though) touch on his
reputation.
'How many slaves does he feed? What's
the extent of his acres?
How big are his platters? How many?
What of his goblets and wine bowls?'
His word is as good as his bond—if he
has enough bonds in his strongbox.
But a poor man's oath, even if sworn
on all altars
All the way from here to the farthest
Dodecanese island,
Has no standing in court. What has he
to fear from the lightnings
Of the outraged gods? He has nothing
to lose; they'll ignore him.

"If you're poor, you're a joke, on each
and every occasion.
What a laugh, if your cloak is dirty or
torn, if your toga
Seems a little bit soiled, if your shoe has
a crack in the leather,
Or if more than one patch attests to
more than one mending!

Poverty's greatest curse, much worse
than the fact of it, is that
It makes men objects of mirth, ridiculed,
humbled, embarrassed.
'Out of the front-row seats!' they cry
when you're out of money,
Yield your place to the sons of some
pimp, the spawn of some cathouse,
Some slick auctioneer's brat, or the louts
some trainer has fathered
Or the well-groomed boys whose sire is
a gladiator.
Such is the law of the place, decreed by
the nitwitted Otho:
*All the best seats are reserved for the classes
who have the most money.*
Who can marry a girl if he has less
money than she does?
What poor man is an heir, or can hope
to be? Which of them ever
Rates a political job, even the meanest
and lowest?
Long before now, all poor Roman descendants of Romans
Ought to have marched out of town in
one determined migration.
Men do not easily rise whose poverty
hinders their merit.
Here it is harder than anywhere else:
the lodgings are hovels,
Rents out of sight; your slaves take
plenty to fill up their bellies
While you make do with a snack. You're
ashamed   of   your   earthenware
dishes—
Ah, but that wouldn't be true if you
lived content in the country,
Wearing a dark-blue cape, and the hood
thrown back on your shoulders.

"In a great part of this land of Italy,
might as well face it,
No one puts on a toga unless he is dead.
On festival days
Where the theater rises, cut from green
turf, and with great pomp
Old familiar plays are staged again, and
a baby,
Safe in his mother's lap, is scared of the
grotesque mask,
There you see all dressed alike, the
balcony and the front rows,

Even His Honor content with a tunic of
simple white.
Here, beyond our means, we have to be
smart, and too often
Get our effects with too much, an elaborate wardrobe, on credit!
This is a common vice; we must keep
up with the neighbors,
Poor as we are. I tell you, everything
here costs you something.
How much to give Cossus the time of
day, or receive from Veiento
One quick glance, with his mouth but-
toned up for fear he might greet you?
One shaves his beard, another cuts off
the locks of his boy friend,
Offerings fill the house, but these, you
find, you will pay for.
Put this in your pipe and smoke it—we
have to pay tribute
Giving the slaves a bribe for the prospect
of bribing their masters.

"Who, in Praeneste's cool, or the
wooded Volsinian uplands,
Who, on Tivoli's heights, or a small town
like Gabii, say,
Fears the collapse of his house? But
Rome is supported on pipestems,
Matchsticks; it's cheaper, so, for the
landlord to shore up his ruins,
Patch up the old cracked walls, and
notify all the tenants
They can sleep secure, though the
beams are in ruins above them.
No, the place to live is out there, where
no cry of *Fire*
Sounds the alarm of the night, with a
neighbor yelling for water,
Moving his chattels and goods, and the
whole third story is smoking.
This you'll never know: for if the
ground floor is scared first,
You are the last to burn, up where the
eaves of the attic
Keep off the rain, and the doves are
brooding over their nest eggs.
Codrus owned one bed, too small for a
midget to sleep on,
Six little jugs he had, and a tankard
adorning his sideboard,
Under whose marble (clay), a bust or a
statue of Chiron,

Busted, lay on its side; an old locker held Greek books
Whose divinest lines were gnawed by the mice, those vandals.
Codrus had nothing, no doubt, and yet he succeeded, poor fellow,
Losing that nothing, his all. And this is the very last straw—
No one will help him out with a meal or lodging or shelter.
Stripped to the bone, begging for crusts, he still receives nothing.

"Yet if Asturicus' mansion burns down, what a frenzy of sorrow!
Mothers dishevel themselves, the leaders dress up in black,
Courts are adjourned. We groan at the fall of the city, we hate
The fire, and the fire still burns, and while it is burning,
Somebody rushes up to replace the loss of the marble,
Some one chips in toward a building fund, another gives statues,
Naked and shining white, some masterpiece of Euphranor
Or Polyclitus' chef d'oeuvre; and here's a fellow with bronzes
Sacred to Asian gods. Books, chests, a bust of Minerva,
A bushel of siver coins. *To him that hath shall be given!*
This Persian, childless, of course, the richest man in the smart set,
Now has better things, and more, than before the disaster.
How can we help but think he started the fire on purpose?

"Tear yourself from the games, and get a place in the country!
One little Latian town, like Sora, say, or Frusino,
Offers a choice of homes, at a price you pay here, in one year,
Renting some hole in the wall. Nice houses, too, with a garden,
Springs bubbling up from the grass, no need for a windlass or bucket,
Plenty to water your flowers, if they need it, without any trouble.

Live there, fond of your hoe, an independent producer,
Willing and able to feed a hundred good vegetarians.
Isn't it something, to feel, wherever you are, how far off,
You are a monarch? At least, lord of a single lizard.

"Here in town the sick die from insomnia mostly.
Undigested food, on a stomach burning with ulcers,
Brings on listlessness, but who can sleep in a flophouse?
Who but the rich can afford sleep and a garden apartment?
That's the source of infection. The wheels creak by on the narrow
Streets of the wards, the drivers squabble and brawl when they're stopped,
More than enough to frustrate the drowsiest son of a sea cow.
When his business calls, the crowd makes way, as the rich man,
Carried high in his car, rides over them, reading or writing,
Even taking a snooze, perhaps, for the motion's composing.
Still, he gets where he wants before we do; for all of our hurry
Traffic gets in our way, in front, around and behind us.
Somebody gives me a shove with an elbow, or two-by-four scantling.
One clunks my head with a beam, another cracks down with a beer keg.
Mud is thick on my shins, I am trampled by somebody's big feet.
Now what?—a soldier grinds his hobnails into my toes.

"Don't you see the mob rushing along to the handout?
There are a hundred guests, each one with his kitchen servant.
Even Samson himself could hardly carry those burdens,
Pots and pans some poor little slave tries to keep on his head, while he hurries
Hoping to keep the fire alive by the wind of his running.

Tunics, new-darned, and ripped to
  shreds; there's the flash of a fir beam
Huge on some great dray, and another
  carries a pine tree,
Nodding above our heads and threat-
  ening death to the people.
What will be left of the mob, if that cart
  of Ligurian marble
Breaks its axle down and dumps its load
  on these swarms?
Who will identify limbs or bones? The
  poor man's cadaver,
Crushed, disappears like his breath.
  And meanwhile, at home, his household
Washes the dishes, and puffs up the
  fire, with all kinds of a clatter
Over the smeared flesh-scrapers, the
  flasks of oil, and the towels.
So the boys rush around, while their
  late master is sitting,
Newly come to the bank of the Styx,
  afraid of the filthy
Ferryman there, since he has no fare,
  not even a copper
In his dead mouth to pay for the ride
  through that muddy whirlpool.

"Look at other things, the various dangers of nighttime.
How high it is to the cornice that breaks,
  and a chunk beats my brains out,
Or some slob heaves a jar, broken or
  cracked, from a window.
Bang! It comes down with a crash and
  proves its weight on the sidewalk.
You are a thoughtless fool, unmindful
  of sudden disaster,
If you don't make your will before you
  go out to have dinner.
There are as many deaths in the night
  as there are open windows
Where you pass by; if you're wise, you
  will pray, in your wretched devotions,
People may be content with no more
  than emptying slop jars.

"There your hell-raising drunk, who has
  had the bad luck to kill no one,
Tosses in restless rage, like Achilles
  mourning Patroclus,
Turns from his face to his back, can't
  sleep, for only a fracas

Gives him the proper sedation. But any
  of these young hoodlums,
All steamed up on wine, watches his
  step when the crimson
Cloak goes by, a lord, with a long, long
  line of attendants,
Torches and brazen lamps, warning
  him, *Keep your distance!*
Me, however, whose torch is the moon,
  or the feeblest candle
Fed by a sputtering wick, he absolutely
  despises.
Here is how it all starts, the fight, if you
  think it is fighting
When he throws all the punches, and
  all I do is absorb them.
He stops. He tells me to stop. I stop. I
  have to obey him.
What can you do when he's mad and
  bigger and stronger than you are?
'Where do you come from?' he cries,
  'you wino, you bean-bloated bastard?
Off what shoemaker's dish have you fed
  on chopped leeks and boiled lamb-
  lip?
What? No answer? Speak up, or take a
  swift kick in the rear.
Tell me where you hang out—in some
  praying-house with the Jew-boys?'
If you try to talk back, or sneak away
  without speaking,
All the same thing: you're assaulted,
  and then put under a bail bond
For committing assault. This is a poor
  man's freedom.
Beaten, cut up by fists, he begs and
  implores his assailant,
Please, for a chance to go home with a
  few teeth left in his mouth.

"This is not all you must fear. Shut up
  your house or your store,
Bolts and padlocks and bars will never
  keep out all the burglars,
Or a holdup man will do you in with a
  switch blade.
If the guards are strong over Pontine
  marshes and pinewoods
Near Volturno, the scum of the swamps
  and the filth of the forest
Swirl into Rome, the great sewer, their
  sanctuary, their haven.

Furnaces blast and anvils groan with the
  chains we are forging:
What other use have we for iron and
  steel? There is danger
We will have little left for hoes and
  mattocks and ploughshares.
Happy the men of old, those primitive
  generations
Under the tribunes and kings, when
  Rome had only one jailhouse!

"There is more I could say, I could give
  you more of my reasons,

But the sun slants down, my oxen seem
  to be calling,
My man with the whip is impatient, I
  must be on my way.
So long! Don't forget me. Whenever
  you come to Aquino
Seeking relief from Rome, send for me.
  I'll come over
From my bay to your hills, hiking along
  in my thick boots
Toward your chilly fields. What's more,
  I promise to listen
If your satirical verse esteems me worthy
  the honor."

The New Testament

In the province of Judaea, tucked away in a far corner of the Roman Empire, was born midway through the reign of Augustus a man whose influence on world history was far to surpass that of the *princeps*—Jesus of Nazareth. We have chosen from the New Testament selections illustrating the teachings of Jesus and the early history and theological doctrines of his followers. From the Gospel of St. Matthew comes the Sermon on the Mount, the most complete and one of the most beautiful statements of the religious views of Jesus. The Acts is a historical book detailing the activities of the founders of the Christian church in the years immediately following the crucifixion of Christ, as seen through the eyes of the early church fathers several years later. Of crucial importance to Western history is the transformation of Christianity from the exclusive possession of an obscure Jewish sect into a message of salvation open to Gentiles as well as to Jews. This was the first step on Christianity's long road to religious domination of the Western world. The selection from Romans contains a statement of Christian doctrine by the Apostle Paul, one of the most influential of all Christian theologians. It was Paul who began the task of developing the teachings of Jesus into an organized and consistent body of theological doctrine.

The cornerstone of Paul's doctrine is the theory of original sin (see p. 23), with its related concepts of predestination, election, and grace. Originated by Paul, elaborated by St. Augustine in the fifth century, and reiterated by the Protestant reformer John Calvin in the sixteenth century, the doctrine of original sin is of fundamental importance in the history of Christian theology. Although of lesser significance, the notion of justification by faith, also included in the selection from Romans, has had a long history. It is associated particularly with the Protestant theology of Martin Luther. The New Testament selections have been taken from the King James Version of the Bible, with slight alterations in form.

St. Matthew

And seeing the multitudes, he went up into a mountain: And when he was set, his disciples came unto him: And he opened his mouth, and taught them, saying, "Bessed are the poor in spirit: for theirs is the kingdom of heaven. Blessed are they that mourn: for they shall be comforted. Blessed are the meek: for they shall inherit the earth. Blessed are they which do hunger and thirst after righteousness: for they shall be filled. Blessed are the merciful: for they shall obtain mercy. Blessed are the pure in heart: for they shall see God. Blessed are the peace-makers: for they shall be called the children of God. Blessed are they which are persecuted for righteousness' sake: for theirs is the kingdom of heaven. Blessed are ye, when men shall revile you, and persecute you, and shall say all manner of evil against you falsely, for my sake. Rejoice, and be exceeding glad: for great is your reward in heaven: for so persecuted they the prophets which were before you.

"Ye are the salt of the earth: but if the salt have lost his savour, wherewith shall it be salted? It is thenceforth good for nothing, but to be cast out, and to be trodden under foot of men. Ye are the light of the world. A city that is set on a hill cannot be hid. Neither do men light a candle, and put it under a bushel, but on a candlestick; and it giveth light unto all that are in the house. Let your light so shine before men, that they may see your good works, and glorify your Father which is in heaven.

"Think not that I am come to destroy the law, or the prophets: I am not come to destroy, but to fulfil. For verily I say unto you, till heaven and earth pass, one jot or one tittle shall in no wise pass from the law, till all be fulfilled. Whosoever therefore shall break one of these least commandments, and shall teach men so, he shall be called the least in the kingdom of heaven: but whosoever shall do and teach them, the same shall be called great in the kingdom of heaven. For I say unto you, that except your righteousness shall exceed the righteousness of the scribes and Pharisees, ye shall in no case enter into the kingdom of heaven.

"Ye have heard that it was said by them of old time, thou shalt not kill; and whosoever shall kill shall be in danger of the judgment. But I say unto you, That whosoever is angry with his brother without a cause shall be in danger of the judgment: and whosoever shall say to his brother, 'Ra-ca,' shall be in danger of the council: but whosoever shall say, 'Thou fool,' shall be in danger of hell fire. Therefore if thou bring thy gift to the altar, and there rememberest that thy brother hath ought against thee; leave there thy gift before the altar, and go thy way; first be reconciled to thy brother, and then come and offer thy gift. Agree with thine adversary quickly, whiles thou art in the way

Chapters 5, 6, 7.

with him; lest at any time the adversary deliver thee to the judge, and the judge deliver thee to the officer, and thou be cast into prison. Verily I say unto thee, Thou shalt by no means come out thence, till thou hast paid the uttermost farthing.

"Ye have heard that it was said by them of old time, Thou shalt not commit adultery. But I say unto you, That whosoever looketh on a woman to lust after her hath committed adultery with her already in his heart. And if thy right eye offend thee, pluck it out, and cast it from thee: for it is profitable for thee that one of thy members should perish, and not that thy whole body should be cast into hell. And if thy right hand offend thee: cut it off, and cast it from thee: for it is profitable for thee that one of thy members should perish, and not that thy whole body should be cast into hell. It hath been said, Whoever shall put away his wife, let him give her a writing of divorcement. But I say unto you, That whosoever shall put away his wife, saving for the cause of fornication, causeth her to commit adultery: and whosoever shall marry her that is divorced committeth adultery.

"Again, ye have heard that it hath been said by them of old time, Thou shalt not forswear thyself, but shalt perform unto the Lord thine oaths. But I say unto you, Swear not at all; neither by heaven; for it is God's throne: nor by the earth; for it is his footstool: neither by Jerusalem; for it is the city of the great King. Neither shalt thou swear by thy head, because thou canst not make one hair white or black. But let your communication be, Yea, yea; Nay,

nay: for whatsoever is more than these cometh of evil.

"Ye have heard that it hath been said, An eye for an eye, and a tooth for a tooth. But I say unto you, That ye resist not evil: but whosoever shall smite thee on thy right cheek, turn to him the other also. And if any man will sue thee at the law, and take away thy coat, let him have thy cloke also. And whosoever shall compel thee to go a mile, go with him twain. Give to him that asketh thee, and from him that would borrow of thee turn not thou away.

"Ye have heard that it hath been said, Thou shalt love thy neighbor, and hate thine enemy. But I say unto you, Love your enemies, bless them that curse you, do good to them that hate you, and pray for them which despitefully use you, and persecute you; that ye may be the children of your Father which is in heaven: for he maketh his sun to rise on the evil and on the good, and sendeth rain on the just and on the unjust. For if ye love them which love you, what reward have ye? Do not even the publicans the same? And if ye salute your brethren only, what do ye more than others? Do not even the publicans so? Be ye therefore perfect, even as your Father which is in heaven is perfect.

"Take heed that ye do not your alms before men, to be seen of them: otherwise ye have no reward of your Father which is in heaven. Therefore when thou doest thine alms do not sound a trumpet before thee, as the hypocrites do in the synagogues and in the streets, that they may have glory of men. Verily I say unto you, they have their reward. But when thou doest alms, let not thy left hand know what thy right hand doeth: that thine alms may be in secret: and thy Father which seeth in secret himself shall reward thee openly.

"And when thou prayest, thou shalt not be as the hypocrites are: for they love to pray standing in the synagogues and in the corners of the street, that they may be seen of men. Verily I say unto you, They have their reward. But thou, when thou prayest, enter into thy closet, and when thou hast shut thy door, pray to thy father which is in secret: and thy Father which seeth in secret shall reward thee openly. But when ye pray, use not vain repetitions, as the heathen do: for they think that they shall be heard for their much speaking. Be not ye therefore like unto them: for your father knoweth what things ye have need of, before ye ask him. After this manner therefore pray ye: Our Father which art in heaven, hallowed be thy name. Thy kingdom come. Thy will be done in earth, as it is in heaven. Give us this day our daily bread. And forgive us our debts, as we forgive our debtors. And lead us not into temptation, but deliver us from evil: For thine is the kingdom, and the power, and the glory, for ever. A-men.

"For if ye forgive men their trespasses, your heavenly Father will also forgive you: But if ye forgive not men their trespasses, neither will your father forgive your trespasses.

"Moreover when ye fast, be not, as the hypocrites, of a sad countenance: for they disfigure their faces, that they may appear unto men to fast. Verily I say unto you, They have their reward. But thou, when thou fastest, anoint thine head, and wash thy face; that thou appear not unto men to fast, but unto thy Father which is in secret: and thy Father, which seeth in secret, shall reward thee openly.

"Lay not up for yourselves, treasures upon earth, where moth and rust doth corrupt, and where thieves break through and steal. But lay up for yourselves treasures in heaven, where neither moth nor rust doth corrupt, and where thieves do not break through nor steal: For where your treasaure is, there will your heart be also. The light of the body is the eye: if therefore thine eye be single thy whole body shall be full of light. But if thine eye be evil, thy whole body shall be full of darkness. If therefore the light that is in thee be darkness, how great is that darkness!

"No man can serve two masters: for either he will hate the one, and love the other; or else he will hold to the one, and despise the other. Ye cannot serve God and mammon. Therefore I say unto you, Take no thought for your life, what ye shall eat, or what ye shall drink; nor yet for your body, what ye shall put on. Is not the life more than meat, and the body than raiment? Behold the fowls of the air: for they sow not, neither do they reap, nor gather into barns; yet your heavenly Father feedeth them. Are ye not much better than they? Which of you by taking thought can add one cubit unto his stature? And why take ye thought for raiment? Consider the lilies of the field, how they grow; they toil not, neither do they spin: And yet I say unto you, That even Solomon in all his glory was not arrayed like one of these. Wherefore, if God so clothe the grass of the field, which today is, and to-morrow is cast into the oven, shall he not much more clothe you, O ye of little faith? Therefore take no thought, saying, What shall we eat? or, What shall we drink? or Wherewithal shall we be clothed? (For after all these things do the Gentiles seek:) for your heavenly Father knoweth that ye have need of all these things. But seek ye first the kingdom of God, and his righteousness; and all these things shall be added unto you. Take therefore no thought for the morrow: for the morrow shall take thought for the things of itself. Sufficient unto the day is the evil thereof.

"Judge not, that ye be not judged. For with what judgment ye judge, ye shall be judged: and with what measure ye mete, it shall be measured to you again. And why beholdest thou the mote that is in thy brother's eye, but considerest not the beam that is in thine own eye? Or how wilt thou say to thy brother, Let me pull out the mote out of thine eye; and, behold, a beam is in thine own eye? Thou hypocrite, first cast out the beam out of thine own eye; and then shalt thou see clearly to cast out the mote out of thy brother's eye.

"Give not that which is holy unto the dogs, neither cast ye your pearls before swine, lest they trample them under their feet, and turn again and rend you.

"Ask, and it shall be given you; seek, and ye shall find; knock, and it shall be opened unto you: For every one that asketh receiveth; and he that seeketh findeth; and to him that knocketh it shall be opened. Or what man is there of you, whom if his son ask bread, will he give him a stone? Or if he ask a fish, will he give him a serpent? If ye then, being evil, know how to give good gifts unto your children, how much more shall your Father which is in heaven give good things to them that ask him? Therefore all things whatsoever ye would that men should do to you, do ye even so to them: for this is the law and the prophets.

"Enter ye in the strait gate: for wide is the gate, and broad is the way, that leadeth to destruction, and many there be which go in thereat: Because strait is the gate, and narrow is the way, which leadeth unto life, and few there be that find it.

"Beware of false prophets, which come to you in sheep's clothing, but inwardly they are ravening wolves. Ye shall know them by their fruits. Do men gather grapes of thorns, or figs of thistles? Even so every good tree bringeth forth good fruit; but a corrupt tree bringeth forth evil fruit. A good tree cannot bring forth evil fruit, neither can a corrupt tree bring forth good fruit. Every tree that bringeth not forth good fruit is hewn down, and cast into the fire. Wherefore by their fruits ye shall know them.

"Not every one that saith unto me, Lord, Lord, shall enter into the kingdom of heaven; but he that doeth the will of my Father which is in heaven. Many will say to me in that day, Lord, Lord, have we not prophesied in thy name? And in thy name have cast out devils? And in thy name done many wonderful works? And then will I profess unto them, I never knew you; depart from me, ye that work iniquity.

"Therefore whosoever heareth these sayings of mine, and doeth them I will liken him unto a wise man, which built his house upon a rock: And the rain descended, and the floods came, and the winds blew, and beat upon that house and it fell not: for it was founded upon a rock. And every one that heareth these sayings of mine, and doeth them not, shall be likened unto a foolish man, which built his house upon the sand: And the rain descended, and the floods came, and the winds blew, and beat upon that house; and it fell: and great was the fall of it." And it came to pass, when Jesus had ended these sayings, the people were astonished at his doctrine: For he taught them as one having authority, and not as the scribes.

The Acts of the Apostles

The former treatise have I made, O Theophilus, of all that Jesus began both to do and teach, until the day in which he was taken up, after that he through the Holy Ghost had given commandments unto the apostles whom he had chosen. To whom also he shewed himself alive after his passion by many infallible proofs, being seen of them forty days, and speaking of the things pertaining to the kingdom of God: And, being assembled together with them, commanded them that they should not depart from Jerusalem, but wait for the promise of the Father, which, saith he, ye have heard of me. For John truly baptized with water; but ye shall be baptized with the Holy Ghost not many days hence.

When they therefore were come together, they asked of him, saying, "Lord, wilt thou at this time restore again the kingdom to Israel?" And he said unto them, "It is not for you to know the times or the seasons, which the Father hath put in his own power. But ye shall receive power, after that the Holy Ghost is come upon you: and ye shall be witnesses unto me both in Jerusa-lem, and in all Judaea, and in Samaria, and unto the uttermost part of the earth." And when he had spoken these things, while they beheld, he was taken up; and a cloud received him out of their sight. And while they looked stedfastly toward heaven as he went up, behold, two men stood by them in white apparel; which also said, "Ye men of Galilee, why stand ye gazing up into heaven? This same Jesus, which is taken up from you into heaven, shall so come in like manner as ye have seen him go into heaven." Then returned they unto Jerusalem from the mount called Olivet, which is from Jerusalem a sabbath day's journey.

And when the day of Pentecost was fully come, they were all with one accord in one place. And suddenly there came a sound from heaven as of a rushing mighty wind, and it filled all the house where they were sitting. And there appeared unto them cloven tongues like as of fire, and it sat upon each of them. And they were all filled with the Holy Ghost, and began to speak with other tongues, as the Spirit gave them utterance. And there were dwelling at Jerusalem Jews, devout

Chapters 1:1–12; 2:1–41; 6:7–15; 7:1–2, 51–60; 8:1–3; 9:1–22; 10.

men, out of every nation under heaven. Now when this was noised abroad, the multitude came together, and were confounded, because that every man heard them speak in his own language. And they were all amazed and marvelled, saying one to another, "Behold are not all these which speak Galilaeans? And how hear we every man in our own tongue, wherein we were born? Parthians, and Medes, and Elamites, and the dwellers in Mesopotamia, and in Judaea, and Cappadocia, in Pontus, and Asia. Phrygia, and Pamphylia, in Egypt, and in the parts of Libya about Cyrene, and strangers of Rome, Jews and proselytes, Cretes and Arabians, we do hear them speak in our tongues the wonderful works of God." And they were all amazed, and were in doubt, saying one to another, "What meaneth this?" Others mocking said, "These men are full of new wine."

But Peter, standing up with the eleven, lifted up his voice, and said unto them, "Ye men of Judaea, and all ye that dwell at Jerusalem, be this known unto you, and hearken to my words. For these are not drunken, as ye suppose, seeing it is but the third hour of the day. But this is that which was spoken by the prophet Joel: 'And it shall come to pass in the last days,' saith God, 'I will pour out of my Spirit upon all flesh: and your sons and your daughters shall prophesy, and your young men shall see visions, and your old men shall dream dreams: And on my servants and on my handmaidens I will pour out in those days of my Spirit; and they shall prophesy. And I will shew wonders in heaven above, and signs in the earth beneath; blood, and fire, and vapour of smoke: The sun shall be turned into darkness, and the moon into blood, before the great and notable day of the Lord come. And it shall come to pass, that whosoever shall call on the name of the Lord shall be saved.' Ye men of Israel, hear these words; Jesus of Nazareth, a man approved of God among you by miracles and wonders and signs, which God did by him in the midst of you, as ye yourselves also know: Him, being delivered by the determinate counsel and foreknowledge of God, ye have taken, and by wicked hands have crucified and slain: Whom God hath raised up, having loosed the pains of death: because it was not possible that he should be holden of it. For David speaketh concerning him, 'I foresaw the Lord always before my face, for he is on my right hand, that I should not be moved. Therefore did my heart rejoice, and my tongue was glad; moreover also my flesh shall rest in hope: Because thou wilt not leave my soul in hell, neither wilt thou suffer thine Holy One to see corruption. Thou hast made known to me the ways of life; thou shalt make me full of joy with thy countenance.' Men and brethren, let me freely speak unto you of the patriarch David, that he is both dead and buried, and his sepulchre is with us unto this day. Therefore being a prophet, and knowing that God had sworn with an oath to him, that of the fruit of his loins, according to the flesh, he would raise up Christ to sit on his throne; he seeing this before spake of the resurrection of Christ, that his soul was not left in hell neither his flesh did see corruption. Thus Jesus hath God raised up, whereof we all are witnesses. Therefore being by the right hand of God exalted, and having received of the Father the promise of the Holy Ghost, he hath shed forth this, which ye now see and hear. For David is not ascended into the heavens: but he saith himself, 'The LORD said unto my Lord, "Sit thou on my right hand, until I make thy foes thy footstool."' Therefore let all the houses of Israel know assuredly, that God hath made that same Jesus, whom ye have crucified, both Lord and Christ."

Now when they heard this, they were pricked in their heart, and said unto Peter and to the rest of the apostles, "Men and brethren, what shall we do?" Then Peter said unto them, "Repent, and be baptized every one of you in the name of Jesus Christ for the remission of sins, and ye shall receive the gift of the Holy Ghost. For the promise is unto you, and to your children, and to all that are afar off, even as many as the Lord our God shall call." And with many other words did he testify and exhort, saying, "Save yourselves from this untoward generation."

Then they that gladly received his word were baptized; and the same day there were added unto them about three thousand souls.

• • •

And the word of God increased; and the number of the disciples multiplied in Jerusalem greatly; and a great company of the priests were obedient to the faith. And Stephen, full of faith and power, did great wonders and miracles among the people.

Then there arose certain of the synagogue, which is called the synagogue of the Libertines, and Cyrenians, and Alexandrians, and of them of Cilicia and of Asia, disput-

ing with Stephen. And they were not able to resist the wisdom and the spirit by which he spake. Then they suborned men, which said, "We have heard him speak blasphemous words against Moses, and against God." And they stirred up the people, and the elders, and the scribes, and came upon him, and caught him, and brought him to the council, and set up false witnesses, which said, "This man ceaseth not to speak blasphemous words against this holy place, and the law: For we have heard him say that this Jesus of Nazareth shall destroy this place, and shall change the customs which Moses delivered us." And all that sat in the council, looking stedfastly on him, saw his face as it had been the face of an angel.

Then said the high priest, "Are these things so?" And he said, "Men, brethren, and fathers, hearken: [*After defending himself by an appeal to the Old Testament, Stephen concludes*] Ye stiffnecked and uncircumcised in heart and ears, ye do always resist the Holy Ghost: as your fathers did, so shall ye. Which of the prophets have not your fathers persecuted? And they have slain them which shewed before of the coming of the Just One; of whom ye have been now the betrayers and murderers: who have received the law by the disposition of angels, and have not kept it."

When they heard these things, they were cut to the heart, and they gnashed on him with their teeth. But he, being full of the Holy Ghost, looked up stedfastly into heaven, and saw the glory of God, and Jesus standing on the right hand of God, and said, "Behold, I see the heavens opened, and the Son of man standing on the right hand of God." Then they cried out with a loud voice, and stopped their ears, and ran upon him with one accord, and cast him out of the city, and stoned him: and the witnesses laid down their clothes at a young man's feet, whose name was Saul. And they stoned Stephen, calling upon God, and saying, "Lord Jesus, receive my spirit." And he kneeled down, and cried with a loud voice, "Lord, lay not this sin to their charge." And when he had said this, he fell asleep.

And Saul was consenting unto his death. And at that time there was a great persecution against the church which was at Jerusalem; and they were all scattered abroad throughout the regions of Judaea and Samaria, except the apostles. And devout men carried Stephen to his burial, and made great lamentation over him. As for Saul, he made havoc of the church, entering into every house, and haling men and women committed them to prison.

•   •   •

And Saul, yet breathing out threatenings and slaughter against the disciples of the Lord, went unto the high priest, and desired of him letters to Damascus to the synagogues, that if he found any of this way, whether they were men or women, he might bring them bound unto Jerusalem. And as he journeyed, he came near Damascus: and suddenly there shined round about him a light from heaven. And he fell to the earth, and heard a voice saying unto him, "Saul, Saul, why persecutest thou me?" And he said, "Who art thou, Lord?" And the Lord said, "I am Jesus whom thou persecutest: it is hard for thee to

kick against the pricks." And he trembling and astonished said, "Lord, what wilt thou have me to do?" And the Lord said unto him, "Arise, and go into the city, and it shall be told thee what thou must do." And the men which journeyed with him stood speechless, hearing a voice, but seeing no man. And Saul arose from the earth; and when his eyes were opened he saw no man: but they led him by the hand, and brought him into Damascus. And he was three days without sight, and neither did eat nor drink.

And there was a certain disciple at Damascus, named Ananias; and to him said the Lord in a vision, "Ananias." And he said, "Behold, I am here, Lord." And the Lord said unto him, "Arise, and go into the street which is called Straight, and enquire in the house of Judas for one called Saul, of Tarsus: for, behold, he prayeth, and hath seen in a vision, a man named Ananias coming in, and putting his hand on him, that he might receive his sight." Then Ananias answered, "Lord, I have heard by many of this man, how much evil he hath done to thy saints at Jerusalem: And here he hath authority from the chief priests to bind all that call on thy name." But the Lord said unto him, "Go thy way: for he is a chosen vessel unto me, to bear my name before the Gentiles, and kings, and the children of Israel: For I will shew him how great things he must suffer for my name's sake." And Ananias went his way and entered into the house; and putting his hands on him said, "Brother Saul, the Lord, even Jesus, that appeared unto thee in the way as thou camest, hath sent me, that thou mightest receive thy sight, and be filled with the Holy Ghost." And immediately there fell from his eyes as it had been scales: and he received sight forthwith, and arose, and was baptized. And when he had received meat, he was strengthened.

Then was Saul certain days with the disciples which were at Damascus. And straightway he preached Christ in the synagogues, that he is the Son of God. But all that heard him were amazed, and said; "Is not this he that destroyed them which called on this name in Jerusalem, and came hither for that intent, that he might bring them bound unto the chief priests?" But Saul increased the more in strength, and confounded the Jews which dwelt at Damascus, proving that this is very Christ.

• • •

There was a certain man in Caesarea called Cornelius, a centurion of the band called the Italian band. A devout man, and one that feared God with all his house, which gave much alms to the people, and prayed to God always. He saw in a vision evidently about the ninth hour of the day an angel of God coming in to him, and saying unto him, "Cornelius." And when he looked on him, he was afraid, and said, "What is it, Lord?" And he said unto him, "Thy prayers and thine alms are come up for a memorial before God. And now send men to Joppa, and call for one Simon, whose surname is Peter: He lodgeth with one Simon a tanner, whose house is by the sea side: he shall tell thee what thou oughtest to do." And when the angel which spake unto

Cornelius was departed, he called two of his household servants, and a devout soldier of them that waited on him continually; and when he had declared all these things unto them, he sent them to Joppa.

On the morrow, as they went on their journey, and drew nigh into the city, Peter went up upon the housetop to pray about the sixth hour. And he became very hungry, and would have eaten: but while they made ready, he fell into a trance, and saw heaven opened, and a certain vessel descending unto him, as it had been a great sheet knit at the four corners, and let down to the earth: wherein were all manner of four-footed beasts of the earth, and wild beasts, and creeping things, and fowls of the air. And there came a voice to him, "Rise, Peter; kill, and eat." But Peter said, "Not so, Lord; for I have never eaten any thing that is common or unclean." And the voice spake unto him again the second time, "What God hath cleansed, that call not thou common." This was done thrice: and the vessel was received up again into heaven. Now while Peter doubted in himself what this vision which he had seen should mean, behold, the men which were sent from Cornelius had made enquiry for Simon's house, and stood before the gate, and called, and asked whether Simon, which was surnamed Peter, were lodged there.

While Peter thought on the vision, the Spirit said unto him, "Behold, three men seek thee. Arise therefore, and get thee down, and go with them, doubting nothing: for I have sent them." Then Peter went down to the men which were sent unto him from Cornelius; and said,

"Behold, I am he whom ye seek: what is the cause wherefore ye are come?" And they said, "Cornelius the centurion, a just man, and one that feareth God, and of good report among all the nation of the Jews, was warned from God by an holy angel to send for thee into his house, and to hear words of thee." Then called he them in, and lodged them. And on the morrow Peter went away with them, and certain brethren from Joppa accompanied him. And the morrow after they entered into Caesarea. And Cornelius waited for them, and had called together his kinsmen and near friends. And as Peter was coming in, Cornelius met him, and fell down at his feet, and worshipped him. But Peter took him up, saying, "Stand up; I myself also am a man." And as he talked with him, he went in, and found many that were come together. And he said unto them, "Ye know how that it is an unlawful thing for a man that is a Jew to keep company, or come unto one of another nation; but God hath shewed me that I should not call any man common or unclean. Therefore came I unto you without gainsaying, as soon as I was sent for: I ask therefore for what intent ye have sent for me? And Cornelius said, "Four days ago I was fasting until this hour; and at the ninth hour I prayed in my house, and, behold, a man stood before me in bright clothing. And said, 'Cornelius, thy prayer is heard, and thine alms are had in remembrance in the sight of God. Send therefore to Joppa, and call hither Simon, whose surname is Peter; he is lodged in the house of one Simon a tanner by the sea side: who, when he cometh, shall speak unto thee.' Immediately therefore I sent to thee; and thou hast well done that thou art come. Now therefore are we all here present before God, to hear all things that are commanded thee of God."

Then Peter opened his mouth, and said, "Of a truth I perceive that God is no respector of persons: But in every nation he that feareth him, and worketh righteousness, is accepted with him. The word which God sent unto the children of Israel, preaching peace by Jesus Christ (He is Lord of all:) That word, I say, ye know, which was published throughout all Judaea, and began from Galilee, after the baptism which John preached; how God anointed Jesus of Nazareth with the Holy Ghost and with power: who went about doing good, and healing all that were oppressed of the devil; for God was with him. And we are witnesses of all things which he did both in the land of the Jews, and in Jerusalem; whom they slew and hanged on a tree: Him God raised up the third day, and shewed him openly; not to all the people, but unto witnesses chosen before of God, even to us, who did eat and drink with him after he rose from the dead. And he commanded us to preach unto the people, and to testify that it is he which was ordained of God to be the Judge of quick and dead. To him give all the prophets witness, that through his name whosoever believeth in him shall receive remission of sins."

While Peter yet spake these words, the Holy Ghost fell on all them which heard the word. And they of the circumcision which believed were astonished, as many as came with Peter, because that on the Gentiles also was poured out the gift of the Holy Ghost. For they heard them speak with tongues, and magnify God. Then answered Peter, "Can any man forbid water, that these should not be baptized, which have received the Holy Ghost as well as we?" And he commanded them to be baptized in the name of the Lord.

The Epistle of Paul the Apostle to the Romans

•   •   •

As it is written, There is none righteous, no, not one: There is none that understandeth, there is none that seeketh after God. They are all gone out of the way, they are together become unprofitable; there is none that doeth good, no, not one. Their throat is an open sepulchre; with their tongues they have used deceit; the poison of asps is under their lips: Whose mouth is full of cursing and bitterness: Their feet are swift to shed blood: Destruction and misery are in their ways: And the way of peace have they not known: There is no fear of God before their eyes.

Now we know that what things soever the law saith, it saith to them who are under the law: that every mouth may be stopped, and all the world may become guilty before God. Therefore by the deeds of the law there shall no flesh be justified in his sight: for by the law is the knowledge of sin. But now the righteousness of God without the law is manifested, being witnessed by the law and the prophets; even the righteousness of God which is by faith of Jesus Christ unto all and upon all them that believe: for there is no difference. For all have sinned, and come short of the glory of God; being justified freely by his grace through the redemption that is in Christ Jesus: Whom God hath set forth to be a propitiation through faith in his blood, to declare his righteousness for the remission of sins that are past, through the forbearance of God; to declare, I say, at this time his righteousness: that he might be just, and the justifier of him which believeth in Jesus. Where is boasting then? It is excluded. By what law? or works? Nay: but by the law of faith. Therefore we conclude that a man is justified by faith without the deeds of the law. Is he the God of the Jews only? Is he not also of the Gentiles? Yes, of the Gentiles also: Seeing it is one God, which shall justify the circumcision by faith, and uncircumcision through faith. Do we then make void the law through faith? God forbid: yea, we establish the law.

•   •   •

Chapters 3:10–31; 5:6; 9:8–21.

Therefore being justified by faith, we have peace with God through our Lord Jesus Christ: By whom also we have access by faith into this grace wherein we stand, and rejoice in hope of the glory of God. And not only so, but we glory in tribulations also: knowing that tribulation worketh patience; and patience, experience; and experience, hope: And hope maketh not ashamed; because the love of God is shed abroad in our hearts by the Holy Ghost which is given unto us. For when we were yet without strength, in due time Christ died for the ungodly. For scarcely for a righteous man will one die: yet peradventure for a good man some would even dare to die. But God commandeth his love toward us, in that, while we were yet sinners, Christ died for us. Much more then, being now justified by his blood, we shall be saved from wrath through him. For if, when we were enemies, we were reconciled to God by the death of his Son, much more, being reconciled, we shall be saved by his life. And not only so, but we also joy in God through our Lord Jesus Christ, by whom we have now received the atonement.

Wherefore, as by one man sin entered into the world, and death by sin; and so death passed upon all men, for that all have sinned. (For until the law sin was in the world: but sin is not imputed when there is no law. Nevertheless death reigned from Adam to Moses, even over them that had not sinned after the similitude of Adam's transgression, who is the figure of him that was to come. But not as the offence, so also is the free gift. For if through the offence of one many be dead, much more the grace of God, and the gift by grace, which is by one man, Jesus Christ, hath abounded unto many. And not as it was by one that sinned, so is the gift: for the judgment was by one to condemnation, but the free gift is of many offences unto justification. For if by one man's offence death reigned by one; much more they which receive abundance of grace and of the gift of righteousness shall reign in life by one, Jesus Christ.) Therefore as by the offence of one judgment came upon all men to condemnation; even so, by the righteousness of one the free gift came upon all men unto justification of life. For as by one man's disobedience many were made sinners, so by the obedience of one shall many be made righteous. Moreover the law entered, that the offence might abound. But where sin abounded, grace did much more abound: That as sin hath reigned unto death, even so might grace reign through righteousness unto eternal life by Jesus Christ our Lord.

What shall we say then? Shall we continue in sin, that grace may abound? God forbid. How shall we, that are dead to sin, live any longer therein? Know ye not, that so many of us as were baptized into Jesus Christ were baptized into his death? Therefore we are buried with him by baptism into death: that like as Christ was raised up from the dead by the glory of the Father, even so we also should walk in newness of life. For if we have been planted together in the likeness of his death, we shall be also in the likeness of his resurrection: Knowing this, that our old man is crucified with him, that the body of sin might be destroyed, that henceforth we should not serve sin. For he that is dead is freed from sin. Now if we be dead with Christ, we believe that we shall also live with him: Knowing that Christ being raised from the dead dieth no more; death hath no more dominion over him. For in that he died, he died unto sin once: but in that he liveth, he liveth unto God. Likewise reckon ye also yourselves to be dead indeed unto sin, but alive unto God through Jesus Christ our Lord.

Let not sin therefore reign in your mortal body, that ye should obey it in the lusts thereof. Neither yield ye your members as instruments of unrighteousness unto sin: but yield yourselves unto God, as those that are alive from the dead, and your members as instruments of righteousness unto God. For sin shall not have dominion over you: for ye are not under the law, but under grace. What then? Shall we sin, because we are not under the law, but under grace? God forbid. Know ye not, that to whom ye yield yourselves servants to obey, his servants ye are to whom ye obey; whether of sin unto death, or of obedience unto righteousness? But God be thanked, that ye were the servants of sin, but ye have obeyed from the heart that form of doctrine which was delivered you. Being then made free from sin, ye became the servants of righteousness.

I speak after the manner of men because of the infirmity of your flesh: for as ye have yielded your members servants to uncleanness and to iniquity unto iniquity; even so now yield your members servants to righteousness unto holiness. For when ye were the servant of sin, ye

were free from righteousness. What fruit had ye then in those things whereof ye are now ashamed? For the end of those things is death. But now being made free from sin, and become servants of God, ye have your fruit unto holiness, and the end everlasting life. For the wages of sin is death; but the gift of God is eternal life through Jesus Christ our Lord.

•   •   •

They which are the children of the flesh, these are not the children of God: but the children of the promise are counted for the seed. For this is the word of promise. At this time will I come, and Sarah shall have a son. And not only this; but when Rebecca also had conceived by one, even by our father Isaac; (for the children being not yet born, neither having done any good or evil, that the purpose of God according to election might stand, not of works, but of him that calleth): it was said unto her, The elder shall serve the younger. As it is written, Jacob have I loved, but Esau have I hated. What shall we say then? Is there unrighteousness with God? God forbid. For he saith to Moses, I will have mercy on whom I will have mercy, and I will have compassion on whom I will have compassion. So then it is not of him that willeth, nor of him that runneth, but of God that sheweth mercy. For the scripture saith unto Pharaoh, Even for this same purpose have I raised thee up, that I might shew my power in thee, and that my name might be declared throughout all the earth. Therefore hath he mercy on whom he will have mercy, and whom he will he hardeneth. Thou wilt say then unto me, Why doth he yet find fault? For who hath resisted his will? Nay but, O man, who are thou that repliest against God? Shall the thing formed say to him that formed it, Why hast thou made me thus? Hath not the potter power over the clay, of the same lump to make one vessel unto honour, and another into dishonour?

Medieval life in town and country. (*Culver Pictures, Inc.*)

THE MIDDLE AGES

When we look back from the twentieth century to the Middle Ages, we are confronted with countless difficulties and contradictions. At times the medieval period seems to have been an age of unrelieved violence and warfare, of treachery, intrigue, and bloodshed. At other times the thousand years from 400 to 1400 seem to have been an "Age of Faith"—an age in which Western humanity sought to relate its life on earth both to God and to its eternal destiny. A third impression is that the Middle Ages was a time when society sought stability and security above all else.

It is difficult to reconcile these three impressions, and perhaps it is futile to try. In a sense, they are all valid; the Middle Ages was bloody, *and* religious, *and* stable. To try to resolve all this diversity into a perfectly understandable whole would be to fall under the criticism of the historian who claimed that "history is a chaos upon which historians impose a pattern."

Yet we can attempt to understand the principles and ideals that were accepted and professed by medieval society. For one segment of the population (roughly one-sixth) the world centered on military life—a life dedicated to concepts of honor, justice, bravery, strength, skill, and loyalty. For another segment (roughly one-tenth) the world centered around a concern for the souls of people. To the friars, the priests, and the clerics, this life was transient and unreal, and only the life hereafter had any real meaning. For the rest of the people who lived during the Middle Ages (certainly the vast majority of the population) life was simply a matter of accepting the four seasons, hard work, the need to cultivate the soil, the dictates of the Church, and the demands of the military caste.

Ideally, every element of the social order had its clearly defined function, which suggests that the Middle Ages at least tried to maintain a stability in which everyone could lead a life in peace, although perhaps not in plenty. But since stability is a difficult ideal to realize, let alone to maintain, the corollary was control over all elements that might tend to disturb the established way of life. The Church tried (though not very successfully) to eliminate the constant fighting of the feudal class by decreeing the Truce and Peace of God which forbade warfare at certain times. The feudal structure itself was designed to define the rank and station of all its members. A knight swore oaths of allegiance and fidelity to a lord and "became his man"; he was obliged to support his lord against enemies, to protect the lord's family, and to serve at the lord's court. In return, the lord granted lands to his vassal and guaranteed him military protection and knightly station. The lands granted were called the "fief" or "feodum" (whence feudalism), and they were actually worked by serfs. The fief was composed of one or more estates called "manors"; there, too, a mutual contractual obligation existed between the lord of the manor and the serf. In return for military protection the serf accepted the jurisdiction of the lord's court, contracted to work a fixed number of days for the lord, and agreed to pay fixed rents to the lord. Legally the serf could not leave the manor without the consent of the lord, but also (and most importantly) the serf could not be put off the land, nor could the fixed rents be raised. In short, the serf had a social and economic status superior to slavery; he was, at least, guaranteed his living, however poor it might have been. His social status was, of course, vastly inferior to that of the vassal who, however subordinate he might be to his liege lord, was still a member of the knightly caste.

In the later Middle Ages, after the revival of trade and of town life, the desire to guarantee a livelihood to everyone was reflected in the gild organization, and in the many regulations that were imposed on the manufacture and distribution of goods. By agreement within the gild, techniques were prescribed, monopoly was forbidden both in buying and selling, prices were fixed, and all gildsmen shared the market; no one was permitted to "get ahead" of his fellow gildsmen. The very concept of the "just price" was an attempt to show that too high a price cheated the buyer and too low a price cheated the seller. In either case, one was deprived of his goods and his well-being.

But stability remained mostly an ideal that was striven for, rather than an actuality that was attained. The failure of the Middle Ages to achieve real stability sprang from the inevitable conflict between medieval political theory and practice on the one hand and medieval theological outlook and organization on the other. Christianity could not be reconciled with militarism; the two were completely antithetical, despite efforts to develop the notion of the "Christian knight" and the "soldiers of God." An even more important source of conflict between the feudal structure and the Catholic hierarchy, however, was the inescapable logic of the situation itself. In a deeply religious age—in any age, for that matter—people are moved to demonstrate their faith and to glorify their God by building beautiful churches or by giving gifts to support the faith. In the Middle Ages, most bequests took the form of land given over to the maintenance of Church officials and functionaries or to provide the necessities of monasteries and nunneries.

This practice created two major difficulties that made conflict between the Church and the feudal system inevitable. First, the land had originally been granted (but not given outright) to a vassal by his liege lord in exchange for military service; if the land was then bequeathed by the vassal to the Church, who was to provide military service to the liege lord? Could a priest or a bishop hire someone to perform the feudal obligations and still remain a Christian?

The second major difficulty arose from the vassal's obligation to swear oaths of allegiance, fidelity, and homage to his liege in order to be "invested" with his fief. Here feudalism ran directly afoul of the Church. A bishop, for instance, had already sworn fidelity to the pope at Rome and could not very well serve two masters, his feudal lord and his ecclesiastical superior.

Out of these difficulties the whole investiture controversy arose, a controversy that developed into a struggle for supreme political power between the feudal monarchs and the popes. The monarchs were victorious, although the question has never been clearly resolved for the hierarchy of the Catholic Church. In the late Middle Ages the Church mobilized all its arsenal of spiritual weapons in an attempt to win the controversy—papal letters, encyclicals, bulls, interdict, and excommunication. All was to no avail, however. And the use of these spiritual weapons to gain political ends itself tended to discredit them and to deprive the Church of its moral authority. So in a real sense the Church itself helped to prepare the way for the secular attitudes that were to characterize the Renaissance.

St. Augustine

For three hundred years after the death of Christ, the Christian churches were engaged in a continuing struggle. Confronted by scores of pagan cults in the Mediterranean world and by the persecution of the Roman government, the new religion was unable to establish its supremacy until the fourth century. Early in that century, under the emperors Galerius and Constantine (himself a convert), Christianity was recognized and tolerated; later in the century, under Theodosius, it was proclaimed as the official religion of the Roman Empire.

But the problems of the churches were far from over, for a host of controversies now arose within the ranks of the Christians themselves. The most critical controversy was over questions of doctrine. Innumerable sects, each preaching its special version of Christian doctrine and combating the views of the others, were scattered throughout the empire. Clearly, if Christianity was to survive, some order had to be brought out of such theological chaos. Into this scene of confusion stepped Augustine (354–430). Highly intelligent, firmly devoted to his conception of the truth, and possessed of unusual administrative ability, Augustine was admirably fitted for the task first of developing a theological doctrine for the Christian religion and then of making that doctrine prevail.

After having been attracted as a youth to various pagan cults, Augustine was converted to Christianity in 386 through the influence of Ambrose, Bishop of Milan. Following his conversion, Augustine devoted most of the rest of his life to formulating and disseminating what he believed to be the true Christian doctrine. The main features of this doctrine are given in the following selection, taken from *The Enchiridion* ("Manual"). The central concept, as with St. Paul, is original sin, but with Augustine the theory becomes systematically articulated. Once he had worked out his doctrine completely, Augustine was in a good position to brand opposing theories as heresies. And he devoted much of his time, thought, and energy, especially in later life, to doctrinal controversies in an effort to purge Christian theology of all heretical elements. He was singularly successful in this endeavor, and orthodox Christianity (even with the later additions made by Thomas Aquinas and others) has remained basically Augustinian.

The Enchiridion

• • •

God's judgments upon fallen men and angels. The death of the body is man's peculiar punishment.

. . . Now the evils I have mentioned are common to all who for their wickedness have been justly condemned by God, whether they be men or angels. But there is one form of punishment peculiar to man—the death of the body. God had threatened him with this punishment of death if he should sin, leaving him indeed to the freedom of his own will, but yet commanding his obedience under pain of death; and He placed him amid the happiness of Eden, as it were in a protected nook of life, with the intention that, if he preserved his righteousness, he should thence ascend to a better place.

Through Adam's sin his whole posterity were corrupted, and were born under the penalty of death, which he had incurred.

Thence, after his sin, he was driven into exile, and by his sin the whole race of which he was the root was corrupted in him, and thereby subjected to the penalty of death. And so it happens that all descended from him, and from the woman who had led him into sin, and was condemned at the same time with him,—being the offspring of carnal lust on which the same punishment of disobedience was visited,—were tainted with the original sin, and were by it drawn through divers errors and sufferings into that last and endless punishment which they suffer in common with the fallen angels, their corrupters and masters, and the partakers of their doom. And thus "by one man sin entered into the world, and death by sin; and so death passed upon all men, for that all have sinned." By "the world" the apostle,[1] of course, means in this place the whole human race.

The state of misery to which Adam's sin reduced mankind, and the restoration effected through the mercy of God.

Thus, then, matters stood. The whole mass of the human race was under condemnation, was lying steeped and wallowing in misery, and was being tossed from one form of evil to another, and, having joined the faction of the fallen angels, was paying the well-merited penalty of that impious rebellion. For whatever the wicked freely do through blind and unbridled lust, and whatever they suffer against their will in the way of open punishment, this all evidently pertains to the just wrath of God. But the goodness of the Creator never fails either to supply life and vital power

---

[1] [St. Paul—*Ed.*]

"The Enchiridion," in *The Works of Aurelius Augustine*, ed. M. Dods, Vol. IX (Edinburgh: T. & T. Clark, 1892), pp. 194–95, 197–200, 206–7, 219, 242–45, 253–55. Courtesy of T. & T. Clark.

to the wicked angels (without which their existence would soon come to an end); or, in the case of mankind, who spring from a condemned and corrupt stock, to impart form and life to their seed, to fashion their members, and through the various seasons of their life, and in the different parts of the earth, to quicken their senses, and bestow upon them the nourishment they need. For He judged it better to bring good out of evil, than not to permit any evil to exist. And if He had determined that in the case of men, as in the case of the fallen angels, there should be no restoration to happiness, would it not have been quite just, that the being who rebelled against God, who in the abuse of his freedom spurned and transgressed the command of his Creator when he could so easily have kept it, who defaced in himself the image of his Creator by stubbornly turning away from His light, who by an evil use of his free-will broke away from his wholesome bondage to the Creator's laws,— would it not have been just that such a being should have been wholly and to all eternity deserted by God, and left to suffer the everlasting punishment he had so richly earned? Certainly so God would have done, had He been only just and not also merciful, and had He not designed that His unmerited mercy should shine forth the more brightly in contrast with the unworthiness of its objects.

· · ·

Men are not saved by good works, nor by the free determination of their own will, but by the grace of God through faith.

But this part of the human race to which God has promised pardon and a share in His eternal kingdom, can they be restored through the merit of their own works? God forbid. For what good work can a lost man perform, except so far as he has been delivered from perdition? Can they do anything by the free determination of their own will? Again I say, God forbid. For it was by the evil use of his free-will that man destroyed both it and himself. For, as a man who kills himself must, of course, be alive when he kills himself, but after he has killed himself ceases to live, and cannot restore himself to life; so, when man by his own free-will sinned, then sin being victorious over him, the freedom of his will was lost. "For of whom a man is overcome, of the same is he brought in bondage." This is the judgment of the Apostle Peter. And as it is certainly true, what kind of liberty, I ask, can the bond-slave possess, except when it pleases him to sin? For he is freely in bondage who does with pleasure the will of his master. Accordingly, he who is the servant of sin is free to sin. And hence he will not be free to do right, until, being freed from sin, he shall begin to be the servant of righteousness. And this is true liberty, for he has pleasure in the righteous deed; and it is at the same time a holy bondage, for he is obedient to the will of God. But whence comes this liberty to do right to the man who is in bondage and sold under sin, except he be redeemed by Him who has said, "If the Son shall make you free, ye shall be free indeed"? And before this redemption is wrought in a man, when he is not yet free to do what is right, how can he talk of the freedom of his will and his good works, except he be inflated by that foolish pride of boasting which the apostle restrains when he says, "By grace are ye saved, through faith."

Faith itself is the gift of God; and good works will not be wanting in those who believe.

And lest men should arrogate to themselves the merit of their own faith at least, not understanding that this too is the gift of God, this same apostle, who says in another place that he had "obtained mercy of the Lord to be faithful," here also adds: "and that not of yourselves; it is the gift of God: not of works, lest any man should boast." And lest it should be thought that good works will be wanting in those who believe, he adds further: "For we are His workmanship, created in Christ Jesus unto good works, which God hath before ordained that we should walk in them." We shall be made truly free, then, when God fashions us, that is, forms and creates us anew, not as men—for He has done that already—but as good men, which His grace is now doing, that we may be a new creation in Christ Jesus, according as it is said: "Create in me a clean heart, O God." For God had already created his heart, so far as the physical structure of the human heart is concerned; but the psalmist prays for the renewal of the life which is still lingering in his heart.

The freedom of the will is also the gift of God, for God worketh in us both to will and to do.

And further, should any one be inclined to boast, not indeed of his works, but of the freedom of his will, as if that first merit belong to him, this very liberty of good action being given to him as a reward he had earned, let him listen to this same preacher of grace, when he says: "For it is God which worketh in you, both to will and to do of His own good pleasure"; and in another place: "So, then, it is not of him that willeth, nor of him that runneth, but of God that showeth mercy." Now as, undoubtedly, if a man is of the age to use his reason, he cannot believe, hope, love, unless he will to do so, nor obtain the prize of the high calling of God unless he voluntarily run for it; in what sense is it "not of him that willeth, nor of him that runneth, but of God that showeth mercy," except that, as it is written, "The preparation of the heart is from the Lord"? Otherwise, if it is said, "it is not of him that willeth nor of him that runneth, but of God that showeth mercy," because it is of both, that is, both of the will of man and of the mercy of God, so that we are to understand the saying, "It is not of him that willeth, nor of him that runneth, but of God that showeth mercy," as if it meant the will of man alone is not sufficient, if the mercy of God go not with in—then it will follow that the mercy of God alone is not sufficient, if the will of man go not with it; and therefore, if we may rightly say, "it is not of man that willeth, but of God that showeth mercy," because the will of man by itself is not enough, why may we not also rightly put it in the converse way: "It is not of God that showeth mercy, but of man that willeth," because the mercy of God by itself does not suffice? Surely, if no Christian will dare to say this, "It is not of God that showeth mercy, but of man that willeth," lest he should openly contradict the apostle, it follows that the true interpretation of the saying, "It is not of him that willeth, nor of him that runneth, but of God that showeth mercy," is that the whole work belongs to God, who both makes the will of man righteous, and thus prepare it for assistance, and assists it when it is prepared. For the man's righteousness of will precedes many of God's gifts, but not all and it must itself be included among those which it does not precede. We read in Holy Scripture, both that God's mercy "shall prevent me," and that His mercy "shall follow me." It prevents the unwilling to make him willing; it follows the willing to make his will effectual. Why are we taught to pray for our enemies, who are plainly unwilling to lead a holy life, unless that God may work willingness in them? And why are we ourselves taught to ask that we may receive, unless that He who has created in us the wish, may Himself satisfy the wish? We pray, then, for our enemies, that the mercy of God may prevent them, as it has prevented us: we pray for ourselves that His mercy may follow us.

Men, being by nature the children of wrath, needed a Mediator. In what sense God is said to be angry.

And so the human race was lying under a just condemnation, and all men were the children of wrath. Of which wrath it is written: "All our days are passed away in Thy wrath; we spend our years as a tale that is told." Of which wrath also Job says: "Man that is born of a woman is of few days, and full of trouble." Of which wrath also the Lord Jesus says: "He that believeth on the Son

hath everlasting life: and he that believeth not the Son shall not see life; but the wrath of God abideth on him." He does not say it will come, but it "abideth on him." For every man is born with it; wherefore the apostle says: "We were by nature the children of wrath, even as others." Now, as men were lying under this wrath by reason of their original sin, and as this original sin was the more heavy and deadly in proportion to the number and magnitude of the actual sins which were added to it, there was need for a Mediator, that is, for a reconciler, who, by the offering of one sacrifice, of which all the sacrifices of the law and the prophets were types, should take away this wrath. Wherefore the apostle says: "For if, when we were enemies, we were reconciled to God by the death of His Son, much more, being reconciled, we shall be saved by His life." Now when God is said to be angry, we do not attribute to Him such a disturbed feeling as exists in the mind of an angry man; but we call His just displeasure against sin by the name "anger," a word transferred by analogy from human emotions. But our being reconciled to God through a Mediator, and receiving the Holy Spirit, so that we who were enemies are made sons ("For as many as are led by the Spirit of God, they are the sons of God"): this is the grace of God through Jesus Christ our Lord.

• • •

Christ, who was Himself free from sin, was made sin for us, that we might be reconciled to God.

Begotten and conceived, then,

without any indulgence of carnal lust, and therefore bringing with Him no original sin, and by the grace of God joined and united in a wonderful and unspeakable way in one person with the Word, the Only-begotten of the Father, a son by nature, not by grace, and therefore having no sin of His own; nevertheless, on account of the likeness of sinful flesh in which He came, He was called sin, that He might be sacrificed to wash away sin. For, under the Old Covenant, sacrifices for sin were call sins. And He, of whom all these sacrifices were types and shadows, was Himself truly made sin. Hence the apostle, after saying, "We pray you in Christ's stead, be ye reconciled to God," forthwith adds: "for He hath made Him to be sin for us who knew no sin; that we might be made the righteousness of God in Him." He does not say, as some incorrect copies read, "He who knew no sin did sin for us," as if Christ had Himself sinned for our sakes; but he says, "Him who knew no sin," that is, Christ, God, to whom we are to be reconciled, "hath made to be sin for us," that is, hath made Him a sacrifice for our sins, by which we might be reconciled to God. He, then being made sin, just as we are made righteousness (our righteousness being not our own, but God's, not in ourselves, but in Him); He being made sin, not His own, but ours, not in Himself, but in us, showed, by the likeness of sinful flesh in which He was crucified, that though sin was not in Him, yet that in a certain sense He died to sin, by dying in the flesh which was the likeness of sin; and that although He himself had never lived the old life of sin, yet by His resurrection He typified our new life springing up out of the old death in sin.

• • •

By the sacrifice of Christ all things are restored, and peace is made between earth and heaven.

And, of course, the holy angels, taught by god, in the eternal contemplation of whose truth their happiness consists, know how great a number of the human race are to supplement their ranks, and fill up the full tale of their citizenship. Wherefore the apostle says, that "all things are gathered together in one in Christ, both which are in heaven and which are on earth." The things which are in heaven are gathered together when what was lost therefrom in the fall of the angels is restored from among men; and the things which are on earth are gathered together, when those who are predestined to eternal life are redeemed from their old corruption. And thus, through that single sacrifice in which the Mediator was offered up, the one sacrifice of which the many victims under the law were types, heavenly things are brought into peace with earthly things, and earthly things with heavenly. Wherefore, as the same apostle says: "For it pleased the Father that in Him should all fulness dwell: and, having made peace through the blood of His cross, by Him to reconcile all things to Himself: by Him, I say, whether they be things in earth or things in heaven."

• • •

Predestination to eternal life is wholly of God's free grace.

And, moreover, who will be so foolish and blasphemous as to say that God cannot change the evil wills of men, whichever, whenever and wheresoever He chooses, and direct them to what is good? But when He does this, He does it of mercy; when He does it not, it is of justice that He does it not; for "He hath mercy on whom He will have mercy, and whom He will He hardeneth." And when the apostle said this, he was illustrating the grace of God, in connection with which he had just spoken of the twins in the womb of Rebecca, "who being not yet born, neither having done any good or evil, that the purpose of God according to election might stand, not of works, but of Him that calleth, it was said unto her, The elder shall serve the younger." And in reference to this matter he quotes another prophetic testimony: "Jacob have I loved, but Esau have I hated." But perceiving how what he had said might affect those who could not penetrate by their understanding the depth of this grace: "What shall we say then?" he says: "Is there unrighteousness with God? God forbid." For it seems unjust that, in the absence of any merit or demerit from good or evil works, God should love the one and hate the other. Now, if the apostle had wished us to understand that there were future good works of the one, and evil works of the other, which of course God foreknew, he would never have said, "not of works," but, "of future works," and in that way would have solved the difficulty, or rather there would then have been no difficulty to solve. As it is, however, after answering, "God forbid"; that is, God forbid that there should be unrighteousness with God; he goes on to prove that there is no unrighteousness in God's doing this, and says: "For he saith to Moses, I will have mercy on whom I will have mercy, and I will have compassion on whom I will have compassion." Now who but a fool would think that God was unrighteous, either in inflicting penal justice on those who earned it, or in extending mercy to the unworthy? Then he draws his conclusion: "So then it is not of him that willeth, nor of him that runneth, but of God that showeth mercy." Thus both the twins were born children of wrath, not on account of any works of their own, but because they were bound in the fetters of that original condemnation which came through Adam. But He who said, "I will have mercy on whom I will have mercy," loved Jacob of His undeserved grace, and hated Esau of His deserved judgment. And as this judgment was due to both, the former learnt from the case of the latter that the fact of the same punishment not falling upon himself gave him no room to glory in any merit of his own, but only in the riches of the divine grace; because "it is not of him that willeth, nor of him that runneth, but of God that showeth mercy." And indeed the whole face, and, if I may use the expression, every lineament of the countenance of Scripture conveys by a very profound analogy this wholesome warning to every one who looks carefully into it, that he who glories should glory in the Lord.

As God's mercy is free, so His judgments are just, and cannot be gainsaid.

Now after commending the mercy of God, saying, "So it is not of him that willeth, nor of him that runneth, but of God that showeth mercy," that he might commend His Justice also (for the man who does not obtain mercy finds, not iniquity, but justice, there being no iniquity with God), he immediately adds: "For the scripture saith unto Pharaoh, Even for this same purpose have I raised thee up, that I might show my power in thee, and that my name might be declared throughout all the earth." And then he draws a conclusion that applies to both, that is, both to His mercy and His justice: "Therefore hath He mercy on whom He will have mercy, and whom He will He hardeneth." "He hath mercy" of His great goodness, "He hardeneth" without any injustice; so that neither can he that is pardoned glory in any merit of his own, nor he that is condemned complain of anything but his own demerit. For it is grace alone that separates the redeemed from the lost, all having been involved in one common perdition through their common origin. Now if any one, on hearing this, should say, "Why doth He yet find fault? for who hath resisted His will?" as if a man ought not to be blamed for being bad, because God hath mercy on whom He will have mercy, and whom He will He hardeneth, God forbid that we should be ashamed to answer as we see the apostle answered: "Nay, but, O man, who are thou that repliest against God? Shall the thing formed say to Him that formed it, Why hast Thou made me thus? Hath not the potter power over the clay, of the same lump to make one vessel unto honour, and another unto dishonour?" Now some foolish people think that in this place the apostle had no answer to give; and for want of a reason to render, rebuked the presumption of his interrogator. But there is great weight in this saying: "Nay, but, O man, who art thou?" and in such a matter as this it suggests to a man in a single word the limits of his capacity, and at the same time does in reality convey an important reason. For if a man does not understand these matters, who is he that he should reply against God? And if he does understand them, he finds no further room for reply. For then he perceives that the whole human race was condemned in its rebellious head by a divine judgment so just, that if not a single member of the race had been redeemed, no one could justly have questioned the justice of God; and that it was right that those who are redeemed should be redeemed in such a way as to show, by the greater number who are unredeemed and left in their just condemnation, what the whole race deserved, and whither the deserved judgment of God would lead even the redeemed, did not His undeserved mercy interpose, so that every mouth might be stopped of those who wish to glory in their own merits, and that he that glorieth might glory in the Lord.

• • •

There is no ground in Scripture for the opinion of those who deny the eternity of future punishments.

It is in vain, then, that some, indeed very many, make moan over the eternal punishment, and perpetual, uninterrupted torments of the lost, and say they do not believe it shall be so; not, indeed, that they directly oppose themselves to Holy Scripture, but, at the suggestion of their own feelings, they soften down everything that seems hard, and give a milder turn to statements which they think are rather designed to terrify than to be received as literally true. For "Hath God," they say, "forgotten to be gracious? hath He in anger shut up His tender mercies?" Now, they read this in one of the holy psalms. But without doubt we are to understand it as spoken of those who are elsewhere called "vessels of mercy," because even they are freed from misery not on account of any merit of their own, but solely through the pity of God. Or, if the men we speak of insist that this passage applies to all mankind, there is no reason why they should therefore suppose that there will be an end to the punishment of those of whom it is said, "These shall go away into everlasting punishment"; for this shall end in the same manner and at the same time as the happiness of those of whom it is said, "but the righteous unto life eternal." But let them suppose, if the thought gives them pleasure, that the pains of the damned are, at certain intervals, in some degree assuaged. For even in this case the wrath of God, that is, their condemnation (for it is this, and not any disturbed feeling in the mind of God that is called His wrath), abideth upon them; that is, His wrath, though it still remains, does not shut up His tender mercies;

though His tender mercies are exhibited, not in putting an end to their eternal punishment, but in mitigating, or in granting them a respite from, their torments; for the psalm does not say, "to put an end to His anger," or, "when His anger is passed by," but "in His anger." Now, if this anger stood alone, or if it existed in the smallest conceivable degree, yet to be lost out of the kingdom of God, to be an exile from the city of God, to be alienated from the life of God, to have no share in that great goodness which God hath laid up for them that fear Him, and hath wrought out for them that trust in Him, would be a punishment so great, that, supposing it to be eternal, no torments that we know of, continued through as many ages as man's imagination can conceive, could be compared with it.

The death of the wicked shall be eternal in the same sense as the life of the saints.

This perpetual death of the wicked, then, that is, their alienation from the life of God, shall abide for ever, and shall be common to them all, whatever men, prompted by their human affections, may conjecture as to a variety of punishments, or as to a mitigation or intermission of their woes; just as the eternal life of the saints shall abide for ever, and shall be common to them all, whatever grades of rank and honour there may be among those who shine with an harmonious effulgence.

Gregory of Tours

The History of the Franks, perhaps the most significant writing in a generally unlettered society, was the work of St. Gregory, Bishop of Tours, a city in the Loire valley of central France. This manuscript has become the most widely known and used source for the history of the Gallo-Roman society of the sixth century. Besides portraying both the violence and the piety of the age, it gives an account of the affairs of kings and armies plus an insight into the customs, beliefs, and manners that then prevailed.

The character of the author undoubtedly contributed mightily to the vigor and the value of the work. Gregory (529–594) was the son of an old, aristocratic Gallo-Roman family of senatorial rank, which had supplied virtually all the bishops of Tours, a fact from which Gregory himself derived much pleasure (and ran the risk of falling into the first of the seven mortal sins). On both sides of his family there was a lengthy tradition of high ecclesiastical office; Gregory was both the great grandson and grandson of bishops and the cousin of the bishop's immediate predecessor. (This was before the principle of sacerdotal celibacy achieved full vigor in the doctrines of the Catholic Church.) He distinguished himself not only by his many courageous defenses of the place and privileges of the Church and by his untiring efforts on behalf of his diocesan flock, but also by his important role as adviser to the Merovingian kings of France. Despite these many and varied duties, Gregory still found time to produce a very large body of literary works which, while of indifferent stylistic merit, are invaluable to the student of the early Middle Ages.

The following selections from *The History of the Franks* are three: the first from the preface, the second from Book II describing the conversion to Christianity of Clovis, an important Frankish king who reigned from 481 to 511, and the third containing Gregory's conclusions from Book X.

The History of the Franks

In these times when the practice of letters declines, nay, rather perishes in the cities of Gaul, there has been found no scholar trained in the art of ordered composition to present in prose or verse a picture of the things that have befallen. Yet there have been done good things many, and evil many; the peoples savagely raged; the fury of kings grew sharp; churches were assailed by heretics and protected by catholics; the faith of Christ that glowed in many hearts was luke-warm in not a few; the faithful enriched the churches while the unbelievers stripped them bare. Wherefore the voice of lament was ofttimes raised, and men said: "Alas! for these our days! The study of letters is perished from us, nor is any found among our peoples able to set forth in a book the events of this present time."

Now when I heard these and like complaints ever repeated, I was moved, with however rude an utterance, to hand down the memory of the past to future generations, in no wise leaving untold the conflicts of the wicked and those who lived in righteousness. I was the more encouraged because I often heard with surprise our people say that while the accomplished writer is understood by few, it is the man of plain speech who has the general ear.

Further, it seemed good to me for the better computation of the years, that in this first book, of which the chapters follow, I should begin from the foundation of the world.

BOOK II

• • •

After this, Childeric died, and Clovis his son reigned in his stead. In the fifth year of his reign, Syagrius, king of the Romans, son of Aegidius, had his residence in the city of Soissons, which had before been the home of the above-mentioned Aegidius. Clovis marched against him, with his relation Ragnachar, himself also a king, and called upon him to fix a field of battle. Syagrius did not seek delay nor did he fear to stand his ground. And so when the battle was joined between them, Syagrius, seeing his army crushed, turned to flight and escaped as fast as he could to Alaric at Toulouse. But Clovis sent to Alaric calling upon him to surrender the fugitive, else he must look to be himself invaded for giving him refuge. Then Alaric, lest he should incur the wrath of the Franks for his sake, was afraid, after the craven habit of the Goths, and handed him over to the messengers in bonds. When Clovis received his prisoner,

Gregory of Tours, *The History of the Franks*, trans. O. M. Dalton (Oxford: The Clarendon Press, 1927), pp. 2, 65–75, 81, 476–78. Reprinted by permission of Oxford University Press.

he ordered him to be imprisoned; had him put to the sword in secret, while he took possession of his kingdom.

At this time many churches were plundered by the troops of Clovis, because he was yet fast held in pagan errors. Thus it happened that a ewer of great size and beauty had been taken, with other ornaments used in the service of the church. But the bishop of that church sent messengers to the king, asking that if no other of the sacred vessels might be restored, his church might at least receive back this ewer. When the king heard this he said to the envoy: "Follow us to Soissons, for there all the booty is to be divided, and if the lot gives me the vessel, I will fulfil the desire of the bishop." When they were at Soissons and all the spoil was laid out in open view, the king said: "I ask you, most valiant warriors, not to refuse to cede me that vessel" (he meant the ewer of which I have spoken) "over and above my share." After this speech all the men of sense replied: "All that is before our eyes, most glorious king, is thine; we ourselves are submitted to thy power. Do now that which seemeth good to thee, for none is so strong as to say thee nay." At these words a soldier of a vain, jealous, and unstable temper raised his axe and smote the ewer, crying with a loud voice: "Naught shalt thou receive of this but that which thine own lot giveth thee." While all stood astounded at this act, the king suppressed his resentment at the wrong under a show of patient mildness; he then took the ewer and restored it to the bishop's envoy. But the wound remained hidden in his heart. After a lapse of a year, he commanded the whole army to assemble with full equipment, and to exhibit their arms in their brightness on the field of March. The king went round inspecting them all; but when he came to the man who struck the ewer he said: "None hath appeared with his arms so ill kept as thou; neither thy lance, nor thy sword, nor thy axe is fit for use." He then seized the axe, and threw it on the ground. As the man bent down a little to take it up, the king swung his own axe high and cleft his skull, saying as he did, "Thus didst thou treat the ewer at Soissons." The man lying dead, he dismissed the rest, having put great fear of him into their hearts by his act. Clovis waged many wars and won many victories. For in the tenth year of his reign he invaded the Thuringians, and subjected them to his rule.

At that time the king of the Burgundians was Gundioc, of the race of the royal persecutor Athanaric whom I have before mentioned. He had four sons, Gundobad, Godigisel, Chilperic, and Gundomar. Gundobad put his brother Chilperic to the sword, and drowned his wife by tying a stone to her neck. Her two daughters he condemned to exile, the elder of whom, Chrona, had adopted the habit of a nun, while the younger was called Clotild. It happened that Clovis used often to send envoys into Burgundy, and they discovered the young Clotild. Observing her grace and understanding, and learning that she was of the blood royal, they spoke of these things to King Clovis, who straightway sent an embassy to Gundobad, asking her in marriage. Gundobad was afraid to refuse, and handed her over to the men, who received her, and with all speed brought her before the king. At sight of her he greatly rejoiced and was united to her in wedlock, having already by a concubine one son named Theuderic.

Of Queen Clotild the king had a first-born son whom the mother wished to be baptized; she therefore persistently urged Clovis to permit it, saying: "The gods whom ye worship are naught; they cannot aid either themselves or others, seeing that they are images of wood, or stone, or metal. Moreover the names which ye have given them are the names of men and not of gods. Saturn was a man, fabled to have escaped by flight from his son to avoid being thrust from his kingdom; Jupiter also, the lewdest practiser of all debaucheries and of unnatural vice, the abuser of the women of his own family, who could not even abstain from intercourse with his own sister, as she herself admitted in the words 'sister and spouse of Jove.' What power had Mars and Mercury? They may have been endowed with magical arts; they never had the power of the divine name. But ye should rather serve Him who at His word created out of nothing the heaven and earth, the sea and all therein; who made the sun to shine and adorned the heaven with stars; who filled the waters with fish, the earth with animals, the air with birds; at whose nod the lands are made fair with fruits, the trees with apples, the vine with grapes; by whose largess every creature was made to render homage and service to the man whom he created." Though the queen ever argued thus, the king's mind was nowise moved toward belief, but he replied: "It is by command of our gods that all things are created and

come forth; it is manifest that thy god availeth in nothing; nay more, he is not even proven to belong to the race of gods." But the queen, true to her faith, presented her son for baptism; she ordered the church to be adorned with hangings and curtains, that the king, whom no preaching could influence, might by this ceremony by persuaded to belief. The boy was baptized and named Ingomer, but died while yet clothed in the white raiment of his regeneration. Thereupon the king was moved to bitter wrath, nor was he slow to reproach the queen, saying: "If the child had been dedicated in the name of my gods, surely he would have survived, but now baptized in the name of thy God, he could not live a day." The queen replied: "I render thanks to Almighty God, Creator of all things, who hath not judged me all unworthy, and deigneth to take into His kingdom this child born of my womb. My mind is untouched by grief at this event, since I know that they which he called from this world in the white robes of baptism shall be nurtured in the sight of God." Afterwards she bore another son, who was baptized with the name of Chlodomer. When he too began to ail, the king said: "It cannot but befall that this infant like his brother shall straightway die, being baptized in the name of thy Christ." But the mother prayed, and God ordained that the child should recover.

Now the queen without ceasing urged the king to confess the true God, and forsake his idols; but in no wise could she move him to this belief, until at length he made war upon a time against the Alamanni, when he was driven of necessity to confess what of his free will he had denied. It befell that when the two hosts joined battle there was grievous slaughter, and the army of Clovis was being swept to utter ruin. When the king saw this he lifted up his eyes to heaven, and knew compunction in his heart, and moved to tears, cried aloud: "Jesus Christ, Thou are proclaimed by Clotild Son of the living God, Thou that are said to give aid to those in stress, and to grant victory to those that hope in Thee, I entreat from a devout heart the glory of Thy succour. If Thou grant me victory over these enemies, and experience confirm that power which the people dedicated to Thy name claimeth to have proved, then will I also believe on Thee and be baptized in Thy name. I have called upon mine own gods, but here is proof that they have withdrawn themselves from helping me; wherefore I believe that they have no power, since they come not to the succour of their servants. Thee do I now invoke, on Thee am I fain to believe, if but I may be plucked out of the hands of mine adversaries." And as he said this, lo, the Alamanni turned their backs and began to flee. And when they saw that their king was slain, they yielded themselves to Clovis, saying: "No longer, we entreat thee, let the people perish; we are now thy men." Then the king put an end to the war, and having admonished the people, returned in peace, relating to the queen how he had called upon the name of Christ and had been found worthy to obtain the victory. This happened in the fifteenth year of his reign.

Then the queen commanded the holy Remigius, bishop of Reims, to be summoned secretly, entreating him to impart the word of salvation to the king. The bishop, calling the king to him in privity, began to instil into him faith in the true God, Maker of heaven and earth, and urged him to forsake his idols, which were unable to help either himself or others. But Clovis replied: "I myself, most holy father, will gladly hearken to thee; but one thing yet remaineth. The people that followeth me will not suffer it that I forsake their gods; yet will I go, and reason with them according to thy word." But when he came before the assembled people, or ever he opened his mouth, the divine power had gone forth from him, and all the people cried with one voice: "O gracious king, we drive forth our gods that perish, and are ready to follow that immortal God whom Remigius preacheth." News of this was brought to the bishop, who was filled with joy, and commanded the font to be prepared. The streets were overshadowed with coloured hangings, the churches adorned with white hangings, the baptistry was set in order, smoke of incense spread in clouds, perfumed tapers gleamed, the whole church about the place of baptism was filled with the divine fragrance. And now the king first demanded to be baptized by the bishop. Like a new Constantine, he moved forward to the water; to blot out the former leprosy, to wash away in this new stream the foul stains borne from old days. As he entered to be baptized the saint of God spoke these words with eloquent lips: "Meekly bow thy proud head, Sicamber; adore that which thou has burned, burn that which thou hast adored." For the holy Remigius, the bishop, was of excellent learning, and above all skilled in the art of rhetoric, and so exemplary in holiness that his miracles were equal to those of the holy Silvester; there is preserved to us a book of his life, in which it is related how he raised a man from the dead. The king, therefore, confessing Almighty God, three in one, was baptized in the name of the Father, the Son, and the Holy Ghost, and anointed with holy chrism, with the sign of the Cross of Christ. Of his army were baptized more than three thousand; and his sister Albofled, who not long after was taken to the Lord, was likewise baptized. And when the king was sorrowing for her death, the holy Remigius sent him a letter of consolation, beginning after this fashion: "The cause of thy sadness doth afflict me with a great affliction, for that thy sister of fair memory hath passed away. But this shall console us, that she hath in such wise left the world as that we should rather lift up our eyes to her than mourn her." And another of his sisters was converted, by name Iahthechild, who had fallen into the heresy of the Arians;[1] she also received the holy chrism, having confessed the Son and the Holy Ghost equal to the Father.

At this time the two brothers, Gundobad and Godigisel, possessed their kingdom about the Rhone and Saone with the territory of Marseilles. They and their people were in the thraldom of the Arian sect. And as the brothers were on terms of hostility, Godigisel, who had heard of the victories won by King Clovis, sent envoys to him by stealth, saying: "If thou afford me aid to pursue my brother, so that I may

either slay him in battle, or drive him from the kingdom, I will pay thee every year such tribute as thou mayest thyself impose." This offer Clovis received gladly, and promised him aid whenever his necessity should demand it. At a time appointed between them he marched an army against Gundobad, who, ignorant of his brother's guile, sent to him upon this news, saying: "Come thou to my deliverance, for the Franks have risen against us, and are come up against our territory to take it. Let us therefore be of one mind against a people that hateth us, for if we hold apart we shall undergo the fate suffered by other peoples." Godigisel made answer: "I will come with my army, and will bring thee succour." So all three kings set their forces in movement together, Clovis marching against Gundobad and Godigisel; they came to Dijon with all the armaments of war. But when they joined battle on the Ouche, Godigisel joined Clovis, and their united armies crushed the force of Gundobad. But he, perceiving the treachery of his brother which till that hour he never suspected, turned his back and fled along the Rhone, until he entered the city of Avignon. After his victory thus gained, Godigisel promised Clovis a part of his kingdom, and went home in peace, entering Vienne in triumph, as though he were master of the entire kingdom. But Clovis reinforced his troops, and followed Gundobad with intent to take him from Avignon and slay him. When Gundobad heard this, he was grievously afraid, dreading to be overtaken by a sudden death. Now he had with him Aridius, a man of rank, who was both strenuous and

---

[1] [A sect that denied the divinity of Jesus—*Ed.*]

astute. Him he summoned and thus addressed: "I am hemmed in by straits upon every side, and know not what to do, for these barbarians are fallen upon me with intent to slay us and lay waste all the land." Aridius answered: "Thou hadst best assuage the savagery of this man, and so preserve thy life. Now therefore, if it be pleasing in thy sight, I will feign to forsake thee and desert to him; once with him I will bring it about that he neither ruin thee nor yet this country. Do thou only have a care to satisfy all the demands which by my advice he shall make of thee, till the Lord of His goodness deign to make thy cause triumph." Gundobad made answer: "I will do all that thou shalt adjoin." Thereupon Aridius bade him farewell and departed, and came to King Clovis, to whom he said: "Behold in me, most pious king, thy humble slave, who hath forsaken the miserable Gundobad to serve thy mightiness. If now thy piety deign to look on me, thou and thy posterity shall find in me an honest and faithful follower." Clovis forthwith took him to himself, and kept him near his person: for he could tell lively tales, was active in counsel, just in judgment, and faithful in every trust. Clovis then continuing to invest the city with his army, Aridius said: "O King, if in the majesty of thy high estate thou deign to hear from me a few words of humble advice, though indeed thou hast small need of counsel, I will offer them in all loyalty; and it shall be useful to thee and to the cities through which it is thy intent to pass. Wherefore dost thou keep afoot this army, when thy foe abideth in an impregnable place? Thou layest waste the fields and devourest the meadows, thou cuttest the vines, thou hewest down the olives, all the fruits of this region thou dost utterly destroy, and yet thou availest not to do him hurt. Send rather envoys to him and impose a yearly tribute, that this region be saved from ruin, and thou be always lord over thy vassal. If he should refuse, then do according to thy pleasure." The king harkened to this counsel, and bade his army return home. And he sent an embassy to Gundobad, commanding him yearly to pay the tribute now to be laid upon him. And he paid it forthwith, and pledged himself to pay it hereafter.

But later, when he had recovered strength, he disdained to pay the promised tribute to King Clovis, and marched an army against Godigisel his brother, besieging him in the city of Vienne. As soon as provisions began to run short among the common people, Godigisel feared the famine might extend even to him, and ordered them to be driven outside the city. It was done; but among the rest was expelled the artificer who had charge of the aqueduct. This man, indignant at his expulsion with the others, went in a fury to Gundobad, and showed him he might break into the city and take vengeance on his brother. Under his guidance armed men were led along the aqueduct, preceded by men with iron crowbars. For there was an outlet covered by a great stone, which was moved away by the crowbars under the direction of the artificer, and so they entered the city, taking in the rear the garrison who were discharging their arrows from the walls. Then at a signal given by a trumpet from the centre of the city, the besiegers seized the gates, threw them open, and crowded in. The inhabitants were caught between two forces and cut to pieces, but Godigisel took refuge in a church of the heretics, and was there put to death with the Arian bishop. The Franks who were with him held together in a tower; Gundobad commanded that none of them should be harmed, and when they were taken, sent them into banishment to King Alaric at Toulouse; but the Gallo-Romans of senatorial family and the Burgundians who had taken part with Godigisel he slew. He restored to his dominion the whole region now known as Burgundy, and instituted milder laws among the Burgundians that there should be no undue oppression of the Romans.

Gundobad, perceiving the doctrines of the heretics to be worthless, confessed that Christ, the Son of God, and the Holy Ghost are both equal to the Father and asked secret baptism of the holy bishop of Vienne. But the bishop replied: "If thou verily believest, it is thy duty to follow the teaching of our Lord Himself, when He said: 'If any man will confess Me before men, him will I also confess before My Father which is in heaven; but whosoever shall deny Me before men, Him will I also deny before my Father which is in heaven.' This also did our Lord urge even upon His holy and beloved, the blessed apostles, when He said: 'But beware of men; for they will deliver you up to councils, and in their synagogues they will scourge you; yea, and before governors and kings shall ye be brought for my sake, for a testimony to them and to the Gentiles.' But thou that art a king, and needest not to fear that any shall lay hands on thee, see how thou dreadest revolt among the people, not daring to confess in public the Creator of all men. Forsake this foolishness, and that which thou professest to believe in thy heart declare with thy lips before the people. For according to the word of the blessed apostle: 'With the heart man believeth unto righteousness, and with the mouth confession is made unto salvation.' Likewise also the prophet saith: 'I will give Thee thanks in the great congregation, I will praise Thee among much people.' And again: 'I will give thanks unto Thee, O Lord, among the peoples; I will sing praises unto Thee among the nations.' Thou fearest the people, O king; but perceivest thou not that it is more meet for the people to follow thy belief, than for thee to indulge their weakness? For thou art the head of thy people; the people is not thy head. If thou goest at warfare, it is thou that goest before the troops of thy host, which follow whither thou leadest. Wherefore it is better that thou shouldst lead them to the knowledge of the truth than that thou shouldst perish and leave them in their error. 'For God is not mocked,' nor doth He love the man who for an earthly kingdom refuseth to confess Him before the world." Though troubled by these arguments, Gundobad persisted to his dying day in this madness, nor ever would publicly confess that the three persons of the Trinity are equal. The blessed Avitus was at this time of great eloquence; for heresy springing up in Constantinople, both that taught by Eutyches and that of Sabellius, to the effect that our Lord Jesus Christ had in Him nothing of the divine nature, at the request of King Gundobad he wrote against them. There are today extant among us his admirable letters, which, as they once quelled heresy, so now they edify the Church of God. He wrote a book of Homilies, six metrical books on the creation of the world and on various other subjects, and nine books of Letters including those just mentioned. In a homily composed on the Rogations, he relates that these solemnities which we celebrate before the triumph of our Lord's Ascension were instituted by Mamertus, bishop of Vienne (his own see when he wrote), at a time when the city was alarmed by many portents. For it was frequently shaken by earthquakes, and wild creatures, stags and wolves, entered the gates, wandering without fear through the whole city. These things befell through the circle of the year, till at the approach of the Easter festival the whole people looked devoutly for the mercy of God, that at last this day of great solemnity might set a term to all their terror. But on the very vigil of that glorious night, while the holy rite of the Mass was being celebrated, on a sudden the royal palace within the walls was set ablaze by fire from heaven. All the congregation, stricken with fear, rushed from the church, believing that the whole city would be consumed in this fire, or that the earth would open and swallow it up. The holy bishop, prostrate before the altar, with groans and tears implored the mercy of God. What need for me to say more? the prayer of the illustrious bishop penetrated to the height of heaven; the river of his flowing tears extinguished the burning palace. When, after these events, the day of the Lord's Ascension drew near, he imposed a fast upon the people, instituted the form of prayer, the order of their repasts, and the manner of their joyful almsgiving to the poor. Thereupon all these terrors ceased; the fame of this deed spread through all the provinces, putting all the bishops in mind to follow the example of his faith. And down to our day these rites are celebrated in all churches in Christ's name, in compunction of the heart and a contrite spirit.

Now when Alaric, king of the Goths, beheld the manner in which King Clovis kept steadily subduing his neighbours in war, he sent envoys to him with this message: "If it please thee, O my brother, I am minded that we two meet by God's grace." Clovis did not refuse, but came to him. They met on an island in the Loire near the village of Amboise in the territory of the city of Tours. There they conversed, ate and drank together, swore mutual friendship, and parted in peace. Many people in Gaul at this time ardently desired to live under the dominion of the Franks.

•   •   •

After these events [*mostly wars—* Ed.] Clovis died at Paris, and was buried in the church of the Holy Apostles which he had himself built, with Clotild his queen. It was the fifth year after the battle of Vouillé that he passed away. And all the days of his reign were thirty years, and of his own age forty-five. From the passing of the holy Martin to the passing of Clovis, which was in the eleventh year of the episcopate of Licinius, bishop of Tours, there are counted one hundred and twelve years. After the death of her lord, Queen Clotild came to Tours, and, save for rare visits to Paris, here she remained all the days of her life, distinguished for her great modesty and kindliness.

BOOK X

• • •

The nineteenth bishop was myself, Gregory, the unworthy. At the time when I succeeded to the cathedral church of Tours, in which the blessed Martin and the other bishops of the Lord were consecrated to the episcopal office, it was all ruined and destroyed by the fire. I rebuilt it greater in size and height than before, and dedicated it in the seventeenth year after my consecration. I learned from priests far advanced in years that the relics of the martyrs of Agaun had been placed in the church by the men of old time. In the treasure of the Church of the holy Martin I discovered the reliquary; the relics had fallen into great decay; they had been translated to this place on account of their miraculous power. While vigils were being celebrated in their honour, the fancy took me to visit them once more by the light of a taper. I was narrowly examining them, when the custodian of the church said to me: "There is here a hollowed stone covered by a lid, but what it may contain I know not at all; I learned that my predecessors in this office were in like manner ignorant. I will bring it, that thou mayest carefully investigate its contents." He brought it, and I of course opened it, when I found within a silver casket containing not only relics of the witnesses of the sacred legion, but also others of divers saints, both martyrs and confessors. We also found other stones hollowed in the same way, in which were relics of the holy apostles and other martyrs. Marvelling at this gift, divinely granted, and rendering thanks to God, after vigils celebrated and masses said, I placed all in the cathedral church. In the cell of the holy Martin close to the cathedral church I placed relics of the martyrs Cosmas and Damian. I found the walls of the holy basilica burned with fire, and ordered them to be painted and decorated by the skill of our craftsmen with a richness equal to that which they had known before. I caused a baptistery to be erected close to the basilica, in which I placed relics of Saint John and of Sergius the martyr; in the earlier baptistery I placed those of Benignus the martyr. In many places within the territory of Tours I dedicated churches and oratories which I enriched with relics of the saints; but it were overlong to recount them in their order.

I have written ten books of History, seven of Miracles, and one on the Lives of the Fathers. I have composed one book of commentaries on the Psalms; I have also written one book on the Offices of the Church. These works may be written in an unpolished style, but I adjure all of you bishops of the Lord, who after me in this my lowliness shall govern the church of Tours, by the coming of our Lord Jesus Christ and by the day of Judgment terrible to all sinners, if ye would not depart confounded from the Judgment, to be condemned with the Evil One, never to let these books be destroyed or rewritten, by choosing out some parts and omitting others, but to leave them all complete and intact in your time just as I myself have left them. But whoever thou art, O priest of God, if our Martianus hath instructed thee in the seven arts, which is to say, if by grammar he hath taught thee to read, by dialectic to discuss propositions for argument, by rhetoric to know the different metres, by geometry to reckon the measurements of surfaces and lines, by astronomy to observe the courses of the stars, by arithmetic to compute the parts of numbers, by music to bring into one harmony songs of sweet accent and modulations of sound; if in all these things thou shalt be so skilled as to hold my style inelegant, even so, I pray thee, remove naught of that which I have written. If aught therein please thee, I refuse thee not permission to translate it into verse, but leave my work complete. I completed the writings of these books in the twenty-first year after my consecration. Although in what has gone before I have set down the list of the bishops of Tours, with the years of their tenure of office, I have not computed the total number as in a chronicle, because I have not been able exactly to discover the intervals between the several consecrations.

The following, then, is the whole sum of the years of the world:

From the beginning to the Deluge, MMCCXLII years.

From the Deluge to the passage of the Red Sea by the children of Israel, MCCCCIV years.

From the passage of the Red Sea to the Resurrection of our Lord, MDXXXVIII years.

From the Resurrection of our Lord to the passing of the holy Martin, CCCCXII years.

From the passing of the holy Martin to the above-mentioned year, I mean the twenty-first of my consecration, which is the fifth of Gregory, pope of Rome, the thirty-first of King Guntram, and the nineteenth of Childebert the young, CXCVII years. The sum of all which years is MMMMMDCCXCII.

Einhard

Rarely do we complain that a biography is too short, that it tantalizes the reader without satisfying his desire to learn more. But this complaint is valid in the case of Einhard's *Life of Charlemagne*. This brief work, one of our major sources of information about ninth-century Europe and about Charlemagne and his court, is reproduced here in its entirety.

Einhard (occasionally called Eginhard) was remarkably well qualified for the task he set himself. Born in 770 of a wealthy landholding family in the eastern part of Charlemagne's territories, he was destined for a career in the Church. At an early age he received his formal education at the monastery of Fulda (in central Germany), which had been heavily endowed by his family, and about 790 he became a member of the court of Charlemagne. Thus began the long association between the emperor and the monk.

Charlemagne loved his circle of intimates—a circle composed of many of the most highly educated and stimulating minds of the times, including the English theologian and teacher, Alcuin of York. Einhard's presence in this company enabled him to observe Charlemagne at short range and to develop the firsthand knowledge of his subject that gives the biography its authenticity. Einhard survived Charlemagne by about twenty-nine years, occupying himself with church building, acquiring holy relics, taking part in public affairs, and writing. The death of his wife and the political disintegration that set in after Charlemagne's death led Einhard finally to withdraw from public life. He died in 844.

Charlemagne, or Charles the Great, was a shining figure in a historical epoch we now often refer to as the "Dark Ages," so shining indeed that his period is frequently called the "Carolingian Renaissance." After his death the advances toward a higher civilization that were made during his lifetime soon dissipated and Europe sank back once again into a state of relative darkness for another two centuries. For most of his long reign Charles made his capital at Aix-la-Chapelle, now named Aachen, a city where present-day Germany, Belgium, and the Netherlands meet. His stone throne can still be seen in the chapel he built there.

The Life of Charlemagne

After I had made up my mind to describe the life and habits and, above all, the deeds of my lord and patron, the illustrious and deservedly famous King Charles, I set about doing so as succinctly as possible. I have tried not to omit anything that has come to my notice, and at the same time not to be long-winded and offend those discerning readers who object to the very idea of a modern history. But I also wanted to keep my new work from displeasing those who disapprove even of the masterpieces of the wisest and most learned authors of antiquity. To be sure, I am fully aware that there are many men of letters who do not regard contemporary matters so far beneath their notice as to treat them with contempt and consider them fit only to sink into silence and oblivion. On the contrary, the enthusiasm for things past leads some writers to recount the famous deeds of other men as best they can, and in this way they hope to insure that their own names will be remembered by posterity.

Be this as it may, none of these possible objections can prevent me from writing on the subject, since I am convinced that no one can describe these events better than I can. For I was there when they took place and I know them as an eyewitness, so to speak. Furthermore, I am not entirely sure if they will be recorded by anyone else. And so I thought it would be better to write down what I had to say even at the risk of duplicating what others might write, rather than to allow the illustrious life of the greatest king of the age and his famous deeds, unmatched by his contemporaries, to disappear forever into forgetfulness.

Besides, there was another reason, important enough in itself, I think, to make me compose this book: namely, that Charles educated me and gave me his life-long friendship and that of his children from the time I came to the court. In this way he attached me to his person and made me so devoted to him in life and death that I might well be called ungrateful if I were to forget everything he did for me and never say a word about his great and magnificent generosity, I, who owe him so much; indeed, that would mean allowing his life to remain unremembered and unpraised, as though he had never lived! To be sure, my abilities, feeble and inadequate as they are—nonexistent even—are incapable of portraying his life as it really ought to be portrayed. Even the eloquence of a Cicero would not have been up to that.

Here, then, is the book containing the life story of a truly great man. You will marvel at his deeds,

Einhard, *The Life of Charlemagne*, trans. E.S. Firchow and E.H. Zeydel (Coral Gables: University of Miami Press, 1972), pp. 31–119. Used by permission of University of Miami Press.

and probably also at the presumption of a barbarous Frank for imagining that he could write tastefully and elegantly in Latin. For I am not much versed in the Roman tongue. Then, too, you will perhaps be amazed at my temerity in ignoring the words of Cicero when, speaking of Latin writers, he said in the first book of his *Tusculan Disputations* that "whoever puts his thoughts in writing and can not arrange and state them clearly, and delight the reader with a pleasant style, makes a complete mockery of the writer's craft." This remark of the famous orator might have kept me from writing if I had not already made up my mind to brave the judgment of the world and take a chance with my feeble talents. I thought this would be better than to allow the memory of so great a man to perish out of petty concern for my own reputation.

1. THE MEROVINGIANS

The family of the Merovingians from which the Franks customarily chose their kings is believed to have ruled until the time of King Hilderich. Hilderich was deposed, tonsured, and sent to a monastery by the command of the Roman Pope Stephen. Although the royal line apparently ended only with him, it had long before ceased to matter and possessed no more except the empty title of king. The real wealth and power of the kingdom were in the hands of the prefects of the palace, the so-called majordomos, and their word was law. The king had no choice but to sit on the throne with flowing hair and full beard, content with his title and the semblance of sovereignty. He would listen to messengers coming from all around and, as they left, give them replies as though they were his own, but in reality, they had been dictated to him or even forced on him.

Except for the empty title of king and an intermittent allowance which the prefect of the palace gave or did not give him at his pleasure, the king owned nothing but a single estate, and that was not a very lucrative one. He lived on it and had a few servants there performing the most necessary duties and making a show of obsequiousness. Wherever he had to go, he went like a farmer in a cart drawn by a span of oxen with a carter driving them. That is how he went to the palace and how he went to the meetings of his people, which took place yearly for the good of the realm. And in this same way he returned home. But the administration of the state and all internal and external business was carried out by the prefect of the palace.

2. CHARLES' ANCESTORS

When Hilderich was deposed, the office of majordomo was already hereditarily held by Pepin, the father of King Charles. For Pepin's father, Charles [*Charles Martel*—Ed.], had in his time crushed the rebels who were trying to take over all of Franconia. He had also defeated the Saracens so badly in two great battles, when they attempted to occupy Gaul, that they had to return to Spain. One of these battles had taken place in Aquitaine near Poitiers [*in 732*—Ed.], the other on the Berre River not far from Narbonne. This same Charles had in turn received the office of majordomo from his father Pepin and had administered it extremely well. It was customary for the people to bestow such an honor only on men of noble birth and great wealth.

When Pepin, the father of King Charles, held this office, bequeathed by his grandfather and father to him and to his brother Carloman, the two of them shared it quite amicably for several years, nominally under King Hilderich. But then for some unknown reason Carloman abandoned the burdensome government of the temporal kingdom—possibly because he longed for a more contemplative life—and went into retirement in Rome. There, giving up his worldly garb, he became a monk and built a monastery on Mt. Soracte near the church of St. Sylvester. For a number of years he enjoyed his longed-for seclusion, along with a few monks who had accompanied him. But when a great many noble Franks came on pilgrimages to Rome to fulfill vows and insisted on paying homage to their former lord, it was impossible for him to get any peace, which he cherished more than anything else, and he decided to move elsewhere. When he saw that the crowds of intruders were interfering with his resolve to be alone, he left the mountain and went away to the province of Samnium, to the monastery of St. Benedict on Monte Cassino, where he spent the rest of his life in prayer.

Waifar, duke of Aquitaine, and then, at the end of the war, he died of dropsy in Paris. His sons Charles and Carloman survived him, and on them, by the will of Providence, the succession devolved. In solemn assembly the Franks appointed them kings on condition that they share the realm equally, Charles ruling the part which had belonged to their father Pepin, Carloman the part formerly controlled by his uncle Carloman. Both accepted these conditions and each one took over that section of the divided kingdom which he had received according to the agreement.

But peace between the two brothers was maintained only with the greatest difficulty since many of Carloman's followers plotted to break up the partnership. A few even tried to provoke a war with their intrigues. The outcome, however, showed that there was more imagined than real danger. When Carloman died, his wife and sons fled to Italy with the most important members of their court. Without any apparent reason she spurned her brother-in-law and placed herself and her children under the protection of Desiderius, king of the Lombards. Carloman had succumbed to an illness after ruling jointly for two years, and at his death Charles was unanimously proclaimed king of the Franks.

3. CHARLES BECOMES KING

Pepin, no longer majordomo but king by authority of the Roman pontiff, ruled alone over the Franks for fifteen years or more. For nine unbroken years he fought against

4. PLAN OF THIS WORK

Because nothing has been recorded in writing about Charles' birth,[1] infancy, or even boyhood, and be-

[1] [The conjectural date of Charlemagne's birth is April 2, 742—Ed.]

cause no survivor has been found who claims to know of these matters, I consider it foolish to write about them. So I have decided to skip what we know nothing about and proceed to recount and describe Charles' exploits, habits, and other facts of his life. First I want to tell of his deeds at home and abroad, then describe his habits and interests, his rulership and finally his death, omitting nothing that is worth mentioning or necessary to know.

5. WAR IN AQUITAINE

Of all the wars Charles waged, the first was the Aquitainian campaign, begun but not finished by his father. Charles believed that it would soon be over. He asked his brother, who was still living at the time, to help him. But although his brother disappointed him and failed to provide the promised support, Charles completed the undertaking with great vigor. He was unwilling to give up what he had begun or to abandon a task once taken on until he had carried out his plans and brought them to a happy conclusion by force of perseverance and steadfastness. He even compelled Hunold, who after Waifar's death had tried to seize Aquitaine and revive a war that was almost finished, to leave the country and flee to the land of the Basques. But Charles gave him no respite. He crossed the Garonne River, built Fort Fronsac, and through diplomatic channels let the Basque Duke Lupus know that he had better return the fugitive speedily or he would come and get Hunold by force. Lupus thought better of it and not only handed over

Hunold but also submitted himself and the province he ruled to the jurisdiction of Charles.

6. WAR WITH THE LOMBARDS

When the affairs of Aquitaine had been settled and the war ended, and after his brother had died, Charles undertook a campaign against the Lombards at the request and pleading of Bishop Hadrian of Rome. His father had once before fought the Lombards, that time in response to the entreaties of Pope Stephen. Pepin had done so under great difficulties, for certain nobles with whom he usually consulted had opposed his wishes so strongly that they openly declared they would desert the king and go home. Nevertheless, arms were taken up against King Aistulf at that time and the war brought to a speedy end. But although the reasons for this conflict seem to have been similar and indeed the same in both Charles' and Pepin's case, the difficulties of seeing it through and settling it varied in each instance. Pepin, after a few days' siege at Pavia, forced Aistulf to give hostages and to return to the Romans the cities and fortresses he had taken. He also made Aistulf swear a sacred oath that he would not try to regain what he had surrendered. Charles, on the other hand, pursued the war more single-mindedly and did not rest until he had forced King Desiderius to surrender unconditionally after weakening him in a lengthy siege. He also ordered Desiderius' son Adalgis, who was the favorite of his people, to leave the kingdom and Italy and to restore everything he had taken from the Romans. Charles then prevented Rotgaud, the duke of Friuli, from starting a revolt. After that he subjected all of Italy to his rule and made his son Pepin king of the conquered Italian territories.

At this point I should describe how difficult it was for Charles to cross the Alps on his way to Italy and how the Franks toiled when crossing the trackless mountain ridges, the rocky cliffs, and the sharp peaks reaching to the sky. But I have decided to describe in this work Charles' way of life rather than the outcome of the wars he waged. Suffice it to say that the end of the campaign resulted in the subjugation of Italy, the deportation of Desiderius into permanent exile, the expulsion of his son Adalgis from Italy, and the restoration of the possessions taken by the Lombard kings to Pope Hadrian of Rome.

7. WAR WITH THE SAXONS

Then the Saxon war—which had merely been interrupted—was taken up again. The Franks have never been involved in any struggle that was more prolonged, more bitter, or more laborious. For the Saxons—like almost all of the nations inhabiting Germania—are savage by nature, given to the cult of demons, and hostile to our religion. They do not find it dishonorable to violate or break divine or human laws. Hardly a day passed without incidents threatening the peace. The border between our land and theirs runs almost entirely through plains, with the exception of a few areas where large forests or mountain ridges provide the territories with natural boundaries. Thus, murder, robbery, and arson never ceased on both sides. Eventually the Franks became so enraged that it no longer seemed enough to retaliate and so they decided to wage open war. Accordingly, war was declared and fought by both parties with great ferocity. It continued for thirty-three years and cost the Saxons far more than the Franks. To be sure, it could have been concluded sooner if the treachery of the Saxons had allowed it. For it is difficult to say how many times they surrendered to the king and promised to do what they were ordered, how often and without delay they furnished hostages that were demanded, and how often they received legates. Many times they were so badly defeated and weakened that they vowed to give up their cult of demons and indicated their willingness to submit to the Christian faith. But just as they were often ready to do this, just as often were they in a hurry to break their promises. Thus, I cannot say with certainty which of these courses of action they more truthfully favored. It is a fact, however, that after the beginning of the war against the Saxons hardly a year passed without some vacillation on their part. And yet the king in his high purpose and unswerving constancy both in success and failure was not to be frustrated by their fickleness, nor could he be made to abandon what he had begun. He never allowed any of them who perpetrated such perfidy to go unpunished. In these instances he either led an army personally or sent one with his counts to avenge the crimes and mete our proper punishment. After he had defeated all of those who had been offering resistance, he subjected them to his power. Then he took ten thousand Saxons who lived on both banks of the Elbe river, with their wives and children, and resettled them in various contingents here and there throughout Gaul and Germania. And so the war which had dragged on for so many years was concluded under the conditions which the king imposed and the Saxons accepted. The conditions were that they give up the cult of demons, abandon the religious practices of their ancestors, adopt the sacraments of the Christian faith and religion, and become a single nation with the Franks.

8. WAR WITH THE SAXONS (continued)

Although this struggle had gone on for many years, the king himself fought the enemy not more than twice during the period, and this within a single month with only a few days intervening: once at the mountain Osning, in a place called Detmold, and once at the river Hase. The enemies were so routed and defeated in these two battles that they subsequently never dared to provoke the king again or to resist him when he approached, unless they were protected by fortifications. In these fights many noblemen and leaders in highest positions were killed, both among the Franks and Saxons. Finally, the strife ended in the thirty-third year. But meanwhile so many other great wars had been declared against the Franks in various parts of the world and were taken up under the king's guidance that anyone considering the matter

might justifiably wonder whether Charles' endurance in time of trouble or his good fortune is more to be admired. The Saxon war had begun two years before the Italian, and, although it was carried on without interruption, none of the other pressing duties were set aside nor other equally difficult struggles dropped for its sake. For the king surpassed everyone in his time in prudence and nobility of mind, and he turned down nothing that had to be undertaken or carried out. He did not shy at the difficulties or fear the dangers involved because he had learned to accept and endure everything in accordance with its nature. Neither in adversity did he yield nor was he misled by good fortune when it beckoned deceptively during times of great success.

9. EXPEDITION TO SPAIN

While Charles was engaged in the strenuous and almost incessant struggle with the Saxons and after he had built fortifications at strategic points along the frontier, he decided to invade Spain with as large an army as he could raise. He crossed the Pyrenees successfully and accepted the surrender of all the towns and castles on his way. Finally, he turned back with his forces safe and intact, but when recrossing the mountains he was made to feel the treachery of the Basques. In a densely wooded area well suited for ambush the Basques had prepared to attack the army from the top of the highest mountain. As the troops were proceeding in a long column through the narrow mountain passes, the Basques descended on the baggage train and the protecting rear guard and forced them into the valley. In the ensuing battle the Basques slaughtered them to a man. They seized the baggage and, under cover of the growing darkness, quickly scattered in all directions. In this encounter the Basques had the advantage of light weapons and a favorable terrain; the Franks on the other hand were hampered by their heavy equipment and the unevenness of the battle ground. Ekkehard, the royal steward, Anshelm, the count of the Palace, and Roland the Margrave of Brittany, as well as many others were killed in the engagement.[2] Unfortunately, the incident could not be avenged since the enemies disappeared without a trace after the attack and there were no signs where they might be found.

10. SUBMISSION OF THE BRETONS AND BENEVENTIANS

Charles also conquered the Bretons, who lived in a certain remote part of Gaul along the west coast and were not subject to him. He sent an expedition against them, which forced them to give hostages and made them promise to do what was expected of them.

Then he entered Italy with an army and, marching through Rome, went as far as Capua, a city in Campania. There he set up a camp and threatened to take up arms against the Beneventians unless they surrendered. Aregis, the duke of Benevento, prevented this by sending

his sons Rumold and Grimold with a large sum of money asking the king to accept them as hostages. He promised that he and his people would do as Charles demanded, on the condition that he would not be forced to appear before the king in person. Charles was more concerned about the good of the people than about the duke's stubbornness, and so he accepted the hostages and agreed that, in view of the large gift of money, the duke should not be compelled to come. He kept one of the two sons of Aregis, not yet of age, as a hostage and sent the older one back to his father. Charles also dispatched legates to receive oaths of loyalty from the Beneventians and from Aregis himself. After that he returned to Rome, spent several days there in worship at the holy places, and finally went back to Gaul.

11. TASSILO AND THE WAR WITH THE BENEVENTIANS

All at once a war broke out in Bavaria which was, however, swiftly concluded. It was caused by the pride and folly of Duke Tassilo. At the urging of his wife, who was a daughter of King Desiderius and who imagined that she could avenge her father's exile through her husband, he made an alliance with the Huns, the neighbors of the Bavarians to the east. According to its terms, Tassilo not only refused to do the king's bidding but also tried his best to challenge him to war. The dauntless king could not tolerate this outrageous insolence. He therefore collected his troops from all over and personally marched to

---

[2] [Battle of Roncesvalles (778), described in the *Song of Roland*—Ed.]

Bavaria with a large army. He reached the river Lech, which separates the Bavarians from the Alemanni, and established his camp there. Before invading the province, however, he decided to find out about the plans of the duke by sending messengers to him. Tassilo realized that there was no point for him or his people to act stubbornly, and so he presented himself to the king to ask for forgiveness. He furnished the hostages that were demanded, among them also his son Theodo, and swore an oath that he would never again be persuaded by anyone to be disobedient to Charles. Thus a speedy end was made to the war which at first had threatened to become one of major proportions. Tassilo, however, was later summoned to the court and not permitted to return. His province was from that time on ruled not by one duke but by several counts.

12. WAR WITH THE SLAVS

After these problems had been solved arms were taken up against the Slavs, who were known to us as Wiltzes but who call themselves Welatabi in their own language. The Saxons fought as auxiliaries in this war, together with other peoples who followed the standards of the king. To be sure, their loyalty was more perfunctory than real. The conflict was caused by the Wiltzes, who were constantly invading and harassing the Abodrites—long-time allies of the Franks—and could not be intimidated by warnings.

A gulf of undetermined length stretches from the western Ocean toward the East, nowhere exceeding a hundred miles across, though narrower at many points [*Baltic Sea*—Ed.]. Numerous nations live around its shores. The Danes, for instance, and the Swedes, whom we call Norsemen, occupy the northern shore and all the islands along it. The southern shore, on the other hand, is inhabited by Slavs, Estes, and various other nationalities. Among these are the Wiltzes whom Charles was attacking now. In a single campaign led by himself, he crushed and conquered them so effectively that they never again dared to refuse his order.

13. WAR WITH THE HUNS

Next to the Saxon the war which now followed was the most important of them all: it was directed against the Avars or Huns. Charles undertook it with greater energy and far better equipment than any other before. He made one expedition himself to Pannonia—the Huns were occupying this province at that time—and the execution of the rest of the campaign he assigned to his son Pepin and to his provincial prefects, counts, and representatives. Although the war was carried on most vigorously, it ended only in the eighth year. The deserted palace of the Khan as well as the way in which Pannonia was divested of all its population, so that not even a trace of human habitation now remains, testify to the many battles fought and the great amount of blood shed there. The entire Hunnish nobility perished during these struggles and their glory vanished. All the money and treasures they had collected over many years were taken away. There is in memory of man no war ever fought against the Franks in which they became richer and accumulated greater wealth. Indeed, although up to that time the Huns had almost seemed to be paupers, so much gold and silver were found in their palace, and so much precious loot captured in the battles, that one can say with good reason: the Franks justly took away from the Huns what the latter had previously unjustly acquired from other peoples.

Only two leaders of the Franks perished in this campaign. Duke Eric of Friuli was killed through the treachery of the townspeople in the seaport town of Tarsatica in Liburnia. Gerold, the prefect of Bavaria, was slain by an unidentified person in Pannonia when he was about to join the attack against the Huns and was marshaling his lines on horseback. He died together with two others who accompanied him while he was exhorting his soldiers one by one to muster their courage for the battle. Otherwise the conflict was practically bloodless and its outcome highly advantageous for the Franks, although because of its magnitude, it lasted for a long time.

14. WAR WITH THE DANES

At long last the Saxon war, too, came to a proper conclusion befitting its long duration. The following wars in Bohemia and Linonia were bound to be brief. Under the leadership of the young King Charles they were quickly settled. Charles' last campaign was directed against those Norsemen who are called Danes. They first were engaged in piracy; later they invaded and devastated the coasts of Gaul and Germania with a rather large fleet. Godofrid, their king, was so filled with vain ambition that he saw himself as the future master over all of Germania. Already he regarded Frisia and Saxony as his own provinces and had subjugated his neighbors, the Abodrites, forcing them to pay tribute. Furthermore, he bragged that in a short time he would be coming with a very large force to the king's court at Aachen. However empty his boasts were, some people did indeed believe them and thought that he was about to do something of this kind. But he was prevented by sudden death from carrying out his plans. He was assassinated by his own guard, and this ended his life and the war he had begun.

15. CONQUESTS

These were the wars which the mighty King Charles planned so carefully and executed so brilliantly in various parts of the world during his reign of forty-seven years. As a result the kingdom of the Franks, which was already great and powerful when Charles inherited it from his father Pepin, was almost doubled in size. Formerly, the Frankish territory had encompassed only that part of Gaul lying between the Rhine and the Loire, the ocean and the Balearic Sea, as well as that part of Germania inhabited by the so-called East Franconians and bordering on Saxony and the Danube, the Rhine and the Saale—a river separating the Thuringians from the Sorbs—and, finally, the land of the Alemanni and Bavarians.

Through the wars described above Charles conquered first Aquitaine, then Gascony and the entire Pyrenees region as far south as the Ebro River. This river originates in Navarre and flows through the most fertile plains of Spain, emptying into the Balearic Sea beneath the walls of the city of Tortosa. Charles also added to his territory all of Italy from Aosta to Lower Calabria, where the border runs between the Beneventians and the Greeks—an area extending over more than a thousand miles. Furthermore, he incorporated Saxony—no small part of Germania and considered equal in length and twice the width of Franconia—and both Upper and Lower Pannonia, as well as Dacia on the other side of the Danube, Istria, Liburnia, and Dalmatia. Only the coastal towns of the latter countries he left to the emperor of Constantinople out of friendship and in consideration of a treaty he had made with him. Finally, Charles subjugated and forced to pay tribute all of the barbarian and savage nations who inhabit Germania between the Rhine and the Vistula rivers, the ocean and the Danube. They speak almost the same language but have quite different customs and habits. The most important of these tribes are the Wiltzes, Sorbs, Abodrites, and Bohemians. With these he was forced to fight, but others, by far the greater number, surrendered without a struggle.

16. FOREIGN RELATIONS

Charles also increased the glory of his empire by establishing friendly relations with many kings and peoples. An example is his close friendship with King Alfons of Galicia and Asturias, who always insisted on calling himself Charles' vassal when sending him letters or ambassadors. Charles also secured the favor of the Scottish kings by his great generosity, so that they always referred to him as their master and called themselves his subjects and servants. To this day there exist letters sent by them which clearly express these feelings.

With King Harun of Persia, who ruled almost all of the Orient except India, he was on such friendly terms that Harun preferred Charles' goodwill to the friendship of all other kings and potentates on earth and considered Charles alone worthy of his respect and homage. At one time the king of the Franks sent messengers with offerings to the most Holy Sepulcher, the site of the Resurrection of our Lord and Savior. When they appeared before Harun to relay their master's wishes, the king not only permitted them to carry out their mission but also gave Charles the jurisdiction over their holy and blessed place. On their return Harun sent along his own messengers with precious gifts, garments, spices, and other riches of the Orient. A few years earlier Charles had asked him for an elephant and Harun had sent him the only one he owned.

The three emperors of Constantinople, Nicephorus, Michael, and Leo, also sought Charles' friendship and alliance and sent numerous legations to his court. Only when Charles assumed the title of emperor did they begin to distrust him out of fear that he would seize their lands. To allay these fears and make sure that there would be no occasion for further trouble, Charles at once concluded a firm treaty with them. But the Greeks and the Romans remained suspicious of Frankish power. Hence the Greek proverb: "Have a Frank as a friend, but not as a neighbor."

17. PUBLIC WORKS

No matter how much time and effort Charles spent on planning and carrying out campaigns to enlarge his realm and subjugate foreign nations, he still was able to begin work on a number of public projects designed to help and beautify his kingdom. Some of them he actually managed to complete. The Basilica of the Holy Mother of God in Aachen, a triumph of the arts of construction, is quite rightly considered among the most remarkable of these. So, too, the bridge spanning the Rhine at Mainz, which is a full five hundred paces long, since the river is that wide at this point [2250 feet—Ed.]. The bridge was destroyed by fire and was not rebuilt because Charles died a year later. He had intended to replace the wooden structure with one of stone. He also began building two magnificent palaces, one near the city of Mainz close to his estate at Ingelheim, the other in Nymwegen on the Waal River, which flows south of the island of the Batavians. But his chief concern was for the churches. When he discovered one in any part of his kingdom that was old and ready to collapse he charged the responsible bishops and priests with restoring it. And he made sure that his instructions were carried out by having his agents check up on them.

He also set up a navy to withstand the attacks of the Norsemen and had the necessary ships built on the rivers which flow from Gaul and Germania into the North Sea. Since the Norsemen were continuously invading and devastating the Gallic and Germanic coasts, he placed guards and fortifications in all harbors and large estuaries where ships could enter. In this way he prevented the enemy from landing and looting. He did the same in the south along the shores of Narbonensis, Septimania, and Italy as far south as Rome to ward off the Moors who had just begun to take up piracy. As a consequence Italy was hardly touched during his reign except for the Etruscan town of Civita Vecchia, which was treacherously captured and plundered by the Moors. Gaul and Germania were likewise spared except for a few Frisian islands along the Germanic coast which were laid waste by the Norsemen.

18. PRIVATE LIFE

This is how Charles defended and enlarged his empire and at the same time made it beautiful. My subject from this point on will be his intellectual abilities and his extraordinary steadfastness both in success and in adversity; and, further, whatever else concerns his private and domestic life.

After the death of his father, Charles ruled the kingdom together with his brother. Everyone was surprised that he bore the latter's animosity and envy with so much patience that he could never be provoked to anger by him. At his mother's request he married a daughter of the Lombard king Desiderius but repudiated her for unknown reasons after one year. Then he married Hildegard, who came from a very noble Swabian family. With her he had three sons, Charles, Pepin, and Louis, and as many daughters, Rotrud, Bertha, and Gisela. He had three more daughters, Theoderada, Hiltrud, and Rotheid, two of them with his [third] wife Fastrada, who came from Eastern Franconia and was therefore Germanic, the third by a concubine whose name I cannot recall at the moment. When Fastrada died he took Liutgard to wife, who was from Alemannia and with whom he had no children. After her death he had four concubines: Madelgard, who bore him a daughter by the name of Rothild; Gerswinda from Saxony, with whom he had another daughter called Adeltrud; Regina, who gave him two sons, Drogo and Hugo; and Adelind, who had Theoderic.

His mother Berthrada spent her old age in great honor in his house. He always treated her with greatest respect; only when he divorced the daughter of King Desiderius, whom he had married to please her, was there any disagreement between them. Berthrada died soon after Hildegard, but she had lived long enough to see three grandsons and three granddaughters in the house of her son. Charles buried her with highest honors in the church of St. Denis, where his father had been laid to rest.

Like his mother, he treated his only sister Gisela, who had entered a convent as a young girl, with the greatest affection. She died a few years before he did in the convent where she had spent most of her life.

19. PRIVATE LIFE
(continued)

For the education of his children Charles made the following provisions: his sons as well as his daughters were to be instructed first in those liberal arts in which he took most interest himself. As soon as the boys were old enough they had to learn how to ride, hunt, and handle weapons in Frankish style. The girls had to get used to carding wool and to the distaff and the spindle. To prevent their becoming bored and lazy he gave orders for them to be taught to engage in these and all other virtuous activities. Of his children, only two sons and one daughter died before him: Charles, who was the oldest; Pepin, whom he had made king of Italy; and his oldest daughter Rotrud, who had been engaged to marry the emperor Constantine of Greece. Pepin was survived by one son, called Bernhard, and five daughters: Adelheid, Atula, Guntrada, Bertheid, and Theoderada. How much Charles cared for his grandchildren was proved after their father's death: he made Bernhard Pepin's successor and raised the five girls together with his own daughters. When his two sons and daughter died, Charles reacted to their deaths with much less equanimity than might have been expected of so strong-minded a man. Because of his deep-seated devotion to them he broke down in tears. Also, when he was told of the death of the Roman Pope Hadrian, who was one of his best friends, he wept as much as if he had lost a brother or a favorite son. For Charles was by nature a man who had a great gift for friendship, who made friends easily and never wavered in his loyalty to them. Those whom he loved could rely on him absolutely.

He supervised the upbringing of his sons and daughters very carefully. When he was at home he never ate his meals without them and when he went away, he always took them along. At such times his sons rode by his side and his daughters followed close behind, protected by a bodyguard of hand-picked men. Although the girls were very beautiful and he loved them dearly, it was odd that he did not permit any of them to get married either to a man of his own nation or to a foreigner. Rather, he kept all of them with him until his death, saying that he could not live without their company. And on account of this, he had to suffer a number of unpleasant experiences, however lucky he was in every other respect. But he never let on that he had heard of any suspicions regarding their chastity or any rumors about them.

20. CONSPIRACIES AGAINST CHARLES

By one of the concubines he had a son whom I have not mentioned along with the others. His name was Pepin and he had a handsome face but was hunchbacked. While his father was wintering in Bavaria during the war against the Huns, Pepin pretended to be ill and became involved with some Frankish nobles in a plot against his father. He had been lured into it by empty promises that they would make him king. But the scheme was discovered and the traitors punished. Pepin was ton-

sured and allowed, on his own free will, to enter the monastery of Pruem, where he spent the rest of his life as a monk.

But even before this there had been a great conspiracy in Germania against Charles. All of the guilty ones were exiled, some of them only after being blinded, but the others were not harmed physically. Only three were killed because they had drawn their swords and tried to resist being taken prisoners. After they had slaughtered a number of men, they were killed themselves since there was no other way to subdue them. It was generally felt that Queen Fastrada's cruelty was responsible for these uprisings. And in both cases the reason they were aimed at Charles was because he apparently acquiesced in his wife's cruelty and seemed to have lost a good deal of his usual kindness and easy disposition. But for the rest, he was deeply loved and respected by everyone at home and abroad during all of his life, and no one ever accused him of being unnecessarily harsh.

21. TREATMENT OF FOREIGNERS

Charles liked foreigners and made every effort to see that they were well received. Often there were so many of them in his palace and kingdom that they were quite rightly considered a nuisance. But, magnanimous as he was, he was never bothered by such annoyances. For he felt that he would be rewarded for his troubles if they praised his generosity and gave him a good reputation.

22. PERSONAL APPEARANCE

Charles had a big and powerful body and was tall but well-proportioned. That his height was seven times the length of his own feet is well known. He had a round head, his eyes were unusually large and lively, his nose a little longer than average, his gray hair attractive, and his face cheerful and friendly. Whether he was standing or sitting his appearance was always impressive and dignified. His neck was somewhat short and thick and his stomach protruded a little, but this was rendered inconspicuous by the good proportions of the rest of his body. He walked firmly and his carriage was manly, yet his voice, though clear, was not as strong as one might have expected from someone his size. His health was always excellent, except during the last four years of his life, when he frequently suffered from attacks of fever. And at the end he also limped with one foot. All the same, he continued to rely on his own judgment more than on that of his physicians, whom he almost hated because they ordered him to give up his customary roast meat and eat only boiled meat instead.

According to Frankish custom, he rode and hunted a great deal. There is probably no nation on earth that can match the Franks in these skills. Charles was also fond of the steam of natural hot springs. He swam a great deal and did it so well that no one could compete with him. This was why he built the palace in Aachen and spent there the last years of his life without interruption until he died. He in-vited not only his sons but also his nobles and friends, sometimes even his retinue and bodyguard, to bathe with him, so that frequently there would be more than a hundred people in the baths.

23. DRESS

He wore the national dress of the Franks. The trunk of his body was covered with a linen shirt, his thighs with linen pants. Over these he put a tunic trimmed at the border with silk. The legs from the knee downward were wound with leggings, fastened around the calves with laces, and on his feet he wore boots. In winter he protected his shoulders and chest with a vest made of otter skins or marten fur, and over that he wrapped a blue cloak. He always carried a sword strapped to his side, and the hilt and belt thereof were made either of gold or silver. Only on special holidays or when ambassadors from foreign nations were to be received did he sometimes carry a jewel-studded saber. He disliked foreign clothes no matter how beautiful they were, and would never allow himself to be dressed in them. Only in Rome was he seen on two occasions in a long tunic, chlamys, and Roman shoes: the first time at the entreaty of Pope Hadrian and the second by request of his successor Leo. On high festival days he wore a suit of golden cloth and boots ornamented with jewels. His cloak was fastened by a golden brooch, and on his head he carried a diadem of gold, embellished with gems. On the other days, however, his dress was not much different from that of the common people.

24. HABITS

Charles was a moderate eater and drinker, especially the latter, because he abominated drunkenness in any man, particularly in himself and in his associates. But he could not easily abstain from eating and often complained that fasting was bad for his health. He rarely gave banquets and then only on special feast days for large numbers of guests. His daily dinner consisted of four courses, besides the roast which the hunters used to bring in on spits and which he loved more than any other food. During the meal he either listened to music or to someone reading aloud. Stories and the deeds of the old heroes were recited to him. He also enjoyed the books of St. Augustine, especially *The City of God.*

He was so temperate in drinking wine or other beverages that he rarely drank more than three times during a meal. After his midday meal in summer he would eat some fruit and take another drink, then remove his clothes and shoes, just as he did at night, and rest for two to three hours. His sleep at night would usually be interrupted four or five times, and as soon as he awoke, he got up. While he was being dressed and having his shoes put on, he would invite his friends to come into the room. If the count of the palace told him of some dispute which could not be settled without his decision, he ordered the litigants brought before him at once and, just as though he were sitting in a court of justice, would hear the case and pronounce judgment. At the same time he would give instructions on what had to be transacted that day, or what his ministers were to be charged with doing.

25. STUDIES

Charles was a gifted speaker. He spoke fluently and expressed whatever he had to say with great clarity. Not only was he proficient in his mother tongue but he also took trouble to learn foreign languages. He spoke Latin as well as his own language, but Greek he understood better than he could speak it. At times he was so eloquent that he almost seemed verbose. He was zealous in his cultivation of the liberal arts, and respected and honored highly those who taught them. He learned grammar from the Deacon Peter of Pisa, who was then already an old man. Another deacon, Albinus, surnamed Alcuin,[3] a man of Saxon origin who came from Britain and was the greatest scholar of his time, taught him the other subjects. Under his direction, the king spent a great deal of time and effort studying rhetoric, logic, and especially astronomy. He learned how to calculate and with great diligence and curiosity investigated the course of the stars. He also tried his hand at writing and to this end always kept writing tablets and notebooks under his pillow in bed in order to practice during spare moments. But since he had only started relatively late in life, he never became very accomplished in this art.

26. PIETY

The king practiced the Christian religion, in which he had been raised since childhood, with the

---

[3] [Alcuin of York (735–804)—*Ed.*]

greatest piety and devotion. That is why he built the beautiful basilica in Aachen and decorated it with gold and silver, candelabras, lattices, and portals of solid bronze. Since he was unable to get the columns and marble for the structure from anywhere else, he had them brought from Rome and Ravenna.

As long as his health permitted, the king attended church regularly in the morning and evening and took part in the late-night hours and morning mass. He was especially concerned that everything done in the church should be carried out with the greatest possible dignity. Often he admonished the sacristans to see to it that nothing unseemly or unclean was brought into the church or left there. He gave many sacred vessels of gold and silver and so many priestly vestments that when services were held not even the doorkeepers—the humblest in ecclesiastical rank—had to perform their duties in everyday clothes.

Charles also worked very hard at improving the quality of liturgical reading and chanting of the psalms. He himself was well versed in both, although he would never read in public or sing, except in a low voice and together with the congregation.

27. GENEROSITY

Charles was especially interested in helping the poor, and his generosity was of the kind for which the Greeks use the word *eleemosyna* (alms). But his charity was not limited to his own country and kingdom, for wherever he heard of Christians living in poverty, he would send them money out of compassion for their wretched lot, even overseas, to Syria and Egypt, as well as to Africa, Jerusalem, Alexandria, and Carthage. This was also the chief reason why he cultivated friendships with kings across the seas, so that the Christians living in need under their jurisdiction would receive some aid and succor.

Of all sacred and hallowed places, he loved the Cathedral of the Holy Apostle Peter in Rome most of all. He endowed its treasure room with great quantities of gold, silver, and precious stones. He sent its pontiffs many, indeed innumerable, gifts. During his entire reign nothing seemed more important to him than to exert himself to restore the city of Rome to its old splendor and to have the Cathedral of St. Peter not only secured and defended but, through his generosity, adorned and enriched beyond all other churches. Although he favored this church so much, he only visited it four times during his reign of forty-seven years, there to fulfill his vows and offer his prayers.

28. CHARLES BECOMES EMPEROR

But there were also other reasons for Charles' last visit to Rome. The Romans had forced Pope Leo, on whom they had inflicted various injuries, like tearing out his eyes and cutting out his tongue, to beg for the king's assistance. Charles therefore went to Rome to put order into the confused situation and reestablish the status of the Church. This took the whole winter. It was on this occasion that he accepted the titles of Emperor and Augustus, which at first he disliked so much that he said he would never have entered the church even on this highest of holy days[4] if he had beforehand realized the intentions of the Pope. Still, he bore with astonishing patience the envy his imperial title aroused in the indignant Eastern Roman emperors. He overcame their stubborn opposition with magnanimity—of which he unquestionably had far more than they did—and sent frequent embassies to them, always calling them his brothers in his letters.

29. REFORMS

After Charles had accepted the imperial title he noticed that there were many flaws in the legal code of his people, for the Franks have two separate sets of laws differing markedly in many details. He planned to fill in the gaps, to reconcile discrepancies, and to correct what was wrongly and improperly stated. But he was unable to get very much done, except for making a very few additions and even those incomplete. Even so, he did order all the unwritten laws of the nations under his rule collected and written down. He also had the same done for the very old heathen songs which tell of the deeds and wars of former kings, so that they might be preserved for posterity. In addition, he began a grammar of his native language.

Charles gave Frankish names to the months. Before that the Franks had used partly Latin, partly barbarian names for them. He also

invited appropriate designations for the twelve winds for which there had previously been barely four words. As for the months, he called January uuintarmanoth, February hornung, March lenzinmanoth, April ostarmanoth, May uuinnemanoth, June brachmanoth, July heuuimanoth, August aranmanoth, September uuitumanoth, October uuindumemanoth, November herbistmanoth, and December heilagmanoth. To the winds he gave the following names: the east wind (subsolanus) he called ostroniuuint, the southeaster (eurus) ostsundroni, the south-southeaster (euroauster) sundostroni, the south wind (auster) sundroni, the south-southwester (austroafricus) sunduuestroni, the southwester (africus) uuestsundroni, the west wind (zephyrus) uuestroni, the northwester (chorus) uuestnordroni, the north-northwester (circius) norduuestroni, the north wind (septentrio) nordroni, the northeaster (aquilo) nordostroni, and the north-northeaster (vulturnus) ostnordroni.

30. CORONATION OF LOUIS AND CHARLES' DEATH

At the end of his life, when he was already beset by illness and old age, Charles summoned Louis, the king of Aquitaine and Hildegard's only surviving son, to his presence. He invited all of the Frankish nobles to a solemn assembly, in which with their consent he appointed Louis co-regent over the entire realm and heir to the imperial title. He crowned his son himself by placing the diadem on his head and ordering that he be addressed Emperor

---

[4] [Charlemagne was crowned Emperor on Christmas day, 800—*Ed.*]

and Augustus. His decision was received by all those present with great acclaim since it seemed to be divinely inspired for the good of the kingdom. It increased his reputation as a ruler and instilled considerable respect among foreign nations. After Charles had sent his son back to Aquitaine, he started out as usual for the hunt paying no heed to his advanced age. Thus occupied, he spent what was left of the autumn not far from Aachen and returned to the palace at approximately the beginning of November. While he was wintering there he was attacked by a high fever during the month of January and had to retire to bed. As he always did when he had a temperature, he began to diet in the belief that he could cure or at least alleviate his illness by abstaining from food. In addition to the fever he developed a pain in his side, which the Greeks call pleurisy, but he kept fasting and did not take any sustenance except for an occasional drink. On the seventh day after he had taken to bed he received the Holy Communion and died on 28 January between eight and nine o'clock in the morning. Charles was then in the seventy-second year of his life and in the forty-seventh year of his reign.

31. BURIAL

His body was washed and prepared for burial in the customary way, then brought to the basilica and buried amid the great lamentations of the entire population. At first there was uncertainty about where he should be laid to rest because he had never given any instructions on this point during his lifetime. Finally everyone agreed that there could be no more appropriate place than the basilica which he had built at his own expense in this city out of love for God and our Lord Jesus Christ and in honor of the Holy and Immaculate Virgin. He was interred there on the same day he died. Above his grave a gilded arch was raised with his image and an inscription reading as follows: "In this tomb lies the body of Charles, the great Christian Emperor, who gloriously increased the kingdom of the Franks and ruled successfully for forty-seven years. He died in his seventies in the seventh year of the indiction, on January 28th in the year of our Lord 814."

32. OMENS OF DEATH

There were many omens indicating the approach of his death, so that not only others but even he himself took note of the forewarnings. During the last three years of his life there were frequent eclipses of the sun and moon, and black spots were seen on the face of the sun for seven days. On Ascension Day the portico between the cathedral and the palace which he had had built with immense effort suddenly came crashing down in complete ruin. The wooden bridge across the Rhine at Mainz, which had taken ten years of hard work to build and which was so cleverly constructed that it seemed as if it would last forever, this bridge accidentally caught fire and burnt to ashes in three hours, so that not a single plank remained except what was under water. During his last campaign in Saxony against Godofrid, the king of the Danes, Charles all at once saw a ball of brilliant fire falling from the sky and flashing from right to left through the clear atmosphere. He had just left his camp before sunrise to start out on the march. While everybody was looking and wondering what this sign meant, his horse suddenly fell headfirst and threw him to the ground so violently that the clasp on his cloak broke and his sword belt burst. The attendants who were near him and rushed to his aid helped him up without his weapons and cloak. The lance which he had been holding tightly in his hand was thrown a distance of more than twenty feet.

In addition to all this there were numerous earth tremors in his palace in Aachen, and in the houses which Charles visited the wooden beams in the ceilings creaked constantly. Furthermore, lightning had struck the basilica in which he was later to be buried and the golden ball which decorated the gable was destroyed and hurled onto the roof of the bishop's house next to the church. In the same basilica there was an inscription written in red ochre naming its builder and running along the edge of the circular space which surrounds the interior part of the building between the upper and lower arches. Its last words read: "Karolus Princeps." Several people noticed that during the last year of his life, only a few months before he died, the letters of the word "Princeps" had become so blurred that they could hardly be deciphered.

But Charles took no notice of these omens; in any case he acted as if they had nothing whatever to do with him.

33. LAST WILL

Charles had decided to draw up a will in which he wanted to make his daughters and illegitimate children heirs to some part of his estate. Since he started too late, however, he was unable to complete it. Nevertheless, three years before his death he made a division of his treasures, money, clothing, and other movable property in the presence of his friends and attendants. He called on them to bear witness that the apportionment which he had planned should be executed faithfully after his death. He had a brief statement prepared summarizing what he wanted done with the property he had divided. This document reads as follows: "In the name of the Almighty Lord God, the Father, the Son, and the Holy Ghost. Here is a description of the division which was made by the most glorious and pious Lord Charles, Emperor and Augustus, in the eight hundred and eleventh year after the incarnation of our Lord Jesus Christ, during the forty-third year of his reign over the Franks, in the thirty-sixth year of his rule over Italy, in the eleventh year of his Imperial sovereignty, and in the fourth indiction. After much pious and prudent deliberation and with the help of God, he has decided to distribute the valuables and money which on this day are on deposit in his treasury. In doing so he wished above all to ensure that in his case the distribution of alms, which among Christians is traditionally made from their own personal belongings, would be carried out in an orderly and reasonable fashion. He also wanted to be certain that his heirs should understand quite clearly and definitely what was to be theirs, so that they could divide up the inheritance properly without any litigation or dispute. Such being his intention and purpose, he first divided all his tangible and movable possessions, consisting of gold and of silver, precious stones and royal vestments, deposited in his treasury on the stipulated day into three main parts. One part he left intact; the other two he subdivided into twenty-one smaller portions, the reason for this being that, as is well known, there are twenty-two capital cities in his realm. One of these portions shall be given for charitable purposes to each of the cities by his heirs and friends. The archbishop responsible for the diocese shall receive the portion and divide it with his suffragans in such a manner that one-third is kept for his church and two-thirds is given to the suffragans. These twenty-one portions into which two-thirds of his property were subdivided to correspond to the number of capital cities in the kingdom have been carefully separated and set aside in individual coffers on which the names of the cities of destination are written. The cities to which these alms and gifts are to be given are as follows: Rome, Ravenna, Milan, Cividale del Friuli, Grado, Cologne, Mainz, Salzburg, Trier, Sens, Besançon, Lyons, Rouen, Rheims, Arles, Vienne, Moûtiers-en-Tarantaise, Embrun, Bordeaux, Tours, and Bourges.

"The third main part which is to be preserved intact shall be dealt with in the following manner: while both of the above-mentioned parts are to be divided in the way stated and are to be kept under seal, the third part is to be used for the defrayment of the daily expenses by

the owner and will constitute property of which he cannot be deprived by any sworn obligation whatsoever. This provision shall remain in force for as long as he lives or for as long as he judges that he has need of it. After his death or voluntary withdrawal from the secular world the said part is to be divided into four shares. One of these shall be added to the above mentioned twenty-one portions; the second share is to go to his sons and daughters and their sons and daughters and shall be distributed in a just and equitable way; the third shall be devoted to the poor in the customary Christian manner; the fourth is to be similarly parceled out in form of a pension, in the name of Christian charity, among the male and female servants of the Palace.

"To this third main part of his fortune, which like the rest consists of gold and silver, he desires that there be added all vessels and utensils made of bronze, iron, and other metal, together with his weapons, clothes, and other movable property, whether valuable or not, and for whatever use intended, such as curtains, coverlets, tapestries, woolens, leather goods, pack saddles, and whatever else might be found that day in the treasury or in his wardrobe. In this way the shares of the third part will be enlarged and the alms distributed among a greater number of people.

"Further, he has given orders that the chapel, that is to say the furnishings which he has donated and collected, or inherited from his father, be kept intact and not be subject to any kind of division. Should there, however, be any vessels, books, or other objects of which it is certainly known that they were not given to the chapel by him, then any person desiring them may buy them, provided a fair price is paid. In the same way he decreed that the large collection of books in his library may be bought by persons who want them and will pay a just price for them. The proceeds shall go to the poor.

"Among his other treasures and valuables there are known to be three silver tables and one of unusual size and weight made of gold. He has stipulated and decreed that one of them, square in shape and decorated with a plan of the city of Constantinople, be sent to Rome to the Cathedral of the Holy Apostle Peter together with the other gifts thereto intended. The second table, round in shape and engraved with a picture of the city of Rome, shall be given to the bishopric of the church of Ravenna. The third, far superior to the others, both in beauty of craftsmanship and in weight, consists of three concentric circles on which a map of the entire world is skillfully traced in great detail. This table together with the golden one, called the fourth, shall be added to the third main part of his fortune which he has allotted to his heirs and to those who are to receive alms.

"These arrangements and stipulations were done in the presence of the following bishops, abbots, and counts who were able to attend on that day, and whose names are herein recorded:

Bishops

Hildebald	John
Richolf	Theodolf
Arno	Jesse
Wolfar	Heito
Bernoin	Waltgaud
Laidrad	

Abbots

Fridugis	Angilbert
Adalung	Irmino

Counts

Walach	Richwin
Meginher	Edo
Otolf	Ercangar
Stephan	Gerold
Otolf	Ercangar
Stephan	Gerold
Unruoch	Bero
Burchard	Hildegern
Meginhard	Hroccolf."
Hatto	

After Charles' death, his son Louis, who succeeded him by divine ordination, examined this document and had its provisions carried out as speedily as possible and with the utmost scrupulousness.

Life in Country and Town

The preceding selections have given us some idea of the life of the clerics and the nobles during the Middle Ages. But we can have no genuine understanding of a society without knowing something about the ways in which the vast majority of the people made their living and about the obligations they had toward the political groups that dominated them. For example, our understanding of the ancient world would be vastly enriched if we had reliable accounts of the slave society of Athens or the small landholders of Sparta, or if we knew more of the causes of the Spartacus revolt under the Roman Republic, or if we had detailed information on the organization of the *latifundia* in the days of the Empire. Happily, our information about the daily life of everyman during the Middle Ages is somewhat more abundant, though still far from plentiful.

Generally, the social and economic historian gleans facts from hundreds of wills, deeds, transaction records, court cases, and the like. From these minuscule and fragmentary records he draws his generalizations. But we must remember that the people who lived during the Middle Ages were not quantitatively and economically oriented, as we in the modern world are. Consequently, we dare not put too much faith in their recorded statistics. The medieval chronicler might, for example, refer to an army of sixty thousand men, but the modern historian would be unwise to accept this figure at face value. Chances are the chronicler picked the number at random to dramatize the notion of a "very large" army. Moreover, general statements and observations on economic matters during the Middle Ages are rare, reflecting perhaps a lack of interest in that realm of human activity.

The first document that follows gives us a glimpse into rural life in the Middle Ages, as it was lived by the common people. A set of instructions for stewards of the royal lands, the *Capitulare de Villis*, was probably prepared by Louis the Pious, king of Aquitaine in southern France, in the late eighth century. The second selection, *Charter of the Liberties of Lorris*, reveals some facets of life in the towns. The charter was granted by Louis VII to the small north-central French town of Lorris in 1155. Historically it is important because it served as a model for numerous town charters in the years that followed.

Capitulare de Villis

1. We wish that our estates which we have instituted to serve our needs discharge their services to us entirely and to no other men.

2. Our people shall be well taken care of and reduced to poverty by no one.

3. Our stewards shall not presume to put our people to their own service, either to force them to work, to cut wood, or to do any other task for them. And they shall accept no gifts from them, either horse, ox, cow, pig, sheep, little pig, lamb, or anything else excepting bottles of wine or other beverage, garden produce, fruits, chickens, and eggs.

4. If any of our people does injury to us either by stealing or by some other offense he shall make good the damage and for the remainder of the legal satisfaction he shall be punished by whipping, with the exception of homicide and arson cases which are punishable by fines. The stewards, for injuries of our people to other men, shall endeavor to secure justice according to the practices which they have, as is the law. Instead of paying fines our people, as we have said, shall be whipped. Freemen who live in our domains or estates shall make good the injuries they do according to their law and the fines which they have incurred shall be paid for our use either in cattle or in equivalent value.

5. When our stewards ought to see that our work is done—the sowing, plowing, harvesting, cutting of hay, or gathering of grapes—let each one at the proper season and in each and every place organize and oversee what is to be done that it may be done well. If a steward shall not be in his district or can not be in some place let him choose a good substitute from our people or another in high repute to direct our affairs that they may be successfully accomplished. And he shall diligently see to it that a trustworthy man is delegated to take care of this work.

6. We wish our stewards to give a tithe of all our products to the churches on our domains and that the tithe not be given to the churches of another except to those entitled to it by ancient usage. And our churches shall not have clerics other than our own, that is, of our people or our palace.

7. Each steward shall perform his services fully, just as it has been prescribed, and if the necessity should arise that more must be done then he shall determine whether he should increase the service or the day-work.

8. Our stewards shall take care of our vines in their district and cultivate them well. And they shall put the wine in good vessels and carefully see to it that none is lost.

"Capitulare de Villis," Introduction to Contemporary Civilization in the West, 2nd ed., eds. Contemporary Civilization Staff of Columbia College (New York: Columbia University Press, 1954), Vol. 1, pp. 5–13. Courtesy of Columbia University Press.

And other required wine which is not from our vines they shall buy for provisioning the royal estates. And when they have bought more than is needed for this provisioning they shall inform us that we can let them know what is to be done with it. For they shall put the product of our vines to our use. The wine which those persons on our estates pay as rent shall be put in our cellars.

9. We wish that each steward in his district have measures of the *modius, sextarius,* the *situla* of eight *sextarii,* and the *corbus,* the same as we have in our palace.

10. Our mayors, foresters, stablemen, cellarers, deans, toll-collectors, and other officers shall do the regular and fixed labor and pay the due of pigs for their holdings and fulfill well their offices in return for the manual labor remitted them. And if any mayor holds a benefice he shall send his representative so that the manual labor and other services will be performed for him.

11. No steward shall take lodging for his own need or for his dogs from our people or from those in the forests.

12. No steward shall maintain at the expense of anyone else our hostages placed on our estates.

13. The stewards shall take good care of the stallions and not allow them to remain in one pasture too long lest they damage it. And if there should be any unsound or too old or about to die they shall inform us in good time before the season for putting them with the mares.

14. They shall take good care of our mares and separate them from the colts at the right time. And when the fillies increase in number they

shall also be separated to form a new herd.

15. Our stewards shall have our foals sent to the palace in the winter at the Feast of Saint Martin.

16. We wish that our stewards fully perform in the manner established for them whatever we or the queen or our officers, the seneschal or the butler, in our name or that of the queen command. If anyone shall not do this through negligence he shall abstain from drink from the time that it is made known to him until he comes into our presence or that of the queen and seeks pardon from us. And if the steward is with the army, on guard duty, or on a mission or otherwise engaged and he commands his assistants to do something and they fail to do it, then they shall come afoot to the palace and abstain from food and drink until they have given their reasons for not doing it. Then they shall receive their sentence, a whipping or whatever we or the queen deem appropriate.

17. Each steward shall have as many men taking care of the bees for our use as he has estates in his district.

18. At our mills the stewards shall have hens and geese according to the nature of the mill or as many more as is possible.

19. In our barns on the chief estates they shall have at least 100 chickens and 30 geese and on our lesser estates at least 50 chickens and 12 geese.

20. Each steward shall have the produce [of the fowl] brought always in abundance to the manor every year and besides shall inspect it three or four or more times.

21. Each steward shall have fishponds on our estates where they

were before and if it is possible to enlarge them, he shall do so. Where there were none before and it is now possible to have them let them be constructed.

22. Those who hold vines from us shall have no less than three or four circles of grapes for our use.

23. On each of our estates the stewards shall have cow-barns, pigsties, sheepfolds, and stables for goats, as many as possible, and never be without them. And they shall further have for performing their services cows furnished by our serfs so that our barns and teams are not in the least diminished by the services of work on our demesne. And when they are charged with furnishing food they shall have lame but healthy oxens and cows, and horses that are not mangy, and other healthy animals. They shall not on that account strip, as we have said, the cow-barns or the plough-beasts.

24. Each steward shall be responsible that whatever ought to be supplied for our table is all good and excellent and prepared carefully and cleanly. And each steward shall have grain for two meals for each day of the service that he is charged with supplying our table. Similarly the other provisions shall be good in all respects, the flour as well as the meat.

25. The stewards shall make known on the first of September whether or not there is pasturage for the hogs.

26. The mayors shall not have more land in their administration than they can get about and oversee in one day.

27. Our houses shall constantly have fire and watch service that they may be safe. And when royal envoys

or legates are coming to or leaving the palace, in no wise shall they exercise the right of bed and board in our manor houses except by our special order or that of the queen. But the count in his district or those persons who have been accustomed of old to caring for envoys and legates shall continue to do so as before. And pack-horses and other necessary things shall be provided in the customary fashion that they may come to the palace or depart in a fashion befitting them.

28. We wish that every year in Lent on Palm Sunday, which is called Hosanna Sunday, our stewards carefully render according to our instructions the money arising from the products of our land after we know for the particular year what our income is.

29. Each steward shall see to it that anyone of our people who have cases to plead shall not of necessity have to come to us so that he will not lose through negligence days on which he ought to be working. And if one of our serfs has some rights to claim outside our lands, his master shall do all that he can to secure justice for him. In case the serf shall not be able to get justice his master shall not permit him to exhaust himself in his efforts but shall see to it that the matter is made known to us by himself or by his representative.

30. Of those things that our stewards ought to provide for our needs, we wish them to put aside all the products due us from them, and what must be placed in the wagons for the army, taking it from the homes as well as from the herdsmen and that they know how much they have reserved for this purpose.

31. They shall set aside each year

what they ought to give as food and maintenance to the workers entitled to it and to the women working in the women's quarters and shall give it fully at the right time and make known to us what they have done with it and where they got it.

32. Each steward shall see to it that he always has the very best seed by purchase or otherwise.

33. After the above things have been set aside and after the sowing and other works have been done, all that remains of all the products shall be preserved until we give word to what extent they shall be sold or stored according to our order.

34. At all times it is to be seen to with diligence that whatever is worked upon or made with the hands such as lard, smoked meat, salted meat, newly salted meat, wine, vinegar, mulberry wine, cooked wine, fermentations, mustard, cheese, butter, malt, beer, mead, honey, wax, and flour shall be prepared or made with the greatest cleanliness.

35. We wish that fat be made of the fat sheep and pigs. Moreover the stewards shall have in each estate not less than two fattened oxen either there to be made into fat or to be sent to us.

36. Our woods and forests shall be well taken care of and where there shall be a place for a clearing let it be cleared. Our stewards shall not allow the fields to become woods and where there ought to be woods they shall not allow anyone to cut too much or damage them. And they shall look carefully after our wild beasts in the forests and also take care of the goshawks and sparrowhawks reserved for our use. They shall collect diligently our tax

for the use of our forests and if our stewards or our mayors or their men put their pigs for fattening in our forests they shall be the first to pay the tenth of them to give a good example so that thereafter the other men will pay the tenth in full.

37. The stewards shall keep our fields and cultivated lands in good shape and care for the meadows at the right time.

38. They shall always have sufficient fat geese and chickens for our use when they ought to provide it or send it to us.

39. We wish that the stewards collect the chickens and eggs which the lesser officials and the holders of *mansi* pay each year and when they are not needed that they have them sold.

40. Each steward shall always have on our estates for the sake of adornment unusual birds, peacocks, pheasants, ducks, pigeons, partridges, and turtledoves.

41. The buildings on our estates and the fences which enclose them shall be well taken care of and the stables and kitchens, bake-houses and presses shall be carefully ordered so that the workers in our service can perform their duties fittingly and very cleanly.

42. Each manor shall have in the store-room counterpanes, bolsters, pillows, bedclothes, table and bench covers, vessels of brass, lead, iron, and wood, andirons, chains, pot-hooks, adzes, axes, augurs, knives, and all sorts of tools so that it will not be necessary to seek them elsewhere or to borrow them. And the stewards shall be responsible that the iron instruments sent to the army are in good condition and when they are returned that they are put back into the store-room.

43. For our women's work-shops the stewards shall provide the materials at the right time as it has been established, that is flax, wool, woad, vermilion dye, madder, wool-combs, teasels, soap, grease, vessels and the other lesser things which are necessary there.

44. Of the minor foods two-thirds shall be sent for our service each year, vegetables as well as fish, cheese, butter, honey, mustard, vinegar, millet, panic, dried and fresh herbs, radishes, and turnips; similarly wax, soap, and other lesser things. Whatever is left shall be made known to us in an inventory as we have said above. The stewards shall by no means neglect to do this as they have up to now because we wish to check by the two-thirds sent to us what that third is which remains.

45. Each steward shall have good workmen in his district—iron-workers, goldsmiths, silversmiths, leather-workers, turners, carpenters, shield-makers, fishermen, fowlers or falconers, soap-makers, brewers who know how to make beer, cider, perry or any other beverage fit to drink, bakers who can make bread for our needs, net-makers who are skilled in making nets for hunting as well as fishing or for taking birds, and other workmen whose listing would be a lengthy matter.

46. They shall take good care of our walled game preserves which the people call parks and always repair them in time and on no account delay so that it becomes necessary to rebuild them. They shall do the same for all the buildings.

47. Our hunters and falconers and other servitors who attend us zealously in the palace shall receive assistance on our estates in carrying out what we or the queen have ordered by our letters when we send them on any of our affairs, or when the seneschal or butler instructs them to do anything on our authority.

48. The wine-presses on our estates shall be well taken care of. The stewards shall see to it that no one presumes to press our grapes with his feet but that all is done cleanly and honestly.

49. The women's quarters, that is, their houses, heated rooms, and sitting-rooms, shall be well ordered and have good fences around them and strong gates that our work may be done well.

50. Each steward shall see to it that there are as many horses in one stable as ought to be there and as many attendants as should be with them. And those stablemen who are free and hold benefices in that district shall live off their benefices. Similarly if they are men of the domain who hold *mansi* they shall live off them. Those who do not have such shall receive maintenance from the demesne.

51. Each steward shall see to it that in no manner wicked men conceal our seed under the ground or do otherwise with the result that our harvests are smaller. And likewise, concerning other misdeeds, they shall watch them so that they can do no harm.

52. We wish that our stewards render justice to our *coloni* and serfs and to the *coloni* living on our estates, to the different men fully and entirely such as they are due.

53. Each steward shall see to it that our men in their districts in no way become robbers or evil-doers.

54. Each steward shall see to it

that our people work well at their tasks and do not go wandering off to markets.

55. We wish that whatever our stewards have sent, supplied, or set aside for our use they shall record in an inventory; whatever they have dispensed in another; and what is left they shall also make known to us in an inventory.

56. Each steward shall hold frequent audiences in his district, administer justice, and see to it that our peoples live uprightly.

57. If any of our serfs wishes to say anything to us about our affairs over and above his steward, the steward shall not obstruct the means of his coming to us. If the steward knows that his assistants wish to come to the palace to speak against him then he shall make known to the palace the arguments against them so that their denunciations in our ears may not engender disgust. Accordingly we wish to know whether they come from necessity or without sufficient cause.

58. When our pups are committed to the stewards to be raised, the steward shall feed them at his own expense or entrust them to his assistants, that is to the mayors and deans or to the cellarers, who shall feed them well at their own expense unless it happens that by our order or that of the queen they are to be fed on our estate at our expense. In that case the steward shall send a man for this work who will feed them well. And he shall set aside what is to be fed them so that it will not be necessary for him to go to the kennels every day.

59. Each steward when he should give service shall send every day three *librae* of wax and eight *sextaria* of soap; besides this he shall do his best to send six *librae* of wax wherever we shall be with our attendants on the Feast of Saint Andrew; he shall do likewise at Mid-Lent.

60. On no account shall mayors be selected from the powerful men but from those of middling estate who are trustworthy.

61. Each steward when he should give service shall have his malt brought to the palace and at the same time have the master brewers come who are to make good beer there.

62. That we may know what and how much of everything we have, each steward every year at Christmas shall report those of our revenues which they hold, everything differentiated clearly and orderly. That is, an accounting of the land cultivated with the oxen which our ploughmen drive and that which is cultivated by the holders of *mansi* who owe us labor-service; of the payments of pigs, the taxes, the income from judgments and fines and from the beasts taken in our forests without our permission and from the other compositions; an accounting of the mills, forests, fields, bridges, and ships; of the free men and the hundred-men who owe service for parts of our domain; of the markets, vineyards and of those who pay us wine; of the hay, firewood, torches, planks and other lumber; of the income from the waste-land; of the vegetables, millet, panic, wool, flax, and hemp; of the fruit of the trees, of the big and little nuts, of the graftings of various trees, of the gardens, turnips, fishponds, hides, skins and horns; of the honey, wax, fat, tallow, and soap; of the mulberry wine, cooked wine, mead, and vinegar; of the

beer, new and old wine, new and old grain, chickens and eggs, and geese; of the fishermen, smiths, shield-makers and leather-workers; of the troughs, boxes, and cases; of the turners and saddlers; of the forges and mines, that is iron, lead, and other mines; of those paying taxes; and of the colts and fillies.

63. Of all the above mentioned things nothing that we require shall seem hard to our stewards for we wish the stewards to require them from their assistants in the same fashion without any hardship. And all things which any man shall have in his house or on his estate our stewards ought also to have on our estates.

64. Our carts which accompany the army, that is, the war-carts, shall be well-constructed, and their coverings be good, with hides on top and so sewn together that if the necessity of swimming waters should arise they can cross rivers without any water getting to the provisions inside and in this fashion our things may, as we said, get across without damage. And we wish that flour for our use be put in each cart, that is 12 *modii*, and that they put in those in which wine is sent 12 *modii* of our measure. In each cart let them have a shield, a lance, a quiver, and a bow.

65. The fish in our fish-ponds shall be sold and others put in their place so that they may always have fish in them. However, when we are not coming to our estates they shall be sold and our stewards shall dispose of them to our advantage.

66. The stewards shall report to us the number of male and female goats and their horns and skins; and they shall bring to us annually newly salted cuts of fat goats.

67. The stewards shall inform us about any vacant *mansi* or any newly acquired serfs if they have any in their district for whom they have no place.

68. We wish that each steward always have ready good barrels bound with iron which they can send to the army or to the palace and that the stewards do not make containers of leather.

69. The stewards at all times shall report to us how many wolves each one has taken and shall send the skins to us. And in the month of May they shall hunt down and destroy the whelps with poison, traps, pits, and dogs.

70. We wish that the stewards have all sorts of plants in the garden, namely, lilies, roses, fenugreek, costmary, sage, rue, southernwood, cucumbers, pumpkins, squash, kidney-beans, cumin, rosemary, caraway, chick-peas, squill, gladiolus, dragonarum, anise, colosynth, heliotrope, spicknel, seseli, lettuce, fennel-flower, rocket, garden cress, burdock, pennyroyal, horse-parsley, parsley, celery, lovage, juniper, dill, sweet-fennel, endive, dittany, mustard, savory, water-mint, garden mint, applemint, tansy, catnip, centaury, garden-poppy, beets, hazel-wort, marshmallows, tree-hibiscus, mallows, carrots, parsnip, garden-orach, amaranth, kohlrabi, cabbages, onions, chives, leeks, radishes, shallots, cibols, garlic, madder, teasel, garden beans, Moorish peas, coriander, chervil, capers, clary. And the gardener shall have house-leek growing on his house.

As for trees, we wish that they have various kinds of apple, pear, and plum trees, sorb, medlar, chestnut, peach trees of different kinds, quince, filbert, almond, mulberry, laurel, pine, fig, walnut, and cherry trees of various kinds.

Names of apple trees: *gozmaringa, geroldinga, crevedella, spirauca*, sweet ones and sour ones, and all the kind that keep, as well as those which are eaten when picked and those that are forced.

They shall have three or four kinds of pears which will keep, sweet ones, cooking, and late pears.

Charter of the Liberties of Lorris

1. Let whoever shall have a house in the parish of Lorris pay a quit-rent of six deniers only for his house, and each acre of land which he shall have in this parish; and if he make such an acquisition, let that be the quit-rent of his house.

2. Let no inhabitant of the parish of Lorris pay a duty of entry nor any tax for his food, and let him not pay any duty of measurement for the corn which his labor, or that of the animals which he may have shall procure him, and let him pay no duty for the wine which he shall get from his vines.

3. Let none of them go on a [military] expedition on foot or horseback, whence he cannot return home the same day if he desire to do so.

4. Let none of them pay toll to Étampes, to Orleans, or to Milly, which is in Gâtinais, or to Melun.

5. Let no one who has property in the parish of Lorris lose any of it for any misdeed whatsoever, unless the said misdeed be committed against us or any of our guests.

6. Let no one going to the fairs or markets of Lorris, or in returning, be stopped or inconvenienced unless he shall have committed some misdeed that same day; and let no one on a fair or market day at Lorris, seize the bail given by his security; unless the bail be given the same day.

7. Let forfeitures of sixty sous be reduced to five, that of five sous to twelve deniers, and the provost's fee in cases of plaint, to four deniers.

8. Let no man of Lorris be forced to go out of it to plead before the lord king.

9. Let no one, neither us nor any other, take any tax, offering, or exaction from the men of Lorris.

10. Let no one sell wine at Lorris with public notice, except the king, who shall sell his wine in his cellar with that notice.

11. We will have at Lorris, for our service and that of the queen, a credit of a full fortnight, in the articles of provisions; and if any inhabitant have received a gage from the lord king, he shall not be bound to keep it more than eight days, unless he please.

12. If any have had a quarrel with another, but without breaking a closed house, and if it be accommodated without plaint brought before the provost, no fine shall be due, on this account, to us or to our

Carta Franchesie Lorriaci, trans. W. Hazlitt.

provost; and if there has been a plaint they can still come to an agreement when they shall have paid the fine. And if any one bear plaint against another, and there has been no fine awarded against either one to the other, they shall not, on that account, owe anything to us or our provost.

13. If any one owe an oath to another, let the latter have permission to remit it.

14. If any men of Lorris have rashly given their pledge of a duel, and if with the consent of the provost they accommodate it before the pledges have been given, let each pay two sous and a half; and if the pledges have been given, let each pay seven sous and a half; and if the duel has been between men having the right of fighting in the lists, then let the hostages of the conquered pay one hundred and twelve sous.

15. Let no man of Lorris do forced work for us, unless it be twice a year to take our wine to Orleans, and nowhere else; and those only shall do this who shall have horses and carts, and they shall be informed of it beforehand; and they shall receive no lodging from us. The laborers also shall bring wood for our kitchen.

16. No one shall be detained in prison if he can furnish bail for his appearance in court.

17. Whoever desires to sell his property may do so; and having received the price, he may leave the town, free and unmolested, if he please so to do, unless he has committed any misdeed in the town.

18. Whoever shall have remained a year and a day in the parish of Lorris without any claim having pursued him thither, and without the right having been interdicted him, whether by us or our provost, he shall remain there free and tranquil.

19. No one shall plead against another unless it be to recover, and ensure the observance of, what is his due.

20. When the men of Lorris shall go to Orleans with merchandise, they shall pay, upon leaving the town, one denier for their cart, when they go not for sake of the fair; and when they go for the sake of the fair and the market, they shall pay, upon leaving Orleans, four deniers for each cart; and on entering, two deniers.

21. At marriages in Lorris, the public cryer shall have no fee, nor he who keeps watch.

22. No cultivator of the parish of Lorris, cultivating his land with the plow, shall give, in the time of harvest, more than one hermine [six bushels] of rye to all the serjeants of Lorris.

23. If any knight or serjeant find, in our forests, horses or other animals belonging to the men of Lorris, he must not take them to any other than to the provost of Lorris; and if any animal of the parish of Lorris, put to flight by bulls, or assailed by flies, have entered our forest, or leaped our banks, the owner of the animal shall owe no fine to the provost, if he can swear that the animal has entered in spite of his keeper. But if the animal entered with the knowledge of his keeper, the owner shall pay twelve deniers, and as much for each animal, if there be more than one.

24. There shall be at Lorris no duty paid for using the oven.

25. There shall be at Lorris no watch rate.

26. All men of Lorris who shall take salt or wine to Orleans, shall pay only one denier for each cart.

27. No men of Lorris shall owe any fine to the provost of Étampes, nor to the provost of Pithiviers nor to any in Gâtinais.

28. None among them shall pay the entry dues in Ferrières, nor in Château-Landon, nor in Puiseaux, nor in Nibelle.

29. Let the men of Lorris take the dead wood in the forest for their own use.

30. Whosoever, in the market of Lorris, shall have bought or sold anything, and shall have forgotten to pay the duty, may pay it within eight days without being troubled, if he can swear that he did not withhold the right wittingly.

31. No man of Lorris having a house or a vineyard, or a meadow, or a field, or any buildings in the domain of St. Benedict, shall be under the jurisdiction of the abbot of St. Benedict or his serjeant, unless it be with regard to the quit-rent in kind, to which he is bound; and, in that case, he shall not go out of Lorris to be judged.

32. If any of the men of Lorris be accused of anything, and the accuser cannot prove it by witness, he shall clear himself by a single oath from the assertion of his accuser.

33. No man of this parish shall pay any duty because of what he shall buy or sell for his use on the territory of the precincts, nor for what he shall buy on Wednesday at the market.

34. These customs are granted to the men of Lorris, and they are common to the men who inhabit Courpalais, Chanteloup, and the bailiwick of Harpard.

35. We order that whenever the provost shall be changed in the town, he shall swear faithfully to observe these customs; and the same shall be done by new serjeants when they shall be instituted.

Given at Orleans in the year of our Lord 1155.

Magna Carta

It is conventional to cite Magna Carta as one of the great charters of liberty in the Anglo-Saxon legal heritage. And yet, if we examine the document with due regard for the time and place of its signing, we may find that the fictions which have grown up around it have obscured its real significance. For example, when English parliamentarians during the civil war of the seventeenth century sought precedents for their invasion of royal prerogatives, they cited the famous Chapter 39 of the Great Charter. According to this section the Crown was to guarantee that "no freeman shall be taken or imprisoned . . . except by the lawful judgment of his peers and by the law of the land." Superficially, this passage may be taken as a guarantee of trial by jury and freedom from arbitrary arrest, and a statement of the subservience of all (including the king) to the law of the land. Thus, Magna Carta becomes a milestone on the high road to democracy.

This fiction is certainly attractive, but it remains only a fiction. In 1215 Magna Carta was imposed upon King John by a group of Anglo-Norman barons who insisted that John live within the framework of the feudal contract. The Charter was a solemn agreement—of debatable legal validity, however, since it was extracted from the king by force—that both king and baron would respect their mutual duties and obligations, as defined in the feudal ceremonies of homage, fealty, and investiture.

Here, of course, lies the real significance of Magna Carta. The document is a clear expression of feudal institutions and ideas, from which we can derive an accurate picture of the mostly highly developed feudal society of Western Europe. The feudalism that the Normans under William the Conqueror brought to England in 1066 reached its clearest expression when it was laid over the indigenous Anglo-Saxon society. The selection that follows contains the most important provisions of Magna Carta.

Magna Carta

John, by the grace of God, King of England, Lord of Ireland, Duke of Normandy and Aquitaine, and Count of Anjou: To the Archbishops, Bishops, Abbots, Earls, Barons, Justiciaries, Foresters, Sheriffs, Reeves, Ministers, and all Bailiffs and others, his faithful subjects, Greeting. Know ye that in the presence of God, and for the health of Our soul, and the souls of Our ancestors and heirs, to the honor of God, and the exaltation of Holy Church, and amendment of Our kingdom, by the advice of Our reverend Fathers, Stephen, Archbishop of Canterbury, Primate of all England, and Cardinal of the Holy Roman Church; Henry, Archbishop of Dublin; William of London, Peter of Winchester, Jocelin of Bath and Glastonbury, Hugh of Lincoln, Walter of Worcester, William of Coventry, and Benedict of Rochester, Bishops; Master Pandulph, the Pope's subdeacon and familiar; Brother Aymeric, Master of the Knights of the Temple in England; and the noble persons, William Marshal, Earl of Pembroke; William, Earl of Salisbury; William, Earl of Warren; William, Earl of Arundel; Alan de Galloway, Constable of Scotland; Warin Fitz-Gerald, Peter Fitz-Herbert, Hubert de Burgh, Seneschal of Poitou, Hugh de Neville, Matthew Fitz-Herbert, Thomas Basset, Alan Basset, Philip Daubeny, Robert de Roppelay, John Marshal, John Fitz-Hugh, and others, Our liegemen:

1. We have, in the first place, granted to God, and by this Our present Charter confirmed for Us and Our heirs forever—That the English Church shall be free and enjoy her rights in their integrity and her liberties untouched. And that We will this so to be observed appears from the fact that We of Our own free will, before the outbreak of the dissensions between Us and Our barons, granted, confirmed, and procured to be confirmed by Pope Innocent III the freedom of elections, which is considered most important and necessary to the English Church, which Charter We will both keep Ourself and will it to be kept with good faith by Our heirs forever. We have also granted to all the free men of Our kingdom, for Us and Our heirs forever, all the liberties underwritten, to have and to hold to them and their heirs of Us and Our heirs.

2. If any of Our earls, barons, or others who hold of Us in chief by knight's service shall die, and at the time of his death his heir shall be of full age and owe a relief [a form of tax], he shall have his inheritance by ancient relief; to wit, the heir or heirs of an earl of an entire earl's barony, £100; the heir or heirs of a baron of an entire barony, £100;

Magna Carta, trans. A. E. Dick Howard (Charlottesville: The University Press of Virginia, 1964), pp. 33–44, 46–52. Courtesy of the Rector and Visitors of the University of Virginia.

the heir or heirs of a knight of an entire knight's fee, 100s. at the most; and he that owes less shall give less, according to the ancient custom of fees.

3. If, however, any such heir shall be under age and in ward, he shall, when he comes of age, have his inheritance without relief or fine.

4. The guardian of the land of any heir thus under age shall take therefrom only reasonable issues, customs, and services, without destruction or waste of men or property; and if We shall have committed the wardship of any such land to the sheriff or any other person answerable to Us for the issues thereof, and he commit destruction or waste, We will take an amends from him, and the land shall be committed to two lawful and discreet men of that fee, who shall be answerable for the issues to Us or to whomsoever We shall have assigned them. And if We shall give or sell the wardship of any such land to anyone, and he commit destruction or waste upon it, he shall lose the wardship, which shall be committed to two lawful and discreet men of that fee, who shall, in like manner, be answerable unto Us as has been aforesaid.

5. The guardian, so long as he shall have the custody of the land, shall keep up and maintain the houses, parks, fishponds, pools, mills, and other things pertaining thereto, out of the issues of the same, and shall restore the whole to the heir when he comes of age, stocked with ploughs and tillage, according as the season may require and the issues of the land can reasonably bear.

6. Heirs shall be married without loss of station, and the marriage shall be made known to the heir's nearest of kin before it be contracted.

7. A widow, after the death of her husband, shall immediately and without difficulty have her marriage portion and inheritance. She shall not give anything for her marriage portion, dower, or inheritance which she and her husband held on the day of his death, and she may remain in her husband's house for forty days after his death, within which time her dower shall be assigned to her.

8. No widow shall be compelled to marry so long as she has a mind to live without a husband, provided, however, that she give security that she will not marry without Our assent, if she holds of Us, or that of the lord of whom she holds, if she holds of another.

9. Neither We nor Our bailiffs shall seize any land or rent for any debt so long as the debtor's chattels are sufficient to discharge the same; nor shall the debtor's sureties be distrained so long as the debtor is able to pay the debt. If the debtor fails to pay, not having the means to pay, then the sureties shall answer the debt, and, if they desire, they shall hold the debtor's lands and rents until they have received satisfaction of the debt which they have paid for him, unless the debtor can show that he has discharged his obligation to them.

10. If anyone who has borrowed from the Jews any sum of money, great or small, dies before the debt has been paid, the heir shall pay no interest on the debt so long as he remains under age, of whomsoever he may hold. If the debt shall fall

into Our hands, We will take only the principal sum named in the bond.

*   *   *

12. No scutage [*a payment in place of a personal service*—Ed.] or aid shall be imposed in Our kingdom unless by common counsel thereof, except to ransom Our person, make Our eldest son a knight, and once to marry Our eldest daughter, and for these only a reasonable aid shall be levied. So shall it be with regard to aids from the City of London.

13. The City of London shall have all her ancient liberties and free customs, both by land and water. Moreover, We will and grant that all other cities, boroughs, towns, and ports shall have all their liberties and free customs.

14. For obtaining the common counsel of the kingdom concerning the assessment of aids (other than in the three cases aforesaid) or of scutage, We will cause to be summoned, severally by Our letters, the archbishops, bishops, abbots, earls, and great barons; We will also cause to be summoned, generally, by Our sheriffs and bailiffs, all those who hold lands directly of Us, to meet on a fixed day, but with at least forty days' notice, and at a fixed place. In all letters of such summons We will explain the cause therof. The summons being thus made, the business shall proceed on the day appointed, according to the advice of those who shall be present, even though not all the persons summoned have come.

15. We will not in the future grant permission to any man to levy an aid upon his free men, except to ransom his person, make his eldest

son a knight, and once to marry his eldest daughter, and on each of these occasions only a reasonable aid shall be levied.

16. No man shall be compelled to perform more service for a knight's fee or other free tenement than is due therefrom.

17. Common Pleas shall not follow Our Court, but shall be held in some certain place.

*   *   *

20. A free man shall be amerced [fined] for a small fault only according to the measure thereof, and for a great crime according to its magnitude, saving his position; and in like manner a merchant saving his trade, and a villein [serf] saving his tillage, if they should fall under Our mercy. None of these amercements shall be imposed except by the oath of honest men of the neighborhood.

21. Earls and barons shall be amerced only by their peers, and only in proportion to the measure of the offense.

22. No amercement shall be imposed upon a clerk's [clergyman's] lay property, except after the manner of the other persons aforesaid, and without regard to the value of his ecclesiastical benefice.

23. No village or person shall be compelled to build bridges over rivers except those bound by ancient custom and law to do so.

*   *   *

28. No constable or other of Our bailiffs shall take corn or other chattels of any man without immediate payment, unless the seller voluntarily consents to postponement of payment.

29. No constable shall compel any knight to give money in lieu of castle-guard when the knight is willing to perform it in person or (if reasonable cause prevents him from performing it himself) by some other fit man. Further, if We lead or send him into military service, he shall be quit of castle-guard for the time he shall remain in service by Our command.

30. No sheriff or other of Our bailiffs, or any other man, shall take the horses or carts of any free man for carriage without the owner's consent.

31. Neither We nor Our bailiffs will take another man's wood for Our castles or for any other purpose without the owner's consent.

· · ·

35. There shall be one measure of wine throughout Our kingdom, and one of ale, and one measure of corn, to wit, the London quarter, and one breadth of dyed cloth, russets, and haberjets, to wit, two ells within the selvages. As with measures so shall it also be with weights.

· · ·

38. In the future no bailiff shall upon his own unsupported accusation put any man to trial without producing credible witnesses to the truth of the accusation.

39. No free man shall be taken, imprisoned, disseised [dispossessed], outlawed, banished, or in any way destroyed, nor will We proceed against or prosecute him, except by the lawful judgment of his peers and by the law of the land.

40. To no one will We sell, to none will We deny or delay, right or justice.

41. All merchants shall have safe conduct to go and come out of and into England, and to stay in and travel through England by land and water for purposes of buying and selling, free of illegal tolls, in accordance with ancient and just customs, except, in time of war, such merchants as are of a country at war with Us. If any such be found in Our dominion at the outbreak of war, they shall be attached, without injury to their persons or goods, until it be known to Us or Our Chief Justiciary how Our merchants are being treated in the country at war with Us, and if Our merchants be safe there, then theirs shall be safe with Us.

42. In the future it shall be lawful (except for a short period in time of war, for the common benefit of the realm) for anyone to leave and return to Our kingdom safely and securely by land and water, saving his fealty to Us. Excepted are those who have been imprisoned or outlawed according to the law of the land, people of the country at war with Us, and merchants, who shall be dealt with as aforesaid.

· · ·

52. If anyone has been disseised or deprived by Us, without the legal judgment of his peers, of lands, castles, liberties, or rights, We will immediately restore the same, and if any dispute shall arise thereupon, the matter shall be decided by judgment of the twenty-five barons mentioned below in the clause for securing the peace. With regard to all those things, however, of which any man was disseised or deprived, with-

out the legal judgment of his peers, by King Henry Our Father or Our Brother King Richard, and which remain in Our hands or are held by others under Our warranty, We shall have respite during the term commonly allowed to the Crusaders, except as to those matters on which a plea had arisen, or an inquisition had been taken by Our command, prior to Our taking the Cross. Immediately after Our return from Our pilgrimage, or if by chance We should remain behind from it, We will at once do full justice.

54. No one shall be arrested or imprisoned upon a woman's appeal for the death of any person other than her husband.

55. All fines unjustly and unlawfully given to Us, and all amercements levied unjustly and against the law of the land, shall be entirely remitted or the matter settled by judgment of the twenty-five barons of whom mention is made below in the clause for securing the peace, or the majority of them, together with the aforesaid Stephen, Archbishop of Canterbury, if he himself can be present, and any others whom he may wish to bring with him for the purpose; if he cannot be present, the business shall nevertheless proceed without him. If any one or more of the said twenty-five barons be interested in a suit of this kind, he or they shall be set aside, as to this particular judgment, and another or others, elected and sworn by the rest of the said barons for this occasion only, be substituted in his or their stead.

· · ·

60. All the customs and liberties aforesaid, which We have granted to be enjoyed, as far as in Us lies, by Our people throughout Our kingdom, let all Our subjects, whether clerks or laymen, observe, as far as in them lies, toward their dependents.

61. Whereas We, for the honor of God and the amendment of Our realm, and in order the better to allay the discord arisen between Us and Our barons, have granted all these things aforesaid, We, willing that they be forever enjoyed wholly and in lasting strength, do give and grant to Our subjects the following security, to wit, that the barons shall elect any twenty-five barons of the kingdom at will, who shall, with their utmost power, keep, hold, and cause to be kept the peace and liberties which We have granted unto them and by this Our present Charter have confirmed, so that if We, Our Justiciary, bailiffs, or any of Our ministers offend in any respect against any man, or shall transgress any of these articles of peace or security, and the offense be brought before four of the said twenty-five barons, these four barons shall come before Us, or Our Chief Justiciary if We are out of the kingdom, declaring the offense, and shall demand speedy amends for the same. If We or, in case of Our being out of the kingdom, Our Chief Justiciary fail to afford redress within the space of forty days from the time the case was brought before Us or, in the event of Our having been out of the kingdom, Our Chief Justiciary, the aforesaid four barons shall refer the matter to the rest of the twenty-five barons, who, together with the commonalty of the whole country, shall distrain and distress Us to the utmost of their power, to wit, by capture of

Our castles, lands, and possessions and by all other possible means, until compensation be made according to their decision, saving Our person and that of Our Queen and children; as soon as redress has been had, they shall return to their former allegiance. Anyone in the kingdom may take oath that, for the accomplishment of all the aforesaid matters, he will obey the orders of the said twenty-five barons and distress Us to the utmost of his power; and We give public and free leave to everyone wishing to take such oath to do so, and to none will we deny the same. Moreover, all such of Our subjects who shall not of their own free will and accord agree to swear to the said twenty-five barons, to distrain and distress Us together with them, We will compel to do so by Our command in the manner aforesaid. If any one of the twenty-five barons shall die or leave the country or be in any way hindered from executing the said office, the rest of the said twenty-five barons shall choose another in his stead, at their discretion, who shall be sworn in like manner as the others. In all cases which are referred to the said twenty-five barons to execute, and in which a difference shall arise among them, supposing them all to be present, or in which not all who have been summoned are willing or able to appear, the verdict of the majority shall be considered as firm and binding as if the whole number should have been of one mind. The aforesaid twenty-five shall swear to keep faithfully all the aforesaid articles and, to the best of their power, to cause them to be kept by others. We will not procure, either by Ourself or any other, anything from any man whereby any of these concessions or liberties may be revoked or abated. If any such procurement be made, let it be null and void; it shall never be made use of either by Us or by any other.

62. We have also wholly remitted and pardoned all ill-will, wrath, and malice which has arisen between Us and Our subjects, both clergy and laymen, during the disputes, to and with all men. Moreover, We have fully remitted and, as far as in Us lies, wholly pardoned to and with all, clergy and laymen, all trespasses made in consequence of the said disputes from Easter in the sixteenth year of Our reign till the restoration of peace. Over and above this, We have caused to be made in their behalf letters patent by testimony of Stephen, Archbishop of Canterbury, Henry, Archbishop of Dublin, the Bishops above-mentioned, and Master Pandulph, for the security and concessions aforesaid.

63. Wherefore We will, and firmly charge, that the English Church shall be free, and that all men in Our kingdom shall have and hold all the aforesaid liberties, rights, and concessions, well and peaceably, freely, quietly, fully, and wholly, to them and their heirs, of Us and Our heirs, in all things and places forever, as is aforesaid. It is moreover sworn, as well on Our part as on the part of the barons, that all these matters aforesaid shall be kept in good faith and without deceit. Witness the above-named and many others. Given by Our hand in the meadow which is called Runnymede, between Windsor and Staines, on the fifteenth day of June in the seventeenth year of Our reign.

Church and State

Throughout the Middle Ages, the Church and the temporal rulers of Europe waged a running battle for political supremacy. For a time, the Church seemed assured of victory. It reached the height of its power during the pontificate of Innocent III (1198–1216), who succeeded in forcing King John to surrender England to him, to be held by John in the future as a fief from the papacy. The final victory, however, went to the secular powers, who gradually effected a separation between political authority and spiritual authority, reserving the former for themselves and permitting the Church to exercise the latter.

The documents that follow reflect the Church's position at two different phases during this long struggle. The first document is concerned with a dispute between the Holy Roman Emperor, Henry IV, and Pope Gregory VII, a dispute that resulted in Henry's famous winter pilgrimage to Canossa to seek absolution from the pope. The document is actually a letter, written in 1081, from Gregory to the Bishop of Metz, who had sought papal aid in combating the emperor. It is important because it contains Gregory's view of the position of the Church relative to the state, as well as the main arguments on which that position rested.

The second document, the papal bull *Unam Sanctam*, was written over two hundred years later (1302), during a controversy between Pope Boniface VIII and King Philip the Fair of France. Philip replied to the bull, which flatly asserts the political supremacy of the Church, by having the pope seized. Although Boniface was soon released, he died almost immediately afterward. Philip again took the initiative and managed to convert the papacy into an adjunct of the French throne. This episode marked the turning point in the political fortunes of the church, for the popes were never able to regain the ascendancy over the secular monarchs that the papacy had enjoyed under Pope Innocent III.

The Second Letter of Gregory VII to Hermann, Bishop of Metz, March 15, 1081

GREGORY, BISHOP, servant of the servants of God, to Our well-beloved brother in Christ, Hermann, Bishop of Metz, health and the Apostolic Benediction.

We know your desire to employ yourself, and to confront dangers, in the defence of truth, and We see in your good-will, the action of Divine Providence. The ineffable grace of God and His marvellous bounty, never permit His chosen ones to lapse into complete error, nor do they allow them to be altogether conquered and enslaved by sin. After the salutary trials of persecution, and the anxieties which they have experienced, the elect come forth stronger than before. Fear makes cowards shamelessly rival one another in flight; in like manner, those inspired by manly courage, strive to be in the front rank and to obtain the palm of valour and bravery. If We address this language to your charity, it is because you too wish to be in the front rank in the Christian army; that is, amongst those who, you know well, are closest to, and most worthy of, the God who gives the Victory.

You ask Us to come to your aid by Our writings and to refute the insanity of those, who maintain with their guilty tongues, that the Holy Apostolic See had not the right to excommunicate King Henry, that despiser of the Christian law, that destroyer of Churches, and of the Empire, that abettor and accomplice of heretics, and that it had not power to absolve from the oath of fidelity, which had been sworn to him. It does not seem very necessary for Us to do this, for this power is established by many authentic texts of Holy Scripture. We cannot indeed believe, that those who, for their own damnation, and with unblushing impudence oppose and fight against truth can, in their ignorance or madness, have had the audacity to use these texts as their justification. There would not, however, be anything astonishing in that, for it is the custom of the wicked to seek protection for their vices, and to defend their accomplices; it matters little to them if they ruin themselves by their lies.

To quote one proof from among many. Who does not know that saying of Our Lord and Savior Jesus Christ, in the Gospel

Thou art Peter, and upon this rock I will build My church; and the gates of hell shall not prevail against it. I will give to you the keys of the Kingdom of Heaven, and whatsoever you shall bind on earth, shall be bound also in heaven, and whatsoever you shall loose upon earth, shall be loosed also in heaven. [Matthew XVI:18, 19]

Are kings an exception? Do they not

Trans. A. H. Mathew.

form part of the flock confided to St. Peter by the Son of God? Then, We ask, who will dare to claim that he has nothing to do with the power of St. Peter, that the universal power of binding and loosing given to St. Peter, has no reference to him? No one would act in this manner, but that unhappy man, who, unwilling to bear the yoke of the Lord, would submit to that of the devil and renounce his right to belong to the fold of Christ. By this proud denial of the power divinely granted to St. Peter, he would obtain liberty, a sad liberty indeed, for the more he denied the power, the more heavily would his eternal damnation weigh upon him, on the day of judgment.

• • •

The blessed Pope Gregory, writing to a certain senator abbot, asserts that kings, who allow themselves to violate the decrees of the Apostolic See, ought to be deprived of their dignities. *If*, he writes,

any king, priest, judge, or any secular, knowing the present decree, dares to offend against it, let him lose his power and dignity, and let him declare himself guilty before God of the iniquity he has committed. If he does not restore what he has unjustly stolen, and do penance in proportion to his fault, let him be deprived of the most holy Body and Blood of our Lord and Redeemer Jesus Christ; and may the vengeance of the eternal judgment fall upon him.

If blessed Gregory, who was the meekest of the doctors, decreed that kings, who violated the statutes, which he gave to a hospital, should not only be deposed, but excommunicated and damned for ever, who would dare to reproach us for having deposed and excommunicated Henry, the despiser of the apostolic judgments, the fierce enemy of Mother Church, the infamous despoiler and merciless scourge of the whole kingdom, and of the churches? Who, but one, who is still more unworthy than he, would dare to cast reproach upon us? We read in a letter of the blessed Peter, concerning the ordination of Clement:

If any one is a friend to those to whom he (Clement) does not speak, through that very fact, he belongs to those who wish to destroy the Church of God; in the body he seems to be with us; but his spirit and his heart are against us.

Such an enemy is to be dreaded more than one whose enmity is open, and apparent to all; for the former works evil under cover of false friendship and causes disunion and destruction in the Church. Remark this well, dearly beloved, the blessed Peter judges him, whose conduct is condemned by the Pope, in so severe a manner, that he even goes so far as to condemn those, who are bound to him by friendship, and even those who hold converse with him.

It is, therefore, impossible for a dignity which owes its origin to men of the world, and even to those ignorant of God, not to be in subjection to that dignity, which the Providence of the all-powerful God instituted, to bring honour to Him, and which, in His mercy, He has granted to the whole world. If the Son of this all-powerful God is undoubtedly God and Man, He is also the High Priest, the chief of all priests, and He is now seated at the right hand of the Father, where He intercedes for us without ceasing.

The Son of God despised the earthly kingdoms, of which the sons of this world are so proud; it was of His own accord that He chose and embraced the priesthood of the Cross. Every one knows that the first kings and the first dukes, were men ignorant of God, who, influenced by blind cupidity, and intolerable presumption, aided, moreover, by the Demon-prince of this world, strove by the help of robbery, lies and homicide, and almost every vice, to have dominion over their equals, that is, over other men. When these kings and dukes sought afterwards to draw the priests of the Lord into their ways, to whom can one more fitly compare them than to him who is the head of all the sons of pride, to him who tried to tempt the Sovereign of Pontiffs Himself, the Chief of Priests, the Son of the Most High, by showing Him all the kingdoms of the world and saying to Him, *I will give you all this if you fall down at my feet and adore me.* Who can doubt that the priests of Christ are the fathers and masters of kings; that they are the princes of all the faithful? Is it not an act of utter madness, when the son tries to rule the father, the disciple the master; when he wishes to reduce him to submission by imposing on him iniquitous conditions, though he knows well that this father and master has the power of binding and loosing on earth, as well as in heaven?

· · ·

Moreover, on his death-bed, every Christian king who wishes to escape hell, to pass from darkness to light, to appear at the judgment-seat of God, after having received absolution for his faults, humbly implores the ministry of the priest. But who is there, I do not say, priest, but even layman, who has ever begged the help of an earthly king, when at the point of death, and filled with anxiety for the salvation of his soul? What king or emperor can, by right of his office, give holy baptism to a Christian, deliver him from the power of the devil, give him entrance among the children of God, or anoint him with the holy chrism? Who, among them, can consecrate the Body and Blood of the Lord, in other words, perform that greatest act of the Christian religion? Has the power of binding and absolving in heaven and on earth been given to any one of them? In all these things, the superiority of the sacerdotal dignity is evident. If not one among them has the power to ordain a cleric of Holy Church, still less have they the right of deposing him for any fault. In ecclesiastical orders, the authority which deposes, ought to be superior to that which ordains. Bishops can consecrate other bishops, but they cannot dispose them, without the authority of the Apostolic See. Very little discernment is therefore necessary to understand the superiority of the priesthood over the royal state. If, in all that concerns their sins, kings are amenable to priests, much more must they be so, to the Roman Pontiff.

On closer examination, the title of king is much better suited to good Christians than to bad princes. The former seek the glory of God, and know how to govern themselves; the latter, preoccupied with their own interests, and not with the interests of God, are enemies to themselves and tyrants to others. The former are part of the Body of Jesus Christ; the latter of the body of the devil. The first-mentioned govern themselves, that they may reign eternally with the Supreme Emperor: the power of the second is exercised in such a way, that they will be lost for ever, with the prince of darkness, the king of all the sons of pride.

It is not surprising if bad bishops make common cause with an impious king; they receive their honours from that king in an unlawful way, hence they both love and dread him at the same time. By their consent to perform simoniacal ordinations, they, as it were, sell God at a low price. The elect are indissolubly united to their head; the reprobate, in like manner clings tenaciously round him who is the author of evil, especially when the matter at stake is to resist the good. To argue with them is of little avail, rather weep over their sad fate, that the all-powerful God may deliver them from the snares of Satan, and that He may in the end open their eyes to the truth.

• • •

What emperor or king ever restored the dead to life, cured lepers or gave sight to the blind? We have the Emperor Constantine, of pious memory, the Emperors Theodosius, Honorius, Charles and Louis, who loved justice, spread the Christian religion, and defended the Church: the Church praises and venerates them, yet she does not say that they had, to a striking extent, the gift of miracles. What altars or basilicas are there dedicated to a king or an emperor; has the church ever allowed Mass to be celebrated in honour of any one of them? Kings and princes, so proud of being above other men, in this life, ought to fear all the more, lest they should be condemned to eternal fire in the life hereafter. Thus it is written: *The mighty shall be mightily tormented.* They will have to render an account of each subject under their sway. If it is no small labour for any ordinary mortal, filled with the spirit of religion, to save one single soul, that is, his own; how great is not the responsibility of princes who have the charge of thousands of souls! Holy Church punishes severely the sinner who has committed homicide; what then will happen to those who have caused death to thousands of persons for the sake of the glory of this world? It sometimes happens that, after having been the cause of death to many, they utter with their lips a *mea culpa;* but in the depths of their hearts, they rejoice at the extension of their glory and power. They are very far from wishing that they had left their great deeds undone; the fact of having sent their fellow-creatures to Tartarus, fills them with no compunction. Their repentance is worthless in the sight of God, it is not inspired by true contrition of heart, as they do not wish to give up what they have acquired by conquest, and at the cost of so much human blood. They have reason to fear; they ought often to recall to their minds what we have already said, that a very small number of saints is to be found amongst the multitude of kings who have succeeded one another, on the different thrones of the earth, since the beginning of the world. On the other hand, in one single line of Pontiffs, as for instance, the Roman Pontiffs from the time of St. Peter, more than a hundred are distinguished for eminent sanctity. What reason is there for this, unless, as has been already said, it is that kings of the earth and princes, fascinated by a vain desire of glory, subordinate their spiritual interests to the temporal interests of themselves and their kingdoms. Truly godly pontiffs, on the contrary, allow no earthly matters to come between them and the cause of God. The first-mentioned are remorseless in avenging personal affronts; but, when the offence is committed against God, they seem to lack energy to punish the offenders: the second easily forget the wrongs done to themselves, but with difficulty pardon the injuries done to God. The former, engrossed in the things of this world, set little value on spiritual things; the latter, having their thoughts constantly directed towards heaven, feel nothing but contempt for all that is of this earth.

• • •

In the name of the Omnipotent God, and through the authority of blessed Peter, prince of apostles, We grant you, brother Hermann, permission to fulfil the Episcopal duties in all the bishoprics of the kingdom of Lorraine in which the Bishops have been excommunicated, for having held intercourse with Henry, formerly called king. This permission will hold good so long as these Bishops remain excommunicated— that is, until they have been absolved, either by Us or by Our lawful successor.

The Bull *Unam Sanctam* of Boniface VIII

That there is one Holy Catholic and Apostolic Church we are impelled by our faith to believe and to hold— this we do firmly believe and openly confess—and outside of this there is neither salvation or remission of sins, as the bridegroom proclaims in Canticles, "My dove, my undefiled is but one; she is the only one of her mother; she is the choice one of her that bare her." The Church represents one mystic body and of this body Christ is the head; of Christ, indeed, God is the head. In it is one Lord, and one faith, and one baptism. In the time of the flood, there was one ark of Noah, prefiguring the one Church, finished in one cubit, having one Noah as steersman and commander. Outside of this, all things upon the face of the earth were, as we read, destroyed. This Church we venerate and this alone, the Lord saying through his prophets, "Deliver my soul, O God, from the sword; my

"The Bull *Unam Sanctam* of Boniface VIII," in *Translations and Reprints from the Original Sources of European History*, Vol. III, No. 6 (Philadelphia: The Department of History of the University of Pennsylvania, 1912), pp. 20–23. Courtesy of the Department of History of the University of Pennsylvania.

darling from the power of the dog." He prays thus for the soul, that is for Himself, as head, and also for the body which He calls one, namely, the Church on account of the unity of the bridegroom, of the faith, of the sacraments, and of the charity of the Church. It is that seamless coat of the Lord, which was not rent, but fell by lot. Therefore, in this one and only Church, there is one body and one head,— not two heads as if it were a monster—namely, Christ and Christ's Vicar, Peter and Peter's successor, for the Lord said to Peter himself, "Feed my sheep": *my* sheep, he said, using a general term and not designating these or those sheep, so that we must believe that all the sheep were committed to him. If, then, the Greeks, or others, shall say that they were not entrusted to Peter and his successors, they must perforce admit that they are not of Christ's sheep, as the Lord says in John, "there is one fold, and one shepherd."

In this Church and in its power are two swords, to wit, a spiritual and a temporal, and this we are taught by the words of the Gospel, for when the Apostles said, "Behold, here are two swords" (in the Church, namely, since the Apostles were speaking), the Lord did not reply that it was too many, but enough. And surely he who claims that the temporal sword is not in the power of Peter has but ill understood the word of our Lord when he said, "Put up the sword in its scabbard." Both, therefore, the spiritual and material swords, are in the power of the Church, the latter indeed to be used for the Church, the former by the Church, the one by the priest, the other by the hand of kings and soldiers, but by the will and sufferance of the priest. It is fitting, moreover, that one sword should be under the other, and the temporal authority subject to the spiritual power. For when the Apostle said, "there is no power but of God and the powers that are of God are ordained," they would not be ordained unless one sword were under the other, and one, as inferior, was brought back by the other to the highest place. For, according to the Holy Dionysius, the law of divinity is to lead the lowest through the intermediate to the highest. Therefore, according to the law of the universe, things are not reduced to order directly, and upon the same footing, but the lowest through the intermediate and the inferior through the superior. It behooves us, therefore, the more freely to confess that the spiritual power excels in dignity and nobility any form whatsoever of earthly power, as spiritual interests exceed the temporal in importance. All this we see fairly from the giving of tithes, from the benediction and sanctification, from the recognition of this power and the control of these same things. For the truth bearing witness, it is for the spiritual power to establish the earthly power and judge it, if it be not good. Thus, in the case of the Church and the power of the Church, the prophecy of Jeremiah is fulfilled: "See, I have this day set thee over the nations and over the kingdoms"—and so forth. Therefore, if the earthly power shall err, it shall be judged by the spiritual power: if the lesser spiritual power err, it shall be judged by the higher. But if the supreme power err, it can be judged by God alone and not by man, the apostles bearing witness saying, the spiritual man judges all things but he himself is judged by no one. Hence this power, although given to man and exercised by man, is not human, but rather divine power, given by the divine lips to Peter, and founded on a rock for Him and his successors in Him whom he confessed, the Lord saying to Peter himself, "Whatsoever thou shalt bind," etc. Whoever, therefore, shall resist this power, ordained by God, resists the ordination of God, unless there should be two beginnings, as the Manichaean imagines. But this we judge to be false and heretical, since, by the testimony of Moses, not in the *beginnings,* but in the *beginning,* God created the heaven and the earth. We, moreover, proclaim, declare, and pronounce that it is altogether necessary to salvation for every human being to be subject to the Roman Pontiff.

Given at the Lateran the twelfth day before the Kalends of December, in our eighth year, as a perpetual memorial of this matter.

St. Thomas Aquinas

St. Thomas Aquinas (1225–1274), the leading philosopher and theologian of medieval scholasticism, was one of the greatest synthesizers the West has ever produced. The task he undertook was to reconcile the philosophy of Aristotle, rediscovered by European scholars through their contacts with the Moslems in Spain and elsewhere, with Christian theology. During a relatively short lifetime, he succeeded in combining these two disparate elements into a single comprehensive system of thought capable in principle of explaining everything in the universe that people could know. Questions have been raised about the logical consistency of the Thomistic synthesis, but, whether fully successful or not, it still stands as a landmark in the intellectual career of the West.

Beyond their general historical importance, the writings of Thomas have a special significance in the history of Catholicism. Although Thomas was opposed during his lifetime by various religious leaders because of his heavy reliance on the pagan Aristotle, and although his writings were even condemned at several theological centers in the years immediately after his death, within a century his system was generally accepted as the basis for orthodox Roman Catholic philosophy.

The authoritativeness of the Thomistic doctrine was formally recognized by the Church in 1879 in the encyclical *Aeterni Patris* of Pope Leo XIII, which ordered all Catholic schools to teach Thomas's position as the true philosophy. Leo's order was reiterated in 1923 by Pius X, who wrote: "The following canon of the Church's code should be held as a sacred command: In the study of rational philosophy and theology and in the instruction of students the professor should follow entirely the method, doctrine and principles of the Angelic Doctor [Thomas], and hold them religiously."

Of noble Italian lineage, Thomas decided early in life to become a Dominican monk, much to the displeasure of his family. As a student, he was nicknamed "the dumb ox" because of his quietness and ponderous bulk. Later, as a teacher in the University of Paris, he was so popular that it was difficult to find a hall large enough to accommodate the students who flocked to his lectures.

The selection that follows illustrates Thomas's attempt to establish the consonance between the philosophers' quest for truth based on reason and the Christians' acceptance of divine truth based on revelation.

Summa Contra Gentiles

CHAPTER III

In What Way It Is Possible to Make Known the Divine Truth

Since, however, not every truth is to be made known in the same way,

and it is the part of an educated man to seek for conviction in each subject, only so far as the nature of the subject allows,

as the Philosopher[1] most rightly observes as quoted by Boethius, it is necessary to show first of all in what way it is possible to make known the aforesaid truth.

Now in those things which we hold about God there is truth in two ways. For certain things that are true about God wholly surpass the capability of human reason, for instance that God is three and one: while there are certain things to which even natural reason can attain, for instance that God is, that God is one, and others like these, which even the philosophers proved demonstratively of God, being guided by the light of natural reason.

That certain divine truths wholly surpass the capability of human reason, is most clearly evident. For since the principle of all the knowledge which the reason acquires about a thing, is the understanding of that thing's essence, because according to the Philosopher's teaching the principle of a demonstration is *what a thing is*, it follows that our knowledge about a thing will be in proportion to our understanding of its essence. Wherefore, if the human intellect comprehends the essence of a particular thing, for instance a stone or a triangle, no truth about that thing will surpass the capability of human reason. But this does not happen to us in relation to God, because the human intellect is incapable by its natural power of attaining to the comprehension of His essence: since our intellect's knowledge, according to the mode of the present life, originates from the senses: so that things which are not objects of sense cannot be comprehended by the human intellect, except in so far as knowledge of them is gathered from sensibles. Now sensibles cannot lead our intellect to see in them what God is, because they are effects unequal to the power of their cause. And yet our intellect is led by sensibles to the divine knowledge so as to know about God that He is, and other such truths, which need to be ascribed to the first principle. Accordingly some divine truths are attainable by human reason, while others altogether surpass the power of human reason.

Again. The same is easy to see from the degrees of intellects. For

---

[1] [Aristotle—*Ed.*]

The *"Summa Contra Gentiles"* of St. Thomas Aquinas, trans. Fathers of the English Dominican Province (London: Burns & Oates, Ltd.; New York: Benziger Brothers, Inc., 1924), I, 4–15. Courtesy of Benziger Brothers, Inc., and Burns & Oates, Ltd.

if one of two men perceives a thing with his intellect with greater subtlety, the one whose intellect is of a higher degree understands many things which the other is altogether unable to grasp; as instanced in a yokel who is utterly incapable of grasping the subtleties of philosophy. Now the angelic intellect surpasses the human intellect more than the intellect of the cleverest philosopher surpasses that of the most uncultured. For an angel knows God through a more excellent effect than does man, for as much as the angel's essence, through which he is led to know God by natural knowledge, is more excellent than sensible things, even than the soul itself, by which the human intellect mounts to the knowledge of God. And the divine intellect surpasses the angelic intellect much more than the angelic surpasses the human. For the divine intellect by its capacity equals the divine essence, wherefore God perfectly understands of Himself what He is, and He knows all things that can be understood about Him: whereas the angel knows not what God is by his natural knowledge, because the angel's essence, by which he is led to the knowledge of God, is an effect unequal to the power of its cause. Consequently an angel is unable by his natural knowledge to grasp all that God understands about Himself: nor again is human reason capable of grasping all that an angel understands by his natural power. Accordingly just as a man would show himself to be a most insane fool if he declared the assertions of a philosopher to be false because he was unable to understand them, so, and much more, a man would be exceedingly foolish,

were he to suspect of falsehood the things revealed by God through the ministry of His angels, because they cannot be the object of reason's investigations.

Furthermore. The same is made abundantly clear by the deficiency which every day we experience in our knowledge of things. For we are ignorant of many of the properties of sensible things, and in many cases we are unable to discover the nature of those properties which we perceive by our senses. Much less therefore is human reason capable of investigating all the truths about that most sublime essence.

With this the saying of the Philosopher is in accord where he says that *our intellect in relation to those primary things which are most evident in nature is like the eye of a bat in relation to the sun.*

To this truth Holy Writ also bears witness. For it is written (Job xi. 7): *Peradventure thou wilt comprehend the steps of God and wilt find out the Almighty perfectly?* and (xxxvi. 26) *Behold God is great, exceeding our knowledge*, and (I Cor. xiii. 9): *We know in part.*

Therefore all that is said about God, though it cannot be investigated by reason, must not be forthwith rejected as false, as the Manicheans and many unbelievers have thought.

CHAPTER IV

That the Truth about Divine Things which Is Attainable by Reason Is Fittingly Proposed to Man as an Object of Belief

While then the truth of the intelligible things of God is twofold, one to which the inquiry of reason can attain, the other which surpasses the whole range of human reason, both are fittingly proposed by God to man as an object of belief. We must first show this with regard to that truth which is attainable by the inquiry of reason, lest it appears to some, that since it can be attained by reason, it was useless to make it an object of faith by supernatural inspiration. Now three disadvantages would result if this truth were left solely to the inquiry of reason. One is that few men would have knowledge of God: because very many are hindered from gathering the fruit of diligent inquiry, which is the discovery of truth, for three reasons. Some indeed on account of an indisposition of temperament, by reason of which many are naturally indisposed to knowledge: so that no efforts of theirs would enable them to reach to the attainment of the highest degree of human knowledge, which consists in knowing God. Some are hindered by the needs of household affairs. For there must needs be among men some that devote themselves to the conduct of temporal affairs, who would be unable to devote so much time to the leisure of contemplative research as to reach the summit of human inquiry, namely the knowledge of God. And some are hindered by laziness. For in order to acquire the knowledge of God in those things which reason is able to investigate, it is necessary to have a previous knowledge of many things: since almost the entire consideration of philosophy is directed to the knowledge of God: for which reason metaphysics, which is about divine things, is the last of the parts of philosophy to be studied. Wherefore it is not possible to arrive at the inquiry about the aforesaid truth except after a most laborious study: and few are willing to take upon themselves this labour for the love of a knowledge, the natural desire for which has nevertheless been instilled into the mind of man by God.

The second disadvantage is that those who would arrive at the discovery of the aforesaid truth would scarcely succeed in doing so after a long time. First, because this truth is so profound, that it is only after long practice that the human intellect is enabled to grasp it by means of reason. Secondly, because many things are required beforehand, as stated above. Thirdly, because at the time of youth, the mind, when tossed about by the various movements of the passions, is not fit for the knowledge of so sublime a truth, whereas *calm gives prudence and knowledge*, as stated in 7 *Phys.* Hence mankind would remain in the deepest darkness of ignorance, if the path of reason were the only available way to the knowledge of God: because the knowledge of God which especially makes men perfect and good, would be acquired only by the few, and by these only after a long time.

The third disadvantage is that much falsehood is mingled with the investigations of human reason, on account of the weakness of our intellect in forming its judgments, and by reason of the admixture of phantasms. Consequently many would remain in doubt about those things even which are most truly demonstrated, through ignoring the force of the demonstration: especially when they perceive that different things are taught by the various men who are called wise. Moreover among the many demonstrated truths, there is sometimes a mixture of falsehood that is not demonstrated, but assumed for some probable or sophistical reason which at times is mistaken for a demonstration. Therefore it was necessary that definite certainty and pure truth about divine things should be offered to man by the way of faith.

Accordingly the divine clemency has made this salutary commandment, that even some things which reason is able to investigate must be held by faith: so that all may share in the knowledge of God easily, and without doubt or error.

Hence it is written (Eph. iv. 17, 18): That *henceforward you walk not as also the Gentiles walk in the vanity of their mind, having their understanding darkened:* and (Isa. liv. 13): *All thy children shall be taught of the Lord.*

CHAPTER V

That Those Things Which Cannot Be Investigated by Reason Are Fittingly Proposed to Man as an Object of Faith

It may appear to some that those things which cannot be investigated by reason ought not to be proposed to man as an object of faith: because divine wisdom provides for each thing according to the mode of its nature. We must therefore prove that it is necessary also for those things which surpass reason to be proposed by God to man as an object of faith.

For no man tends to do a thing by his desire and endeavour unless it be previously known to him. Wherefore since man is directed by divine providence to a higher good than human frailty can attain in the present life, as we shall show in the sequel, it was necessary for his mind to be bidden to something higher than those things to which our reason can reach in the present life, so that he might learn to aspire, and by his endeavours to tend to something surpassing the whole state of the present life. And this is especially competent to the Christian religion, which alone promises goods spiritual and eternal: for which reason it proposes many things surpassing the thought of man: whereas the old law which contained promises of temporal things, proposed few things that are above human inquiry. It was with this motive that the philosophers, in order to wean men from sensible pleasures to virtue, took care to show that there are other goods of greater account than those which appeal to the senses, the taste of which things affords much greater delight to those who devote themselves to active or contemplative virtues.

Again it is necessary for this truth to be proposed to man as an object of faith in order that he may have truer knowledge of God. For then alone do we know God truly, when we believe that He is far above all that man can possibly think of God, because the divine essence surpasses man's natural knowledge, as stated above. Hence by the fact that certain things about God are proposed to man, which surpass his reason, he is strengthened in his opinion that God is far above what he is able to think.

There results also another advantage from this, namely, the checking of presumption which is the mother of error. For some there are who presume so far on their wits that they think themselves capable of measuring the whole nature of things by their intellect, in that they esteem all things true which they see, and false which they see not. Accordingly, in order that man's mind might be freed from this presumption, and seek the truth humbly, it was necessary that certain things far surpassing his intellect should be proposed to man by God.

Yet another advantage is made apparent by the words of the Philosopher (10 *Ethic.*). For when a certain Simonides maintained that man should neglect the knowledge of God, and apply his mind to human affairs, and declared that *a man ought to relish human things, and a mortal, mortal things:* the Philosopher contradicted him, saying that *a man ought to devote himself to immortal and divine things as much as he can.* Hence he says (11 *De Anima.*) that though it is but little that we perceive of higher substances, yet that little is more loved and desired than all the knowledge we have of lower substances. He says also (2 *De Coelo et Mundo*) that when questions about the heavenly bodies can be answered by a short and probable solution, it happens that the hearer is very much rejoiced. All this shows that however imperfect the knowledge of the highest things may be, it bestows very great perfection on the soul: and consequently, although human reason is unable to grasp fully things that are above reason, it nevertheless acquires much perfection, if at least it hold things, in any way whatever, by faith.

Wherefore it is written (Eccles. iii. 25): *Many things are shown to thee above the understanding of men*, and (I Cor. ii. 10, 11): *The things . . . that*

are of God no man knoweth, but the Spirit of God: but to us God hath revealed them by His Spirit.

CHAPTER VI

That It Is Not a Mark of Levity to Assent to the Things That Are of Faith, Although They Are Above Reason

Now those who believe this truth, *of which reason affords a proof*, believe not lightly, as though *following foolish fables* (2 Pet. i. 16). For divine Wisdom Himself, Who knows all things most fully, designed to reveal to man *the secrets of God's wisdom:* and by suitable arguments proves His presence, and the truth of His doctrine and inspiration, by performing works surpassing the capability of the whole of nature, namely, the wondrous healing of the sick, the raising of the dead to life, a marvellous control over the heavenly bodies, and what excites yet more wonder, the inspiration of human minds, so that unlettered and simple persons are filled with the Holy Ghost, and in one instant are endowed with the most sublime wisdom and eloquence. And after considering these arguments, convinced by the strength of the proof, and not by the force of arms, nor by the promise of delights, but— and this is the greatest marvel of all—amidst the tyranny of persecutions, a countless crowd of not only simple but also of the wisest men, embraced the Christian faith, which inculcates things surpassing all human understanding, curbs the pleasures of the flesh, and teaches contempt of all worldly things. That the minds of mortal beings should assent to such things, is both the greatest of miracles, and the evident work of divine inspiration, seeing that they despise visible things and desire only those that are invisible. And that this happened not suddenly nor by chance, but by the disposition of God, is shown by the fact that God foretold that He would do so by the manifold oracles of the prophets, whose books we hold in veneration as bearing witness to our faith. This particular kind of proof is alluded to in the words of Heb. ii, 3, 4: *Which,* namely the salvation of mankind, *having begun to be declared by the Lord, was confirmed with us by them that heard Him, God also bearing witness by signs and wonders, and divers . . . distributions of the Holy Ghost.*

Now such a wondrous conversion of the world to the Christian faith is a most indubitable proof that such signs did take place, so that there is no need to repeat them, seeing that there is evidence of them in their result. For it would be the most wondrous sign of all if without any wondrous signs the world were persuaded by simple and lowly men to believe things so arduous, to accomplish things so difficult, and to hope for things so sublime. Although God ceases not even in our time to work miracles through His saints in confirmation of the faith.

On the other hand those who introduced the errors of the sects proceeded in contrary fashion, as instanced by Mohammed, who enticed peoples with the promise of carnal pleasures, to the desire of which the concupiscence of the flesh instigates. He also delivered commandments in keeping with his promises, by giving the reins to carnal pleasure, wherein it is easy for carnal men to obey: and the lessons of truth which he inculcated were only such as can be easily known to any man of average wisdom by his natural powers: yea rather the truths which he taught were mingled by him with many fables and most false doctrines. Nor did he add any signs of supernatural agency, which alone are a fitting witness to divine inspiration, since a visible work that can be from God alone, proves the teacher of truth to be invisibly inspired: but he asserted that he was sent in the power of arms, a sign that is not lacking even to robbers and tyrants. Again, those who believed in him from the outset were not wise men practised in things divine and human, but beastlike men who dwelt in the wilds, utterly ignorant of all divine teaching; and it was by a multitude of such men and the force of arms that he impelled others to submit to his law.

Lastly, no divine oracles or prophets in a previous age bore witness to him; rather did he corrupt almost all the teaching of the Old and New Testaments by a narrative replete with fables, as one may see by a perusal of his law. Hence by a cunning device, he did not commit the reading of the Old and New Testament Books to his followers, lest he should thereby be convicted of falsehood. Thus it is evident that those who believe his words believe lightly.

CHAPTER VII

That the Truth of Reason Is Not in Opposition to the Truth of the Christian Faith

Now though the aforesaid truth of the Christian faith surpasses the ability of human reason, nevertheless those things which are naturally instilled in human reason cannot be opposed to this truth. For it is clear that those things which are implanted in reason by nature, are most true, so much so that it is impossible to think them to be false. Nor is it lawful to deem false that which is held by faith, since it is so evidently confirmed by God. Seeing then that the false alone is opposed to the true, as evidently appears if we examine their definitions, it is impossible for the aforesaid truth of faith to be contrary to those principles which reason knows naturally.

Again. The same thing which the disciple's mind receives from its teacher is contained in the knowledge of the teacher, unless he teach insincerely, which it were wicked to say of God. Now the knowledge of naturally known principles is instilled into us by God, since God Himself is the author of our nature. Therefore the divine Wisdom also contains these principles. Consequently whatever is contrary to these principles, is contrary to the divine Wisdom; wherefore it cannot be from God. Therefore those things which are received by faith from divine revelation cannot be contrary to our natural knowledge.

Moreover. Our intellect is stayed by contrary arguments, so that it cannot advance to the knowledge of truth. Wherefore if conflicting knowledges were instilled into us by God, our intellect would thereby be hindered from knowing the truth. And this cannot be ascribed to God.

Furthermore. Things that are natural are unchangeable so long as nature remains. Now contrary opinions cannot be together in the same subject. Therefore God does not instil into man any opinion or belief contrary to natural knowledge.

Hence the Apostle says (Rom. x. 8): *Thy word is nigh thee even in thy heart and in thy mouth. This is the word of faith which we preach.* Yet because it surpasses reason some look upon it as though it were contrary thereto; which is impossible.

This is confirmed also by the authority of Augustine who says *That which truth shall make known can nowise be in opposition to the holy books whether of the Old or of the New Testament.*

From this we may evidently conclude that whatever arguments are alleged against the teachings of faith, they do not rightly proceed from the first self-evident principles instilled by nature. Wherefore they lack the force of demonstration, and are either probable or sophistical arguments, and consequently it is possible to solve them.

Medieval Secular Poetry

The medieval period in Western history is often referred to as the "Age of Faith." The characterization is apt—as long as it is not taken too literally. However, if one assumes that thought and action during these centuries were wholly dominated by the Church and by visions of life in the hereafter to the consequent denigration of this life and its interests, the result will be a one-sided view of an age that in truth was remarkably varied. The poems in this selection should provide a counterbalance to such a distortion by suggesting some of the secular interests that concerned at least certain groups within medieval society (and even within the Church itself).

Secular poetry, of the type illustrated by the poems included here, developed concurrently, but far from coincidentally, with the beginnings of European universities in the twelfth century. It flourished for over a century but gradually disappeared, largely as a result of ecclesiastical suppression, around the beginning of the fourteenth century. Much of this poetry was the work of a group of writers who became known as the Goliard poets, or the tribe of Golias. The origin of the name is obscure, but it could have been derived from the Old Testament Goliath, who was a Philistine giant sent to wage war against the children of Israel. The poets themselves were wandering scholars, young men who had usually taken some work in one or more of the universities but who found themselves unwilling to endure the rigors of sustained intellectual endeavor so dropped out to join the ranks of academic flotsam drifting about the environs of the major medieval centers of learning. Rebels against the established clerical order, they wrote verses that were almost invariably irreverent and sometimes blatantly blasphemous. Yet the poems have a positive side as well, although their attitude is pagan rather than Christian. Almost always we find in them a glorification of nature, of life, of pleasures (particularly those of table and bed), and of the flesh in general.

The selection includes four poems, chosen to reveal different facets of the writers' interests and attitudes. None of the authors is known; however the first piece is generally ascribed to a man who flourished in the mid-twelfth century and referred to himself, with becoming modesty, as the archpoet of Cologne. All have been translated into English from their original Latin. They were written to be enjoyed.

The Confession of Golias

Boiling in my spirit's veins
  With fierce indignation,
From my bitterness of soul
  Springs self-revelation:
Framed am I of flimsy stuff,
  Fit for levitation,
Like a thin leaf which the wind
  Scatters from its station.

While it is the wise man's part
  With deliberation
On a rock to base his heart's
  Permanent foundation,
With a running river I
  Find my just equation,
Which beneath the self-same sky
  Hath no habitation.

Carried am I like a ship
  Left without a sailor,
Like a bird that through the air
  Flies where tempests hale her;
Chains and fetters hold me not,
  Naught avails a jailer;
Still I find my fellows out
  Toper, gamester, railer.

To my mind all gravity
  Is a grave subjection;
Sweeter far than honey are
  Jokes and free affection.
All that Venus bids me do,
  Do I with erection,
For she ne'er in heart of man
  Dwelt with dull dejection.

Down the broad road do I run,
  As the way of youth is;
Snare myself in sin, and ne'er
  Think where faith and truth is,
Eager far for pleasure more
  Than soul's health, the sooth is,
For this flesh of mine I care,
  Seek not ruth where ruth is.

Prelate, most discreet of priests,
  Grant me absolution!

Dear's the death whereof I die,
  Sweet my dissolution;
For my heart is wounded by
  Beauty's soft suffusion;
All the girls I come not nigh,
  Mine are in illusion.

'Tis most arduous to make
  Nature's self surrender;
Seeing girls, to blush and be
  Purity's defender!
We young men our longings ne'er
  Shall to stern law render,
Or preserve our fancies from
  Bodies smooth and tender.

Who, when into fire he falls,
  Keeps himself from burning?
Who within Pavia's walls
  Fame of chaste is earning?
Venus with her finger calls
  Youth at every turning,
Snares them with her eyes, and thralls
  With her amorous yearning.

If you brought Hippolitus
  To Pavia Sunday,
He'd not be Hippolitus
  On the following Monday;
Venus there keeps holiday
  Every day as one day;
'Mid these towers in no tower dwells
  Venus Verecunda.

In the second place I own
  To the vice of gaming:
Cold indeed outside I seem,
  Yet my soul is flaming:
But when once the dice-box hath
  Stripped me to my shaming,
Make I songs and verses fit
  For the world's acclaiming.

In the third place, I will speak
  Of the tavern's pleasure;
For I never found nor find
  There the least displeasure;

Trans. John Addington Symonds.

337

Nor shall find it till I greet
  Angels without measure,
Singing requiems for the souls
  In eternal leisure.

In the public-house to die
  Is my resolution;
Let wine to my lips be nigh
  At life's dissolution:
That will make the angels cry,
  With glad elocution,
"Grant this toper, God on high,
  Grace and absolution!"

With the cup the soul lights up,
  Inspirations flicker;
Nectar lifts the soul on high
  With its heavenly ichor:
To my lips a sounder taste
  Hath the tavern's liquor
Than the wine a village clerk
  Waters for the vicar.

Nature gives to every man
  Some gift serviceable;
Write I never could nor can
  Hungry at the table;
Fasting, any stripling to
  Vanquish me is able;
Hunger, thirst, I liken to
  Death that ends the fable.

Nature gives to every man
  Gifts as she is willing:
I compose my verses when
  Good wine I am swilling,
Wine the best for jolly guest
  Jolly hosts are filling:
From such wine rare fancies fine
  Flow like dews distilling.

Such my verse is wont to be
  As the wine I swallow;
No ripe thoughts enliven me
  While my stomach's hollow;
Hungry wits on hungry lips
  Like a shadow follow,
But when once I'm in my cups,
  I can beat Apollo.

Never to my spirit yet
  Flew poetic vision

Until first my belly had
  Plentiful provision;
Let but Bacchus in the brain
  Take a strong position,
Then comes Phoebus flowing in
  With a fine precision.

There are poets, worthy men,
  Shrink from public places,
And in lurking-hole or den
  Hide their pallid faces;
There they study, sweat, and woo
  Pallas and the Graces,
But bring nothing forth to view
  Worth the girls' embraces.

Fasting, thirsting, toil the bards,
  Swift years flying o'er them;
Shun the strife of open life,
  Tumults of the forum;
They, to sing some deathless thing,
  Lest the world ignore them,
Die the death, expend their breath,
  Drowned in dull decorum.

Lo! my frailties I've betrayed,
  Shown you every token,
Told you what your servitors
  Have against me spoken;
But of those men each and all
  Leave their sins unspoken,
Though they play, enjoy to-day:
  Scorn their pledges broken.

Now within the audience-room
  Of this blessed prelate,
Sent to hunt out vice, and from
  Hearts of men expel it;
Let him rise, nor spare the bard,
  Cast at him a pellet:
He whose heart knows not crime's
    smart,
  Show my sin and tell it!

I have uttered openly
  All I knew that shamed me,
And have spued the poison forth
  That so long defamed me;
Of my old ways I repent,
  New life hath reclaimed me;
God beholds the heart—'twas man
  Viewed the face and blamed me.

Goodness now hath won my love,
 I am wroth with vices;
Made a new man in my mind,
 Lo, my soul arises!
Like a babe new milk I drink—
 Milk for me suffices,
Lest my heart should longer be
 Filled with vain devices.

Thou Elect of fair Cologne,
 Listen to my pleading!
Spurn not thou the penitent;
 See, his heart is bleeding!

Give me penance! what is due
 For my faults exceeding
I will bear with willing cheer,
 All thy precepts heeding.

Lo, the lion, king of beasts,
 Spares the meek and lowly;
Toward submissive creatures he
 Tames his anger wholly.
Do the like, ye powers of earth,
 Temporal and holy!
Bitterness is more than's right
 When 'tis bitter solely.

Let's Away with Study

Let's away with study,
 Folly's sweet.
Treasure all the pleasure
 Of our youth:
Time enough for age
 To think on Truth.
So short a day,
And life so quickly hasting,
And in study wasting
 Youth that would be gay!

'Tis our spring that slipping,
 Winter draweth near,
Life itself we're losing,
 And this sorry cheer
Dries the blood and chills the heart,
 Shrivels all delight.
Age and all its crowd of ills
 Terrifies our sight.
So short a day,
And life so quickly hasting,
And in study wasting
 Youth that would be gay!

Let us as the gods do,
 'Tis the wiser part:
Leisure and love's pleasure
 Seek the young in heart
Follow the old fashion,
 Down into the street!
Down among the maidens,
 And the dancing feet!
So short a day,
And life so quickly hasting,
And in study wasting
 Youth that would be gay!

There for the seeing
 Is all loveliness,
White limbs moving
 Light in wantonness.
Gay go the dancers,
 I stand and see,
Gaze, till their glances
 Steal myself from me.
So short a day,
And life so quickly hasting,
And in study wasting
 Youth that would be gay!

Helen Waddell, *Mediaeval Latin Lyrics*, 5th ed. (London: Constable and Company, Ltd., 1948), p. 221. Courtesy of Constable and Company, Ltd.

Flora

Rudely blows the winter blast,
  Withered leaves are falling fast,
Cold hath hushed the birds at last.
    While the heavens were warm and
      glowing,
      Nature's offspring loved in May;
    But man's heart no debt is owing
      To such change of month or day
      As the dumb brute-beasts obey.
Oh, the joys of this possessing!
How unspeakable the blessing
    That my Flora yields to-day!

Labour long I did not rue,
Ere I won my wages due,
And the prize I played for drew.
    Flora with her brows of laughter,
      Gazing on me, breathing bliss,
    Draws my yearning spirit after,
      Sucks my soul forth in a kiss:
      Where's the pastime matched with
      this:
Oh, the joys of this possessing!
How unspeakable the blessing
    Of my Flora's loveliness!

Truly mine is no harsh doom,
While in this secluded room
Venus lights for me the gloom!
    Flora faultless as a blossom
      Bares her smooth limbs for mine
      eyes;

Softly shines her virgin bosom,
    And the breasts that gently rise
    Like the hills of Paradise.
Oh, the joys of this possessing!
How unspeakable the blessing
    When my Flora is the prize!

From her tender breasts decline,
In a gradual curving line,
Flanks like swansdown white and fine.
    On her skin the touch discerneth
      Naught of rough; 'tis soft as snow:
    'Neath the waist her belly turneth
      Unto fulness, where below
      In Love's garden lilies blow.
Oh, the joys of this possessing!
How unspeakable the blessing!
    Sweetest sweets from Flora flow.

Ah, should Jove but find my fair,
He would fall in love, I swear,
And to his old tricks repair:
    In a cloud of gold descending
      As on Danae's brazen tower,
    Or the sturdy bull's back bending,
      Or would veil his godhood's power
      In a swan's form for one hour.
Oh, the joys of this possessing!
How unspeakable the blessing!
    How divine my Flora's flower!

Trans. John Addington Symonds.

Gaudeamus Igitur

Let us live, then, and be glad
  While young life's before us!
    After youthful pastime had,
    After old age hard and sad,
  Earth will slumber o'er us.

Where are they who in this world,
  Ere we kept, were keeping?
    Go ye to the gods above;
    Go to hell; inquire thereof:
  They are not; they're sleeping.

Trans. John Addington Symonds.

Brief is life, and brevity
  Briefly shall be ended:
    Death comes like a whirlwind
      strong,
    Bears us with his blast along;
  None shall be defended.

Live this university,
  Men that learning nourish;
    Live each member of the same,
    Long live all that bear its name:
  Let them ever flourish!

Live the commonwealth also,
  And the men that guide it!
    Live our town in strength and
      health,
    Founders, patrons, by whose wealth
  We are here provided!

Live all girls! A health to you
  Melting maids and beauteous!
    Live the wives and women too,
    Gentle, loving, tender, true,
  Good, industrious, duteous!

Perish cares that pule and pine!
  Perish envious blamers!
    Die the Devil, thine and mine!
    Die the starch-necked Philistine!
  Scoffers and defamers!

Jean, Sire de Joinville

The *Memoirs, or History and Chronicle of the Very Christian King Saint Louis* by Jean, Sire de Joinville, one of the great contemporary accounts of the Crusades, provides a most valuable portrayal of French feudalism at its height. It is, as well, a very human document, for in it the author writes of his fear in battle (hardly a knightly virtue), his love of wine (preferably undiluted with water), and his doubts about his Christian faith, revealing his essential humanity. Despite his fears and misgivings, however, Joinville was a capable and brave knight, deeply dedicated to his religious beliefs.

Joinville (1224–1319) accompanied King Louis IX of France on the Crusade that sailed from southern France in 1248 bound for Cyprus. Louis, a profoundly religious man, had earlier conceived the Crusade and had decided that the way to free the Holy Land from the grip of the Saracens was by the conquest of Egypt. Such a stratagem, he believed, would severely truncate Moslem power and thus lead to reestablishment of Christian control over Jerusalem. After a nine-month delay at Cyprus waiting for a great number of French knights to join him—and incidentally giving the Moslems that much more time to prepare a warm reception for the Crusaders—Louis finally crossed the Mediterranean to the mouths of the Nile. At Damietta the royal army forced its way ashore but failed to follow up this success, with disastrous results. When Louis did push across and up the Nile toward Cairo, he was utterly defeated and his army destroyed. The king himself was captured and later ransomed. Louis and Joinville spent about four more years in Syria, returning to France in 1254.

The *Memoirs* of Joinville were written nearly sixty years (circa 1300–1309) after the events he describes. They are thus the reminiscences of an old man and as such tend to be garrulous, repetitious, and vaguely petulant. But withal they accurately depict both the grandeur and the frailty of the feudal Christian ideology.

Memoirs

• • •

Joinville Leaves His Castle

After these things I returned to our county, and we agreed, the Count of Sarebruck and I, that we should send our baggage in carts to Ausonne, thence to be borne on the river Saône, and to Arles by the Saône, and the Rhône.

The day that I left Joinville I sent for the Abbot of Cheminon, who was held to be one of the most worthy of the order of the white monks (Cistercians). (I heard this witness regarding him given at Clairvaux on the festival of our Lady, when the saintly king was present, by a monk, who showed the abbot to me, and asked if I knew who he was; and I inquired why he asked me this, and he answered, "because I think he is the worthiest monk in all the white order. For listen," said he, "what I heard tell by a worthy man who slept in the same dormitory as the Abbot of Cheminon. The abbot had bared his breast because of the great heat; and this did the worthy man see who lay in the same dormitory: he saw the Mother of God go to the abbot's bed, and draw his garment over his breast, so that the wind might do him no hurt.")

This Abbot of Cheminon gave me my scarf and staff of pilgrimage; and then I departed from Joinville on foot, barefoot, in my shirt—not to reenter the castle till my return; and thus I went to Blécourt, and Saint-Urbain, and to other places thereabouts where there are holy relics. And never while I went to Blécourt and Saint-Urbain would I turn my eyes towards Joinville for fear my heart should melt within me at thought of the fair castle I was leaving behind, and my two children.

I and my companions ate that day at Fontaine-l'Archevêque before Donjeux; and the Abbot Adam of Saint-Urbain—whom God have in His grace!—gave a great quantity of fair jewels to myself and the nine knights I had with me. Thence we went to Auxonne, and thence again, with the baggage, which we had placed in boats, from Auxonne to Lyons down the river Saône; and along by the side of the boats were led the great warhorses.

At Lyons we embarked on the Rhône to go to Arles the White; and on the Rhône we found a castle called Roche-de-Glun, which the king had caused to be destroyed, because Roger, the lord of the castle, was accused of robbing pilgrims and merchants.

The Crusaders Embark, August 1248

In the month of August we entered into our ship at the Roche-de-Marseille. On the day that we entered into our ship, they opened the door of the ship and put therein all the horses we were to take overseas;

From *Memoirs of the Crusades* by Villehardouin and de Joinville, translated by Sir Frank T. Marzials.

and then they reclosed the door, and caulked it well, as when a cask is sunk in water, because, when the ship is on the high seas, all the said door is under water.

When the horses were in the ship, our master mariner called to his seamen, who stood at the prow, and said: "Are you ready?" and they answered, "Aye, sir—let the clerks and priests come forward!" As soon as these had come forward, he called to them, "Sing, for God's sake!" and they all, with one voice, chanted: *"Veni Creator Spiritus."*

Then he cried to his seamen "Unfurl the sails, for God's sake!" and they did so.

In a short space the wind filled our sails and had borne us out of sight of land, so that we saw naught save sky and water, and every day the wind carried us further from the land where we were born. And these things I tell you, that you may understand how foolhardy is that man who dares, having other's chattels in his possession, or being in mortal sin, to place himself in such peril, seeing that, when you lie down to sleep at night on shipboard, you lie down not knowing whether, in the morning, you may find yourself at the bottom of the sea.

At sea a singular marvel befell us; for we came across a mountain, quite round, before the coast of Barbary. We came across it about the hour of vespers, and sailed all night, and thought to have gone about fifty leagues: and, on the morrow, we found ourselves before the same mountain; and this same thing happened to us some two or three times. When the sailors saw this, they were all amazed, and told us we were in very great peril; for we were nigh unto the land of the Saracens of Barbary.

Then spake a certain right worthy priest, who was called the Dean of Maurupt; and he told us that never had any mischance occurred in his parish—whether lack of water, or overplus of rain, or any other mischance—but so soon as he had made three processions, on three Saturdays, God and His mother sent them deliverance. It was then a Saturday. We made the first procession round the two masts of the ship. I had myself carried in men's arms, because I was grievously sick. Never again did we see the mountain, and on the third Saturday we came to Cyprus.

Sojourn in Cyprus— Embassage from the Tartars—Joinville Takes Service with the King

When we came to Cyprus, the king was already there, and we found great quantities of the king's supplies, that is to say, the cellarage of the king, and his treasure, and his granaries. The king's cellarage was set in the middle of the fields, on the shore by the sea. There his people had stacked great barrels of wine, which they had been buying for two years before the king's arrival; and the barrels were stacked one upon the other in such sort that when you looked at them in front, the stacks seemed as if they were barns.

The wheat and the barley they had set in heaps in the midst of the fields, and when you looked at them, it seemed as if they were mountains, for the rain, which had long been beating on the grain, had caused it to sprout, so that the outside looked like green grass. Now it happened that when they wished to take the grain into Egypt, they took away the upper crust with the green grass, and found the wheat and barley within as fresh as if newly threshed.

The king himself, as I heard tell in Syria, would very willingly have gone on to Egypt, without stopping, had it not been for his barons, who advised him to wait for such of his people as had not yet arrived.

While the king was sojourning in Cyprus, the great king of the Tartars sent envoys to him, with many good and gracious words. Among other things, he signified that he was ready to help the king to conquer the Holy Land, and to deliver Jerusalem from the hands of the Saracens.

The king received the envoys in very friendly fashion, and set other envoys in return, who remained away two years. And the king, by his envoys, sent to the King of the Tartars a tent made like a chapel, very costly, for it was all of fair, fine scarlet cloth. The king, moreover, to see if he could draw the Tartars to our faith, caused images to be graven in the said chapel, representing the Annunciation of our Lady, and all the other points of the faith. And these things he sent by two brothers of the order of Preachers, who knew the Saracen language, and could show and teach the Tartars what they ought to believe.

The two brothers came back to the king at the time when the king's brothers were returning to France; and they found the king, who had left Acre, where his brothers had parted from him, and had come to Caesarea, which he was fortifying; nor was there at that time any truce or peace with the Saracens. How the king's envoys were received will I tell you, as they themselves told it to the king; and in what they reported you may hear much that is strange and marvellous; but I will not tell you of it now, because, in order to do so, I should have to interrupt matters already begun;—so to proceed.

I, who had not a thousand *livres* yearly in land, had undertaken, when I went oversea, to bear, beside my own charges, the charges of nine knights, and two knights-banneret; and so it happened, when I arrived in Cyprus, that I had no more left, my ship being paid for, than twelve score *livres tournois;* wherefore some of my knights apprised me that if I did not provide myself with moneys, they would leave me. But God, who never failed me yet, provided for me in such fashion that the king, who was at Nicosia, sent for me, and took me into his service, and placed eight hundred livres in my coffers; and thus I had more moneys than I required.

• • •

The Host Leaves Cyprus— 1249

As soon as we entered into the month of March, by the king's command the king, the barons, and the other pilgrims ordered that the ships should be re-laden with wine and provisions, so as to be ready to move when the king directed. And when the king saw that all had been duly ordered, the king and queen embarked on their ships on the Friday before Pentecost (21st May 1249), and the king told his barons to follow in their ships straight to

Egypt. On the Saturday the king set sail and all the others besides, which was a fair thing to look upon, for it seemed as if all the sea, so far as the eye could reach, were covered with the canvas of the ships' sails; and the number of the ships, great and small, was reckoned at eighteen hundred.

The king anchored at the head of a hillock which is called the Point of Limassol, and all the other vessels anchored round about him. The king landed on the day of Pentecost. After we had heard mass a fierce and powerful wind, coming from the Egyptian side, arose in such sort that out of two thousand eight hundred knights, whom the king was taking into Egypt, there remained no more than seven hundred whom the wind had not separated from the king's company and carried away to Acre and other strange lands; nor did they afterwards return to the king for a long while.

The day after Pentecost the wind had fallen. The king and such of us as had, according to God's will, remained with him, set sail forthwith, and met the Prince of Morea, and the Duke of Burgundy, who had been sojourning in Morea. On the Thursday after Pentecost the king arrived before Damietta, and we found there, arrayed on the sea-shore, all the power of the soldan—a host fair to look upon, for the soldan's arms are of gold, and when the sun struck upon them they were resplendent. The noises they made with their cymbals and horns was fearful to listen to.

The king summoned his barons to take counsel what they should do. Many advised that he sould wait till his people returned, seeing that no

more than a third part had remained with him; but to this he would by no means agree. The reason he gave was, that to delay would put the foe in good heart, and, particularly, he said that there was no port before Damietta in which he could wait for his people, and that, therefore, any strong wind arising might drive the ships to other lands, like as the ships had been driven on the day of Pentecost.

Preparation for Disembarkation in Egypt

It was settled that the king should land on the Friday before Trinity and do battle with the Saracens, unless they refused to stand. The king ordered my Lord John of Beaumont to assign a galley to my Lord Everard of Brienne and to myself, so as that we might land, we and our knights, because the great ships could not get close up to the shore.

As God so willed, when I returned to my ship, I found a little ship that my Lady of Beyrout, who was cousin-german to my Lord of Montbéliard and to myself, had given me, and that carried eight of my horses.

When the Friday came I and my Lord Everard went, fully armed, to the king and asked for the galley; whereupon my Lord John of Beaumont told us that we should not have it. When our people saw that they would get no galley, they let themselves drop from the great ship into the ship's boat, pell-mell, and as best they could, so that the boat began to sink. The sailors saw that the boat was sinking, little by little, and they escaped into the big ship and left my knights in the boat. I asked the master how many more people there were in the boat than the boat could hold. He told me twenty men-at-arms; and I asked him whether he could take our people to land if I relieved him of so many, and he said, "Yes." So I relieved him in such sort that in three journeys he took them to the ship that had carried my horses.

While I was conducting these people a knight belonging to my Lord Everard of Brienne, and whose name was Plonquet, thought to go down from the great ship into the boat; but the boat moved away, and he fell into the sea and was drowned.

When I came back to my ship I put into my little boat a squire whom I made a knight, and whose name was my Lord Hugh of Vaucouleurs, and two very valiant bachelors—of whom the one had the name my Lord Villain of Versey, and the other my Lord William of Dammartin—who were at bitter enmity the one against the other. Nor could any one make peace between them, because they had seized each other by the hair in Morea. And I made them forgive their grievances and embrace, for I swore to them on holy relics that we should not land in company of their enmity.

Then we set ourselves to get to land, and came alongside of the barge belonging to the king's great ship, there where the king himself was. And his people began to cry out to us, because we were going more quickly than they, that I should land by the ensign of St. Denis, which was being borne in another vessel before the king. But I heeded them not, and caused my people to land in front of a great body of Turks, at a place where there were full six thousand men on horseback.

So soon as these saw us land, they came toward us, hotly spurring. We, when we saw them coming, fixed the points of our shields into the sand and the handles of our lances in the sand with the points set towards them. But when they were so near that they saw the lances about to enter into their bellies, they turned about and fled.

The Crusaders Disembark in Front of the Saracens

My Lord Baldwin of Rheims, a right good man, who had come to land, requested me, by his squire, to wait for him; and I let him know I should do so willingly, for that a right good man such as he ought surely to be waited for in like case of need,— whereby I had his favour all the time that he lived. With him came to us a thousand knights; and you may be assured that, when I landed, I had neither squire, no knight, no varlet that I had brought with me from my own country, and yet God never left me without such as I needed.

At our left hand landed the Count of Jaffa, who was cousin-german to the Count of Montbéliard, and of the lineage of Joinville. It was he who landed in greatest pride, for his galley came all painted, within and without, with escutcheons of his arms, which arms are *or* with a cross of gules *patée*. He had at least three hundred rowers in his galley, and for each rower there was a targe with the count's arms thereon, and to each targe was a pennon attached with his arms wrought in gold.

While he was coming it seemed

as if his galley flew, so did the rowers urge it forward with their sweeps; and it seemed as if the lightning were falling from the skies at the sound that the pennants made, and the cymbals, and the drums, and the Saracenic horns that were in his galley. So soon as the galley had been driven into the sand as far up as they could drive it, both he and his knights leapt from the galley, well armed and well equipped, and came and arrayed themselves beside us.

I had forgotten to tell you that when the Count of Jaffa landed he immediately caused his tents and pavilions to be pitched; and so soon as the Saracens saw them pitched, they all came and gathered before us, and then came on again, spurring hotly, as if to run in upon us. But when they saw that we should not fly, they shortly turned and went back again.

On the right hand, at about a long-crossbow-shot's distance, landed the galley that bore the ensign of St. Denis. And there was a Saracen who, when they had landed, came and charged in among them, either because he could not hold in his horse, or because he thought the other Saracens would follow him; but he was hacked in pieces.

St. Louis Takes Possession of Damietta

When the king heard tell that the ensign of St. Denis was on shore he went across his ship with large steps; and maugre the legate who was with him he would not leave from following the ensign, but leapt into the sea, which was up to his armpits. So he went, with his shield hung to his neck, and his helmet on his head, and his lance in his hand, till he came to his people who were on the shore. When he reached the land, and looked upon the Saracens, he asked what people they were, and they told him they were Saracens; and he put his lance to his shoulder, and his shield before him, and would have run in upon the Saracens if the right worthy men who were about him would have suffered it.

The Saracens sent thrice to the soldan, by carrier-pigeons, to say that the king had landed, but never received any message in return, because the soldan's sickness was upon him. Wherefore they thought that the soldan was dead, and abandoned Damietta. The king sent a knight forward to know if it was sooth that Damietta was so abandoned. The knight returned to the king and said it was sooth and that he had been into the houses of the soldan. Then the king sent for the legate and all the prelates of the host, and all chanted with a loud voice *Te Deum laudamus*. Afterwards the king mounted his horse, and we all likewise, and we went and encamped before Damietta.

Very unadvisedly did the Turks leave Damietta, in that they did not cut the bridge of boats, for that would have been a great hindrance to us; but they wrought us very much hurt in setting fire to the bazaar, where all the merchandise is collected, and everything that is sold by weight. The damage that followed from this was as great as if—which God forbid!—some one were, tomorrow, to set fire to the Petit-Pont in Paris.

Now let us declare that God Almighty was very gracious to us when He preserved us from death and peril on our disembarkation, seeing that we landed on foot and affronted our enemies who were mounted. Great grace did our Lord also show us when He delivered Damietta into our hands, for otherwise we could only have taken it by famine, and of this we may be fully assured, for it was by famine that King John had taken it in the days of our fathers (in 1219).

Mistake of St. Louis— Disorder Among the Crusaders

Our Lord can say of us, as He said of the children of Israel—*et pro nihilo habuerunt terram desiderabilem.*[1] And what does He say afterwards? He says that they forgot God their Saviour. And so did we forget Him as I will shortly tell you.

But first I will tell you of the king who summoned his barons, the clerks, and the laymen, and asked them to help him to decide how the booty taken in the city should be divided. The patriarch was the first to speak, and he spoke thus: "Sire, methinks it were well that you should keep the wheat, and the barley, and the rice, and whatever is needed to sustain life, so as to provision the city; and that you should have it cried throughout the host that all other goods are to be brought to the legate's quarters, under pain of excommunication." To this advice all the other barons assented. Now, as it fell out, all the goods brought to the legate's quarters did not amount in value to more than six thousand livres.

When this had been done, the king and the barons summoned John of Valery, the right worthy man, and spoke to him thus: "Sir of Valery," said the king, "we are agreed that the legate should hand over to you the six thousand livres, so that you may divide them as may seem best to you." "Sire," replied the right worthy man, "you do me much honour, and great thanks be yours! But, please God! that honour can I not accept, nor can I carry out your wish, for by so doing I should make null the good customs of the Holy Land, whereby, when the cities of the enemy are captured, the king takes a third of the goods found therein, and the pilgrims take two thirds. And this custom was well observed by King John when he took Damietta, and as old folks tell us, the same custom was observed by the kings of Jerusalem, who were before King John. If then it pleases you to hand over to me the two parts of the wheat, and the barley, and the rice, and the other provisions, then shall I willingly undertake to make division among the pilgrims."

The king did not decide to do this; so matters remained as they were; and many were ill-pleased that the king should set aside the good old customs.

The king's people, who ought, by liberal dealing, to have retained the merchants, made them pay, so it was said, the highest rents they could exact for the shops in which to sell their goods; and the rumour of this got abroad to foreign lands, so that many merchants forbore to come and bring supplies to the host.

The barons, who ought to have kept what was theirs so as to spend it in fitting time and place, took to giving great feasts, and an outrageous excess of meats. The common

---

[1] "They despised the pleasant land."

people took to consorting with lewd women; whereby it happened, after we returned from captivity, that the king discharged a great many of his people. And when I asked him why he had done this, he told me that he had found, of a certainty, that those whom he had discharged held their ill places of assemblage at a short stone's throw from his pavilion, and that at a time when the host was in greatest distress and misery.

The Saracens Attack the Camp—Death of Walter of Autrèche

Now let us go back to the matter in hand, and tell how, shortly after we had taken Damietta, all the horsemen of the soldan came before the camp, and attacked it from the land side. The king and all the horsemen armed themselves. I, being in full armour, went to speak to the king, and found him fully armed, sitting on a settle, and round him were the right worthy knights belonging to his own division, all in full armour. I asked if he desired that I and my people should issue from the camp, so that the Saracens should not fall upon our tents. When my Lord John of Beaumont heard my question, he cried to me in a very loud voice, and commanded me, in the king's name, not to leave my quarters till the king so ordered.

I have told you of the right worthy knights who were of the king's special following, for there were eight of them, all good knights who had won prizes for arms on the further or hither side of the seas, and such knights it was customary to call good knights. These are the names of the knights about the king:—my Lord Geoffry of Sargines, my Lord Matthew of Marly, my Lord Philip of Nanteuil, and my Lord Imbert of Beaujeu, Constable of France; but the last was not then present, he was outside the camp—he and the master of the crossbowmen, with most of the king's sergeants-at-arms—to guard the camp so that the Turks might not do any mischief thereto.

Now it happened that my Lord Walter Autrèche got himself armed at all points in his pavilion; and when he was mounted upon his horse, with his shield at his neck and his helmet on his head, he caused the flaps of his pavilion to be lifted, and struck spurs into his horse to ride against the Turks; and as he left his pavilion, all alone, all his men shouted with a loud voice, "Chatillon." But so it chanced that or ever he came up to the Turks he fell, and his horse flew over his body; and the horse went on, covered with his arms, to our enemies, because the Saracens were, for the most part, mounted on mares, for which reason the horse drew to the side of the Saracens.

And those who looked on told us that four Turks came by Lord Walter, who lay upon the ground, and as they went by, gave him great blows with their maces there where he lay. Then did the Constable of France and several of the king's sergeants deliver him, and they brought him back in their arms to his pavilion. When he came there he was speechless. Several of the surgeons and physicians of the host went to him, and because it did not seem to them that he was in danger of death, they had him blooded in both arms.

That night, very late, my Lord

Aubert of Narcy proposed that we should go and see him, for as yet we had not seen him, and he was a man of great name and of great valour. We entered into his pavilion, and the chamberlain came to meet us, and asked us to move quietly, so as not to wake his master. We found him lying on coverlets of miniver, and went to him very softly, and found him dead. When this was told to the king, he replied that he would not willingly have a thousand such men acting contrary to his orders as this man had done.

Renewed Attacks on the Part of the Saracens—the King Decides to Await the Arrival of the Count of Poitiers

The Saracens entered every night into the camp on foot and killed our people there where they found them sleeping, whereby it chanced that they killed the sentinel of the lord of Courtenay, and left him lying on a table, and cut off his head, and took it away with them. And this they did because the soldan gave a besant of gold for every Christian man's head.

And we were at this disadvantage because the battalions guarded the camp, each one its night, on horseback; and when the Saracens wished to enter into the camp, they waited till the noise of the horses and of the battalions had passed, and then crept into the camp behind the horses, making their way out before it was day. So the king ordered that the battalion which had been used to keep guard on horseback should keep guard on foot, whereby all the camp was in safety, because of our men who kept guard, and were spread out in such wise that one man touched the other.

After this was done, the king decided not to leave Damietta till his brother, the Count of Poitiers, had arrived with the remaining forces of France. And so that the Saracens might not charge on their horses into the midst of the camp, the king caused all the camp to be enclosed with great earthworks, and on the earthworks were set crossbowmen to watch every night, and sergeants; and such were set also at the entrance to the camp.

St. Catherine of Siena

It is relatively easy to analyze the structure of the medieval church, to describe its long struggle for political supremacy with the secular rulers of Western Europe, and even to grasp the main points of its theology. But what of the central fact that lay behind all of these things—the religious beliefs and practices of ordinary Christians during the Middle Ages? What did the religious life really mean to the average person? Obviously, we can never fully answer this question. Nevertheless, we do have numerous accounts written by or about individuals that describe in detail their inner lives of faith and devotion: people like St. Francis of Assisi, St. Bonaventure, St. Catherine of Siena, and many others. In most of these accounts we can discern, in various degrees, a strain of mysticism, or the individual's experience of having, as he or she sincerely believed, a direct, personal contact with the divine. Usually this meant a form of mystical communion, in which the person's soul experienced a direct union with God. An even stronger, physical connection was experienced by St. Francis; he had imprinted on his body the stigmata, or the wounds suffered by Jesus on the cross. In the case of St. Catherine, she believed that in her mystical experiences she was having direct conversations with God. As Raymond of Capua, her religious superior, describes these experiences:

So about two years before her death, such a clarity of Truth was revealed to her from Heaven that Catherine was constrained to spread it about by means of writing, asking her secretaries to stand ready to take down whatever came from her mouth as soon as they noticed that she had gone into ecstasy. Thus in a short time was composed a dialogue between a soul who asks the Lord four questions, and the Lord himself who replies to the soul.

The selection that follows contains excerpts from the beginning and end of the mystical dialogue between St. Catherine and God.

St. Catherine was born in Siena, in northern Italy, in 1347, the twenty-fourth of twenty-five children; she died in Rome in 1380, while serving on a mission for Pope Urban VI, to try to heal schisms within the church. Although she was a mystic, she was also a tireless social worker, an able theologian, a political negotiator, and a religious administrator; in other words, a gifted woman of practical affairs. Her greatest mystical experience, her "mystical death," occurred in 1368, when for four hours she experienced mystical union with God, while her body lay seemingly lifeless to those around her.

The Dialogue

Catherine of Siena, *The Dialogue*, trans. Suzanne Noffke (Mahwah, N. J.: Paulist Press, 1980), pp. 25–27, 363–366. Used by permission of Paulist Press.

PROLOGUE

In the Name of Christ Crucified and of Gentle Mary

A soul rises up, restless with tremendous desire for God's honor and the salvation of souls. She has for some time exercised herself in virtue and has become accustomed to dwelling in the cell of self-knowledge in order to know better God's goodness toward her, since upon knowledge follows love. And loving, she seeks to pursue truth and clothe herself in it.

But there is no way she can so savor and be enlightened by this truth as in continual humble prayer, grounded in the knowledge of herself and of God. For by such prayer the soul is united with God, following in the footsteps of Christ crucified, and through desire and affection and the union of love he makes of her another himself. So Christ seems to have meant when he said, "If you will love me and keep my word, I will show myself to you, and you will be one thing with me and I with you."[1] And we find similar words in other places from which we can see it is the truth that by love's affection the soul becomes another himself.

To make this clearer still, I remember having heard from a certain servant of God[2] that, when she was at prayer, lifted high in spirit, God would not hide from her mind's eye his love for his servants. No, he would reveal it, saying among other things, "Open your mind's eye and look within me, and you will see the dignity and beauty of my reasoning creature. But beyond the beauty I have given the soul by creating her in my image and likeness, look at those who are clothed in the wedding garment of charity, adorned with many true virtues: They are united with me through love. So I say, if you should ask me who they are, I would answer," said the gentle loving Word, "that they are another me; for they have lost and drowned their own will and have clothed themselves and united themselves and conformed themselves with mine."

It is true, then, that the soul is united to God through love's affection.

Now this soul's will was to know and follow truth more courageously. So she addressed four petitions to the most high and eternal Father, holding up her desire for herself first of all—for she knew that she could be of no service to

---

[1] Cf. Jn. 14:21–23.

[2] Catherine refers to herself in the third person throughout The *Dialogue*. Almost imperceptibly at this point she changes from present to past tense, a perspective she maintains in the narrative passages throughout the rest of the work.

353

her neighbors in teaching or example or prayer without first doing herself the service of attaining and possessing virtue.

Her first petition, therefore, was for herself. The second was for the reform of holy Church. The third was for the whole world in general, and in particular for the peace of Christians who are rebelling against holy Church with great disrespect and persecution. In her fourth petition she asked divine providence to supply in general and in particular for a certain case which had arisen.

This desire of hers was great and continuous. But it grew even more when First Truth [*God*—Ed.] showed her the world's need and how storm-tossed and offensive to God it is. And she had on her mind, besides, a letter she had received from her spiritual father, a letter in which he expressed pain and unbearable sadness over the offense against God, the damnation of souls, and persecutions against holy Church. All of this stirred up the flame of her holy desire with grief for the offense but with gladness in the hope by which she waited for God to provide against such great evils.

She found herself eager for the next day's Mass—it would be Mary's day[3]—because in communion the soul seems more sweetly bound to God and better knows his truth. For then the soul is in God and God in the soul, just as the fish is in the sea and the sea in the fish. So when it was morning and time for Mass she took her place with eager desire. From her deep knowledge of herself, a holy justice gave birth to hatred and displeasure against herself, ashamed as she was of her imperfection, which seemed to her to be the cause of all the evils in the world. In this knowledge and hatred and justice she washed away the stains of guilt, which it seemed to her were, and which indeed were, in her own soul, saying, "O eternal Father, I accuse myself before you, asking that you punish my sins in this life. And since I by my sins am the cause of the sufferings my neighbors must endure, I beg you in mercy to punish me for them."

• • •

CONCLUSION

• • •

Now that soul had seen the truth and the excellence of obedience with the eye of her understanding, and had known it by the light of most holy faith; she had heard it with feeling and tasted it with anguished longing in her will as she gazed into the divine majesty. So she gave him thanks, saying:

Thanks, thanks be to you, eternal Father, that you have not despised me, your handiwork, nor turned your face from me, nor made light of these desires of mine. You, Light, have disregarded my darksomeness; you, Life, have not considered that I am death; nor you, Doctor, considered these grave weaknesses of mine. You, eternal Purity, have disregarded my wretched filthiness; you who are infinite have overlooked the fact that I am finite, and you, Wisdom, the fact that I am foolishness.

[3] Saturday, the day traditionally dedicated to Mary.

For all these and so many other endless evils and sins of mine, your wisdom, your kindness, your mercy, your infinite goodness have not despised me. No, in your light you have given me light. In your wisdom I have come to know the truth; in your mercy I have found your charity and affection for my neighbors. What has compelled you? Not my virtues, but only your charity.

Let this same love compel you to enlighten the eye of my understanding with the light of faith, so that I may know your truth, which you have revealed to me. Let my memory be great enough to hold your favors, and set my will ablaze in your charity's fire. Let that fire burst the seed of my body and bring forth blood; then with that blood, given for love of your blood, and with the key of obedience, let me unlock heaven's gate.

I heartily ask the same of you for every reasoning creature, all and each of them, and for the mystic body of holy Church. I acknowledge and do not deny that you loved me before I existed, and that you love me unspeakably much, as one gone mad over your creature.

O eternal Trinity! O Godhead! That Godhead, your divine nature, gave the price of your Son's blood its value. You, eternal Trinity, are a deep sea: The more I enter you, the more I discover, and the more I discover, the more I seek you. You are insatiable, you in whose depth the soul is sated yet remains always hungry for you, thirsty for you, eternal Trinity, longing to see you with the light in your light. Just as the deer longs for the fountain of living water, so does my soul long to escape from the prison of my darksome body and see you in truth.

O how long will you hide your face from my eyes?

O eternal Trinity, fire and abyss of charity, dissolve this very day the cloud of my body! I am driven to desire, in the knowledge of yourself that you have given me in your truth, to leave behind the weight of this body of mine and give my life for the glory and praise of your name. For by the light of understanding within your light I have tasted and seen your depth, eternal Trinity, and the beauty of your creation. Then, when I considered myself in you, I saw that I am your image. You have gifted me with power from yourself, eternal Father, and my understanding with your wisdom—such wisdom as is proper to your only-begotten Son; and the Holy Spirit, who proceeds from you and from your Son, has given me a will, and so I am able to love.

You, eternal Trinity, are the craftsman; and I your handiwork have come to know that you are in love with the beauty of what you have made, since you made of me a new creation in the blood of your Son.

O abyss! O eternal Godhead! O deep sea! What more could you have given me than the gift of your very self?

You are a fire always burning but never consuming; you are a fire consuming in your heat all the soul's selfish love; you are a fire lifting all chill and giving light. In your light you have made me know your truth: You are that light beyond all light who gives the mind's eye supernatural light in such fullness and perfection that you bring clarity even to the light of faith. In that faith I see that my soul has life, and in that light receives you who are Light.

In the light of faith I gain wisdom in the wisdom of the Word your Son, in the light of faith I am strong, constant, persevering; in the light of faith I have hope: It does not let me faint along the way. This light teaches me the way, and without this light I would be walking in the dark. This is why I asked you, eternal Father, to enlighten me with the light of most holy faith.

Truly this light is a sea, for it nourishes the soul in you, peaceful sea, eternal Trinity. Its water is not sluggish; so the soul is not afraid because she knows the truth. It distills, revealing hidden things, so that here, where the most abundant light of your faith abounds, the soul has, as it were, a guarantee of what she believes. This water is a mirror in which you, eternal Trinity, grant me knowledge; for when I look into this mirror, holding it in the hand of love, it shows me myself, as your creation, in you, and you in me through the union you have brought about of the Godhead with our humanity.

This light shows you to me, and in this light I know you, highest and infinite Good: Good above every good, joyous Good, Good beyond measure and understanding! Beauty above all beauty; Wisdom above all wisdom—indeed you are wisdom itself! You who are the angels' food are given to humans with burning love. You, garment who covers all nakedness, pasture the starving within your sweetness, for you are sweet without trace of bitterness.

O eternal Trinity, when I received with the light of most holy faith your light that you gave me, I came to know therein the way of great perfection, made smooth for me by so many wonderful explanations. Thus I may serve you in the light, not in the dark; and I may be a mirror of a good and holy life; and I may rouse myself from my wretched life in which, always through my own fault, I have served you in darkness. I did not know your truth, and so I did not love it. Why did I not know you? Because I did not see you with the glorious light of most holy faith, since the cloud of selfish love darkened the eye of my understanding. Then with your light, eternal Trinity, you dispelled the darkness.

But who could reach to your height to thank you for so immeasurable a gift, for such generous favors, for the teaching of truth that you have given me? A special grace, this, beyond the common grace you give to other creatures. You willed to bend down to my need and that of others who might see themselves mirrored here.

You responded, Lord; you yourself have given and you yourself answered and satisfied me by flooding me with a gracious light, so that with that light I may return thanks to you. Clothe, clothe me with yourself, eternal Truth, so that I may run the course of this mortal life in true obedience and in the light of most holy faith. With that light I sense my soul once again becoming drunk! Thanks be to God! Amen.

Giovanni Boccaccio

It is a commonplace that medieval civilization reached its apex in the thirteenth century and then went into decline in the fourteenth. Many explanations have been offered for this historical phenomenon, their diversity emphasizing the complexity of the causes at work. Among these certainly must be included a natural catastrophe that overwhelmed Europe in the middle years of the fourteenth century—the Black Death.

We now know, what the millions of victims of the Black Death did not, that their disease was bubonic plague, a highly infectious and usually fatal illness caused by contact with infected rats or the fleas they carried. The Black Death, so named because its victims were marked with dark, purplish spots, originated in Asia and was brought to Europe by Genoese ships from the east in 1347. During the next four years it decimated the population of Europe, spreading in all directions outward from Italy. Although the toll of its victims varied from locality to locality and estimates of total fatalities must be received with discretion, scholars have concluded that the plague (along with several recurrences later in the century) probably claimed the lives of some 25 million people, or roughly one-fourth of the population of Europe.

Only a little thought is needed to appreciate the effects on the survivors of such an overwhelming catastrophe. Some of these, as well as a vivid account of the plague, are described by Giovanni Boccaccio (1313–1375) in the Prelude to his *The Decameron*, which was itself, at least in conception, a consequence of the Black Death. Boccaccio, in his descriptions, knew whereof he spoke, for he was in Florence himself when the Black Death struck there with devastating force in the spring of 1348.

The Decameron itself consists of a series of stories told by members of an imaginary group of Florentines who had fled the city, to pass the time during their exile.

The Decameron

Whenever, fairest ladies, I pause to consider how compassionate you all are by nature, I invariably become aware that the present work will seem to you to possess an irksome and ponderous opening. For it carries at its head the painful memory of the deadly havoc wrought by the recent plague, which brought so much heartache and misery to those who witnessed, or had experience of it. But I do not want you to be deterred, for this reason, from reading any further, on the assumption that you are to be subjected, as you read, to an endless torrent of tears and sobbing. You will be affected no differently by this grim beginning than walkers confronted by a steep and rugged hill, beyond which there lies a beautiful and delectable plain. The degree of pleasure they derive from the latter will correspond directly to the difficulty of the climb and the descent. And just as the end of mirth is heaviness, so sorrows are dispersed by the advent of joy.

This brief unpleasantness (I call it brief, inasmuch as it is contained within few words) is quickly followed by the sweetness and the pleasure which I have already promised you, and which, unless you were told in advance, you would not perhaps be expecting to find after such a beginning as this. Believe me, if I could decently have taken you whither I desire by some other route, rather than along a path so difficult as this, I would gladly have done so. But since it is impossible without this memoir to show the origin of the events you will read about later, I really have no alternative but to address myself to its composition.

I say, then, that the sum of thirteen hundred and forty-eight years had elapsed since the fruitful Incarnation of the Son of God, when the noble city of Florence, which for its great beauty excels all others in Italy, was visited by the deadly pestilence. Some say that it descended upon the human race through the influence of the heavenly bodies, others that it was a punishment signifying God's righteous anger at our iniquitous way of life. But whatever its cause, it had originated some years earlier in the East, where it had claimed countless lives before it unhappily spread westward, growing in strength as it swept relentlessly on from one place to the next.

In the face of its onrush, all the wisdom and ingenuity of man were unavailing. Large quantities of refuse were cleared out of the city by officials specially appointed for the purpose, all sick persons were forbidden entry, and numerous instructions were issued for safeguarding the people's health, but all to no avail. Nor were the countless petitions humbly directed to God by the pious, whether by means of formal processions or in any other guise, any less ineffectual. For in the early spring of the year we have mentioned, the plague began, in a terrifying and extraordinary manner, to make its disastrous effects apparent. It did not take the form it had assumed in the East, where if anyone bled from the nose it was an obvious portent of certain death. On the contrary, its earliest symptoms, in men and women alike, was the appearance of certain swellings in the groin or the armpit, some of which were egg-shaped whilst others were roughly the size of the common apple. Sometimes the swellings were large, sometimes not so large, and they were referred to by the populace as *gavòccioli*. From the two areas already mentioned, the deadly *gavòcciolo* would begin to spread, and within a short time it would appear at random all over the body. Later on, the symptoms of the disease changed, and many people began to find dark blotches and bruises on their arms, thighs, and other parts of the body, sometimes large and few in number, at other times tiny and closely spaced. These, to anyone unfortunate enough to contract them, were just as infallible a sign that he would die as the *gavòcciolo* had been earlier, and as indeed it still was.

Against these maladies, it seemed that all the advice of physicians and all the power of medicine were prof-itless and unavailing. Perhaps the nature of the illness was such that it allowed no remedy: or perhaps those people who were treating the illness (whose numbers had increased enormously because the ranks of the qualified were invaded by people, both men and women, who had never received any training in medicine), being ignorant of its causes, were not prescribing the appropriate cure. At all events, few of those who caught it ever recovered, and in more cases death occurred within three days from the appearance of the symptoms we have described, some people dying more rapidly than others, the majority without any fever or other complications.

But what made this pestilence even more severe was that whenever those suffering from it mixed with people who were still unaffected, it would rush upon these with the speed of a fire racing through dry or oily substances that happened to be placed within its reach. Nor was this the full extent of its evil, for not only did it infect healthy persons who conversed or had any dealings with the sick, making them ill or visiting an equally horrible death upon them, but it also seemed to transfer the sickness to anyone touching the clothes or other objects which had been handled or used by its victims.

It is a remarkable story that I have to relate. And were it not for the fact that I am one of many people who saw it with their own eyes, I would scarcely dare to believe it, let alone commit it to paper, even though I had heard it from a person whose word I could trust. The plague I have been describing was of so contagious a nature that very often it visibly did more than simply pass from one person to another. In other words, whenever an animal other than a human being touched anything belonging to a person who had been stricken or exterminated by the disease, it not only caught the sickness, but died from it almost at once. To all of this, as I have just said, my own eyes bore witness on more than one occasion. One day, for instance, the rags of a pauper who had died from the disease were thrown into the street, where they attracted the attention of two pigs. In their wonted fashion, the pigs first of all gave the rags a thorough mauling with their snouts after which they took them between their teeth and shook them against their cheeks. And within a short time they began to writhe as though they had been poisoned, then they both dropped dead to the ground, spread-eagled upon the rags that had brought about their undoing.

These things, and many others of a similar or even worse nature, caused various fears and fantasies to take root in the minds of those who were still alive and well. And almost without exception, they took a single and very inhuman precaution, namely to avoid or run away from the sick and their belongings, by which means they all thought that their own health would be preserved.

Some people were of the opinion that a sober and abstemious mode of living considerably reduced the risk of infection. They therefore formed themselves into groups and lived in isolation from everyone else.

Having withdrawn to a comfortable abode where there were no sick persons, they locked themselves in and settled down to a peaceable existence, consuming modest quantities of delicate foods and precious wines and avoiding all excesses. They refrained from speaking to outsiders, refused to receive news of the dead or the sick, and entertained themselves with music and whatever other amusements they were able to devise.

Others took the opposite view, and maintained that an infallible way of warding off this appalling evil was to drink heavily, enjoy life to the full, go round singing and merrymaking, gratify all of one's cravings whenever the opportunity offered, and shrug the whole thing off as one enormous joke. Moreover, they practised what they preached to the best of their ability, for they would visit one tavern after another, drinking all day and night to immoderate excess; or alternatively (and this was their more frequent custom), they would do their drinking in various private houses, but only in the ones where the conversation was restricted to subjects that were pleasant or entertaining. Such places were easy to find, for people behaved as though their days were numbered, and treated their belongings and their own persons with equal abandon. Hence most houses had become common property, and any passing stranger could make himself at home as naturally as though he were the rightful owners. But for all their riotous manner of living, these people always took good care to avoid any contact with the sick.

In the face of so much affliction and misery, all respect for the laws of God and man had virtually broken down and been extinguished in our city. For like everybody else, those ministers and executors of the laws who were not either dead or ill were left with so few subordinates that they were unable to discharge any of their duties. Hence everyone was free to behave as he pleased.

There were many other people who steered a middle course between the two already mentioned, neither restricting their diet to the same degree as the first group, nor indulging so freely as the second in drinking and other forms of wantonness, but simply doing no more than satisfy their appetite. Instead of incarcerating themselves, these people moved about freely, holding in their hands a posy of flowers, or fragrant herbs, or one of a wide range of spices, which they applied at frequent intervals to their nostrils, thinking it an excellent idea to fortify the brain with smells of that particular sort; for the stench of dead bodies, sickness, and medicines seemed to fill and pollute the whole of the atmosphere.

Some people, pursuing what was possibly the safer alternative, callously maintained that there was no better or more efficacious remedy against a plague than to run away from it. Swayed by this argument, and sparing no thought for anyone but themselves, large numbers of men and women abandoned their city, their homes, their relatives, their estates and their belongings, and headed for the countryside, either in Florentine territory or, better still, abroad. It was as though

they imagined that the wrath of God would not unleash this plague against men for their iniquities irrespective of where they happened to be, but would only be aroused against those who found themselves within the city walls; or possibly they assumed that the whole of the population would be exterminated and that the city's last hour had come.

Of the people who held these various opinions, not all of them died. Nor, however, did they all survive. On the contrary, many of each different persuasion fell ill here, there, and everywhere, and having themselves, when they were fit and well, set an example to those who were as yet unaffected, they languished away with virtually no one to nurse them. It was not merely a question of one citizen avoiding another, and of people almost invariably neglecting their neighbours and rarely or never visiting their relatives, addressing them only from a distance; this scourge had implanted so great a terror in the hearts of men and women that brothers abandoned brothers, uncles their nephews, sisters their brothers, and in many cases wives deserted their husbands. But even worse, and almost incredible, was the fact that fathers and mothers refused to nurse and assist their own children, as though they did not belong to them.

Hence the countless numbers of people who fell ill, both male and female, were entirely dependent upon either the charity of friends (who were few and far between) or the greed of servants, who remained in short supply despite the attraction of high wages out of all pro-

portion to the services they performed. Furthermore, these latter
were men and women of coarse
intellect and the majority were un-
used to such duties, and they did
little more than hand things to the
invalid when asked to do so and
watch over him when he was dying.
And in performing this kind of service, they frequently lost their lives
as well as their earnings.

As a result of this wholesale desertion of the sick by neighbours,
relatives and friends, and in view of
the scarcity of servants, there grew
up a practice almost never previously heard of, whereby when a
woman fell ill, no matter how gracious or beautiful or gently bred she
might be, she raised no objection to
being attended by a male servant,
whether he was young or not. Nor
did she have any scruples about
showing him every part of her body
as freely as she would have displayed it to a woman, providing that
the nature of her infirmity required
her to do so; and this explains why
those women who recovered were
possibly less chaste in the period
that followed.

Moreover a great many people
died who would perhaps have survived had they received some assistance. And hence, what with the
lack of appropriate means for tending the sick, and the virulence of
the plague, the number of deaths
reported in the city whether by day
or night was so enormous that it
astonished all who heard tell of it,
to say nothing of the people who
actually witnessed the carnage. And
it was perhaps inevitable that among
the citizens who survived there
arose certain customs that were

quite contrary to established tradition.

It had once been customary, as it
is again nowadays, for the women
relatives and neighbours of a dead
man to assemble in his house in
order to mourn in the company of
the women who had been closest to
him; moreover his kinsfolk would
forgather in front of his house along
with his neighbours and various
other citizens, and there would be
a contingent of priests, whose numbers varied according to the quality
of the deceased; his body would be
taken thence to the church in which
he had wanted to be buried, being
borne on the shoulders of his peers
amidst the funeral pomp of candles
and dirges. But as the ferocity of
the plague began to mount, this
practice all but disappeared entirely
and was replaced by different customs. For not only did people die
without having many women about
them, but a great number departed
this life without anyone at all to
witness their going. Few indeed
were those to whom the lamentations and bitter tears of their relatives were accorded; on the contrary, more often than not
bereavement was the signal for
laughter and witticisms and general
jollification—the art of which the
women, having for the most part
suppressed their feminine concern
for the salvation of the souls of the
dead, had learned to perfection.
Moreover it was rare for the bodies
of the dead to be accompanied by
more than ten or twelve neighbours
to the church, nor were they borne
on the shoulders of worthy and
honest citizens, but by a kind of
gravedigging fraternity, newly come

into being and drawn from the lower orders of society. These people assumed the title of sexton, and demanded a fat fee for their services, which consisted in taking up the coffin and hauling it swiftly away, not to the church specified by the dead man in his will, but usually to the nearest at hand. They would be preceded by a group of four or six clerics, who between them carried one or two candles at most, and sometimes none at all. Nor did the priests go to the trouble of pronouncing solemn and lengthy funeral rites, but, with the aid of these so-called sextons, they hastily lowered the body into the nearest empty grave they could find.

As for the common people and a large proportion of the bourgeoisie, they presented a much more pathetic spectacle, for the majority of them were constrained, either by their poverty or the hope of survival, to remain in their houses. Being confined to their own parts of the city, they fell ill daily in their thousands, and since they had no one to assist them or attend to their needs, they inevitably perished almost without exception. Many dropped dead in the open streets, both by day and by night, whilst a great many others, though dying in their own houses, drew their neighbours' attention to the fact more by the smell of their rotting corpses than by any other means. And what with these, and the others who were dying all over the city, bodies were here, there and everywhere.

Whenever people died, their neighbours nearly always followed a single, set routine, prompted as much by their fear of being contaminated by the decaying corpse as by any charitable feelings they may have entertained towards the deceased. Either on their own, or with the assistance of bearers whenever these were to be had, they extracted the bodies of the dead from their houses and left them lying outside their front doors, where anyone going about the streets, especially in the early morning, could have observed countless numbers of them. Funeral biers would then be sent for, upon which the dead were taken away, though there were some who, for lack of biers, were carried off on plain boards. It was by no means rare for more than one of these biers to be seen with two or three bodies upon it at a time; on the contrary, many were seen to contain a husband and wife, two or three brothers and sisters, a father and son, or some other pair of close relatives. And times without number it happened that two priests would be on their way to bury someone, holding a cross before them, only to find that bearers carrying three or four additional biers would fall in behind them; so that whereas the priests had thought they had only one burial to attend to, they in fact had six or seven, and sometimes more. Even in these circumstances, however, there were no tears or candles or mourners to honour the dead; in fact, no more respect was accorded to dead people than would nowadays be shown toward dead goats. For it was quite apparent that the one thing which, in normal times, no wise man had ever learned to accept with patient resignation (even though it struck so seldom and unobtrusively), had now been brought home to the feeble-minded as well, but the scale of the calamity caused them to regard it with indifference.

Such was the multitude of corpses (of which further consignments were arriving every day and almost by the hour at each of the churches), that there was not sufficient consecrated ground for them to be buried in, especially if each was to have its own plot in accordance with long-established custom. So when all the graves were full, huge trenches were excavated in the churchyards, into which new arrivals were placed in their hundreds, stowed tier upon tier like ships' cargo, each layer of corpses being covered over with a thin layer of soil till the trench was filled to the top.

But rather than describe in elaborate detail the calamities we experienced in the city at that time, I must mention that, whilst an ill wind was blowing through Florence itself, the surrounding region was no less badly affected. In the fortified towns, conditions were similar to those in the city itself on a minor scale; but in the scattered hamlets and the countryside proper, the poor unfortunate peasants and their families had no physicians or servants whatever to assist them, and collapsed by the wayside, in their fields, and in their cottages at all hours of the day and night, dying more like animals than human beings. Like the townspeople, they too grew apathetic in their ways, disregarded their affairs, and neglected their possessions. Moreover they all behaved as though each day was to be their last, and far from making provision for the future by tilling their lands, tending their flocks, and adding to their previous labours, they tried in every way they could think of to squander the assets already in their possession. Thus it came about that oxen, asses, sheep, goats, pigs, chickens, and even dogs (for all their deep fidelity to man) were driven away and allowed to roam freely through the fields, where the crops lay abandoned and had not even been reaped, let alone gathered in. And after a whole day's feasting, many of these animals, as though possessing the power of reason, would return glutted in the evening to their own quarters, without any shepherd to guide them.

But let us leave the countryside and return to the city. What more remains to be said, except that the cruelty of heaven (and possibly, in some measure, also that of man) was so immense and so devastating that between March and July of the year in question, what with the fury of the pestilence and the fact that so many of the sick were inadequately cared for or abandoned in their hour of need because the healthy were too terrified to approach them, it is reliably thought that over a hundred thousand human lives were extinguished within the walls of the city of Florence? Yet before this lethal catastrophe fell upon the city, it is doubtful whether anyone would have guessed it contained so many inhabitants.

Ah, how great a number of splendid palaces, fine houses, and noble dwellings, once filled with retainers, with lords and with ladies, were bereft of all who had lived there, down to the tiniest child! How numerous were the famous families, the vast estates, the notable fortunes, that were seen to be left without a rightful successor! How many gallant gentlemen, fair ladies, and sprightly youths, who would have been judged hale and hearty by Galen, Hippocrates and Aesculapius (to say nothing of others), having breakfasted in the morning with their kinfolk, acquaintances and friends, supped that same evening with their ancestors in the next world!

Benvenuto Cellini at work. (*Culver Pictures, Inc.*)

RENAISSANCE AND REFORMATION

The Renaissance was a cultural and intellectual revival that began in the city-states of northern Italy during the fourteenth and fifteenth centuries. The gradual change from the medieval outlook was probably caused by several factors: the great economic prosperity of these city-states, their contacts through trade with other cultures, the reduction of the papacy to the role of an Italian principality, and the Church's loss of emotional prestige. These elements combined to produce the highly secular outlook that is the essence of the Renaissance.

This secular outlook is commonly referred to as "humanism," a term that may be defined in two ways. According to the narrower definition, humanism was a rebirth, or renaissance, of interest in classical antiquity. People turned to a rereading of the great (and not so great) works of Greek and Roman literature, a reexamination and preservation of classical architecture and sculpture, and a restudy of the classical languages themselves. This very interest in the glories of Greece and Rome, however, exacted its price, for Renaissance literature and some of its art tended to be imitative, to rely too heavily on the models of a bygone day. The conviction that it was impossible to surpass or even to equal the achievements of the ancients tended to inhibit the mind and imagination of the people of the Renaissance.

The broader definition of humanism states the typically Renaissance notion that people and their activities are the most important and interesting elements of the universe. Thus, humankind, rather than God, is the proper subject of contemplation and examination. This secular, humanistic outlook posed many interesting problems. If humankind and human life on this earth are the most important concern, how may the "good" person or the "good" life be determined? Castiglione, in his manual on conduct, *The Book of the Courtier*, claimed that virtue is its own reward, that one does not do good out of hope for reward or fear of punishment in an afterlife, but only because it is good to be good. Some of the same secular ethic is implied in the political theories of Machiavelli, whose ideal prince was not concerned with or troubled by an angry or beneficent God but only with the problems of acquiring and maintaining power to ensure a stable political order in which the citizenry could live in peace and plenty.

During the fifteenth and sixteenth centuries the Renaissance spread from Italy to France, England, Spain, the Lowlands, and throughout Germany and

Poland. Italian manners and customs were widely adopted; it became fashionable to build "in the Italian fashion" and to dress "in the Italian mode." More important, however, than the adoption of these cultural superficialities was the ready acceptance by scholars in northern Europe of the critical methods developed by Italian humanists of reading and analyzing documents, literature, and writings of all kinds. Moreover, the scientific attitude and the widespread curiosity about the physical world led many Europeans to inquire, to study, to dissect, to experiment, and to seek a fuller understanding of the nature of the universe and their place in it.

Among the leaders of the New Learning in the North was Sir Thomas More of England, who looked closely at his society and found it mean and corrupt. This conclusion he elaborated in his brilliant and immensely popular satire, *Utopia*, which was published in 1516 in Latin and subsequently translated into English, French, Spanish, German, and Italian. More's close friend, Erasmus of Rotterdam, was also deeply influenced by the skeptical, critical thought of the Renaissance. Erasmus translated the New Testament from Greek into Latin, wrote various *Colloquies* containing observations and commentaries on the contemporary world, and, more lasting perhaps, published his penetrating analysis of people and affairs under the title *The Praise of Folly*.

Not everyone, however, received the New Learning with the same enthusiasm. A German monk, Martin Luther, though he accepted the typically humanistic ideas regarding the critical examination of texts, could not accept the Renaissance notion that this world and its affairs were of primary importance. He was unwilling to divorce himself from the crucial problem of the salvation of people's souls. Most of the people of the Renaissance simply shelved the problem of salvation—for them, life was for the living, to be enjoyed and possibly to be remembered without remorse or regret. Benvenuto Cellini, an Italian goldsmith, was a perfect example of this attitude. But for Luther (a contemporary of Cellini) life on this earth was merely a transient aspect of the eternal life of the soul. In this one sense, Luther represented a reversion to the medieval outlook. But at the same time he shared in the new intellectual movements, being convinced that everyone was competent to read and understand the holy writings and to find salvation through faith.

Justification by faith lay at the heart of the Lutheran break with the Catholic Church. Originally, Luther sought only the reform of church practice, not of doctrine. But the indifference of the church leaders, together with what seemed to him an almost institutionalized acceptance of abuses, made Luther's outcries go unheard. The Church finally became seriously enough concerned over Luther's protests to excommunicate him, thereby laying the ground for the Protestant movement. Launched by Luther, Protestantism quickly gained adherents in many parts of Europe. The most influential of these was a Frenchman transplanted to Geneva, John Calvin, who supplied the movement with a theology. Anything but an innovator, Calvin returned to the writings of St. Paul and St. Augustine and the doctrine of original sin, which he reiterated with a rare combination of legalistic precision and evangelical fervor.

For centuries, the Catholic Church had been flexible enough in its thinking and its practices to adjust to reform movements from within—for example, the Cluniac movement of the eleventh century, the Cistercian of the twelfth, and the Franciscan of the thirteenth. But by the end of the fifteenth century the Church was no longer able to provide the spiritual comfort required to sustain a great number of loyal and devoted followers. During the fifteenth century a group of mystics, who dedicated their lives to poverty and the education of the youth, had appeared in Germany: the Brotherhood of the Common Life. This relatively obscure group felt that the conventional Catholic Church was somehow failing in its purposes, and sought to restore a measure of fervor to the traditional faith. Even Erasmus was concerned about the abuses in church practice and the indifference of church leadership to the needs of the people. He presented his solutions to these problems in what he called "the philosophy of Christ."

One of the outcomes of the conflict between the Protestant movement and the Catholic Church was a revitalization of the Catholic faith. Led mostly by the militant order of the Society of Jesus, founded in 1540 by a Spanish soldier, St. Ignatius of Loyola, the Catholics reconverted Poland, Bohemia, and large areas of France and Germany. Of course, this revitalization was not accomplished without bitterness, heroism, and conflict from both Protestant and Catholic. The Peasants Revolt in Germany in the early sixteenth century, the religious wars in France in the late sixteenth century, and the Thirty Years' War in the early seventeenth century were only outstanding examples of the hatred, fear, and bloodshed provoked by conflicting religious opinions.

During the Renaissance, then, Europe was expanding intellectually and culturally through scientific investigation and literary and artistic innovation, and was attempting to find some solution to religious controversy. Europe was expanding geographically as well, for the time of the Renaissance and Reformation was also the age of exploration and commercial revolution. To the west new continents were discovered, new colonies planted, and new empires created. The discovery of a sea route around Africa immensely stimulated traffic between western Europe and the Orient, leading finally to a relative decline in the economic status of the great Italian cities and the emergence of Portugal, Spain, the Dutch Republic, and finally France and England as world powers with great fleets and vast overseas holdings. The influx of wealth (both in goods and precious metals) from East and West created severe economic dislocations and upheavals in Europe, adding another source of strife and discontent to a culture already troubled by the ferment of Renaissance skepticism and Reformation religious enthusiasm. It was from this matrix that the modern Western world began to emerge, a world no longer completely dominated by Europe but gradually and increasingly influenced in its history by the cultures that developed in the vast and virgin continents discovered by Christopher Columbus and rapidly explored by his followers.

Pico della Mirandola

Giovanni Pico, the Count of Mirandola (1463–1494), epitomized both in his life and in his writings the Renaissance ideal of manhood. Nobly born, wealthy, handsome, and brilliant, he was well embarked on a distinguished intellectual career which would certainly have made him the undisputed leader of the humanistic movement when he unfortunately fell victim to fever at the age of thirty.

Unwilling to limit himself, as many other humanists did, to translating and imitating the literature of classical Greece and Rome, Pico undertook the task of assimilating all the great writings of the past, searching out the elements of truth contained in each of them, and assembling these truths into a new philosophical synthesis of his own. The *Oration on the Dignity of Man* is a part of his ambitious project. After seven years of study in various European universities, Pico arrived in Rome at the age of twenty-three and announced that he was prepared to defend in public debate against anyone in Europe a list of nine hundred theses representing the conclusions that he had derived from his studies. (He even offered to pay the travel expenses of scholars coming long distances.) The debate, scheduled for January 1487, never took place. Pope Innocent VIII, suspicious that Pico was straying from orthodoxy, appointed a commission to examine the list of theses. When the commission confirmed the pope's suspicions by labeling a number of them heretical, Innocent forced the debate to be canceled.

The nature of the *Oration*, which Pico had intended as an introductory address for the debate, is evident from its title. Apart from the intrinsic interest of the discussion itself, including the many references which Pico makes to the most diverse literary sources, the significance of the *Oration* lies in its eloquent summation of the Renaissance interest in humans and the belief in the dignity of human life. The selection that follows includes the first seven sections of the *Oration*.

On the Dignity of Man

Most reverend fathers: I have read in the writings of the Arabs that Azdallah the Saracen, when asked what thing on this worldly stage appeared most marvelous to him, replied that he perceived nothing more wonderful than Man. This opinion is concurred in by that famous statement of Hermes Trismegistus:

Man, Asclepius, is a great miracle.

As I pondered the sense of these sayings, I became dissatisfied with those arguments which are brought forth in profusion by many people to establish the excellence of Humanity: namely, that Man is the intermediary of all created things, slave to those above him, king to those below; that Man is the interpreter of nature, by virtue of the sharpness of his senses, the searching of his reason, and the light of his understanding; that Man is the interval between time and eternity, the copula of the universe (as the Persians say), or even its wedding, a little lower, on David's authority, than the angels. These are great things, certainly, but not of prime importance; not so great that they lay just claim to the highest admiration. For, under these conditions, why should we not give even greater admiration to the angels themselves, and to the blessed choir of Heaven? At length, I felt that I had come to understand both why Man is the most fortunate of creatures, and thus worthy of all admiration, and what, finally, this situation is which he has received in the scheme of the universe—a position to be envied, not only by the beasts, but by the stars, by the spirits beyond the world. The answer is marvelous and incredible. How could it be otherwise? For it is on this account that Man is rightly said and believed to be a great miracle, truly a being to be admired.

Hear now, Fathers, what this solution is, and, in your courtesy, grant my discourse a friendly audience.

The Supreme Father, God the Creator, had already fashioned this worldly residence which we see about us, the majestic temple of His Godhood, after the laws of His secret wisdom. He had adorned the zone beyond the heavens with intellects; He had quickened the ethereal spheres into life with eternal souls; He had filled the foul and filthy regions of the lower world with a multitude of animals of every sort. But, His work completed, the Demiurge desired that there be someone to contemplate the reason of such a great work, to love its beauty, to wonder at its vastness. Thus, when everything had been finished (as Moses and Timaeus bear witness), He turned His thoughts last of all to bringing forth Man. But there remained no archetype on which to pattern the new creature, no treasure to bestow on the new son as an inheritance, no place in all the new world where

Giovanni Pico della Mirandola, *De Hominis Dignitate*, trans. Douglass S. Parker.

that contemplator of the universe might sit. By this time, all things were full; all things had been distributed in the highest, middle, and lowest orders. But it was not the nature of the Father's power to fail, as though exhausted, in the last act of creation; nor of His wisdom, to waver in a necessary deed through lack of a plan; nor of His beneficent love, to compel the very being who was to praise the divine generosity in other things to impugn that generosity in himself. At length the Greatest Craftsman decided that this being, to whom He could give nothing of its own, should share in everything which he had assigned to each of the other beings. Thus he received Man as a work of undefined pattern, and placing him in the center of the world, addressed him as follows:

I have given you, O Adam, neither a fixed location, nor an especial appearance, nor any gift peculiarly your own; therefore, you may attain and possess, as you wish and as you will, whatever location, whatever appearance, whatever gifts you yourself desire. The nature of all other things is limited and confined within laws which I have laid down. You, confined by no limits, will determine your nature for yourself by your judgment, into whose power I have consigned you. I have placed you in the middle of the world, whence you may survey the more conveniently everything which is in the world. I have made you neither heavenly nor earthly, neither mortal nor immortal; thus, as a free and sovereign craftsman, you may mold yourself whatever form you choose. You will be able to degenerate into those lower creatures, which are brutes; you will be able, by the determination of your mind, to be reborn into those higher creatures, which are divine.

How great is the generosity of God the Father! How great and admirable is the happiness of Man, whose gift it is to have that which he wishes! Upon their birth, beasts bring with them from their mother's bag (as Lucilius says) all that they will ever possess. From the beginning of time, or soon after, the supreme spirits have been that which they will be throughout all eternity. But as Man is born, the Father has planted in him seeds of every sort, shoots of every life; those which each man cultivates will grow, and bear their fruits in him. If these are vegetable, he will become a plant; if sensual, a brute; if rational, a heavenly being; if intellectual, an angel and son of God. But if Man, not contented with any creature's lot, betakes himself into the center of his oneness, then, made one with God, in the solitary darkness of the Father he who was created above all things will excell all things.

Who would not admire this chameleon of ours? Or, rather, who would admire anything else more greatly? Asclepius of Athens does no wrong when he says of man that, in accordance with his changing aspect and his self-transforming nature, he was symbolized in the mysteries of Proteus. Hence those metamorphoses celebrated among the Hebrews and the Pythagoreans: indeed, the most secret Hebrew theology makes transformations, now of holy Enoch into an angel of the divinity, now of other men into other divine spirits; the Pythagoreans transform evildoers into beasts, and even (if we may believe Empedocles) into plants. Imitating this, Mohammed would often say, "He who departs from the divine law becomes a beast," and rightly so. For not the bark, but the dull and insensible nature makes the plants; not the hide, but the brutish and sensual soul the beast; not the circular body, but correct reason the heavens; not separation from the body, but spiritual intelligence the angel. For should you see a man given up to his belly and creeping on the ground, you see a plant, not a man; should you see someone blinded by the empty illusions of an apparition like Calypso, enticed by titillating allurements, a slave to his senses, you see a beast, not a man; should you see a philosopher perceiving all by his correct reasoning, you would revere him—he is a being of heaven, not of earth; should you see a pure contemplator, unconscious of his body, completely withdrawn into the sanctuary of his mind, this is no earthly, no celestial being:—this is a most majestic spirit dressed in human flesh.

Is there anyone, then, who would not admire man? Not wrongly, in both the Mosaic and the Christian scriptures, he is called now by the name of "all flesh," now by the name of "every creature," since he molds, fashions, and transforms himself after the appearance of all flesh and after the nature of every creature. Therefore Evanthes the Persian, in his account of the Chaldean theology, writes that Man possesses no innate form of his own, but many extraneous and foreign ones, whence that saying of the Chaldeans that man is an animal of varied and manifold and unstable nature.

But to what end do I record this? So that, after we have been born in this condition—that of being what we wish—we shall understand that we must take especial care that it not be said against us, that we were in honor and knew it not, and became as brutes and foolish beasts. Rather, may the words of the prophet Asaph apply—"Ye are gods, and all of you are children of the most High,"—lest we, abusing the Father's most indulgent generosity, render that unfettered choice which He gave us harmful rather than beneficial. May some holy aspiration enter our hearts, so that we are not content with middling things, but pant for the highest and strain to achieve them, since we can if we will.

Let us scorn the earthly, despise the heavenly, and thus, disdaining everything which is of the world, fly to that assembly beyond the world which is nearest God, who towers over all. There, as the holy mysteries tell, Seraphim, Cherubim, and Thrones occupy the first place; let us strive to equal their dignity and glory. And, if we wish it, we shall be in no wise lower than they.

Christopher Columbus

Although the fact is well-known, it is easily forgotten that Christopher Columbus, when he set sail across the "Western Ocean" with his three tiny ships on August 3, 1492, was bound not for a new world but for "the Indies" (India, China, and the islands of East Asia). His venture was a prosaic even though a hazardous one. He hoped to discover a sea route that would make trade with the East, with its highly desired silks, rugs, jewelry, drugs, and spices, easier than the long and arduous caravan treks across Asia. According to Columbus' (mis)calculations his destination could be reached by sailing some three thousand miles due west around the world, a distance which, as it turned out, was just that to the islands of the new world that he discovered.

In 1484 Columbus submitted his proposal of reaching the east by sailing west to the king of Portugal, hoping to receive financial support for the project. But the Portuguese were already deeply committed to an attempt to reach the same destination by sailing south, around Africa and thence east to India and beyond, so Columbus' appeal was rejected. From there Columbus went to Spain and, after two years of effort, gained an audi-

ence with King Ferdinand and Queen Isabella. After six more years spent in negotiations, the monarchs finally agreed to underwrite the venture and Columbus set off on his epochal voyage. The crossing of the Atlantic, from the Canary Islands (the last port of call on the European side) to the island of San Salvador in the Bahamas (northeast of Cuba), where Columbus landed on October twelfth and took possession in the name of Ferdinand and Isabella, occupied a total of thirty-six days.

Over a period of twelve years Columbus made four voyages to the new world, discovering many of the Caribbean Islands and establishing several colonies. His voyages took him to the mainland of both South and Central America as well. And, although he heard tales of a great ocean farther to the west, he never realized that the lands he had discovered were not a part of the orient but of a new continent.

The two selections that follow consist of the initial entry Columbus made in a journal he kept of his first voyage and a letter he wrote as he neared the end of the voyage, describing some of the sights he had seen and the things he had done.

Journal and Letter

Because, most Christian and very exalted and very excellent and very powerful Princes, King and Queen of the Spains and of the Islands of the Sea, our Lords, in this present year of 1492 after your Highnesses had made an end to the war of the Moors, who were reigning in Europe, and having finished the war in the very great city of Granada, where in this present year on the 2nd day of the month of January, I saw the Royal banners of your Highnesses placed by force of arms on the towers of the Alhambra, which is the fortress of the said City: and I saw the Moorish King come out to the gates of the City and kiss the Royal hands of your Highnesses, and the hands of the Prince, my Lord: and then in that present month, because of the information which I had given your Highnesses about the lands of India, and about a Prince who is called Great Khan, which means in our Romance language, King of Kings,—how he and his predecessors had many times sent to Rome to beg for men learned in our Holy Faith that they might be instructed therein, and that the Holy Father had never furnished them, and so, many peoples believing in idolatries and receiving among themselves sects of perdition, were lost:—your Highnesses, as Catholic Christians and Princes, loving the Holy Christian faith and the spreading of it, and enemies of the sect of Mahomet and of all idolatries and heresies, decided to send me, Christopher Columbus, to the said regions of India, to see the said Princes and the peoples and lands, and learn of their disposition, and of everything, and the measures which could be taken for their conversion to our Holy Faith: and you ordered that I should not go to the east by land, by which it is customary to go, but by way of the west, whence until to-day we do not know certainly that any one has gone. So that, after having banished all the Jews from all your Kingdoms and realms, in the same month of January, your Highnesses ordered me to go with a sufficient fleet to the said regions of India: and for that purpose granted me great favours and ennobled me, that from then henceforward I might entitle myself *Don* and should be High Admiral of the Ocean-Sea [*Atlantic*—Ed.] and Viceroy and perpetual Governor of all the islands and continental land which I might discover and acquire, and which from now henceforward might be discovered and acquired in the Ocean-Sea, and that my eldest son should succeed in the same manner, and thus from generation to generation for ever after: and I started from the city of Granada on Saturday, the 12th day of the month of May in the same year 1492: I came to the village of Palos, which is a sea-port, where I fitted out three vessels, very suitable for a similar undertaking: and I left the

Trans. J. B. Thacher.

375

said port, well supplied with a large quantity of provisions and with many seamen, on the 3rd day of the month of August in the said year on a Friday at the half hour before sunrise, and took my way to the Canary Islands of your Highnesses, which are in the said Ocean-Sea, in order to set out on my voyage from there and sail until I arrived at the Indies, and make known the message of your Highnesses to those Princes, and fulfil the commands which had thus been given me: and for this purpose, I decided to write everything I might do and see and which might take place on this voyage, very punctually from day to day, as will be seen henceforth. Also, Lords and Princes, besides describing each night what takes place during the day, and during the day, the sailings of the night, I propose to make a new chart for navigation, on which I will locate all the sea and the lands of the Ocean-Sea, in their proper places, under their winds; and further, to compose a book and show everything by means of drawing, by the latitude from the equator and by longitude from the west, and above all, it is fitting that I forget sleep, and study the navigation diligently, in order to thus fulfil these duties, which will be a great labour.

LETTER

Sir:

As I know that you will have pleasure of the great victory which our Lord hath given me in my voyage, I write you this, by which you shall know that, in twenty days I passed over to the Indies with the fleet which the most illustrious King and Queen, our Lords, gave me:

where I found very many islands peopled with inhabitants beyond number. And, of them all, I have taken possession for their Highnesses, with proclamation and the royal standard displayed; and I was not gainsaid. On the first which I found, I put the name San Salvador, in commemoration of His high Majesty, who marvellously hath given all this: the Indians call it Guanahani. The second I named the Island of Santa Maria de Concepcion, the third Ferrandina, the fourth Isabella, the fifth La Isla Juana [Cuba]; and so for each one a new name. When I reached Juana, I followed its coast westwardly, and found it so large that I thought it might be the mainland province of Cathay. And as I did not thus find any towns and villages on the seacoast, save small hamlets with the people whereof I could not get speech, because they all fled away forthwith, I went on farther in the same direction, thinking I should not miss of great cities or towns. And at the end of many leagues, seeing that there was no change, and that the coast was bearing me northwards, whereunto my desire was contrary since the winter was already confronting us, I formed the purpose of making from thence to the South, and as the wind also blew against me, I determined not to wait for other weather and turned back as far as a port agreed upon; from which I sent two men into the country to learn if there were a king, or any great cities. They travelled for three days, and found interminable small villages and a numberless population, but nought of ruling authority; wherefore they returned. I understood sufficiently from other Indians whom I had already taken, that this land, in its continuousness, was an island; and so I followed its coast eastwardly for a hundred and seven leagues as far as where it terminated; from which headland I saw another island to the east, ten *or* eight leagues distant from this, to which I at once gave the name La Spañola. And I proceeded thither, and followed the northern coast, as with La Juana, eastwardly for a hundred and seventy-eight great leagues in a direct easterly course, as with La Juana. The which, and all the others, are very large to an excessive degree, and this extremely so. In it, there are many havens on the seacoast, incomparable with any others that I know in Christendom, and plenty of rivers so good and great that it is a marvel. The lands thereof are high, and in it are very many ranges of hills, and most lofty mountains incomparably beyond the Island of Centrefrei; all most beautiful in a thousand shapes, and all accessible, and full of trees of a thousand kinds, so lofty that they seem to reach the sky. And I am assured that they never lose their foliage; as may be imagined, since I saw them as green and as beautiful as they are in Spain during May. And some of them were in flower, some in fruit, some in another stage according to their kind. And the nightingale was singing, and other birds of a thousand sorts, in the month of November, round about the way that I was going. There are palm-trees of six or eight species, wondrous to see for their beautiful variety; but so are the other trees, and fruits, and plants therein. There are wonderful pinegroves, and very large plains of verdure, and there is honey, and many kinds of birds, and many various fruits.

In the earth there are many mines of metals; and there is a population of incalculable number. Spañola is a marvel; the mountains and hills, and plains and fields, and land, so beautiful and rich for planting and sowing, for breeding cattle of all sorts, for building of towns and villages. There could be no believing, without seeing, such harbours as are here, as well as the many and great rivers, and excellent waters, most of which contain gold. In the trees and fruits and plants, there are great differences from those of Juana. In this, there are may spiceries, and great mines of gold and other metals. The people of this island, and of all the others that I have found and seen or not seen, all go naked, men and women, just as their mothers bring them forth; although some women cover a single place with the leaf of a plant, or a cotton something which they make for that purpose. They have no iron or steel, nor any weapons; nor are they fit thereunto; not because they be not a well-formed people and of fair stature, but that they are most wondrously timorous. They have no other weapons than the stems of reeds in their seeding state, on the end of which they fix little sharpened stakes. Even these, they dare not use; for many times has it happened that I sent two or three men ashore to some village to parley, and countless numbers of them sallied forth, but as soon as they saw those approach, they fled away in such wise that even a father would not wait for his son. And this was not because any hurt had ever been done to any of them:—on the contrary, at every headland where I have gone and been able to hold speech with them, I gave them of everything which I had, as well cloth as many other things, without accepting aught therefor; but such they are, incurably timid. It is true that since they have become more assured, and are losing that terror, they are artless and generous with what they have, to such a degree as no one would believe but he who had seen it. Of anything they have, if it be asked for, they never say no, but do rather invite the person to accept it, and show as much lovingness as though they would give their hearts. And whether it be a thing of value, or one of little worth, they are straightways content with whatsoever trifle of whatsoever kind may be given them in return for it. I forbade that anything so worthless as fragments of broken platters, and pieces of broken glass, and strapbuckles, should be given them; although when they were able to get such things they seemed to think they had the best jewel in the world, for it was the hap of a sailor to get, in exchange for a strap, gold to the weight of two and a half castellanos, and others much more for other things of far less value; while for new blancas they gave every thing they had, even though it were the worth of two or three gold castellanos, or one or two arrobas of spun cotton. They took even pieces of broken barrel-hoops, and gave whatever they had, like senseless brutes; insomuch that it seemed to me ill. I forbade it, and I gave gratuitously a thousand useful things that I carried, in order that they may conceive affection, and furthermore may be made Christians; for they are inclined to the love and service of their Highnesses and of all the Castilian nation, and they strive to combine in giving us things which they have in abundance, and of which we are in need. And they know no sect, or idolatry; save that they all believe that power and goodness are in the sky, and they believed very firmly that I, with these ships and crew, came from the sky; and in such opinion, they received me at every place where I landed, after they had lost their terror. And this comes not because they are ignorant; on the contrary, they are men of very subtle wit, who navigate all those seas, and who give a marvellously good account of everything—but because they never saw men wearing clothes or the like of our ships. And as soon as I arrived in the Indies, in the first island that I found, I took some of them by force, to the intent that they should learn our speech and give me information of what there was in those parts. And so it was, that very soon they understood us and we them, what by speech or what by signs; and those Indians have been of much service. To this day I carry them with me who are still of the opinion that I come from heaven, as appears from much conversation which they have had with me. And they were the first to proclaim it wherever I arrived; and the others went running from house to house and to the neighbouring villages, with loud cries of "Come! come to see the people from heaven!" Then, as soon as their minds were reassured about us, every one came, men as well as women, so that there remained none behind, big or little; and they all brought something to eat and drink, which they gave with wondrous lovingness. They have in all the islands very many canoes, after the manner of rowing-galleys, some larger, some smaller; and a good many are larger than a galley of eighteen benches. They are not so wide, because they are made of a single log of timber, but a galley could not keep up with them in rowing, for their motion is a thing beyond belief. And with these, they navigate through all those islands which are numberless, and ply their traffic. I have seen some of those canoes with seventy and eighty men in them, each one with his oar. In all those islands, I saw not much diversity in the looks of the people, or in their manners and language; but they all understand each other, which is a thing of singular towardness for what I hope their Highnesses will determine, as to making them conversant with our holy faith, unto which they are well disposed. I have already told how I had gone a hundred and seven leagues, in a straight line from West to East, along the seacoast of the Island of Juana; according to which itinerary, I can declare that that island is larger than England and Scotland combined; as, over and above those hundred and seven leagues, there remains for me, on the western side, two provinces whereto I did not go—one of which they call Anan, where the people are born with tails—which provinces cannot be less in length than fifty or sixty leagues, according to what may be understood from the Indians with me, who know all the islands. This other, Española, has a greater circumference than the whole of Spain from Colibre in Catalunya, by the seacoast, as far as Fuente Ravia in Biscay; since, along one of its four sides, I went for a hundred and eight-eight great leagues in a straight line from West to East. This is a land to be desired,—and once seen, never to be relinquished—in which—although, indeed, I have taken possession of them all for their Highnesses, and all are more richly endowed than I have skill and power to say, and I hold them all in the name of their Highnesses who can dispose thereof as much and as completely as of the kingdoms of Castile—in this Española, in the place most suitable and best for its proximity to the gold mines, and for traffic with the continent, as well on this side as on the further side of the Great Can, where there will be great commerce and profit, I took possession of a large town which I named the city of Navidad. And I have made fortifications there, and a fort which by this time will have been completely finished and I have left therein men enough for such a purpose, with arms and artillery, and provisions for more than a year, and a boat, and a man who is master of all sea-craft for making others; and great friendship with the King of that land, to such a degree that he prided himself on calling and holding me as his brother. And even though his mind might change towards attacking those men, neither he nor his people know what arms are, and go naked. As I have already said, they are the most timorous creatures there are in the world, so that the men who remain there are alone sufficient to destroy all that land, and the island is without personal danger for them if they know how to behave themselves. It seems to me that in all those islands, the men are all content with a single wife; and to their chief or king they give as many as twenty. The women, it appears to me, do more work than the men.

Nor have I been able to learn whether they held personal property, for it seemed to me that whatever one had, they all took shares of, especially of eatable things. Down to the present, I have not found in those islands any monstrous men, as many expected, but on the contrary all the people are very comely; nor are they black like those in Guinea, but have flowing hair; and they are not begotten where there is an excessive violence of the rays of the sun. It is true that the sun is there very strong, notwithstanding that it is twenty-six degrees distant from the equinoctial line. In those islands, where there are lofty mountains, the cold was very keen there, this winter; but they endure it by being accustomed thereto, and by the help of the meats which they eat with many and inordinately hot spices. Thus I have not found, nor had any information of monsters, except of an island which is here the second in the approach to the Indies, which is inhabited by a people whom, in all the islands, they regard as very ferocious, who eat human flesh. These have many canoes with which they run through all the islands of India, and plunder and take as much as they can. They are no more ill-shapen than the others, but have the custom of wearing their hair long, like women; and they use bows and arrows of the same reed-stems, with a point of wood at the top, for lack of iron which they have not. Amongst those other tribes who are excessively cowardly, these are ferocious; but I hold them as nothing more than the others. These are they who have to do with the women of Matremonio—which is the first island that is encountered in the passage from Spain to the Indies— in which there are no men. Those women practise no female usages, but have bows and arrows of reeds such as above mentioned; and they arm and cover themselves with plates of copper of which they have much. In another island, which they assure me is larger than Española, the people have no hair. In this, there is incalculable gold; and concerning these and the rest I bring Indians with me as witnesses. And in conclusion, to speak only of what has been done in this voyage, which has been so hastily performed, their Highnesses may see that I shall give them as much gold as they may need, with very little aid which their Highnesses will give me; spices and cotton at once, as much as their Highnesses will order to be shipped, and as much as they shall order to be shipped of mastic,—which till now has never been found except in Greece, in the island of Xio, and the Seignory sells it for what it likes; and aloe-wood as much as they shall order to be shipped; and slaves as many as they shall order to be shipped—and these shall be from idolaters. And I believe that I have discovered rhubarb and cinnamon, and I shall find that the men whom I am leaving there will have discovered a thousand other things of value; as I made no delay at any point, so long as the wind gave me an opportunity of sailing, except only in the town of Navidad till I had left things safely arranged and well established. And in truth I should have done much more if the ships had served me as well as might reasonably have been expected. This is enough; and thanks to eternal God our Lord who gives to all those who walk His way, victory over things which seem impossible; and this was signally one such, for although men have talked or written of those lands, it was all by conjecture, without confirmation from eyesight, importing just so much that the hearers for the most part listened and judged that there was more fable in it than anything actual, however trifling. Since thus our Redeemer has given to our most illustrious King and Queen, and to their famous kingdoms, this victory in so high a matter, Christendom should take gladness therein and make great festivals, and give solemn thanks to the Holy Trinity for the great exaltation they shall have by the conversion of so many peoples to our Holy faith; and next for the temporal benefit which will bring hither refreshment and profit, not only to Spain, but to all Christians. This briefly, in accordance with the facts. Dated on the caravel, off the Canary Islands, the 15 February of the year 1493.

At your command,

The Admiral

Niccolò Machiavelli

A reading of *The Prince* by Machiavelli (1469–1527) makes it easy to understand the evil connotations that have come to surround the term "Machiavellian." Written as a handbook for political leaders, *The Prince* is most famous as the source of the doctrine that, in politics, the end always justifies the means. With Machiavelli, this doctrine was no theoretical assumption; it was a conclusion derived from acute observation and analysis of the political practices of the day. As a diplomat in the service of his native city of Florence, Machiavelli was able to observe the tactics of the men who were struggling for control of the Italian peninsula in the early sixteenth century. The most colorful of these power-hungry men was the notorious Caesar Borgia, son of Pope Alexander VI, whom Machiavelli met on numerous occasions during his diplomatic career. For Borgia, power clearly was an end in itself.

Although, in *The Prince*, Machiavelli praises Borgia and advocates the pursuit of power without regard to the methods employed, to be fair we must realize that Machiavelli himself was not an unqualified Machiavellian. In the final chapter of *The Prince*, he urges Lorenzo de' Medici to exert his princely power to unify Italy and drive out foreign oppressors, an end that Machiavelli valued more highly than the mere pursuit of power for its own sake. And in his *Discourses* he concludes that the best-governed state is a state ruled, not by a Machiavellian prince, but by the people themselves. Despite these qualifications, however, Machiavelli's reputation in history is that of the champion of power politics.

To capture something of the flavor and diversity of the Italian Renaissance, we have only to realize that Machiavelli and Pico della Mirandola were contemporaries living in the city of Florence. Yet, while Pico was writing on the dignity of man, Machiavelli was observing, "for it may be truly affirmed of mankind in general, that they are ungrateful, fickle, timid, dissembling, and self-interested. . . ."

The Prince

Niccolò Machiavelli, Citizen and Secretary of Florence, to the Most Magnificent Lorenzo de' Medici

Those who court the favour of princes generally present them with whatever they possess that is most rare, curious, or valuable; as horses, armour, embroidered cloths, precious stones, &c., according to the dignity of the personage they seek to propitiate. For my part, my anxiety to present myself to the notice of your highness, with the best proof of my devotion, has not enabled me to discover, amongst all I possess, anything that I esteem more, or account so valuable, as a knowledge of the actions of celebrated men; a knowledge acquired by a long experience of modern times, and a diligent perusal of the ancients. The observations which I have made with all the accuracy, reflection, and care of which I am capable, are contained in the small volume now addressed to you. And although I have not the vanity to deem it worthy of your acceptance, yet I am persuaded that your goodness will not refuse the offering, since it is impossible to present you with anything more valuable than a work which will place before you, in a small compass, all the experience I have acquired during many years of continual meditation and suffering in the school of adversity.

You will find in this fragment neither a glowing and lofty style, nor any of those meretricious ornaments with which authors seek to embellish their works. Its interest must depend upon the importance of the subject, the solidity of the reflections, and the truth of the facts recorded.

It will, perhaps, appear presumptuous in me, a man of humble birth, to propose rules of conduct to those who govern; but as the painter when about to sketch a mountainous country places himself in the plain, and in order to draw the scenery of a vale, ascends an eminence, even so, I conceive, that a person must be a prince to discover the nature and character of a people, and one of the people to judge properly of a prince.

I am therefore bold enough to hope that you will accept this feeble tribute in reference to the intention with which it is offered; and if you condescend to read it with attention, you will have evidence of my ardent desire to see you fill with glory those high destinies, to which fortune and your splendid talents have called you.

If from your elevated position you should condescend to look down on a person in my lowly station, you will see how long and how unworthily I have been persecuted by the extreme and unrelenting malevolence of fortune.

Niccolò Machiavelli

• • •

Niccolò Machiavelli, "The Prince," from *The History of Florence and the Affairs of Italy.*

CHAPTER XIV

Of the Duties of a Prince Relative to His Military Force

Princes ought ... to make the art of war their sole study and occupation, for it is peculiarly the science of those who govern. War, and the several sorts of discipline and institutions relative to it, should be his only study, the only profession he should follow, and the object he ought always to have in view. By this means princes can maintain possession of their dominions; and private individuals are sometimes raised thereby to supreme authority; whilst, on the other hand, we frequently see princes shamefully reduced to nothing, by suffering themselves to be enfeebled by slothful inactivity. I repeat, therefore, that by a neglect of this art it is that states are lost, and by cultivating it they are acquired.

Francis Sforza, from a private station, attained the rank of duke of Milan, by having an army always at his disposal; and by a deviation from this rule his children, who succeeded to the dukedom, were reduced to the station of private individuals. And this is not surprising: for, in the first place, nothing is so likely to impair our esteem for the character of a prince as to see him destitute of a military force; and, as I shall endeavour to prove hereafter, that a prince should most particularly beware of falling into general contempt.

We cannot establish a comparison between men who are armed, and those who are not so; and it would be equally absurd to suppose that the disarmed should command, and the others obey. A prince who is ignorant of the art of war can never enjoy repose or safety amongst armed subjects; he will always be to them an object of contempt, as they to him will justly be subjects of suspicion; how is it possible then that they should act in concert? In short, a prince who does not understand the art of war can never be esteemed by his troops, nor can he ever confide in them.

It is necessary therefore that princes should pay their whole attention to the art of war, which includes mental labour and study as well as the military exercise. To begin with the latter, the prince should take the utmost care that his troops be well disciplined and regularly exercised. The chase is well adapted to inure the body to fatigue, and to all the intemperances of weather. This exercise will also teach him to observe the sources and situations, as well as the nature of rivers and marshes; to measure the extent of plains, and the declivity of mountains. By these means he will acquire a knowledge of the topography of a country which he has to defend, and will easily habituate himself to select the places where war may be best carried on. For the plain and valleys of Tuscany resemble more or less those of other countries; so that a perfect knowledge of one will enable them to form a tolerably accurate judgment of the other.

This study is particularly useful to commanders. A general who neglects it will never know where to look for an enemy, nor how to conduct his troops, nor to encamp, nor the proper time to attack. The Greek and Roman historians deservedly praised Philopomenes, prince of Achaia, for his application to the study of war in time of peace. He was accustomed in his travels to stop and ask his friends, which of two armies would have the advantage, if one posted on such or such a hill, and the other in such a particular place? In what manner this, if commanded by himself, should join and give battle to the other? What steps he ought to take in order to secure a retreat, or pursue the enemy, in case he should retire? He thus proposed to them in every case which might happen in war, listened attentively to their opinion, and then gave his own, together with the reasons on which it was founded. By these means he was always prepared to meet unforeseen events.

As to that part of military science which is learned in the closet, a prince ought to read history, and to pay particular attention to the achievements of great generals, and the cause of their victories and defeats; but above all he should follow the example of those great men who, when they select a model, resolve to follow in his steps. It was thus that Alexander the Great immortalized himself by following the example of Achilles, Caesar by imitating Alexander, and Scipio by copying Cyrus. If we take the trouble to compare the life of the latter Roman with that of Cyrus, we shall see how nearly Scipio copied the modesty, affability, humanity, liberality, and the other virtues with which Xenophon adorns his hero.

It is thus a wise prince should conduct himself, and so employ his time during peace, that if fortune should change, he may be prepared equally for her frowns or her favours.

CHAPTER XV

What Deserves Praise or Blame in Men, and Above All in Princes

It now remains to show in what manner a prince should behave to his subjects and friends. This matter having been already discussed by others, it may seem arrogant in me to pursue it farther, especially if I should differ in opinion from them; but as I write only for those who possess sound judgment, I thought it better to treat this subject as it really is, in fact, than to amuse the imagination with visionary models of republics and governments which have never existed. For the manner in which men now live is so different from the manner in which they ought to live, that he who deviates from the common course of practice, and endeavours to act as duty dictates, necessarily ensures his own destruction. Thus, a good man, and one who wishes to prove himself so in all respects, must be undone in a contest with so many who are evilly disposed. A prince who wishes to maintain his power ought therefore to learn that he should not be always good, and must use that knowledge as circumstances and the exigencies of his own affairs may seem to require.

Laying aside, then, the false ideas which have been formed as to princes, and adhering only to those which are true, I say, that all men, and especially princes, are marked and distinguished by some quality or other which entails either reputation or dishonour. For instance, men are liberal or parsimonious, honourable or dishonourable, effeminate or pusillanimous, courageous or enterprising, humane or cruel, affable or haughty, wise or debauched, honest or dishonest, good tempered or surly, sedate or inconsiderate, religious or impious, and so forth.

It would, doubtless, be happy for a prince to unite in himself every species of good quality; but as our nature does not allow so great a perfection, a prince should have prudence enough to avoid those defects and vices which may occasion his ruin; and as to those which can only compromise his safety and the possession of his dominions, he ought, if possible, to guard against them; but if he cannot succeed in this, he need not embarrass himself in escaping the scandal of those vices, but should devote his whole energies to avoid those which may cause his ruin. He should not shrink from encountering some blame on account of vices which are important to the support of his states; for everything well considered, there are some things having the appearance of virtues, which would prove the ruin of a prince, should he put them in practice, and others, upon which, though seemingly bad and vicious, his actual welfare and security entirely depend.

CHAPTER XVI

Of Liberality and Economy

To begin with the first qualities of the above-mentioned, I must observe that it is for the interest of a prince to be accounted liberal, but dangerous so to exercise his liberality, that he is thereby neither feared nor respected. I will explain myself. If a prince be only liberal,

as far as it suits his purposes, that is to say, within certain bounds, he will please but few, and will be called selfish. A prince who wishes to gain the reputation of being liberal, should be regardless of expense; but then to support this reputation, he will often be reduced to the necessity of levying taxes on his subjects, and adopting every species of fiscal resource which cannot fail to make him odious. Besides exhausting the public treasure by his prodigality, his credit will be destroyed, and he will run the risk of losing his dominions on the first reverse of fortune, his liberality, as it always happens, having ensured him more enemies than friends. And which is worse, he cannot retrace his steps and replenish his finances, without being charged with avarice.

A prince, therefore, who cannot be liberal without prejudicing his state, should not trouble himself much about the imputation of being covetous; for he will be esteemed liberal in time, when people see that by parsimony he has improved his revenue, become able to defend his dominions, and even to undertake useful enterprises without the aid of new taxes; then the many from whom he takes nothing will deem him sufficiently liberal, and the few only, whose expectations he has failed to realize, will accuse him of avarice. In our own times we have seen no great exploits performed, except by those who have been accounted avaricious; all the others have failed. Julius II attained the pontifical chair by means of his bounty; but he judged rightly in supposing, that in order to enable him to prosecute the war against France, it would do him injury to preserve his reputation for liberality. By his parsimony he was able to support the expense of all his wars without the imposition of new taxes. The present king of Spain could never have accomplished all his great enterprises, if he had felt any ambition to be thought liberal.

A prince, then, who would avoid poverty, and always be in a condition to defend his dominions without imposing new taxes on his subjects, should care little for being charged with avarice, since the imputed vice may be the very means of incurring the prosperity and stability of his government.

It may however be alleged that Caesar would never have attained the empire but by his liberality, and that many others have arrived at the highest honours by the same means. I answer, you are either in possession of dominion already, or you are not. In the first place, liberality would be prejudicial; in the second, the reputation of it is serviceable and necessary. Caesar endeavoured to appear liberal whilst he aspired to the empire of Rome. But if he had lived longer, he would have lost that reputation for liberality which had paved him the way to empire, or he would have lost himself in the attempt to preserve it.

There have been, however, some princes who have performed splendid actions, and who have distinguished themselves by their liberality; but then their prodigality did not come from the public purse. Such were Cyrus, Alexander, and Caesar. A prince ought to be very sparing of his own and his subjects' property; but he should be equally lavish of that which he takes from the enemy, if he desires to be popular with his troops; for that will not diminish his reputation, but

rather add to it. He who is too liberal cannot long continue so; he will become poor and contemptible unless he grinds his subjects with new taxes—which cannot fail to render him odious to them. Now there is nothing a prince ought to dread so much as his subjects' hatred; unless, indeed, it be their contempt. And both these evils may be occasioned by over liberality. If he must choose between extremes, it is better to submit to the imputation of parsimony than to make a show of liberality; since the first, though it may not be productive of honour, never gives birth to hatred and contempt.

CHAPTER XVII

On Cruelty and Clemency, and Whether It Is Better to Be Loved Than Feared

To proceed to other qualities which are requisite in those who govern. A prince ought unquestionably to be merciful, but should take care how he executes his clemency. Caesar Borgia was accounted cruel; but it was to that cruelty that he was indebted for the advantage of uniting Romagna to his other dominions, and of establishing in that province peace and tranquillity, of which it had been so long deprived. And, every thing well considered, it must be allowed that this prince showed greater clemency than the people of Florence, who, to avoid the reproach of cruelty, suffered Pistoia to be destroyed. When it is necessary for a prince to restrain his subjects within the bounds of duty, he should not regard the imputation of cruelty, because by making a few examples, he will find that he really showed more humanity in the end, than he, who by too great indulgence, suffers disorders to arise, which commonly terminate in rapine and murder. For such disorders disturb a whole community, whilst punishments inflicted by the prince affect only a few individuals.

This is particularly true with respect to a new prince, who can scarcely avoid the reproach of cruelty, every new government being replete with dangers. Thus Virgil makes Dido excuse her severity, by the necessity to which she was reduced of maintaining the interests of a throne which she did not inherit from her ancestors:—

Res dura et regni novitas me talia cogunt
Moliri, et late fines custode tueri.

A prince, however, should not be afraid of phantoms of his own raising; neither should he lend too ready an ear to terrifying tales which may be told him, but should temper his mercy with prudence, in such a manner, that too much confidence may not put him off his guard, nor causeless jealousies make him insupportable. There is a medium between a foolish security and an unreasonable distrust.

It has been sometimes asked, whether it is better to be loved than feared; to which I answer, that one should wish to be both. But as that is a hard matter to accomplish, I think, if it is necessary to make a selection, that it is safer to be feared than be loved. For it may be truly affirmed of mankind in general, that they are ungrateful, fickle, timid, dissembling, and self-interested; so long as you can serve them, they are entirely devoted to you; their wealth, their blood, their lives, and even their offspring are at your disposal, when you have no occasion for them; but in the day of need, they turn their back upon you. The prince who relies on professions, courts his own destruction, because the friends whom he acquires by means of money alone, and whose attachment does not spring from a regard for personal merit, are seldom proof against reverse of fortune, but abandon their benefactor when he most requires their services. Men are generally more inclined to submit to him who makes himself dreaded, than to one who merely strives to be beloved; and the reason is obvious, for friendship of this kind, being a mere moral tie, a species of duty resulting from a benefit, cannot endure against the calculations of interest: whereas fear carries with it the dread of punishment, which never loses its influence. A prince, however, ought to make himself feared, in such a manner, that if he cannot gain the love, he may at least avoid the hatred, of his subjects; and he may attain this object by respecting his subjects' property and the honour of their wives. If he finds it absolutely necessary to inflict the punishment of death, he should avow the reason for it, and above all things, he should abstain from touching the property of the condemned party. For certain it is that men sooner forget the death of their relations than the loss of their patrimony. Besides, when he once begins to live by means of rapine, many occasions offer for seizing the wealth of his subjects; but there will be little or no necessity for shedding blood.

But when a prince is at the head of his army, and has under his command a multitude of soldiers, he should make little account of being esteemed cruel; such a character will be useful to him, by keeping his troops in obedience, and preventing every species of faction.

Hannibal, among many other admirable talents, possessed in a high degree that of making himself feared by his troops; insomuch, that having led a very large army, composed of all kinds of people, into a foreign country, he never had occasion, either in prosperity or adversity, to punish the least disorder or the slightest want of discipline: and this can only be attributed to his extreme severity, and such other qualities as caused him to be feared and respected by his soldiers, and without which his extraordinary talents and courage would have been unavailing.

There have been writers notwithstanding, but, in my opinion, very injudicious ones who, whilst they render every degree of justice to his talents and his splendid achievements, still condemn the principle on which he acted. But nothing can in this respect more fully justify him than the example of Scipio, one of the greatest generals mentioned in history. His extreme indulgence towards the troops he commanded in Spain occasioned disorders, and at length a revolt, which drew on him from Fabius Maximus, in full senate, the reproach of having destroyed the Roman soldiery. This general having suffered the barbarous conduct of one of his lieutenants toward the Locrians to go unpunished, a senator, in his justification, observed that there were some men who knew better how to avoid doing ill themselves than to punish it in others. This excess of indulgence would in time

have tarnished the glory and reputation of Scipio, if he had been a prince; but as he lived under a republican government, it was not only connived at, but redounded to his glory.

I conclude, then, with regard to the question, whether it is better to be loved than feared,—that it depends on the inclinations of the subjects themselves, whether they will love their prince or not; but the prince has it in his own power to make them fear him, and if he is wise, he will rather rely on his own resources than on the caprice of others, remembering that he should at the same time so conduct himself as to avoid being hated.

CHAPTER XVIII

Whether Princes Ought to Be Faithful to Their Engagements

It is unquestionably very praiseworthy in princes to be faithful to their engagements; but among those of the present day, who have been distinguished for great exploits, few indeed have been remarkable for this virtue, or have scrupled to deceive others who may have relied on their good faith.

It should therefore be known, that there are two ways of deciding any contest: the one by laws, the other by force. The first is peculiar to men, the second to beasts; but when laws are not sufficiently powerful, it is necessary to recur to force: a prince ought therefore to understand how to use both these descriptions of arms. This doctrine is admirably illustrated to us by the ancient poets in the allegorical history of the education of Achilles, and many other princes of antiquity, by the centaur Chiron, who, under the double form of man and beast, taught those who were destined to govern, that it was their duty to use by turns the arms adapted to both these natures, seeing that one without the other cannot be of any durable advantage. Now, as a prince must learn how to act the part of a beast sometimes, he should make the fox and the lion his patterns. The first can but feebly defend himself against the wolf, and the latter readily falls into such snares as are laid for him. From the fox, therefore, a prince will learn dexterity in avoiding snares; and from the lion, how to employ his strength to keep the wolves in awe. But they who entirely rely upon the lion's strength, will not always meet with success: in other words, a prudent prince cannot and ought not to keep his word, except when he can do it without injury to himself, or when the circumstances under which he contracted the engagement still exist.

I should be cautious in inculcating such a precept if all men were good; but as the generality of mankind are wicked, and ever ready to break their words, a prince should not pique himself in keeping his more scrupulously, especially as it is always easy to justify a breach of faith on his part. I could give numerous proofs of this, and show numberless engagements and treaties which have been violated by the treachery of princes, and that those who enacted the part of the fox, have always succeeded best in their affairs. It is necessary, however, to disguise the appearance of craft, and thoroughly to understand the art of feigning and dissembling; for men are generally so simple and so weak, that he who wishes to deceive easily finds dupes.

One example, taken from the history of our own times, will be sufficient. Pope Alexander VI played during his whole life a game of deception; and notwithstanding his faithless conduct was extremely well known, his artifices always proved successful. Oaths and protestations cost him nothing; never did a prince so often break his word or pay less regard to his engagements. This was because he so well understood this chapter in the art of government.

It is not necessary, however, for a prince to possess all the good qualities I have enumerated, but it is indispensable that he should appear to have them. I will even venture to affirm, that it is sometimes dangerous to use, though it is always useful to seem to possess them. A prince should earnestly endeavour to gain the reputation of kindness, clemency, piety, justice, and fidelity to his engagements. He ought to possess all these good qualities, but still retain such power over himself as to display their opposites whenever it may be expedient. I maintain, that a prince, and especially a new prince, cannot with impunity exercise all the virtues, because his own self-preservation will often compel him to violate the laws of charity, religion, and humanity. He should habituate himself to bend easily to the various circumstances which may from time to time surround him. In a word, it will be as useful to him to persevere in the path of rectitude, while he feels no inconvenience in doing so, as to know how to deviate from it when circumstances dictate such a course. He should make it a rule above all things, never to utter anything which does not breathe of kindness, justice, good faith, and piety: this last quality it is most important for him to appear to possess, as men in general judge more from appearances than from reality. All men have eyes, but few have the gift of penetration. Every one sees your exterior, but few can discern what you have in your heart; and those few dare not oppose the voice of the multitude, who have the majesty of their prince on their side. Now, in forming a judgment of the minds of men, and more especially of princes, as we cannot recur to any tribunal, we must attend only to results. Let it then be the prince's chief care to maintain his authority; the means he employs, be what they may, will, for this purpose, always appear honourable and meet applause; for the vulgar are ever caught by appearances, and judge only by the event. And as the world is chiefly composed of such as are called the vulgar, the voice of the few is seldom or never heard or regarded.

There is a prince now alive (whose name it may not be proper to mention) who ever preaches the doctrines of peace and good faith; but if he had observed either the one or the other, he would long ago have lost both his reputation and dominions [*Ferdinand of Spain*— Ed.].

•   •   •

CHAPTER XXV

How Far Fortune Influences the Things of This World, and How Far She May Be Resisted

I know that several have thought, and many still are of opinion, that all sublunary events are governed either by Divine Providence or by chance, in such a manner that human wisdom has no share in their direction; and hence they infer that man should abstain from interfering with their course, and leave everything to its natural tendency.

The revolutions which in our times are of such frequent recurrence, seem to support this doctrine, and I own, that I, myself, am almost inclined to favour such opinions, particularly when I consider how far those events surpass all human conjecture; yet, as we confessedly possess a free will, it must, I think, be allowed, that chance does not so far govern the world as to leave no province for the exercise of human prudence.

For my own part, I cannot help comparing the blind power of chance to a rapid river, which, having overflowed its banks, inundates the plains, uproots trees, carries away houses and lands, and sweeps all before it in its destructive progress; everybody flies possessing neither resolution nor power to oppose its fury. But this should not discourage us, when the river has returned within its natural limits, from constructing dykes and banks to prevent a recurrence of similar disasters. It is the same with fortune; she exercises her power when we oppose no barrier to her progress.

If we cast our eyes on Italy, which has been the theatre of these revolutions, and consider the causes by which they have been provoked, we shall find it to be a defenceless country. If she had been properly fortified like Germany, Spain, or France, such inundations of foreigners would never have happened, or at least their irruptions would have been attended with less devastation.

Let this suffice in general concerning the necessity of opposing fortune. But to descend to particulars. It is no uncommon thing to see a prince fall from prosperity to adversity, without our being able to attribute his fate to any change in conduct or character; for, as I have already shown at large, he who relies solely on fortune must be ruined inevitably whenever she abandons him.

Those princes who adapt their conduct to circumstances are rarely unfortunate. Fortune is only changeable to those who cannot conform themselves to the varying exigencies of the times; for we see different men take different courses to obtain the end they have in view; for instance, in pursuit of riches or glory, one prosecutes his object at random, the other with caution and prudence: one employs art, the other force; one is impetuosity itself, the other all patience; means by which each may severally succeed. It also happens that of two who follow the same route, one may arrive at his destination, and the other fail; and that if two other persons, whose dispositions are diametrically opposite, pursue the same object by wholly different means, yet both shall equally prosper; which is entirely owing to the temper of the times, which always prove favourable or adverse, according as men conform to them.

Circumstances also frequently decide whether a prince conducts himself well or ill on any particular occasion. There are times when an extraordinary degree of prudence is necessary; there are others when the prince should know how to trust some things to chance; but there is nothing more difficult than suddenly to change his conduct and character; sometimes from inability to resist his old habits and inclinations, at others, from want of resolution to quit a course in which he had always been successful.

Julius II, who was of a fiery and violent disposition, succeeded in all his enterprises; doubtless, because a prince of such a character was best adapted to the circumstances under which the church was then governed by this pontiff. Witness his first invasion of the territory of Bologna, in the life of John Bentivoglio, which gave great umbrage to the Venetians and the kings of France and Spain, but none of them dared to interfere. The first, because they did not feel themselves strong enough to cope with a pontiff of his character; Spain, because she was engaged in the conquest of Naples: and France, besides having an interest in keeping fair with Julius, wished still to humble the Venetians; so that she, without hesitation, granted the pope all the assistance he required.

Julius II, therefore, by a precipitate mode of proceeding, succeeded in an enterprise which could not have been accomplished by cool and deliberate measures. He would unquestionaly have failed had he given Spain and the Venetians time to reflect on his designs, and if he had allowed France the opportunity of amusing him by excuses and delays.

Julius II displayed in all his enterprises the same character of violence; and his successes have in that respect fully justified him; but he did not perhaps live long enough to experience the inconstancy of fortune; for had an occasion unexpectedly occurred in which it would have been necessary to act with prudence and circumspection, he would infallibly have been ruined, in consequence of that impetuosity and inflexibility of character which wholly governed him.

From all these circumstances we may conclude, that those who cannot change their system when occasion requires it, will no doubt continue prosperous as long as they glide with the stream of fortune; but when that turns against them, they are ruined, from not being able to follow that blind goddess through all her variations.

Besides, I think that it is better to be bold than too circumspect; because fortune is of a sex that likes not a tardy wooer, and repulses all who are not ardent, she declares also, more frequently, in favour of those who are young, because they are bold and enterprising.

CHAPTER XXVI

Exhortation to Deliver Italy from Foreign Powers

When I take a review of the subject matter treated of in this book, and examine whether the circumstances in which we are now placed would be favourable to the establishment of a new government, honourable alike to its founder and advantageous to Italy, it appears to me that there never was, nor ever will be, a period more appropriate for the execution of so glorious an undertaking.

If it was necessary that the people of Israel should be slaves to Egypt, in order to elicit the rare talents of Moses; that the Persians should groan under the oppression of the Medes, in order to prove the cour-age and magnanimity of Cyrus; and that the Athenians should be scattered and dispersed, in order to make manifest the rare virtues of Theseus, it will be likewise necessary, for the glory of some Italian hero, that his country should be reduced to its present miserable condition, that they should be greater slaves than the Israelites, more oppressed than the Persians, and still more dispersed than the Athenians; in a word, that they should be without laws and without chiefs, pillaged, torn to pieces, and enslaved by foreign powers.

And though it has sometimes unquestionably happened that men have risen, who appeared to be sent by Heaven to achieve our deliverance; yet jealous fortune has ever abandoned them in the midst of their career; so that our unfortunate country still groans and pines away in the expectation of a deliverer, who may put an end to the devastations in Lombardy, Tuscany, and the kingdom of Naples. She supplicates Heaven to raise up a prince who may free her from the odious and humiliating yoke of foreigners, who may close the numberless wounds with which she has been so long afflicted, and under whose standard she may march against her cruel oppressors.

But on whom can Italy cast her eyes except upon your illustrious house, which, visibly favoured by Heaven and the church, the government of which is confided to its care, possesses also the wisdom and the power necessary to undertake so glorious an enterprise? and I cannot think that the execution of this project will seem difficult if you reflect on the actions and conduct of the heroes whose examples I have above adduced. Though their exploits were indeed wonderful, they were still but men; and although their merit raised them above others, yet none of them certainly were placed in a situation so favourable as that in which you now stand. You have justice on your side; their cause was not more lawful than yours, and the blessing of God will attend you no less than them. Every war that is necessary is just; and it is humanity to take up arms for the defence of a people to whom no other resource is left.

All circumstances concur to facilitate the execution of so noble a project, for the accomplishment of which it will only be necessary to tread in the steps of those great men whom I have had an opportunity of mentioning in the course of this work. For though some of them, it is true, were conducted by the hand of God in a wonderful manner, though the sea divided to let them pass, a cloud directed their course, a rock streamed with water to assuage their thirst, the manna fell from heaven to appease their hunger, yet there is no occasion for such miracles at present, as you possess in yourself sufficient power to execute a plan you ought by no means to neglect. God will not do everything for us; much is left to ourselves, and the free exercise of our will, that so our own actions may not be wholly destitute of merit.

If none of our princes have hitherto been able to effect what is now expected from your illustrious house, and if Italy has continually been unfortunate in her wars, the evil has arisen from the defects in military discipline, which no person has possessed the ability to reform. Nothing reflects so much honour on a new prince as the new laws and institutions established under his direction, especially when they are good, and bear the character of grandeur. Now it must be acknowledged that Italy soon accommodates herself to new forms. Her inhabitants are by no means deficient in courage, but they are destitute of proper chiefs; the proof of this is in the duels and other individual combats in which the Italians have always evinced consummate ability, whilst their valour in battles has appeared well-nigh extinguished. This can only be attributed to the weakness of the officers, who are unable to ensure obedience from those who know, or think they know, the art of war. Thus we have seen the greatest generals of the present day, whose orders were never executed with exactness and celerity. These are the reasons why, in the wars in which we have been for the last twenty years engaged, the armies raised in Italy have been almost always beaten. Witness Tarus, Alexandria, Capua, Genoa, Vaila, Bologna, and Mestri.

If therefore your illustrious house is willing to regulate its conduct by the example of our ancestors, who have delivered their country from the rule of foreigners, it is necessary, above all things, as the only true foundation of every enterprise, to set on foot a national army; you cannot have better or more faithful soldiers, and though every one of them may be a good man, yet they will become still better when they are all united, and see themselves honoured, caressed, and rewarded by a prince of their own.

It is therefore absolutely necessary to have troops raised in our own country, if we wish to protect it from the invasion of foreign powers. The Swiss as well as the Spanish infantry are highly esteemed, but both have defects which may be avoided in the formation of our troops, which would render them superior to both of those powers. The Spaniards cannot support the shock of cavalry, and the Swiss cannot maintain their ground against infantry that is equally resolute with themselves.

Experience has fully shown that the Spanish battalions cannot resist the French cavalry, and that the Swiss have been beaten by the infantry of Spain. And though there has not been any thorough trial with regard to the Swiss on this point, yet there was a sort of specimen at the battle of Ravenna, where the Spanish infantry came in contact with the German troops, who fought in the same order as the Swiss. Upon that occasion, the Spaniards, having with their accustomed vivacity, and under the protection of their bucklers, thrown themselves across the pikes of the Germans, the latter were obliged to give way, and would have been entirely defeated, if their cavalry had not come to their relief.

It is necessary therefore to institute a military force possessing neither the defects of the Swiss nor the Spanish infantry, and that may be able to maintain its ground against the French cavalry, and this is to be effected, not by changing their arms, but by altering their discipline. Nothing is more likely to make a new prince esteemed, and to render his reign illustrious.

Such an opportunity ought eagerly to be embraced, that Italy, after her long sufferings, may at last behold her deliverer appear. With what demonstrations of joy and gratitude, with what affection, with what impatience for revenge, would he not be received by those unfortunate provinces, who have so long groaned under such odious oppression. What city would shut her gates against him, and what people would be so blind as to refuse him obedience? What rivals would he have to dread? Is there one Italian who would not hasten to pay him homage? All are weary of the tyranny of these barbarians. May your illustrious house, strong in all the hopes which justice gives our cause, deign to undertake this noble enterprise, that so, under your banners, our nation may resume its ancient splendour, and, under your auspices, behold the prophecy of Petrarch at last fulfilled.

When virtue takes the field,
  Short will the conflict be,
Barbarian rage shall yield
  The palm to Italy:
For patriot blood still warms Italian veins,
Though low the fire, a spark at least remains.

Benvenuto Cellini

The term "Renaissance man" has come to suggest one who has an almost universal genius, an ability to do all things well. It also implies a confidence in the human potential, a conviction that someone with reason and taste can do anything if he merely applies his human resources to the task at hand. Leonardo da Vinci once wrote a letter to Lodovico Sforza, who afterward became the Duke of Milan, applying for a job. In cataloging his abilities, Leonardo exudes self-confidence. He claims that he can ". . . construct very light bridges, easy to transport from one place to another . . . [in case of siege] remove the water from the ditches, and make an infinite variety of scaling-ladders . . . [make] a kind of cannon that is easy and convenient to carry, and that will throw out inflammable matters, causing great affright and damage to the enemy . . . make cannon, mortars, and field pieces of beautiful and useful shape, and different from those in common use . . . equal all others in architecture, in designing both public and private edifices, and in conducting water from one place to another . . . undertake in sculpture works in marble, bronze, or terra-cotta; likewise in painting can do what can be done equal to any other, whoever he may be. . . ." The letter closes with this assurance: "And if any of the above-mentioned things seem to any impossible and impracticable, I offer to make trial of them in your park, or in any other place that may please your Excellency, to whom I commend myself with all possible humility." And the remarkable thing is that Leonardo could actually do what he said he could.

Another Renaissance figure with the same kind of brash assurance was Benvenuto Cellini (1500–1571), who, though a lesser artist than Leonardo, was his equal in confidence and probably his superior in the ability to live life to its fullest. Actually, Cellini was a semi-frustrated sculptor who is best known for his work as a goldsmith. Although little of his work has survived, Cellini's great masterpiece, the gold salt-cellar made for Francis I of France, is preserved at the Kunsthistorisches Museum in Vienna.

Cellini's *Autobiography*, from which the following selections are taken, was written between 1558 and 1562, but was not published until the early eighteenth century. It enjoyed enormous popularity as a highly revealing personal document and as an intimate portrait of the sixteenth century—nor has it lost its fascination for modern readers.

The Life of Benvenuto Cellini

BOOK FIRST

I

All men of whatsoever quality they be, who have done anything of excellence, or which may properly resemble excellence, ought, if they are persons of truth and honesty, to describe their life with their own hand; but they ought not to attempt so fine an enterprise till they have passed the age of forty. This duty occurs to my own mind, now that I am travelling beyond the term of fifty-eight years, and am in Florence, the city of my birth. Many untoward things can I remember, such as happen to all who live upon our earth; and from those adversities I am now more free than at any previous period of my career—nay, it seems to me that I enjoy greater content of soul and health of body than ever I did in by-gone years. I can also bring to mind some pleasant goods and some inestimable evils, which, when I turn my thoughts backward, strike terror in me, and astonishment that I should have reached this age of fifty-eight, wherein, thanks be to God, I am still traveling prosperously forward.

II

It is true that men who have laboured with some show of excellence, have already given knowledge of themselves to the world; and this alone ought to suffice them; I mean the fact that they have proved their manhood and achieved renown. Yet one must needs live like others; and so in a work like this there will always be found occasion for natural bragging, which is of divers kinds, and the first is that a man should let others know he draws his lineage from persons of worth and most ancient origin.

I am called Benvenuto Cellini, son of Maestro Giovanni, son of Andrea, son of Cristofano Cellini; my mother was Madonna Elisabetta, daughter to Stefano Granacci; both parents citizens of Florence. It is found written in chronicles made by our ancestors of Florence, men of old time and of credibility, even as Giovanni Villani writes, that the city of Florence was evidently built in imitation of the fair city of Rome; and certain remnants of the Colosseum and the Baths can yet be traced. These things are near Santa Croce. The capital was where is now the Old Market. The Rotonda is entire, which was made for the temple of Mars, and is now dedicated to our Saint John. That thus it was, can very well be seen, and cannot be denied; but the said buildings are much smaller than those of Rome. He who caused them to be built, they say, was Julius Caesar, in concert with some noble Romans, who, when Fiesole had been stormed and taken, raised a city in this place, and each of them took in hand to erect one of these notable edifices.

• • •

The Life of Benvenuto Cellini, 4th ed. [autobiography], trans. J. A. Symonds.

Thus then we find; and thus we believe that we are descended from a man of worth. Furthermore, we find that there are Cellinis of our stock in Ravenna, that most ancient town of Italy, where too are plenty of gentle folk. In Pisa also there are some, and I have discovered them in many parts of Christendom; and in this state also the breed exists, men devoted to the profession of arms; for not many years ago a young man, called Luca Cellini, a beardless youth, fought with a soldier of experience and a most valorous man, named Francesco da Vicorati, who had frequently fought before in single combat. This Luca, by his own valour, with sword in hand, overcame and slew him, with such bravery and stoutness that he moved the folk to wonder, who were expecting quite the contrary issue; so that I glory in tracing my descent from men of valour.

As for the trifling honours which I have gained for my house, under the well-known conditions of our present ways of living, and by means of my art, albeit the same are matters of no great moment, I will relate these in their proper time and place, taking much more pride in having been born humble and having laid some honourable foundation for my family, than if I had been born of great lineage and had stained or so overclouded that by my base qualities. So then I will make a beginning by saying how it pleased God I should be born.

• • •

When I reached the age of fifteen, I put myself, against my father's will, to the goldsmith's trade with a man called Antonio, son of Sandro, known commonly as Marcone the goldsmith. He was a most excellent craftsman and a very good fellow to boot, high-spirited and frank in all his ways. My father would not let him give me wages like the other apprentices; for having taken up the study of this art to please myself, he wished me to indulge by whim for drawing to the full. I did so willingly enough; and that honest master of mine took marvellous delight in my performances. He had an only son, a bastard, to whom he often gave his orders, in order to spare me. My liking for the art was so great, or, I may truly say, my natural bias, both one and the other, that in a few months I caught up the good, nay, the best young craftsmen in our business, and began to reap the fruits of my labours. I did not, however, neglect to gratify my good father from time to time by playing on the flute or cornet. Each time he heard me, I used to make his tears fall accompanied with deep-drawn sighs of satisfaction. My filial piety often made me give him that contentment, and induced me to pretend that I enjoyed the music too.

• • •

XII

When I had recovered my health, I returned to my old friend Marcone, the worthy goldsmith, who put me in the way of earning money, with which I helped my father and our household. About that time there came to Florence a sculptor named Piero Torrigiani; he arrived from England, where he had resided many years; and being intimate with my master, he daily visited his house; and when he saw my drawings and the things which I was making, he said: "I have come to Florence to enlist as many young men as I can; for I have undertaken to execute a great work for my king, and want some of my own Florentines to help me. Now your method of working and your designs are worthy rather of a sculptor than a goldsmith; and since I have to turn out a great piece of bronze, I will at the same time turn you into a rich and able artist." This man had a splendid person and a most arrogant spirit, with the air of a great soldier more than of a sculptor, especially in regard to his vehement gestures and his resonant voice, together with a habit he had of knitting his brows, enough to frighten any man of courage. He kept talking every day about his gallant feats among these beasts of Englishmen.

In course of conversation he happened to mention Michel Agnolo Buonarroti, led thereto by a drawing I had made from a cartoon of the divinest painter. This cartoon was the first masterpiece which Michel Agnolo exhibited, in proof of his stupendous talents. He produced it in competition with another painter, Lionardo da Vinci, who also made a cartoon; and both were intended for the council-hall in the palace of the Signory. They represented the taking of Pisa by the Florentines; and our admirable Lionardo had chosen to depict a battle of horses, with the capture of some standards, in as divine a style as could possibly be imagined. Michel Agnolo in his cartoon portrayed a number of foot-soldiers, who, the season being summer, had gone to bathe in Arno. He drew

them at the very moment the alarm is sounded, and the men all naked run to arms; so splendid in their action that nothing survives of ancient or of modern art which touches the same lofty point of excellence; and as I have already said, the design of the great Lionardo was itself most admirably beautiful. These two cartoons stood, one in the palace of the Medici, the other in the hall of the Pope. So long as they remained intact, they were the school of the world. Though the divine Michel Agnolo in later life finished that great chapel of Pope Julius, he never rose half-way to the same pitch of power; his genius never afterwards attained to the force of those first studies.

XIII

Now let us return to Piero Torrigiani, who, with my drawing in his hand, spoke as follows: "This Buonarroti and I used, when we were boys, to go into the Church of the Carmine, to learn drawing from the chapel of Masaccio. It was Buonarroti's habit to banter all who were drawing there; and one day, among others, when he was annoying me, I got more angry than usual, and clenching my fist, gave him such a blow on the nose, that I felt bone and cartilage go down like biscuit beneath my knuckles; and this mark of mine he will carry with him to the grave." These words begat in me such hatred of the man, since I was always gazing at the masterpieces of the divine Michel Agnolo, that although I felt a wish to go with him to England, I now could never bear the sight of him.

All the while I was in Florence, I

studied the noble manner of Michel Agnolo, and from this I have never deviated. About that time I contracted a close and familiar friendship with an amiable lad of my own age, who was also in the goldsmith's trade. He was called Francesco, son of Filippo, and grandson of Fra Lippo Lippi, that most excellent painter. Through intercourse together, such love grew up between us that, day or night, we never stayed apart. The house where he lived was still full of the fine studies which his father had made, bound up in several books of drawings by his hand, and taken from the best antiquities of Rome. The sight of these things filled me with passionate enthusiasm; and for two years or thereabouts we lived in intimacy. At that time I fashioned a silver bas-relief of the size of a little child's hand. It was intended for the clasp to a man's belt; for they were then worn as large as that. I carved on it a knot of leaves in the antique style, with figures of children and other masks of great beauty. This piece I made in the workshop of one Francesco Salimbene; and on its being exhibited to the trade, the goldsmiths praised me as the best young craftsman of their art.

There was one Giovan Battista, surnamed Il Tasso, a woodcarver, precisely of my own age, who one day said to me that if I was willing to go to Rome, he should be glad to join me. Now we had this conversation together immediately after dinner; and I being angry with my father for the same old reason of the music, said to Tasso: "You are a fellow of words, not deeds." He answered: "I too have come to anger with my mother; and if I had cash enough to take me to Rome, I would not turn back to lock the door of that wretched little workshop I call mine." To these words I replied that if that was all that kept him in Florence I had money enough in my pockets to bring us both to Rome. Talking thus and walking onwards, we found ourselves at the gate San Piero Gattolini without noticing that we had got there; whereupon I said: "Friend Tasso, this is God's doing that we have reached this gate without either you or me noticing that we were there; and now that I am here, it seems to me that I have finished half the journey." And so, being of one accord, we pursued our way together, saying "Oh, what will our old folks say this evening?" We then made an agreement not to think more about them till we reached Rome. So we tied our aprons behind our backs, and trudged almost in silence to Siena. When we arrived at Siena, Tasso said (for he had hurt his feet) that he would not go farther, and asked me to lend him money to get back. I made answer: "I should not have enough left to go forward; you ought indeed to have thought of this on leaving Florence; and if it is because of your feet that you shirk the journey, we will find a return horse for Rome, which will deprive you of the excuse." Accordingly I hired a horse; and seeing that he did not answer, I took my way toward the gate of Rome. When he knew that I was firmly resolved to go, muttering between his teeth, and limping as well as he could, he came on behind me very slowly and at a great distance. On reaching the gate, I felt pity for my comrade, and waited for him, and took him on the crupper, saying: "What would our friends speak of us to-morrow, if, having left for Rome, we had not pluck to get beyond Siena?" Then the good Tasso said I spoke the truth; and as he was a pleasant fellow, he began to laugh and sing; and in this way, always singing and laughing, we travelled the whole way to Rome. I had just nineteen years then, and so had the century.

When we reached Rome, I put myself under a master who was known as Il Firenzuola. His name was Giovanni, and he came from Firenzuola in Lombardy, a most able craftsman in large vases and big plate of that kind. I showed him part of the model for the clasp which I had made in Florence at Salimbene's. It pleased him exceedingly; and turning to one of his journeymen, a Florentine called Giannotto Giannotti, who had been several years with him, he spoke as follows: "This fellow is one of the Florentines who know something, and you are one of those who know nothing." Then I recognised the man, and turned to speak with him; for before he went to Rome, we often went to draw together, and had been very intimate comrades. He was so put out by the words his master flung at him, that he said he did not recognise me or know who I was; whereupon I got angry, and cried out: "O Giannotto, you who were once my friend—for have we not been together in such and such places, and drawn, and ate, and drunk, and slept in company at your house in the country? I don't want you to bear witness on my behalf to this worthy man, your master, because I hope my hands are such that without aid from you they will declare what sort of a fellow I am."

XIV

When I had thus spoken, Firenzuola, who was a man of hot spirit and brave, turned to Giannotto, and said to him, "You vile rascal, aren't you ashamed to treat a man who has been so intimate a comrade with you in this way?" And with the same movement of quick feeling, he faced round and said to me: "Welcome to my workshop; and do as you have promised; let your hands declare what man you are."

He gave me a very fine piece of silver plate to work on for a cardinal. It was a little oblong box, copied from the prophyry sarcophagus before the door of the Rotonda. Beside what I copied, I enriched it with so many elegant masks of my invention, that my master went about showing it through the art, and boasting that so good a piece of work had been turned out from his shop. It was about half a cubit in size, and was so constructed as to serve for a salt-cellar at table. This was the first earning that I touched at Rome, and part of it I sent to assist my good father; the rest I kept for my own use, living upon it while I went about studying the antiquities of Rome, until my money failed, and I had to return to the shop for work. Battista del Tasso, my comrade, did not stay long in Rome, but went back to Florence.

After undertaking some new commissions, I took it into my head, as soon as I had finished them, to change my master; I had indeed been worried into doing so by a certain Milanese, called Pagolo Arsago. My first master, Firenzuola, had a great quarrel about this with Arsago, and abused him in my presence; whereupon I took up speech in defence of my new master. I said that I was born free, and free I meant to live, and that there was no reason to complain of him, far less of me, since some few crowns of wages were still due to me; also that I chose to go, like a free journeyman, where it pleased me, knowing I did wrong to no man. My new master then put in with his excuses, saying that he had not asked me to come, and that I should gratify him by returning to Firenzuola. To this I replied that I was not aware of wronging the latter in any way, and as I had completed his commissions, I chose to be my own master and not the man of others, and that he who wanted me must beg me of myself. Firenzuola cried: "I don't intend to beg you of yourself; I have done with you; don't show yourself again upon my premises." I reminded him of the money he owed me. He laughed me in the face; on which I said that if I knew how to use my tools in handicraft as well as he had seen, I could be quite as clever with my sword in claiming the just payment of my labour. While we were exchanging these words, an old man happened to come up, called Maestro Antonio, of San Marino. He was the chief among the Roman goldsmiths, and had been Firenzuola's master. Hearing what I had to say, which I took good care that he should understand, he immediately espoused my cause, and bade Firenzuola pay me. The dispute waxed warm, because Firenzuola was an admirable swordsman, far better than he was a goldsmith. Yet reason made itself heard; and I backed my cause with the same spirit, till I got myself paid. In course of time Firenzuola and I became friends, and at his request

I stood godfather to one of his children.

XV

I went on working with Pagolo Arsago, and earned a good deal of money, the greater part of which I always sent to my good father. At the end of two years, upon my father's entreaty, I returned to Florence, and put myself once more under Francesco Salimbene, with whom I earned a great deal, and took continual pains to improve in my arts. I renewed my intimacy with Francesco di Filippo; and though I was too much given to pleasure, owing to that accursed music, I never neglected to devote some hours of the day or night to study. At that time I fashioned a silver heart's-key (*chiavaquore*), as it was then called. This was a girdle three inches broad, which used to be made for brides and was executed in half relief with some small figures in the round. It was a commission from a man called Raffaello Lapaccini. I was very badly paid; but the honour which it brought me was worth far more than the gain I might have justly made by it. Having at this time worked with many different persons in Florence, I had come to know some worthy men among the goldsmiths, as, for instance, Marcone, my first master; but I also met with others reputed honest, who did all they could to ruin me, and robbed me grossly. When I perceived this, I left their company, and held them for thieves and blackguards. One of the goldsmiths, called Giovanbattista Sogliani, kindly accommodated me with part of his shop, which stood at the side of the New Market near the Landi's bank. There I finished several pretty pieces, and made good gains, and was able to give my family much help. This roused the jealousy of the bad men among my former masters, who were called Salvadore and Michele Guasconti. In the guild of the goldsmiths they had three big shops, and drove a thriving trade. On becoming aware of their evil will against me, I complained to certain worthy fellows, and remarked that they ought to have been satisfied with the thieveries they practised on me under the cloak of hypocritical kindness. This coming to their ears, they threatened to make me sorely repent of such words; but I, who knew not what the colour of fear was, paid them little or no heed.

* * *

XIX

At Siena I waited for the mail to Rome, which I afterwards joined; and when we passed the Paglia, we met a courier carrying news of the new Pope Clement VII. Upon my arrival in Rome, I went to work in the shop of the master-goldsmith Santi. He was dead; but a son of his carried on the business. He did not work himself, but entrusted all his commissions to a young man named Lucagnolo from Iesi, a country fellow, who while yet a child had come into Santi's service. This man was short but well proportioned, and was a more skilful craftsman than any one whom I had met with up to that time; remarkable for facility and excellent in design. He executed large plate only; that is to say, vases of the utmost beauty, basins, and such pieces. Having put myself to work there, I began to make some candelabra for the Bishop of Salamanca, a Spaniard. They were richly chased, so far as the sort of work admits. A pupil of Raffaello da Urbino called Gian Francesco, and commonly known as Il Fattore, was a painter of great ability; and being on terms of friendship with the Bishop, he introduced me to his favour, so that I obtained many commissions from that prelate, and earned considerable sums of money.

During that time I went to draw sometimes in Michel Agnolo's chapel, and sometimes in the house of Agostino Chigi of Siena, which contained many incomparable paintings by the hand of that great master Raffaello. This I did on feast-days, because the house was then inhabited by Messer Gismondo, Agostino's brother. They plumed themselves exceedingly when they saw young men of my sort coming to study in their palaces. Gismondo's wife, noticing my frequent presence in that house—she was a lady as courteous as could be, and of surpassing beauty—came up to me one day, looked at my drawings, and asked me if I was a sculptor or a painter; to whom I said I was a goldsmith. She remarked that I drew too well for a goldsmith; and having made one of her waiting-maids bring a lily of the finest diamonds set in gold, she showed it to me, and bade me value it. I valued it at 800 crowns. Then she said that I had very nearly hit the mark, and asked me whether I felt capable of setting the stones really well. I said that I should much like to do so, and began before her eyes to make a little sketch for it, working all the better because of the pleasure I took in conversing with so lovely and agreeable a gentlewoman. When the sketch was finished, another Roman lady of great beauty joined us; she had been above, and now descending to the ground-floor, asked Madonna Porzia what she was doing there. She answered with a smile: "I am amusing myself by watching this worthy young man at his drawing; he is as good as he is handsome." I had by this time acquired a trifle of assurance, mixed, however, with some honest bashfulness; so I blushed and said: "Such as I am, lady, I shall ever be most ready to serve you." The gentlewoman, also slightly blushing, said: "You know well that I want you to serve me"; and reaching me the lily, told me to take it away; and gave me besides twenty golden crowns which she had in her bag, and added: "Set me the jewel after the fashion you have sketched, and keep for me the old gold in which it is now set." On this the Roman lady observed: "If I were in that young man's body, I should go off without asking leave." Madonna Porzia replied that virtues rarely are at home with vices, and that if I did such a thing, I should strongly belie my good looks of an honest man. Then turning round, she took the Roman lady's hand, and with a pleasant smile said: "Farewell, Benvenuto." I stayed on a short while at the drawing I was making, which was a copy of a Jove by Raffaello. When I had finished it and left the house, I set myself to making a little model of wax, in order to show how the jewel would look when it was completed. This I took to Madonna Porzia, whom I found with the same Roman lady. Both of them were highly satisfied

with my work, and treated me so kindly that, being somewhat emboldened, I promised the jewel should be twice as good as the model. Accordingly I set hand to it, and in twelve days I finished it in the form of a fleur-de-lys, as I have said above, ornamenting it with little masks, children, and animals, exquisitely enamelled, whereby the diamonds which formed the lily were more than doubled in effect.

XX

While I was working at this piece, Lucagnolo, of whose ability I have before spoken, showed considerable discontent, telling me over and over again that I might acquire far more profit and honour by helping him to execute large plate, as I had done at first. I made him answer that, whenever I chose, I should always be capable of working at great silver pieces; but that things like that on which I was now engaged were not commissioned every day; and beside their bringing no less honour than large silver plate, there was also more profit to be made by them. He laughed me in the face, and said: "Wait and see Benvenuto; for by the time that you have finished that work of yours, I will make haste to have finished this vase, which I took in hand when you did the jewel; and then experience shall teach you what profit I shall get from my vase, and what you will get from your ornament." I answered that I was very glad indeed to enter into such a competition with so good a craftsman as he was, because the end would show which of us was mistaken. Accordingly both the one and the other of us, with a scornful smile upon our lips, bent our heads in grim earnest to the work, which both were now desirous of accomplishing; so that after about ten days, each had finished his undertaking with great delicacy and artistic skill.

Lucagnolo's was a huge silver piece, used at the table of Pope Clement, into which he flung away bits of bone and the rind of divers fruits, while eating; an object of ostentation rather than necessity. The vase was adorned with two fine handles, together with many masks, both small and great, and masses of lovely foliage, in as exquisite a style of elegance as could be imagined; and seeing which I said it was the most beautiful vase that ever I set eyes on. Thinking he had convinced me, Lucagnolo replied: "Your work seems to me no less beautiful, but we shall soon perceive the difference between the two." So he took his vase and carried it to the Pope, who was very well pleased with it, and ordered at once that he should be paid at the ordinary rate of such large plate. Meanwhile I carried mine to Madonna Porzia, who looked at it with astonishment, and told me I had far surpassed my promise. Then she bade me ask for my reward whatever I liked; for it seemed to her my desert was so great that if I craved a castle she could hardly recompense me; but since that was not in her hands to bestow, she added laughing that I must beg what lay within her power. I answered that the greatest reward I could desire for my labour was to have satisfied her ladyship. Then, smiling in my turn, and bowing to her, I took my leave, saying I wanted no reward but that. She turned to the Roman lady and said: "You see

that the qualities we discerned in him are companied by virtues, and not vices." They both expressed their admiration, and then Madonna Porzio continued: "Friend Benvenuto, have you never heard it said that when the poor give to the rich, the devil laughs?" I replied: "Quite true! and yet, in the midst of all his troubles, I should like this time to see him laugh"; and as I took my leave, she said that this time she had no will to bestow on him that favour.

When I came back to the shop, Lucagnolo had the money for his vase in a paper packet; and on my arrival he cried out: "Come and compare the price of your jewel with the price of my plate." I said that he must leave things as they were till the next day, because I hoped that even as my work in its kind was not less excellent than his, so I should be able to show him quite an equal price for it.

XXI

On the day following, Madonna Porzia sent a major-domo of hers to my shop, who called me out, and putting into my hands a paper packet full of money from his lady, told me that she did not choose the devil should have his whole laugh out; by which she hinted that the money sent me was not the entire payment merited by my industry, and other messages were added worthy of so courteous a lady. Lucagnolo, who was burning to compare his packet with mine, burst into the shop, then in the presence of twelve journeymen and some neighbours, eager to behold the result of this competition, he seized his packet, scornfully exclaiming "Ou! Ou!" three or four times, while he poured his money on the counter with a great noise. They were twenty-five crowns in giulios; and he fancied that mine would be four or five crowns *di moneta*. I for my part, stunned and stifled by his cries, and by the looks and smiles of the bystanders, first peeped into my packet; then, after seeing that it contained nothing but gold, I retired to one end of the counter, and, keeping my eyes lowered and making no noise at all, I lifted it with both hands suddenly above my head, and emptied it like a mill hopper. My coin was twice as much as his; which caused the onlookers, who had fixed their eyes on me with some derision, to turn round suddenly to him and say: "Lucagnolo, Benvenuto's pieces, being all of gold and twice as many as yours, make a far finer effect." I thought for certain that, what with jealousy and what with shame, Lucagnolo would have fallen dead upon the spot; and though he took the third part of my gain, since I was a journeymen (for such is the custom of the trade, two-thirds fall to the workman and one-third to the masters of the shop), yet inconsiderate envy had more power in him that avarice: it ought indeed to have worked quite the other way, he being a peasant's son from Iesi. He cursed his art and those who taught it to him, vowing that thenceforth he would never work at large plate, but give his whole attention to those whoreson gewgaws, since they were so well paid. Equally enraged on my side, I answered that every bird sang its own note; that he talked after the fashion of the hovels he came from; but that I dared swear that I should

succeed with ease in making his lubberly lumber, while he would never be successful in my whoreson gewgaws. Thus I flung off in a passion, telling him that I would soon show him that I spoke truth. The bystanders openly declared against him, holding him for a lout, as indeed he was, and me for a man, as I had proved myself.

XXII

Next day, I went to thank Madonna Porzia, and told her that her ladyship had done the opposite of what she said she would; for that while I wanted to make the devil laugh, she had made him once more deny God. We both laughed pleasantly at this, and she gave me other commissions for fine and substantial work.

Meanwhile, I contrived, by means of a pupil of Raffaello da Urbino, to get an order from the Bishop of Salamanca for one of those great water-vessels called *acquereccia*, which are used for ornaments to place on sideboards. He wanted a pair made of equal size; and one of them he intrusted to Lucagnolo, the other to me. Giovan Francesco, the painter I have mentioned, gave us the design. Accordingly I set hand with marvellous good-will to this piece of plate, and was accommodated with a part of his workshop by a Milanese named Maestro Giovan Piero della Tacca. Having made my preparations, I calculated how much money I should need for certain affairs of my own, and sent all the rest to assist my poor father.

It so happened that just when this was being paid to him in Florence, he stumbled upon one of those Radicals who were in the Eight at the time when I got into that little trouble there. It was the very man who had abused him so rudely, and who swore that I should certainly be sent into the country with the lances. Now this fellow had some sons of very bad morals and repute; wherefore my father said to him: "Misfortunes can happen to anybody, especially to men of choleric humour when they are in the right, even as it happened to my son; but let the rest of his life bear witness how virtuously I have brought him up. Would God, for your well-being, that your sons may act neither worse nor better towards you than mine do to me. God rendered me able to bring them up as I have done; and where my own power could not reach, 'twas He who rescued them, against your expectation, out of your violent hands." On leaving the man, he wrote me all this story, begging me for God's sake to practise music at times, in order that I might not lose the fine accomplishment which he had taught me with such trouble. The letter so overflowed with expressions of the tenderest fatherly affection, that I was moved to tears of filial piety, resolving before he died, to gratify him amply with regard to music. Thus God grants us those lawful blessings which we ask in prayer, nothing doubting.

XXIII

While I was pushing forward Salamanca's vase, I had only one little boy as help, whom I had taken at the entreaty of friends, and half against my own will, to be my workman. He was about fourteen years of age, bore the name of Paulino, and was son to a Roman burgess, who lived upon the income of his property. Paulino was the best-mannered, the most honest, and the most beautiful boy I ever saw in my whole life. His modest ways and actions, together with his superlative beauty and his devotion to myself, bred in me as great an affection for him as a man's breast can hold. This passionate love led me oftentimes to delight the lad with music; for I observed that his marvellous features, which by complexion wore a tone of modest melancholy, brightened up, and when I took my cornet, broke into a smile so lovely and sweet, that I do not marvel at the silly stories which the Greeks have written about the deities of heaven. Indeed, if my boy had lived in those times, he would probably have turned their heads still more. He had a sister, named Faustina, more beautiful, I verily believe, than that Faustina about whom the old books gossip so. Sometimes he took me to their vineyard, and, so far as I could judge, it struck me that Paulino's good father would have welcomed me as a son-in-law. This affair led me to play more than I was used to do.

It happened at that time that one Giangiacomo of Cesena, a musician in the Pope's band, and a very excellent performer, sent word through Lorenzo, the trumpeter of Lucca, who is now in our Duke's service, to inquire whether I was inclined to help them at the Pope's Ferragosto, playing soprano with my cornet in some motets of great beauty selected by them for that occasion. Although I had the greatest desire to finish the vase I had begun, yet, since music has a wondrous charm of its own, and also because I wished to please my old father, I consented to join them. During eight days before the festival we practised two hours a day together; then on the first of August we went to the Belvedere, and while Pope Clement was at table, we played those carefully studied motets so well that his Holiness protested he had never heard music more sweetly executed or with better harmony of parts. He sent for Giangiacomo, and asked him where and how he had procured so excellent a cornet for soprano, and inquired particularly who I was. Giangiacomo told him my name in full. Whereupon the Pope said: "So, then, he is the son of Maestro Giovanni?" On being assured I was, the Pope expressed his wish to have me in his service with the other bandsmen. Giangiacomo replied: "Most blessed Father, I cannot pretend for certain that you will get him, for his profession, to which he devotes himself assiduously, is that of a goldsmith, and he works in it miraculously well, and earns by it far more than he could do by playing." To this the Pope added: "I am the better inclined to him now that I find him possessor of a talent more than I expected. See that he obtains the same salary as the rest of you; and tell him from me to join my service, and that I will find work enough by the day for him to do at his other trade." Then stretching out his hand, he gave him a hundred golden crowns of the Camera in a handkerchief, and said: "Divide these so that he may take his share."

When Giangiacomo left the Pope, he came to us, and related in detail all that the Pope had said, and after dividing the money between the

eight of us, and giving me my share, he said to me: "Now I am going to have you inscribed among our company." I replied: "Let the day pass; to-morrow I will give my answer." When I left them, I went meditating whether I ought to accept the invitation, inasmuch as I could not but suffer if I abandoned the noble studies of my art. The following night my father appeared to me in dream, and begged me with tears of tenderest affection, for God's love and his, to enter upon this engagement. Methought I answered that nothing would induce me to do so. In an instant he assumed so horrible an aspect as to frighten me out of my wits, and cried: "If you do not, you will have a father's curse; but if you do, may you be ever blessed by me!" When I awoke, I ran, for very fright, to have myself inscribed. Then I wrote to my old father, telling him the news, which so affected him with extreme joy that a sudden fit of illness took him, and well-nigh brought him to death's door. In his answer to my letter, he told me that he too had dreamed nearly the same as I had.

XXIV

Knowing now that I had gratified my father's honest wish, I began to think that everything would prosper with me to a glorious and honourable end. Accordingly, I set myself with indefatigable industry to the completion of the vase I had begun for Salamanca. That prelate was a very extraordinary man, extremely rich, but difficult to please. He sent daily to learn what I was doing; and when his messenger did not find me at home, he broke into fury, saying that he would take the work out of my hands and give it to others to finish. This came of my slavery to that accursed music. Still I laboured diligently night and day, until, when I had brought my work to a point when it could be exhibited, I submitted it to the inspection of the Bishop. This so increased his desire to see it finished, that I was sorry I had shown it. At the end of three months I had it ready, with little animals and foliage and masks, so beautiful as one could hope to see. No sooner was it done than I sent it by the hand of my workman, Paulino, to show that able artist Lucagnolo, of whom I have spoken above. Paulino, with the grace and beauty which belonged to him, spoke as follows: "Messer Lucagnolo, Benvenuto bids me say that he has sent to show you his promises and your lumber, expecting in return to see from you his gewgaws." This message given, Lucagnolo took up the vase, and carefully examined it; then he said to Paulino: "Fair boy, tell your master that he is a great and able artist, and that I beg him to be willing to have me for a friend, and not to engage in aught else." The mission of that virtuous and marvellous lad caused me the greatest joy; and then the vase was carried to Salamanca, who ordered it to be valued. Lucagnolo took part in the valuation, estimating and praising it far above my own opinion. Salamanca, lifting up the vase, cried like a true Spaniard: "I swear by God that I will take as long in paying him as he has lagged in making it." When I heard this, I was exceedingly put out, and fell to cursing all Spain and every one who wished well to it.

Amongst other beautiful ornaments, this vase had a handle, made all of one piece, with most delicate mechanism, which, when a spring was touched, stood upright above the mouth of it. While the prelate was one day ostentatiously exhibiting my vase to certain Spanish gentlemen of his suite, it chanced that one of them, upon Monsignor's quitting the room, began roughly to work the handle, and as the gentle spring which moved it could not bear his loutish violence, it broke in his hand. Aware what mischief he had done, he begged the butler who had charge of the Bishop's plate to take it to the master who had made it, for him to mend, and promised to pay what price he asked, provided it was set to rights at once. So the vase came once more into my hands, and I promised to put it forthwith in order, which indeed I did. It was brought to me before dinner; and at twenty-two o'clock the man who brought it returned, all in a sweat, for he had run the whole way, Monsignor having again asked for it to show to certain other gentlemen. The butler, then, without giving me time to utter a word, cried: "Quick, quick, bring me the vase." I, who wanted to act at leisure and not to give it up to him, said that I did not mean to be so quick. The serving-man got into such a rage that he made as though he would put one hand to his sword, while with the other he threatened to break the shop open. To this I put a stop at once with my own weapon, using therewith spirited language, and saying: "I am not going to give it to you! Go and tell Monsignor, your master, that I want the money for my work before I let it leave this shop." When the fellow saw he could not obtain it by swaggering, he fell to praying me, as one prays to the Cross, declaring that if I would only give it up, he would take care I should be paid. These words did not make me swerve from my purpose; but I kept on saying the same thing. At last, despairing of success, he swore to come with Spaniards enough to cut me in pieces. Then he took to his heels; while I, who inclined to believe partly in their murderous attack, resolved that I would defend myself with courage. So I got an admirable little gun ready, which I used for shooting game, and muttered to myself: "He who robs me of my property and labour may take my life, too, and welcome." While I was carrying on this debate in my own mind, a crowd of Spaniards arrived, led by their major-domo, who, with the head-strong rashness of his race, bade them go in and take the vase and give me a good beating. Hearing these words, I showed them the muzzle of my gun, and prepared to fire, and cried in a loud voice: "Renegade Jews, traitors, is it thus that one breaks into houses and shops in our city of Rome? Come as many of you thieves as like, an inch nearer to this wicket, and I'll blow all their brains out with my gun." Then I turned the muzzle toward their major-domo, and making as though I would discharge it, called out: "And you big thief, who are egging them on, I mean to kill you first." He clapped spurs to the jennet he was riding, and took flight head-long. The commotion we were making stirred up all the neighbours, who came crowding round, together with some Roman gentlemen who chanced to pass and cried: "Do but kill the renegades, and we will stand

by you." These words had the effect of frightening the Spaniards in good earnest. They withdrew, and were compelled by the circumstances to relate the whole affair to Monsignor. Being a man of inordinate haughtiness, he rated the members of his household, both because they had engaged in such an act of violence, and also because, having begun, they had not gone through with it. At this juncture the painter, who had been concerned in the whole matter, came in, and the Bishop bade him go and tell me that if I did not bring the vase at once, he would make mincemeat for me; but if I brought it, he would pay its price down. These threats were so far from terrifying me, that I sent him words I was going immediately to lay my case before the Pope.

In the meantime, his anger and my fear subsided; whereupon, being guaranteed by some Roman gentlemen of high degree that the prelate would not harm me, and having assurance that I should be paid, I armed myself with a large poniard and my good coat of mail, and betook myself to his palace, where he had drawn up all his household. I entered, and Paulino followed with the silver vase. It was just like passing through the Zodiac, neither more nor less; for one of them had the face of the lion, another of the scorpion, a third of the crab. However, we passed onward to the presence of the rascally priest, who spouted out a torrent of such language as only priests and Spaniards have at their command. In return I never raised my eyes to look at him, nor answered word for word. That seemed to augment the fury of his anger; and causing paper to be put before me, he commanded me to write an acknowledgement to the effect that I had been amply satisfied and paid in full. Then I raised my head and said I should be very glad to do so when I had received the money. The Bishop's rage continued to rise; threats and recriminations were flung about; but at last the money was paid, and I wrote the receipt. Then I departed, glad at heart and in high spirits.

Desiderius Erasmus

In contrast to the Italian Renaissance, which became quite secular and pagan in temper, the Renaissance in northern Europe retained more of the medieval Christian outlook. The combination of Renaissance humanism with Christianity, characteristic of the northern Renaissance, is exemplified most clearly in the writings of Erasmus of Rotterdam (1466–1536). Intensely aware of the shortcomings of the Catholic Church of his day, Erasmus was nevertheless convinced that the elimination of these evils lay not in a rejection of Christianity but rather in a return to it. Believing that the Church had departed from the true teachings of its founder, he urged a reform of religious beliefs and practices based on a return to the gospel of the New Testament or, as he called it, the "philosophy of Christ." Erasmus felt that such a reform should be inaugurated and carried forward by the Church itself through a program of widespread education. He parted company with Martin Luther because he was unwilling to go along with Luther's insistence that, since gradual reform from within based on an appeal to reason was futile, the only solution lay in violent revolt against the Church. Although Erasmus refused to join the Protestant movement, he contributed significantly to the Reformation by appealing for a return to the original teachings of Christ and by directing pointed satires against abuses within the Church.

The selection that follows describes some of the more blatant abuses prevalent in the Church during the early sixteenth century. It consists of a conversation between a pious believer and his less gullible friend, in which the former relates his adventures during pilgrimages he has made to three holy sites: the shrine of Santiago de Compostella (in Spain), dedicated to St. James the Apostle; the shrine of our Lady of Walsingham (in eastern England), dedicated to the Virgin Mary; and the shrine of the martyr, Thomas Becket, at Canterbury, England. Taken from Erasmus' book, *The Colloquies*, the dialogue was first published in 1526. Erasmian irony is evident throughout the selection, sometimes in a gentle form in the asides of Menedemus (which Ogygius usually misunderstands) and once, quite directly and forcefully, in his short speech near the end of the dialogue condemning the physical embellishment of churches at the expense of the poor.

A Pilgrimage for Religion's Sake
Menedemus, Ogygius

MENEDEMUS: What marvel is this? Don't I see my neighbor Ogygius, whom nobody's laid eyes on for six whole months? I heard he was dead. It's his very self, unless I'm losing my mind completely. I'll go up to him and say hello.—Greetings, Ogygius.

OGYGIUS: Same to you, Menedemus.

MEN.: Where in the world do you return from, safe and sound? A sad rumor spread here that you'd sailed in Stygian waters.

OGYG.: No, thank heaven; I've seldom enjoyed better health.

MEN.: I hope you'll always be able to refute silly rumors of that sort! But what's this fancy outfit? You're ringed with scallop shells, choked with tin and leaden images on every side, decked out with straw necklaces, and you've snake eggs on your arms.[1]

OGYG.: I've been on a visit to St. James of Compostella and, on my way back, to the famous Virgin-by-the-Sea, in England; or rather I revisited her, since I had gone there three years earlier.

MEN.: Out of curiosity, I dare say.

OGYG.: On the contrary, out of devotion.

---

[1] Shells, traditional symbols of pilgrims, were connected especially with St. James and the pilgrimage to Compostella. The "snake eggs" are beads, *i.e.*, a rosary.

MEN.: Greek letters, I suppose, taught you that devotion.

OGYG.: My wife's mother had bound herself by a vow that if her daughter gave birth to a boy and he lived, I would promptly pay my respects to St. James and thank him in person.

MEN.: Did you greet the saint only in your own name and your mother-in-law's?

OGYG.: Oh, no, in the whole family's.

MEN.: Well, I imagine your family would have been no less safe even if you had left James ungreeted. But do please tell me: what answer did he make when you thanked him?

OGYG.: None, but he seemed to smile as I offered my gift, nodded his head slightly, and at the same time held out these scallop shells.

MEN.: Why does he give these rather than something else?

OGYG.: Because he has plenty of them; the sea nearby supplies them.

MEN.: Generous saint, who both delivers those in labor and gives presents to callers! But what new kind of vowing is this, that some lazy person lays the work on others? If you bound yourself by a vow that, should your affairs prosper, I would fast twice a week, do you think I'd do what you had vowed?

OGYG.: No, I don't, even if you'd sworn in your own name. For you

---

The Colloquies of Erasmus, trans. Craig R. Thompson (Chicago: The University of Chicago Press, 1965), pp. 287–289, 291–300, 303–309.

enjoy mocking the saints. But she's my mother-in-law; custom had to be kept. You're acquainted with women's whims, and besides I had an interest in it too.

MEN.: If you hadn't kept her vow, what risk would there have been?

OGYG.: The saint couldn't have sued me at law, I admit, but he could have been deaf thereafter to my prayers or secretly have brought some disaster upon my family. You know the ways of the mighty.

MEN.: Tell me, how is the excellent James?

OGYG.: Much colder than usual.

MEN.: Why? Old age?

OGYG.: Joker! You know saints don't grow old. But this new-fangled notion that pervades the whole world results in his being greeted more seldom than usual. And if people do come, they merely greet him; they make no offering at all, or only a very slight one, declaring it would be better to contribute that money to the poor.

MEN.: A wicked notion!

OGYG.: And thus so great an apostle, accustomed to shine from head to foot in gold and jewels, now stands a wooden figure with hardly a tallow candle to his name.

· · ·

MEN.: But what fortune brought you back to England?

OGYG.: An unexpectedly favorable breeze carried me there, and I had virtually promised the Virgin-by-the-Sea that I would pay her another visit in two years.

MEN.: What were you going to ask of her?

OGYG.: Nothing new, just the usual things: family safe and sound, a larger fortune, a long and happy life in this world, and eternal bliss in the next.

MEN.: Couldn't the Virgin Mother here at home see to those matters? At Antwerp she has a church much grander than the one by the sea.

OGYG.: I can't deny that, but different things are bestowed in different places, either because she prefers this or (since she is obliging) because she accommodates herself to our feelings in this respect.

MEN.: I've often heard about James, but I beg you to describe for me the domain of the Virgin-by-the-Sea.

OGYG.: Well, I'll do the best I can in brief. She has the greatest fame throughout England, and you would not readily find anyone in that island who hoped for prosperity unless he greeted her annually with a small gift, according to his means.

MEN.: Where does she live?

OGYG.: By the northwest[2] coast of England, only about three miles from the sea. The village has scarcely any means of support apart from the tourist trade. There's a college of canons, to whom, however, the Latins add the title of Regulars: an order midway between monks and the canons called Seculars.

MEN.: You tell me of amphibians, such as the beaver.

OGYG.: Yes, and the crocodile. But details aside, I'll try to satisfy you in a few words. In unfavorable matters, they're canons; in favorable ones, monks.

---

[2] A slip: Walsingham is in northern Norfolk.

MEN.: So far you're telling me a riddle.

OGYG.: But I'll add a precise illustration. If the Roman pontiff assailed all monks with a thunderbolt,[3] then they'd be canons, not monks. Yet if he permitted all monks to take wives, then they'd be monks.

MEN.: Strange favors. I wish they'd take mine, too.

OGYG.: But to get to the point. This college depends almost entirely on the Virgin's generosity for its support. The larger gifts are reserved, to be sure, but any small change, anything of trifling value, goes toward feeding the community and their head, whom they call the prior.

MEN.: Do they live holy lives?

OGYG.: They're not without praise. They're richer in piety than income. The church is fine and splendid, but the Virgin doesn't dwell there; in honor of her Son she yields that to him. She has her own church, that she may be on the right of her Son.

MEN.: The right? Which direction does the Son face, then?

OGYG.: I'm glad you remind me. When he faces west he has his mother on his right; when he turns to the east she's on his left. However, she doesn't dwell here, either, for the building is not yet finished, and the place is quite airy—windows and doors open, and Ocean, father of the winds, nearby.

MEN.: Too bad. So where does she live?

OGYG.: In that church, which as I said is unfinished, is a small chapel built on a wooden platform. Visitors are admitted through a narrow door on each side. There's very little light: only what comes from tapers, which have a most pleasing scent.

MEN.: All this is appropriate to religion.

OGYG.: Yes, and if you peered inside, Menedemus, you would say it was the abode of the saints, so dazzling is it with jewels, gold, and silver.

MEN.: You make me impatient to go there.

OGYG.: You won't regret the trip.

MEN.: Is there no holy oil there?

OGYG.: Silly! That oil exudes only from the tombs of saints, such as Andrew and Catherine. Mary isn't buried.

MEN.: My mistake, I admit. But finish your story.

OGYG.: As the cult spreads more widely, different things are displayed in different places.

MEN.: In order, perhaps, that the giving may be more generous; as it is said, "Loot quickly comes when sought by many hands."

OGYG.: And custodians are always present.

MEN.: Some of the canons?

OGYG.: No, they're not used, lest on a favorable opportunity for religious devotion they might stray from devoutness, and while honoring the Virgin pay too little regard to their own virginity. Only in the interior chapel, which I said is the inner sanctum of the Holy Virgin, a canon stands by the altar.

MEN.: What for?

OGYG.: To receive and keep the offering.

MEN.: Do people contribute whether they want to or not?

OGYG.: Not at all, but a certain sense of duty impels some to give when a person's standing by; they

---

[3] Excommunication.

wouldn't give if no one were present to watch them. Or sometimes they give more liberally than they would otherwise.

MEN.: That's human nature. I'm no stranger to it.

OGYG.: Nay, there are some so devoted to the Most Holy Virgin that while they pretend to lay an offering on the altar, they steal, with astonishing nimbleness, what somebody else had placed there.

MEN.: Suppose there's no witness: would the Virgin strike them dead on the spot?

OGYG.: Why would the Virgin do that, any more than does the heavenly Father himself, whom men aren't afraid to rob of treasures, even digging through the church wall for the purpose?

MEN.: I can't tell which to be the more astonished at, their impious audacity or God's mildness.

OGYG.: Then, on the north side—not of the church (don't mistake me) but of the wall enclosing the whole area adjacent to the church—is a certain gateway. It has a tiny door, the kind noblemen's gates have, so that whoever wants to enter must first expose his shins to danger and then stoop besides.

MEN.: Certainly it wouldn't be safe to go at an enemy through such a door.

OGYG.: Right. The custodian told me that once a knight on horseback escaped through this door from the hands of an enemy who was on the point of overtaking him in his flight. In despair he commended himself then and there to the Holy Virgin, who was close by. For he had determined to take refuge at her altar if the door was open. And mark this wonder: suddenly the knight was entirely within the churchyard and the other man outside, furious.

MEN.: And was this wondrous tale of his believed?

OGYG.: Of course.

MEN.: A rational chap like you wouldn't accept it so easily.

OGYG.: He showed me on the door a copper plate, fastened by nails, containing a likeness of the knight who was saved, dressed in the English fashion of that period as we see it in old pictures—and if pictures don't lie, barbers had a hard time in those days, and so did weavers and dyers.

MEN.: How so?

OGYG.: Because the knight was bearded like a goat, and his clothing didn't have a single pleat and was so tight that it made the body itself thinner. There was another plate, too, showing the size and shape of the shrine.

MEN.: You had no right to doubt after that!

OGYG.: Beneath the little door was an iron grating, admitting you only on foot. It was not seemly that a horse should afterward trample the spot the horseman had consecrated to the Virgin.

MEN.: And rightly consecrated.

OGYG.: To the east is a small chapel, filled with marvels. I betake myself to it. Another custodian receives us. After we've prayed briefly, we're immediately shown the joint of a human finger (the largest of three). I kiss it and then ask whose relics these are, "Saint Peter's," he says. "Not the apostle Peter's?" "Yes." Then looking at the great size of the joint, which might have been a giant's, I said, "Peter must have been an extremely big man." At this one of my companions burst into a loud laugh, which annoyed me no end, for if he had been quiet the attendant would have kept none of the relics from our inspection. However, we appeased him with some coins.

In front of the little building was a structure that during the wintertime (he said), when everything was covered by snow, had been brought there suddenly from far away. Under this were two wells, filled to the top. They say the stream of water is sacred to the Holy Virgin. It's a wonderfully cold fluid, good for headache and stomach troubles.

MEN.: If cold water cures headache and stomach troubles, oil will put out fire next.

OGYG.: You're hearing about a miracle, my good friend—besides, what would be miraculous about cold water quenching thirst?

MEN.: Clearly this is only one part of the story.

OGYG.: That stream of water, they declared, suddenly shot up from the ground at the command of the Most Holy Virgin. Inspecting everything carefully, I inquired how many years it was since the little house had been brought there. "Some ages," he replied. "In any event," I said, "the walls don't look very old." He didn't dissent. "Even these wooden posts don't look old." He didn't deny they had been placed there recently, and the fact was self-evident. "Then," I said, "the roof and thatch of the horse seem rather recent." He agreed. "Not even these crossbeams, nor the very rafters supporting the roof, appear to have been put here many years ago." He nodded. "But since no part of the building has survived, how is it known for certain," I asked, "that this is the cottage brought here from so far away?"

MEN.: How did the attendant get out of that tangle, if you please?

OGYG.: Why, he hurriedly showed us an old, worn-out bearskin fastened to posts and almost laughed at us for our dulness in being slow to see such a clear proof. So, being persuaded, and excusing our stupidity, we turned to the heavenly milk of the Blessed Virgin.

MEN.: O Mother most like her Son! He left us so much of his blood on earth; she left so much of her milk that it's scarcely credible a woman with only one child could have so much, even if the child had drunk none of it.

OGYG.: The same thing is said about the Lord's Cross, which is exhibited publicly and privately in so many places that if the fragments were joined together they'd seem a full load for a freighter. And yet the Lord carried his whole cross.

MEN.: Doesn't it seem amazing to you, too?

OGYG.: Unusual, perhaps, but by no means amazing, since the Lord, who multiplies these things as he wills, is omnipotent.

MEN.: You explain it reverently, but for my part I'm afraid many such affairs are contrived for profit.

OGYG.: I don't think God will stand for anybody mocking him in that way.

MEN.: On the contrary, though Mother and Son and Father and Spirit are robbed by the sacrilegious, sometimes they don't even bestir themselves slightly enough to frighten off the criminals by a nod or a noise. So great is the mildness of divinity.

OGYG.: That's true. But hear the rest. This milk is kept on the high altar, in the midst of which is Christ; on the right, for the sake of honor, is his Mother. For the milk represents his Mother.

MEN.: So it's in plain sight.

OGYG.: Enclosed in crystal, that is.

MEN.: Therefore liquid.

OGYG.: What do you mean, liquid, when it flowed fifteen hundred years ago? It's hard: you'd say powdered chalk, tempered with white of egg.

MEN.: Why don't they display it exposed?

OGYG.: To save the virginal milk from being defiled by the kisses of men.

MEN.: Well said, for in my opinion there are those who would bring neither clean nor chaste mouths to it.

OGYG.: When the custodian saw us, he rushed up, donned a linen vestment, threw a sacred stole round his neck, prostrated himself devoutly, and adored. Next he held out the sacred milk for us to kiss. We prostrated ourselves devoutly on the lowest step of the altar and, after first saluting Christ, uttered to the Virgin a short prayer I had prepared for this occasion: "Virgin Mother, who hast had the honor of suckling at thy maidenly breast the Lord of heaven and earth, thy Son Jesus, we pray that, cleansed by his blood we may gain that blessed infancy of dovelike simplicity which, innocent of all malice, deceit, and guile, longs without ceasing for the milk of gospel doctrine until it attains to the perfect man, to the measure of the fulness of Christ, whose blessed company thou enjoyest forever, with the Father and Holy Spirit. Amen."

MEN.: Certainly a devout intercession. What effect did it have?

OGYG.: Mother and Son both seemed to nod approval, unless my eyes deceived me. For the sacred milk appeared to leap up, and the Eucharistic elements gleamed somewhat more brightly. Meanwhile the custodian approached us, quite silent, but holding out a board like those used in Germany by toll collectors on bridges.

MEN.: Yes, I've often cursed those greedy boards when traveling through Germany.

OGYG.: We gave him some coins, which he offered to the Virgin. Next, through an interpreter who understands the language well (a smooth-tongued young man named Robert Aldridge, I believe), I tried as civilly as I could to find out what proof he had that this was the Virgin's milk. I wanted to know this clearly for the pious purpose of stopping the mouths of certain unbelievers who are accustomed to laugh at all these matters. At first the custodian frowned and said nothing. I told the interpreter to press him, but even more politely. He did so with the utmost grace, such that if with words of that sort he had entreated the Mother herself, recently out of childbed, she would not have taken offense. But the custodian, as if possessed, gazed at us in astonishment, and as though horrified by such a blasphemous speech, said, "What need is there to inquire into that when you have an authentic record?" And it looked very much as if he would throw us out for heretics, except that we calmed the fellow's wrath with money.

MEN.: What did you do then?

OGYG.: What do you suppose we did? As though beaten with a club, or struck by a thunderbolt, we took ourselves out of there, humbly begging pardon (as one should in sacred matters) for such outrageous presumption. Then on to the little chapel, the shrine of the Holy Virgin. At our approach a custodian turns up, a Minorite, and gazes at us as though studying us; after we go a little farther a second one turns up, likewise staring at us; then a third.

MEN.: Perhaps they wanted to draw you.

OGYG.: But I suspected something very different.

MEN.: What was that?

OGYG.: That a sacrilegious person had filched something from the Holy Virgin's ornaments, and that their suspicion was directed against me. So when I entered the chapel I greeted the Virgin Mother with a short prayer, like this: "O thou alone of all womankind Mother and Virgin, Mother most blessed, purest of maidens, we who are unclean come unto thee who art pure. We bless thee, we worship thee as best we can with our poor gifts. May thy Son grant us that, by emulating thy most blessed life, we too, through the grace of the Holy Spirit, may be made worthy to conceive the Lord Jesus spiritually in our inmost hearts, and never lose him once conceived. Amen." Kissing the altar at the same time, I laid some coins upon it and went away.

MEN.: What did the Virgin do at this? Didn't she indicate by the slightest nod that your short prayer was heard?

OGYG.: As I told you, there was a dim religious light, and she stood in the shadows, to the right of the altar. Finally, the first custodian's harangue had so squelched me that I didn't dare lift my eyes.

MEN.: So this expedition didn't end very happily.

OGYG.: On the contrary, quite happily.

MEN.: You've brought me back to life, for "my heart had fallen to my knees," as your Homer says.

OGYG.: After lunch we went back to the church.

MEN.: You dared to, when you were suspected of sacrilege?

OGYG.: That may be, but I was not suspect in my own eyes. A good conscience knows no fear. I wanted to see the "record" to which the guide had referred us. After searching for it a long time, we found it, but the board was hung so high nobody could possibly read it. I'm no Lynceus so far as eyes are concerned, nor am I totally blind, either. So as Aldridge read, I followed along, not trusting him completely in so vital a matter.

MEN.: Were all your doubts cleared up?

OGYG.: I was ashamed of having doubted, so clearly was the whole thing set forth before my eyes—the name, the place, the story, told in order. In a word, nothing was omitted. There was said to be a certain William of Paris, a holy man, inasmuch as from time to time he was remarkably devoted to searching the world over for saints' relics. After traveling through many lands, visiting monasteries and churches everywhere, he came at length to Constantinople, where his brother was bishop. When William was preparing to return, his brother confided to him that a certain nun had the milk of the Virgin Mother and that he would be extremely blessed ever afterward if by prayer, purchase, or artifice he could get hold of a portion of it. All other relics he had collected to date were as nothing compared with this sacred milk. From that moment William could not rest until by his begging he won a little of the milk. With this treasure he thought himself richer than Croesus.

MEN.: Why not? And beyond expectation, too.

OGYG.: He hurried straight home, but a fatal illness stopped him short.

MEN.: How slight, brief, and limited is human happiness!

OGYG.: Aware of the danger, he summons a fellow pilgrim, a most reliable Frenchman. Swearing him to secrecy, he entrusts the milk to him on condition that if he reaches home safely he is to place this treasure on the altar of the Holy Virgin who dwells in the great church in Paris [*Notre Dame de Paris*—Ed.], overlooking the Seine that flows by on each side—the river itself seems to give way in honor of the Virgin's sanctity. To make a long story short, William is buried; the other hurries on; and disease takes him, too. In despair of his life, he gives the milk to an English companion but binds him by many oaths to do what he himself had intended to do. He dies; the other takes the milk and places it on the altar in the presence of the canons there (formerly called Regulars, as they are yet at St. Genevieve's). From them he begged a little of the milk. This he carried to England and finally brought to St. Mary-by-the-Sea, summoned to this place by divine inspiration.

MEN.: Surely this story is very consistent.

OGYG.: More than that: lest any uncertainty remain, there were inscribed, above, the names of suffragan bishops who grant indulgences as extensive as their supply affords to those who come to see the milk and don't neglect to leave a small offering.

MEN.: How much can they grant?

OGYG.: Forty days.

MEN.: Are there days even in the underworld?

OGYG.: There's time, certainly.

MEN.: When the whole supply's been granted, is there none left to give out?

OGYG.: On the contrary: what they grant is inexhaustible. And obviously this is different from what happens to the jar of the Danaides, since that, though continuously filled, is always empty; but as for this, if you always drain it, still the jar's no emptier.

MEN.: If forty days apiece are granted to a hundred thousand men, each man has so much?

OGYG.: Yes.

MEN.: And if those who received forty days before lunch were to ask for the same number again at dinner time it would be at hand to bestow?

OGYG.: Oh, yes, even if they asked for it ten times an hour.

MEN.: Wish I had such a money box at home! I'd ask merely for three drachmas if only they renewed themselves.

OGYG.: If the answer to your prayer is to be so large as that, you're hoping to turn into gold completely. But to resume the story. This "proof" was added, with pious simplicity: that although the Virgin's milk shown in a great many other places was of course to be reverenced, nevertheless this was to be venerated more than that elsewhere, because that was scraped from rocks whereas this flowed from the Virgin's own breasts.

MEN.: How was this known?

OGYG.: Oh, the nun of Constantinople, who gave the milk, said so.

MEN.: And perhaps St. Bernard informed her?

OGYG.: That's what I think.

MEN.: The one who in old age was privileged to taste milk from that same breast which the child Jesus sucked. Hence I'm surprised he's called "the mellifluous" instead of "the lactifluous." But how can that be called the Virgin's milk which did not flow from her breasts?

OGYG.: It did flow, but falling on the rock where she happened to be sitting when giving suck, it hardened and then, by God's will, so increased.

MEN.: Right. Continue.

OGYG.: After this, while we're strolling about, looking at sights of interest before departing, the custodians turn up again, glance at us, point with the finger, run up, go away, rush back, nod; they seemed to be on the point of accosting us if they could find courage enough.

MEN.: Weren't you at all scared then?

OGYG.: Oh, no, I looked them straight in the eye, smiling and gazing at them as if inviting them to address me. At last one comes near and asks my name. I give it. He asks if I was the man who two years earlier had put up a votive tablet in Hebrew. I admit it.

MEN.: Do you write Hebrew?

OGYG.: Of course not, but anything they don't understand they call Hebrew. Soon the protos-hysteros of the college comes—having been sent for, I imagine.

MEN.: What title is that? Haven't they an abbot?

OGYG.: No.

MEN.: Why?

OGYG.: Because they don't know Hebrew.

MEN.: Nor a bishop?

OGYG.: No.

MEN.: Why?

OGYG.: Because the Virgin is still too hard up to buy an expensive staff and miter.

• • •

MEN.: Go on; continue what you began.

OGYG.: Next he shows us gold and silver statues. "This one," says he, "is all gold; the other one, silver gilded." He adds the weight and worth of each, and the name of the donor. When, marveling at every one, I was congratulating the Virgin on such fortunate wealth, the guide said: "Since I notice you're a devout sightseer, I don't think it right to keep anything from you: you shall see the Virgin's very greatest secrets." At the same time he takes down from the altar itself a world of wonderful things. If I tried to enumerate them all, the day would not be long enough. Thus the pilgrimage ended very happily for me. I had my fill of sights, and I brought away with me this priceless gift, a pledge from the Virgin herself.

MEN.: Didn't you test the power of your piece of wood?

OGYG.: I did. Before three days passed, I found at a certain inn a man who had gone mad; they were ready to chain him. I slipped this wood under his pillow secretly. He fell into a long, deep sleep. In the morning he woke up as sound as ever.

MEN.: Maybe it wasn't insanity but delirium tremens from drink. Sleep usually helps that malady.

OGYG.: Joke as you please, Menedemus, but about something else. To make fun of the saints is neither reverent nor prudent. Why, the man himself said that a woman of marvelous beauty had appeared to him in a dream and held out a cup to him.

MEN.: Hellebore, I dare say.

OGYG.: I don't know about that, but I do know the man's in his right mind.

MEN.: Did you overlook Thomas, Archbishop of Canterbury:

OGYG.: By no means. No pilgrimage is more devout.

MEN.: I long to hear about it, if that's not too much trouble.

OGYG.: Oh, no, I want you to hear. There's a part of England called Kent, facing France and Flanders; its chief city is Canterbury. In it are two monasteries, almost adjacent, both of them Benedictine houses. That named for St. Augustine is evidently the older; the one now called after St. Thomas appears to have been the Archbishop's see, where he used to live with a few chosen monks; just as today, too, bishops have residences adjoining the churches but separate from the houses of other canons. (In old times both bishops and canons were usually monks; evidence abounds to prove that.) The church sacred to St. Thomas [*Canterbury Cathedral*—Ed.] rises to the sky so majestically that it inspires devotion even in those who see it from afar. Thus by its splendor it now dims the glory of the neighboring one and, so to speak, overshadows the spot that was anciently the most sacred. It has two huge towers, as though greeting visitors a long way off and making the region ring far and wide with the wonderful sound of its bronze

bells. At the south entrance of the church are stone statues of three armed men, who with sacrilegious hands murdered the blessed saint. Their surnames are added: Tusci, Fusci, Berri.[4]

MEN.: Why is so much honor paid to impious men?

OGYG.: Obviously they have the same honor as Judas, Pilate, and Caiaphas, that wicked band whom you see carefully carved on gilded altars. The surnames are added lest anybody in the future speak well of them. Attention is called to them in order that hereafter no courtier lift a hand against bishops or Church property. For those three conspirators went mad after committing their crime, and would not have recovered had they not begged help of the most holy Thomas.

MEN.: O the everlasting mercy of martyrs!

OGYG.: When you enter, the spacious grandeur of the building is disclosed. This part is open to the public.

MEN.: Is there nothing to see there?

OGYG.: Nothing but the mass of the structure and some books—among them the Gospel of Nicodemus—chained to pillars, and a tomb, I don't know whose.

MEN.: Then what?

OGYG.: Iron screens prevent you from going further, but they permit a view of the space between the end of the building and the choir, as it is called. This is ascended by many steps, under which a certain vault gives access to the north side. A

---

[4] De Tracy, Fitzurse, and Le Breton or Brito; Erasmus omits the name of the fourth, De Morville.

wooden altar sacred to the Holy Virgin is shown there; a very small one, not worth seeing except as a monument of antiquity, a rebuke to the luxury of our times. There the holy man is said to have spoken his last farewell to the Virgin when death was at hand. On the altar is the point of the sword with which the crown of the good bishop's head was cut off; and his brain, evidently smashed to make death come more quickly. Out of love for the martyr we reverently kissed the sacred rust of this sword.

Leaving this place, we went into the crypt. It has its own custodians. First is shown the martyr's skull, pierced through. The top of the cranius is bared for kissing, the rest covered with silver. Along with this is displayed a leaden plate with "Thomas of Acre" carved on it. The hair shirt, girdle, and drawers by which the bishop used to subdue his flesh hang in the gloom there— horrible even to look at and a reproach to our softness and delicacy.

MEN.: Perhaps to the monks themselves, too.

OGYG.: From here we return to the choir. On the north side mysteries are laid open. It is wonderful how many bones were brought forth—skulls, jaws, teeth, hands, fingers, whole arms, all of which we adored and kissed. This would have gone on forever if my fellow pilgrim, an unobliging chap, had not cut short the enthusiasm of the guide.

MEN.: Who was this?

OGYG.: An Englishman named Gratian Pullus, a learned and upright man but less respectful toward this side of religion than I liked.

MEN.: Some Wycliffite, I suppose.[5]

OGYG.: I don't think so, though he had read his books. Where he got hold of them isn't clear.

MEN.: Did he offend the guide?

OGYG.: An arm was brought forth, with the bloodstained flesh still on it. He shrank from kissing this, looking rather disgusted. The custodian soon put his things away. Next we viewed the altar table and ornaments; then the objects that were kept under the altar—all of them splendid; you'd say Midas and Croesus were beggars if you saw the quantity of gold and silver.

MEN.: No kisses here?

OGYG.: No, but a different sort of desire came to my mind.

MEN.: What?

OGYG.: I was sad because I had no such relics at home.

MEN.: An impious thought!

OGYG.: Admitted, and I begged the saint's forgiveness before I left the church. After this we were conducted to the sacristy. Good Lord, what an array of silk vestments there, what an abundance of gold candelabra! There too we saw St. Thomas' staff. It looked like a cane plated with silver. It was not at all heavy, had no ornamentation, and was no more than waist-high.

MEN.: No cross?[6]

OGYG.: None that I saw. We were shown a pallium, silk to be sure, but coarse, without gold or jewels, and there was a facecloth, soiled by sweat from his neck and preserving ob-

[5] [Follower of John Wycliffe, English religious reformer (1320?–1384)—Ed.]

[6] I.e., "No cross on the staff?" An archbishop's staff is surmounted by a cross.

vious spots of blood. These memorials of the plain living of olden times we gladly kissed.

MEN.: They're not shown to everyone?

OGYG.: Certainly not, my good friend.

MEN.: How did you manage to make such an impression of devoutness that no secrets were kept from you?

OGYG.: I had some acquaintance with the Reverend Father William Warham, the Archbishop. He gave me a note of recommendation.

MEN.: I hear from many persons that he is a man of remarkable kindness.

OGYG.: More than that: you would call him kindness itself if you knew him. His learning, integrity, and holiness of life are so great that you would find him lacking in no quality befitting a perfect prelate. Next we were led up above, for behind the high altar you ascend as though into a new church. There in a small chapel is shown the entire face[7] of the saint, gilded and ornamented with jewels. Here a certain unlooked-for accident almost upset all our good luck.

MEN.: I'm waiting to hear what misfortune you mean.

OGYG.: My friend Gratian was anything but ingratiating on this occasion. After a short prayer he asked the keeper, "I say, good father, is it true, as I've heard, that in his lifetime Thomas was most generous to the poor?" "Very true," the man replied, and began to rehearse the saint's many acts of kindness to them. Then Gratian: "I don't suppose his disposition changed in this matter, unless perhaps for the better." The custodian agreed. Gratian again: "Since, then, the saint was so liberal toward the needy, though he was still poor himself and lacked money to provide for the necessities of life, don't you think he'd gladly consent, now that he's so rich and needs nothing, if some poor wretched woman with hungry children at home, or daughters in danger of losing their virtue because they have no money for dowries, or a husband sick in bed and penniless—if, after begging the saint's forgiveness, she carried off a bit of all this wealth to rescue her family, as though taking from one who wanted her to have it, either as a gift or a loan?" When the keeper in charge of the gilded head made no reply to this, Gratian, who's impulsive, said, "For my part, I'm convinced the saint would even rejoice that in death, too, he could relieve the wants of the poor by his riches." At this the custodian frowned and pursed his lips, looking at us with Gorgon eyes, and I don't doubt he would have driven us from the church with insults and reproaches had he not been aware that we were recommended by the archbishop. I managed to placate the fellow by smooth talk, affirming that Gratian hadn't spoken seriously but liked to joke; and at the same time I gave him some coins.

MEN.: I quite approve of your sense of duty. But seriously, I wonder sometimes what possible excuse there could be for those who spend so much money on building, decorating, and enriching churches that there's simply no limit to it. Granted that the sacred vestments and vessels of the church must have a dignity appropriate to their liturgical

_____

[7] "Facies"; here a bust.

use; and I want the building to have grandeur. But what's the use of so many baptistries, candelabra, gold statues? What's the good of the vastly expensive organs, as they call them? (We're not content with a single pair, either). What's the good of that costly musical neighing when meanwhile our brothers and sisters, Christ's living temples, waste away from hunger and thirst?

OGYG.: Every decent, sensible man favors moderation in these matters, of course. But since the fault springs from excessive devotion, it merits applause; especially when one thinks of the opposite vice in those who rob churches of their wealth. These gifts are generally given by kings and potentates and would be worse spent on gambling and war. And if you divert anything, that, in the first place, is regarded as sacrilege; next, those who are regular contributors stop their giving; above all, men are incited to robbery. Hence churchmen are custodians of these things rather than owners of them. In short, I'd rather see a church abounding in sacred furnishings than bare and dirty, as some are, and more like stables than churches.

MEN.: Yet we read that in former times bishops were praised for selling the sacred vessels and using the money to relieve the poor.

OGYG.: They're praised today, too, but only praised. In my judgment, to imitate them is neither allowable nor agreeable.

MEN.: I'm holding up your story. Let's have the conclusion.

OGYG.: Hear it, then; I'll be brief. While this was going on, the chief official came forward.

MEN.: Who? The abbot of the place?

OGYG.: He has a miter and abbatial revenue; he lacks only the name of abbot and is called prior, because the archbishop serves instead of an abbot. In ancient times whoever was archbishop of this diocese was also a monk.

MEN.: Well, I wouldn't mind being called camel if I had an abbot's income.

OGYG.: He seemed to me a good, sensible man; something of a Scotist[8] theologian, too. He opened for us the chest in which the rest of the holy man's body is said to lie.

MEN.: You saw the bones?

OGYG.: No, that's not permitted, nor would it be possible without the use of ladders. But within the wooden chest is a golden chest; when this is drawn up by ropes, it reveals inestimable treasure.

MEN.: What do I hear?

OGYG.: The cheapest part was gold. Everything shone and dazzled with rare and surpassingly large jewels, some bigger than a goose egg. Some monks stood about reverently. When the cover was removed, we all adored. The prior pointed out each jewel by touching it with a white rod, adding its French name, its worth, and the name of the donor. The principal ones were gifts from kings.

MEN.: He must have a remarkable memory.

OGYG.: Your guess is correct, though practice helps too, for he often does this. From here he leads the way back to the crypt. There the Virgin Mother has a residence, but a somewhat dark one, enclosed by a double row of iron rails.

---

[8] [Apparently a reference to the medieval theologian, John Duns Scotus (1265?–1308)—*Ed.*]

MEN.: What's she afraid of?

OGYG.: Only robbers, I suppose, for I've never seen anything more loaded with riches.

MEN.: You tell me of dark riches.

OGYG.: When the lanterns were brought closer, we saw a more than regal sight.

MEN.: More wealth than that of St. Mary-by-the-Sea?

OGYG.: It looks like much more. She alone knows her secret wealth. It isn't shown to any but persons of the highest importance or to special friends. At last we were led back to the sacristy. There a chest with a black leather cover was brought out, placed on the table, and opened. Immediately everyone worshiped on bended knee.

MEN.: What was inside?

OGYG.: Some linen rags, many of them still showing traces of snivel. With these, they say, the holy man wiped the sweat from his face or neck, the dirt from his nose, or whatever other kinds of filth human bodies have. At this point my friend Gratian again displayed something less than graciousness. To him, since he was English and a well-known person of considerable standing, the prior kindly offered one of the rags as a gift, thinking he was making him a present that would please him very much. But Gratian was hardly grateful for it. He touched the piece with his fingers, not without a sign of disgust, and put it back scornfully, puckering his lips as though whistling. (This is what he ordinarily did if he came across anything he thought contemptible.) Shame and alarm together embarrassed me dreadfully. But the prior, no boor, pretended not to notice this incident, and after offering us a glass of wine dismissed us kindly, for we were returning to London.

Martin Luther

The theory that all events are inter-related receives dramatic confirmation in the relationship between the Renaissance and the Reformation. To raise money to build St. Peter's Cathedral in Rome, the greatest monument of Renaissance art, Pope Leo X authorized the granting of papal indulgences in return for suitable donations to the Church. In 1517, one of the papal agents, a Dominican friar named John Tetzel, appeared in central Germany, to grant these indulgences. Martin Luther (1483–1546), a professor at the University of Wittenberg, responded by posting on the door of the Castle Church a list of Ninety-Five Theses, in which he attacked the entire theory and practice of indulgences. Luther's act, in turn, set in motion a series of events that resulted finally in the Protestant Reformation.

Although Tetzel's activities had set him off, Luther based his opposition to the Church on grounds far deeper than the problem of indulgences. Basically, the question centered on the salvation of people's souls. From his studies of St. Paul and St. Augustine, Luther became convinced that, since all people are utterly condemned and lost as a result of original sin, it is impossible for them to achieve salvation by any works of their own. Rather, salvation is the free gift of God's grace through faith. This doctrine of justification by faith rather than by works undercut the position of the Catholic Church, which maintained that, since the works necessary to salvation (e.g., the sacraments) could be performed only with the aid of the priesthood, the Church provided the sole means to salvation. In place of the priestly hierarchy, Luther substituted the notion of "the priesthood of all believers."

An Open Letter to the Christian Nobility of the German Nation Concerning the Reform of the Christian Estate, 1520

To His Most Illustrious and
Mighty Imperial Majesty,
and to the Christian
Nobility of the German
Nation,

DOCTOR MARTIN LUTHER

Grace and power from God, Most illustrious Majesty, and most gracious and dear Lords.

It is not out of sheer forwardness or rashness that I, a single, poor man, have undertaken to address your worships. The distress and oppression which weigh down all the Estates of Christendom, especially of Germany, and which move not me alone, but everyone to cry out time and again, and to pray for help, have forced me even now to cry aloud that God may inspire some one with His Spirit to lend this suffering nation a helping hand. Ofttimes the councils have made some pretence at reformation, but their attempts have been cleverly hindered by the guile of certain men and things have gone from bad to worse. I now intend, by the help of God, to throw some light upon the wiles and wickedness of these men, to the end that when they are known, they may not henceforth be so hurtful and so great a hindrance. God has given us a noble youth to be our head and thereby has awakened great hopes of good in many hearts; wherefore it is meet that we should do our part and profitably use this time of grace.

In this whole matter the first and most important thing is that we take earnest heed not to enter on it trusting in great might or in human reason, even though all power in the world were ours; for God cannot and will not suffer a good work to be begun with trust in our own power or reason. Such works He crushes ruthlessly to earth, as it is written in the xxxiii Psalm, "There is no king saved by the multitude of an host: a mighty man is not delivered by much strength." On this account, I fear, it came to pass of old that the good Emperors Frederick I and II, and many other German emperors were shamefully oppressed and trodden under foot by the popes, although all the world feared them. It may be that they relied on their own might more than on God, and therefore they had to fall. In our own times, too, what was it that raised the bloodthirsty Julius II to such heights? Nothing else, I fear, except that France, the Germans, and Venice relied upon themselves. The children of Benjamin slew forty-two thousand Israelites

"An Open Letter to the Christian Nobility of the German Nation Concerning the Reform of the Christian Estate," trans. C. M. Jacobs, in *Works of Martin Luther* (Philadelphia: Muhlenberg Press, 1915), II, 63–84. Courtesy of the Fortress Press.

because the latter relied on their own strength.

That it may not so fare with us and our noble young Emperor Charles, we must be sure that in this matter we are dealing not with men, but with the princes of hell, who can fill the world with war and bloodshed, but whom war and bloodshed do not overcome. We must go at this work despairing of physical force and humbly trusting God; we must seek God's help with earnest prayer, and fix our minds on nothing else than the misery and distress of suffering Christendom, without regard to the deserts of evil men. Otherwise we may start the game with great prospect of success, but when we get well into it the evil spirits will stir up such confusion that the whole world will swim in blood, and yet nothing will come of it. Let us act wisely, therefore, and in the fear of God. The more force we use, the greater our disaster if we do not act humbly and in God's fear. The popes and the Romans have hitherto been able, by the devil's help, to set kings at odds with one another, and they may well be able to do it again, if we proceed by our own might and cunning, without God's help.

I. The Three Walls of the Romanists

The Romanists, with great adroitness, have built three walls about them, behind which they have hitherto defined themselves in such wise that no one has been able to reform them; and this has been the cause of terrible corruption throughout all Christendom.

First, when pressed by the temporal power, they have made decrees and said that the temporal power has no jurisdiction over them, but, on the other hand, that the spiritual is above the temporal power. Second, when the attempt is made to reprove them out of the Scriptures, they raise the objection that the interpretation of the Scriptures belongs to no one except the pope. Third, if threatened with a council, they answer with the fable that no one can call a council but the pope.

In this wise they have slyly stolen from us our three rods, that they may go unpunished, and have ensconced themselves within the safe stronghold of these three walls, that they may practise all the knavery and wickedness which we now see. Even when they have been compelled to hold council they have weakened its power in advance by previously binding the princes with an oath to let them remain as they are. Moreover, they have given the pope full authority over all the decisions of the council, so that it is all one whether there are many councils,—except that they deceive us with puppet-shows and sham-battles. So terribly do they fear for their skin in a really free council! And they have intimidated kings and princes by making them believe it would be an offence against God not to obey them in all these knavish, crafty deceptions.

Now God help us, and give us one of the trumpets with which the walls of Jericho were overthrown, that we may blow down these walls of straw and paper, and may set free the Christian rods for the punishment of sin, bringing to light the craft and deceit of the devil, to the end that through punishment we may reform ourselves, and once more attain God's favor.

Against the first wall we will direct our first attack.

It is pure invention that pope, bishops, priests and monks are to be called the "spiritual estate"; princes, lords, artisans, and farmers the "temporal estate." That is indeed a fine bit of lying and hypocrisy. Yet no one should be frightened by it; and for this reason— *viz.*, that all Christians are truly of the "spiritual estate," and there is among them no difference at all but that of office, as Paul says in I Corinthians xii, We are all one body, yet every member has its own work, whereby it serves every other, all because we have one baptism, one Gospel, one faith, and are all alike Christians; for baptism, Gospel and faith alone make us "spiritual" and a Christian people.

But that a pope or a bishop anoints, confers, tonsures, ordains, consecrates, or prescribes dress unlike that of the laity,—this may make hypocrites, and graven images, but it never makes a Christian or "spiritual" man. Through baptism all of us are consecrated to the priesthood, as St. Peter says in I Peter ii, "Ye are a royal priesthood, a priestly kingdom," and the book of Revelation says, "Thou hast made us by Thy blood to be priests and kings." For if we had no higher consecration than pope or bishop gives, the consecration by pope or bishop would never make a priest, nor might anyone either say mass or preach a sermon or give absolution. Therefore when the bishop consecrates it is the same thing as if he, in the place and stead of the whole congregation, all of whom have like power, were to take one out of their number and charge him to use this power for the others; just as though ten brothers, all king's sons and equal heirs, were to choose one of themselves to rule the inheritance for them all,—they would all be kings and equal in power, though one of them would be charged with the duty of ruling.

To make it still clearer. If a little group of pious Christian laymen were taken captive and set down in a wilderness, and had among them no priest consecrated by a bishop, and if there in the wilderness they were to agree in choosing one of themselves, married or unmarried, and were to charge him with the office of baptising, saying mass, absolving and preaching, such a man would be as truly a priest as though all bishops and popes had consecrated him. That is why in cases of necessity any one can baptise and give absolution, which would be impossible unless we were all priests. This great grace and power of baptism and of the Christian Estate they have well-nigh destroyed and caused us to forget through the canon law. It was in the manner aforesaid that Christians in olden days chose from their number bishops and priests, who were afterwards confirmed by other bishops, without all the show which now obtains. It was thus that Sts. Augustine, Ambrose, and Cyprian became bishops.

Since, then, the temporal authorities are baptised with the same baptism and have the same faith and Gospel as we, we must grant that they are priests and bishops, and count their office one which has a proper and a useful place in the Christian community. For whoever comes out of the water of baptism can boast that he is already conse-crated priest, bishop, and pope, though it is not seemly that every one should exercise the office. Nay, just because we are all in like man-ner priests, no one must put himself forward and undertake, without our consent and election, to do what is in the power of all of us. For what is common to all, no one dare take upon himself without the will and the commands of the community; and should it happen that one cho-sen for such an office were deposed for malfeasance, he would then be just what he was before he held office. Therefore a priest in Chris-tendom is nothing else than an of-fice-holder. While he is in office, he has precedence; when deposed, he is a peasant or a townsman like the rest. Beyond all doubt, then, a priest is no longer a priest when he is deposed. But now they have in-vented *characteres indelebiles*, and prate that a deposed priest is never-theless something different from a mere layman. They even dream that a priest can never become a layman, or be anything else than a priest. All this is mere talk and manmade law.

From all this it follows that there is really no difference between lay-men and priests, princes and bish-ops, "spirituals" and "temporals," as they call them, except that of office and work, but not of "estate"; for they are all of the same estate,— true priests, bishops, and popes,— though they are not all engaged in the same work, just as all priests and monks have not the same work. This is the teaching of St. Paul in Romans xii and I Corinthians xii, and of St. Peter in I Peter ii, as I have said above, *viz.*, that we are all one body of Christ, the Head, all members

one of another. Christ has not two different bodies, one "temporal," the other "spiritual." He is one Head, and He has one body.

Therefore, just as those who are now called "spiritual"—priests, bishops or popes—are neither dif-ferent from other Christians nor superior to them, except that they are charged with the administration of the Word of God and the sacra-ments, which is their work and of-fice, so it is with the temporal au-thorities,—they bear sword and rod with which to punish the evil and to protect the good. A cobbler, a smith, a farmer, each has the work and office of his trade, and yet they are all alike consecrated priests and bishops, and every one by means of his own work or office must benefit and serve every other, that in this way many kinds of work may be done for the bodily and spiritual welfare of the community, even as all the members of the body serve one another.

See, now, how Christian is the decree which says that the temporal power is not above the "spiritual estate" and may not punish it. That is as much as to say that the hand shall lend no aid when the eye is suffering. Is it not unnatural, not to say unchristian, that one member should not help another and pre-vent its destruction? Verily, the more honorable the member, the more should the others help. I say then, since the temporal power is ordained of God to punish evildoers and to protect them that do well, it should therefore be left free to per-form its office without hindrance through the whole body of Chris-tendom without respect of persons, whether it affect pope, bishops, priests, monks, nuns or anybody else. For if the mere fact that the temporal power has a smaller place among the Christian offices than has the office of preachers or confessors, or of the clergy, then the tailors, cobblers, masons, carpenters, potboys, tapsters, farmers, and all the secular tradesmen, should also be prevented from providing pope, bishops, priests and monks with shoes, clothing, houses, meat and drink, and from paying them tribute. But if these laymen are allowed to do their work unhindered, what do the Roman scribes mean by their laws, with which they withdraw themselves from the jurisdiction of the temporal Christian power, only so that they may be free to do evil and to fulfill what St. Peter has said: "There shall be false teachers among you, and through covetousness shall they with feigned words make merchandise of you."

On this account the Christian temporal power should exercise its office without let or hindrance, regardless whether it be pope, bishop, or priest whom it affects; whoever is guilty, let him suffer. All that the canon law has said to the contrary is sheer invention of Roman presumption. For thus saith St. Paul to all Christians: "Let every soul (I take that to mean the pope's soul also) be subject unto the higher powers; for they bear not the sword in vain, but are the ministers of God for the punishment of evil-doers, and for the praise of them that do well." St. Peter also says: "Submit yourselves unto every ordinance of man for the Lord's sake, for so is the will of God." He has also prophesied that such men shall come as will despise the temporal authorities, and this has come to pass through the canon law.

So then, I think this first paperwall is overthrown, since the temporal power has become a member of the body of Christendom, and is of the "spiritual estate," though its work is of a temporal nature. Therefore its work should extend freely and without hindrance to all the members of the whole body; it should punish and use force whenever guilt deserves or necessity demands, without regard to pope, bishops, and priests,—let them hurl threats and bans as much as they will.

This is why guilty priests, if they are surrendered to the temporal law, are first deprived of their priestly dignities, which would not be right unless the temporal sword had previously had authority over them by divine right.

Again, it is intolerable that in the canon law so much importance is attached to the freedom, life and property of the clergy, as though the laity were not also as spiritual and as good Christians as they, or did not belong to the Church. Why are your life and limb, your property and honor so free, and mine not? We are all alike Christians, and have baptism, faith, Spirit, and all things alike. If a priest is killed, the land is laid under interdict,—why not when a peasant is killed? Whence comes this great distinction between those who are equally Christians? Only from human laws and inventions!

Moreover, it can be no good spirit who has invented such exceptions and granted to sin such license and impunity. For if we are bound to strive against the works and words of the evil spirit, and to drive him out in whatever way we can, as Christ commands and His Apostles, ought we, then, to suffer it in silence when the pope or his satellites are bent on devilish words and works? Ought we for the sake of men to allow the suppression of divine commandments and truths which we have sworn in baptism to support with life and limb? Of a truth we should then have to answer for all the souls that would thereby be abandoned and led astray.

It must therefore have been the very prince of devils who said what is written in the canon law: "If the pope were so scandalously bad as to lead souls in crowds to the devil, yet he could not be deposed." On this accursed and devilish foundation they build at Rome, and think that we should let all the world go to the devil, rather than resist their knavery. If the fact that one man is set over others were sufficient reason why he should escape punishment, then no Christian could punish another, since Christ commands the lowliest and the least.

Where sin is, there is no escape from punishment; as St. Gregory also writes that we are indeed all equal, but guilt puts us in subjection one to another. Now we see how they whom God and the Apostles have made subject to the temporal sword deal with Christendom, depriving it of its liberty by their own wickedness, without warrant of Scripture. It is to be feared that this is a game of Antichrist or a sign that he is close at hand.

The second wall is still more flimsy and worthless. They wish to be the only Masters of the Holy Scriptures, even though in all their lives they learn nothing from them. They assume for themselves sole authority, and with insolent juggling of words they would persuade us that the pope, whether he be a bad man or a good man, cannot err in matters of faith; and yet they cannot prove a single letter of it. Hence it comes that so many heretical and unchristian, nay, even unnatural ordinances have a place in the canon law, of which, however, there is no present need to speak. For since they think that the Holy Spirit never leaves them, be they ever so unlearned and wicked, they make bold to decree whatever they will. And if it were true, where would be the need or use of the Holy Scriptures? Let us burn them, and be satisfied with the unlearned lords at Rome, who are possessed of the Holy Spirit,—although He can possess only pious hearts! Unless I had read it myself, I could not have believed that the devil would make such clumsy pretensions at Rome, and find a following.

But, not to fight them with mere words, we will quote the Scriptures. St. Paul says in I Corinthians xiv: "If to anyone something better is revealed, though he be sitting and listening to another in God's Word, then the first, who is speaking, shall hold his peace and give place." What would be the use of this commandment, if we were only to believe him who does the talking or who has the highest seat? Christ also says in John vi, that all Christians shall be taught of God. Thus it may well happen that the pope and his followers are wicked men, and no true Christians, not taught of God, not having true understanding. On the other hand, an ordinary man may have true understanding; why then should we not follow him? Has not the pope erred many times? Who would help Christendom when the pope errs, if we were not to believe another, who had the Scriptures on his side, more than the pope?

Therefore it is a wickedly invented fable, and they cannot produce a letter in defence of it, that the interpretation of Scripture or the confirmation of its interpretation belongs to the pope alone. They have themselves usurped this power; and although they allege that this power was given to Peter when the keys were given to him, it is plain enough that the keys were not given to Peter alone, but to the whole community. Moreover, the keys were not ordained for doctrine or government, but only for the binding and loosing of sin, and whatever further power of the keys they arrogate to themselves is mere invention. But Christ's word to Peter, "I have prayed for thee that thy faith fail not," cannot be applied to the pope, since the majority of the popes have been without faith, as they must themselves confess. Besides, it is not only for Peter that Christ prayed, but also for all Apostles and Christians, as he says in John xvii: "Father, I pray for those whom Thou hast given Me, and not for these only, but for all who believe on Me through their word." Is not this clear enough?

Only think of it yourself! They must confess that there are pious Christians among us, who have the true faith, Spirit, understanding, word and mind of Christ. Why, then, should we reject their word and understanding and follow the pope, who has neither faith nor Spirit? That would be to deny the whole faith and the Christian Church. Moreover, it is not the pope alone who is always in the right, if the article of the Creed is correct: "I believe in one holy Christian Church"; otherwise the prayer must run: "I believe in the pope at Rome," and so reduce the Christian Church to one man,—which would be nothing else than a devilish and hellish error.

Besides, if we are all priests, as was said above, and all have one faith, one Gospel, one sacrament, why should we not also have the power to test and judge what is correct or incorrect in matters of faith? What becomes of the words of Paul in I Corinthians ii: "He that is spiritual judgeth all things, yet he himself is judged of no man," and II Corinthians iv: "We have all the same Spirit of faith"? Why, then, should not we perceive what squares with faith and what does not, as well as does an unbelieving pope?

All these and many other texts should make us bold and free, and we should not allow the Spirit of liberty, as Paul calls Him, to be frightened off by the fabrications of the popes, but we ought to go boldly forward to test all that they do or leave undone, according to our interpretation of the Scriptures, which rests on faith, and compel them to follow not their own interpretation, but the one that is better. In the olden days Abraham had to listen to his Sarah, although she was in more complete subjection to him than we are to anyone on earth. Balaam's ass, also, was wiser than the prophet himself. If God then spoke by an ass against a prophet, why should He not be able even now to speak by a righteous man against the pope? In like manner St. Paul rebukes St. Peter as a man in error. Therefore it behooves every Christian to espouse the cause of the faith, to understand and defend it, and to rebuke all errors.

The third wall falls of itself when the first two are down. For when the pope acts contrary to the Scriptures, it is our duty to stand by the Scriptures, to reprove him, and to constrain him, according to the word of Christ in Matthew xviii: "If thy brother sin against thee, go and tell it him between thee and him alone; if he hear thee not, then take with thee one or two more; if he hear them not, tell it to the Church; if he hear not the Church, consider him a heathen." Here every member is commanded to care for every other. How much rather should we do this when the member that does evil is a ruling member, and by his evil-doing is the cause of much harm and offence to the rest! But if I am to accuse him before the Church, I must bring the Church together.

They have no basis in Scripture for their contention that it belongs to the pope alone to call a council or confirm its actions; for this is based merely upon their own laws, which are valid only in so far as they are not injurious to Christendom or contrary to the laws of God. When the Pope deserves punishment, such laws go out of force, since it is injurious to Christendom not to punish him by means of a council.

Thus we read in Acts xv that it was not St. Peter who called the Apostolic Council, but the Apostles and elders. If, then, that right had belonged to St. Peter alone, the council would not have been a Christian council, but an heretical *conciliabulum*. Even the Council of Nicaea—the most famous of all— was neither called nor confirmed by the Bishop of Rome, but by the Emperor Constantine, and many other emperors after him did the like, yet these councils were the most Christian of all. But if the pope alone had the right to call councils, then all these councils must have been heretical. Moreover, if I consider the councils which the pope has created, I find that they have done nothing of special importance.

Therefore, when necessity demands, and the pope is an offence to Christendom, the first man who is able should, as a faithful member of the whole body, do what he can to bring about a truly free council. No one can do this so well as the temporal authorities, especially since now they also are fellow-Christians, fellow-priests, "fellow-spirituals," fellow-lords over all things, and whenever it is needful or profitable, they should give free course to the office and work in which God has put them above every man. Would it not be an unnatural thing, if a fire broke out in a city, and every body were to stand by and let it burn on and on and consume everything that could burn, for the sole reason that nobody had the authority of the burgomaster, or because, perhaps, the fire broke out in the burgomaster's house? In such case is it not the duty of every citizen to arouse and call the rest? How much more should this be done in the spiritual city of Christ, if a fire of offence breaks out, whether in the papal government, or anywhere else? In the same way, if the enemy attacks a city, he who first rouses the others deserves honour and thanks; why then should he not deserve honour who makes known the presence of the enemy from hell, and awakens the Christians, and calls them together?

But all their boasts of an authority which dare not be opposed amount to nothing after all. No one in Christendom has authority to do injury, or to forbid the resisting of injury. There is no authority in the Church save for edification. Therefore, if the pope were to use his authority to prevent the calling of a free council, and thus became a hindrance to the edification of the Church, we should have regard neither for him nor for his authority; and if he were to hurl his bans and thunderbolts, we should despise his conduct as that of a madman, and relying on God, hurl back the ban on him, and coerce him as best we could. For this presumptuous authority of his is nothing; he has no such authority; and he is quickly overthrown by a text of Scripture; for Paul says to the Corinthians; "God has given us authority not for the destruction, but for the edification of Christendom." Who is ready to overleap this text? It is only the power of the devil and of Antichrist which resists the things that serve for the edification of Christendom; it is, therefore, in no wise to be obeyed, but is to be opposed with life and goods and all our strength.

Even though a miracle were to be done in the pope's behalf against the temporal powers, or though someone were to be stricken with a plague—which they boast has sometimes happened—it should be considered only the work of the devil, because of the weakness of our faith in God. Christ Himself prophesied in Matthew xxiv: "There shall come in My Name false Christs and false prophets, and do signs and wonders, so as to deceive even the elect," and Paul says in II Thessalonians ii, that Antichrist shall, through the power of Satan, be mighty in lying wonders.

Let us, therefore, hold fast to this: No Christian authority can do anything against Christ; as St. Paul says, "We can do nothing against Christ, but for Christ." Whatever does aught against Christ is the power of Antichrist and of the devil, even though it were to rain and hail wonders and plagues. Wonders and plagues prove nothing, especially in these evil times, for which all the Scriptures prophesy false wonders. Therefore we must cling with firm faith to the words of God, and then the devil will cease from wonders.

Thus I hope that the false, lying terror with which the Romans have this long time made our conscience timid and stupid, has been allayed. They, like all of us, are subject to the temporal sword; they have no power to interpret the Scriptures by mere authority, without learning; they have no authority to prevent a council or, in sheer wantonness, to pledge it, bind it, or take away its liberty; but if they do this, they are in truth in the communion of Antichrist and of the devil, and have nothing at all of Christ except the name.

II. Abuses To Be Discussed in Councils

We shall now look at the matters which should be discussed in the councils, and with which popes, cardinals, bishops, and all the scholars ought properly to be occupied day and night if they love Christ and His Church. But if they neglect this duty, then let the laity and the temporal authorities see to it, regardless of bans and thunders; for an unjust ban is better than ten just releases, and an unjust release worse than ten just bans. Let us, therefore, awake, dear Germans, and fear God rather than men, that we may not share the fate of all the poor souls who are so lamentably lost through the shameful and devilish rule of the Romans, in which the devil daily takes a larger and larger place—if indeed, it were possible that such a hellish rule could grow worse, a thing I can neither conceive nor believe.

1. It is a horrible and frightful thing that the ruler of Christendom, who boasts himself vicar of Christ and successor of St. Peter, lives in such worldly splendor that in this regard no king nor emperor can equal or approach him, and that he who claims the title of "most holy" and "most spiritual" is more worldly than the world itself. He wears a triple crown, when the greatest kings wear but a single crown; if that is like the poverty of Christ and of St. Peter, then it is a new kind of likeness. When a word is said against it, they cry out "Heresy!" but that is because they do not wish to hear how unchristian and ungodly such a practice is. I think, however, that if the pope were with tears to pray to God he would have to lay aside these crowns, for our God can suffer no pride, and his office is nothing else than this,—daily to weep and pray for Christendom, and to set an example of all humility.

However that my be, this splendour of his is an offence, and the pope is bound on his soul's salvation to lay it aside, because St. Paul says, "Abstain from all outward shows, which give offence," and in Rom. xii, "We should provide good, not

only in the sight of God, but also in the sight of all men." An ordinary bishop's crown would be enough for the pope; he should be greater than others in wisdom and holiness, and leave the crown of pride to Antichrist, as did his predecessors several centuries ago. They say he is a lord of the world; that is a lie; for Christ, Whose vicar and officer he boasts himself to be, said before Pilate, "My kingdom is not of this world," and no vicar's rule can go beyond his lord's. Moreover, he is not the vicar of the glorified, but of the crucified Christ, as Paul says, "I was willing to know nothing among you save Christ, and Him only as the Crucified"; and in Philippians ii, "So think of yourselves as ye see in Christ, Who emptied Himself and took upon Him the appearance of a servant"; and again in I Corinthians i, "We preach Christ, the Crucified." Now they make the pope a vicar of the glorified Christ in heaven, and some of them have allowed the devil to rule them so completely that they have maintained that the pope is above the angels in heaven and has authority over them. These are indeed the very works of the very Antichrist.

2. What is the use in Christendom of these people who are called the cardinals? I shall tell you. Italy and Germany have many rich monasteries, foundations, benefices, and livings. No better way has been discovered to bring all these to Rome than by creating cardinals and giving them the bishoprics, monasteries, and prelacies, and so overthrowing the worship of God. For this reason we now see Italy a very wilderness—monasteries in ruins, bishoprics devoured, the prelacies

and the revenues of all the churches drawn to Rome, cities decayed, land and people laid waste, because there is no more worship or preaching. Why? The cardinals must have the income. No Turk could have so devastated Italy and suppressed the worship of God.

Now that Italy is sucked dry, they come into Germany, and begin oh so gently. But let us beware, or Germany will soon become like Italy. Already we have some cardinals: what the Romans seek by that the "drunken Germans" are not to understand until we have not a bishopric, a monastery, a living, a benefice, a *heller* or a *pfennig* left. Antichrist must take the treasures of the earth, as it was prophesied. So it goes on. They skim the cream off the bishoprics, monasteries, and benefices, and because they do not yet venture to turn them all to shameful use, as they have done in Italy, they only practise for the present the sacred trickery of coupling together ten or twenty prelacies and taking a yearly portion from each of them, so as to make a tidy sum after all. The priory of Würzburg yields a thousand *gulden*; that of Bamberg, something; Mainz, Trier and the others, something more; and so from one to ten thousand *gulden* might be got together, in order that a cardinal might live at Rome like a rich king.

"After they are used to this, we will create thirty or forty cardinals in a day, and give to one Mount St. Michael at Bamberg and the bishopric of Würzburg to boot, hang on to these a few rich livings, until churches and cities are waste, and after that we will say, 'We are Christ's vicars and shepherds of Christ's sheep; the mad, drunken Germans must put up with it.'"

I advise, however, that the number of cardinals be reduced, or that the pope be made to keep them at his own expense. Twelve of them would be more than enough, and each of them might have an income of a thousand *gulden* a year. How comes it that we Germans must put up with such robbery and such extortion of our property, at the hands of the pope? If the Kingdom of France has prevented it, why do we Germans let them make such fools and apes of us? It would all be more bearable if in this way they only stole our property; but they lay waste the churches and rob Christ's sheep of their pious shepherds, and destroy the worship and the Word of God. Even if there were not a single cardinal, the Church would not go under. As it is they do nothing for the good of Christendom; they only wrangle about the incomes of bishoprics and prelacies, and that any robber could do.

3. If ninety-nine parts of the papal court were done away and only the hundredth part allowed to remain, it would still be large enough to give decisions in matters of faith. Now, however, there is such a swarm of vermin yonder in Rome, all boasting that they are "papal," that there was nothing like it in Babylon. There are more than three thousand papal secretaries alone; who will count the other offices, when they are so many that they scarcely can be counted? And they all lie in wait for the prebends and benefices of Germany as wolves lie in wait for the sheep. I believe that Germany now gives much more to the pope at Rome than it gave in former times to the emperors. In-

deed, some estimate that every year more than three hundred thousand *gulden* find their way from Germany to Rome, quite uselessly and fruitlessly; we get nothing for it but scorn and contempt. And yet we wonder that princes, nobles, cities, endowments, land, and people are impoverished! We should rather wonder that we still have anything to eat!

John Calvin

The success of Protestantism as an international reform movement was due largely to the work of a younger contemporary of Luther, the Frenchman John Calvin. Born Jean Cauvin in Picardy in 1509, Calvin went to Paris in 1523 to study first for a clerical and later for a legal career. During his student days he became acquainted with the writings of Luther, which were beginning to circulate through France at the time. His growing sympathy for the German "heresies" brought him to the attention of the authorities and he was forced to flee from the country. After some wandering he established himself permanently in the small city of Geneva, Switzerland. Thus began one of the most remarkable social and political experiments of modern times. Under Calvin's leadership Geneva was organized as a theocratic state. The clergy assumed control not only of the political affairs of the city but of the moral life of its citizens as well. In his attempts to realize a society of saints, Calvin systematically set about to banish gaiety, frivolity, and sin from the city. Although he was unusually successful, and Geneva became a city of piety and sobriety, Calvin was never fully satisfied. Sin, he discovered, could not be eradicated

completely but would periodically rear its ugly head in the midst of his saintly society.

From Geneva, which came to be known as the Protestant Rome, Calvinism spread throughout most of Europe, into Germany, Poland, Bohemia, Hungary, and the Low Countries. The French Huguenots were Calvinists as were the Scottish Presbyterians and the English Puritans, who brought both the religious doctrines and the theocratic social organization of Calvin across the Atlantic to the colony of Massachusetts.

Calvin was not only a religious and social reformer but also one of the greatest of all Christian theologians. In his *Institutes of the Christian Religion*, which he first published at the age of twenty-seven, he reiterated and defended the Augustinian doctrine of original sin, with its implied notions of election, faith, and grace. On the subject of predestination, about which most theologians had spoken in muted tones, Calvin was particularly vehement. God in his omnipotence has decreed from all eternity the ultimate destiny of every individual soul. We, guilty sinners, can do nothing to alter this divine decree; all that rests with us is to praise God's infinite grace if he h?s elected us for salvation or to accept his just condemnation if he has damned us to hell.

The selection from the *Institutes* that follows outlines the main features of Calvin's theology.

Institutes of the Christian Religion

Discussion of Human Nature as Created, of the Faculties of the Soul, of the Image of God, of Free Will, and of the Original Integrity of Man's Nature

We must now speak of the creation of man: not only because among all God's works here is the noblest and most remarkable example of his justice, wisdom, and goodness; but because, as we said at the beginning, we cannot have a clear and complete knowledge of God unless it is accompanied by a corresponding knowledge of ourselves. This knowledge of ourselves is twofold: namely, to know what we were like when we were first created and what our condition became after the fall of Adam. While it would be of little benefit to understand our creation unless we recognized in this sad ruin what our nature in its corruption and deformity is like, we shall nevertheless be content for the moment with the description of our originally upright nature. And to be sure, before we come to the miserable condition of man to which he is now subjected, it is worth-while to know what he was like when first created. Now we must guard against singling out only those natural evils of man, lest we seem to attribute them to the Author of nature. For in this excuse, impiety thinks it has sufficient defense, if it is able to claim that whatever defects it possesses have in some way proceeded from God. It does not hesitate, if it is reproved, to contend with God himself, and to impute to him the fault of which it is deservedly accused. And those who wish to seem to speak more reverently of the Godhead still willingly blame their depravity on nature, not realizing that they also, although more obscurely, insult God. For if any defect were proved to inhere in nature, this would bring reproach upon him.

Since, then, we see the flesh panting for every subterfuge by which it thinks that the blame for its own evils may in any way be diverted from itself to another, we must diligently oppose this evil intent. Therefore we must so deal with the

From *Calvin: Institutes of the Christian Religion*, LCC, Vols. XX and XXI, ed. John T. McNeill and trans. Ford Lewis Battles. Published simultaneously in the U.S.A. by The Westminster Press and in Great Britain by S.C.M. Press, Ltd., London.

calamity of mankind that we may cut off every shift, and may vindicate God's justice from every accusation. Afterward, in the proper place, we shall see how far away men are from the purity that was bestowed upon Adam. . . .

In this integrity man by free will had the power, if he so willed, to attain eternal life. Here it would be out of place to raise the question of God's secret predestination because our present subject is not what can happen or not, but what man's nature was like. Therefore Adam could have stood if he wished, seeing that he fell solely by his own will. But it was because his will was capable of being bent to one side or the other, and was not given the constancy to persevere, that he fell so easily. Yet his choice of good and evil was free, and not that alone, but the highest rectitude was in his mind and will, and all the organic parts were rightly composed to obedience, until in destroying himself he corrupted his own blessings.

Hence the great obscurity faced by the philosophers, for they were seeking in a ruin for a building, and in scattered fragments for a well-knit structure. They held this principle, that man would not be a rational animal unless he possessed free choice of good and evil; also it entered their minds that the distinction between virtues and vices would be obliterated if man did not order his life by his own planning. Well reasoned so far—if there had been no change in man. But since this was hidden from them, it is no wonder they mix up heaven and earth! They, as professed disciples of Christ, are obviously playing the fool when, by compromising between the opinions of the philoso-

phers and heavenly doctrine, so that these touch neither heaven nor earth, in man—who is lost and sunk down into spiritual destruction—they will seek after free choice. But these matters will be better dealt with in their proper place. Now we need bear only this in mind: man was far different at the first creation from his whole posterity, who, deriving their origin from him in his corrupted state, have contracted from him a hereditary taint. For, the individual parts of his soul were formed to uprightness, the soundness of his mind stood firm, and his will was free to choose the good. If anyone objects that his will was placed in an insecure position because its power was weak, his status should have availed to remove any excuse; nor was it reasonable for God to be constrained by the necessity of making a man who either could not or would not sin at all. Such a nature would, indeed, have been more excellent. But to quarrel with God on this precise point, as if he ought to have conferred this upon man, is more than iniquitous, inasmuch as it was in his own choice to give whatever he pleased. But the reason he did not sustain man by the virtue of perseverance lies hidden in his plan; sobriety is for us the part of wisdom. Man, indeed, received the ability provided he exercised the will; but he did not have the will to use his ability, for this exercising of the will would have been followed by the perseverance. Yet he is not excusable, for he received so much that he voluntarily brought about his own destruction; indeed, no necessity was imposed upon God of giving man other than a mediocre and even transitory will, that from man's Fall he might gather occasion for his own glory.

God by His Power Nourishes and Maintains the World Created by Him, and Rules Its Several Parts by His Providence

Moreover, to make God a momentary Creator, who once for all finished his work, would be cold and barren, and we must differ from profane men especially in that we see the presence of divine power shining as much in the continuing state of the universe as in its inception. For even though the minds of the impious too are compelled by merely looking upon earth and heaven to rise up to the Creator, yet faith has its own peculiar way of assigning the whole credit for Creation to God. To this pertains that saying of the apostle's to which we have referred before, that only "by faith we understand that the universe was created by the word of God." For unless we pass on to his providence—however, we may seem both to comprehend with the mind and to confess with the tongue—we do not yet properly grasp what it means to say: "God is Creator." Carnal sense, once confronted with the power of God in the very Creation, stops there, and at most weighs and contemplates only the wisdom, power and goodness of the author in accomplishing such handiwork. (These matters are self-evident, and even force themselves upon the unwilling.) It contemplates, moreover, some general preserving and governing activity, from which the force of motion derives. In short, carnal sense thinks there is an energy divinely bestowed

from the beginning, sufficient to sustain all things.

But faith ought to penetrate more deeply, namely, having found him Creator of all, forthwith to conclude he is also everlasting Governor and Preserver—not only in that he drives the celestial frame as well as its several parts by a universal motion, but also in that he sustains, nourishes, and cares for everything he has made, even to the least sparrow. Thus David, having briefly stated that the universe was created by God, immediately descends to the uninterrupted course of His providence, "By the word of Jehovah the heavens were made, and all their host by the breath of his mouth." Soon thereafter he adds, "Jehovah has looked down upon the sons of men," and what follows is in the same vein. For although all men do not reason so clearly, yet, because it would not be believable that human affairs are cared for by God unless he were the Maker of the universe, and nobody seriously believes the universe was made by God without being persuaded that he takes care of his works, David not inappropriately leads us in the best order from the one to the other. In general, philosophers teach and human minds conceive that all parts of the universe are quickened by God's secret inspiration. . . .

But because we know that the universe was established especially for the sake of mankind, we ought to look for this purpose in his governance also. The prophet Jeremiah exclaims, "I know, O Lord, that the way of man is not his own, nor is it given to man to direct his own steps." Moreover, Solomon says, "Man's steps are from the Lord and how may man dispose his way?" Let them now say that man is moved by God according to the inclination of his nature, but that he himself turns that motion whither he pleases. Nay, if that were truly said, the free choice of his ways would be in man's control. Perhaps they will deny this because he can do nothing without God's power. Yet they cannot really get by with that, since it is clear that the prophet and Solomon ascribe to God not only might but also choice and determination. Elsewhere Solomon elegantly rebukes this rashness of men, who set up for themselves a goal without regard to God, as if they were not led by his hand. "The disposition of the heart is man's, but the preparation of the tongue is the Lord's." It is an absurd folly that miserable men take it upon themselves to act without God, when they cannot even speak except as he wills!

Indeed, Scripture, to express more plainly that nothing at all in the world is undertaken without his determination, shows that things seemingly most fortuitous are subject to him. For what can you attribute more to chance than when a branch breaking off from a tree kills a passing traveler? But the Lord speaks far differently, acknowledging that he has delivered him to the hand of the slayer. Likewise, who does not attribute lots to the blindness of fortune? But the Lord does not allow this, claiming for himself the determining of them. He teaches that it is not by their own power that pebbles are cast into the lap and drawn out, but the one thing that could have been attributed to chance he testifies to come from himself. In the same vein is that saying of Solomon, "The poor man and the usurer meet together; God

illumines the eyes of both." He points out that, even though the rich are mingled with the poor in the world, while to each his condition is divinely assigned, God, who lights all men, is not at all blind. And so he urges the poor to patience; because those who are not content with their own lot try to shake off the burden laid upon them by God. Thus, also, another prophet rebukes the impious who ascribe to men's toil, or to fortune, the fact that some lie in squalor and others rise up to honors. "For not from the east, nor from the west, nor from the wilderness comes lifting up; because God is judge, he humbles one and lifts up another." Because God cannot put off the office of judge, hence he reasons that it is by His secret plan that some distinguish themselves, while others remain contemptible. . . .

How We May Apply This Doctrine to Our Greatest Benefit

. . . All who will compose themselves to his moderation will not murmur against God on account of their adversities in time past, nor lay the blame for their own wickedness upon him as did the Homeric Agamemnon, saying: "I am not the cause, but Zeus and fate." And they will not, as if carried off by the fates, out of desperation cast themselves to destruction like that youth of Plautus: "Unstable is the lot of things, the fates drive men according to their own pleasure. I will betake myself to the precipice, that there I may lose my goods with my life." And they will not follow the example of another, and cover up their own evil deeds with the name

"God." For thus Lyconides says in another comedy: "God was the instigator; I believe the gods willed it. For I know if they had not so willed, it would not have happened." But rather let them inquire and learn from Scripture what is pleasing to God so that they may strive toward this under the Spirit's guidance. At the same time, being ready to follow God wherever he calls, they will show in very truth that nothing is more profitable than the knowledge of this doctrine.

Profane men with their absurdities foolishly raise an uproar, so that they almost, as the saying is, mingle heaven and earth. If the Lord has indicated the point of our death, they say, we cannot escape it. Therefore it is vain for anyone to busy himself in taking precautions. One man does not dare take a road that he hears is dangerous, lest he be murdered by thieves; another summons physicians, and wears himself out with medicines to keep himself alive; another is afraid of living in tumble-down houses. In short, all devise ways and forge them with great purpose of mind, to attain what they desire. Now either all these remedies which attempt to correct God's will are vain; or else there is no fixed decree of God that determines life and death, health and disease, peace and war, and other things that men, as they desire or hate them, so earnestly try by their own toil either to obtain or to avoid. Also they conclude that believers' prayers, by which the Lord is asked to provide for things that he has already decreed from eternity, are perverse, not to say superfluous. To sum up, they cancel all those plans which have to do with the future, as militating against God's providence, which, without their being consulted, has decreed what he would have happen. Then whatever does happen now, they so impute to God's providence that they close their eyes to the man who clearly has done it. Does an assassin murder an upright citizen? He has carried out, they say, God's plan. Has someone stolen, or committed adultery? Because he has done what was foreseen and ordained by the Lord, he is the minister of God's providence. Has a son, neglecting remedies, with never a care awaited the death of a parent? He could not resist God, who had so appointed from eternity. Thus all crimes, because subject to God's ordinance, they call virtues. . . .

The same men wrongly and rashly lay the happenings of past time to the naked providence of God. For since on it depends everything that happens, therefore, say they, neither thefts, nor adulteries, nor murders take place without God's will intervening. Why therefore, they ask, should a thief be punished, who has plundered someone whom the Lord would punish with poverty? Why shall a murderer be punished, who has killed one whose life the Lord has ended? If all such men are serving God's will, why shall they be punished? On the contrary, I deny that they are serving God's will. For we shall not say that one who is motivated by an evil inclination, by only obeying his own wicked desire, renders service to God, at His bidding. A man, having learned of His will, obeys God in striving toward the goal to which he is called by that same will. From what source do we learn but from his Word? In such fashion we must in our deeds search out God's will which he declares through his Word. God requires of us only what he commands. If we contrive anything against his commandment, it is not obedience but obstinacy and transgression. Yet, unless he willed it, we would not do it. I agree. But do we do evil things to the end that we may serve him? Yet he by no means commands us to do them; rather we rush headlong, without thinking what he requires, but so raging in our unbridled lust that we deliberately strive against him. And in this way we serve his just ordinance by doing evil, for so great and boundless is his wisdom that he knows right well how to use evil instruments to do good. And see how absurd their argument is: they would have transgressors go unpunished, on the ground that their misdeeds are committed solely by God's dispensation.

I grant more: thieves and murderers and other evildoers are the instruments of divine providence, and the Lord himself uses these to carry out the judgments that he has determined with himself. Yet I deny that they can derive from this any excuse for their evil deeds. Why? Will they either involve God in the same iniquity with themselves, or will they cloak their own depravity with his justice? They can do neither.

• • •

By the Fall and Revolt of Adam the Whole Human Race Was Delivered to the Curse, and Degenerated from Its Original Condition; the Doctrine of Original Sin

With good reason the ancient proverb strongly recommended knowledge of self to man. For if it is considered disgraceful for us not to know all that pertains to the business of human life, even more detestable is our ignorance of ourselves, by which, when making decisions in necessary matters, we miserably deceive and even blind ourselves!

But since this precept is so valuable, we ought more diligently to avoid applying it perversely. This, we observe, has happened to certain philosophers, who, while urging man to know himself, propose the goal of recognizing his own worth and excellence. And they would have him contemplate in himself nothing but what swells him with empty assurance and puffs him up with pride.

But knowledge of ourselves lies first in considering what we were given at creation and how generously God continues his favour toward us, in order to know how great our natural excellence would be if only it had remained unblemished; yet at the same time to bear in mind that there is in us nothing of our own, but that we hold on sufferance whatever God has bestowed upon us. Hence we are ever dependent on him. Secondly, to call to mind our miserable condition after Adam's fall; the awareness of which, when all our boasting and self-assurance are laid low, should truly humble us and overwhelm us with shame. In the beginning God fashioned us after his image that he might arouse our minds both to zeal for virtue and to meditation upon eternal life. Thus, in order that the great nobility of our race (which distinguishes us from brute beasts) may not be buried beneath our own dullness of wit, it behooves us to recognize that we have been endowed with reason and understanding so that, by leading a holy and upright life, we may press on to the appointed goal of blessed immortality.

But that primal worthiness cannot come to mind without the sorry spectacle of our foulness and dishonour presenting itself by way of contrast, since in the person of the first man we have fallen from our original condition. From this source arise abhorrence and displeasure with ourselves, as well as true humility; and thence is kindled a new zeal to seek God, in whom each of us may recover those good things which we have utterly and completely lost. . . .

Because what God so severely punished must have been no light sin but a detestable crime, we must consider what kind of sin there was in Adam's desertion that enkindled God's fearful vengeance against the whole of mankind. To regard Adam's sin as gluttonous intemperance (a common notion) is childish. As if the sum and head of all virtues lay in abstaining solely from one fruit, when all sorts of desirable delights abounded everywhere; and not only abundance but also magnificent variety was at hand in that blessed fruitfulness of earth!

We ought therefore to look more deeply. Adam was denied the tree of the knowledge of good and evil to test his obedience and prove that he was willingly under God's command. The very name of the tree shows the sole purpose of the precept was to keep him content with his lot and to prevent him from becoming puffed up with wicked lust. But the promise by which he was bidden to hope for eternal life so long as he ate from the tree of life, and conversely, the terrible threat of death once he tasted of the tree of knowledge of good and

evil, served to prove and exercise his faith. Hence it is not hard to deduce by what means Adam provoked God's wrath upon himself. Indeed, Augustine speaks rightly when he declares that pride was the beginning of all evils. For if ambition had not raised man higher than was meet and right, he could have remained in his original state.

But we must take a fuller definition from the nature of the temptation which Moses describes. Since the woman through unfaithfulness was led away from God's Word by the serpent's deceit, it is already clear that disobedience was the beginning of the Fall. This Paul also confirms, teaching that all were lost through the disobedience of one man. Yet it is at the same time to be noted that the first man revolted from God's authority, not only because he was seized by Satan's blandishments, but also because, contemptuous of truth, he turned aside to falsehood. And surely, once we hold God's Word in contempt, we shake off all reverence for him. For, unless we listen attentively to him, his majesty will not dwell among us, nor his worship remain perfect. Unfaithfulness, then, was the root of the Fall. But thereafter ambition and pride, together with ungratefulness, arose, because Adam by seeking more than was granted him shamefully spurned God's great bounty, which had been lavished upon him. To have been made in the likeness of God seemed a small matter to a son of earth unless he also attained equality with God—a monstrous wickedness! If apostasy, by which man withdraws from the authority of his Maker—indeed insolently shakes off his yoke—is a foul and detestable offense, it is vain to extenuate Adam's sin. Yet it was not simply apostasy, but was joined with vile reproaches against God. These assented to Satan's slanders, which accused God of falsehood and envy and ill will. Lastly, faithlessness opened the door to ambition, and ambition was indeed the mother of obstinate disobedience; as a result, men, having cast off the fear of God, threw themselves wherever lust carried them. Hence Bernard rightly teaches that the door of salvation is opened to us when we receive the gospel today with our ears, even as death was then admitted by those same windows when they were opened to Satan. For Adam would never have dared oppose God's authority unless he had disbelieved in God's Word. Here, indeed, was the best bridle to control all passions: the thought that nothing is better than to practice righteousness by obeying God's commandments; then, that the ultimate goal of the happy life is to be loved by him. Therefore Adam, carried away by the devil's blasphemies, as far as he was able extinguished the whole glory of God.

As it was the spiritual life of Adam to remain united and bound to his Maker, so estrangement from him was the death of his soul. Nor is it any wonder that he consigned his race to ruin by his rebellion when he perverted the whole order of nature in heaven and on earth. "All creatures," says Paul, "are groaning," "subject to corruption, not of their own will." If the cause is sought, there is no doubt that they are bearing part of the punishment deserved by man, for whose use they were created. Since, therefore, the curse, which goes about through all the regions of the world, flowed hither and yon from Adam's guilt,

it is not unreasonable if it is spread to all his offspring. Therefore, after the heavenly image was obliterated in him, he was not the only one to suffer this punishment—that, in place of wisdom, virtue, holiness, truth, and justice, with which adornments he had been clad, there came forth the most filthy plagues, blindness, impotence, impurity, vanity, and injustice—but he also entangled and immersed his offspring in the same miseries.

This is the inherited corruption, which the church fathers termed "original sin," meaning by the word "sin" the depravation of a nature previously good and pure. There was much contention over this matter, inasmuch as nothing is farther from the usual view than for all to be made guilty by the guilt of one, and thus for sin to be made common. This seems to be the reason why the most ancient doctors of the church touched upon this subject so obscurely. At least they explained it less clearly than was fitting. Yet this timidity could not prevent Pelagius from rising up with the profane fiction that Adam sinned only to his own loss without harming his posterity. Through this subtlety Satan attempted to cover up the disease and thus to render it incurable. But when it was shown by the clear testimony of Scripture that sin was transmitted from the first man to all his posterity, Pelagius quibbled that it was transmitted through imitation, not propagation. Therefore, good men (and Augustine above the rest) labored to show us that we are corrupted not by derived wickedness, but that we bear inborn defect from our mother's womb. . . .

So that these remarks may not be made concerning an uncertain and unknown matter, let us define original sin. It is not my intention to investigate the several definitions proposed by various writers, but simply to bring forward the one that appears to me most in accordance with truth. Original sin, therefore, seems to be a hereditary depravity and corruption of our nature, diffused into all parts of the soul, which first makes us liable to God's wrath, then also brings forth in us those works which Scripture calls "works of the flesh." And that is properly what Paul often calls sin. The works that come forth from it—such as adulteries, fornications, thefts, hatreds, murders, carousings—he accordingly calls "fruits of sin," although they are also commonly called "sins" in Scripture, and even by Paul himself.

We must, therefore, distinctly note these two things. First, we are so vitiated and perverted in every part of our nature that by this great corruption we stand justly condemned and convicted before God, to whom nothing is acceptable but righteousness, innocence, and purity. And this is not liability for another's transgression. For, since it is said that we became subject to God's judgment through Adam's sin, we are to understand it not as if we, guiltless and undeserving, bore the guilt of his offense but in the sense that, since we through his transgression have become entangled in the curse, he is said to have made us guilty. Yet not only has punishment fallen upon us from Adam, but a contagion imparted by him resides in us, which justly deserves punishment. For this reason, Augustine, though he often calls sin "another's" to show more clearly that it is distributed among us

through propagation, nevertheless declares at the same time that it is peculiar to each. And the apostle himself most eloquently testifies that "death has spread to all because all have sinned." That is, they have been enveloped in original sin and defiled by its stains. For that reason, even infants themselves, while they carry their condemnation along with them from the mother's womb, are guilty not of another's fault but of their own. For, even though the fruits of their iniquity have not yet come forth, they have the seed enclosed within them. Indeed, their whole nature is a seed of sin; hence it can be only hateful and abhorrent to God. From this it follows that it is rightly considered sin in God's sight, for without guilt there would be no accusation.

Then comes the second consideration: that this perversity never ceases in us, but continually bears new fruits—the works of the flesh that we have already described— just as a burning furnace gives forth flame and sparks, or water ceaselessly bubbles up from a spring. Thus those who have defined original sin as "the lack of the original righteousness, which ought to reside in us," although they comprehend in this definition the whole meaning of the term, have still not expressed effectively enough its power and energy. For our nature is not only destitute and empty of good, but so fertile and fruitful of every evil that it cannot be idle. . . .

Man Has Now Been Deprived of Freedom of Choice and Bound Over to Miserable Servitude

We have now seen that the domination of sin, from the time it held the first man bound to itself, not only ranges among all mankind, but also completely occupies individual souls. It remains for us to investigate more closely whether we have been deprived of all freedom since we have been reduced to this servitude; and, if any particle of it still survives, how far its power extends. But in order that the truth of this question may be more readily apparent to us, I shall presently set a goal to which the whole argument should be directed. The best way to avoid error will be to consider the perils that threaten man on both sides. (1) When man is denied all uprightness, he immediately takes occasion for complacency from the fact; and, because he is said to have no ability to pursue righteousness on his own, he holds all such pursuit to be of no consequence, as if it did not pertain to him at all. (2) Nothing, however slight, can be credited to man without depriving God of his honour, and without man himself falling into ruin through brazen confidence. Augustine points out both these precipices.

Here, then, is the course that we must follow if we are to avoid crashing upon these rocks: when man has been taught that no good thing remains in his power, and that he is hedged about on all sides by most miserable necessity, in spite of this he should nevertheless be instructed to aspire to a good of which he is empty, to a freedom of which he has been deprived. In fact, he may thus be more sharply aroused from inactivity than if he were supposed that he was endowed with the highest virtues. Everyone sees how necessary this second point is. I observe that too many persons have doubts about the first point. For since this is an undoubted fact, that nothing

of his own ought to be taken away from man, it ought to be clearly evident how important it is for him to be barred from false boasting. At the time when man was distinguished with the noblest marks of honour through God's beneficence, not even then was he permitted to boast about himself. How much more ought he now to humble himself, cast down as he has been—due to his own ungratefulness—from the loftiest glory into extreme disgrace! At that time, I say, when he had been advanced to the highest degree or honor, Scripture attributed nothing else to him than that he had been created in the image of God, thus suggesting that man was blessed, not because of his own actions, but by participation in God. What, therefore, now remains for man, bare and destitute of all glory, but to recognize God for whose beneficence he could not be grateful when he abounded with the riches of this grace; and at least, by confessing his own poverty, to glorify him in whom he did not previously glory in recognition of his own blessings?

Also, it is no less to our advantage than pertinent to God's glory that we be deprived of all credit for our wisdom and virtue. Thus those who bestow upon us anything beyond the truth add sacrilege to our ruin. When we are taught to wage our own war, we are but borne aloft on a reed stick, only to fall as soon as it breaks! Yet we flatter our strength unduly when we compare it even to a reed stick! For whatever vain men devise and babble concerning these matters is but smoke. . . .

If this be admitted, it will be indisputable that free will is not sufficient to enable man to do good works, unless he be helped by grace, indeed by special grace, which only the elect receive through regeneration. For I do not tarry over those fanatics who babble that grace is equally and indiscriminately distributed. But it has not yet been demonstrated whether man has been wholly deprived of all power to do good, or still has some power, though meager and weak; a power, indeed, that can do nothing of itself, but with the help of grace also does its part. The Master of the Sentences meant to settle this point when he taught: "We need two kinds of grace to render us capable of good works." He calls the first kind "operating," which ensures that we effectively will to do good. The second he calls "co-operating," which follows the good will as a help. The thing that displeases me about this division is that, while he attributes the effective desire for good to the grace of God, yet he hints that man by his very own nature somehow seeks after the good—though ineffectively. Thus Bernard declares the good will is God's work, yet concedes to man that of his own impulse he seeks this sort of good will. But this is far from Augustine's thought, from whom Peter Lombard pretended to have taken this distinction. The ambiguity in the second part offends me, for it has given rise to a perverted interpretation. They thought we cooperate with the assisting grace of God, because it is our right either to render it ineffectual by spurning the first grace, or to confirm it by obediently following it. This the author of the work *The Calling of the Gentiles* expresses as follows: "Those who employ the judgment of reason are free to forsake grace, so that not to have for-saken it is a meritorious act; and what could not be done without the co-operation of the Spirit is counted meritorious for those whose own will could not have accomplished it." I chose to note these two points in passing that you, my reader, may see how far I disagree with the sounder Schoolmen. I differ with the more recent Sophists to an even greater extent, as they are farther removed from antiquity. However, we at least understand from this division in what way they grant free will to man. For Lombard finally declares that we have free will, not in that we are equally capable of doing or thinking good and evil, but merely that we are freed from compulsion. According to Lombard, this freedom is not hindered, even if we be wicked and slaves of sin, and can do nothing but sin.

Man will then be spoken of as having this sort of free decision, not because he has free choice equally of good and evil, but because he acts wickedly by will, not by compulsion. Well put, indeed, but what purpose is served by labeling with a proud name such a slight thing? A noble freedom, indeed—for man not to be forced to serve sin, yet to be such a willing slave that his will is bound by the fetters of sin!

• • •

Eternal Election, by Which God Has Predestined Some to Salvation, Others to Destruction

In actual fact, the covenant of life is not preached equally among all men, and among those to whom it is preached, it does not gain the same acceptance either constantly or in equal degree. In this diversity the wonderful depth of God's judgment is made known. For there is no doubt that this variety also serves the decision of God's eternal election. If it is plain that it comes to pass by God's bidding that salvation is freely offered to some while others are barred from access to it, at once great and difficult questions spring up, explicable only when reverent minds regard as settled what they may suitably hold concerning election and predestination. A baffling question this seems to many. For they think nothing more inconsistent than that out of the common multitude of men some should be predestined to salvation, others to destruction. But how mistakenly they entangle themselves will become clear in the following discussion. Besides, in the very darkness that frightens them not only is the usefulness of this doctrine made known but also its very sweet fruit. We shall never be clearly persuaded, as we ought to be, that our salvation flows from the wellspring of God's free mercy until we come to know his eternal election, which illuminates God's grace by this contrast: that he does not indiscriminately adopt all into the hope of salvation but gives to some what he denies to others.

How much the ignorance of this principle detracts from God's glory, how much it takes away from true humility, is well known. Yet Paul denies that this which needs so much to be known can be known unless God, utterly disregarding works, chooses those whom he has decreed within himself. "At the present time," he says, "a remnant has been saved according to the election of grace. But if it is by grace, it is no more of works; otherwise grace would no more be grace. But if it is of works, it is no more of grace; otherwise work would not be work." If—to make it clear that our salvation comes about solely from God's mere generosity—we must be called back to the course of election, those who wish to get rid of all this are obscuring as maliciously as they can what ought to have been gloriously and vociferously proclaimed, and they tear humility up by the very roots. Paul clearly testifies that, when the salvation of a remnant of the people is ascribed to the election of grace, then only is it acknowledged that God of his mere good pleasure preserves whom he will, and moreover that he pays no reward, since he can owe none.

They who shut the gates that no one may dare seek a taste of this doctrine wrong men no less than God. For neither will anything else suffice to make us humble as we ought to be nor shall we otherwise sincerely feel how much we are obliged to God. And as Christ teaches, here is our only ground for firmness and confidence: in order to free us of all fear and render us victorious amid so many dangers, snares, and mortal struggles, he promises that whatever the Father has entrusted into his keeping will be safe. From this we infer that all those who do not know that they are God's own will be miserable through constant fear. Hence, those who by being blind to the three benefits we have noted would wish the foundation of our salvation to be removed from our midst, very badly serve the interests of themselves and of all other believers. How is it that the church becomes manifest to us from this, when, as Bernard rightly teaches, "it could not otherwise be found or recognized among creatures, since it lies marvelously hidden . . . both within the bosom of a blessed predestination and within the mass of a miserable condemnation?"

But before I enter into the matter itself, I need to mention by way of preface two kinds of men.

Human curiosity renders the discussion of predestination, already somewhat difficult of itself, very confusing and even dangerous. No restraints can hold it back from wandering in forbidden bypaths and thrusting upward to the heights. If allowed, it will leave no secret to God that it will not search out and unravel. Since we see so many on all sides rushing into this audacity and impudence, among them certain men not otherwise bad, they should in due season be reminded of the measure of their duty in this regard.

First, then, let them remember that when they inquire into predestination they are penetrating the sacred precincts of divine wisdom. If anyone with carefree assurance breaks into this place, he will not succeed in satisfying his curiosity and he will enter a labyrinth from which he can find no exit. For it is not right for man unrestrainedly to search out things that the Lord has willed to be hid in himself, and to unfold from eternity itself the sublimest wisdom, which he would have us revere but not understand that through this also he should fill us with wonder. He has set forth by his Word the secrets of his will that he has decided to reveal to us. These he decided to reveal in so far as he

foresaw that they would concern us and benefit us. . . .

Profane men, I admit, in the matter of predestination abruptly seize upon something to carp, rail, bark, or scoff at. But if their shamelessness deters us, we shall have to keep secret the chief doctrines of the faith, almost none of which they or their like leave untouched by blasphemy. An obstinate person would be no less insolently puffed up on hearing that within the essence of God there are three Persons than if he were told that God foresaw what would happen to man when he created him. And they will not refrain from guffaws when they are informed that but little more than five thousand years have passed since the creation of the universe, for they ask why God's power was idle and asleep for so long. Nothing, in short, can be brought forth that they do not assail with their mockery. Should we, to silence these blasphemies, forbear to speak of the deity of Son and Spirit? Must we pass over in silence the creation of the universe? No! God's truth is so powerful, both in this respect and in every other, that it has nothing to fear from the evil-speaking of wicked men.

So Augustine stoutly maintains in his little treatise *The Gift of Perseverance*. For we see that the false apostles could not make Paul ashamed by defaming and accusing his true doctrine. They say that this whole discussion is dangerous for godly minds—because it hinders exhortations, because it shakes faith, because it disturbs and terrifies the heart itself—but this is nonsense! Augustine admits that for these reasons he was frequently charged with preaching predestination too freely, but, as it was easy for him, he over-whelmingly refuted the charge. We, moreover, because many and various absurdities are obtruded at this point, have preferred to dispose of each in its own place. I desire only to have them generally admit that we should not investigate what the Lord has left hidden in secret, that we should not neglect what he has brought into the open, so that we may not be convicted of excessive curiosity on the one hand, or of excessive ingratitude on the other. For Augustine also skillfully expressed this idea: we can safely follow Scripture, which proceeds at the pace of a mother stooping to her child, so to speak, so as not to leave us behind in our weakness. But for those who are so cautious or fearful that they desire to bury predestination in order not to disturb weak souls—with what color will they cloak their arrogance when they accuse God indirectly of stupid thoughtlessness, as if he had not foreseen the peril that they feel they have wisely met? Whoever, then, heaps odium upon the doctrine of predestination openly reproaches God, as if he had unadvisedly let slip something hurtful to the church.

No one who wishes to be thought religious dares simply deny predestination, by which God adopts some to hope of life, and sentences others to eternal death. But our opponents, especially those who make foreknowledge its cause, envelop it in numerous petty objections. We, indeed, place both doctrines in God, but we say that subjecting one to the other is absurd.

When we attribute foreknowledge to God, we mean that all things always were, and perpetually remain, under his eyes, so that to his knowledge there is nothing future or past, but all things are present. And they are present in such a way that he not only conceives them through ideas, as we have before us those things which our minds remember, but he truly looks upon them and discerns them as things placed before him. And this foreknowledge is extended throughout the universe to every creature. We call predestination God's eternal decree, by which he determined with himself what he willed to become of each man. For all are not created in equal condition; rather, eternal life is foreordained for some, eternal damnation for others. Therefore, as any man has been created to one or the other of these ends, we speak of him as predestined to life or to death. . . .

As Scripture, then, clearly shows, we say that God once established by his eternal and unchangeable plan those whom he long before determined once for all to receive into salvation, and those whom, on the other hand, he would devote to destruction. We assert that, with respect to the elect, this plan was founded upon his freely given mercy, without regard to human worth; but by his just and irreprehensible but incomprehensible judgment he has barred the door of life to those whom he has given over to damnation. Now among the elect we regard the call as a testimony of election. Then we hold justification another sign of its manifestation, until they come into the glory in which the fulfillment of that election lies. But as the Lord seals his elect by call and justification, so, by shutting off the reprobate from knowledge of his name or from the sanctification of his Spirit, he, as it were, reveals by these marks what sort of judgment awaits them. Here I shall pass over many fictions that stupid men have invented to overthrow predestination. They need no refutation, for as soon as they are brought forth they abundantly prove their own falsity.

The Counter Reformation

The Counter Reformation of the Catholic Church—or the Catholic Reformation, as it is sometimes called—expressed itself in three major institutions: the Society of Jesus (usually called the Jesuits), the Inquisition (or Holy Office), and the Council of Trent. The Company or Society of Jesus was founded by St. Ignatius of Loyola (1491–1556), an unlettered Spanish soldier who, as the result of a religious experience he underwent after being wounded in battle, resolved to become a "soldier of Christ." Once he had recovered, he set about educating himself, starting with elementary school and continuing through the University of Paris, where he began organizing the Jesuit order. Loyola's new Society was established along military lines; an iron discipline demanded that each member show complete obedience to his immediate superiors and ultimately to his supreme commander, the pope. During the religious conflicts of the sixteenth and seventeenth centuries, the Jesuits were always to be found on the side of the papal forces, in opposition primarily to the Protestants but to Catholic liberals as well.

The Inquisition was an old organization, which had been developed by the Dominican order in the thirteenth century primarily to combat the Albigensian heresy in southern France. It gained its greatest strength, however, in Spain, where it was used as the prime agent of persecution against the Moors and Jews, particularly under the leadership of the notorious Torquemada. After the Reformation the Inquisition joined forces with the Jesuits to combat the "Protestant heresy."

The Council of Trent, called originally by Pope Paul III in 1545, met at irregular intervals over a period of nearly twenty years under three different popes in the capital of the Italian Tyrol. The Council responded to the Protestant movement by reaffirming the basic doctrines of the Catholic Church while at the same time calling for a reform of abuses within the Church. The selection that follows includes some of the more important decrees, concerning both doctrine and practice, adopted by the Council.

The Canons and Decrees of the Council of Trent

Decree Touching the Opening of the Council

Doth it please you,—unto the praise and glory of the holy and undivided Trinity, Father, and Son, and Holy Ghost; for the increase and exaltation of the Christian faith and religion; for the extirpation of heresies; for the peace and union of the Church; for the reformation of the Clergy and Christian people; for the depression and extinction of the enemies of the Christian name,—to decree and declare that the sacred and general council of Trent do begin, and hath begun?

They answered: It pleaseth us.

Decree Concerning the Canonical Scriptures

The sacred and holy, oecumenical, and general Synod of Trent,—lawfully assembled in the Holy Ghost, the same three legates of the Apostolic See presiding therein,—keeping this always in view, that, errors being removed, the purity itself of the Gospel be preserved in the Church; which (Gospel), before promised through the prophets in the holy Scriptures, our Lord Jesus Christ, the Son of God, first promulgated with His own mouth, and then commanded to be preached by His Apostles to every creature, as the fountain of all, both saving truth, and moral discipline; and seeing clearly that this truth and books, and the unwritten traditions which, received by the Apostles from the mouth of Christ himself, or from the Apostles themselves, the Holy Ghost dictating, have come down even unto us, transmitted as it were from hand to hand; (the Synod) following the examples of the orthodox Fathers, receives and venerates with an equal affection of piety, and reverence, all the books both of the Old and the New Testament—seeing that one God is the author of both—as also the said traditions, as well those appertaining to faith as to morals, as having been dictated, either by Christ's own word of mouth, or by the Holy Ghost, and preserved in the Catholic Church by a continuous succession.

Decree Concerning the Edition, and the Use, of the Sacred Books

Moreover, the same sacred and holy Synod,—considering that no small utility may accrue to the Church of God, if it be made known which out of all the Latin editions, now in circulation, of the sacred books, is to be held as authentic,—ordains and declares, that the said old and vulgate edition, which, by the lengthened usage of so many ages, has been approved of in the Church, be, in public lectures, disputations, sermons and expositions, held as

The Canons and Decrees of the Sacred and Oecumenical Council of Trent, trans. J. Waterworth.

authentic; and that no one is to dare, or presume to reject it under any pretext whatever.

Furthermore, in order to restrain petulant spirits, It decrees, that no one, relying on his own skill, shall,— in matters of faith, and of morals pertaining to the edification of Christian doctrine,—wresting the sacred Scripture to his own senses, presume to interpret the said sacred Scripture contrary to that sense which holy mother Church,—whose it is to judge of the true sense and interpretation of the holy Scriptures,—hath held and doth hold;— or even contrary to the unanimous consent of the Fathers; even though such interpretations were never (intended) to be at any time published. . . .

Decree Concerning Original Sin

That our Catholic *faith, without which it is impossible to please God,* may, errors being purged away, continue in its own perfect and spotless integrity, and that the Christian people may not *be carried about with every wind of doctrine;* whereas that old serpent, the perpetual enemy of mankind, amongst the very many evils with which the Church of God is in these our times troubled, has also stirred up not only new, but even old, dissensions touching original sin, and the remedy thereof; the sacred and holy, oecumenical and general Synod of Trent,—lawfully assembled in the Holy See presiding therein,—wishing now to come to the reclaiming of the erring, and the confirming of the wavering—following the testimonies of the sacred Scriptures, of the holy Fathers, or the most approved coun-

cils, and the judgment and consent of the Church itself, ordains, confesses, and declares these things touching the said original sin:

1. If any one does not confess that the first man, Adam, when he had transgressed the commandment of God in Paradise, immediately lost the holiness and justice wherein he had been constituted; and that he incurred, through the offence of that prevarication, the wrath and indignation of God, and consequently death, with which God had previously threatened him, and, together with death, captivity under his power who thenceforth *had the empire of death, that is to say, the devil,* and that the entire Adam, through that offence of prevarication, was changed, in body and soul, for the worse; let him be anathema.

2. If any one asserts, that the prevarication of Adam injured himself alone, and not his posterity; and that the holiness and justice, received of God, which he lost, he lost for himself alone, and not for us also; or that he, being defiled by the sin of disobedience, has only transfused death, and pains of the body, into the whole human race, but not sin also, which is the death of the soul; let him be anathema:— whereas he contradicts the apostle who says; *By one man sin entered into the world, and by sin death, and so death passed upon all men, in whom all have sinned.*

3. If any one asserts, that this sin of Adam,—which in its origin is one, and being transfused into all by propagation, not by imitation, is in each one as his own,—is taken away either by the powers of human nature, or by any other remedy than the merit of the *one mediator, our Lord Jesus Christ, who hath reconciled us to*

God in his own blood, made unto us justice, sanctification, and redemption; or if he denies that the said merit of Jesus Christ is applied, both to adults and to infants, by the sacrament of baptism rightly administered in the form of the Church; let him be anathema: *For there is no other name under heaven given to men, whereby we must be saved.* Whence that voice; *Behold the lamb of God, behold him who taketh away the sins of the world*; and that other; *As many as have been baptized, have put on Christ.*

• • •

That a Rash Presumptuousness in the Matter of Predestination Is to Be Avoided

No one, moreover, so long as he is in this mortal life, ought so far to presume as regards the secret mystery of divine predestination, as to determine for certain that he is assuredly in the number of the predestinate; as if it were true, that he that is justified, either cannot sin any more, or, if he do sin, that he ought to promise himself an assured repentance; for except by special revelation, it cannot be known whom God hath chosen unto Himself.

• • •

On the Sacraments in General

Canon I. If any one saith, that the sacraments of the New Law were not all instituted by Jesus Christ, our Lord; or, that they are more, or less, than seven, to wit, Baptism, Confirmation, the Eucharist, Penance, Extreme Unction, Order, and Matrimony; or even that any one of these seven is not truly and properly a sacrament; let him be anathema.

Canon II. If any one saith, that these said sacraments of the New Law do not differ from the sacraments of the Old Law, save that the ceremonies are different, and different the outward rites; let him be anathema.

Canon III. If any one saith, that these seven sacraments are in such wise equal to each other, as that one is not in any way more worthy than another; let him be anathema.

Canon IV. If any one saith, that the sacraments of the New Law are not necessary unto salvation, but superfluous; and that, without them, or without the desire thereof, men obtain of God, through faith alone, the grace of justification;— though all (the sacraments) are not indeed necessary for every individual; let him be anathema.

Canon V. If any one saith, that these sacraments were instituted for the sake of nourishing faith alone; let him be anathema.

Canon VI. If any one saith, that the sacraments of the New Law do not contain the grace which they signify; or, that they do not confer that grace on those who do not place an obstacle thereunto; as though they were merely outward signs of grace or justice received through faith, and certain marks of the Christian profession, whereby believers are distinguished amongst men from unbelievers; let him be anathema.

Canon VII. If any one saith, that grace, as far as God's part is concerned, is not given through the said sacraments, always, and to all men, even though they receive them rightly, but (only) sometimes, and to some persons; let him be anathema.

Canon VIII. If any one saith, that by the said sacraments of the New Law grace is not conferred through the act performed, but that faith alone in the divine promise suffices for the obtaining of grace; let him be anathema.

Canon IX. If any one saith, that, in the three sacraments, Baptism, to wit, Confirmation, and Order, there is not imprinted in the soul a character, that is, a certain spiritual and indelible sign, on account of which they cannot be repeated; let him be anathema.

Canon X. If any one saith, that all Christians have power to administer the word, and all the sacraments; let him be anathema.

Canon XI. If any one saith, that, in ministers, when they effect, and confer the sacraments, there is not required the intention at least of doing what the Church does; let him be anathema.

Canon XII. If any one saith, that a minister, being in mortal sin,—if so be that he observe all the essentials which belong to the effecting, or conferring of, the sacrament,—neither effects, nor confers the sacrament; let him be anathema.

Canon XIII. If any one saith, that the received and approved rites of the Catholic Church, wont to be used in the solemn administration of the sacraments, may be condemned, or without sin be omitted at pleasure by the ministers, or be changed, by every pastor of the churches, into other new ones; let him be anathema.

• • •

On the Real Presence of Our Lord Jesus Christ in the Most Holy Sacrament of the Eucharist

In the first place, the holy Synod teaches, and openly and simply professes, that, in the august sacrament of the holy Eucharist, after the consecration of the bread and wine, our Lord Jesus Christ, true God and man, is truly, really, and substantially contained under the species of those sensible things. For neither are these things mutually repugnant,—that our Saviour Himself always sitteth at the right hand of the Father in heaven, according to the natural mode of existing, and that, nevertheless, He be, in many other places, sacramentally present to us in his own substance, by a manner of existing, which, though we can scarcely express it in words, yet can we, by the understanding illuminated by faith, conceive, and we ought most firmly to believe, to be possible unto God: for thus all our forefathers, as many as were in the true Church of Christ, who have treated of his most holy Sacrament have most openly professed, that our Redeemer instituted this so admirable a sacrament at the last supper, when, after the blessing of the bread and wine, He testified, in express and clear words, that He gave them His own very Body, and His own Blood; words which,— recorded by the holy Evangelists, and afterwards repeated by Saint Paul, whereas they carry with them that proper and most manifest meaning in which they were understood by the Fathers,—it is indeed a crime the most unworthy that they should be wrested, by certain contentious and wicked men, to fictitious and imaginary tropes, whereby the verity of the flesh and blood of Christ is denied, contrary to the universal sense of the Church, which, as *the pillar and ground of truth*, has detested, as satanical, these inventions devised by impious men; she recognising, with a mind ever grateful and unforgetting, this most excellent benefit of Christ.

• • •

On the Most Holy Sacrament of the Eucharist

Canon I. If any one denieth, that, in the sacrament of the most holy Eucharist, are contained truly, really, and substantially, the body and blood together with the soul and divinity of our Lord Jesus Christ, and consequently the whole Christ; but saith that He is only therein as in a sign, or in figure, or virtue; let him be anathema.

Canon II. If any one saith, that, in the sacred and holy sacrament of the Eucharist, the substance of the bread and wine remains conjointly with the body and blood of our Lord Jesus Christ, and denieth that wonderful and singular conversion of the whole substance of the bread into the Body, and of the whole substance of the wine into the Blood—the species only of the bread and wine remaining—which conversion indeed the Catholic Church most aptly calls Transubstantiation; let him be anathema.

• • •

Canon IX. If any one denieth, that all and each of Christ's faithful of both sexes are bound, when they

have attained to years of discretion, to communicate every year, at least at Easter, in accordance with the precept of the holy Mother Church; let him be anathema.

• • •

Canon XI. If any one saith, that faith alone is a sufficient preparation for receiving the sacrament of the most holy Eucharist; let him be anathema. And for fear lest so great a sacrament may be received unworthily, and so unto death and condemnation, this holy Synod ordains and declares, that sacramental confession, when a confessor may be had, is of necessity to be made beforehand, by those whose conscience is burthened with mortal sin, how contrite even soever they may think themselves. But if any one shall presume to teach, preach, or obstinately to assert, or even in public disputation to defend the contrary, he shall be thereupon excommunicated.

• • •

On the Ecclesiastical Hierarchy, and on Ordination

But, forasmuch as in the sacrament of Order, as also in Baptism, and Confirmation, a character is imprinted, which can neither be effaced nor taken away; the holy Synod with reason condemns the opinion of those, who assert that the priests of the New Testament have only a temporary power; and that those who have once been rightly ordained, can again become laymen, if they do not exercise the ministry of the word of God. And if any one affirm, that all Christians indiscriminately are priests of the New Testament, or that they are all mutually endowed with an equal spiritual power, he clearly does nothing but confound the ecclesiastical hierarchy, which is *as an army set in array*; as if, contrary to the doctrine of blessed Paul, *all* were *apostles, all prophets, all evangelists, all pastors, all doctors.* Wherefore, the holy Synod declares that, besides the other ecclesiastical degrees, bishops, who have succeeded to the place of the apostles, principally belong to this hierarchical order; that they are *placed*, as the same apostle says *by the Holy Ghost, to rule the Church of God*; that they are superior to priests; administer the sacrament of Confirmation; ordain the ministers of the Church; and that they can perform very many other things; over which functions others of an inferior order have no power. Furthermore, the sacred and holy Synod teaches, that, in the ordination of bishops, priests, and of the other orders, neither the consent, nor vocation, nor authority, whether of the people, or of any civil power or magistrate whatsoever, is required in such wise as that, without this, the ordination is invalid; yea rather doth It decree, that all those who, being only called and instituted by the people, or by the civil power and magistrate, ascend to the exercise of these ministrations, and those who of their own rashness assume them to themselves, are not ministers of the Church, but are to be looked upon as *thieves and robbers, who have not entered by the door.* These are the things which it hath seemed good to the sacred Synod to teach the faithful

of Christ, in general terms, touching the sacrament of Order.

• • •

On the Sacrament of Matrimony

• • •

Canon IX. If anyone saith, that clerics constituted in sacred orders or Regulars, who have solemnly professed chastity, are able to contract marriage, and that being contracted it is valid, notwithstanding the ecclesiastical law, or vow; and that the contrary is nothing else than to condemn marriage; and, that all who do not feel that they have the gift of chastity, even though they have made a vow thereof, may contract marriage; let him be anathema: seeing that God refuses not that gift to those who ask for it rightly, neither does *He suffer us to be tempted above that which we are able.*

Canon X. If any one saith, that the marriage state is to be placed above the state of virginity, or of celibacy, and that it is not better and more blessed to remain in virginity, or in celibacy, than to be united in matrimony; let him be anathema.

• • •

On the Invocation, Veneration, and Relics, of Saints, and on Sacred Images

The holy Synod enjoins on all bishops, and others who sustain the office and charge of teaching, that, agreeably to the usage of the Catholic and Apostolic Church, received from the primitive times of the

Christian religion, and agreeably to the consent of the holy Fathers, and to the decrees of sacred Councils, they especially instruct the faithful diligently concerning the intercession and invocation of saints; the honour (paid) to relics; and the legitimate use of images: teaching them, that the saints, who reign together with Christ, offer up their own prayers to God for men; that it is good and useful suppliantly to invoke them, and to have recourse to their prayers, aid, (and) help for obtaining benefits from God, through His Son, Jesus Christ our Lord, who is our alone Redeemer and Saviour; but that they think impiously, who deny that the saints, who enjoy eternal happiness in heaven, are to be invocated; or who assert either that they do not pray for men; or, that the invocation of them to pray for each of us even in particular, is idolatry: or that it is repugnant to the word of God; and is opposed to the honour of the *one mediator of God and men, Christ Jesus*; or, that it is foolish to supplicate, vocally, or mentally, those who reign in heaven. Also, that the holy bodies of holy martyrs, and of others now living with Christ—which bodies were the living members of Christ, and *the temple of the Holy Ghost*, and which are by Him to be raised unto eternal life, and to be glorified— are to be venerated by the faithful; through which (bodies) many benefits are bestowed by God on men; so that they who affirm that veneration and honour are not due to the relics of saints; or, that these, and other sacred monuments, are uselessly honoured by the faithful; and that the places dedicated to the memories of the saints are in vain visited with the view of obtaining

their aid; are wholly to be condemned, as the Church has already long since condemned, and now also condemns them.

Moreover, that the images of Christ, of the Virgin Mother of God, and of the other saints, are to be had and retained particularly in temples, and that due honour and veneration are to be given them; not that any divinity, or virtue, is believed to be in them, on account of which they are to be worshipped; or that anything is to be asked of them; or, that trust is to be reposed in images, as was of old done by the Gentiles who placed their hope in idols; but because the honour which is shown them is referred to the prototypes which those images represent; in such wise that by the images which we kiss, and before which we uncover the head, and prostrate ourselves, we adore Christ; and we venerate the saints, whose similitude they bear: as by the decrees of Councils, and especially of the second Synod of Nicaea, has been defined against the opponents of images.

• • •

Cardinals and All Prelates of the Churches Shall Be Content with Modest Furniture and a Frugal Table: They Shall Not Enrich Their Relatives or Domestics Out of the Property of the Church

It is to be wished, that those who undertake the office of a bishop should understand what their portion is; and comprehend that they are called, not to their own convenience, not to riches or luxury, but to labours and cares for the glory of God. For it is not to be doubted, that the rest of the faithful also will be more easily excited to religion and innocence, if they shall see those who are set over them, not fixing their thoughts on the things of this world, but on the salvation of souls, and on their heavenly country. Wherefore the holy Synod, being minded that these things are of the greatest importance toward restoring ecclasiastical discipline, admonishes all bishops, that, often meditating thereon, they show themselves conformable to their office, by their actual deeds, and the actions of their lives; which is a kind of perpetual sermon; but above all that they so order their whole conversation, as that others may thence be able to derive examples of frugality, modesty, continency, and of that holy humility which so much recommends us to God.

Wherefore, after the example of our fathers in the Council of Carthage, it not only orders that bishops be content with modest furniture, and a frugal table and diet, but that they also give heed that in the rest of their manner of living, and in their whole house, there be nothing seen that is alien from this holy institution, and which does not manifest simplicity, zeal toward God, and a contempt of vanities. Also, it wholly forbids them to strive to enrich their own kindred or domestics out of the revenues of the church: seeing that even the canons of the Apostles forbid them to give to their kindred the property of the church, which belongs to God: but if their kindred be poor, let them distribute to them thereof as poor, but not misapply, or waste, it for their sakes: yea, the holy Synod with the utmost

earnestness, admonishes them completely to lay aside all this human and carnal affection toward brothers, nephews, and kindred, which is the seed-plot of many evils in the Church. And what has been said of bishops, the same is not only to be observed by all who hold ecclesiastical benefices, whether Secular or Regular, each according to the nature of his rank, but the Synod decrees that it also regards the cardinals of the holy Roman Church; for whereas, upon their advice to the most holy Roman Pontiff, the administration of the universal Church depends, it would seem to be a shame, if they did not at the same time shine so pre-eminent in virtue and in the discipline of their lives, as deservedly to draw upon themselves the eyes of all men.

•   •   •

Decree Concerning Indulgences

Whereas the power of conferring Indulgences was granted by Christ to the Church; and she has, even in the most ancient times, used the said power, delivered unto her of God; the sacred holy Synod teaches, and enjoins, that the use of Indulgences, for the Christian people most salutary, and approved of by the authority of sacred Councils, is to be retained in the Church; and It condemns with anathema those who either assert, that they are useless; or who deny that there is in the Church the power of granting them. In granting them, however, It desires that, in accordance with the ancient and approved custom in the Church, moderation be observed; lest, by excessive facility, ecclesiastical discipline be enervated. And being desirous that the abuses which have crept therein, and by occasion of which this honourable name of Indulgences is blasphemed by heretics, be amended and corrected, It ordains generally by this decree, that all evil gains for the obtaining thereof,—whence a most prolific cause of abuses amongst the Christian people has been derived,—be wholly abolished. But as regards the other abuses which have proceeded from superstition, ignorance, irreverence, or from whatsoever other source, since, by reason of the manifold corruptions in the places and provinces where the said abuses are committed, they cannot conveniently be specially prohibited; It commands all bishops, diligently to collect, each in his own church, all abuses of this nature, and to report them in the first provincial Synod; that, after having been reviewed by the opinions of the other bishops also, they may forthwith be referred to the Sovereign Roman Pontiff, by whose authority and prudence that which may be expedient for the universal Church will be ordained; that thus the gift of holy Indulgences may be dispensed to all the faithful, piously, holily, and incorruptly.